JOSEPH H. MAYFIELD

Vice-president for Campus Life, Professor of Philosophy and New Testament Greek, Northwest Nazarene College, Nampa, Idaho. A.B., Pasadena College; M.A., University of Southern California; D.D., Pasadena College. Graduate studies at Columbia University and Claremont Graduate School.

RALPH EARLE

Professor of New Testament, Nazarene Theological Seminary, Kansas City, Missouri. A.B., Eastern Nazarene College; M.A., Boston University; B.D., Th.D., Gordon Divinity School. Postdoctoral studies have been taken at Harvard and Edinburgh universities.

BEACON
BIBLE COMMENTARY

In Ten Volumes

Volume VII

JOHN

Joseph H. Mayfield, M.A., D.D.

ACTS

Ralph Earle, B.D., M.A., Th.D.

BEACON HILL PRESS OF KANSAS CITY
Kansas City, Missouri

BEACON BIBLE COMMENTARY

In Ten Volumes

Preface

"All scripture is given by inspiration of God, and is profitable for doctrine, for reproof, for correction, for instruction in righteousness: that the man of God may be perfect, throughly furnished unto all good works" (II Tim. 3:16-17).

We believe in the plenary inspiration of the Bible. God speaks to men through His Word. He hath spoken unto us by His Son. But without the inscripted Word how would we know the Word which was made flesh? He does speak to us by His Spirit, but the Spirit uses the written Word as the vehicle of His revelation, for He is the true Author of the Holy Scriptures. What the Spirit reveals is in agreement with the Word.

The Christian faith derives from the Bible. It is the Foundation for faith, for salvation, and sanctification. It is the Guide for Christian character and conduct. "Thy word is a lamp unto my feet, and a light unto my path" (Ps. 119:105).

The revelation of God and His will for men is adequate and complete in the Bible. The great task of the Church, therefore, is to communicate the knowledge of the Word, to enlighten the eyes of their understanding, and to awaken and to illuminate the conscience that men may learn "to live soberly, righteously, and godly, in this present world." This leads to the possession of that "inheritance [that is] incorruptible, and undefiled, and that fadeth not away, reserved in heaven."

When we consider the translation and interpretation of the Bible, we admit we are guided by men who are not inspired. Human limitation, as well as the plain fact that no scripture is of private or single interpretation, allows variation in the exegesis and exposition of the Bible.

Beacon Bible Commentary is offered in ten volumes with becoming modesty. It does not supplant others. Neither does it purport to be exhaustive or final. The task is colossal. Assignments have been made to thirty-nine of the ablest writers available. They are trained men with serious purpose, deep dedication, and supreme devotion. The sponsors and publishers, as well as the contributors, earnestly pray that this new offering among Bible commentaries will be helpful to preachers, teachers, and laymen in discovering the deeper meaning of God's Word and in unfolding its message to all who hear them.

—G. B. WILLIAMSON

Quotations and References

Boldface type in the exposition indicates a quotation from the King James Version of the passage under discussion. Readings from other versions are put in quotation marks and the version is indicated.

In scripture references a letter (*a*, *b*, etc.) indicates a clause within a verse. When no book is named, the book under discussion is understood.

Bibliographical data on a work cited by a writer may be found by consulting the first reference to the work by that writer, or by turning to the bibliography.

The bibliographies are not intended to be exhaustive but are included to provide complete publication data for volumes cited in the text.

References to authors in the text, or inclusion of their books in the bibliography, does not constitute an endorsement of their views. All reading in the field of biblical interpretation should be discriminating and thoughtful.

Acknowledgments

Permission to quote from copyrighted material is gratefully acknowledged, as follows:

Abingdon Press: *The Interpreter's Bible.*

Association Press: Studdert-Kennedy, "The Gambler," *Christ in Poetry.*

Cambridge University Press: C. H. Dodd, *Interpretation of the Fourth Gospel.*

William B. Eerdmans Publishing Co.: E. M. Blaiklock, *Acts of the Apostles.* F. F. Bruce, *Commentary on the Book of Acts.*

Harper and Row: F. J. Foakes-Jackson, *Acts of the Apostles.* Henry J. Cadbury, *Book of Acts in History.*

Inter-Varsity Press: F. F. Bruce, *Acts of the Apostles.*

University of Chicago Press: W. F. Arndt and F. W. Gingrich, *Greek-English Lexicon of the New Testament.*

Scripture quotations have been used from the following sources:

The Amplified New Testament. Copyright 1958, The Lockman Foundation, La Habra, California.

The Berkeley Version in Modern English. Copyright 1958, 1959, Zondervan Publishing House.

The Bible: A New Translation, James Moffatt. Copyright 1950, 1952, 1953, 1954, by James A. R. Moffatt. Used by permission of Harper and Row.

The Bible: An American Translation, J. M. Powis Smith, Edgar J. Goodspeed. Copyright 1923, 1927, 1948 by The University of Chicago Press.

New American Standard Bible. Copyright 1960, 1962, 1963, The Lockman Foundation, La Habra, California.

The New English Bible. © The Delegates of the Oxford University Press and the Syndics of the Cambridge University Press, 1961.

The New Testament in Modern English. © J. B. Phillips, 1958. Used by permission of The Macmillan Company.

Revised Standard Version of the Holy Bible, copyrighted 1946 and 1952 by the Division of Christian Education of the National Council of Churches.

The editors as well as the writers have shared in selecting or contributing the homiletical suggestions and teaching outlines throughout the volume.

Maps and charts appearing at the end of the volume are adapted and reproduced from the Beacon Hill Press of Kansas City line of *Bible Maps and Charts,* or are specially prepared for this volume.

How to Use the "Beacon Bible Commentary"

The Bible is a Book to be read, to be understood, to be obeyed, and to be shared with others. *Beacon Bible Commentary* is planned to help at the points of understanding and sharing.

For the most part, the Bible is its own best interpreter. He who reads it with an open mind and receptive spirit will again and again become aware that through its pages God is speaking *to him*. A commentary serves as a valuable resource when the meaning of a passage is not clear even to the thoughtful reader. Also after one has seen his own meaning in a passage from the Bible, it is rewarding to discover what truth others have found in the same place. Sometimes, too, this will correct possible misconceptions the reader may have formed.

Beacon Bible Commentary has been written to be used with your Bible in hand. Most major commentaries print the text of the Bible at the top of the commentary page. The editors decided against this practice, believing that the average user comes to his commentary from his Bible and hence has in mind the passage in which he is interested. He also has his Bible at his elbow for any necessary reference to the text. To have printed the full text of the Bible in a work of this size would have occupied approximately one-third of the space available. The planners decided to give this space to additional resources for the reader. At the same time, writers have woven into their comments sufficient quotations from the passages under discussion that the reader maintains easy and constant thought contact with the words of the Bible. These quoted words are printed in boldface type for quick identification.

ILLUMINATION FROM RELATED PASSAGES

The Bible is its own best interpreter when a given chapter or a longer section is read to find out what it says. This book is also its own best interpreter when the reader knows what the Bible says in other places about the subject under consideration. The writers and editors of *Beacon Bible Commentary* have constantly striven to give maximum help at this point. Repeated and carefully chosen cross-references have been included in order that the reader may thus find the Bible interpreted and illustrated by the Bible itself.

Paragraph Treatment

The truth of the Bible is best understood when we grasp the thought of the writer in its sequence and connections. The verse divisions with which we are familiar came into the Bible late (the sixteenth century for the New Testament and the seventeenth century for the Old). They were done hurriedly and sometimes missed the thought pattern of the inspired writers. The same is true of the chapter divisions. Most translations today arrange the words of the sacred writers under our more familiar paragraph structure.

It is under this paragraph arrangement that our commentary writers have approached their task. They have tried always to answer the question, What was the inspired writer saying in this passage? Verse numbers have been retained for easy identification but basic meanings have been outlined and interpreted in the larger and more complete thought forms.

Introductions to Bible Books

The Bible is an open Book to him who reads it thoughtfully. But it opens wider when we gain increased understanding of its human origins. Who wrote this book? Where was it written? When did the writer live? What were the circumstances that caused him to write? Answers to these questions always throw added light on the words of the Scripture.

These answers are given in the Introductions. There also you will find an outline of each book. The Introduction has been written to give an overview of the whole book; to provide you with a dependable road map before you start your trip—and to give you a place of reference when you are uncertain as to which way to turn. Don't ignore the flagman when he waves his warning sign, "See Introduction." At the close of the commentary on each book you will find a bibliography for further study.

Maps and Charts

The Bible was written about people who lived in lands that are foreign and strange to most English-speaking readers. Often better understanding of the Bible depends on better knowledge of Bible geography. When the flagman waves his other sign, "See map," you should turn to the map for a clearer understanding of locations, distances, and related timing of the experiences of the men with whom God was dealing.

This knowledge of Bible geography will help you to be a better Bible preacher and teacher. Even in the more formal presentation of the sermon it helps the congregation to know that the flight into Egypt was "a journey on foot, some 200 miles to the southwest." In the less formal and smaller groups such as Sunday school classes and prayer meeting Bible study, a large classroom map enables the group to see the locations as well as to hear them mentioned. When you have seen these places on your commentary maps, you are better prepared to share the information with those whom you lead in Bible study.

Charts which list Bible facts in tabular form often make clear historical relationships in the same way that maps help with understanding geography. To see listed in order the kings of Judah or the Resurrection appearances of Jesus often gives clearer understanding of a particular item in the series. These charts are a part of the resources offered in this set.

Beacon Bible Commentary has been written for the newcomer to Bible study and also for those long familiar with the written Word. The writers and editors have probed each chapter, each verse, every clause, phrase, and word in the familiar King James Version. We have probed with the question, What do these words mean? If the answer is not self-evident, we have How well we have succeeded the reader must judge, but we invite you to explore these words or passages that puzzle you when you are reading God's written Word.

EXEGESIS AND EXPOSITION

Bible commentators often use these words to describe two ways of making clear the meaning of a passage in the Scriptures. *Exegesis* is a study of the original Greek or Hebrew words to understand what meanings those words had when they were used by men and women in Bible times. To know the meaning of the separate words, as well as their grammatical relationship to charged ourselves to give the best explanation known to us. each other, is one way to understand more clearly what the inspired writer meant to say. You will often find this kind of enriching help in the commentary. But word studies alone do not always give true meaning.

Exposition is a commentator's effort to point out the meaning of a passage as it is affected by any one of several facts known to the writer but perhaps not familiar to the reader. These facts may be (1) the context (the surrounding verses or chapters), (2) the historical background, (3) the related teachings from other parts of the Bible, (4) the significance of these messages from God as they relate to universal facts of human life, (5) the relevance of these truths to unique contemporary human situations. The commentator thus seeks to explain the full meaning of a Bible passage in the light of his own best understanding of God, man, and the world in which we live.

Some commentaries separate the exegesis from this broader basis of explanation. In *Beacon Bible Commentary* writers have combined the exegesis and exposition. Accurate word studies are indispensable to a correct understanding of the Bible. But such careful studies are today so thoroughly reflected in a number of modern English translations that they are often not necessary except to enhance the understanding of the theological meaning of a passage. The writers and editors seek to reflect a true and accurate exegesis at every point, but specific exegetical discussions are introduced chiefly to throw added light on the meaning of a passage, rather than to engage in scholarly discussion.

The Bible is a practical Book. We believe that God inspired holy men of old to declare these truths in order that the readers might better understand and do the will of God. *Beacon Bible Commentary* has been undertaken only for the purpose of helping men to find more effectively God's will for them as revealed in the Scripture—to find that will and to act upon that knowledge.

Helps for Bible Preaching and Teaching

We have said that the Bible is a Book to be shared. Christian preachers and teachers since the first century have sought to convey the gospel message by reading and explaining selected passages of Scripture. *Beacon Bible Commentary* seeks to encourage this kind of expository preaching and teaching. The set contains more than a thousand brief expository outlines that have been used by outstanding Bible teachers and preachers. Both writers and editors have assisted in contributing or selecting these homiletical suggestions. It is hoped that the outlines will suggest ways in which the reader will want to try to open the Word of God to his class or congregation. Some of these analyses of preachable passages have been contributed by our contemporaries. When the outlines have appeared in print, authors and references are given in order that the reader may go to the original source for further help.

In the Bible we find truth of the highest order. Here is given to us, by divine inspiration, the will of God for our lives. Here we have sure guidance in all things necessary to our relationships to God and under Him to our fellowman. Because these eternal truths come to us in human language and through human minds, they need to be put into fresh words as languages change and as thought patterns are modified. In *Beacon Bible Commentary* we have sought to help make the Bible a more effective Lamp to the paths of men who journey in the twentieth century.

A. F. Harper

Table of Contents

VOLUME VII

Abbreviations and Explanations

The Books of the Bible

Gen.	Job	Jonah	I or II Cor.
Exod.	Ps.	Mic.	Gal.
Lev.	Prov.	Nah.	Eph.
Num.	Eccles.	Hab.	Phil.
Deut.	Song of Sol.	Zeph.	Col.
Josh.	Isa.	Hag.	I or II Thess.
Judg.	Jer.	Zech.	I or II Tim.
Ruth	Lam.	Mal.	Titus
I or II Sam.	Ezek.	Matt.	Philem.
I or II Kings	Dan.	Mark	Heb.
I or II Chron.	Hos.	Luke	Jas.
Ezra	Joel	John	I or II Pet.
Neh.	Amos	Acts	I, II, or III John
Esther	Obad.	Rom.	Jude
			Rev.

Vulg.	The Vulgate
LXX	The Septuagint
ASV	American Standard Revised Version
ERV	English Revised Version
RSV	Revised Standard Version
Amplified NT	Amplified New Testament
NASB	New American Standard Bible
NEB	New English Bible
Beginnings	Beginnings of Christianity, by Lake and Cadbury
EGT	Expositor's Greek Testament
HDB	Hastings' Dictionary of the Bible
IB	Interpreter's Bible
IDB	The Interpreter's Dictionary of the Bible
VGT	Vocabulary of Greek Testament, by Moulton and Milligan

c.	chapter	OT	Old Testament
cc.	chapters	NT	New Testament
ca.	about		
v.	verse	Heb.	Hebrew
vv.	verses	Gk.	Greek
MS, MSS	manuscript manuscripts		

The Gospel According to

JOHN

Joseph H. Mayfield

Introduction

The Fourth Gospel is a word portrait of the greatest of historical events. In fact, this event is the theme of the Gospel. "And the Word was made flesh, and dwelt among us" (1:14). Everything the author wrote was to make this clear and meaningful to the reader.

The first readers of the Fourth Gospel were most likely second- or third-generation Christians. What they knew about Jesus' life, ministry, death, and resurrection they had learned either by word of mouth or the reading of earlier Gospel accounts. There is evidence that among some of these early Christians there were misconceptions about these facts and meanings, giving rise to certain heresies.

A. AUTHORSHIP

Early external evidence points to the Apostle John as the author. The testimony of the Church fathers is nearly unanimous in favor of this position. The internal evidence is dual in kind. Indirect evidence indicates that the author was a Jew, a Jew of Palestine, an eyewitness, an apostle, and that the apostle was John.[1]

Internal direct evidence is in itself inconclusive except for the fact that it is clear the author himself witnessed much of what he recorded. It is inconclusive in that the witness is not named. He writes that "the Word was made flesh, and dwelt among us" (1:14), indicating the Incarnate One to be among those with whom the writer was himself associated. Again he declares himself to be a witness at the scene of the Crucifixion. When the soldier pierced the Lord's side, blood and water came out. The writer attests his witness: "And he that saw it bare record, and his record is true" (19:35). Without giving his name the author at the very conclusion of the Gospel identifies himself as a witness: "This is that disciple which testifieth of these things, and wrote these things" (21:24).

B. THE AUTHOR

John was the son of Zebedee, a fisherman, and Salome (Mark 15:40; 16:1; cf. Matt. 27:56). It is thought that he was younger than his brother James. Evidently the members of the Zebedee

---

[1]B. F. Westcott, *The Gospel According to St. John* (London: John Murray, 1908), pp. v-xxv.

family were people of some means. They had hired servants (Mark 1:20), and according to John 19:27, John cared for Mary after Jesus' death.

Though the apostle is not mentioned by name as a disciple of John the Baptist, there is reason to believe that he was one of the two of John's disciples alluded to in John 1:35-40. If such is the case, it is evident that the apostle was first a disciple of John the Baptist. Later he left John to follow Jesus and became a full-time disciple of the Master (Matt. 4:18-22; Mark 1:19-20; Luke 5:1-11; cf. John 1:29-46).

John was one of the inner circle of disciples along with his brother James and Peter. On several occasions, during the last half of Jesus' ministry, these three were drawn into a more intimate relationship with Jesus than were the other disciples (Matt. 17:1-8; Mark 9:2-8; Luke 9:28-36, 49 ff.; 22:8). Peter and John were the only disciples to follow Jesus to the place of judgment (John 18:15-16), and John alone went with Jesus to Golgotha (John 19:26). It was John and Peter who had a footrace to the tomb on the first Easter morning (John 20:3-4).

The apostle is mentioned in the Book of Acts nine times. There he is overshadowed by the leadership of Peter. Paul names him as one of the leaders in the Jerusalem church (Gal. 2:9).

The Revelation, commonly held to have been written by John, is the only other scripture reference to the apostle. His self-portrayal there shows him on the Isle of Patmos (Rev. 1:9) as prophet and seer.

Early patristic literature makes occasional reference to the apostle. From these it is evident that he was a resident of Ephesus. Westcott quotes Jerome as saying of him that "when he tarried at Ephesus to extreme old age, and could only with difficulty be carried to the church in the arms of his disciples, and was unable to give utterance to many words, he used to say no more at their several meetings than this, 'Little children, love one another.' At length the disciples and fathers who were there, wearied with hearing always the same words, said, 'Master, why dost thou always say this?' 'It is the Lord's command,' was his worthy reply, 'and if this alone be done, it is enough.' "[2]

Since the apostle hailed from Galilee and was of Jewish parentage, his background gave to him the breadth of experience

[2]*Ibid.*, p. xxxiv.

to understand and interpret Jesus' life, teachings, ministry, death, and resurrection from both the Judaic and Hellenistic points of view.

C. Date

Estimates as to the date of writing have varied from the middle of the first century to the middle of the second. Those who discount the Johannine authorship tend to favor the later date. Some recent scholarship argues for the earlier date on the basis of archaeological findings at the ancient Greek colony of Pella. However, both internal and external evidence quite consistently point to a date around A.D. 95.

D. Purpose

The purpose of the author is clearly stated: "And many other signs truly did Jesus in the presence of his disciples, which are not written in this book: but these are written, that ye might believe that Jesus is the Christ, the Son of God; and that believing ye might have life through his name" (John 20:30-31). In order better to understand this statement an analysis of key ideas will help.

1. *The Miracles (Signs)*

The Greek word used here is *semeion*. In its classical use the word meant: (a) a mark, sign, or token by which something is known; a trace, track; (b) a sign from the gods, an omen; (c) a sign or signal to do anything; the signal for battle.[3] In the Koine Greek the word came to mean "miracle" or "wonder" as well as "sign." The King James Version translates the word "sign" four times and "miracle" thirteen times. As it is used in John's statement of purpose, the word calls forth two distinct ideas. Certainly it refers to the miracles performed by Jesus, some of which are recorded exclusively in the Fourth Gospel. But it also gives a clue for an answer to the question, Why did he record these miracles as signs? Translated literally the answer is, "That you may have faith that Jesus is the Christ, the Son of God." John saw the miracles of Jesus as signals for action, and he designated the act of faith to be the action desired.

2. *Faith*

The noun "faith" (*pistis*) does not appear in the Gospel of John. However, the verb "believe" (*pisteuo*) is used in various

---

[3]Liddell and Scott, *Greek-English Lexicon* (Abridged, Twenty-fifth edition; Chicago: Follett Publishing Company, 1927), p. 633.

21

forms ninety-four times. It is a key word in the Gospel. Faith is an act that is a total, personal response to the One whom God has sent, the Incarnate Word. Faith has three clearly discernible elements according to L. H. Marshall.[4] These are belief, trust, and loyalty. Just as gunpowder is not gunpowder if any of its three elements—carbon, saltpeter, or sulphur—is missing, so is faith a genuine faith only if all its elements are present. An excellent example of this is found in John 11.

3. Jesus Is the Christ

Both the product and the object of faith are fused into one. The product of an achieving faith is a correct understanding of the historical fact of Messianic fulfillment in the Incarnation. But faith is at its highest achievement when its Object is Jesus, the Christ, the Son of God.

John also has purposefully designed his writing, both by selection and by ordering of events and sayings, to show that God's *Logos,* the Incarnate Word, is the complete and final Fulfillment of all that is foreshadowed in the law and the prophets. Though John does not record Jesus' own statement (Matt. 5:17) in this regard, he demonstrates by carefully selected "signs" that Jesus came not to destroy the law and the prophets but to fulfill them.

4. Life

The word life (*zoe*) is used thirty-six times. In seventeen of these it is used with the adjective eternal (*aionios*), but without any evident change of meaning.[5] Further, the verb to live (*zen*) occurs sixteen times, and there are three occurrences of *zoopoiein,* meaning "to make alive." Thus it is evident that "life" is a major theme of the fourth Gospel. The noun form (*zoe*) is defined by Arndt and Gingrich to mean "life in the physical sense," "a *means of sustenance or livelihood.*" It also means "the life of believers which proceeds from God and Christ" and refers to the "life of grace and holiness . . . Especially in Johannine usage the concept *zoe* is copiously employed, as a rule to designate the result of faith in Christ; in most cases it is stated expressly that

[4]*The Challenge of New Testament Ethics* (London: Macmillan and Co., 1950), p. 271.

[5]C. H. Dodd, *The Interpretation of the Fourth Gospel* (Cambridge: The University Press, 1954), p. 144.

the follower of Jesus possesses life even in this world."[6] In many passages, as here, the word life (*zoe*) is used synonymously with eternal life (*zoe aionios*). Thus it is seen that John's purpose in writing is that the reader, through achieving faith, might become the recipient of eternal life, a present life of grace and holiness.

E. KEY WORDS

Vivid contrasts provide much of the background imagery and symbolism in the Gospel. One of these contrasts is light and darkness—"And the light shineth in the darkness" (1:5). The word "light" (*phos*) appears twenty-one times and "darkness" (*skotia*) is used six times. Jesus is the Light (8:12), and He came to drive out the darkness (1:5), which represents evil in all its forms, both in the individual and in the cosmic sense. There is the assurance that ultimately in God's purpose and time all that the light represents will triumph, and all that darkness stands for will be removed and defeated (cf. Rev. 20:10). It is quite evident that the author had in mind writing a polemic against the Gnostic belief. This was a philosophical doctrine of a metaphysical dualism of light and darkness, good and evil, with no assurance of the ultimate triumph of God and right.

Another set of key words is "truth" and "witness." Jesus said before Pilate, "For this cause came I into the world, that I should bear witness unto the truth" (18:37). The word "truth" (*aletheia*) or a cognate form is used forty-nine times, while "witness," often in the same context as the word "truth," appears forty-two times. Jesus is himself God's Truth manifest in the flesh, a true Witness (3:33), for He himself is the Truth (14:6). Then there are those who bear witness to Jesus: the Father (5:37); Jesus' own witness concerning himself (8:14); the witness of John the Baptist (1:15); the witness of Jesus' own works or signs (10:25); the Scriptures (5:39-40); the disciples (15:27; 21:24); the Spirit (15:26; 16:14).

"Life" and "judgment" (*krisis*) also represent key ideas. The word "life" has been discussed above. Just as it is used with the adjective "eternal" with richness of meaning, it is also set in contrast to judgment or death. The word "judgment" is used twenty-six times and consistently portrays the present condition of those who have refused to believe (3:18-19) in the One who is the Light (9:39-41). The coming of the Light constitutes the final judgment on sin and death (16:8-11).

[6]*A Greek-English Lexicon of the New Testament and Other Early Christian Literature* (Chicago: The University of Chicago Press, 1952), p. 341.

23

Outline

I. Prologue, 1:1-18
  A. The Word: Essential Nature and Relations, 1:1-5
  B. John the Baptist and the Light, 1:6-8
  C. The Word Among Men, 1:9-13
  D. The Incarnation, 1:14-18
II. The Witnesses, 1:19-51
  A. John the Baptist, 1:19-42
  B. Philip and Nathanael, 1:43-51
III. The Signs, 2:1—12:50
  A. The New Wine, 2:1-12
  B. The New Temple, 2:13-22
  C. The New Insight into Man, 2:23—5:47
  D. The New Bread, 6:1-71
  E. The New Outpouring, 7:1-52
  F. The Section on Adultery, 7:53—8:11
  G. A Series of Controversies, 8:12-59
  H. The New Congregation, 9:1—10:42
  I. From Death to Life, 11:1-57
  J. The Universal Christ, 12:1-50
IV. The Last Supper and Last Discourses, 13:1—16:33
  A. The Supper, 13:1-30
  B. The Last Discourses, 13:31—16:33
V. The Lord's Prayer, 17:1-26
  A. Jesus Prays for Himself, 17:1-8
  B. Jesus Prays for His Disciples, 17:9-19
  C. Jesus Prays for Future Believers, 17:20-26
VI. Arrest and Trial, 18:1—19:16
  A. The Arrest, 18:1-14
  B. The Trial, 18:15—19:16
VII. The Crucifixion and Burial, 19:17-42
  A. The Crucifixion, 19:17-37
  B. The Burial, 19:38-42
VIII. Resurrection and Appearances, 20:1—21:25
  A. The Resurrection Evidence, 20:1-10
  B. Personal Appearance to Mary Magdalene, 20:11-18
  C. Personal Appearance to the Ten, 20:19-23
  D. Personal Appearance to the Eleven, 20:24-29
  E. A Delayed Preface, 20:30-31
  F. Personal Appearance by the Sea of Tiberias, 21:1-23
  G. Finis, 21:24-25

Section I Prologue

The prologue is at once a clear statement of the great themes of the Gospel, and a fusion of the best in both Hellenic thought and Judaic religion. The Logos (Word) of the Stoics and Philo is here presented, not as a "cold philosophical abstraction,"[1] but as the person of God living among men who came to recognize and worship Him, and to bear witness concerning Him. Though the word *logos* appears only in 1:1 and 1:14, it is evident that the idea of God's personal revelation described in the Word is never far from the author's mind (cf. Rev. 19:13). These first eighteen verses, with the exception of vv. 6-8 and 15, are sometimes called the "Logos Hymn."

A. THE WORD: ESSENTIAL NATURE AND RELATIONS, 1:1-5

The opening words, **In the beginning was the Word, and the Word was with God, and the Word was God** (1), remind the reader of Gen. 1:1. There is no more appropriate way to begin the account of the greatest event in history. This is where the Hebrew religion began—"In the beginning God . . ." (cf. I John 1:1). Just as God is eternal, so is the Word. He is "Alpha and Omega, the beginning and the ending" (Rev. 1:8). The verb **was,** used three times in this first verse, describes continuous action without regard to beginning or ending. As Westcott well says, "The imperfect tense of the original suggests in this relation, as far as human language can do so, the notion of absolute supra-temporal existence."[2]

The eternal Word is described as **with God.** The preposition **with** loses some of the force of the original language, which indicates "motion toward" or "face-to-face." Thus the **Word** is in a most intimate relationship with God.

The last clause, **and the Word was God,** raises the question: What is the essential nature of the Word? There have been many attempts to identify **the Word** with the universal reason of

[1]Richard Francis Weymouth, revised by James Alexander Robertson, *The New Testament in Modern Speech* (5th ed.; Boston: Pilgrim Press, 1943), p. 212.

[2]*Op. cit.,* p. 2.

the Stoics, or with Plato's use of the "word," or even the Hebrew concept, sometimes personalized, of wisdom. However, all these fall short of the Johannine use of the term. When John wrote, **And the Word was God,** he meant the reader to understand that the essential nature of the Word is Deity, God speaking to man. It is a description of "God's self-disclosure."[3] Further, in the Greek the definite article is not used with the word **God** (*theos*). This omission of the definite article emphasizes kind or quality. Thus the essential nature of the Word is described. John's portrayal of the Word as eternal and as God should serve to answer those who insist that He (the Word) was only a firstborn creature who is divine!

Verse 2 emphatically reiterates the eternality of the Word. As literally translated, it reads: "This One (the Word) was in the beginning face-to-face with God."

Four relationships of the Word are described in 1:3-5:

1. *To the world*

All things were made by him; and without him was not any thing made that was made (3; cf. Ps. 33:6, 9; Col. 1:15-17; Heb. 1:2). The last clause, which is emphatic, was added to guard against first-century false doctrines "which attributed the origin of certain existences to inferior creators, or regarded matter as self existent."[4]

2. *To life and light*

In him was life; and the life was the light of men (4). Here the Word is seen as the Source of life. Biological life comes from Him to be sure, but there is more. As regularly used in this Gospel the word **life** (*zoe*, thirty-six times; never *bios*, biological life) refers to life "from above" (3:3), "eternal life" (3:15-16; 20:31), abundant life (10:10). As He is the Source of all life, He is also the Source of all light. The first creation of the Divine Word was light (Gen. 1:3). Likewise the Psalmist speaks of life and light together. "For with thee is the fountain of life: in thy light shall we see light" (Ps. 36:9). The Word incarnate describes himself as "the light of the world" (John 8:12). Light and life are on the offensive. Death is destined to defeat (11:26); the darkness of the tomb is dispelled by the penetrating and shining light.

[3]C. H. Dodd, *op. cit.*, p. 330.
[4]*Ibid.*, p. 269.

3. *To men*

And the life was the light of men (4). The Word is God's
personal Revelation to men. This Revelation is personal in that
it proceeds from God and is directed to men. The Word is "the
true Light, which lighteth every man that cometh into the world"
(1:9).

4. *To darkness*

**And the light shineth in the darkness; and the darkness
comprehended it not** (5). The eternal Word, in figures of light
and life, has come to men who are sitting in darkness and death.
All through the fourth Gospel are the portrayals of the consequent struggle between Light and darkness, usually crowned
with victory for Light, but sometimes not. Jesus gave sight
(light) to a man blind from birth (c. 9). He brought Lazarus
from the tomb of death and darkness (c. 11). But one who was
close to Him, Judas Iscariot, went out into the night of eternal
darkness (13:30). The word translated **comprehended**, meaning
"to grasp" or "to understand," also means "to overcome." Although John may have intended both meanings, the latter, coupled
with the aorist tense[5] of the verb, is the promise of ultimate and
final victory for the light and all for which it stands.

B. JOHN THE BAPTIST AND THE LIGHT, 1:6-8

**There was a man sent from God, whose name was John.
The same came for a witness, to bear witness of the Light, that
all men through him might believe. He was not that Light, but
was sent to bear witness of that Light** (6-8). The Baptist is
introduced early in the story. In his recital of the Logos Hymn,
at the mention of the Light the author wants it clearly understood
that John the Baptist is not the Light. Then too, as will be seen
later, the writer John was a disciple of the Baptist before he left
to follow Jesus. Hence, being close to John the Baptist, he knew
well the relationship sustained between the Baptist and Jesus.

The author is careful in his selection of a verb to describe the
coming of John. **There was a man** literally means "there came
into being (or history) a man." His "becoming" is not to be confused with the "being" of the eternal Word (1:1).

John the Baptist stood for the old order as prophet and priest
(Matt. 11:9-10), but for the new order as herald. The witness of

---

[5]The aorist tense in Greek defines an act as one and simple without
any reference to its being continued or repeated. So here, the inability of
the evil to overcome the good is ultimate, final, and absolute.

the Baptist himself (1:33) makes it clear that thus he conceived his role. Men would believe through him. He was to be the occasion for men to have faith. But the Object of men's faith must ever and always be the eternal Word, Jesus Christ.

C. THE WORD AMONG MEN, 1:9-13

That was the true Light, which lighteth every man that cometh into the world (9). Isaiah, the prophet, cried, "Arise, shine; for thy light is come, and the glory of the Lord is risen upon thee" (60:1). Prophecy is fulfilled; the true Light has come. Christ is the Light. The meaning of **true** needs clarification. To say that Christ is the **true Light** suggests that all other lights are misleading or false. But this is not what John is saying. Rather, Christ is the real, perfect, genuine Light. Others by comparison (e.g., the Baptist) are imperfect, shadowy, or unsubstantial. Though not the true Light, they are nevertheless not false.[6]

The Gospel of John has often been called the Universal Gospel, and so it is. Here the author writes that the Logos, the Christ, is the **Light, which lighteth every man that cometh into the world.**

He was in the world, and the world was made by him, and the world knew him not. He came unto his own, and his own received him not (10-11). In majestic style, using the most simple language, John portrays the fact, purpose, and outcome of the Incarnation. The fact is, **He was in the world,** a world and people of His own creation. The purpose is, **He came unto his own.** But the outcome, man's response to God's move toward man, was failure to know Him, refusal to receive Him. God's purpose and man's refusal are here set in vivid contrast. A literal translation would read, "He came into His own things, and His own people did not receive Him." It is not the natural world that refused to accept Him. Refusal and rebellion are from the hearts of men. John uses the word "know" to embrace more than intellectual understanding. "Failure to know God is a failure on an ethical plane. It is willful rejection of God, and repudiation of his righteousness."[7] No doubt the consummate rejection of God's best

---

[6]J. H. Bernard, *A Critical and Exegetical Commentary on the Gospel According to St. John,* ed. A. H. McNeile ("The International Critical Commentary"; Edinburgh: T. & T. Clark, 1928), I, 11.

[7]C. H. Dodd, *op. cit.,* p. 159.

and highest disclosure was on the part of the leaders of Israel, usually described by John as "the Jews."[8]

But as many as received him, to them gave he power to become the sons of God, even to them that believe on his name: which were born, not of blood, nor of the will of the flesh, nor of the will of man, but of God (12-13).

Though many rejected the shining Light, God's personal disclosure, many received Him. The word translated **power** (better, "right") "does not describe mere ability, but legitimate, rightful authority, derived from a competent source which includes the idea of power"[9] (cf. 5:27; 10:18; 17:2; 19:10-11). God in the Incarnation has made adequate provision for men to have the right, based on proper authority and power, to become the "children" (RSV) of God. This right to become children of God is not an inherent human capacity apart from the grace of God. It is given of God. Only men who receive Him, i.e., those who have faith, are the children of God. God's self-disclosure is universal, it is to all men (9), but man's response is not. Not all men have faith.

There is only one way to become a child of God; that is to be begotten *"out of* God." Even the most illustrious and religious human ancestry is not sufficient for membership in the society of God's family. The Samaritan woman (4:12) resorted to Jacob as certification for her religious standing, and the Jews frequently talked to Jesus about their father Abraham (8:33, 39, 53, 57) as a sufficient reason for their standing before God. Jesus' teaching to Nicodemus, himself a teacher of Israel, centered in this fact (3:3, 5). Only God can give spiritual life.

A sermon entitled "The True Light" describing the mission of the living Word could be constructed around these points: (1) The Word is life, 4; (2) The Word conquers all, 5; (3) The Word is God among men, 1, 14.

D. THE INCARNATION, 1:14-18

And the Word was made flesh, and dwelt among us, (and we beheld his glory, the glory as of the only begotten of the Father,) full of grace and truth (14).

---

[8]The word *Jew* or *Jewish* appears sixty-nine times in this Gospel compared with fifteen times in the Synoptics. The refusal of the Jews to believe on Jesus and their rejection of Him are major ideas in John.

[9]Westcott, *op. cit.,* p. 9.

Westcott[10] points out the four essential parts of this great declaration.

1. *The Nature of the Incarnation*

The Word was made flesh. The verb here translated **was made** actually means "became" (cf. 1:6); hence it accurately describes that which came into history. Speaking to the Greek world of his day, John said in the best terms possible that "the Logos of philosophy is the Jesus of History."[11] Further, the Docetic Gnostics of that day were claiming that there was no real incarnation: Jesus' body was only an "appearance." At the most the Christ was a theophany—an appearance of God in human form. The Word never really became flesh. Against this John made the simple, forthright, and powerful declaration, **The Word became flesh** (cf. I John 4:2; II John 7). Hoskyns says:

> The Word became flesh—dangerous language when divorced from its context in the Fourth Gospel, for the author does not mean that Spirit was turned into flesh and therefore became profitless, or that the Spirit or the Word of God became a thing visible to the historical eye. He does, however, mean that the flesh of Jesus was the place where men did, and still do, believe and disbelieve; where the division between those who believe and those who do not believe becomes an ultimate division between the children of God and the children of the Devil. Any relative distinction between faith and unbelief is unthinkable.[12]

The nature of the Incarnation as here set forth makes several things clear. According to Westcott:

> a. The Lord's humanity was complete . . . (The Word became *flesh,* and not *a body* or the like.) b. The Lord's humanity was real and permanent . . . (The Word *became* flesh, and did not *clothe himself in* flesh.) c. The Lord's human and divine natures remained without change, each fulfilling its part according to its proper laws . . . (The *Word* became *flesh,* both terms being preserved side by side.) d. The Lord's humanity was universal and not individual, as including all that belongs to the essence of man, without regard to sex or race or time. (The Word became *flesh* and not *a man.*) e. The Lord's human and divine natures were united in one person . . . f. The Word did not acquire personality by the Incarnation.[13]

[10]*Op. cit.,* p. 10.

[11]Bernard, *op. cit.,* p. 19.

[12]Edwyn Clement Hoskyns, *The Fourth Gospel,* ed. Francis Noel Davey (London: Faber and Faber Limited, 1947), p. 85.

[13]*Op. cit.,* p. 11.

A. T. Robertson contends that the statement, **The Word became flesh,** is an allusion to the Virgin Birth. He asks the rhetorical question, "What intelligent meaning can one give to John's language here apart from the Virgin Birth? What ordinary mother or father speaks of a child 'becoming flesh'?"[14]

2. *The Historical Life of the Incarnate Word* (1:14b)

He **dwelt among us.** The temporality of the Incarnation is shown in the figure of a tent for temporary dwelling. John wrote literally, "The Word tabernacled or set up a tent among us." The historicity of the Incarnation is certified in the place of the habitation—**among us** (cf. Ps. 85:9-10).

3. *Personal Witness to the Human-Divine Life* (1:14c)

We **beheld his glory.** Perhaps the best comment on this is made by John himself in his First Epistle. "That which was from the beginning, which we have heard, which we have seen with our eyes, which we have looked upon, and our hands have handled of the Word of life" (1:1). The clause "we have looked upon" is exactly the same form used in 1:14 for **we beheld.** This is the historical aorist and refers to a definite moment in the past. What these apostolic witnesses beheld was **his glory.** John "speaks for those who have faith, and therefore vision."[15] They saw the manifestation of God's presence and power at work among men. It was everywhere present in His life, work, death, and resurrection. His disciples saw His glory and believed in Him (2:14; 11:4, 40; 12:41; 17:5, 22, 24).

4. *The Incarnate Word as the Revealer of God* (1:14d-18)

A word needs to be said about the phrase **the only begotten of the Father.** This, compared with Col. 1:15, where Christ is described as "the firstborn of every creature," presents His sonship under complementary aspects. "The first marks His relation to God as absolutely without parallel, the other His relation to creation as preexistent and sovereign."[16] The meaning is clear and forceful. "The glory of the Incarnate Word was such glory

---

[14]A. T. Robertson, *Word Pictures in the New Testament* (Nashville: Broadman Press, 1930), V, 12.

[15]C. H. Dodd, *op. cit.,* p. 186.

[16]Westcott, *op. cit.,* p. 12.

as the only Son of the Eternal Father would derive from Him and so could exhibit to the faithful."[17]

The word **grace** appears only here and in 1:16-17. It is grace that He came to give to men. **And of his fulness have all we received, and grace for grace (16).** The companion word to **grace** is **truth** (17), and truth is the essential character of the Word. This is truth in the philosophical sense of reality, the ethical sense of holiness, and the moral sense of love. Jesus said of himself, "I am ... the truth" (14:6).

Verse 15 is a reiteration concerning John the Baptist. In 1:7 he bears witness to the Light; here he makes a witness or affirmation that heralds the coming of the Christ while asserting His eternal existence. **John bare witness of him, and cried, saying, This was he of whom I spake, He that cometh after me is preferred before me: for he was before me.**

The idea of abundance from the rich storehouse of God's infinite grace is prominent in John. It is keynoted here in the prologue, **And of his fulness have all we received, and grace for grace (16).** This idea of abundance recurs again and again in the words and works of Jesus. At Cana of Galilee there was sufficient of the best wine (2:10). He gave the Samaritan woman "a well of water springing up into everlasting life" (4:14). For the hungry multitude there was more than enough (6:13). To the thirsty soul He promised not only enough to satisfy but an overflow of "rivers of living water" (7:38). Life abundant for the true believers is made possible by His coming into the world (10:10). John exhibits not only a universal gospel in the explicit sense (i.e., a gospel for "whosoever will") but one that is universal in an implicit sense. Every area of the life of the man of faith is permeated by God's abundant grace.

The expression **grace for grace** is literally "grace taking the place of grace." Robertson remarks that it is "like the manna fresh each morning, new grace for the new day and the new service."[18]

For the law was given by Moses, but grace and truth came by Jesus Christ (17). This vivid contrast at once provides: (1) a plan for the organization of the materials in the fourth Gospel and (2) sets the stage for the conflict and controversy that culminated in the Cross.

[17]Bernard, *op. cit.*, p. 24.
[18]*Op. cit.*, p. 16.

The organization of the materials in John's Gospel shows that the revelation through the Word is superior to that of the Law, that in Jesus Christ alone the Law finds complete fulfillment (He came not to destroy but to fulfill). This superior revelation is God's full, personal, and final disclosure (14:9).

Jesus was not in conflict with the Law. But those who represented the Law were in conflict with Him. This resulted in prolonged controversy between Jesus and the Jews. It began over the Sabbath laws (5:10) and culminated in the Cross (19:18).

It is not that John thought of Law and grace as antithetical, or that the Law was untrue. It was true as far as it went. But it was insufficient for man's deepest needs, whereas Christ is adequate since He is the Source of all truth and grace.

Here John uses the full historical name **Jesus Christ.** It is found in the Synoptics only in Matt. 1:1; Mark 1:1; and again in John only in 17:3.

It was firm Jewish tradition that no one had ever seen God with the physical sight (Exod. 33:20; Deut. 4:12). Hence John wrote, **No man hath seen God at any time** (18). But this does provide the occasion for him to declare the full truth of what he is about to describe in detail. **The only begotten Son, which is in the bosom of the Father, he hath declared him.** Here are described in majestic statements Christ's preexistence with and unique relationship to the Father, **the only begotten Son;** His incarnation, **he hath declared him;** and His eternal being and exaltation, **which is in the bosom of the Father.** The best comment on the expression **in the bosom of the Father** was made by John himself when he wrote, as literally translated, "The Word was face-to-face with God" (1:1).

Section **II** The Witnesses

John 1: 19-51

A. JOHN THE BAPTIST, 1: 19-42

1. *John's Testimony Concerning Himself* (1: 19-23)

The Gospel story actually begins with 1: 19. In the prologue the author has mentioned in a general way the Baptist and his witness (1: 6-7, 15), but here he moves into some detail about him within a historical setting. The theme for the section is the opening statement, "This is the testimony of John" (19, RSV).

No one was in a more favorable position than John the Baptist to give witness concerning the incarnate Word. It was prophesied that he would come to prepare "the way of the Lord" (Isa. 40: 3). According to Jesus' own words this prophecy was fulfilled in the coming of John. When speaking of him Jesus said, "And if ye will receive it, this is Elias, which was for to come" (Matt. 11: 14).

The careful scrutiny of the **priests and Levites**[1]—an official delegation from the Temple, sent by the Jews from Jerusalem to discover if possible the origin and mission of John—marks the beginning of an ever-increasing hostility, first to John and later to Jesus. This culminated in the early assassination of John the Baptist (Matt. 14: 3-10) and the crucifixion of Jesus.

The first conversation of the fourth Gospel (there are many dialogues in the book) begins with the question put by the priests and Levites, **Who art thou?** (19) John's first reply, **I am not the Christ** (20), is most explicit in that it affirms what he himself is not. In no case were men to think of him as the promised and expected Messiah (Isa. 7: 14; 9: 6).

The questioners pursued the matter further. **What then? Art thou Elias?** (21) On the basis of Mal. 4: 5, the Jews expected the coming of Elijah (Elias) "before the coming . . . of the day of the Lord"; hence theirs was an appropriate question. John's answer, **I am not** (21), is in no way a contradiction of the words of Jesus in Matt. 11: 14; for, while the Baptist fulfilled the pre-

---

[1]The Levites were commissioned to teach the Law (II Chron. 35: 3; Neh. 8: 7-9). Levites are not mentioned in the Synoptics, except in Luke 10: 32 (only elsewhere in NT in Acts 4: 36).

liminary ministry of which Malachi had spoken, he was not Elijah returned to the earth in bodily form.

John's negative answer evoked a further question, **Art thou that prophet?**—literally, "the prophet," the one predicted in Deut. 18:15. That the Jews looked for **that prophet** is evident from John 6:14 and 7:40. But the Baptist's answer was another resounding **No!** The three answers to the various questions became consistently shorter, less explanatory, more to the point of denial. The interrogators then told why they needed an answer to their question, **Who art thou?** It was **that we may give an answer to them that sent us.** They then persisted, **What sayest thou of thyself?** (22) John's answer to this is both an affirmation and a denial: **I am the voice of one crying in the wilderness, Make straight the way of the Lord, as said the prophet Esaias** (Isaiah, 23). The denial is implied. He was not the Word, but a voice to declare the Word, hence both an affirmation and a fulfillment.

2. John's Relationship to the Coming One (1:24-28)

And they which were sent were of the Pharisees (24) is better translated: "Now they had been sent from the Pharisees" (NASB). Again the question was pressed in such a manner as to review ground already covered and yet designed to introduce a new query concerning baptism. **Why baptizest thou then, if thou be not that Christ, nor Elias, neither that prophet?** (25) Since the inquiring group had originated in Jerusalem with the Pharisees, it is only natural that this should be a point of question, for it was they who thought of themselves as the guardians of Jewish orthodoxy, particularly as related to forms and practices having to do with baptisms.

John's answer is a ready admission of his practice of baptism with water, a symbolic rite of purification (cf. Matt. 3:6; Mark 1:8; Luke 3:3, 12; 7:29). Evidently Jesus was in the company of those present when John talked about baptism, for he added, **But there standeth one among you, whom ye know not (26).** The NASB translation of 1:27 is better attested in the Greek manuscripts. It reads, ". . . he who comes after me, the thong of whose sandal I am not worthy to untie." John fulfilled his mission of herald as he recognized Him who is of true and ultimate worth, even as he was keenly aware of his own unworthiness in such a Presence.

The author makes note of the location where these events took place. **These things were done in Bethabara beyond Jordan, where John was baptizing** (28). Such indications of place are characteristic of the fourth Gospel and are evidence that the author was certainly an eyewitness. The exact location of the place here mentioned is not known today, and the problem is somewhat complicated by the fact that the oldest manuscripts read, "Bethany beyond Jordan." "Origen, a third century scholar residing in Palestine, insisted that the name was Bethabara."[2] Probably he is responsible for the change in the Greek text. Since early manuscripts do not support Origen's position it may be concluded that a place named Bethany is what the author had in mind. **Beyond Jordan** would be east of the Jordan, perhaps on the east bank of the river (see map 1).

3. *John's Witness Concerning the Lamb of God* (1:29-34)

The next day John seeth Jesus coming unto him, and saith, Behold the Lamb of God, which taketh away the sin of the world (29). **The next day** was the day after the opening events of the account (1:19). **Behold the Lamb of God.** The title here ascribed to Jesus quickly calls to mind the Suffering Servant prophecy in Isaiah 53, particularly the words in 53:7, "He is brought as a lamb to the slaughter" (cf. Jer. 11:19). In the New Testament, allusions to this idea abound (cf. Acts 8:32; I Cor. 5:7; I Pet. 1:19; Rev. 5:6, 8, 13; 6:16; 7:9; 12:11). It is evident from these that the title here ascribed to Jesus implies the idea of vicarious suffering and patient endurance as well as appropriate sacrifice. How could it be otherwise? Man has not made the provision for redemption; it proceeds from God. Hence the Baptist declares "Jesus to be the property of God, by whose complete obedience the normal sacrifices in the temple . . . were fulfilled and superseded"[3] (cf. Exod. 29:38-46; John 2:18-22).

It is true that the paschal Lamb was not either a sacrifice "to take away sin" in an expiatory sense, nor was it to carry away sin as did the scapegoat. Yet the full symbolism of the Passover along with the slain lamb portrayed the struggle between life and death, purity and uncleanness, wholeness and imperfection. The

[2]George Ernest Wright and Floyd Vivian Filson, *The Westminster Historical Atlas of the Bible* (Philadelphia: The Westminster Press, 1946), p. 85.

[3]Hoskyns, *op. cit.,* p. 176.

root is sin. Christ came from God to take away the sin of the world. "The *sin* of the world—not *sins* in the plural—is here contemplated . . . The *sin of the world* is a deeper stain than the sins of individual men and women; and the fourth Evangelist, who views the mission *sub specie aeternitatis*, sees that it is the sin of the *kosmos* (cf. v. 9), the lawlessness and rebellion of all created beings, that is the subject of redemption."[4]

John refers to his witness of the previous day (cf. 1:27, 30) with a reaffirmation of: (1) Jesus' absolutely superior and eternal being, **After me cometh a man which is preferred before me: for he was before me,** 30; (2) His own human limitation, **I knew him not,** 31, 33; (3) His favorable position as a witness, **I saw the Spirit descending from heaven like a dove,** 32, **And I saw, and bare record that this is the Son of God,** 34.

I knew him not (31, 33) probably means that John did not have the full assurance that Jesus was the Messiah. Being related to Jesus, he was probably acquainted with Him (cf. Matt. 3:14). But complete certainty as to His messiahship came only with the sign of the Spirit descending as a dove.

And John bare record, saying, I saw the Spirit descending from heaven like a dove, and it abode upon him (32). This is the first mention of the Spirit in the Gospel of John. Experience of and teaching about the Spirit were central in the life of the Early Church. These are evident in this Gospel. The Baptist predicted a baptism with the Holy Spirit (Matt. 3:11; Mark 1:8; Luke 3:16; John 1:33); Jesus was himself anointed by the Holy Spirit (Matt. 3:16; Mark 1:10; Luke 3:22; John 1:32); He promised the disciples that He would send to them the Holy Spirit (John 14:16-17; 15:26; 16:7); and the promise was fulfilled (20:22; Acts 1:8).

The witness of John the Baptist concerning Jesus' anointing sets the visible occurrence and the invisible truth side by side.[5] This marks the beginning of Jesus' public ministry and "for that receives, as true Man, the appropriate gifts. The Spirit by whom men are subjectively united to God descends upon the Word made Flesh, by whom objectively God is revealed to men."[6]

And I knew him not; but he that sent me to baptize with water, the same said unto me, Upon whom thou shalt see the

⁴Bernard, *op. cit.*, p. 47.
⁵Hoskyns, *op. cit.*, p. 177.
⁶Westcott, *op. cit.*, p. 21.

Spirit descending, and remaining on him, the same is he which baptizeth with the Holy Ghost (33). This declaration is one of vivid contrasts. In bold statements John at once affirms his genuine human ignorance, **I knew him not,** and the full assurance of certain and understandable revelation, **the same said unto me.** Then there is the contrast of the two baptisms: one with water, the other with the Spirit. The first speaks of the old order—the Law, prophets, Jewish rites and ceremonies. It was to this order that John belonged in part. But his baptism of repentance (Luke 3:3) and confession (Mark 1:5) leads to the new and fulfilling order centered in the person and work of Jesus Christ and climaxed in the baptism with the Holy Spirit (cf. Joel 2:28; Acts 2:17). John's is a "baptism with water only, which cannot purify the people of God. It can only make known the universal need of sanctification. The baptism of John can only direct men to Christ."[7]

This contrast between the old and the new (the latter always as the complete and perfect fulfillment of all that is foreshadowed in the former) is a regularly recurring pattern in both dialogue and event throughout the entire fourth Gospel. Though Jesus' statement, "I am not come to destroy, but to fulfil" (Matt. 5:17), does not appear in John as a parallel passage, its meaning is illustrated time and again by word and deed.

The veracity of John's witness concerning Jesus is certified by his recognition of the person of Jesus as the Son of God. **And I saw, and bare record that this is the Son of God (34).** This title **Son of God** is ascribed to Jesus by Nathanael (1:49) and Martha (11:27), and is used by the Synoptists (Matt. 14:33; 26:63; 27:40; Mark 3:11; Luke 22:70). It was a title that had "a definite meaning to Jewish ears, and was applied in the sense of 'Messiah.' "[8]

4. *John's Witness to His Disciples* (1:35-42)

Again the next day after John stood, and two of his disciples; and looking upon Jesus as he walked, he saith, Behold the Lamb of God! (35-36) This, the third day of these opening scenes, marks the actual beginning of Jesus' ministry. The transition from the personage and work of the Baptist to that of Jesus

[7]Hoskyns, *op. cit.,* p. 169.
[8]Bernard, *op. cit.,* p. 52.

is depicted in graphic style. John fades into the background; Jesus quickly takes the place of prominence (3:30).

The witness of John concerning Jesus, **Behold the Lamb of God!** was made in the presence of two of John's disciples, one of whom was Andrew (1:41). The identity of the second disciple is not directly given, but it is conjectured that he was John the Apostle. The following reasons are given: (1) The use of the word "first" in 1:41 **(He,** i.e., Andrew, **first findeth his own brother Simon)** implies either that Andrew first found his brother and then second, by implication, the other disciple found his brother, or that Andrew first found Simon before he himself did anything else. Many scholars (e.g., Westcott, Hoskyns) favor the former interpretation, which points to John and his brother James. (2) According to the Synoptic account the call of Andrew and Peter is closely related to the call of the other pair of brothers, James and John (Matt. 4:18-22; Mark 1:16-20; Luke 5:4-11). (3) The anonymity of the other disciple is in keeping with the author's consistent reluctance to use his own name (cf. John 13:23; 19:26; 20:2; 21:20).

Having established the identity of the two disciples of John the Baptist, it is now appropriate to follow the sequence of events on this momentous third day. When John made his witness concerning Jesus, apparently it was not addressed to his two disciples, although we read: **And the two disciples heard him (John) speak** (37). Neither was John's witness addressed to Jesus. He saw **Jesus as he walked** (36), gave his witness, and the two disciples **followed Jesus** (37), evidently away from John. This is the last we read of John, the forerunner, until 3:23, where there is an allusion to his baptizing.

As the two disciples followed Jesus, He turned and asked, **What seek ye?** (38) These first words of Jesus in John's Gospel are a question to the two disciples. The words are an appropriate beginning for meaningful dialogue. Were the disciples looking for something for themselves? Was their search born of selfishness? Was their shift from the Baptist to Jesus a seeking for advantage? Did they expect to find satisfaction for physical appetites (cf. 6:26), or an easy discipleship that involved no repentance or confession? The answer of the two shows insight. They were looking for Someone rather than something. **Rabbi, where dwellest thou?** was their fine response, at once an answer to Jesus' question and an affirmation of their deep concern. "For a thing (*what?*) these first disciples substituted a Person. They were in need of Christ first and not any special gift of Christ."⁓ The title by which they addressed Jesus, **Rabbi**, John translates to mean **Master** (Gk., "teacher"). The title occurs frequently in the fourth Gospel, and it is usually used to introduce "an unintelligent or at least an inadequate question or action"[10] (cf. 1:49; 3:2; 4:31; 6:25; 9:2; 11:8; 20:16).

Jesus' answer to the disciples is both an imperative and an invitation: **Come and see.** The imperative **Come** they matched with obedience: **They came.** The invitation **see** was rewarded with **They . . . saw where he dwelt** (39).

Alexander Maclaren finds, in vv. 37-39, "The First Disciples": (1) **What seek ye?** 3; (2) **Come and see,** 39; (3) **They came and saw,** 39.

The brothers, Andrew and Peter, were fishermen, as were James and John (Matt. 4:18, 21; Mark 1:16; Luke 5:3-10). It was Andrew, himself a new disciple of Jesus, who **findeth his own brother** (41). What a wonderful place to make a witness— in one's own home, to one's own loved ones! There is also implied a searching witness. Some have to be sought out. The lost must be found. Further, Andrew's witness was clear. **We have found the Messias.** Long looked for, promised by God through the prophets, the Messiah has been identified, He has been found! Andrew's witness was not only personal and clear, but it was forceful. **He brought him to Jesus** (42). Men have to be brought to the place of confrontation with Jesus the Christ.

John gives no indication that Peter said anything at this first meeting with Jesus. There is a time when God speaks and all man needs to do is to hear what He says. **And when Jesus beheld him, he said, Thou art Simon the son of Jona: thou shalt be called Cephas, which is by interpretation, A stone** (42). Jesus saw Peter not only as he was but as he could become through God's transforming grace—**Thou art . . . thou shalt be.** By natural name **Simon**, the new man would be **Cephas** (Aramaic) or **Peter** (Gk.), signifying the new nature, a rock. The name Simon he received from his parents; the name Peter (a new nature) he received as God's gift, a gift that goes to all who respond in faith. What God wants to do, is able to do, and will do for any

⁹Westcott, *op. cit.*, p. 24.
¹⁰Hoskyns, *op. cit.*, p. 179.

man who responds in submissive faith is prefigured here in what happened to Peter.

B. PHILIP AND NATHANAEL, 1:43-51

Jesus now takes the initiative. It is His desire to go from Bethany to Galilee (see map 1), where with purposeful intent He **findeth Philip, and saith unto him, Follow me** (43).[11] The call to Philip, whom John describes to be of the same Galilean city (Bethsaida) as Andrew and Peter, issued in Philip's personal search for and witness to Nathanael. **Philip findeth Nathanael, and saith unto him, We have found him, of whom Moses in the law, and the prophets, did write, Jesus of Nazareth, the son of Joseph** (45). In this statement it is important to note (1) the wording of Philip's witness, and (2) the person to whom the witness was made.

Philip's witness indicated that he himself had been searching the Old Testament scriptures, and this search had disclosed that Moses and the prophets had alike written about One who was to come. The Messianic hope burned within Philip's bosom. It is also evident that Philip recognized Jesus of Nazareth to be this One. However, his witness fell short of the full truth concerning Jesus' nature, for he described Him as **"Jesus . . . son of Joseph."**[12]

Nathanael means "gift of God" and is comparable to the Greek name Theodore. Some have identified him with the Bartholomew of the Synoptics, particularly in view of the fact that Bartholomew is not mentioned in John nor is Nathanael named except in John.

That he was a student of the Old Testament scriptures is evident from the fact that Philip's statement about Moses and the Law was meaningful to him. Also he had no reason based on prophecy to expect the Messiah to come from so poor a village —**Can there any good thing come out of Nazareth?** (46) Nathanael's skepticism was quickly matched by Philip's insistence, **Come and see** (46). Such action always provides the setting for the human-divine encounter.

Nathanael's question, **Can there any good thing come out of**

---

[11]The reading of the best Greek text would allow Peter to be the subject of the verbs "would" and "find," which would make a most interesting sequence: Andrew finds and brings Peter; Peter finds Philip; and Philip finds Nathanael. All these were fellow Galileans and friends.

[12]Bernard, *op. cit.,* p. 62.

Nazareth? (46) provokes the question to the modern mind, Who is Jesus? The context of the question provides an illuminating answer: (1) He is the adequate Sacrifice for man's sin, 29; (2) He is the One who baptizes with the Holy Spirit, 33; (3) He is the great Teacher of men, 38; (4) He is the King, the only One worthy of man's highest allegiance, 49.

Nathanael is the image of the ideal son of Jacob, **an Israelite indeed, in whom is no guile!** (47) He is pictured sitting under his fig tree, a symbol of the highest and best that the old order of law and prophets could possibly produce (cf. I Kings 4:25; Mic. 4:4). It was this kind of man that Jesus saw in Nathanael, and it was this kind of man (a true Israelite) who would dare to make the great confession, **Rabbi, thou art the Son of God; thou art the King of Israel** (49).

Jesus put the question to Nathanael: **Because I said unto thee, I saw thee under the fig tree, believest thou? Thou shalt see greater things than these** (50). A man does not have real faith because he sees, or receives. Rather, a man of faith knows, and because he knows, he sees greater things—an open heaven, even God's full revelation in the Son of Man. So Jesus said to Nathanael, **Verily, verily, I say unto you, Hereafter ye shall see heaven open, and the angels of God ascending and descending upon the Son of man** (51).

The phrase **Verily, verily** is found only in John's Gospel— always on the lips of Jesus. It means "truly, truly."

The imagery of v. 51 recalls that of Jacob's vision (Gen. 28:12). In both cases the angels, who have been ministering to men, are seen as first ascending to heaven and then descending again to earth.

The ladder which Jacob saw reaching from earth to heaven typified Christ Jesus, the "one mediator between God and men" (I Tim. 2:5). The ministering angels are thought of as ascending and descending upon Him. Jacob's ancient dream was fulfilled in Israel's Messiah.

In this first chapter of John there are eight highly descriptive and different titles ascribed to the Incarnate One. He is Logos, the living "Word" (1, 14); "the Lamb of God," the perfect Sacrifice (29); "Son of God," very God (34, 49); "Rabbi," the Master Teacher (38); "Messias," "Christ," the Anointed One (41); "Jesus of Nazareth," the God-man in history (45); "King of Israel," the One crowned King by those who put their faith in Him (49); and, "the Son of man," very man (51).

Section **III** *The Signs*

Beginning with chapter two there is recorded a series of miracles or signs. These signs are given for a specific purpose, which is stated in the theme of the Gospel, that the reader "might believe that Jesus is the Christ, the Son of God" (20:31).

Since this part of the Gospel of John comprises about one-half the entire content (cc. 2—12), it is important to note some of its general characteristics. It is clearly evident that the author organized his materials around the mighty works and deeds of Jesus, beginning with the turning of water into wine and culminating with the raising of Lazarus from the dead. However the incident of the cleansing of the Temple, though recorded early in John's account (2:13-21), is an action that Jesus clearly and intentionally associated with the greatest of signs and miracles, His resurrection from the dead (2:18-22).

The relating of some of the signs to the national feasts of the Jews is with point and purpose, and is a frequently recurring pattern (5:1; 6:4; 7:14, 37; 12:1). This may be due in part to the fact that the preponderance of the events took place in Judea, but such could not be the reason for the comment preceding the feeding of the five thousand by the Sea of Galilee—"And the passover, a feast of the Jews, was nigh" (6:4). It is quite evident that this part of the author's plan was to show Jesus Christ as the perfect Fulfillment of everything foreshadowed in the Law as portrayed in the feasts.

Another general characteristic of John's record of the signs is that proportionately the account of the event itself is quite brief when compared to the comment, discourse, dialogue, or debate that follows. In fact, dialogue is a prominent feature in this section (cc. 3—4). The elements of debate (6:22-65; 8:12-59) and drama (9:1-41) are used to heighten the meaning and significance of the signs and miracles.

The reader of this section of the Gospel will do well to keep in mind that there is the constantly recurring theme of the contrast between the old way of the Law, and the new way; that is, faith in Jesus Christ. The old way is regularly symbolized by water—e.g., "six waterpots" (2:6); "born of water" (3:5); "Jacob

. . . gave us the well" (4:12); "there is at Jerusalem . . . a pool"
(5:2); "Go, wash in the pool of Siloam" (9:7). The new way is
evident in each instance, for the coming of Jesus into the event
always meant fulfillment and completion—e.g., "thou hast kept
the good wine until now" (2:10); "born . . . of the Spirit" (3:5);
"the water that I shall give him shall be in him a well of water
springing up into everlasting life" (4:14); "And immediately the
man was made whole" (5:9); "He went his way therefore, and
washed, and came seeing" (9:7).

Beginning with the account of the healing of the impotent
man in chapter five the signs become occasions for debate about
the meaning and purpose of the Law, and Jesus' relationship to
it. It is usually the Sabbath laws that are the point of issue.
Further, this conflict over the healing of the impotent man marks
the beginning of the hostility of the Jews, which increases and
finally culminates in the Cross.

A. THE NEW WINE, 2:1-12

This beginning of miracles (2:11), recorded only in the
fourth Gospel, is a fitting introduction to all that is to follow.

> No other miracle has so much of prophecy in it; no other, there-
> fore, would have inaugurated so fitly the whole future work of the
> Son of God. For that work might be characterized throughout as
> an ennobling of the common, and a transmuting of the mean; a
> turning of the water of life into the wine of heaven.[1]

And the third day there was a marriage in Cana of Galilee
(1). The timing of this event has a dual significance. The first,
purely chronological, relates this to the event of the conversation
with Nathanael. The literal translation would be "the day after
tomorrow" or "two days later." The promise to Nathanael that
he would see an open heaven could not be delayed in its fulfillment. It was on this **third day** that **Jesus . . . manifested his
glory; and his disciples believed on him** (11).

The miracle took place at Cana, about nine miles north of
the city of Nazareth (see map 1).[2] The designation **Cana of
Galilee** is probably to distinguish it from another Cana near

---

[1]Richard Chenevix Trench, *The Miracles of Our Lord* (New York:
D. Appleton and Company, 1873), p. 105.

[2]The traditional site is Kefr Kenna, four miles northeast of Nazareth,
on the road to Capernaum. But most scholars today prefer Khirbet Qana,
about nine miles north of Nazareth. The name means "place of reeds."

Tyre, or possibly to mark the change of the place of events from Perea to Galilee.

There was a marriage. Though this was a historical event, the wedding is a frequently used metaphor in Jesus' teaching about the nature of the coming Kingdom. The Kingdom is compared to a royal marriage (Matt. 22:2). Jesus describes himself as a Bridegroom and His disciples as guests (Mark 2:19-20). In another setting Jesus is the Bridegroom and John the Baptist is the friend or "best man" (3:29). In other New Testament figures the Church is the bride and Christ is the Bridegroom (II Cor. 11:2; Rev. 21:2). In an extended metaphor Paul speaks of the Church as the bride of Christ (Eph. 5:22-32).

And the mother of Jesus was there. And both Jesus was called, and his disciples, to the marriage (1-2). The mother of Jesus is not mentioned by name in this Gospel, a fact which is of interest when one remembers that the disciple John is also not mentioned by name. Her presence at the wedding seems to have been prior to the coming of Jesus and the disciples. This, with her later remark to Jesus about the lack of wine, indicates that she was in some way related to the family. It would in turn explain why Jesus and His disciples were invited.

And when they wanted wine, the mother of Jesus saith unto him, They have no wine (3). The first clause may be translated literally, "And when the wine had run out." This amounted to a social catastrophe for the families of the bride and groom. There is a Jewish saying, "Without wine there is no joy," and this would be particularly true at a festive occasion such as a wedding. The fact that the wedding celebration lasted over a period of several days only complicated the already embarrassing situation.

Mary's report to Jesus, **They have no wine,** supports the literal translation "when the wine had run out." The question is, Why did she tell this to Jesus? Was it a subtle suggestion that they should leave? Did she say it loudly enough that others could hear, and all the guests could make preparation to leave in order to avoid embarrassment for the bride and groom? Or did she have an idea that Jesus, her Son whom she knew so well, had a solution for the problem? In any case, there is a very practical lesson here. Learn to tell Him every need, even though the need seems to be ever so mundane.

Jesus saith unto her, Woman, what have I to do with thee? mine hour is not yet come (4). Jesus' response to His mother is by no means brusque, crude, or unkind. The word **woman** as used in that day was "perfectly respectful and even intimate."[3]

What have I to do with thee? Again, these words as they appear in the KJV seem to be somewhat abrupt, even to the point of being harsh. But such is not the case. A literal translation would be, "What to Me and to you?" or, "What is there in common between My point of view and your point of view?" Jesus was asking His mother if she really understood His nature, mission, and ultimate sacrifice.

This is made even more evident by the explanatory statement which He added, **mine hour is not yet come.** What did Jesus mean? Two ideas are clear when one examines the other passages where this expression occurs. First, it is evident that no man could alter God's plan and purpose of redemption (7:30; 8:20). Second, in some mysterious and yet glorious way Jesus' "finest hour" was the Cross. That which evil men intended as death and shame was transmuted into life and glory (12:23; 13:1; 17:1).

His mother saith unto the servants, Whatsoever he saith unto you, do it (5). Whatever else may be conjectured about Mary's estimate of Jesus' nature and mission, one thing is certain here: He is worthy of trust and obedience.

And there were set there six waterpots of stone, after the manner of the purifying of the Jews, containing two or three firkins apiece. Jesus saith unto them, Fill the waterpots with water. And they filled them up to the brim (6-7). These were large stone jars holding between eighteen and twenty-seven gallons each. All the guests were supposed to wash their feet when entering. It is not accidental that John tells of their function as related to **the manner of the purifying of the Jews.** For these vessels represent the whole way of the Law, legalism, which is shown to be: (1) inadequate for the real needs of man (**They have no wine,** 2:3); (2) limited in comparison with the full scope and abundant joy in the gospel as symbolized by wine in such a large quantity (cf. 1:16; 7:38; 16:24); (3) less than God's best for man (cf. 2:10; Heb. 10:1). "The old legal religion 'lacks wine', all the life energy is gone from it."[4]

And he saith unto them, Draw out now, and bear unto the governor of the feast. And they bare it. When the ruler of the

---

[3]G. H. C. Macgregor, *The Gospel of John,* "The Moffatt New Testament Commentary" (New York: Harper and Brothers Publisher, n.d.), p. 51.

[4]Macgregor, *loc. cit.*

feast had tasted the water that was made wine, and knew not whence it was: (but the servants which drew the water knew;) the governor of the feast called the bridegroom, and saith unto him, Every man at the beginning doth set forth good wine; and when men have well drunk, then that which is worse: but thou has kept the good wine until now (8-10). The presence of the Lord of life and Giver of true joy transformed the whole scene. Resources that had been inadequate for man's needs (3) now became abundant. Resources that had been limited in scope and a threat to man's real joy now flowed in rich profusion. Resources that were less than the best, **that which is worse**, are now God's best for man, **thou hast kept the good wine until now**. At its best, the Law was "a shadow of good things to come" (Heb. 10:1); but now, in Jesus Christ, the good things have come, available to all men, adequate for man's deepest needs (cf. 1:17).

It is evident that "Man's Disappointment Is God's Appointment." (1) Man's insufficiency is met by divine adequacy, 3, 7, 10; (2) Sorrow is turned to joy, 3, 10; (3) Man's own shabby resources are supplanted by God's best, 10.

This beginning of miracles did Jesus in Cana of Galilee, and manifested forth his glory; and his disciples believed on him (11). The initial purpose of the sign or miracle was immediately accomplished. It is twofold. **Jesus . . . manifested forth his glory.** Concerning this Lightfoot comments:

> . . . any action of the Lord, the Word become flesh, is of necessity a manifestation of His glory; but . . . a full revelation of that glory is only made with the completion of His work, upon the cross. Hence in our thought of the Lord's one work, His life and His death cannot be separated.[5]

The manifestation of Jesus' glory produced the desired results: **and his disciples believed on him.** Here is the culmination of a typical sequence in John's Gospel—a sign, evident glory, faith (cf. 20:31). This account of the disciples' response could well be translated, "And his disciples put their faith into Him." Here discipleship becomes personal faith, faith that is dynamic, faith that is "the absolute transference of trust from oneself to another."[6]

Under "The First Miracle in Cana," Alexander Maclaren notes (1) The revelation of our Lord's creative power, 8-10;

[5]*Op. cit.*, p. 102.
[6]Westcott, *op. cit.*, p. 39.

(2) Our Lord's purpose to hallow all family life, 1-2; (3) Our Lord as the One who transforms the water of earthly gladness into the wine of heavenly blessedness, 6-8; (4) Our Lord's glory as supplying the deficiencies of earthly sources, 3.

After this he went down to Capernaum, he, and his mother, and his brethren, and his disciples: and they continued there not many days (12). This note of transition seems simply a geographical observation. Leaving Cana of Galilee, those who had been guests at the wedding journeyed to Capernaum (see map 1) on the north shore of the Sea of Galilee, where they remained only a few days.

B. The New Temple, 2:13-22

And the Jews' passover was at hand, and Jesus went up to Jerusalem (13). What is about to take place is carefully described as to time and place, for both are important. The beginning and ending of Jesus' public ministry are associated with the Jews' Passover at Jerusalem. It is evident that part of John's plan is to show Jesus the Christ as the complete and perfect Fulfillment of the Law, the best and highest in Judaism. It is therefore appropriate that this opening public event in Jesus' ministry should be associated with the Passover, the greatest of feasts of the Jews, and that it should take place at Jerusalem, the only and true Zion for every child of Israel.

1. *The Cleansing of the Old* (2:14-17)

And (He) found in the temple those that sold oxen and sheep and doves, and the changers of money sitting: and when he had made a scourge of small cords, he drove them all out of the temple, and the sheep, and the oxen; and poured out the changers' money, and overthrew the tables; and said unto them that sold doves, Take these things hence; make not my Father's house an house of merchandise (14-16). God's house had become corrupted. That which was to be holy, set apart for sacred uses only, had been profaned. This is what Jesus found when He went to the holy place in the Holy City. The Law, with all its safeguards against profanation of the sacred and holy, had not been able to cope with evil and selfish men. So here they were, merchants and money changers with their wares—Roman coins, and Tyrian half shekels for payment of the annual head tax into the Temple treasury.

What Jesus did here is entirely in keeping with His nature and character. There are some who think that all that can be said about Him is "gentle Jesus, meek and mild." It is true that He is loving and forgiving. He does describe himself as "meek and lowly in heart" (Matt. 11:29). But there is more than that, and in this incident one sees another aspect of His nature. He does not deal easily nor light-handedly with evil. He is a Light that shines in darkness (John 1:5). He sent word to Herod, "Go ye, and tell that fox" (Luke 13:32). The Pharisees did not find His words soothing, or His appellations pleasing. "You . . . white-washed tombs" (Matt. 23:27, RSV); "You serpents, you brood of vipers, how are you to escape being sentenced to hell?" (Matt. 23:33, RSV); "You blind guides" (Matt. 23:24, RSV). So here, evil men were confronted by Jesus, the Source of light, right, good, and integrity. He took the **scourge of small cords** and **drove them all out of the temple.** The word translated **drove** is a strong term that means "He threw them out of the Temple." This has been described as "a wild scene, with cowering figures clutching desperately at their tables, as these were flung here and there; or running after their spilled coins, as these rolled hither and thither; or shrinking from the lash that had no mercy till the holy place was cleansed."[7]

And his disciples remembered that it was written, The zeal of thine house hath eaten me up (17). The scripture is taken from Ps. 69:9. The tense in the original is the future: "will consume me." It is as though the disciples saw that Jesus' struggle with evil would eventuate in a cross, yet they did not realize that the Cross was the complement of the empty tomb.

2. *The Sign of the New* (2:18-22)

Then answered the Jews and said unto him, What sign shewest thou unto us, seeing that thou doest these things? (18) Though they are described here by the general term **Jews,** the question evidently came from the high priest's party, the Sadducees, who controlled the Temple revenues.[8] Their question was more than a request for a sign. It was also a challenge of Jesus' authority to do what He had just done in the Temple (cf. Mat-

---

[7]Arthur John Gossip, "The Gospel According to St. John" (Exposition), *The Interpreter's Bible,* ed. George A. Buttrick, *et al.,* VIII (New York: Abingdon-Cokesbury Press, 1952), 497.

[8]*Ibid.,* p. 499.

thew 23; Mark 11:28; Luke 20:2). The Jews had an inclination
to demand a miracle as a basis for their acceptance of the reality
of the divine truth. They would believe only if they could see
(John 6:30).

Jesus' answer to their question was simple, yet in language
with double meaning. **Destroy this temple, and in three days I
will raise it up** (19). The word used for **temple** in the account
of the cleansing is *hieron* (2:14). This is "the whole sacred enclosure, with the courts and porticoes [see Chart *A*], which is
never used metaphorically," while *naos* (2:19) is "the actual
sacred building, used below of the body of Christ (v. 21), and of
Christians who form His spiritual body"[9] (cf. I Cor. 3:16-17;
6:19; II Cor. 6:16). It is evident from the response of **the Jews**
(20) that they took Jesus to mean the restored Temple, the actual
building. But He was speaking **of the temple** (*naos*) **of his body**
(21).

Further, what Jesus said here (19) was used as a part of the
accusation against Him by the false witnesses at His trial. One
said, "We heard him say, I will destroy this temple that is made
with hands, and within three days I will build another made
without hands" (Mark 14:58). Another said, "This fellow said,
I am able to destroy the temple of God, and to build it in three
days" (Matt. 26:61). The hecklers at the Cross repeated the
accusations (Matt. 27:40; Mark 15:29). Jesus actually said
neither, "I will destroy," nor, "I am able to destroy," nor, "I will
build another," nor, "I am able to build another." Rather He
said, **Destroy this temple** (i.e., "If you destroy this temple") . . .
I will raise it up. It is obvious that Jesus spoke about the role
of the Jews in the event of the Cross, the Resurrection, the end
of the old Jewish system of sacrifice and ritual, the institution of
the new order with all the meanings that belong to the body of
Christ. "His cleansing of the temple, therefore, dramatically signifies that Jesus' very body is the place where God is propitiated.
Without this atonement, all the temple sacrifices become empty;
with it, they become superfluous."[10]

**Then said the Jews, Forty and six years was this temple
in building, and wilt thou rear it up in three days? But he
spake of the temple of his body** (20-21). "It has taken forty-six

[9]Westcott, *op. cit.*, p. 41.

[10]Carl F. H. Henry, "John," *The Biblical Expositor*, consulting editor,
Carl F. H. Henry (Philadelphia: A. J. Holman Company, 1960), III, 163.

years to build this temple" (RSV) reflects the true state of affairs. Herod's Temple was begun in 19-20 B.C., and at the time of this incident it was not complete. But it had taken forty-six years to bring it to its current state. **Three days** obviously refers to the time between the Crucifixion and the Resurrection, though it was by no means evident to the Jews who heard, nor even to the disciples until after Jesus' resurrection, as John makes clear. **When therefore he was risen from the dead, his disciples remembered that he had said this unto them; and they believed the scripture, and the word which Jesus had said (22).** It is conjectured in the light of Acts 13:35 that **the scripture** John meant was Ps. 16:10: "For thou wilt not leave my soul in hell; neither wilt thou suffer thine Holy One to see corruption."

C. The New Insight into Man, 2:23—5:47

The three concluding verses of chapter two are at once a transition and an introduction. They are a transition in that, whereas Jesus has been dealing with groups of persons (at the wedding and in the Temple), He now focuses attention and discourse on the individual man and his basic needs. It is an introduction in that it opens the door to dialogue, a new and important style in the Gospel.

Now, when he was in Jerusalem at the passover, in the feast day, many believed in his name, when they saw the miracles which he did (23). It is evident that, at the Passover, Jesus did many signs that appealed to the people. What the miracles were John does not say (cf. 20:30). But the response was a quality of faith that is less than the best. In fact, it is thought by some to be a false faith.[11] There is no doubt that faith based only on signs is less than Jesus demands, and there is no indication that such faith issues in life (cf. 3:16; 6:29, 35). As it was then, so it is now: some will believe only if they can see a sign—the unusual or spectacular.

But Jesus did not commit himself unto them, because he knew all men, and needed not that any should testify of man: for he knew what was in man (24-25). Several of the newer translations say that Jesus did "not trust himself to them" (NEB). The reserve with which Jesus held himself in His self-revelation is evident here. Miracles and signs—these He would

---

[11]Westcott, *op. cit.*, p. 45.

do. But, even as He told His mother (2:4), His "hour"—the Cross, the full revelation—had not yet come. He knew that when He did commit himself fully to men, because of man's evil heart, the Cross would be inevitable. When God did His best, the Incarnation, Satan and evil men did their worst, the Cross.

Jesus' divine knowledge about men is a startling fact. John wanted his readers to know that, whenever a man is confronted by Jesus of Nazareth, that man's deepest needs and darkest sins are laid bare. Nicodemus could not hide the deadness of his soul. The Samaritan woman found no cover for the shame of her guilt-ridden past. The man by the pool could not help but disclose his own utter helplessness. **He knew what was in man** (25). In our day of humanism man is taught early and late that he is responsible only to himself and to his fellowmen. Though this may sound good, it is only a half-truth. The other half is that man is responsible to God, and any sin is first a sin against God (Ps. 51:4).

1. *New Life for a Dead Man—Nicodemus* (3:1-21)

One of the occasional misfortunes of chapter divisions in the Bible is a break in the thought where there ought not to be one. The beginning of chapter three is an excellent example of this. John wrote of Jesus that "he knew what was in man" (2:25). But John went right on and wrote without any break in line or thought, **There was a man of the Pharisees, named Nicodemus, a ruler of the Jews** (1). It is as though John were saying, "Jesus had perfect insight into man's deepest need. Let me cite a few examples, beginning with a man, the Pharisee Nicodemus." So Nicodemus becomes "Exhibit *A*" to illustrate what Jesus knows about man.

The word for **man** in both 2:25 and 3:1 is *anthropos,* which basically refers to man as a class. It is a generic word. So what is said here about Nicodemus, an individual man, is said of all men. This is one of the many universalizations in the Gospel of John. It is not only that salvation is for "whosoever" (16), but it is also true that all men are in need of the birth from above (cf. Rom. 3:23).

The care with which Nicodemus' station in Jewish religious life is described is not accidental. He was **a man of the Pharisees . . . a ruler of the Jews.** If any man in the old order knew the meaning of God and His plans and purposes for man, it should have been Nicodemus—deeply saturated in the monotheistic tradition, along with the teachings of the Law, the history of Israel, and the proclamations of the prophets. But somewhere, somehow, he had missed the way, and in that same measure he typifies what had happened to Judaism. So once again John sets forth here a vivid contrast between the old order with all of its inadequacies, misunderstandings, and failures, and the new order that insures abundance of life that has the true and living God as its Source.

The same came to Jesus by night (2). There has been a great deal of speculation about why Nicodemus came **by night**. Some have said that it was because he was fearful of the opinions of others, particularly his peers. There is something to be said for this in the light of the other two occasions where he appears in this Gospel. His defense of Jesus in 7:50 seems to be somewhat impersonal, and it was Joseph of Arimathaea who initiated the request for the body of Jesus (19:39). Perhaps Nicodemus wanted a quiet, nighttime conference. But a better question about his coming would be, Why did he come at all? The answer to this may explain why he came **by night**. Because of the deep hunger of his soul he came to the Lord out of darkness in which he and his peers were immersed. Compare this with Judas' action. When he left Jesus to identify himself with the Jews, he went out, "and it was night" (13:30). The vivid contrast between light and darkness appears regularly throughout the Gospel (cf. 1:5, 9; 3:19; 8:12; 9:4-5; 12:35).

Nicodemus said, **Rabbi, we know that thou art a teacher come from God: for no man can do these miracles that thou doest, except God be with him** (2). The signs that Jesus had performed (2:23) pointed the way for Nicodemus and those whom he represented (note the plural **we know**). Because of these miracles they thought Jesus to be a special, divinely sent teacher. **Rabbi . . . thou art . . . come from God**. But this was not to recognize him as Messiah.[12]

Jesus answered and said unto him, Verily, verily, I say unto thee, Except a man be born again, he cannot see the kingdom of God (3). With unhampered insight Jesus went right to the heart of Nicodemus' problem. There must be a new kind of life if one is even to see God's presence, His plan and purpose for man. Westcott says:

[12]Bernard, *op. cit.,* p. 101.

53

> Without this new birth—this introduction into a vital con-
> nexion with a new order of being, with a corresponding endowment
> of faculties—no man can see—can outwardly apprehend—the king-
> dom of God. Our natural powers cannot realise that which is essen-
> tially spiritual. A new vision is required for the objects of a new
> order.[13]

But such new vision is impossible apart from new life. Jesus
is careful to designate the source of this new life. **Except a man
be born again** really has a double meaning. The word translated
again is *anothen*, and has the various meanings, "from above,"
"again," and "anew."[14] The word is used by John with the
obvious meaning "from above" in 3:31 and 19:11. Such could
have been Jesus' intention here. If man is to have life in the
eternal and real sense, it must come from above. Biological life
is passed to offspring by parents, but God's life He alone can
give (1:13) and it is from above. The meaning **again** is given
credence because Nicodemus' reply uses the words **a second time.**
Evidently this is what Nicodemus understood Jesus to say. The
meaning "anew" (RSV) provides a fortunate translation here,
for it combines the idea of something new and different—"from
above"—as well as the idea of **again.**

**Nicodemus saith unto him, How can a man be born when
he is old? can he enter the second time into his mother's womb,
and be born? Jesus answered, Verily, verily, I say unto thee,
Except a man be born of water and of the Spirit, he cannot enter
into the kingdom of God** (4-5). Nicodemus' questions reflect
more than simply his misunderstanding of Jesus' declaration. It
could be that he understood too well! How could he believe that
a man **when he is old** could be transformed into a new creature?
It might even reflect his own feeling of lostness in the night of sin
and death, where not even the highest form of religion had been
able to bring light and life. Inadequate and false indeed is that
religion which does not transform a man even as a birth anew!

Jesus' response to Nicodemus' questions at once fortifies His
earlier declaration, and sums up in one pregnant statement the
whole plan of redemption for man. **Except a man be born of
water and of the Spirit, he cannot enter into the kingdom of
God** (5). The word here translated **a man** is the indefinite pro-

[13]*Op. cit.,* p. 48.

[14]Arndt and Gingrich, *op. cit.,* p. 76.

noun *tis* and could well read, "any man." What is said here is a universalization. It is true for any man, not just Nicodemus. But why the shift from **born anew** (3) to **born of water and of the Spirit** (5)? A quick look at the use of the word **water** in its contexts (1:33; 2:6-7; 4:6-7; 5:2-3; 7:38-39) discloses that in this Gospel it is a symbol of the old order of the Law with its ritual of baptisms, purifications, and cleansings. One must keep in mind that (1) Jesus declared He came to fulfill and not to destroy the Law (Matt. 5:17); (2) in each of these instances referred to above, the order represented by water was not destroyed—e.g., the six water jars were not broken but filled; (3) in each, water is set in context with a new order—e.g., Spirit (1:33), the new wine (2:10), "a well of water springing up into everlasting life" (4:14), wholeness (5:9), Spirit (7:39); (4) in this instance (3:10) He was talking to "the teacher of Israel" (ASV). In view of this it is easy to understand why He said **born of water and of the Spirit.** It is as though He said: "Nicodemus, begin where you are. But fulfillment, life, the solving of your innermost problem will come only with birth from above, the birth of the Spirit!" Compare 3:5 with 19:34 and I John 5:6-8.

That which is born of the flesh is flesh; and that which is born of the Spirit is spirit (6). Like produces like. The old order could produce only the old life. Darkness begets darkness. The Law, which is for the lawless, cannot give birth to the good life. If one is to have life, the source must be the Spirit. The preposition used in this last clause is most graphic. A literal translation would read, "That which is born *out of* the Spirit is spirit."

Marvel not that I said unto thee, Ye must be born again. The wind bloweth where it listeth, and thou hearest the sound thereof, but canst not tell whence it cometh, and whither it goeth: so is every one that is born of the Spirit (7-8). The argument by analogy here is particularly potent because it is based on a play on the word *pneuma,* which means both "wind" and "spirit." The fact of wind no one can deny; its behavior—whence and whither—no one, not even the teacher, fully knows. There is an element of mystery. So why should one be "stopped" by the element of mystery in the new birth? "The great mystery of religion is not the punishment, but the forgiveness of sin: not the natural permanence of character, but spiritual regeneration."[15]

[15]Westcott, *op. cit.,* p. 49.

Nicodemus answered and said unto him, How can these things be? Jesus answered and said unto him, Art thou a master of Israel, and knowest not these things? (9-10). Jesus' thrice repeated declaration of the theme, "Ye must be born again" (3, 5, 7), along with His illustration of the natural phenomenon of the wind, left Nicodemus filled with wonder and amazement. Likewise, Jesus seemed not a little taken back by the lack of spiritual understanding on the part of "the teacher of Israel" (ASV). The use of the definite article with "teacher," which appears in the Greek, is not accidental. Since Nicodemus represented the best in Judaism, failure at this point speaks of the spiritual deadness, darkness, and ignorance which characterized the old order. It was to this order as well as to Nicodemus that Jesus came to give life, even abundant life (10:10).

Verily, verily, I say unto thee, We speak that we do know, and testify that we have seen; and ye receive not our witness. If I have told you earthly things, and ye believe not, how shall ye believe, if I tell you of heavenly things? (11-12). The use of the plurals we and ye provides some problems for the exegete. We speak . . . and testify, according to Westcott, alludes to Jesus and those whom He had gathered around Him.[16] Bernard rejects this on the ground that this linking of Jesus' witness with that of His disciples is not characteristic of John's record. He contends rather that this use of the plural we is editorial.[17] In either case it is instructive to note that the we is set in vivid contrast with ye. The giving of the witness is parallel with the rejection of the witness. Thus the totality of the witness (i.e., the Incarnation and those who believe) is set in contrast with the rejection of the witness by the Jews (cf. 1:10-11).

There are many who dichotomize the world and spiritual experience. Earthly things speak to them of certainty and reality. Heavenly things speak to them of mystery, the unreal, and superstition. But, as Jesus so clearly pointed out to Nicodemus, all of life is a matter of some mystery. Even the most learned scientists stand in awe when faced with the problem of the meaning of the universe. No man can live without some kind of faith in someone or something.

And no man hath ascended up to heaven, but he that came down from heaven, even the Son of man which is in heaven

[16]*Ibid.*, p. 52.
[17]*Op. cit.*, p. 110.

(13). The last clause, **which is in heaven,** does not appear in many of the oldest MSS. The verse speaks of the Incarnation as being the exclusive authoritative witness about heavenly things (i.e., the things of the Spirit). The expression **he that came down from heaven** is peculiar to John, and clearly refers to the Incarnation (6:33, 38, 41-42, 50-51, 58). The use of the title **Son of man** simply fortifies this statement.

And as Moses lifted up the serpent in the wilderness, even so must the Son of man be lifted up: that whosoever believeth in him should not perish, but have eternal life (14-15). Because the children of Israel "spake against God, and against Moses . . . the Lord sent fiery serpents among the people" (Num. 21:5-6). The repentant survivors, threatened with death, appealed to Moses. At the Lord's instruction Moses provided a serpent of brass fixed to a pole, which was raised up for the smitten to see. Those who looked lived. Jesus knew that **even so must the Son of man be lifted up.** The necessity of the Cross is twofold. The first is the kind of world into which Christ came. "The Incarnation, under the actual circumstances of humanity, carried with it the necessity of the Passion."[18] The second is the love that sent Him. Such love is the expression of the divine nature, a supreme effort to reach and redeem lost men who are under the sting and sentence of death. The whole figure is a kind of paradox that says, Though it be an instrument of death, there is life in the Cross.

The **whosoever believeth** speaks of the universal gospel, that is, the good news for all men. There are no barriers of nation, race, or time. The perfect sacrifice has been made. It is for man to respond, to have faith. The Greek uses the preposition *eis,* meaning "into," with the verb *believe.* A literal translation would be "that whosoever puts faith into Him." Faith is man's perfect response to God's call and claim on him.

This is the first mention of **eternal life,** the gift that goes to those who have faith. What a fitting climax to Jesus' discourse with Nicodemus, who had come out of darkness and death to Him who is Light and Life! The reward is life eternal.

Authorities differ as to where the discourse of Jesus and Nicodemus ends. Some see the end at 13, others 15, and still others 21. However most scholars feel that 16 begins John's reflection and comment on what Jesus had said.

[18]Westcott, *op. cit.,* p. 53.

From the story of Nicodemus (3:1-15) Alexander Maclaren raises the question "Teacher or Saviour?" (1) The imperfect confession, 1-2; (2) Jesus Christ deals with the imperfect confession, 3-15; (3) The courageous confessor, John 7:50-52; 19:38-39.

For God so loved the world, that he gave his only begotten Son, that whosoever believeth in him should not perish, but have everlasting life (16). This is the first mention of God's love in this Gospel. It is a dominant theme in the book, though little more is said of it until chapter 13. **God so loved the world.** Here again is the universal outreach. It is to all men. None are excluded. This describes why God did what He did. He loved! The word in the Greek is *egapesen.* This is the love that moves in the interest of others with no thought for self. It is a love willing to risk all for the possible advantage of another, that counts no price too great if another can receive benefit. The aorist tense of the verb indicates that God's act of love is without limitation of time while also being one and complete. It is love absolute!

He gave his only begotten Son. Though this act is much more frequently described by the verb "sent" (e.g., 3:17, 34; 6:29, 38-40), here the idea emphasized is God's gift to man (cf. 4:10). Again, the tense of the verb **gave** speaks of the absolute and complete act of giving (cf. Heb. 10:14). He gave **his only begotten Son**; i.e., the Gift was most precious, and "the title 'only begotten' is added to enhance this conception."[19]

That whosoever believeth in him should not perish, but have everlasting life. The alternatives are set. They are life and death! God's Gift has made it possible for man to make the choice, the response of faith. The verbs **perish** and **have** are in different tenses. The former is in the aorist tense and means "once for all" banished into outer darkness. The latter is in the present tense, indicating a present and abiding eternal life.

For God sent not his Son into the world to condemn the world; but that the world through him might be saved (17). The word **condemn** may be translated "judge" (ASV), and this applies to its use in the following two verses. The purpose of God's Gift was not to bring men to judgment but to salvation. Yet judgment is inevitable, and it is man who brings it on himself when he refuses to accept God's mediating and atoning

[19]*Ibid.,* p. 55.

Gift. "Man is free to choose torment without God rather than happiness in God; he has a right to hell, as it were."[20]

Judgment and condemnation do not come to the man who has faith, for **he that believeth on him is not condemned** (18). Literally translated it says, "He who puts his faith into Him [i.e., Jesus Christ] is not being judged." In vivid contrast to this state of blessedness for the man of faith is the man who refuses to believe. **He that believeth not is condemned already, because he hath not believed in the name of the only begotten Son of God.** This already strong statement takes on new weight and warning when one considers the tense of the two verbs, **is condemned** and **hath not believed.** In the Greek both are perfect tense, which portrays a present state that is the result of past action. So in this life, condemnation is now a fact because **he that believeth not** has been judged already. Condemnation is a present state because the unbeliever has refused to believe.

There is "An Open Door to Life," God's life for men. It has three characteristics: (1) It is God's gift from above, 3, 16; (2) It comes only to the one who has faith, 15-16; (3) The alternative to life is God's judgment, 18.

With verse 19 the figure shifts from life to light and from unbelief to darkness. The reason that men have come into judgment and condemnation is **that light is come into the world, and men loved darkness rather than light, because their deeds were evil** (19; cf. 1:4, 9-11; 8:12; 9:4-5).

Unbelief and faith have their natural and inevitable consequents. These are carefully traced in verses 20 and 21. Unbelief issues in evil deeds. **For every one that doeth evil hateth the light, neither cometh to the light, lest his deeds should be reproved** (20). The sequence is clear—unbelief, darkness, evil deeds. Unbelief and evil living go hand in hand. The man who says that it makes no difference what he believes is also saying that actions do not have moral value or meaning. On the other hand, and in vivid contrast, is the man of faith. **But he that doeth truth cometh to the light, that his deeds may be made manifest, that they are wrought in God** (21). Note the sequence —faith, life, light, good deeds. To have a holy life there must be a holy man (cf. Matt. 7:16-20). The two are inseparable. One of the key words in the Gospel of John is *truth*. It is always per-

[20]Nicholas Berdyaev, *Freedom and the Spirit* (New York: Charles Scribner's Sons, 1935), p. 324.

sonal, grounded in the nature and character of God, and is a way for man to live in his relationship both to God and to man. Truth is something to be done—**he that doeth truth**—as well as something to be said.

2. *The New Master* (3:22-36)

The first three verses in this section mark a transition of both place and persons. Jesus has been in Jerusalem, where He wrought many miracles, and then talked at length with Nicodemus. So **after these things came Jesus and his disciples into the land of Judaea; and there he tarried with them, and baptized (22)**. The expression **into the land of Judaea** appears only here in the New Testament, and probably refers "to the country districts of Judea . . . somewhere near the fords in the neighborhood of Jericho."[21] (See map 1.)

Since this whole section is devoted to an expanded explanation of the relationship between John the Baptist and Jesus, these two occupy the center stage while the Jews, John's disciples, and Jesus' disciples appear only on the periphery. **And John also was baptizing in Aenon near to Salim, because there was much water there: and they came, and were baptized. For John was not yet cast into prison (23-24)**. The location of the place of John's baptizing as described here is not known, except that it probably was not at the Jordan. **Salim** is commonly placed "four or five miles east of Shechem where today there is a small village of the same name."[22] Two or three possible locations of **Aenon** have been suggested, but none is fixed with certainty. The word perhaps means "abounding in springs" (cf. **there was much water there**).

The timing of the conversation that follows is made clear by the statement, **John was not yet cast into prison (24;** cf. Matt. 4:12; Mark 1:14).

The witness which John the Baptist is about to make is set against the background of a question about purifying. **Then there arose a question between some of John's disciples and the Jews about purifying. And they came unto John, and said unto him, Rabbi, he that was with thee beyond Jordan, to whom thou barest witness, behold, the same baptizeth, and all men come to him (25-26)**. The old way of ritualistic, but empty and

---

[21]Bernard, *op. cit.*, p. 127.
[22]Macgregor, *op. cit.*, p. 89.

powerless, religion is represented by the Jews (cf. 2:6). They put much emphasis on the **purifying** (ceremonial washing) of the body. The dawning of a new day, a better way, a prophetic proclamation is represented by John (cf. 1:33). The consummation is found in the person of the One who was with John beyond Jordan.

John's answer to the Jews indicates that he knew immediately what they really wanted to know. "What is your estimate of this Man who is competing with you, a Man whom you baptized, a Man who is taking your crowd?" His response was in four parts. First, he reminded them that all men are in the last analysis subject to the sovereign will of God. **A man can receive nothing, except it be given him from heaven** (27; cf. 3:3). Second, he made clear his real relationship to the Christ, reminding his questioners of an earlier statement, **I am not the Christ** (28; cf. 1:20). As will be seen later (see comment on 4:26), the author uses the "I am" statements as direct affirmations of Jesus' deity. Likewise, here, John's negative form of the statement, **I am not,** or literally, "not I am," is a firm and clear disclaiming of the messiahship. But he does recognize and affirm his own role as related to the Christ, **I am sent before him** (28). Third, he used the figure of the bridegroom, bride, and friend of the bridegroom. Because of who the bridegroom is, there is real delight and joy for the friend. Complete fulfillment and fullness of joy belong to those who recognize Jesus for who He is, and who find in His voice the source of pure delight. **The friend . . . rejoiceth greatly because of the bridegroom's voice: this my joy therefore is fulfilled** (29; cf. 16:24).

Finally, the whole relationship is summed up in John's self-effacing declaration, made in the true spirit of the holy life: **He must increase, but I must decrease** (30).

Some scholars agree that v. 31 begins the author's comments on what has just transpired, while others argue that this (31-36) is a displaced section and should immediately follow v. 21. Lightfoot defends the existing location of the passage. He declares it is "a suitable appendix to 3:22-30."[23] A good look at the content of the section sustains his position. **He that cometh from above is above all** and **he that cometh from heaven is above all** (31) obviously relate to Jesus, while **he that is of the earth is earthly, and speaketh of the earth** clearly refers to John.

[23]*Op. cit.,* p. 120.

Then there follows a description of the One **from above** who is **above all.**

He is, first, a Witness of **what he hath seen and heard** (32). "The change of tense appears to mark a contrast between that which belonged to the existence (*hath seen,* ἑώρακεν), and to the mission (*heard,* ἤκουσεν, not *hath heard*) of the Son."[24] The witness, rejected by some (32), has been received by others (33). Anyone who receives the "witness has set his seal to this, that God is true" (33, NASB), "feeling that he whose word is truth is absolutely dependable, and will stand to his promises, however impossible they sound; and testifying later that they have tried this thing and it works, that God means what he says, and does it."[25]

He whom God hath sent speaketh the words of God (34). This One is the living Word (1:14), making a full revelation of God (1:18). There is a threefold reason for this. (1) When God gives, it is freely and without limitation. "For it is not by measure that he gives the Spirit" (34, RSV; cf. 1:16; 4:10; 7:38-39). (2) **The Father loveth the Son** (35). The full, free gift of the Incarnate One was born of love (cf. 3:16). (3) The whole mission of redeeming man was made the responsibility of the Son. No other way was provided. **The Father . . . hath given all things into his hand** (35).

Finally, the author makes the alternative clear by comparing faith and unbelief, with their certain and sure consequents: eternal life and the wrath of God. **He that believeth on the Son hath everlasting life: and he that believeth not the Son shall not see life; but the wrath of God abideth on him** (36). Faith issues in eternal life, which is the present possession of the believer, for the tense of the verb **hath** is present (cf. 5:24; 6:47, 54; Rom. 8:2-4). The expression **he that believeth not** is better translated, "he who does not obey" (RSV). The opposite of faith is actually "refusal to obey." When faith is weak or faltering, it is well to give attention to obedience. When one obeys, faith is a natural consequent. For those who refuse or neglect to obey, there is the inevitable **wrath of God.** This language is somewhat surprising after the high expression of God's love to man. But it points up the fact that man's gravest sin is unbelief, which is disobedience. Nor would God's love be more than weak indul-

---

[24]Westcott, *op. cit.,* p. 61.
[25]Gossip, *op. cit.,* p. 517.

gence if He were not true to His word and His holy nature. It is as Gossip well says:

> . . . Christ is never kinder than when his eyes, as he looks at us, are as a flame of fire, and he speaks to us terrible words; when he will make no compromise with us, but demands instant obedience, here and now, on pain of parting with him. If he had not loved us enough to be severe with us, he would have lost our souls. With awe and humility we need to give God thanks no less really for his wrath than for his mercy.[26]

3. *The New Worship* (4:1-30)

The opening verses of this section are a carefully written transition giving explanations of Jesus' work and walk. The sequence is simple. **The Pharisees** heard that Jesus was making and baptizing **more disciples than John.** When the Lord learned about this He left Judea for Galilee (1, 3; see map 1). Three things are of interest here. First, it is the Pharisees who represent the hostile Jews; the Sadducees or Herodians are not mentioned by name in the Gospel of John. Second, there is no indication that the author intended to describe supernatural knowledge on Jesus' part. **The Lord knew** (1) indicates only that the reports of His work were widely known. Third, the parenthesis **though Jesus himself baptized not, but his disciples** (2) was intended to correct the rumor that was abroad (3:26; 4:1).

And he must needs go through Samaria (4). The **must needs** expresses obligation, which may be of a dual nature. The shortest route from Judea to Galilee was through Samaria. However, because of the deep animosity between the Jews and the Samaritans, many Jews going from Judea to Galilee went east across the Jordan, north through Perea, and back across the Jordan into Galilee. It could have been that in the interest of time Jesus went through Samaria. However, more likely the necessity expressed here is related to His purpose and mission. Samaria, and specifically a Samaritan woman, needed Him.

Then cometh he to a city of Samaria, which is called Sychar, near to the parcel of ground that Jacob gave to his son Joseph. Now Jacob's well was there (5-6). Centuries of history are brought into the setting (cf. Gen. 33:19; 48:22; Josh. 24:32). The evident purpose is to show that the old way identified with Jacob and Joseph, and even Jacob's Well, comes to meaning and

---

[26]*Ibid.,* p. 519.

fulfillment only in Christ Jesus. Most authorities agree that
Sychar is identified as the present village Askar at the foot of
Mount Ebal. It is about half a mile north of Jacob's Well (see
map 1).

**Jesus therefore, being wearied with his journey, sat thus
on the well: and it was about the sixth hour** (6). Even as John
is careful to show Jesus' deity, so he takes care to point up
His perfect humanity. Jesus was wearied with the journey
and sat down (cf. 1:14; 19:28; Heb. 4:15). The expression **sat
thus** contains an adverb meaning "in this manner." It has provoked various interpretations. One is that this story about Jesus
and the Samaritan woman was told and retold many times. The
storyteller would illustrate as he spoke, and when he came to
this point, he would sit down, demonstrating Jesus' posture.
Jesus . . . sat thus—i.e., in this manner—**on the well. It was
about the sixth hour**—i.e., it was about noon, the heat of the
day, and time for the noon meal (cf. 4:8).

a. The Old and New Water (4:7-15). The setting of time
and place is clear. On stage, as it were, is the central Figure,
very God and very man, the One who knows all men (2:25).
To the well comes **a woman of Samaria to draw water** (7).
Little did the woman suspect that on this day, while engaged
in the tiresome routine of carrying water, there would come to
her life's greatest gift (cf. Matt. 13:44). Still less could she have
guessed that she would be "Exhibit B" in the Gospel of John
illustrating that Jesus did in fact know "what was in man"
(2:25).

The word **water** introduces the theme of the dialogue that
follows, and at the end is elevated "to mean the water of eternal
life" (cf. 1:33; 2:6-7; 3:5).[27] **Jesus saith unto her, Give me
to drink** (7). In this superb example of personal witness Jesus
began the conversation at a point where the woman could
understand in terms of something about which she was already
thinking.

As if to explain why Jesus asked only for himself, the
author inserted an explanatory note about the disciples who
had gone into the village to buy food (8).

**Then saith the woman of Samaria unto him, How is it
that thou, being a Jew, askest drink of me, which am a woman
of Samaria? for the Jews have no dealings with the Samari-**

---

[27]Dodd, *op. cit.*, p. 311.

tans (9). The woman's response to Jesus was natural because of the historical feud between Jews and Samaritans, and also because of a shocked custom morality that He, a man, should ask a kindness of a strange woman. The original word for **have dealings with** "suggests the relations of familiar intercourse and not of business."[28]

Jesus' response to the woman at once affirmed her ignorance of His real nature, and at the same time deeply aroused her curiosity. **If thou knewest the gift of God, and who it is that saith to thee, Give me to drink; thou wouldest have asked of him, and he would have given thee living water (10).** The word for **gift**, *dorea*, carries the idea of "free gift"; that is, a gift with no strings attached (cf. 3:16). *"Gift* here is a regal word, used of the benefactions of a king, or a rich man. It is always applied to the gift of the Spirit in the Book of Acts."[29] He is that kind of Gift! But this woman did not know. Had she known, she would have done the asking, He the giving. What she, and all who ask in faith, could receive would be **living water.** How carefully Jesus led her from the place she was—thinking about water in Jacob's Well—to a higher and more satisfying concept! **Living water** is that which is "perennial, springing from an unfailing source, ever flowing fresh."[30] This **he would have given** to her. So her attention is drawn from water to Him —which placed Him in immediate contrast with Jacob and all the things associated with him. Hence her question: **Sir, thou hast nothing to draw with, and the well is deep: from whence then host thou that living water? Art thou greater than our father Jacob? (11-12)**

The contrast between the old way as represented by Jacob's Well and the new way, **the water that I shall give him (14),** is vivid and clear in the words of Jesus to the woman. The old way of law, prophets, and specifically the Samaritan emphasis on the Pentateuch, was not good enough to satisfy and meet man's deepest needs. **Whosoever drinketh of this water shall thirst again (13).** The Samaritan woman knew well that Jesus spoke the truth about her. It was not only that she had come daily for years to Jacob's Well for water; the real problem was that

[28]Westcott, *op. cit.*, p. 69.

[29]R. H. Strachan, *The Fourth Gospel* (3rd ed.; London: Student Christian Movement Press, Ltd., 1941), p. 151.

[30]Westcott, *ibid.*

all her life her religion had not satisfied the thirst of her withered soul. Many people perform all that their religion requires, but having never drunk deeply of Him who is the Living Water, their lives are unchanged, dry, and fruitless. Jesus' promise to the woman is universal: **Whosoever drinketh of the water that I shall give him shall never thirst; but the water that I shall give him shall be in him a well of water springing up into everlasting life (14).** Here it is! Life's superlative offered to a sinful, needy, benighted creature. Outward form is replaced by a new and inner source. Stagnant pools in the soul are transformed into a gushing well. The withered, dead soul of man comes to partake of and participate in "eternal life." Little did the woman comprehend the full import of such a promise. Still thinking in terms of her dull, dead world of materialism, she replied, **Sir, give me this water, that I thirst not, neither come hither to draw (15).** She had a glimpse of light. The expression **that I thirst not** could well be much more than a description of physical craving for water.

b. *The Old and New Life* (4:16-30). With sudden abruptness Jesus changed the conversation. From appeal and promise He shifted to probe and command. One cannot claim the benefits of the gospel—a well of water and eternal life—without meeting the demands of the gospel, confession and repentance. **Go, call thy husband, and come hither (16).** The probe was sharp, reaching to the innermost core of her being, searching out the story of her sorry past. Her confession was simple, and yet evasive. **Sir, I have no husband (17).** Reflecting perfectly Jesus' knowledge of men (2:25), the probe went deeper. **Thou hast well said, I have no husband: for thou hast had five husbands; and he whom thou now hast is not thy husband: in that saidst thou truly (17-18).** Apparently the woman was now living with a lover without the benefit of marriage rite, possibly without divorce from the last of her five husbands. The evidence all points to a woman of loose morals whose form of religion had never been able to free her from the chains of evil habit. Jesus recognized her admission, not as an evasion, but as a confession. He said literally, "This word you have spoken is true." There is an old cliché that it is the truth that hurts. It would better be said, "It is the truth that helps!" No man has ever lost by facing up to the full demands of truth (cf. 1:14, 19; 3:21; 4:24; 14:6).

Him whom she first recognized only as a Jew (4:9), the woman now acclaimed to be more. **Sir, I perceive that thou art** a prophet (19). "Such insight, and not merely foresight, is the chief characteristic of the prophets."[31] In this dialogue there is an excellent example of the progression in teaching by steps— water (4:7), living water (4:10), a well of water (4:14). It is matched by a progression in understanding of the nature of Jesus—a Jew (4:9), a prophet (4:19), the Christ (4:29) (cf. 9:11, 17, 38).

Having recognized Jesus' knowledge about her, the woman quickly shifted the topic of conversation to one that would be safer for her and at the same time would be within the province of a prophet. **Our fathers worshipped in this mountain; and ye say, that in Jerusalem is the place where men ought to worship** (20). Her statement reflects an appeal to her own religion, **Our fathers worshipped in this mountain.** It reflects also an attempt to use the diversities and divisions within religion, **and ye say,** as an excuse for her own dismal failure in life. This is an old pattern that is very modern.

This mountain, Gerizim, had a significant role in the tradition of the Samaritans. Here "Abraham prepared the sacrifice of Isaac, and here also . . . he met Melchisedek. . . . And in the Samaritan Pentateuch, Gerizim and not Ebal is the mountain on which the altar was erected, Deut. xxviii: 4."[32]

The question of where to worship was answered by Jesus' classic statement about the nature of true worship as related to His mission. **The hour cometh** (21, 23) is to be understood in terms of His completed sacrifice that would make possible true worship (cf. 2:4; 7:30; 8:20; 12:23; 13:1; 17:1). **The hour cometh, when ye shall neither in this mountain, nor yet at Jerusalem, worship the Father** (21). This statement was also related to the destruction of the actual temples of worship. The Temple in Jerusalem was destroyed in A.D. 70, and Hyrcanus had destroyed the Samaritans' temple on Gerizim in 129 B.C.

Ye worship ye know not what (22). The Samaritans rejected all of the Old Testament except the Pentateuch. Jesus' appraisal of the inferiority of their rites and worship is reflected in the use of the neuter pronoun **what.** The object of their worship was impersonal, little understood, and vague, not only for the woman but for all in her nation. There is no such thing as genuine worship based on ignorance or what one does not know.

---

[31]Macgregor, *op. cit.,* p. 102.
[32]Westcott, *op. cit.,* pp. 72-73.

Such practices lead either to fanaticism or humanistic legalism. On the other hand, the Jews, with whom Jesus identifies himself, are recognized as the instrument of God's revelation: **We know what we worship: for salvation is of the Jews** (22).

But the hour cometh, and now is, when the true worshippers shall worship the Father in spirit and in truth: for the Father seeketh such to worship him (23). Now is the time for old forms limited to place and nation to be transformed into a worship that is at once personal, **in spirit,** and intelligent, **in truth.** "To worship *in spirit* means that we yield our wills to God's will, our thoughts and plans to God's for us and for the world. . . . *In truth* means that we are not worshipping an 'Image' of God, made out of our own ideas. . . . Christ alone has introduced us to the real or 'true' God."[33] The key word in this whole idea is **Father.** He is the Object of worship and the One who seeks true worshipers. "Once God is revealed to be the universal Father . . . the limitations of place are done away, and both the knowledge and the worship of God are mediated by purely spiritual means."[34] The nature of the object of worship, **God is a Spirit** (24; cf. I John 1:5; 4:8), determines the necessary conditions of worship. **They that worship him must worship him in spirit and in truth** (24).

The woman saith unto him, I know that Messias cometh, which is called Christ: when he is come, he will tell us all things (25). Samaritan Messianic expectation was not based on the great wealth of predictions in the prophets, since they accepted only the Pentateuch. These hopes were probably founded on scriptures such as Gen. 3:15 and Deut. 18:15. The woman's mention of the Messiah, "the Anointed One," opened the door for Jesus' great self-disclosure, **I that speak unto thee am he** (26), or literally, "I am, the one speaking to you!" This is the first occurrence of the expression, "I am," which Jesus uses many times in John's Gospel to disclose His true nature. Some are direct statements like this one (e.g., 6:20; 8:24, 58). Others appear in metaphor (e.g., 6:35; 8:12; 14:6). The expression in one form or the other occurs twenty-seven times in John's Gospel. The Greek form is *ego eimi,* and is the first person, singular, present, indicative form of the verb *eimi,* which portrays essential existence or being. The personal existence is intensified by the

[33]Strachan, *op. cit.,* p. 157.
[34]Macgregor, *op. cit.,* p. 103.

use of the first person, singular, personal pronoun, *ego.* This takes on tremendous meaning when compared with God's self-disclosure to Moses as "I am" (Exod. 3:14). Jesus was saying to this Samaritan woman, "The one speaking with you is the I am, the very God himself!" Thus ended the conversation, and so appropriately, for there was nothing more to be said. God himself had spoken.

And upon this came his disciples, and marvelled that he talked with the woman: yet no man said, What seekest thou? or, Why talkest thou with her? (27) The surprise of the disciples was not because of the woman's character, for they knew nothing of her past, nor because of her nationality. It was because Jesus talked with a woman. "A man should hold no conversation with a woman in the street, not even with his own wife, still less with any other woman, lest men should gossip."[35] The disciples asked no questions. There is no need of questioning one whom you trust.

The conversation had ended, but for this woman a new life had begun. The new life was marked by three things. First, there was the forsaking of the old life, a meaningless religion, a never satisfied thirst—she **left her waterpot** (28). She no longer needed it, for she had within an inexhaustible well of water (4:14). Second, her witness was personal and productive. She said to the men in the city, **Come, see a man, which told me all things that ever I did . . . Then they went out of the city, and came unto him** (29-30; cf. 39, 42). Finally, the question which she posed to her listeners was a display of her own utter amazement, surprise, and lingering doubt—"This is not the Christ, is it?" (4:29, NASB) It served also to raise an important question in the minds of the men of the village.

The fact that the woman left her water jar at the well suggests that she left her old manner of living. A message titled "Leaving the Old Life" could be structured on three ideas: (1) A new source of joy and life, 14; (2) A new witness, 29-31; (3) From moral disgrace to productive living, 18, 39-42.

4. *The New Harvest Fields* (4:31-42)

The conversation between Jesus and the Samaritan woman began about physical thirst and concluded with the gift of life-giving water. So here physical appetite—**Master, eat** (31)—pro-

---

[35]Strack and Billerbeck, *Kommentar zum N.T. aus Talmud und Midrasch,* II, 438.

vides the occasion for teaching the disciples about true satisfaction of life's deepest need. **I have meat to eat that ye know not of. My meat (food) is to do the will of him that sent me, and to finish his work** (32, 34). For the Son to accomplish His mission He must derive strength from the Father, who sent Him (cf. 5:19, 26; 6:57; 8:29). This divine food by which the Son lives is dual in its nature. First, it **is to do the will of him that sent** the Son (cf. Ps. 40:8; Heb. 10:7-10). It is evident that God's will is to make provision for and to call man to the sanctified life (I Thess. 4:3). Second, it is God's will that the Son "should bring to completion His work" (34, lit. translation; cf. 17:4). "His mission is, not only to teach or to 'announce', but to complete the work of man's salvation; that is . . . to effect the transformation of water into wine, to raise the new temple, to bring (through His descent and ascent) the possibility of birth ἐκ πνεύματος, to give living water which springs up to eternal life—in a word, to open to mankind a truly spiritual or divine life."[36]

To finish his work necessarily involves taking a hard, realistic look at the task at hand. One Samaritan woman had come, but out there lay **fields . . . white already to harvest** (35). A whole nation was in need of and ready for the gift of eternal life. Procrastination or rationalized delays are unrealistic. "Do you not say" (NEB), **There are yet four months, and then cometh harvest?** The time is now! If this generation is to receive the gospel, this generation must get it to the people.

If there is to be a harvest, there must be sowing as well as reaping, and both of these involve hard labor. The one sowing sees the promise of the end in the beginning; the one reaping realizes the results of the beginning in the end. So both **may rejoice together** (36), for the fruit of their mutual labors is **life eternal** (36). "There will be no need to speak, in this connexion, of a before and after, of this man or of that, since the work will be seen as one" (cf. 17:20-23).[37] Although there is a division of work, **One soweth, and another reapeth** (37), there is unity in that the end product is one. **I sent you to reap that whereon ye bestowed no labour: other men laboured, and ye are entered into their labours** (38). "All, in so far as they are reapers, owe the reward, which they are receiving, to the labours of others."[38]

[36]Dodd, *op. cit.*, p. 316.
[37]Lightfoot, *op. cit.*, p. 126.
[38]*Ibid.*

The perfect example of the harvest field is found in what happened in Samaria. The woman **testified, He told me all that ever I did** (39), with the result that **many of the Samaritans of that city believed on him for** (lit., "because of") **the saying of the woman** (39). The sowing, a personal testimony, brought forth fruit, faith in Him. Such was the impact of the woman's witness that the Samaritans came to see Jesus, and **they besought him that he would tarry with them: and he abode there two days** (40).

However important witness is in bringing men to Christ, in the last analysis it is only a mediary. Each man has to come to his own personal confrontation where his faith is based, not on what some other has said, but in Christ and His eternal Word. So it was with these men. **Many more believed because of his own word; and said unto the woman, Now we believe, not because of thy saying: for we have heard him ourselves, and know that this is indeed the Christ, the Saviour of the world** (41-42). What happened here was at once intensely personal—**we believe . . . we have heard him ourselves . . .** we **know**—and also characterized by the breaking down of the barriers of nationalism and religious sectarianism. They recognized this One in whom they believed as **the Saviour of the world** (42), not just a messiah for the Samaritans. The first and last thought of the believer in Christ is worldwide missions.

5. *A New Level of Faith* (4:43-54)

Now after two days he departed thence, and went into Galilee (43). The **two days** refers to His stay in Samaria (40), and **thence,** His leaving Samaria. **For Jesus himself testified, that a prophet hath no honour in his own country** (44). **His own country** has been interpreted to mean (1) Galilee in general, (2) Nazareth, (3) lower Galilee not including Capernaum, (4) Judea. The first three of these seem to be unlikely meanings in John, in the light of 1:11 and 7:41-42. Judea seems the most probable meaning. Westcott writes: "The Lord had not been received with due honor in Jerusalem. His Messianic claim had not been welcomed. He did not trust himself to the Jews there. He was forced to retire. If many followed Him, they were not the representatives of the people, and their faith reposed on miracles."[39]

---

[39]*Op. cit.*, p. 77.

In contrast to this artificial response and ultimate rejection in Judea was the open-armed welcome in the north. **The Galilaeans received him, having seen all the things that he did at Jerusalem at the feast: for they also went unto the feast (45).**

In introducing the setting of the event about to be described the author makes mention of the earlier sign that Jesus performed in **Cana of Galilee, where he made the water wine (46).** This seems to be an invitation to compare the two miracles, and indeed they do have striking points of similarity. There (2:1-11) the account centers around water becoming wine; here (49) near-death is turned into life. There it is Jesus' mother's faith which achieves; here, the faith of the nobleman. There the servants carry water that becomes wine; here they bring good news of life. In both, the event moves from sorrow to joy, and becomes the occasion for others to believe—there the disciples (2:11), here the nobleman and **his whole house (53).**

And there was a certain nobleman, whose son was sick at Capernaum (46). According to Arndt and Gingrich the word translated **nobleman** could refer to "a relative of the royal (Herodian) family" but more probably refers "to a royal official."[40]

Reports of Jesus' works in Jerusalem (2:23) had evidently gone before Him into Galilee, and the earlier miracle at Cana had no doubt been the topic of more than one conversation in Capernaum, which was only fifteen miles away (see map 1). So when the official **heard that Jesus was come out of Judaea into Galilee, he went unto him, and besought him that he would come down, and heal his son: for he was at the point of death (47).** The word translated **he went** literally means "he went away," indicating that the father left the son, ill as he was, to make his plea to Jesus. The verb **besought** is in the imperfect tense in the Greek, thus indicating repeated and continued asking.

Jesus' answer, though apparently a refusal, was in reality a test of the official's faith. **Except ye see signs and wonders, ye will not believe (48).** This is a searching question. Are the signs and wonders the occasion for faith, or are they the result of faith? Is the spectacular event, the miracle, the ecstatic experience a thing to be sought for itself alone, or are these the by-products of, or open doors to, a dynamic and properly placed faith; that is, faith in Him and His Word? The word **wonders** appears only

[40]*Op. cit.,* p. 136.

here in John. The two words **signs and wonders** combined "mark the two chief aspects of miracles: the spiritual aspect, whereby they suggest some deeper truth than meets the eye, of which they are in some sense symbols and pledges; and the external aspect, whereby their strangeness arrests attention."[41]

The renewed plea of the official was based on the question of life and death. He was not prepared to enter into a theological discussion when his immediate need loomed so large. **Sir, come down ere my child die** (49). Jesus' reply was a further and more pressing test of the man's faith. **Go thy way; thy son liveth** (50). The official had come to get Jesus (47, 49); now all he was getting was Jesus' promise of life for his son. Could he believe, having not seen? (Cf. 20:29.) Is it possible to take God at His word without hesitation? This man did! **And the man believed the word that Jesus had spoken unto him, and he went his way** (50). His unhesitating faith is emphasized by the tense of the verb **he went.** It could be translated literally, "He was on his way."

Verses 51-53 are a kind of epilogue that serves to certify what has already been accomplished. The report of the servants to the official, **Thy son liveth** (51), appears in better readings as indirect discourse—literally, "that his child was living." What Jesus had promised was exactly fulfilled! Just as the test to the official's faith was pressed a second time, so now the certification is made sure beyond doubt. The father's inquiry about **the hour when** the boy **began to amend** (52) disclosed the fact **that it was at the same hour, in the which Jesus said unto him, Thy son liveth** (53). What had been belief in Jesus' specific promise (50) now takes on the deeper and broader aspect of personal faith. **He himself believed, and his whole house** (53).

This is the second miracle (sign) **that Jesus did, when he was come out of Judaea into Galilee** (54). The notation of the series of signs at Cana of Galilee is to mark the visits of Jesus there as related to the intervening trip to Jerusalem (cf. 2:11, 13; 4:3).

In 4:46-54 we find (1) Our Lord lamenting over an inadequate faith, 46-48; (2) Our Lord testing and thus strengthening a growing faith, 49-50; (3) The absent Christ rewarding the faith that has been tested, 51-53 (Alexander Maclaren).

[41]Westcott, *op. cit.,* p. 78.

6. *The New Walk* (5:1-47)

a. *The Sign and Its Sequel* (5:1-18). On His previous visit to Jerusalem (2:13-22), Jesus had met opposition and hostility from the Jews. Now His second visit is to be the occasion for the beginning of the Sabbath controversy which issues in argument, open hostility from the Jews, and the final rejection, with Calvary as the culmination. "Throughout this gospel the greater His work for men, the greater the cost to Himself, and the greater the manifestation of His glory."[42] His earlier visit had been at the time of the Passover (2:13); now Jesus' journey to Jerusalem was occasioned by an unnamed feast. **After this there was a feast of the Jews; and Jesus went up to Jerusalem** (1; cf. 6:4; 7:37; 13:1).

The setting for the episode is described as to place, time, name, persons, and tradition. The place is in Jerusalem at a pool **by the sheep market** ("gate," ASV, 2). The time was **a feast of the Jews** (1). Both of these facts provide a background of symbolism quite in keeping with other settings for Jesus' miracles (cf. 2:6, 13; 3:5; 4:13-14; 6:4; 9:7). The name of the place has come through the texts with a variety of spellings, hence various meanings. Some of the spellings are: **Bethesda,** "house of mercy"; Bethzatha (RSV), "house of the olive," well attested by good MSS and generally accepted; and Bethsaida, "house of fishing," a rather inappropriate name for a place in Jerusalem.[43] The pool is described as **having five porches** in which **lay a great multitude of impotent folk, of blind, halt, withered** (2-3). The best MSS do not include the last part of 3 nor any of 4; hence they are usually not found in modern translations. Most authorities agree that these were a later addition, probably in keeping with Jewish tradition. Some copyist added these explanations to make clear the reason for sick people being there, and to explain the meaning of v. 7. The whole scene—the pool, the multitude of sick people—is one of misery, disappointment, and failure.

A certain man was there, which had an infirmity thirty and eight years (5). The method of introducing the central figure into the episode is characteristic of John (cf. 3:1; 4:7). Further, this man is presented as a type of all men. **A certain**

[42]Lightfoot, *op. cit.,* p. 138.
[43]Macgregor, *op. cit.,* pp. 167-68.

man, nameless to be sure, yet describing something about all men
—man's utter inability to help himself. Thus the account here
becomes "Exhibit C" of what Jesus knows about man (cf. 2:25,
Nicodemus; 4:7, the Samaritan woman). The man is described
as having had his **infirmity thirty and eight years.** The mention
of the period of time has been interpreted by some to be a reference to the period of the punishment of the Israelites in the
wilderness (Deut. 2:14). Most likely it was added "simply to
mark the inveteracy of the disease" (cf. 9:1).[44]

**When Jesus saw him lie, and knew that he had been now a
long time in that case, he saith unto him, Wilt thou be made
whole?** (6) Jesus' compassion and His knowledge of the man's
deepest needs (cf. 5:14) combined to prompt the question. At
first glance this appears to be silly. Of course the man wanted to
be well, else he would not have been at the pool, a source of
supposed healing. Yet Jesus knew that people become inured
to a life of woe and misery, losing their will to respond to an
adequate source of help. So it was a good question!

**The impotent man answered him, Sir, I have no man, when
the water is troubled, to put me into the pool: but while I am
coming, another steppeth down before me** (7). What a picture!
He was friendless—**I have no man.** He was **impotent,** unable to
help himself, yet struggling—**while I am coming.** It was not that
he had lost his will; he had not yet come to the right source, or
rather the right source of help had not yet come to him. Here
is portrayed, in the figure of the pool, the inadequacy of the Law
(Judaism) to meet man's real needs. Man's most intense strug-
gles cannot save him from the crippling paralysis of sin.

Jesus saith unto him, Rise, take up thy bed, and walk (8).
Take up thy bed meant, "Pick up your mat" (Berk.). Three
imperatives in a row! And every one of them is a preposterous
command for a paralytic. It is easy to imagine how the impotent
man must have felt. For thirty-eight years as a victim of this
crippling disease he had been able to move only with difficulty.
And now he is to rise, take up his bed, and walk. Impossible?
Yes, it was impossible from every purely human point of view.
But to Jesus this man was the object of His compassion, and His
command meant His enablement. Struggling for release, the man
saw a gleam of hope and took Jesus at His word.

[44]Westcott, *op. cit.,* p. 82.

And immediately the man was made whole, and took up his bed, and walked (9). The healing was immediate and complete, as indicated by the aorist tense of the verb **was made**. The man's obedient response to Jesus' command was the occasion for his healing. Everything that Jesus requested, the man obediently carried through: **Rise,** he arose (by implication); **take up thy bed** (aorist tense), he **took up his bed** (aorist); **walk** (present tense); he **walked** (imperfect tense, better translated "he was walking"). The use of the aorist here indicates that the old life which had been victimizing him for these thirty-eight years was no longer to have dominion over him (cf. Rom. 6:14). The walk, portrayed by the present imperative (8), and the imperfect indicative (9), was to be a new way of continuous and customary living.

And on the same day was the sabbath (9). This notation is important, for it marks the beginning of a long, sustained, and ever sharper controversy about Jesus' relationship to the Law and to the Jews (cf. 5:16; 7:23; 8:5; 9:14).

The Jews therefore said unto him that was cured, It is the sabbath day: it is not lawful for thee to carry thy bed (10). The **bed** (pallet) was a light, flexible mat used by the poor people. It could be rolled up and easily carried, but even this was not to be carried on the Sabbath (cf. Neh. 13:19; Jer. 17:21). According to the Mishnah, thirty-nine works were forbidden on the Sabbath.[45]

The human inclination to shift blame from oneself to another is reflected in the man's response to the Jews: **He that made me whole, the same said unto me, Take up thy bed, and walk** (11). But even if the healed man had an inclination to shift blame for a violation of the Sabbath law, he also made a clear witness about what he knew—he had been healed. The man's experience with Jesus was unequivocal—**He . . . made me whole.** The Jews pressed their investigation. **What man is that which said unto thee, Take up thy bed, and walk?** (12) They would not grant that this One responsible for Sabbath desecration could be Lord of the Sabbath; hence they asked, **What man?** (Cf. 9:11, 24.)

Here the author puts in an explanatory note. **And he that was healed wist** (knew) **not who it was: for Jesus had conveyed**

---

[45]Wilbert F. Howard, "The Gospel According to St. John" (Introduction and Exegesis), *The Interpreter's Bible*, ed. George A. Buttrick, *et al.*, VIII (New York: Abingdon-Cokesbury Press, 1952), 542.

himself away— (lit., "to bend the head aside, to avoid a blow") [46] **—a multitude being in that place** (13). Jesus simply slipped away and lost himself in the crowd. His hour had not yet come when He would bring to full issue the conflict between the old and the new. But there was a point of conflict, an important issue that had to be brought into the open. It was the relationship of the healed man to Jesus. So, **afterward Jesus findeth him in the temple, and said unto him, Behold, thou art made whole: sin no more, lest a worse thing come unto thee** (14). The ever-seeking Lord (cf. Luke 15:3-10) **findeth him.** At least the man had not gone back to the old place, the pool. Rather he was **in the temple,** possibly offering thanks for his restoration. Jesus first reminded him of what he now knew so well, **thou art made whole,** and then passed to the great imperative, **sin no more** (present tense, lit., "no longer continue to sin"). We need to remember that: (1) it was Jesus who gave the command; (2) what He commands He enables one to do; (3) He would not require something of one person that He would not ask of all; (4) living above sin is God's plan for man. The last part of Jesus' statement reflects two things. First, it seems to imply that the thirty-eight years of sickness had been the result of the man's own folly and sin, without implying that such is the case with all sickness (cf. 9:3). Second, there is suggested an element of judgment (cf. 3:18-19; 5:22-29).

A development under the title "God's Power Meets Man's Impotence" could have three parts: (1) Man's impotence, 8; (2) God's command is man's enablement, 8-9, 14; (3) Obedient faith is the key, 9, 14.

At this, the man took the initiative, went back to the Jews, and told them **that it was Jesus, which had made him whole** (15; cf. 9:35-38; Rom. 10:9). The man's confession to the Jews precipitated a continuing crisis. **And therefore did the Jews persecute Jesus, and sought to slay him, because he had done these things on the sabbath day** (16). The first clause could be literally translated, "The Jews used to persecute, or were persecuting, Jesus," indicating that such was a continuing pattern. This is matched by the tense of the verb in the last clause, which could read, "He [i.e., Jesus] used to do, or continually did, these things on the Sabbath." Evidently there were many more "Sab-

---

[46]Westcott, *op. cit.,* p. 83.

bath violations" in the works of Jesus than are recorded (cf. 20: 30).

Jesus' answer to the Jews added fuel to the fires. He said, **My Father worketh hitherto, and I work** (17). The whole point of the previous argument had been work on the Sabbath. Now, did Jesus imply that it was not only a question of His own activity on the Sabbath, but also the activity of His Father? Their work is one (19); hence what is predicated of the one belongs to the other. "The sabbath rest of the Father, rightly understood, is the unimpeded activity of love, so that in deeds of mercy wrought on the sabbath the work of the Father and the Son is at one."[47]

Such a claim by Jesus provided the ground for a further accusation to be made against Him. **Therefore the Jews sought the more to kill him, because he not only had broken the sabbath, but said also that God was his Father, making himself equal with God** (18). "By placing His action on the same level with the action of God" He was making **himself equal with God.**[48] Such a claim raised serious questions in the minds of Jews dedicated to a belief in and defense of a rigorous monotheism. So in a very profound sense Jesus' teaching that follows (5:19-47) is a thoroughgoing defense of Christian monotheism in which Father and Son are one.

b. *The Relation of the Father to the Son* (5:19-24). This very closely reasoned paragraph was most likely addressed to a small, trained audience, perhaps even the Sanhedrin.[49] The point of the argument is **that all men should honour the Son, even as they honour the Father** (23). To come to this conclusion, Jesus presented four steps, each introduced by the word *for*. First, the Son in all His activity and work is absolutely dependent on the Father, **for what things soever he** (i.e., the Father) **doeth, these also doeth the Son likewise** (19). Second, the bond of the union is love and perfect confidence; the fruit of the union is **greater works. For the Father loveth the Son, and sheweth him all things that himself doeth: and he will shew him greater works than these, that ye may marvel** (20). That is, God would show greater works through Christ, that unbelievers might marvel. Third, the unity is evident in the great issue of life and death. **For as the Father raiseth up the dead, and quickeneth them; even so the**

[47]Lightfoot, *op. cit.*, p. 140.

[48]Westcott, *op. cit.*, p. 84.

[49]*Ibid.*, pp. 81, 84.

Son quickeneth whom he will (21). Evidences of this kind of quickening are seen in Jesus' teaching to Nicodemus (3:3); here in vv. 24, 26; in the figure of the bread (6:27); and most graphically in the death and life scene at Lazarus' tomb (11:25-26; cf. 1:4; 3:36). Fourth, **because he is the Son of man** (27) the prerogative of judgment has been given to Him by the Father. **For the Father judgeth no man, but hath committed all judgment unto the Son** (22; cf. 5:30; 8:16). He did this **that all men should honour the Son, even as they honour the Father** (23). "Positively, the work of Christ is to bring life and light; negatively, it results in judgment upon those who refuse the life and turn away from the light."[50]

The Son is absolutely dependent on the Father and is so united to Him by the perfect bond of love and confidence that the issues of life, death, and judgment find a perfect solution. The Son is deserving of honor even as is the Father. In fact, the unity is so perfect that **he that honoureth not the Son honoureth not the Father which hath sent him** (23).

These deep theological reasonings are followed by a warm and personal appeal, **Verily, verily, I say unto you, He that heareth my word, and believeth on him that sent me, hath everlasting life** (eternal life, 24). The three verbs are present tense; so hearing, believing, and possessing all have present reality. Eternal life begins when one hears and believes (cf. 20:31). Further, because of the union described above, to believe on the Father, who sent the Son, is tantamount to faith in the Son (cf. 3:16; 6:29).

c. *The Relation of the Son of Man* (5:25-29). The statement, **Verily, verily, I say unto you** (25) "always in this Gospel introduces a majestic claim" (cf. 1:51).[51] Majestic claim it is indeed, for **the hour is coming, and now is, when the dead shall hear the voice of the Son of God: and they that hear shall live** (25). "The new order is breaking through into the old" (cf. 4:23).[52] Those who are spiritually dead will hear, and those who respond in faith will live (cf. 5:21, 24). What they hear, **the voice of the Son of God,** is the speaking Word, the full revelation and consummation of God's reach to men dead in trespasses and sins.

[50]C. H. Dodd, *op. cit.,* p. 256.
[51]*Ibid.*
[52]Macgregor, *op. cit.,* p. 178.

This reach to man is possible because of the unity of action in the Father and the Son. **For as the Father hath life in himself; so hath he given to the Son to have life in himself** (26). It is because of this unity as evident in the works of the incarnate Son that the Father **hath given him authority to execute judgment also, because he is the Son of man** (27). In view of the fact that the definite article is absent from both nouns in **Son of man** (lit. translation), it is evident that "the prerogative of judgment is connected with the true humanity of Christ (*Son of Man*) and not with the fact that he is the representative of humanity (*the Son of Man*)." [53]

The ideas of life and judgment in the new order (25) are now carried one step further. **Marvel not at this: for the hour is coming, in the which all that are in the graves shall hear his voice, and shall come forth; they that have done good, unto the resurrection of life; and they that have done evil, unto the resurrection of damnation** ("judgment," ASV; 28-29). **The hour is coming,** that is, not the present hour with the promise and realization of spiritual life (cf. 5:25), but the time when **all that are in the graves shall hear his voice.** Here man responds—**shall come forth**—not because he wills or believes, but because God has called him to an accounting of "the things done in his body . . . whether it be good or bad" (II Cor. 5:10). "The Christian conception is that men are held responsible for deeds done in the flesh. The casting away of the flesh at death does not mean the shedding of the evil and gross side of a man's nature, while their souls are saved."[54]

d. *Witnesses of the Son* (5:30-47). The argument thus far (5:19-29) has shown (1) that the Son is dependent on the Father in a dynamic unity, and (2) that man must find life in the Son if he is to live either now (5:24) or in the future (5:29). This has been described by some as the witness of the Father to the Son. So it is that the Son seeks not His own will, **but the will of the Father which hath sent** Him (30). And it is because of this that His **judgment is just.** If He alone were to bear witness of himself, His witness would not be true (31)[55]—that is, "admissible as legal evidence" (NASB, margin).

[53]Westcott, *op. cit.,* p. 87.
[54]Strachan, *op. cit.,* p. 172.
[55]Westcott, *op. cit.,* p. 89.

Another witness to the Son is that by John the Baptist. **And I know that the witness which he witnesseth of me is true** (32). Jesus reminds His listeners of their earlier questioning of John and his response. **Ye sent unto John, and he bare witness unto the truth** (33; cf. 1:15, 19, 27, 32). But as clear and certain as was John's witness, it was not his witness to the Son that certified the Son's relationship to the Father. **I receive not testimony from man** (34). Rather, Jesus was making every appeal He could to His hearers to bring them to salvation—**these things** (cf. 24) **I say, that ye might be saved** (34). **He** (i.e., John) **was a burning and a shining light: and ye were willing for a season to rejoice in his light** (35). The verb **was** reflects Jesus' recognition of the imprisonment or death of John. The last clause reminds His hearers of their vacillating attitude toward John, first acccepting him and then turning against him when his call to repentance became altogether inconvenient for them.

Another witness, **greater . . . than that of John,** is the witness of works: **for the works which the Father hath given me to finish, the same works that I do, bear witness of me, that the Father hath sent me** (36; cf. 10:25). By the works is meant "the whole outward manifestation of Christ's activity, both those acts which we call supernatural and those we call natural. All alike are wrought in fulfillment of one plan and by one power."[56] Rejection of Jesus' works, which in the plan included the Cross, was a rejection not only of the Father's witness (37) but also of the Son, **for whom he** (i.e., the Father) **hath sent, him ye believe not** (38).

The final witness of the Son which Jesus calls to the attention of His listeners is the witness of the Scriptures. **Search the scriptures; for in them ye think ye have eternal life** (39). The initial verb could be either indicative or imperative, but the indicative seems to make better sense in this context. It would read literally, "You are searching the Scriptures, because in them you think you have eternal life."

In this section (39-47) the Scriptures are described: (1) as a Witness of the Son—**they are they which testify of me** (39); (2) as that which accuses the unbelieving hearers—**there is one that accuseth you, even Moses, in whom ye trust. For had ye believed Moses, ye would have believed me: for he wrote of me**

[56]*Ibid.,* p. 90.

(45-46). The Son, of whom the Scriptures witness (39), is seen as: (1) the Source of life (40); (2) the One who has come in the Father's name (43), and does not receive honor from men (41). Against this background the hearers, the Jews (see comment on 5:19-24), are described in vivid language. In spite of their much searching of the Scriptures, the Witness to the Son, they refuse to come to Jesus, the true Source of life (40), they do not love God (42), they are apt to believe impostors (43), they have a wrong scale of values (44), and, quite ironically, they do not even believe the Scriptures which they continually are searching (38, 46).

Verse 41 seems to mean that Christ did not seek honor (Gk., "glory") from men. But He knew that if they had **the love of God** (42) in them, they would honor Him.

D. THE NEW BREAD, 6:1-71

1. *The Sign of the Loaves* (6:1-14)

After these things Jesus went over the sea of Galilee, which is the sea of Tiberias (1, see map 1). Again the scene shifts from Jerusalem (5:1-2) to Galilee, where now for the third time He has gone (2:1; 4:3). The expression **after these things** is characteristic of John, and here sums up what had recently transpired in Jerusalem. Jesus' stay in Galilee on this occasion was longer, evidently because of the opposition which He had been encountering in Jerusalem (5:16; 7:1). The use of **sea of Tiberias** is peculiar to John (6:23; 21:1). This was a later name that began to be used following the founding of the city of Tiberias on the west shore of the Sea of Galilee by Herod Antipas (*ca.* A.D. 25).

And a great multitude followed him, because they saw his miracles which he did on them that were diseased (2). Both of the verbs **followed** and **did** are in the imperfect tense in the Greek. They could well be translated "were continually following" and "was continually doing." Jesus' healing activity was regularly attracting crowds to Him in Galilee.

And Jesus went up into a mountain, and there he sat with his disciples (3). This, with the statement in v. 1 and compared to Luke 9:10, indicates the setting to be near Bethsaida Julias on the northeast shore of the Sea of Galilee. By **a mountain** "is meant the plateau-land above the lake, not any particular summit."[57]

And the passover, a feast of the Jews, was nigh (4). This is a rather surprising statement, because Galilee is far from Jerusalem, where the Passover was traditionally celebrated. The best explanation seems to be that the author calls attention to this greatest feast of the Jews in order to put Judaism in sharp contrast with what Jesus says to the same multitude in Capernaum (6:24, 59). Much that our Lord said there is of a highly sacramental nature (e.g., 53). The old bread (manna, 31) and all it stands for (Judaism, the Law) are inadequate for man's real need of eternal life, whereas Jesus proclaims himself to be "the bread which came down from heaven" (41), the "bread of life" (48).

This is the only miracle of Jesus that is recorded in all four Gospels (cf. Matt. 14:13-21; Mark 6:30-44; Luke 9:10-17). **When Jesus then lifted up his eyes, and saw a great company come unto him, he saith unto Philip, Whence may we buy bread, that these may eat?** (5) The record here makes no mention that Jesus had compassion on the multitude (cf. Matt. 14:14; Mark 6:34). Rather, their coming is the occasion for Philip to be put to the test. **This he said to prove him** (6). John's notation—**for he himself knew what he would do**—is typical. "Throughout the Gospel the Evangelist speaks as one who had an intimate knowledge of the Lord's mind."[58]

Philip's response, **two hundred pennyworth of bread is not sufficient for them, that every one of them may take a little** (7), deals with the problem "at the level of the market-place."[59] **Pennyworth** is literally "denarii." The denarius was a Roman silver coin worth about eighteen or twenty cents, "a workman's average daily wage."[60] Two hundred of these, even if the disciples had them, would be insufficient. So the question still stands, "Whence bread for the multitude?" Philip, and every Christian, "must be brought to realize that all missionary enterprise originates in an adequate human interpretation of the

---

[57]Macgregor, *op. cit.*, p. 127.
[58]Westcott, *op. cit.*, p. 96.
[59]Lightfoot, *op. cit.*, p. 157.
[60]Arndt and Gingrich, *op. cit.*, p. 178.

Divine purpose, and is not merely a human desire to spread our own religious convictions limited by our material resources."[61]

Philip's response was calculating and hesitating. Andrew's suggestion was optimistic, indicating the possibility of taking full advantage of the opportunity at hand (cf. 1:41-42), unpromising as it might seem on the surface. **There is,** he said, **a lad here, which hath five barley loaves, and two small fishes: but what are they among so many?** (9) The quantity of food was very small and the quality was not the best. **Barley loaves** were the coarse food of poor people, and the **two small fishes** were sardine-like pickled or dried fish.

At this Jesus took full command: **Make the men sit down** (10). The fact that **there was much grass in the place** suggests the spring of the year (cf. 6:4), which harmonizes with the reference to the Passover (4). The word used for **men** indicates that the **five thousand** were exclusive of women and children (cf. Matt. 14:21). **Jesus took the loaves; and when he had given thanks, he distributed . . . to them that were set down; and likewise of the fishes as much as they would** (11). The words **to the disciples, and the disciples** are not in the best MSS, and so are omitted in recent versions. But the Synoptic accounts indicate that Jesus used the disciples to feed the crowd. The word translated **when he had given thanks,** *eucharistesas,* is at once beautiful and highly significant. From it comes the word Eucharist, meaning the Lord's Supper. Much that follows (6:51-58) is eucharistic in its tone and meaning (cf. Matt. 26:27; Mark 14:23; Luke 22:19).

The oft recurring theme of the abundance of God's gift of grace and His Spirit to man shines forth here—**they were filled** (12; cf. 1:16; 2:7; 4:14; 7:38-39). So when all had eaten, at Jesus' command, the disciples **filled twelve baskets with the fragments of the five barley loaves, which remained over and above unto them that had eaten** (13).

Then those men, when they had seen the miracle (sign) **that Jesus did, said, This is of a truth that prophet that should come into the world** (14, cf. Deut. 18:15). This response to the sign is typical of other responses in this Gospel (cf. 4:19; 7:40; 9:17). It was also the motivating force that caused them to try **to take him by force, to make him a king** (15), and having failed

---

[61]Strachan, *op. cit.,* p. 179.

in that, to seek Him out on the other side of the lake (6:24-25). To avoid a possible Messiah-King uprising—for such are the connotations of the words **prophet** and **king**—Jesus **departed again into a mountain himself alone** (15).

2. *The Sign of the Stilled Sea* (6:15-24)

This section is a kind of transitional interlude in the major theme—Bread of Life. It has at least three main purposes. First, it gives the account of the change of scene from Bethsaida Julias, the place of the sign of the loaves and fishes, to Capernaum (see map 1), the scene of the discourse concerning the Bread of Life. This is of particular interest, since the disciples first went **over the sea** (17) westward in a storm-tossed boat (16-19). Later Jesus crossed over, **walking on the sea** (19) and riding in the boat with the disciples (21). Still later (the next day) the people **took shipping, and came to Capernaum** (24).

A second purpose is to show man's utter inadequacy in the face of adversity when left to his own resources. The picture is graphic and clear. **It was now dark** (17), with the consequent inability of the disciples to keep a sure course. They were alone, separated from the Source of adequate help—**Jesus was not come to them** (17). The natural adversities of life overtook them— **And the sea arose by reason of a great wind that blew** (18). Their fears multiplied at the appearance of the unrecognized Presence—**they were afraid** (19). **Twenty or thirty furlongs** would be about three or four miles.

Finally, it is the setting in which the disciples learned that the Divine Presence comes to man, not only in the hour of worship in the holy place, but in the unexpected moment of man's greatest need (cf. Heb. 4:16). Jesus came saying, **It is I** (lit., "I am"); the Divine Presence is here; do not be afraid (20).

Then they willingly received him into the ship: and immediately the ship was at the land whither they went (21). Here is a beautiful epilogue to the whole drama. **Immediately** probably means "quickly."

3. *The Eternal Bread* (6:25-65)

a. True Labor (6:25-34). The multitudes who ate of the miraculous loaves and fishes were not easily daunted. They must not lose contact with One who had provided a meal for them at no cost or labor on their part. Reasoning that He had left Beth-saida Julias for Capernaum, they followed, seeking for Him (24). **And when they had found him on the other side of the sea, they said unto him, Rabbi, when camest thou hither?** (25) Since it was the next day **when they had found him,** these people were hungry for food again. They tried to make it appear that they followed across the lake because of who He was, but the real reason was that they hoped to get something for themselves. And Jesus, knowing it (cf. 2:25), said, **Verily, verily, I say unto you, Ye seek me, not because ye saw the miracles, but because ye did eat of the loaves, and were filled** (26). Jesus then laid down for them both a command and a promise. The command is both negative and positive. **Labour not for the meat** (food) **which perisheth, but for that meat which endureth unto everlasting** (eternal) **life** (27). The promise is that belief on the Son (27) provides more than perishing food; it brings a gift that **endureth unto everlasting life, which the Son of man shall give unto you** (27). The contrast of the two words **labour** and **give** "is essential to the sense of the passage. The believer's work does not earn a recompense at the last but secures a gift."[62] The Giver of the gift is also himself the Gift (cf. 6:51), **for him hath God the Father sealed** (27); that is, "commissioned him for this very purpose."[63]

The next question asked by the people is a deliberative question—one that expects an answer in the imperative mood. It could be translated literally "What should we do in order that we may be working the works of God?" (28) Enigmatic as it may sound, Jesus' answer was simply, "To have faith in Christ is the work that really counts" (cf. Acts 16:30-31): **This is the work of God, that ye believe on him whom he hath sent** (29). The present tense of the verb **believe** is important here. It means "that you may have faith continually, that you may live the life of faith."[64]

Jesus' request for them to have faith **on him whom** God **hath sent** caused them to challenge His authority (cf. 2:18; 4:11). Why should they believe in **him? What sign shewest thou then, that we may see, and believe thee? what dost thou work?** (30) Their resort to traditional but meaningless religion is typical in John's record. **Our fathers did eat manna in the desert; as it is written,**

[62]Westcott, *op. cit.,* p. 100.
[63]Macgregor, *op. cit.,* p. 138.
[64]Bernard, *op. cit.,* p. 193.

86

He gave them bread from heaven to eat (31; cf. 4:12, 20; 5:10;
9:16). It is as if these people were saying to Jesus, "Yesterday
You fed us. Today we have sought You out for another meal and
all You give us is talk about having faith. Moses did better than
that. The manna was fresh every morning. So either produce or
we will not follow You any longer!"

At this Jesus set the record straight. Even the gifts, **manna,**
of the old covenant were not from Moses but from God—**Moses
gave you not that bread from heaven** (32). And even God's gift
of the old covenant, here the manna, was intended but to fore-
shadow the **true bread** (cf. Heb. 10:1). **For the bread of God is
he which cometh down from heaven, and giveth life unto the
world** (33; cf. 4:14).[65] Just as the Samaritan woman had asked,
"Sir, give me this water, that I thirst not, neither come hither to
draw" (4:15), so these people said, **Lord, evermore give us this
bread** (34).[66]

b. *"True Bread"* (6:35-40). What had been hidden in sign
and symbol Jesus now declared to them openly. If they really
wanted the bread He would give, they must know that He is that
Bread. **I am the bread of life: he that cometh to me shall never
hunger; and he that believeth on me shall never thirst** (35; cf.
4:14; 6:48, 58; 7:37-38). Thus far in the Gospel of John, **I am**
has occurred twice in Jesus' forthright declarations of His deity
(4:26; 6:20). Here begins the use of strong and expressive meta-
phors. They recur seventeen times, and in changing figure: e.g.,
I am the bread of life; "I am the light of the world" (8:12);
"I am the door" (10:9). Westcott writes, "The figures with which
it [I am] is connected furnish a complete study of the Lord's
work."[67]

The present tense of the verbs **cometh** and **believeth,** portraying continued and persistent action, is important in this section.
The full implication is that cessation of coming or having faith

[65]No doubt the reader has noted the striking similarity of style and
structure between this dialogue and the one between Jesus and the Samaritan woman in chapter four.

[66]The word here translated **Lord** is *kyrie,* the same word which is
translated "Sir" in 4:15. In this context it seems that the polite form "sir"
would be a better translation because these people were not recognizing
Jesus as Lord. This would suggest that the request, **Evermore give us this
bread,** was a cynical response rather than a sincere request.

[67]*Op. cit.,* p. 102.

would also mean discontinuance of the satisfaction for hunger and thirst.

The people had requested a sign (6:30) and now Jesus tells them that they have the sign—the Incarnation—yet they are not believing. **Ye also have seen me, and believe not** (36).

There are two main themes in verses 37-40. First, the will of the Father is made effective to man through the Son, with the result of eternal life. The Son does the will of the Father—**For I came down from heaven, not to do mine own will, but the will of him that sent me** (38; cf. Matt. 26:39, 42). Because of the Son's perfect performance of the Father's will, God's plan for man is: (1) full fellowship with Christ (37); (2) guidance and grace for those who come (37) and thus "keep on having faith in Him" (lit., 40); and (3) eternal life, that is, life at its highest here and now—the sanctified life (cf. I Thess. 4:3). Later there will be the full transformation (cf. II Cor. 3:18) at participation in His resurrection. The clause **and I will raise him up at the last day** (40) appears as a kind of refrain throughout this section (39-40, 44, 54).

The second theme is that eternal life, in both its present and its eschatological meanings, is open to man. This is not because of man's merit but only by God's grace. To interpret negatively the clause, **All that the Father giveth me shall come to me** (37), as the basis for a doctrine of reprobation is resorting to grim logic. Gossip comments: "There are truer things in life than that. . . . All it says is that if we are Christ's at all, then we are his not because of anything we have done . . . but solely because God set himself to win us."[68]

c. *Objections Met* (6:41-51). The Jews objected to Jesus' claim that He was **the bread which came down from heaven** (41) on the ground that they knew His human parentage (42). How could He be Bread from heaven? Jesus met their objection by pointing out that it is the Father who has taken the initiative to redeem man (44), and that what they see or ought to see is God's full revelation to man in the One whom God has sent (44, 46). This, He said, they should have known by reading the prophets (Isa. 54:13; Jer. 31:34). Had they followed the teaching of the prophets they would have **learned of the Father** and come unto the Son (45). So perfect and adequate is the revelation of God

[68]*Op. cit.*, pp. 569-70.

in the Son that He could say, **Verily, verily, I say unto you, He that believeth on me hath everlasting** (eternal) **life** (47).

The Jews had appealed to their traditional religion as more adequate than Jesus' promise (6:31). Now Jesus, while declaring himself to be the **bread of life** (48), with subtle humor added, **Your fathers did eat manna in the wilderness, and are dead** (49). The old covenant did not meet man's deepest need. But the new, eternal Bread is that which **a man may eat . . . and not die** (50). Further, the new Bread is here, available for all men through the Cross. **The bread that I will give is my flesh, which I will give for the life of the world** (51).

d. *True Food and Drink* (6:52-59). The promise of Jesus that He would give His **flesh . . . for the life of the world** (6:51) caused strife ("a fierce dispute," NEB) among the Jews, and they asked, **How can this man give us his flesh to eat?** (52) Jesus was of course speaking figuratively of His atonement but they stumbled, and men still stumble, at the idea of the Cross, and its highest provision. They did not ask, "How can we eat?" They asked, "Is God able?"[69] Men still ask the question in a slightly different form, "Is God able to sanctify a man wholly?"

Jesus' answer at once describes the exclusive way of Christian holiness and proclaims the great promise of the possibility of eternal life, the life of holiness. **Except** (i.e., there is no alternative) **ye eat the flesh of the Son of man, and drink his blood, ye have no life in you. Whoso eateth my flesh, and drinketh my blood, hath** (present tense) **eternal life; and I will raise him up at the last day** (53-54). The one who through faith partakes of His nature, the life of holiness, *has* eternal life. Holiness of heart is at the center of the meaning of the Eucharist.

Two themes for later development appear in Jesus' answer. **He that eateth my flesh, and drinketh my blood, dwelleth in me, and I in him** (56). The same word here translated **dwelleth** appears as the theme "abiding" in the figure of the vine and branches in c. 15. The theme of the unity of the Father, the Son, and the believer is evident in v. 57: **As the living Father hath sent me, and I live by the Father: so he that eateth me, even he shall live by me** (cf. 17:21).

The final summation of Jesus' answer shows the ultimate inadequacy of the old covenant and the enduring satisfaction in

[69]The word translated **can** in 6:52 is *dynatai,* and means "to have ability or power to perform."

89

the new Bread. **Your fathers did eat manna, and are dead: he that eateth of this bread shall live for ever** (58).

e. *A Hard Saying* (6:60-65). **Many therefore of his disciples, when they had heard this, said, This is an hard saying; who can hear it?** (60) The saying was hard, not in that it was unintelligible, but because it carried the high and full demands of the cross. "It made claims on the complete submission, self-devotion, self-surrender of the disciples. It pointed significantly to death."[70] **Who can hear it?** means, "Who could accept that?" (Phillips)

Jesus' answer (61-64) to their complaint was really a turn on their question. If they stumbled at the full implications of the Incarnation, what would they do if they saw **the Son of man ascend up where he was before?** (62) If it is hard to believe that God has come in the flesh (cf. 1:14), how could one believe that **it is the spirit that quickeneth** (63) and that even in death on a cross there is glory (cf. Phil. 2:8-9)? **The flesh profiteth nothing** (63); that is, "The new age which Jesus inaugurates . . . is not to be defined in terms of crude miracles on the phenomenal level, the plane of σάρξ . . . but in terms of that order of being which is real and eternal."[71]

In spite of the fact that Jesus' words are **spirit** and **life** (63), He knew that some were not responding in faith; **Jesus knew from the beginning who they were that believed not, and who (Judas Iscariot) should betray him** (64; cf. 2:25). In v. 65 Jesus repeats what He had already said in v. 44. Here we find again the reality of divine sovereignty at work with human freedom.

4. *Disciples at the Crossroads* (6:66-71)

There are no more startling words in John's Gospel than these: **From that time many of his disciples went back, and walked no more with him** (66). Some had followed Him for the wrong reason (6:26); others were too willing to retreat into a traditional religion (6:31); still others found the call to holiness of heart and life too demanding for them (6:53)—so they **went back!**

Why did they go back? A development titled "Disciples at the Crossroads" could be structured around three basic ideas:

---

[70]Westcott, *op. cit.,* p. 109.
[71]Dodd, *op. cit.,* p. 336.

(1) Some were more interested in material gain (loaves) than in letting Jesus master their lives, 26-27; (2) Some were completely satisfied with a form of religion devoid of commitment, 30-31; (3) Some, particularly Judas, saw the real cost of discipleship, holiness of heart, 53, 70-71.

At this Jesus turned to the twelve and said, **Will ye also go away?** (67) Peter had had a firsthand look at the "possibilities of grace"—the promise of becoming a partaker of His nature (6:54) and the guarantee of sharing in His resurrection (6:39-40, 44, 54). With this background Peter utttered those memorable words, **Lord, to whom shall we go? thou hast the words of eternal life. And we believe and are sure that thou art that Christ, the Son of the living God** ("the Holy One of God," ASV; 68-69).

Judas and his betrayal of Jesus is mentioned twice in this section (64, 70-71). Could it be that, just as Peter saw "the possibilities of grace" leading to heart holiness, Judas saw that a cross and not an earthly kingdom lay ahead? That there is no way to serve God except to become a partaker of His nature (6:53)? Could it be that, from this day when he came to the light of holiness of heart, he set his direction to rejection of the light, which culminated in final separation? "He . . . went immediately out: and it was night" (13:30).

E. THE NEW OUTPOURING, 7:1-52

1. *Jesus and His Brothers* (7:1-9)

After these things (the events of chapter 6) **Jesus walked** (lit., was walking) **in Galilee: for he would not walk in Jewry** (Judea), **because the Jews sought to kill him** (1). This takes the reader back to the events in 5:10-47, when Jesus was in Judea. Because He had healed the impotent man on the Sabbath and had declared that God was His Father, "the Jews sought the more to kill him" (5:18). This rejection in Judea explains why Jesus went to Galilee. The time of His departure was sometime in the spring of the year, before the Passover (6:4), and evidently He had stayed in Galilee until the fall of the same year. **Now the Jews' feast of tabernacles was at hand** (2). Again the author associates Jesus' activity in Jerusalem with one of the national feasts (cf. 2:13, 23; 5:1; 13:1). The Feast of Tabernacles was celebrated for seven days in the fall of the year to commemorate the wilderness wanderings (Lev. 23:33-43; Num. 29:12-39; Deut.

16:13-17). This was one of the great feasts of the Jews, second only to the Passover. Josephus described it as "a most holy and most eminent feast."[72]

His brethren therefore said unto him, Depart hence, and go into Judaea, that thy disciples also may see the works that thou doest. For there is no man that doeth any thing in secret, and he himself seeketh to be known openly. If thou doest these things, shew thyself to the world (3-4). His brethren may refer to "the children of the sisters of his mother Mary,"[73] or they may have been sons of Joseph by a former wife.[74] But the simplest and best interpretation is to take them as children of Joseph and Mary. Their suggestion that he **depart hence,** with the reasons given, was a subtle temptation to substitute man's applause and demands for the divine will, to follow man's calendar rather than God's appointed times, "to do the right deed for the wrong reason."[75] In this Gospel the purpose of signs, **works,** is that people may see and believe. However the brethren of Jesus had missed the point. Their request was only **that thy disciples also may see the works that thou doest.** No mention is made of faith. They had completely misjudged Jesus' motives for performing miracles. "For," they said, "no man works in secret if he seeks to be known openly" (4, RSV). The words here translated "openly" literally mean "with boldness." How utterly opposite to the spirit of the Christ of the Cross!

It was true then as it is now that things of the Spirit must be spiritually perceived. So these brethren of Jesus were not able to understand, "for not even His brothers were believing in Him" (5, NASB).

Jesus' answer to the demands of His brethren at once declares to them the reason for their lack of understanding and the divine order of His own life. Their failure to understand was because of their affinity with the world, their lack of spiritual sensitivity to God's plan. To them Jesus said, "Your time is always opportune" (6, NASB), and, **The world cannot hate you** (7).

---

[72]Flavius Josephus, *Antiquities of the Jews,* trans. William Whiston (Philadelphia: David McKay), p. 253.

[73]Adam Clarke, *The New Testament with a Commentary and Critical Notes* (New York: Abingdon Press, n.d.), I, 567.

[74]Westcott, *op. cit.,* p. 116. For further discussion, see notes on Matt. 13:55 (BBC, VI, 139-40).

[75]T. S. Eliot, *Murder in the Cathedral* (New York: Harcourt, Brace, c. 1935) p. 44.

In vivid contrast to this attitude of Jesus' brethren is His own awareness of and submission to the will of God. To their demand that He go up to the feast He responded, **My time is not yet come** (6, cf. 8; 2:4; 7:30; 8:20; 12:23; 17:1). "The feast of Tabernacles was a festival of peculiar joy for work accomplished. At such a feast Christ now had no place."[76] Rather, it was to the Cross that all His life pointed. Hoskyns well says, "The time of His Jerusalem is the time of His death, the Time laid upon Him by the Father."[77] His unbelieving brothers sought to persuade Him to seek the acclaim of men but they could not fathom the truth that the Incarnation must inevitably have its cross. These differences between Jesus' point of view and that of His brothers evoked different responses from the world. **The world cannot hate you; but me it hateth, because I testify of it, that the works thereof are evil** (7).

Likewise these differences must issue in divergent actions by Jesus and His brothers. **Go ye up unto this feast: I go not up yet unto this feast; for my time is not yet full come** (8). The meaning of this verse hinges very much on the negative used by Jesus in His declaration of purpose. The RSV reads, "I am not going up to the feast." This, based on good MS evidence, provides a problem in view of the fact that Jesus did later go to the feast (10). However, there is also good MS evidence (including the earliest witness, Papyrus 66) that the negative is "not yet" (*ouro*). Inasmuch as it makes for consistency, this reading should probably be adopted.

2. Jesus Departs from Galilee (7:10-13)

But when his brethren were gone up, then went he also up unto the feast, not openly, but as it were in secret (10). This is Jesus' farewell to Galilee, the scene of much of His public ministry. He went **in secret**, not with the great company of pilgrims who were journeying to the feast. His arrival at the feast occasioned a search for Him by the Jews (probably the hostile leaders); also **there was much murmuring** ("undercurrent of discussion," Phillips) **among the people concerning him: for some said, He is a good man: others said, Nay; but he deceiveth the people** (12). Even the better estimate of the people was neither good enough nor wholly accurate. Jesus is more

---

[76]Westcott, *op. cit.*, p. 117.
[77]*Op. cit.*, p. 312.

than a good man, and those who acclaim Him only as such have missed altogether the meaning of His incarnation, life, crucifixion, and resurrection (cf. Mark 10:18). The charge that He was "leading the people astray" (NEB) was most likely made because of His having healed the impotent man on the Sabbath (5:10), and then having claimed God to be His Father (5:17-18). Though the people differed in their estimates of Jesus, they were united in keeping their discussions about Him quiet: **no man spake openly of him for fear of the Jews (13).**

3. *Conversations in the Midst of the Feast* (7:14-36)

a. *Jesus Teaches the People* (7:14-24). The feast proper lasted seven days; an eighth was added as a holy convocation (Lev. 23:36), and was called the "great day of the feast" (cf. John 7:37). Jesus' actual appearance at the feast was perhaps on the fourth day, **about the midst of the feast (14). He went up into the temple, and taught** (lit. "and He was teaching"). This is the first reference in John's Gospel to Jesus' teaching in Jerusalem.

And the Jews marvelled, saying, How knoweth this man letters, having never learned? (15) Those who raised the question, the Jews, were Jesus' opposition (cf. 5:16, 18; 7:1, 13; 9:22; 10:31). The implication of their query is not so much that Jesus was illiterate as that in comparison with their learning in the Rabbinical schools He was an uneducated fellow, ignorant of the Law and its meaning. Man's presumption based on human wisdom is a shocking thing!

Jesus' answer to their question at once identifies the source of His teaching and declares His relationship to the Father. **My doctrine** (Gk., "teaching") **is not mine, but his that sent me (16).** His learning and teaching, in contrast with that of the Jews, has its origin and foundation in God. If any man questions the veracity of Jesus' statement, it can be put to the test. **If any man will do his will, he shall know of the doctrine** (teaching), **whether it be of God, or whether I speak of myself (17).** The absolute and final test of veracity and authority is God's will. Knowledge of the will of God and doing His will are inseparable. Action and belief go together.

The one who speaks and acts on the authority of another reflects the character of the one whom he represents and at the same time certifies his own veracity and integrity. So Jesus, sent by God (16, 28-29), is not like a teacher who **speaketh of himself** and seeketh his own glory (18). Rather, **he that seeketh his glory that sent him, the same is true, and no unrighteousness** (lit., "falsehood") [78] **is in him** (18).

For the moment Jesus forsook the subject at hand—defense of His right and ability to speak—and turned on His opponents. It was a twofold attack. First, He asked the rhetorical question, **Did not Moses give you the law?** followed by the devastating charge against them, **and yet none of you keepeth the law** (19). As evidence of their failure to keep the whole law perfectly, Jesus cited their practice of circumcising a male child on the eighth day even if it were a Sabbath: **And ye on the sabbath day circumcise a man** (22). Second, though they may have made right judgment where conflicting laws were involved, they had made wrong judgment where real values were at stake. **If a man on the sabbath day receive circumcision, that the law of Moses should not be broken; are ye angry at me, because I have made a man every whit whole on the sabbath day?** (23) The Jews in keeping the Law placed restraint on a man; Jesus, in doing **one work** (21),[79] fulfilled the highest law, liberating a man. An emphasis on legalistic morality leads one easily to wrong judgments that issue in destruction of real values. Hence Jesus' summation of the matter, **Judge not according to the appearance, but judge righteous judgment** (24).

In the course of the argument Jesus asked the question, **Why go ye about to kill me?** (19) Though the people denied the charge (20), probably due to their lack of information about the designs of the religious leaders, it is evident as seen above that the plan to kill Jesus was already well under way (cf. 1, 25). But "the people knew nothing of it"[80]; that is, the Galilean pilgrims were ignorant about it.

b. *The People Respond* (7:25-31). **Then said some of them at Jerusalem, Is not this he, whom they seek to kill? But, lo, he speaketh boldly, and they say nothing unto him** (25-26). Evidently some of the Jewish leaders at Jerusalem were among the

---

[78]Clarke, *op. cit.*, p. 569.

[79]**One work**, *hen ergon*, refers not so much to the deed as one among many, but rather to the fact that the healing of the impotent man (cf. 5), though a violation of the Sabbath laws, was a fulfilling of His mission as One sent of the Father (cf. 4:34; 9:4; 10:25; 17:4).

[80]Bernard, *op. cit.*, p. 262.

group of people with whom Jesus talked. In any case they knew of the plot to kill Him and were amazed that He was bold and open in His speech. Even more amazing to the people was the fact that **they say nothing unto him.** This paradoxical situation prompted the people to ask several questions. Their first question was designed to establish the identity of Jesus with the one **whom they seek to kill.** The second raised a question about whether or not He was able to speak openly and boldly because the rulers recognized Him as the Messiah. **Do the rulers know indeed that this is the very Christ?** (26) The form of the question in the Greek indicates that the people expected a negative answer. It was a query of doubting and casual interest rather than a serious quest for truth. To bolster their doubt they made a claim to knowledge of Jesus' origin—Nazareth. **Howbeit we know this man whence he is** (27). But did they really know whence Jesus came? Their partial knowledge led them to an entirely wrong conclusion about Jesus' real nature, the fact that He is Messiah, Jesus, the Son of God (cf. 8:14; 9:29-30; 19:9; Heb. 4:14).[81] They also argued that the Messiah's coming would be something mysterious. **But when Christ cometh, no man knoweth whence he is** (27). There is a Jewish saying that "three things come wholly unexpected, Messiah, a god-send, and a scorpion."[82]

In response to their assertion about the Messiah's coming, Jesus affirmed their partial knowledge of Him, and declared His origin to be from the One that sent Him. **Then cried** (cf. 7:37; 12:44) **Jesus in the temple as he taught, saying, Ye both know me, and ye know whence I am: and I am not come of myself, but he that sent me is true, whom ye know not. But I know him: for I am from him, and he hath sent me** (28-29). The Incarnation they could see; Jesus' human origin they knew. But His relationship to the One who **is true** (genuine, real) and from whom He came they knew not. So they knew neither Jesus the Christ nor the One who sent Him, as any true Jew should have known (cf. 14:9). Here "God is described as . . . a real Father, as it were, sending a real Son."[83] **I am from** (*para*) **him** (29) implies "a community of being between the Father and the Son."[84]

[81]Dodd, *op. cit.,* p. 258.

[82]Westcott, *op. cit.,* p. 120.

[83]*Ibid.,* p. 121.

[84]Bernard, *op. cit.,* p. 275.

The reaction of the people was divided. Some **sought to take him** (30) while others **believed on him** (31). The first group was deterred from its action because **his hour was not yet come** (30; cf. 2:4; 8:20; 12:23; 13:1; 17:1). In this Gospel, Jesus' **hour** is His death, which issued in "the hour of His exaltation and glorification, and the power of light, rather than the power of darkness."[85]

Those who believed on Him did so because they reasoned, **When Christ cometh, will he do more miracles than these which this man hath done?** (31) "The reason given . . . for belief on the Lord may be regarded as typically inadequate . . . But belief on the ground of the number of His signs is especially imperfect."[86]

c. *The Attempt to Arrest Jesus* (7:32-36). On hearing **that the people murmured such things**—literally, they "heard the crowd muttering these things"—concerning Jesus (31), **the Pharisees and the chief priests sent officers to take him** (32). This is the first mention of an organized attempt, probably instigated by the Sanhedrin, to take Jesus by force.[87] Jesus met this extremely tense situation with "an utterance sufficiently enigmatic to disturb His enemies, but transparently clear and pregnant with consolation to the readers of the gospel."[88] His answer was, **Yet a little while am I with you, and then I go unto him that sent me. Ye shall seek me, and shall not find me** (33-34). The **little while,** frequently appearing in this Gospel (12:35; 13:33; 14:19; 16:16), is historical in that it refers to the brevity of the Incarnation, and is prophetic in that it is a warning to the Jews that their time to respond is short. Though Jesus had said, "Seek, and ye shall find" (Matt. 7:7), here He warned that even their seeking in the hour of coming distress would be futile, for "the seeking may be so long delayed that the promise cannot be claimed. So, here, the warning is of the danger of delay."[89]

And where I am, thither ye cannot come (34). Many have taken this as referring to Jesus' departure into heaven, and the interpretation is probably correct. However, a close comparison

---

[85]Lightfoot, *op. cit.,* p. 180.

[86]*Ibid.*

[87]The Sanhedrin was composed of three major groups: the chief priests (ex-high priests and probably sons), elders, and scribes (mostly Pharisees). The chief priests were Sadducees. Perhaps elders belonged to both parties.

[88]Hoskyns, *op. cit.,* p. 319.

[89]Bernard, *op. cit.,* p. 279.

of this with other passages in John where the same idea is expressed (8:21; 13:33, 36-37) indicates that much more is intended. The verb (with negative) **cannot** is literally "lack power" or "be unable." If the problem is to be where He is, or to be like Him (cf. 6:53), then the demand is holiness of heart, and this can be wrought only by God's Spirit through Christ. So here, "when the Lord is standing before His opponents, they cannot come where He is, because they do not share His mind . . . Separation from Him is caused not by distance in space, but by unlikeness of heart and mind and spirit."[90]

The questions raised by the Jews in verses 35 and 36 indicate that they missed the real point of Jesus' statement. Yet their question, **Will he go unto the dispersed among the Gentiles (Jews scattered in Gentile countries), and teach the Gentiles?** (35) was highly prophetic (cf. 11:49-52). This accurately describes the course taken by early Christianity.

4. *The Last Day of the Feast* (7:37-52)

a. The Living Stream (7:37-39). The climax of the meaning of Jesus' life, teachings, and death as related to the Feast of the Tabernacles came **in the last day, that great day of the feast** (37). The fact that Jesus came to this feast where people were busily erecting booths of branches in remembrance of God's leading and protecting presence in the wilderness reminds us that "the Word was made flesh" (1:14) and "veritably *tabernacled* in the midst of His people."[91]

The ritual of the last day of the feast, symbolic of the entrance of the Israelites into Canaan, was characterized by a carefully worked plan. The multitude of pilgrims were all in festive array. Each carried in his right hand the *lulabh,* a myrtle and willow branch tied on each side of a palm branch. In his left hand was the *ethrog,* boughs of goodly trees, the so-called paradise apple, a species of citron (Lev. 23:40). The pilgrims were in three companies. One made preparation for the morning sacrifice at the Temple. Another gathered willow branches to adorn the altar. The third, and most important, went to the Pool of Siloam (cf. 9:7), whence the priest brought water in a golden pitcher to the Temple, where he poured the water at the base of the altar as a drink offering. As the water was poured, the great Hallel (Psalms

---

[90]Lightfoot, *op. cit.,* p. 181.
[91]Hoskyns, *op. cit.,* p. 310.

113—118) was chanted antiphonally.[92] It is thought by some that it was immediately after the symbolic rite of pouring water, with the antiphonal response, that **Jesus stood and cried, saying, If any man thirst, let him come unto me, and drink. He that believeth on me, as the scripture hath said, out of his belly** (heart) **shall flow rivers of living water** (37-38).

This event on the **last . . . great day of the feast** (37) points up several ideas of importance. First, there is Siloam (sent), which reminds us that in the new order Jesus is the One sent from and by the Father (cf. 3:17, 34; 5:38; 6:29, 57; 7:29; 8:24; 10:36; 11:42; 17:3, 8, 18, 21, 23, 25) and He fulfills everything foreshadowed by the pool and the water-pouring ceremony. Second, here one sees that what was external and limited, brought to the Temple from without, now becomes internal, dynamic, outflowing, and abundant. Third, the Spirit-filled life is characterized by abundance, both as to its Source, Jesus, the smitten Rock, whence flows the life stream (Num. 20:8; I Cor. 10:4), and as to its outflow, which is to reach every man of every nation (Luke 24:47-49; Acts 1:8). Finally, the account prefigures the fact that what Jesus did made Pentecost possible. "The whole symbolism of the Feast, beginning with the completed harvest, for which it was a thanksgiving, pointed to the future . . . The ceremony of the out-pouring of water, which was considered of such vital importance as to give the whole festival the name 'House of Out-pouring,' was symbolical of the outpouring of the Holy Spirit."[93] This is the obvious intent of the writer of the Gospel, for he commented: **But this spake he of the Spirit, which they that believe on him should receive: for the Holy Ghost was not yet given; because that Jesus was not yet glorified** (39).

A sermon for Pentecost Sunday titled "Pentecost Prophesied" is clearly depicted here. (1) Pentecost in symbol, 37; (2) Pentecost is God's Spirit within, 37-38; (3) Pentecost is life, God's life, abundant, 38.

b. *Divisions in Response* (7:40-52). The claim of Jesus to be the full and complete Source of satisfaction for man's deepest longings was met with various responses from the people. Some said, **Of a truth this is the Prophet. Other said, This is the Christ** (40-41). Because of these conflicting estimates of the person and

[92]Alfred Edersheim, *The Life and Times of Jesus the Messiah* (Grand Rapids: Wm. B. Eerdmans Publishing Company, 1943), pp. 157-60.

[93]*Ibid.*, pp. 149-50.

nature of Jesus, some tried to resolve the problem by the application of Messianic prophecies. **Shall Christ come out of Galilee? Hath not the scripture said, That Christ cometh of the seed of David, and out of the town of Bethlehem, where David was?** (41-42; cf. Ps. 132:11; Jer. 23:5; Mic. 5:2). The scriptures cited were right and true, but as is often the case, these people failed to investigate the facts of Jesus' origin, and based their conclusions only on hearsay. Hence, using only half the truth, they came to wrong conclusions and **there was a division among the people because of him** (43). Feelings ran so high that **some of them would have taken him** (lit., "laid hold of with hostile intent"); **but no man laid hands on him** (44).

Among those who heard Jesus in the Temple were officers commissioned by the chief priests and Pharisees to arrest Him (32). When these men reported back to headquarters, the chief priests and Pharisees asked, **Why have ye not brought him? The officers answered, Never man spake like this man** (45-46). "Having heard His words [they were] powerless in His presence" (cf. 18:1-9).[94] Evil men with evil designs are subject to God's plans and purposes, and even their most powerful exploits are always and only within God's permissive will. The simple and positive response of the officers in no way softened the malice of these evil men. The rhetorical questions put to the officers could be literally translated, "It can't be that you too are led astray, can it? No one of the rulers [probably Sanhedrin] or of the Pharisees has believed in him, has he?" (47-48) Even officers whose lives are highly regimented must make a personal decision when it comes to the question, What will I do with Christ? No moral being can evade this issue. The statement, **But this people who knoweth not the law are cursed** (49), reflects the Jewish reliance on law for salvation. People who knew not the Law (Torah, Mishnah) were under God's judgment.

But among the rulers there was one who was interested in justice, and who also knew of Jesus personally. **Nicodemus saith unto them, (he that came to Jesus by night** [rather, "before"], **being one of them,) Doth our law judge any man, before it hear him, and know what he doeth?** (50-51; cf. Deut. 1:16; Exod. 23:1) This was a challenge to the statement of the Pharisees in 48-49. Here was one ruler who knew the Law, and one who, though somewhat feebly, came to the defense of Jesus. The response of

[94]Lightfoot, *op. cit.*, p. 185.

the Pharisees, **Art thou also of Galilee?** (52) was a taunt, for they knew perfectly well that Nicodemus was not from Galilee. And their further self-defense, evidently made in fury, was not the truth. **Search, and look:** they said, **for out of Galilee ariseth no prophet** (52). How could those men have overlooked Jonah, Hosea, Nahum, and other prophets of the north? Emotional explosions do not yield truth!

F. THE SECTION ON ADULTERY, 7: 53—8: 11

The twelve verses in this section are not found in any of the oldest uncial MSS except Bezae (D), a sixth-century MS. Two MSS (L and Delta) of the eighth and ninth centuries omit it but leave a blank space. It does appear in Jerome's Vulgate (late fourth century) and some late Syriac and Coptic versions. However, none of the Greek commentators for a thousand years after Christ made mention of it. Among these are Origen and Chrysostom. A careful analysis of the vocabulary and style seems to show it not to be Johannine. It is also evident that the text has been poorly transmitted in the copying process; where the section is retained "the various readings are more numerous than in any other part of the N.T."[95] In different MSS it is found after 7:36; 21:24; and Luke 21:38. In the Nestle Greek text it is retained in a footnote, as it is also in the RSV.

However, there is nothing in the account that need bring it into question as to authenticity or historicity. As Bernard says, it "is very like the Synoptic stories about Jesus; while its tenderness and gravity commend it as faithfully representing what Jesus said and did when a woman who had sinned unchastely was brought before him."[96] So the incident may well be used for homiletical purposes.

Now to the episode. **And every man went unto his own house** (53). The divisions and differences had been so deep that now in a very literal sense each went his own way. This is made clearly evident by the fact that **Jesus went unto the mount of Olives** (1). Here is the only mention of this Mount in the fourth Gospel.

[95]J. H. Bernard, *A Critical and Exegetical Commentary on the Gospel According to St. John,* ed. A. H. McNeile ("The International Critical Commentary"; Edinburgh: T. & T. Clark, 1928), II, 717.

[96]*Ibid.,* p. 716.

And early in the morning he came again into the temple, and all the people came unto him; and he sat down, and taught them (2). The word used here for early (*orthrou*) is not characteristically Johannine. Also, this is the only place in John's Gospel where Jesus is seen sitting while teaching the people. The verb for **taught** is in the imperfect tense, and would be better translated "was teaching," indicating that this was habitual and customary for Jesus.

And the scribes and Pharisees brought unto him a woman taken in adultery; and when they had set her in the midst, they say unto him, Master, this woman was taken in adultery, in the very act (3-4). Only here in John is mention made of the scribes, though the expression **scribes and Pharisees** occurs frequently in the Synoptics. The picture is graphic. Jesus and many people were sitting as He taught in the Temple; into their midst these pompous personages came with a wretched creature and **set her in the midst.** Their action was not in the interests of justice, nor is there a shred of evidence that it was born of compassion. It was of no concern to them that such public display would bring embarrassment to both the soiled woman and the sinless Jesus. The accusers continued their charge. **Now Moses in the law commanded us, that such should be stoned: but what sayest thou? (5)** "The woman was not brought before Jesus for formal trial, but in order to get His expression of opinion on a point of the Mosaic law, which might afterwards be used against Him . . ."[97] A look at the Mosaic code indicates that stoning as a penalty for adultery was commanded only in the cases of a betrothed virgin or a married woman found guilty (Deut. 22:21-24).

John makes it clear that the sole intent of the scribes and Pharisees who brought the woman was to set a trap for Jesus: **This they said, tempting him, that they might have to accuse him** (6, "some grounds for accusation"). The trap was set in the form of a dilemma. If Jesus had said she was guilty and they had carried out the penalty, they could have brought Him before the Romans for inciting murder. But if He inclined toward merciful treatment, "He would have been declared by His critics to be a blasphemous person who did not accept the enactments of the sacred law."[98]

[97]Bernard, *op. cit.*, p. 717.
[98]*Ibid.*, p. 718.

But Jesus stooped down, and with his finger wrote on the ground, as though he heard them not (6). Jesus' stooping is not at all unnatural here, for He was sitting as He taught (2); He simply leaned forward to write on the ground. This is the only record of Jesus' writing, and what He wrote was soon erased by passing feet, wind, or rain. Hence it is futile to try to determine with certainty what He wrote, though there have been many interesting conjectures. Some say He wrote no message, but was only diverting attention from the woman to himself; hence the words, most certainly a late gloss, **as though he heard them not.** Others say He stooped to write because of His embarrassment both for the woman and for himself. Others note that the word translated **wrote** (*kategraphen*) may also mean "register," and on this basis conjecture that (1) He was registering the complaint against the woman, which would be no more permanent (in His presence) than the writing in the dust, or (2) He was registering the sins of those who made the accusation. The latter is reflected in a gloss in MS *U* and some cursives that read, "the sins of each one of them." Still others contend that this was Jesus' way of declaring that no answer would be given. T. W. Manson is quoted as saying, "The Lord by His action says in effect, 'You are inviting me to usurp the functions of the procurator. Very well, I will do so; and I will do it in the regular Roman way.' He then stoops down and appears to write down the sentence, after which he reads it out: 'Whoever among you is without sin, let him be the first to cast a stone at her.' The Lord defeats His adversaries by adopting the form of pronouncing sentence in the Roman manner, but by act and word He ensures that it cannot be carried out."[99]

So when they continued asking him, he lifted up himself, and said unto them, He that is without sin among you, let him first cast a stone at her. And again he stooped down, and wrote on the ground (7-8). The persistent insistence of the scribes and Pharisees evoked from Jesus His only words to them on this occasion. His answer was the *coup de grace* to their neatly laid plan and snare. His reply is an excellent example of argument *ad hominem* (i.e., He attacked His opponents rather than dealing with the question of what to do with the woman). The key words in His answer are **without sin** (*anamartetos*).

Is this a reference to absolute sinlessness, or does it refer to

[99]Lightfoot, *op. cit.*, pp. 347-48.

sins of a special kind? It is not likely the latter, as many have taken it, implying that all the men were guilty of the sin of adultery in either thought or act. It is more likely an allusion to the fact that only the sinless One in that circle could pronounce judgment. "The only question raised by His answer is the capacity of sinful men to act as the agents of God's dealing with men and women."[100] These men were unfit to be God's agents, for they would die in their sins (cf. 8:15, 21, 24). And as though to separate himself from their hypocritical arrogance, **again (Jesus) stooped down, and wrote on the ground (8).**

And they which heard it . . . went out one by one, beginning at the eldest . . . and Jesus was left alone, and the woman standing in the midst (9). The two clauses, **being convicted by their own conscience** and **even unto the last,** are clearly interpolations, indicated in part by the italics in KJV. The order of exit, beginning with the eldest, was probably no more than a matter of deference to age on the part of the younger men.

When Jesus had lifted up himself, and saw none but the woman, he said unto her, Woman, where are those thine accusers? (lit., "where are they?") **hath no man condemned thee? She said, No man, Lord (Sir). And Jesus said unto her, Neither do I condemn thee: go, and sin no more (10-11;** cf. 5:14). There is no indication here that mercy extended is license to sin! Grace is never increased or exalted by multiplication of sin. Rather, the Christ of the Cross makes it possible for men to abstain from the sins which He commands men to forsake. For this woman there was now an open door. "His final word is neither of condemnation nor of forgiveness, but a charge to forsake her former way of life."[101] In the final analysis of the account, it is clear that the Law is seen as inadequate for the needs of either the woman or her accusers.

G. A Series of Controversies, 8:12-59

1. *"I Am the Light of the World"* (8:12-20)

The scribes and Pharisees made their hasty exit from the Temple, while Jesus continued His teaching there. He said, **I am the light of the world: he that followeth me shall not walk in darkness, but shall have the light of life (12).** His claim on this

---

[100]Hoskyns, *op. cit.,* p. 570.
[101]Lightfoot, *op. cit.,* p. 348.

occasion to be the **light of the world** is best understood when it is remembered that great golden candelabra were lighted in the Temple during the Feast of Tabernacles. This was done in remembrance of the pillar of fire which directed the children of Israel by night in their wilderness experiences (Exod. 13:21). Even as Jehovah was their illuminating Guide then, so now Jesus is the **I am**, ever present, ever illuminating, dispelling the darkness (cf. 1:5, 9; 3:19; 9:5; 12:46; also 4:26; 6:35, 48; 10:7-9; 11:25; 13:19; 14:6; 15:1; 18:5-6, 8). C. H. Dodd says, "The determining fact of the Gospel . . . is that the archetypal light was manifested in the person of Jesus Christ. He is the Light in which we see light . . . Thus when John speaks of the light coming into the world he is always thinking of the appearance of Jesus Christ in history."[102] **He that followeth me shall not walk in darkness** (i.e., in ignorance, sin, limitation, and death), for he **shall have the light of life.** Light and life go together (cf. 1:4) and it is eternal life which He came to bring to men (3:16; 20:31).

Jesus' claim concerning himself sets the stage for the controversy. **The Pharisees therefore said unto him, Thou bearest record** (witness) **of thyself; thy record** (witness) **is not true** (13). In a sense their claim was correct, for certification of character in a formal or legal manner is not sought from the person in question but from another, and it was to this point that Jesus gave His twofold answer. In the first place, theirs was a wrong judgment in that they did not know His real nature. **Ye cannot tell** (know) **whence I come, and whither I go** (14). Further, their judgment was based on appearance only. **Ye judge after the flesh** (15). Jesus said, **I judge no man**—that is, **after the flesh,** as you do. Second, in contrast to their ignorance of His real nature, He had perfect understanding concerning himself. **I know whence I came, and whither I go** (14). Also their ready judgment, based on appearance only, misread Jesus' real mission, which was one "not of condemnation but of salvation (iii. 17, xii. 47, xx. 31). And yet, since the rejection of the Jews involves present (iii. 18) and ultimate (xii. 48) condemnation the work of salvation is inevitably also a work of condemnation; and if He condemns, His condemnation is true and genuine; there is no escape from it."[103] Finally, He answered their objection to His self-certification by showing that in fact He does

---

[102]*Op. cit.,* p. 204.
[103]Hoskyns, *op. cit.,* p. 331.

have another and adequate Witness. **And yet if I judge, my judgment is true: for I am not alone, but I and the Father that sent me. It is also written in your law, that the testimony of two men is true. I am one that bear witness of myself, and the Father that sent me beareth witness of me (16-18).**

When Jesus claimed His Father as Witness, the Pharisees raised the question, **Where is thy Father? (19)** Even as His questioners knew not His real nature, neither did they begin to comprehend His inseparable union with the Father. **Ye neither know me, nor my Father: if ye had known me, ye should have known my Father also (19; cf. 14:7-9).**

At this point John makes it clear that Jesus' claim to union with the Father was made **in the treasury, as he taught in the temple (20).** Even though Jesus' claim was of great offense to the Jews, yet **no man laid hands on him; for his hour was not yet come (20;** cf. 2:4; 7:30; 12:23; 13:1). It is well to remember that no man can ultimately frustrate the divine plan!

2. *"Whither I Go, Ye Cannot Come"* (8:21-30)

This section is at once a declaration of Jesus' deity (24, 28), and man's greatest sin—the sin of unbelief, which issues in death (21, 24). The chasm between God and sinful man cannot be bridged by man. **I go my way** ("I am going away," NEB), **and ye shall seek me, and shall die in your sins** (lit., "sin"): **whither I go ye cannot come (21;** cf. 7:34, 36; 13:33, 36-37; 14:6). Westcott says: "The search was the search of despair under the pressure of overwhelming calamity; and the issue was not failure only but death, and death in sin, for the search under false motives, with false ends, was itself sin, an open utter abandonment of the divine will."[104] The question of the Jews, **Will he kill himself? (22)** was an unwitting prophecy of Jesus' voluntary sacrificial death (10:18; cf. 11:51; 12:24-25).

Ye are from beneath; I am from above: ye are of this world; I am not of this world (23). Vivid contrasts—**beneath** and **above, this world** and **not of this world**—are characteristic of John's Gospel (cf. light, darkness; truth, falsity; life, death; sight, blindness; day, night). They always depict, as here, that man apart from God is hopelessly lost: **I said therefore unto you, that ye shall die in your sins (24).** In v. 21 the word sin is singular, show-

---

[104]*Op. cit.,* p. 142.

ing sin as one in its essence; here it is plural, **sins,** manifold in its manifestation.[105] That which has separated man from God and keeps him from God has only one antidote. Jesus said literally, "For except you have faith that I am, you shall die in your sins" (24). "The absolute claim of Jesus is denoted by the majestic *I am:* majestic and numinous, because of its Old Testament background."[106] (Cf. 8:28, 58; 20:31; Exod. 3:14; Deut. 32:39; Isa. 43:10.) The only way from death to life is through faith in Christ, very God as well as very man.

The persistence of the Jews in asking, **Who art thou?** (25) was indicative of their continuing ignorance of His real nature. Jesus' response is one of those passages that by change of punctuation in later MSS or versions may be read with different meanings. It may be correctly interpreted, **Even the same that I said unto you from the beginning** (25), or "Why do I talk to you at all?" (RSV, footnote), or "Primarily, I am what I am telling you."[107] **I have many things to say and to judge of you** (26) means, "There is much in you that I could speak about and condemn" (Phillips). What Jesus had to say was true because He spoke **to the world** the things which He had heard from the Father, who sent Him and who **is true.** Yet **they understood not that he spake to them of the Father** (27).

Then said Jesus unto them, When ye have lifted up the Son of man, then shall ye know that I am he (lit., "I am"), **and that I do nothing of myself; but as my Father hath taught me, I speak these things** (28). This is exaltation by way of the Cross, a cross prepared by the Jews. But this became the occasion for all men to know Christ's real nature. Though **Son of man,** He is the eternal **I am.** Oh, glorious mystery and meaning of the Incarnation with its inevitable Cross!

Although the Incarnation meant in one sense a separation of Father—**He that sent me** (29)—and Son, yet the Son is certain of the Father's presence: **he . . . is with me: the Father hath not left me alone; for I do always those things that please him.** "The Father was personally present with the Son . . . There remained perfect unbroken fellowship."[108] **As he spake these words, many believed on him** (lit., "many put their faith into

[105]*Ibid.,* p. 130.
[106]Hoskyns, *op. cit.,* p. 334.
[107]Bernard, *op. cit.,* p. 302.
[108]Westcott, *op. cit.,* p. 132.

Him," 30). "Belief in Christ is due to what He said rather than to the 'signs' which He wrought."[109]

3. *"The Truth Shall Make You Free"* (8:31-38)

Then said Jesus to those Jews which believed on him, If ye continue (lit., "abide") **in my word, then are ye my disciples indeed** (31). It is not accidental that John here describes the response of the **Jews which believed on him** (lit., "believed him") differently from the response mentioned in v. 30 (see NASB; NEB). This distinction points to levels of faith. To believe Him (31) implies a favorable impression, an intellectual assent to what Jesus said, but not necessarily a decision of commitment to discipleship. To believe in (into) Him (30) is to put faith in Him for who He is more than for what He does, and is the way to true discipleship. So it is that while continuing in His word one is His disciple indeed. This relationship is one of truth and freedom. **And ye shall know the truth, and the truth shall make you free** (32). What is it that makes a man truly free? An interesting combination of important factors is given here in 30-32. To have faith in Him (30), to abide in His word (31), true discipleship (31), and knowledge of the truth (32)—these make a man free. Truth which gives birth to freedom is living and personal, and cannot be other than truth incarnate, the Son (36).

Jesus' mention of freedom evoked from the Jews a question. They, the ones who believed Him (31), said: **We be Abraham's seed, and were never in bondage to any man: how sayest thou, Ye shall be made free?** (33) Without knowing it the Jews were in bondage, and that of the worst kind. What is it that makes a man a slave? Three things are evident: (1) sin—**Whosoever committeth sin is the servant of sin** (lit., "is a slave of sin," the definite article in Gk. suggesting the personification of sin as the master, 34); (2) separation from the only true source of freedom —**And the servant abideth not in the house for ever** (35);[110] i.e., **the servant of sin** (34) by his very status as a slave is not

---

[109]Bernard, *op. cit.*, p. 304.

[110]Westcott (*op. cit.*, p. 134) gives this explanation for the problem of correlating 34 and 35: "The transition from the thought of bondage to sin to that of freedom through the Son is compressed. . . . Thus there is a twofold change in thought, (1) from bondage to sin [34] to the idea of bondage [35], and (2) from the idea of sonship (contrasted with the idea of bondage) **to the Son."**

entitled to any of the privileges that belong to a son, e.g., inheritance, permanence of residence (abiding), freedom; (3) utterly wrong motivation—**but ye seek to kill me, because my word hath no place in you** (lit., "My word makes no headway among you," 37). Here is "the picture of men who believe Him, acknowledge the power of personality and message, but are fiercely resentful when they are told that their defence of the conventional and traditional morality is inspired by sinful motives. They are deluded into thinking that even a deep concern for high morality carries with it freedom from sin."[111]

The final and ultimate difference between freedom and slavery is traceable to the source of each. **I speak that which I have seen with my Father: and ye do that which ye have seen with** ("what you have heard from," RSV) **your father** (38). "The perfect revelation through the Son rests upon perfect and direct knowledge."[112] No doubt the allusion to **your father** is not to Abraham but to "your father the devil," made explicit in v. 44.

Never in bondage was the false claim of the Jews and of many another proud and sinful spirit. In this section (29-36) Alexander Maclaren points out: (1) Our bondage, 34; (2) Our ignorance of our slavery, 33; (3) The consequent indifference to Christ's offer of freedom, 33.

4. *"Before Abraham Was, I Am"* (8:39-59)

a. True Fatherhood (8:39-47). The Jews were in no doubt about their parentage.[113] **Abraham is our father** (39). This was true as far as their physical descent was concerned. But as sons of Abraham their lives should have been characterized by obedience to the truth, faith in God, and absolute trust. **Jesus saith unto them, If ye were Abraham's children, ye would do the works of Abraham** (39). A better translation based on good MS evidence would be, "If you are Abraham's children, be doing the works of Abraham." **But now ye seek to kill me, a man that hath told you the truth, which I have heard of God** (40). This is the only place where Jesus applies to himself the title **man**. The expression is of particular interest here, for this section is one in

---

[111]Strachan, *op. cit.*, p. 212.

[112]Westcott, *op. cit.*, p. 135. In this verse the MS evidence for **seen** and "heard" is almost evenly balanced.

[113]The disputation here is about the Jews' relationship to Abraham, the father of Israel, rather than to Moses, the giver of the Law.

which the primary argument is that Jesus is sent out from God
(42), God is His Father (49), and He himself is Deity (58). So
in a highly dramatic way the reader sees the Word which has
become flesh (1:14) meeting evil men on their own ground
(41, 44) as well as making a full confrontation of cosmic evil in
the person of the devil (44). Blessed truth—He is very God *and*
very man! The last clause, **this did not Abraham** (40), means
that Abraham welcomed the heavenly messengers who came with
truth to be believed (Gen. 18:1-8). But these men, purporting
to be sons of Abraham, **seek to kill** the One whom God has sent
(42), and in this **do the deeds of** their **father** (41), the devil (44).

The Jews, now beginning to understand that Jesus was
speaking of spiritual fatherhood, said, **We be not born of fornication; we have one Father, even God** (41). They were saying,
using Old Testament metaphor, "We do not owe our position to
idolatrous desertion of Jehovah."[114] Jesus answered, **If God
were your Father, ye would love me** (42). Such would be the
case because of the inseparable oneness of Father and Son. **I proceeded forth and came from God** (lit., "I am here"); **neither came
I of myself, but he sent me** (42). Rejection of the Son is rejection
of the Father (cf. 15:23).

Jesus, seeing their lack of understanding, raised the question,
Why do ye not understand my speech? (43) and then proceeded
systematically to answer it. There are five reasons. (1) "It is
because you cannot bear to hear my word" (RSV, 43). "Their
incapacity was . . . a spiritual deafness, and not merely an intellectual stupidity."[115] (2) Without equivocation, it was a matter of spiritual lineage. **Ye are of your father the devil, and
the lusts of your father ye will do** (44). To fortify this Jesus
gave a pointed description of their father. **He was a murderer
from the beginning**—no doubt an allusion to the spiritual death
of Adam and Eve (Gen. 2:17); he is incapable of telling the truth
because he abides **not in the truth** (44); and what he speaks is
"from his own nature, for he is a liar and the father of lies" (44,
NASB). (3) They were unable to face the truth. **And because I
tell you the truth, ye believe me not** (45). (4) Because of their
perverse nature they could only be blinded by the pure brilliance
of His utter holiness. **Which of you convinceth me** (can prove
Me guilty) **of sin?** (46; cf. Heb. 4:15) (5) Finally, as a kind of

[114]Westcott, *op. cit.*, p. 136.
[115]Bernard, *op. cit.*, p. 313.

capsheaf, Jesus summed up the whole matter by one question which He himself answered, **And if I say the truth, why do ye not believe me?** He that is of God heareth God's words: ye therefore hear them not, because ye are not of God (46-47).

b. *True Life* (8:48-59). Just as Jesus has declared His true relationship with the Father (38), He now makes known to the Jews His own true nature (58) and what it is that He came to give to men (51). The Jews did not accept Jesus' judgment that they were not of God (47) and retorted, **Say we not well that thou art a Samaritan, and hast a devil?** (48) Evidently Jesus was frequently called a Samaritan as a derogatory epithet. As though that were not severe enough, they accused Him also of being possessed of an evil spirit. **Jesus answered, I have not a devil** (demon, 49). But He made no answer to the charge of being a Samaritan. Some things are better ignored. "He would not recognize the meaning which they attached to a difference of race."[116] **But I honour my Father, and ye do dishonour me. And I seek not mine own glory: there is one that seeketh and judgeth** (49-50). Father and Son are one. To dishonor one is to dishonor the other. Jesus did not take the intended insult as detracting from Him, for He was not seeking His own glory. In the last analysis, their wrong judgment counted naught because God is the **one that seeketh and judgeth** (50). The hate and dishonor of men do not count when God approves.

The **Verily, verily** of 51 is used in John whenever a new and important idea is forthcoming. Here is the promise of victory over death. **I say unto you, If a man** (lit., "any man") **keep my saying** (word), **he shall never see death** (51). The converse of this has been set forth in 8:24, for failure to believe in Jesus means to die in one's sins. This failure to believe has been the continuing position of the Jews throughout the argument. Trust in Abraham they would; but accept Jesus, never! Yet the promise is for any man, Jew or Gentile, who will keep Jesus' word. **Keep** here carries the idea of intent watching, "the observance of the whole revelation in its organic completeness."[117] The "word" (note the singular) to be kept is Christ himself (cf. 1:1, 18; 14:23). "The sayings and the personality must be taken as a living whole."[118] Obviously, the clause **shall never see death** (51) does

[116]Westcott, *op. cit.*, p. 138.
[117]*Ibid.*
[118]Strachan, *op. cit.*, p. 215.

not refer to continuation of biological existence, but rather to eternal life, which begins when one believes.

What had previously been only an opinion of the Jews about Jesus (48), they now declared as certain fact. **Now we know that thou hast a devil** (demon, 52). They based their judgment on Jesus' declaration that those who kept His sayings would never see death. They said, **Abraham is dead, and the prophets; and thou sayest, If a man keep my saying, he shall never taste of death** (52). Actually, Jesus had said **shall never see death** (51). Either they misunderstood or misquoted Jesus, or as some contend, they simply used an expression that is quite synonymous in meaning. They had already pronounced their final judgment on Jesus—**Thou hast a devil** (52), yet they raised another question. It was a taunt rather than honest inquiry, for the form of the question implied that there could be only a negative answer. "You are not greater, are You, than our father Abraham, who died? [cf. 4:12] The prophets died too! Whom are you making yourself to be?" (53, lit. translation) Jesus' answer to their last question centers around the idea that His **Father that honoureth** Him is the same One whom the Jews say is their **God** (54). But both could not be the truth. Then Jesus said, **Yet ye have not known him; but I know him: and if I should say, I know him not, I shall be a liar like unto you: but I know him, and keep his saying** (word, 55). The veracity of Jesus' claim is grounded in His nature, and is expressed in His own personal activity, **I know** and **I keep**. These are the same requirements for the believer to possess eternal life (cf. 51; 17:3). If Jesus had denied His knowledge of the Father, He would have betrayed His own nature. He could not but speak that which He knew.

If the Jews had really been like their father Abraham, they would have known the Father (55), and would have honored the Son (49, 54). Jesus said, **Your father Abraham rejoiced to see my day: and he saw it, and was glad** (56). How great a contrast there is between the blasphemy of the Jews and Abraham's recognition of Jesus! There are two views about **Abraham rejoiced . . . he saw . . . was glad**. Some say that in view of the three past tenses (aorist) this is historical and refers to Abraham's act of faith by which he saw fulfillment of God's promises to him. Others contend that this is Jesus' rebuttal to the statement of the Jews that Abraham had died (52-53); rather, Abraham is alive, even as Moses and Elijah (cf. Matt. 17:3; Mark 9:4; Luke

9:30) and is a rejoicing witness to the fullfillment of God's promises to him.

The Jews, literalists to the bitter end, said, **Thou art not yet fifty years old, and hast thou seen Abraham?** (57) The last clause, on the basis of variant textual readings, could be translated, "Has Abraham seen you?" (RSV, footnote) This reading would tend to substantiate the second interpretation of verse 56 expressed above. The Jews had understood Jesus to refer to Abraham as still living.

Jesus' answer was also His supreme self-disclosure. **Verily, verily, I say unto you, Before Abraham was, I am** (58). The two verbs **was** and **am** are different words in the Greek. The word here translated **was** literally means "came into history," and has a temporal connotation. The verb **am** carries none of the temporal idea, but refers to being in an ultimate sense. Hence the vivid contrast between Abraham and Jesus (cf. 1:1 and 1:6, where there is the same contrast between the Word and John the Baptist).

Then took they up stones to cast at him: but Jesus hid himself, and went out of the temple, going through the midst of them, and so passed by (59). Strachan's comment is most fitting: "It is as though the angry waves reared themselves to put out the stars."[119]

H. THE NEW CONGREGATION, 9:1—10:42

Chapters nine and ten are a unit, and so are best considered together. The giving of sight to the man born blind not only illustrates the shining of the Light into the darkness (1:5), but also becomes the occasion for the beginning of the new community (9:34). This community is composed of those who believe in Jesus as Lord (9:38), and whose Lord is the Shepherd of the sheep (10:2).

1. *From Blindness to Sight* (9:1-7)

And as Jesus passed by, he saw a man which was blind from his birth (1). Some take this to follow immediately the Feast of Tabernacles and the events recorded in chapter eight,[120] while others think it more likely to be associated with the Feast of

---

[119]*Op. cit.*, p. 217.
[120]Hoskyns, *op. cit.*, p. 352.

Dedication (10:22), some weeks later in the winter.[121] When one considers the close relationship of chapters nine and ten, the latter view seems the more plausible. In any case, this opening verse sets the stage for the drama that is to unfold. The two main characters come into full attention—a beggar, blind from birth, and Jesus passing along the road.

And his disciples asked him, saying, Master, who did sin, this man, or his parents, that he was born blind? (2) This tells us that the disciples were present, though the question they asked here is the only role they played other than being bystanders in the unfolding events. Their question reflects the current Jewish belief that the sins of parents are visited on their children (cf. Exod. 20:5; 34:7; Num. 14:18; Deut. 5:9). It also suggests the view held by some that it was possible for the man to have sinned while "still in his mother's womb, or in some previous existence . . . Both these speculations are found in Jewish literature."[122]

Jesus answered, Neither hath this man sinned, nor his parents (3). Here the case is different from that of the impotent man whose illness was evidently related to his own personal sin (5:14). This man and his parents were both victims of a sin-cursed society where the innocent often suffer with the guilty. In such cases there is no necessary connection between the ills and misfortunes of the individual and his own sin. Moral men are all too often the victims of an immoral society. The clause, **but that the works of God should be made manifest in him (3)** could be translated, "But this has come to pass with the result that the works of God may be made manifest in him." God is not to be charged with causing man's misfortunes, sins, and sufferings. Rather, prideful, sinful man, in dire difficulty, can be rescued only by God, which is to God's glory.

I must work the works of him that sent me, while it is day: the night cometh, when no man can work. As long as I am in the world, I am the light of the world (4-5). In some texts the first clause reads, "We must work" (NASB), which would indicate that Jesus included the disciples and perhaps even the blind man (7) in the divine imperative to do the works of God. The phrase **him that sent me,** referring to God, and often occurring in this

---

[121]Westcott, *op. cit.,* p. 143.
[122]Hoskyns, *op. cit.,* p. 353.

Gospel,[123] is of particular importance here in view of the meaning of Siloam ("sent," see comment on v. 7).

There are contrasts here which depict in graphic form the cosmic struggle between good and evil—work, no work; day, night; darkness, light; blindness, sight; spiritual blindness, spiritual sight (9:39-41). God's work and man's work are for the light and all its corollaries; they are against darkness and all that it represents. The apostles ". . . by the power of the Spirit and as witnesses of what they had seen, became Sons of light for the illumination of the world."[124] It was the habit of Phineas Bresee, regardless of the time of day, to use the greeting, "Good morning." It is well to remember that "for the believer it is always day."[125]

The expression **as long as I am in the world** (5) literally translated would read, "Whensoever I am in the world." This is the idea of the universality of Jesus' mission, and is reminiscent of the prologue statement concerning the Light (1:5, 7-9).

When he had thus spoken, he spat on the ground, and made clay of the spittle, and he anointed the eyes of the blind man with the clay (6). During this whole first episode the blind man says absolutely nothing. Jesus, the Light, is in full command! (Cf. Rev. 1:13-18.) "The light cannot but shine."[126]

Various suggestions as to the reason for the use of the clay and spittle have been given. One is that spittle was thought to have healing power; hence Jesus used the means at hand. Irenaeus suggests that the first man was made of the clay of the earth, so here "that which the artificer—the Word—had omitted to form in the womb (i.e., the man's eyes) He then supplied in public."[127] Another explanation is that clay and spittle actually were used to seal the man's eyes, thus providing the occasion for the man to be sent to the Pool of Siloam. This was done, first, to test the man's faith and obedience; second, to say to all that "the truly sent One" fulfilled all that was foreshadowed by Siloam. So it was that Jesus said to him, **Go, wash in the pool of Siloam, (which is by interpretation, Sent)** (7).

---

[123]The phrase "he who sent me" occurs twenty-six times as spoken by Jesus, and another eighteen times in synonymous expressions.

[124]Hoskyns, *op. cit.*, p. 153.

[125]Strachan, *op. cit.*, p. 218.

[126]Macgregor, *op. cit.*, p. 226.

[127]Hoskyns, *op. cit.*, p. 354.

The pool was located in the southeast of Jerusalem (outside the present wall; see map 2) and was fed by a spring. A tunnel one-third of a mile long connects the two. The use of the symbol of water had occurred regularly in the Gospel, always representing the imperfection and inadequacy of Judaism, yet finding fulfillment in the person of Jesus (cf. 1:33; 2:6-7; 3:5; 4:13; 5:3-4, 7; 7:38-39). "The stream which issued from the heart of the rock was an image of Christ . . . So therefore here Christ works through 'the pool,' the 'Sent,' sent, as it were directly from God, that He may lead the disciples once again to connect Him and His working with the promises of the prophets."[128]

He went his way therefore, and washed, and came seeing (7). Even as Naaman went to wash at the command of Elisha, so this man obeyed, and received sight. It was not a case of recovering something that had been lost, for he was born blind. "To become a Christian is not to recover . . . but to receive a wholly new illumination."[129]

And he said unto him, Go, wash in the pool of Siloam . . . He went his way therefore, and washed, and came seeing (7). In this text Norman R. Oke finds the theme "Misfortune Can Be Turned into Fortune." (1) The man born blind was faced with inherited problems, 9:1; (2) The man was also faced with difficult circumstances, 8:59; 9:2; (3) He found that opened eyes lead to an opened heart, 9:34-38.

2. *From Darkness to Light* (9:8-41)

Evidently, on receiving his sight, the man went to his home, where the present scene takes place. The healed man now becomes the central figure in the drama, while neighbors, parents, Pharisees, Jews, officials in the synagogue come and go. It is only at the last that he and Jesus meet again. During these rapidly changing scenes there are two trends that are evident. One is the increasing awareness on the part of the healed man as to who Jesus is. The increasing awareness progresses from **man** (11), to **prophet** (17), to **Lord** (38). The other trend is the increasing unbelief and prejudiced judgment on the part of the Jews. The unbelief, beginning at the same place, **man** (16), moves to calling Jesus a **sinner** (24), and finally accusing Him of being possessed of a "devil" (demon, 10:20). When men are confronted by Jesus,

[128]Westcott, *op. cit.*, p. 145.
[129]Hoskyns, *op. cit.*, p. 352.

something inevitably happens. They are either better or worse; they believe, or refuse to believe; they step out into the light, or retreat into an outer darkness (13:30). There is no neutral ground when one stands before Him who is the Light (5).

a. He Is a Man (9:8-12). **The neighbours therefore, and they which before had seen him that he was blind, said, Is not this he that sat and begged?** (8) This identifies the man who had been blind as a beggar, and one with whom the neighbors were acquainted. Yet the fact that he was now able to see caused some speculative division among those who knew him. **Some said, This is he: others said, He is like him** (9). But there was no doubt in the mind of the man himself. Though the world as he knew it had suddenly changed, he knew his own identity, and so set the record straight by saying, **I am he** (9). This fact having been fully established, his neighbors, with natural curiosity, asked, **How were thine eyes opened?** (10) He immediately identified his Benefactor as **a man that is called Jesus** (11), and proceeded to recite the events in order—clay, anointed eyes, washing in Siloam, sight. It would appear that the report of making the clay, which constituted a violation of the Sabbath laws, was the reason for pressing the further question, **Where is he?** (12) For when the man answered, **I know not** (12), they brought him **to the Pharisees** (13).

b. He Is a Prophet (9:13-17). What the neighbors had asked before, the Pharisees now asked about the event—**how he had received his sight** (15). The answer—being the truth—was the same: clay, anointed eyes, washing, sight. When the Pharisees heard this, their judgment was immediate. **This man is not of God, because he keepeth not the sabbath day** (16). Little did they know that they were pronouncing judgment about the Lord of the Sabbath! Bystanders other than the Pharisees, with a degree of good reasoning, said, **How can a man that is a sinner do such miracles** (lit., "signs")? **And there was a division among them** (16).

The first question of the Pharisees was directed toward the event. Now their inquiry concerned the person of Jesus. **What sayest thou of him, that he hath opened thine eyes?** (17) There can be no real separation of what Jesus does from who He is if one is to have a true appraisal of either His work or His person. The healed man had an experiential acquaintance with Jesus' work, hence was moving in the direction of true understanding

117

of Jesus' nature when he responded to their question, **He is a prophet (17).**

c. He Is Lord (9:18-41). When confronted with evidence contrary to one's prejudices, one's first inclination is to call into question the evidence. So **the Jews** (meaning the Jewish leaders) **did not believe concerning him, that he had been blind, and received his sight, until they called the parents of him that had received his sight. And they asked them, saying, Is this your son, who ye say was born blind? how then doth he now see?** (18-19) The two questions provoked very different answers. The first the parents could not deny. **We know that this is our son, and that he was born blind.** But with the second question they dealt gingerly. Faced with the threat on which **the Jews** (Pharisees) **had agreed already, that if any man did confess that he** (Jesus) **was Christ, he should be put out of the synagogue (22),** they gave their cautious answer: **But by what means he now seeth, we know not; or who hath opened his eyes, we know not: he is of age; ask him: he shall speak for himself (21).** These "pleaders of the fifth amendment" were motivated by fear of excommunication, which was no light matter. To be **put out of the synagogue** meant social, economic, and family ostracism as well as the anathema of the officials of the synagogue. But the healed man was subject to the same threat and fear, and because his parents slid out from under their responsibility, the full weight of decision fell on him.

Since the Pharisees were unable to shake the evidence on the basis of questioning the man's identity, they now turned to him and said, **Give God the praise: we know that this man is a sinner (24).** The phrase **Give God the praise** was used as "a technical term in appealing for truthfulness,"[130] and means simply, "Now tell the truth!" But their own concept of truth was so warped that they called Him who is the Truth a sinner. The truth is a way, and the healed man was on that way. With great insight he answered, **Whether he be a sinner or no, I know not: one thing I know, that, whereas I was blind, now I see (25).** There is something that is absolutely unequivocal about genuine religious experience. And if one has had an experience that transforms from spiritual blindness to spiritual insight, a sound theology must follow. The skeptic or inveterate doubter is hard put to find an answer to the witness of the transformed life.

[130]Wilbert F. Howard, *op. cit.*, p. 617.

The insistent questioning of the Pharisees, **What did he to thee? how opened he thine eyes?** (26) evoked a commitment and a taunt from their would-be victim. Phillips renders it, "Weren't you listening? Why do you want to hear it all over again?" **Will ye also be his disciples?** (lit. translated, "You are not wanting to become His disciples too, are you?" 27). The form of the question indicates that he expected a negative answer from them. He knew full well that they were not about to become disciples. However, his use of the word **also** (too) indicates that he himself was committed to be a disciple.

Then they reviled him, and said, Thou art his disciple; but we are Moses' disciples. We know that God spake unto Moses: as for this fellow, we know not from whence he is (28-29). The verb translated **reviled** (cf. I Pet. 2:23) is a strong word, meaning "to abuse." These men were forcefully contending for their form of religion, while marking themselves off from both Jesus and His new disciple. If any knew whence Jesus came, it should have been Moses' disciples. But the whole trouble lay in the fact that they were not even followers of Moses (cf. 8:39). Their claim to valid religious experience in terms of ancient authentic origin was false.

The Jews' rejection of Jesus and their professed ignorance of His origin (29) seemed to the new disciple to be a most illogical position in the light of what had happened to him. Using a bit of logic based on experience, he attacked their position. **Why herein is a marvellous thing, that ye know not from whence he is, and yet he hath opened mine eyes** (30). Beginning with what he knew for a fact (sight instead of blindness), he argued that such a consequent must have an adequate cause. Jesus could not be a sinner as they had contended (24), for **God heareth not sinners** (31). This observation was more than casual or the result of pragmatic considerations. It was well grounded in Old Testament teaching (see Job 27:9; Ps. 66:18; Isa. 1:15; 59:2; Mic. 3:4; Zech. 7:13). On the other hand, God hears **any man** who is a **worshipper of God** and who does **his will** (31). Added to this is the fact of the unprecedented happening—the opening of the eyes of one that was born blind (32). Only God, or One who has intimate relationship with Him, could be the adequate cause of what had happened. **If this man were not of God, he could do nothing** (33).

Evidently his point was well made. The evidence of his experience, the forcefulness of his logic, and the not too subtle humor in his thrusts (27) constituted a threat to the Jews' prestige and position. Downgrade him they must, because they could not answer either his testimony or his logic. **Thou wast altogether born in sins, and dost thou teach us?** (34) They took his blindness at birth, which they themselves had previously questioned, to be sure proof that his origin was "utter sin" (RSV). They thus tried desperately to disparage the veracity of his testimony and the validity of his logic. Maybe they knew full well that truth does win, and this they could not tolerate, so **they cast him out** (lit., "threw him out," 34). "The 'Pharisees' have expelled from God's flock the man whom Christ Himself enlightened."[131]

For the man born blind this marked the beginning of a new personal relationship. It involved deliberate separation from the old way of darkness; it meant commitment to Jesus as Lord (38). It also was "the beginning of a new Society distinct from the dominant Judaism,"[132] again illustrating the contrast between the old and the new (cf. 1:33; 2:10, 18, 22; 3:5; 4:13-14; 5:8-9; 6:49-50). This new society becomes the theme in c. 10 under the figure of flock, fold, and shepherd.

When any man makes a deliberate decision for what he knows to be the right, and especially when he does so under severe duress and against great opposition, all the forces of truth and right are on his side and come to his aid. **Jesus heard that they had cast him out; and when he had found him, he said unto him, Dost thou believe on the Son of God?** (35) Jesus found him! Oh, blessed thought! The Hound of Heaven will not let go the honest, truth-seeking soul. Jesus' question literally translated would be, "Are you putting your faith into the Son of Man?" The reading "Son of Man" is very strongly supported textually, and fits particularly well into the context which follows, where the dominant theme is of judgment. "For the first time the Lord offers Himself as the object of faith, and that in His universal character in relation to humanity, as 'the Son of man.' He had before called men to follow Him: He had revealed Himself, and accepted the spontaneous homage of believers: but now He proposes a test of fellowship. The universal society is based on the confession of a new truth."[133]

---

[131]Dodd, *op. cit.*, p. 359.

[132]Westcott, *op. cit.*, p. 149.

[132]*Ibid.*

In response to Jesus' question the man answered by a question, **Who is he, Lord** ("sir," RSV), **that I might believe on him? (36)** The RSV translation of *kyrie*, which may mean either "Lord" or "sir," is perhaps preferable, for the association of Jesus with the title "Lord" had apparently not yet dawned on this man's consciousness (cf. 38). **And Jesus said unto him, Thou hast both seen him, and it is he that talketh with thee** (37). "Jesus reveals Himself as the Christ. To see Him and recognize Him is perfect sight and enlightenment, is, in fact, the vision of God" (cf. 14:9).[134] The climax to the whole account is the pointed and dynamic statement of the man, **Lord, I believe** (lit., "I am having faith, Lord"). **And he worshipped him** (38). Practical religious faith often outruns technical theological knowledge. Here the man acclaims Jesus as Lord. He affirms his faith in Jesus for who He is, not simply for what He has done. Recognition led to faith, and faith issued in worship. The tense (aorist) of the verb **worshipped** indicates an attitude and posture of life once for all. With that the healed man is mentioned no more. But what has happened to him has shown the path from darkness to Him who is the Light, and the way from a dead, meaningless, legalistic institution (Judaism) into the society and communion of the redeemed, where Christ is the Shepherd (c. 10). Here strangers (10:5) and hirelings (10:12-13) have no place.

A brief review of vv. 8-41 shows the progression of the healed man's faith. Beginning with his own experience he answered the question, "What think ye of Christ?" in a threefold response: (1) He is a Man, 8-12; (2) He is a Prophet, 13-17; (3) He is Lord, 18-41.

Further, what has happened in the episode has shown judgment to be the inevitable result of the coming of Him who is the Light. **And Jesus said, For judgment I am come into the world, that they which see not might see; and that they which see might be made blind** (39). The Pharisees suspected that they came under this judgment and asked, **Are we blind also?** (lit., "We are not blind too, are we?" 40). Their question implied an anticipated negative answer. But Jesus said, **If ye were blind, ye should have no sin: but now ye say, We see; therefore your sin remaineth** (41). Lightfoot comments: "When the Lord enunciates the cardinal truth that His Gospel involves a discrimination which confounds all the judgments and standards accepted by the

[134]Hoskyns, *op. cit.*, p. 359.

world, the Pharisees, who perceive that His words involve the challenge whether they themselves are in the Light or in darkness, learn, on putting the question to the Lord, that their claim to sight, their belief that they see, is in fact their condemnation."[135]

3. *The Shepherd of the Sheep* (10:1-42)

The opening **Verily, verily** (1) is characteristically used in John to introduce a shift in argument rather than a new episode. So here, Jesus' words are intimately tied to what has gone immediately before. The **I say unto you** (1) addresses the following discourse to both the healed man (9:35) and the Pharisees who were with him (9:40). For the man He had words of comfort and strength (3-4, 7, 9-10); for the Pharisees, words of condemnation and judgment (1, 5, 10-13).

a. The New Society (10:1-18). The parable or figure (1-5) which Jesus used was not at all new to His hearers. In Ezekiel 34 the same figure of shepherd and flock appears. There the rulers are condemned as negligent, tyrannous, careless of their responsibilities (4). They abuse their office (3), and feed themselves rather than the sheep (2-3, 8). As a result the sheep are scattered (5), and have become a prey to every beast of the field (8). Consequently God will judge the unworthy shepherds (10), and will himself gather the scattered sheep (12) and will feed them (14) and give them rest (15). God will appoint one Shepherd, David (Messiah), and He shall feed the flock, and be their Shepherd (23). Then the flock will have peace, enjoy safety (25), and possess the full blessing of the well-watered earth (26). The flock is Israel (30) and belongs to the Lord God (31).

Other Old Testament usages of the same basic figure are found in Psalms 23; 74:1; 78:52, 71; 79:13; 80:1; 95:7; 100:3; Isa. 40:11; Jer. 23:1-4. False shepherds appear in some of the figures; e.g., Jer. 2:8 (RSV, footnote); 10:21; 12:10; Zech. 11:3-9, 15-17. The same metaphorical language appears also elsewhere in the New Testament; e.g., Mark 6:34; 14:27; Luke 12:32; 15:3-7; Matt. 9:36; 15:24; 18:11-13; 26:31; Heb. 13:20; I Pet. 2:25; 5:4.

The reason for the frequent use of the shepherd-sheep figure is, no doubt, that the Jews had been a pastoral people for

---

[135]*Op. cit.*, p. 137.

generations. This kind of language was understandable to all. As Jesus used the figure here, the essential elements all appear: flock, fold, door, shepherd, thieves, robbers, and strangers. It would do violence to the parable to try to find an exact and constant equivalent for each of these; yet some things are evident.

First, there is only one true entrance into the sheepfold. **He that entereth not by the door into the sheepfold, but climbeth up some other way, the same is a thief and a robber (1).** The motive and the method of approach to the flock mark the differences between robber and shepherd. Sin and its agents are set to deceive and destroy, whereas the Good Shepherd (14) lays down His life for the sheep (15).

Second, there is the Good Shepherd (11), who enters the fold by the door—**But he that entereth in by the door is the shepherd of the sheep (2).** The word **shepherd** is *anarthrous* in the Greek, and consequently "fixes attention on the character as distinct from the person."[136] "The shepherd is not *a* figure in the parable, he is *the* figure; and it is upon the description of his behavior that the narrative lingers, in order that the attention of the readers may be concentrated there. Not only are the sheep his own sheep, not only has he full authority to approach them, not only does he call his sheep by name, not only do they hear his voice; but he leads them out, and, when he has put forth all his sheep, he goes before them, and the sheep follow him."[137]

Third, He is the Creator of the new society of believers, i.e., those who believe in Him. **To him the porter openeth; and the sheep hear his voice; and he calleth his own sheep by name, and leadeth them out. And when he putteth forth his own sheep, he goeth before them, and the sheep follow him (3-4).** The mention of the **porter** or gatekeeper is incidental to the story. But one thing stands out. There is a relationship between Shepherd and sheep that is based on the nature of the Shepherd—His voice, His knowledge of the sheep, His leading, His guidance. These words must have meant much to the man who had been healed of his blindness, and who had been excommunicated from his synagogue (9:34) and family. Now he was a member of the new society, a follower of the Good Shepherd. The word for **putteth forth** is the same as that translated "cast out" in 9:34. So really, to be cast out is, from God's point of view, to be called out. Such

[136]Westcott, *op. cit.*, p. 152.
[137]Hoskyns, *op. cit.*, p. 372.

is the *ekklesia* (lit., "the called-out ones"), the Church, the new society.

Fourth, those who belong to this new society, the Church, are amenable to only one voice, **for they know his voice. And a stranger will they not follow, but will flee from him: for they know not the voice of strangers (4-5).** There is a glorious exclusiveness about being a member of Christ's flock—there is only one voice, one way, one will that really counts. In a day of exceedingly complex living the sure way to peace of mind, focus of purpose, and meaningful commitment is found in knowing only his voice. Such "singleness of hearing" is a safeguard not only against heterodoxy but also personality disintegration (cf. 14-15). Thomas R. Kelly calls this the "habitual orientation of all one's self about Him who is the Focus."[138]

Having recorded the parable, the author inserted a note about the reaction of some of the hearers. **This parable spake Jesus unto them: but they understood not what things they were which he spake unto them (6).** The word here translated **parable** occurs only five times in the New Testament, four of them in John (16:25, 29; II Pet. 2:22). It means a symbolic word picture, and especially in Johannine usage a dark saying, a "figure of speech" (NASB) "in which especially lofty ideas are concealed."[139] It is perhaps best translated "allegory" (Moffatt). **They understood not** stands in interesting contrast to John's more usual expression, "they believed not" (cf. 38). Direct acquaintance with (knowledge) and personal commitment to (faith) God's call (voice) and claim (ownership) are definite corollaries in the divine-human encounter.

There now follows an explanation of the parable (vv. 7-18), and yet the explanation is given in highly figurative language (cf. parable of the sower and explanation, Matt. 13:3-23). **Then said Jesus unto them again, Verily, verily, I say unto you, I am the door of the sheep (7).** The **Verily, verily** notes the shift from parable to explanation, which begins with Jesus' self-disclosure of His divine nature (cf. comments on 4:26; 6:20; also of 6:35, 41, 48, 51; 7:34, 36; 8:12, 24, 28, 58; 10:9, 11, 14, 36; 11:25; 13:19; 14:6; 15:1, 5; 17:24; 18:8). The exclusiveness of the way of faith in Christ has never been better put than when

---

[138]*A Testament of Devotion* (New York: Harper and Brothers, 1941), p. 44.

[139]Arndt and Gingrich, *op. cit.*, p. 634.

Jesus said, **I am the door.** Christ is the Way to Christ, for He is both Door and Fold. It sounds attractive when men say that all are Christians who have high ethical ideals comparable to those of the Sermon on the Mount. But how empty it sounds when placed beside the personal challenge, **I am the door!** There is no other! So it follows that **all that ever came before me are thieves and robbers: but the sheep did not hear them** (8). Certainly this is not to be taken as referring to those true messengers of God in the Old Testament, but it does include all who falsely purport to be God's messengers. Even the Pharisees, who perverted Moses' teachings as though they were life-giving, came under this condemnation. "There is no point in human history which lies beyond the horizon of the thieves and robbers of the parables. Whenever men have claimed to announce the gift of life, or shall claim to announce it, apart from faith in Jesus, they proclaim themselves as thieves and robbers, and their activity has been, and is, and will be, a destructive activity."[140]

Again Jesus declared himself to be **the door** (9), but this time to portray the benefits that come to the one who enters. **By me, if any man enter in, he shall be saved, and shall go in and out, and find pasture** (9). It is now a matter of life and death for the sheep. The true and only entrance means life— salvation, security, sustenance. But death attends the false way, for **the thief cometh not, but for to steal, and to kill, and to destroy** (10)—lostness, death, destruction. Against this background is cast the supreme theme of the Gospel—life abundant through faith in Christ. **I am come** ("I came," Phillips) **that they might have life, and that they might have it more abundantly.** The whole purpose of Jesus' mission was to impart life (20:31), and that this life should be of supreme quality (eternal) as well as infinite in quantity (cf. 1:16; 2:6 ff.; 4:14; 6:13; 7:38). God's purpose and plan are not only to save man from death, destruction, and guilt, but to make him holy, "conformed to the image of his Son" (Rom. 8:29). Such purpose could be achieved in only one way, the voluntary death of Jesus. Simply because He is **the good shepherd,** He gives **his life for the sheep** (11). Literally, **the good shepherd** may be translated, "The shepherd, the good one." His goodness so excels that He is singled out—there is no shepherd like Him. Some have raised the question how Christ can be both Door and Shepherd. But that is to strain at the details of

---

[140]Hoskyns, *op. cit.,* pp. 368-69

the parable, for surely He is Door to the fold, the only Entrance to life, and He is Shepherd to the sheep, the only One who cares enough to lay down His life for the sheep (cf. 6:51).

A new figure is introduced with 12—the hireling. **But he that is an hireling, and not the shepherd, whose own the sheep are not, seeth the wolf coming, and leaveth the sheep, and fleeth: and the wolf catcheth them, and scattereth the sheep. The hireling fleeth, because he is an hireling, and careth not for the sheep (12-13).** There is no more intensive or concentrated examination of motive for service than this. One does not have to be a thief, robber, or wolf to destroy the sheep—just a wage worker, i.e., one who thinks only in terms of what he can get, never in terms of what he can give. Unless one keeps a close guard on his motives to keep them pure, when the crisis comes **(the wolf)** a man is overwhelmed and flees, forsaking responsibility and the flock.

The relationship between the Good Shepherd and His flock is grounded in the nature of the relationship between Jesus and the Father. **I am the good shepherd, and know my sheep, and am known of mine** ("My own know Me," NASB). **As the Father knoweth me, even so know I the Father: and I lay down my life for the sheep (14-15).** Each of the six verbs in these verses is in the present tense, thus making the portrayal graphic. The verb **know** in the present tense particularly means to know by acquaintance, experience. The sheep "have experimental knowledge of Jesus as their own shepherd. Here (in this mutually reciprocal knowledge) lies the secret of their love and loyalty."[141]

The universal note of the fourth Gospel shines forth in Jesus' statement, **And other sheep I have, which are not of this fold: them also I must bring, and they shall hear my voice; and there shall be one fold, and one shepherd (16).** Note that it is **other sheep**, not goats. "The flock of Christ is not confined to those enclosed in the Jewish fold, whether in Palestine or elsewhere"[142] (cf. 11:52; 12:32). God's love is to *all* the world (3:16). The moral urgency to bring these other sheep into the fold is expressed in **them also I must bring.** The verb **hear** "takes the genitive, as it does when it connotes hearing with understanding and obedience."[143] **There shall be one fold** should be literally

---

[141]A. T. Robertson, *op. cit.*, p. 180.
[142]Westcott, *op. cit.*, p. 155.
[143]Bernard, *op. cit.*, p. 363.

translated, "They shall be one flock."[144] The verb is plural in the best MSS, and the word "flock" is the correct translation of the Greek *poimne* (cf. Ezek. 34:20-24). "All (Jews and Gentiles) will form one flock under one shepherd."[145]

Jesus' voluntary, self-giving sacrifice provides not only a trend of thought in this section, but is a kind of climax in His interpretation of the parable. The idea has been mentioned before, but now the whole matter is made explicit. The Father's love and the self-giving of the Son are inextricably bound together (6:51; 10:11, 15). **Therefore doth my Father love me, because I lay down my life, that I might take it again. No man taketh it from me, but I lay it down of myself. I have power to lay it down, and I have power to take it again** (17-18). For the first time in this section the idea of the Resurrection is introduced, and is seen to be "the inevitable consequence of the obedience of Jesus."[146]

There is no conflict between Jesus' voluntary self-giving and His statement, **This commandment have I received of my Father** (18). Self-chosen goals in terms of God's perfect will constitute life's highest and best freedom. When Jesus aligned himself with the will of the Father, resurrection was made possible and actual. "The concrete community of Christians in the world has been brought into being by a concrete historical set of obedience, and the whole life of the Church must be controlled by faith in Jesus. In Him the love of God and the faith of men meet, and they meet in the death of Jesus, because there the will of God was finally accomplished: accomplished, because His death was neither the result of the manoeuvres of the Jews nor of some impetuous or capricious decision of Jesus to surrender Himself to His enemies. It was the climax of a divine necessity, and His whole life and ministry moved steadily towards it."[147]

b. *Divisions* (10:19-21). Jesus' declarations concerning himself, as well as His act of healing the man born blind, brought a **division ... among the Jews** (19). This cleavage was deeper than ever before (cf. 9:16). Some raised the question as to Jesus' nature, implying that He was a sinner for having broken the

[144]"A certain disturbance in the understanding of v. 16 was caused by the translation in the Vulgate of the Greek word meaning a *flock* by the Latin word meaning a *fold*" (Hoskyns, *op. cit.*, p. 379).
[145]Robertson, *op. cit.*, p. 181.
[146]Hoskyns, *op. cit.*, p. 379.
[147]*Ibid.*

Sabbath laws, while others contended that no sinner could open
the eyes of a blind man. The **division** (dissension, schism) here
was so sharp that **many of them said, He hath a devil** (demon),
and is mad (20).[148] In the divine-human encounter there is a
law that men cannot be the same when they have met the Man
of Galilee. The response is either faith or unbelief. Faith issues
in a true concept of who Jesus is, as was the case with the healed
man. Unbelief—beginning at the same place, Jesus the Incarnate
(9:15-16)—progressed to the point where they called Him a
sinner (9:24), and now to the supreme blasphemy, **He hath a
devil** (cf. 7:20; 8:48, 52).

Since His enemies believed Jesus to be demon-possessed,
their question put to the opposition was natural: **Why hear ye
him? (20)** The verb **hear** as used in this place means "a hearing
with attention and appreciation,"[149] hence making the schism
among the Jews more understandable.

The retort of the opposition was based purely on pragmatic
premises. Their conclusion was placed squarely on what they
themselves had seen, and that Jesus' statements about himself
could not be the **words** of one **that hath a devil.** They clinched
their argument with the rhetorical question, **Can a devil open
the eyes of the blind? (21)**

c. *Last Public Testimony* (10:22-42). The place is the same
as in 7:10—10:21, **Jerusalem,** but the time is now **winter** and the
occasion **the feast of the dedication (22)**. These few verses (10:
22-42) are all that John has to say about the time between the
events and discourses surrounding the Feast of Tabernacles (7:8)
and the events and discourses close to the last Passover Feast
during Jesus' earthly ministry (12:1). The **feast of the dedication**
was the latest of the great Jewish festivals to be founded. It was
held in commemoration of the purification of the Temple in
164 or 165 B.C. by Judas Maccabaeus and his brothers, bringing to
an end the profanation of the Temple under the Syrian king Anti-
ochus Epiphanes. Still celebrated today by the Jews, it is called
Hanukkah, and falls near Christmastime.[150] It is also known as
the Festival of Lights.

[148]The verb **is mad** means literally "to be out of one's mind" (Arndt
and Gingrich, *op. cit.,* p. 487).

[149]Bernard, *op. cit.,* p. 342.

[150]William Barclay, *The Gospel of John,* II (2nd ed.; "The Daily Study
Bible"; Philadelphia: Westminster Press, 1956), 80-81.

Here, as elsewhere in John, the discourse is associated with a festival (cf. 2:23; 5:1; 6:4; 7:2, 38-39), and has special meaning in terms of the purpose of the festival. It has been suggested that "here the Lord's ministry, which will reach its climax in the passion, is set forth as the true dedication, which is to supersede and replace the Jewish festival."[151] Likewise, the writer's mention of the fact that **it was winter** seems to be more than a casual remark, for it was "the season of death, without and within"[152] (cf. 13:30).

The fact that **Jesus walked in the temple in Solomon's porch** (23, see Chart *A*) may have been because of the cold weather. It was there the rabbis talked with their students and discussed the Law. As Jesus mingled with them, there came the inevitable question. **How long dost thou make us to doubt?** is also translated, "How long dost thou hold us in suspense?" (ASV) Though these translations are acceptable, the Greek verb *aireis* used here is the same word as in 18, and is there translated "taketh." It has been suggested that a fitting translation here could be, "How long dost thou continue to take away our life?" Hoskyns comments: "The ministry and death of Jesus involve the destruction of Judaism . . . Jesus is taking away their life."[153]

In response to the Jews' demand, **If thou be the Christ, tell us plainly** (24), Jesus gave a fourfold reply. (1) The Jews **believed not**, even though the Word had come to them, **I told you**, and His works had borne **witness** of Him (25). God's personal communication to men at its best had not issued in faith on the part of the Jews. (2) The reason for their not having faith, **ye believe not** (26), was that they were **not** His **sheep**. (3) In contrast with those who believe not, there are those He calls **my sheep** (27). Four things characterize His sheep: (*a*) they **hear His voice**, and as here written, they hear with attention and appreciation (20); (*b*) He knows them (lit., "I am personally acquainted with them"; 14-15); (*c*) they follow Him (lit., "they are following Me"); and (*d*) He gives **unto them eternal life** (27-28).[154] (4) Those who hear, with whom He is personally acquainted, and to whom He gives eternal life, **shall never perish, neither shall any man pluck them out of my hand** (28). Some

---

[151]Lightfoot, *op. cit.,* p. 212.

[152]*Ibid.*

[153]*Op. cit.,* pp. 386-87.

[154]See Introduction, sec. 4, "Life," for the meaning of eternal life.

have taken this to mean that one is eternally secure regardless of what a man does himself in respect to his relationship to God. But the guarantee of security—it is a wondrous and adequate promise—is that nothing outside a man can destroy him while he is putting his faith in God. Westcott says: "If man falls at any stage in his spiritual life, it is not from want of divine grace, nor from the overwhelming power of adversaries, but from his neglect to use that which he may or may not use. We cannot be protected against ourselves in spite of ourselves."[155]

This guarantee to the one who has faith is grounded in the very nature of God, for Jesus said, **My Father, which gave them me, is greater than all; and no man is able to pluck them out of my Father's hand (29).** There is a textual problem in the KJV rendering of the first part of 29. The most ancient authority reads, "That which the Father has given me," and this is preferred by some commentators. The same idea is also expressed in 6:39 and 17:2. Both readings, however, convey the same basic idea. "The Father is the only source of the ultimate security of the believers in Jesus. They belong to Jesus because they have been given to Him by the Father."[156]

Further, the guarantee to the believer is grounded in the relationship between the Father and Jesus, for He said, **I and my Father are one (30).** What is the nature of this relationship? In what sense are the Father and Son one? A literal translation would be, "I and the Father, we are one." Westcott says: "Every word in this pregnant clause is full of meaning. It is *I,* not *the Son; the Father,* not *my Father;* one essence, not one person; *are,* not *am.* The revelation is of the nature of Christ in the fulness of His double nature, of the incarnate Son in the fulness of His manifested being, and that in relation to *the Father,* to God as He is Father at once of the Son and of men."[157] Barclay, using other statements of Jesus concerning the unity between Jesus and the Father and believers (17:11, 20-22), argues that the unity here described is basically a moral union. He says: "The bond of unity is love; the proof of love is obedience. Christians are one with each other when they are bound by the bond of unity, and obey the words of Christ. Jesus is one with God, because as no other person ever did, He obeyed God and He loved God. His

---

[155]*Op. cit.,* p. 158.
[156]Hoskyns, *op. cit.,* p. 389.
[157]*Op. cit.,* p. 159.

unity with God is a unity of perfect love, issuing in a perfect obedience."[158] Though this moral union is a fact, it is based on the assumption of the truth of a union of natures.

When **the Jews took up stones again to stone him** (31), it was not a new attitude on their part (cf. 1:11; 5:17-18; 6:40-43, 51-52, 60, 66; 7:29-30; 8:58-59), and it reached its climax in the Crucifixion. The alleged reason for their action was **for blasphemy,** because, they said, **thou, being a man, makest thyself God** (33). Jesus' response to this was an appeal to their reverence for the Scriptures. He quoted from Ps. 82:6, **I said, Ye are gods** (34). This applied "to all the inspired men of the Old Testament, including the prophets, and prepares the way for the contrast between those to whom the word of God came and Jesus, who is veritably the Son of God."[159] Since **the scripture cannot be broken** (35), why should not the title **Son of God** (36) apply to the One **whom the Father hath sanctified, and sent into the world** (36)?[160]

Jesus was willing to submit His claim to the pragmatic test. If His claim, **I am the Son of God** (36), is true, His works should be commensurate with such a claim. **If I do not the works of my Father, believe me not** (37). The Jews had not disclaimed the good works of Jesus (cf. 33), but they had stumbled in unbelief with respect to His true nature. It is easy for man to accept God's blessings and benefits, but it is more difficult to place faith in Christ for who He is. It is the constant theme of John's Gospel that the faith which issues in eternal life is never less than faith in Him for who He is. This is not to say that the works of Jesus have no instrumental value. He exhorted the people to **believe the works: that ye may know, and believe** ("realize," NEB), **that the Father is in me, and I in him** (38). Bernard translates the **know, and believe** more accurately: "that you may perceive, and so reach the fixed conviction of knowledge."[161] But the Jews would brook no compromise and **they sought again to take him** (39). However, since His hour had not yet come (cf. 7:30; 8:20), **he escaped out of their hand.**

[158]*Op. cit.,* p. 87.

[159]Hoskyns, *op. cit.,* p. 391.

[160]The word here translated **sanctified** is a form of the Greek *hagiazo,* meaning "to set apart for sacred use," "consecrate," "make holy." As applied to Jesus, its meaning is "consecrate," "set apart" (cf. 17:19). Here, in the aorist tense, it shows the timelessness of the eternal sacrifice.

[161]*Op. cit.,* p. 369.

This is the "last direct encounter of the Lord with the Jews during the ministry."[162] Argument having ceased, He **went away again beyond Jordan into the place where John at first baptized; and there he abode** (40; cf. 1:28). This location cannot be identified exactly but it would be somewhere east of the Jordan in Perea or Decapolis (see map 1). This return to the place of the beginning of His public ministry was no accident. The quietude of the solitary place and the memory of a great visitation from God are necessary in the life of any person who is facing a crisis as was Jesus (cf. Gen. 35:1-5). But even in this place there was no respite for our Lord from the crowds, **for many resorted unto him** (41) and **believed on him there** (42). In this setting there is a last mention of John the Baptist in this Gospel. It is a kind of comparative evaluation between the works and words of John and Jesus. **John did no miracle: but all things that John spake of this man were true** (41).

I. FROM DEATH TO LIFE, 11:1-57

This is the last of the "signs" recorded by John as evidence that Jesus is the Christ, and as another occasion for faith on the part of those who read (cf. 20:30-31). This miracle, often called the greatest, is a fitting climax to the earthly work of Jesus. It is the example par excellence of what Jesus came to do for men—to bring them from death to life. "I am come that they might have life, and that they might have it more abundantly" (10:10).

The question has frequently been raised concerning the fact that this miracle is recorded only in John and is not mentioned in the Synoptics. We should remember that there are other raising-from-the-dead miracles recorded in the Synoptics: the daughter of Jairus (Matt. 9:18-26; Mark 5:22-43; Luke 8:40-56) and the widow's son (Luke 7:11-17). The Synoptics also make general statements about such miracles characterizing the work and ministry of Jesus (Matt. 11:4-5; Luke 7:22).

At least three things need to be said. First, John makes no mention of these two miracles recorded in the Synoptics; neither does any writer except Luke tell of the widow's son. To discount Lazarus' resurrection solely on the basis of lack of supporting evidence would require the discounting of the raising of

[162]Lightfoot, *op. cit.*, p. 211.

the widow's son also. Second, there is the record of an eyewitness, John; so the burden of proof lies with the man who says, "It didn't happen." Finally, if Jesus was God incarnate, there are no insurmountable difficulties in the account. If He is less than that, the whole New Testament story is entirely incredible. So the question really is: Whom do you think Him to be?

1. *The Death of Lazarus* (11:1-16)

The introduction of the narrative presents the main personages. There are the two sisters, Mary and Martha (cf. Luke 10:38-42). They are identified as residents of Bethany (see map 2), a village on the southeast slope of Olivet, about two miles from Jerusalem. Mary is described as **that Mary which anointed the Lord with ointment, and wiped his feet with her hair** (2, cf. Matt. 26:6-13; Mark 14:3-9). Lazarus,[163] the brother of the two women, is not mentioned elsewhere in the New Testament. But here he is an important, though passive, figure. In characteristic Johannine style he is first introduced as **a certain man** and as **sick** (1), "the fact of chief importance."[164] The sickness of Lazarus depicts the condition of every man apart from God. The affliction is sin, it is universal (Rom. 3:23), and its end is always death (Rom. 6:23).

In their hour of distress, because of the dire sickness of Lazarus, the sisters sent word to Jesus, who was in Perea (10:40), perhaps twenty or thirty miles distant (see map 1), saying, **Lord, behold, he whom thou lovest is sick** (3). The message was sent "with the natural affection of personal attachment."[165] Jesus' initial response said three things: First, **this sickness is not unto death** (4). These words "mean to the hearers that the malady is temporary, but to Jesus they mean that the death of Lazarus is but a temporary death,"[166] for He knew what He would do (cf. 6:6). Second, this sickness is **for the glory of God.** "The cure would undoubtedly enable men to see the glory of God in action."[167] Third, this sickness is **that the Son of God might be glorified thereby.** The miracle of raising Lazarus from the dead is, in John's Gospel, the occasion for Jesus' trial and death

---

[163]A shortened form of Eleazar, meaning the man whose *help is God.*
[164]Hoskyns, *op. cit.*, p. 399.
[165]Westcott, *op. cit.*, p. 165.
[166]Hoskyns, *op. cit.*, p. 399.
[167]Barclay, *op. cit.*, p. 94.

(see 11:47-48, 57), which is also His hour of glorification (12:23; 17:1).

Some have stumbled at what seems to be a paradox. **Jesus loved Martha, and her sister, and Lazarus** (5), and yet **when he heard . . . he abode two days still in the same place where he was** (6). If He **loved**, why did He delay? This is not an unusual question in the minds of men beset by sorrow and death. But Jesus had His reasons. "Because the Lord loved the family He went at the exact moment when His visit would be most fruitful, and not just when He was invited."[168] Elsewhere in the fourth Gospel, Jesus also takes action strictly on His own initiative, never simply at the invitation or behest of men (cf. 2:4; 7:3-10). So here, at the right time He said to His disciples, **Let us go into Judaea again** (7).

This proposal to go back to Judea prompted a considerable discussion between Jesus and His disciples. Its content provides a thought background for the miracle and its consequences that were about to take place. It is evident that the disciples were well aware of the deep hostility of the Jews who **of late sought to stone** Jesus (cf. 10:31, 39). Naturally they asked, **Goest thou thither again?** (8)

Jesus' response to this objection is in highly figurative language. **Are there not twelve hours in the day?** (9)[169] Trench comments by paraphrase thus: "So long as the day, the time appointed by my Father for my earthly walk, endures, so long as there is any work for Me to accomplish, I am safe, and you are safe in my company."[170] Even in the face of life's most formidable enemy, death, one must not submit to the despair born of apparent delay nor to the anxiety which breeds so readily in the hour of crisis. Jesus knew His hour and He was ready at the appointed time.

The idea suggested by the word **day** is developed in figures characteristic of John: **light,** a **walk** without stumbling, made possible because a man **seeth the light of this world** (9, cf. 1:5, 9; 9:5). These positive figures are closely associated with life (1:4; 8:12). They are to overcome the night and darkness, where men stumble (10), and where death reigns (13-14). Verses 9-14 set

---

[168]Westcott, *op. cit.,* p. 165.

[169]The Jewish day was divided into twelve equal hours from sunrise to sunset. Thus the length of the hour varied with the seasons.

[170]*Op. cit.,* p. 420.

the theme for the entire chapter. There is a cosmic struggle between darkness and light, death and life, evil and good. It is particularized here in one man—Lazarus. He **is dead** (14). Into this human situation Jesus was set to go—to evoke faith in those who live, to impart life to the one who was dead.

When Jesus said, **Our friend Lazarus sleepeth; but I go, that I may awake him out of sleep** (11), He was using the word sleep with a dual meaning. As used in the New Testament, it has the euphemistic sense of "death" thirteen times as against only three times the meaning of "normal sleep."[171] But the disciples took Jesus to mean normal sleep; hence their observation, **If he sleep, he shall do well** ("he will recover," NEB, 12). To make the situation perfectly clear to the disciples Jesus said **plainly, Lazarus is dead** (14).[172] The absence of Jesus from that deathbed would be turned into a good thing for the disciples. Jesus said, **I am glad for your sakes that I was not there, to the intent that** ("so that," Berk.) **ye may believe; nevertheless let us go unto him** (15). To raise Lazarus from the dead would be a more convincing miracle than to have healed his illness.

There was no longer a protest from the disciples because of the lurking danger in Judea, but Thomas, characteristically pessimistic, in a kind of loyal despair urged the disciples to share their Master's fate:[173] **Let us also go, that we may die with him** (16). Of Thomas, Westcott says, "He will die for the love which he has, but he will not affect the faith which he has not."[174]

2. *Jesus and Martha* (11:17-27)

The journey from Perea (beyond Jordan, see map 1) to Bethany took about two days. Jesus had stayed where He was for **two days** (6) after He received the message from the sisters. So when He came to Bethany, **he found that he** (i.e., Lazarus) **had lain in the grave four days already** (17).

The proximity of Bethany to Jerusalem, **fifteen furlongs** (18; see map 2), about two miles, made it convenient for **many of the Jews** to come **to Martha and Mary, to comfort them concerning their brother** (19).

---

[171]Bernard, *op. cit.*, p. 378.

[172]The use of the aorist tense of the verb translated **is dead** indicates that at that time Lazarus had already died.

[173]Strachan, *op. cit.*, p. 234.

[174]*Op. cit.*, p. 167.

The two sisters are found to respond to the coming of Jesus in this instance in much the same character as they appear in Luke 10:38-42. Martha is busy, active, taking the lead, while Mary is pensive, devoted, and waiting. So it is that **Martha, as soon as she heard that Jesus was coming, went and met him: but Mary sat still in the house** (20).

The dealings of Jesus with Martha in this incident might be called a lesson in the meaning of faith. For faith to be effective it must be not only dynamic but also complete; i.e., it must be characterized by those responses that involve the whole person. L. H. Marshall likens faith to gunpowder, which is composed of carbon, sulphur, and saltpeter, and each must be in the mixture before there can be an explosion. Likewise genuine faith has its elements of trust, the emotional response; belief, the understanding or intellectual response; and loyalty, the exercise of the will.[175] Jesus challenges Martha to that kind of faith.

There was no question about her trust, for her first words to Jesus were, **Lord, if thou hadst been here, my brother had not died. But I know, that even now, whatsoever thou wilt ask of God, God will give it thee** (21-22). This initial act of trusting faith was reaching "forth to that which it does not grasp."[176] It must have been little consolation or hope to Martha when Jesus suggested that her **brother** would **rise again.** She immediately gave expression to her Jewish hope when she said, **I know that he shall rise again in the resurrection at the last day** (24). She did not yet realize that "in the presence of Jesus resurrection is a present imminent reality, and that what to the Jews is a future hope, is to the Christians a present reality."[177]

In order to bring Martha to understand the immediate presence of the Resurrection, Jesus declared, **I am the resurrection, and the life** (25).[178] Though this statement is cast in the form of the many similitudes in John which express the idea of Deity— e.g., "I am the bread of life" (6:48), or "I am the true vine" (15:1)—this is not a similitude. Rather "it is the reference to

[175]*Op. cit.,* pp. 271 ff.

[176]Westcott, *op. cit.,* p. 168.

[177]Hoskyns, *op. cit.,* p. 402.

[178]It should be noted that the word **life** does not appear in the Chester-Beatty papyrus of the third century, though included in other sources, and fully supported by Jesus' teaching elsewhere in this Gospel.

Himself of what Martha had said about the final Resurrection
. . . the Resurrection of which He is potentially the Source as
well as the Agent."[179] Thus, Jesus is himself the gift of Life, both
present and future, to man, for **he that believeth in me, though
he were dead, yet shall he live: and whosoever liveth and
believeth in me shall never die** (25-26; cf. 6:39-40, 44, 54). Dodd,
making a literal translation, puts these verses in an interesting
correlative form:

> I am the resurrection: he who has faith in me, even if he dies, will
>   live again.
> I am the life: he who is alive and has faith in me will never
>   die.

He then compares Jesus' statement in 5:28 with the event of
chapter eleven, showing this to be a "picture of resurrection."

Those who are in the tombs	He found Lazarus in the tomb (11:17)
will hear his voice	He cried with a loud voice, "Lazarus, come out!" (11:43)
and come out	The dead man came out (11:44)[180]

Thus it is seen that "the Resurrection is . . . a personal communication of the Lord Himself, and not a grace which He has
to gain from another. Martha had spoken of a gift to be obtained
from God and dispensed by Christ . . . He *is* that which men need.
He does not procure the blessing for them."[181]

The prime question for Martha was now not whether Jesus
could do anything, but whether she really knew who He was. So
He asked, **Believest thou this?** (26) This is a further test of her
faith, an examination of her intellectual response. Her answer
was ready and forthright. **Yea, Lord: I believe**[182] **that thou art
the Christ, the Son of God, which should come into the world**
(27; cf. 1:49; 6:69; Matt. 16:16; Mark 8:29). It is not accurate
to speak of a blind or ignorant faith. Such expressions too easily
excuse lazy minds and dull wits. The believer must know by
acquaintance the object of his faith. Too often what is called
faith is simply misplaced trust or foolish guessing. Paul said, "I
know whom I have believed" (II Tim. 1:12).

[179]Bernard, *op. cit.*, p. 387.

[180]*Op. cit.*, p. 365.

[181]Westcott, *op. cit.*, p. 168.

[182]The verb is *pepisteuka*, perfect tense, and literally means, "I have
believed, and still have faith." The perfect tense describes a present state
resulting from past action.

3. *Jesus and Mary* (11: 28-32)

One of the most beautiful personal messages ever sent was taken by Martha from Jesus to Mary. Having left Jesus where she had met Him, Martha said **secretly to Mary, The Master is come, and calleth for thee** (28). The word *didaskalos*, here translated **Master**, literally means "teacher," but **Master** is a good translation because Martha "is speaking of one whom she believed to be Master of the whole painful and distressing situation."[183] As soon as Mary heard the call **she arose quickly, and came to him** (29), meeting Him at the same **place where Martha met him** (30).

Since burial places were outside the city, it may be that the place where Martha met Jesus was near the place where Lazarus was buried. Hence Jesus waited where He first met Martha while she went to call Mary (28). When Mary left so quickly, the Jews of Jerusalem who had come out to comfort the sisters assumed that she had gone to **the grave to weep there** (31). Verse 31 is a kind of footnote which is designed to account for their movement out to the grave where Lazarus was buried.

The meeting of Jesus and Mary reminds the reader of an earlier scene in the home in Bethany when "Mary . . . sat at Jesus' feet, and heard his word" (Luke 10:39); here **she fell down at his feet** (32). It is difficult to think of Mary in any other position before Jesus than in the posture of worship, expectancy, and humility. Her words to Jesus were exactly the same as those of Martha—**Lord, if thou hadst been here, my brother had not died** (32).

The meeting between Jesus and Mary (28-33) could be titled "The Call of the Master," with three aspects: (1) The call is personal, 28; (2) The call comes to men where they are, 28-29; (3) The call grows out of Christ's desire for man and man's need of Him, 32-33.

4. *Jesus and the Jews* (11:33-37)

The scene along the road where Jesus met Mary was one of weeping, on the part of both Mary and **the Jews . . . which came with her** (33). When Jesus saw this **he groaned** (was moved with indignation, ASV, margin) **in the spirit, and was troubled** (33). These words have been variously interpreted by commentators. What did John mean to say? It is evident that "his grief is de-

---

[183]Strachan, *op. cit.*, p. 237.

scribed in language far more intense than that which depicts the grief of Mary and of the Jews."[184] The word translated **groaned** is strong and graphic, meaning here "be deeply moved."[185] But the question remains, What was it that caused Jesus to be so moved? Some consider it to be basically a picture of Jesus' perfect humanity (Bernard, Lagrange). Others see it as grief over human sin that has issued in death (Zahn, Loisy). Still others consider it to be the result of Jesus' "indignation" (ASV) at the hypocrisy and unbelief of the "mourning" Jews (Plummer, Bauer).[186]

At Jesus' question, **Where have ye laid him?** (34) the response came, **Lord, come and see** (34). It was evidently on the way to the grave that **Jesus wept**[187] (35; cf. Luke 19:41) and the Jews exclaimed, **Behold how he loved him!** (36) The next remark from the bystanders was only a backward look. **Could not this man,** they said, **which opened the eyes of the blind, have caused that even this man should not have died?** (37) In their unbelief little did they know the great truth revealed to Martha— the personal and present Resurrection—Jesus Christ the Lord.

5. *Jesus and Lazarus* (11:38-44)

When the company arrived at **the grave,** it was seen to be **a cave, and a stone lay upon it** (38). "The usual Palestinian tomb . . . had no door, but in front of the opening there ran a groove and in the groove there was set a great stone like a cartwheel, and the stone was rolled across the entrance so that the cave was sealed."[188]

When Jesus saw the tomb He said, **Take ye away the stone** (39). Why would the One by whom "all things were made" (1:3) and who was about to bring to life a man four days dead ask someone else to **take . . . away the stone?** Could it have been a challenge to Martha's growing, yet inadequate and incomplete, faith? It was Martha who responded, **Lord, by this time he stinketh: for he hath been dead four days** (39). Her objection, from the human point of view, was well founded, for in a warm climate where they did not practice embalming the processes of

---

[184]Strachan, *op. cit.,* p. 403.
[185]Arndt and Gingrich, *op. cit.,* p. 254.
[186]Hoskyns, *op. cit.,* pp. 403 ff.
[187]This may be translated, "Jesus burst into tears" (Moffatt).
[188]Barclay. *op. cit.,* p. 115.

decay would have taken over completely. Facing life's impossible, she forgot the One who specializes in things thought impossible. This was the acid test to her faith. Would she be loyal, that is, obedient to His command? Dare one suggest that there can be no resurrection from the dead, no impartation of life to men long dead in trespasses and sins unless God's colaborers (I Cor. 3:9) put their shoulders to the gravestone of the impossible and take it away?

Speaking to the question "How Is Your Faith?" a possible outline would be: (1) Trust, the response of emotions, 21-22; (2) Belief, the response of the mind, 23-27; (3) Loyalty, the response of the will, 38-41.

Jesus' assuring word to Martha was, **Said I not unto thee, that, if thou wouldest believe, thou shouldest see the glory of God?** (40) These are like the words spoken to the disciples in Perea (11:4), and they reflect Jesus' self-disclosure to Martha in 25-27. "Whatever this promised vision was to be, it was a *spiritual* vision that is meant, for the verb (see, *optomai*) is always used in John of seeing spiritual or heavenly realities."[189] At that further word from Jesus **they took away the stone from the place where the dead was laid** (41).

Then Jesus, the Son of God, prayed: **Father, I thank thee that thou hast heard me. And I knew that thou hearest me always** (41-42). "His life is a life of complete obedience to the will of God, and his prayer admits of no uncertainty of answer."[190] So it is that true prayer is "the conscious realization of the divine will."[191] **Because of the people which stand by I said it, that they may believe that thou hast sent me** (42). It is evident that Jesus wanted all to understand that God's great power flows through the life of the one who is in perfect accord with God's will.

"The Prayer That Is Heard" (1) Arises out of the cry of the heart, 33-35; (2) Accords with the will of God, 42; and (3) Is assured of the divine response, 43.

Every item of the preliminary countdown having been cared for—Martha's faith, Mary's weeping and worshipful devotion, the unbelief of the Jews, assurance of God's will—**Jesus cried with a loud voice, Lazarus, come forth** (43). God does call forth His own (cf. 5:28; 10:3), and when He calls, there is no power

---

[189]Bernard, *op. cit.*, p. 396.
[190]Hoskyns, *op. cit.*, p. 406.
[191]Westcott, *op. cit.*, p. 173.

that can hold them, not even death itself. The miracle here is "the story of Jesus going to face death in order to conquer death"[192] (cf. I Cor. 15:26-27, 55).

Death did not hold Lazarus, for he **came forth, bound hand and foot with graveclothes: and his face was bound about with a napkin** (44). The question is sometimes raised, How could Lazarus, bound in this fashion, have come forth from the tomb? We may assume that his limbs were swathed separately, as was the Egyptian custom. Or, if we prefer, we may accept Westcott's comment: "It is unnecessary to speculate how Lazarus so bound came forth."[193] It is all a part of the miracle of the defeat of death and deliverance from the darkness and night of the tomb (11:10). But even as in the case of taking away the stone, here now there is work for man to do. Jesus said, **Loose** ("unbind," Phillips) **him, and let him go** (44).[194] God's power alone can bring life and light to dead and benighted souls. But man's task is essential —the untying of knots and healing of scars left by the ravages of sin, which is death.

6. *Jesus and the High Priest* (11:45-57)

There were opposite reactions to the miracle. **Many of the Jews which came to Mary . . . believed on him** (lit., "put their faith into Him"), while others **went their ways to the Pharisees, and told them what things Jesus had done** (45-46). It was the action of this latter group which precipitated the great hostility against Jesus and the decision of the council which finally culminated in His crucifixion.

The chief priests and the Pharisees (i.e., the principal members of the Sanhedrin)[195] **gathered together** in a meeting of the **council** (Sanhedrin) for the express purpose of deciding what to do about the miracle-working Jesus. **What do we?** i.e., "What can we do?" (Phillips, 47) They were faced with two alternatives. **If we let him . . . alone,** they said, **all men will believe on him.** The inevitable consequent of this would be **the Romans**

---

[192]Dodd, *op. cit.,* p. 367.

[193]*Op. cit.,* p. 173.

[194]Comparable to "Let him go home."

[195]The Sanhedrin was the highest court and council of the Jews. It was composed of seventy-one members (both Sadducees and Pharisees), and was presided over by the high priest. It was abolished with the destruction of Jerusalem in A.D. 70.

taking **away both our place** (the Temple) **and nation (48)**. The other alternative was expressed by **Caiaphas, being the high priest that same year (49)**.[196] The expression **that same year** is distinctly Johannine and refers to the year when the sacrifice was made once for all (Heb. 10:10-12). The expression also places Caiaphas in the prophetic role where he as high priest, "whose duty it was to enter the holy of holies and offer the atonement for *that* year, should unconsciously utter a prophecy of the efficacy of the Atonement which was presently to be offered on the cross. This was the acceptable year of the Lord."[197] Caiaphas' proposition was simple. He said, **It is expedient for us, that one man should die for the people, and that the whole nation perish not (50)**. What he meant was: "Better sacrifice one man than let the whole nation suffer."

John noted two important things in the statement of the high priest: (1) It was actually a prophecy, uttered by the high priest in the true function of his office. **This spake he not of himself: but being high priest that year, he prophesied (51)**. (2) It implied a universal sacrifice. Jesus would die not only for the Jews (51) but **that also he should gather together in one the children of God that were scattered abroad (52; cf. 3:16; 10:16; 12:32)**.

The council made the decision **to put Jesus to death (53)**, and for that reason He **walked no more openly among the Jews (54)**. He left the vicinity of Bethany and went **unto a country near to the wilderness,**[198] **into a city called Ephraim, and there continued** ("stayed," NASB) **with his disciples (54)**. Ephraim "lies about fifteen miles north of Jerusalem and some six miles east-northeast of Bethel . . . and is now called Et-Taiyibeh."[199]

Verses 55-57 are a setting of the scene for the events related to the passion, trial, and death of Jesus. The occasion is first mentioned here; **the Jews' passover was nigh at hand (55; cf. 12:1; 13:1; 18:28)**. Because of the proximity of this great feast **many went out of the country up to Jerusalem . . . to purify themselves (55; cf. Acts 21:24)**; that is, be declared ceremonially

---

[196]The office of the high priest was for life. But under Roman rule men held the position for varying lengths of time according to the whim of the imperial authority.

[197]Bernard, *op. cit.*, p. 404.

[198]The wild country northeast of Jerusalem.

[199]Macgregor, *op. cit.*, p. 257.

clean before the Passover began (cf. 18:28; Lev. 7:21; Num. 9:10). It is only natural, in the light of the recent miracle and subsequent events, that the crowds would look **for Jesus** around the Temple, and discuss the improbability that He would come to the feast. Phillips has it, "What do you think? Surely he won't come to the festival?" (56) Evidently, the decision of the council was known to the people, for they gave **a commandment, that, if any man knew where he were, he should shew it** ("report it," NASB), **that they might take him** (57).

J. THE UNIVERSAL CHRIST, 12:1-50

1. *Homage by Anointing* (12:1-11)

It was only a short time after the events of chapter eleven **and just six days before the passover** that Jesus returned to **Bethany** (1). The account immediately calls attention to **Lazarus . . . whom he raised from the dead** as though he were the central attraction. The occasion was **a supper** at which **Martha,** in her characteristic role, **served** (2).[200] Special attention is called to the fact that Lazarus, in normal good health, **was one of them that sat at the table with him** (2). Evidently, "the feast was a grateful recognition of the work done among them."[201]

Though Mary is the last to be introduced into the scene, it is her act of loving devotion that is the central theme of the whole account.[202] She took **a pound**—Roman pound of about twelve ounces—**of ointment of spikenard** ("pure nard," RSV), **very costly,**[203] **and anointed the feet of Jesus, and wiped his feet with her hair** (3). Whatever other members of the Bethany household may have thought of Jesus, one word describes Mary's feeling—love.

Here is seen "The Gift of Love": (1) In lavish extravagance, **very costly . . . ointment**; (2) In humility, she **anointed His feet**;

---

[200]"The feast took place in the evening after the close of the Sabbath" (Westcott, *op. cit.*, p. 176).

[201]*Ibid.*

[202]Similar scenes are recorded in Mark 14:3-9 and Luke 7:36-50. For an excellent discussion of likenesses and differences see the exhaustive work of Bernard, *op. cit.*, pp. 409-14. There is strong evidence that John was well acquainted with Mark's account.

[203]According to Judas' estimate the value was three hundred denarii (5). A denarius, a Roman silver coin, is about eighteen cents, a day's wage; hence Mary's gift was equal to about a year's earnings (Arndt and Gingrich, *op. cit.*, p. 178).

(3) In entire unselfconsciousness, she **wiped his feet with her hair.**[204] There is a universal quality about love like that. John wrote it in poetic language—**and the house was filled with the odour of the ointment (3)** [205]—better, "the fragrance of the perfume."

Judas Iscariot, who was also at the supper, raised an objection to Mary's act. He said, **Why was not this ointment sold for three hundred pence** (denarii), **and given to the poor?** (5) John is quick to add his view. He questioned Judas' motive. It was **not that he cared for the poor** (6). He then named the problem. **Judas was a thief** (6). As treasurer of the group of disciples ("he had the money box," NASB), it was his practice "to pilfer what was put into it" (6, lit. translation). The question has been raised as to why Judas was chosen for that position since it would provide unusual temptations for him. Westcott's reply is, "Temptation commonly comes to us through that for which we are naturally fitted."[206]

Mary and Judas stand in vivid contrast. "Mary in her devotion unconsciously provides for the honour of the dead. Judas in his selfishness unconsciously brings about the death itself."[207]

Jesus quickly came to Mary's defense. **Let her alone:** He said, **against the day of my burying hath she kept this** (7)—lit., "in order that she may keep it for the day of My burial" (NASB). The language at this point is difficult, but seems to indicate, according to Hoskyns, that "Mary consciously recognized the necessity of the death of Jesus, and also, recognizing that the Hour had come, anticipated His burial by an act of intelligent devotion."[208]

Judas' plea for the poor did not escape Jesus' answer. **The poor always ye have with you; but me ye have not always** (8; cf. Deut. 15:11). Mary's keen sense of proper timing cannot go unnoticed. "There are some things which we can do almost any

---

[204]Barclay, *op. cit.*, pp. 127–28.

[205]Bernard rejects any allegorical interpretation of this clause (*op. cit.*, p. 418; cf. Mark 14:9). The statement reflects John's "personal impression at the time" (Westcott, *op. cit.*, p. 177).

[206]*Op. cit.*, p. 177.

[207]*Ibid.*

[208]*Op. cit.*, p. 416. Plummer (*op. cit.*, p. 252) helpfully suggests: "The words are spoken from the point of view of the past, when Mary's act was still only a purpose."

time; and there are some things which we will never do, unless we grasp the chance to do them when it comes."[209]

When word got out that Jesus was with Lazarus in Bethany, **much people** ("the large crowd," Phillips) **came not for Jesus' sake only, but that they might see Lazarus also (9). Because . . . many of the Jews . . . believed on Jesus (11), the chief priests consulted that they might put Lazarus also to death (10).** It is clear that these chief priests, being of the Sadducean party and not believing in the resurrection, felt obligated to get rid of evidence that was contrary to their doctrine.

2. *Homage by Acclamation* (12:12-19)

In a manner characteristic of John, he notes the time of the Triumphal Entry[210] **On the next day (12)**—i.e., the day after the anointing by Mary, or five days before the Passover (cf. 12:1). This means that the entry took place on Sunday. "Christian tradition has followed John in putting the triumphal entry on Palm Sunday."[211]

The news that **Jesus was coming to Jerusalem (12)** soon got around, and **much people that were come to the feast . . . went forth to meet him (12-13)**. As they went they **took branches of palm trees (13)**, "the symbol of regal triumph,"[212] **and cried, Hosanna**, which is the Hebrew for "Save now!" Here the cry was almost equivalent to "God save the King!" The **Hosanna**, along with **Blessed is the King of Israel that cometh in the name of the Lord**, is taken from Ps. 118:25-26, which is purported to have been written "for the Feast of Tabernacles after the Return."[213] (See Neh. 8:14-18.) So the people were filled with high expectancy.[214] In Jesus, after what had happened at Bethany, they saw the conquering Hero, the Anointed One, the Deliverer, and they were acclaiming Him as such.

[209]Barclay, *op. cit.*, pp. 130-31.

[210]The Synoptic accounts of the entry into Jerusalem are found in Matt. 21:4-9; Mark 11:7-10; Luke 19:35-38.

[211]Bernard, *op. cit.*, p. 423.

[212]Hoskyns, *op. cit.*, p. 420.

[213]Westcott, *op. cit.*, p. 179.

[214]"These very verses had been sung by the people as they welcomed Simon Maccabaeus "after he had conquered Acra and wrested it from Syrian domain more than a hundred years before" (Barclay, *op. cit.*, p. 136).

In one brief statement John tells about Jesus procuring a **young ass** (cf. the detailed Synoptic account, Matt. 21:1-11; Mark 11:1-10; Luke 19:29-38), and He **sat thereon** (14). This action was a fulfilling of the prophecy in Zech. 9:9: "Rejoice greatly, O daughter of Zion; shout, O daughter of Jerusalem: behold, thy King cometh unto thee: he is just, and having salvation; lowly, and riding upon an ass, and upon a colt the foal of an ass."

By what He did, He laid unmistakable claim to be the Messiah, God's Anointed One. The action also showed Him to be a spiritual, not a military, Messiah, for "the ass, in contrast to the usual war-horse of a victorious leader, is symbolic of lowliness and peace"[215] (cf. Judg. 10:4; II Sam. 17:23; 19:26).

While all this was taking place, **at the first** it was beyond the disciples' comprehension, **but when Jesus was glorified** (16) the pieces of the puzzle fitted together, and they began to understand. The glorification of Jesus undoubtedly has two meanings in John. One refers to the exaltation by the way of the Cross (12:23-25; 13:31-32; 17:1). The other exaltation is the Resurrection (12:32), Jesus going to the Father (15:26), and the sending of the Paraclete (16:7), all of which showed "the spiritual nature of the Lord's sovereignty."[216]

John adds some comments at the end of the account that are of interest. It was the crowds who were with Him **when he called Lazarus out of his grave, and raised him from the dead** (17), that "were giving witness" to what had happened. Evidently it was this witness that brought the acclaiming crowd from Jerusalem, for **they heard that he had done this miracle** (18).

All of this added up to a desperate situation for the Pharisees. Their neatly laid plans to put a stop to Jesus and His work had ended in what appeared to be complete frustration. **Behold, the world is gone after him** (19), they said. The failure of their malicious scheme caused them to turn on and blame each other; so they said, **Perceive ye how ye prevail nothing?** (19)

3. *Arrival of the Greeks* (12:20-36)

It is not certain whether the Greeks who were **among them that came up to worship at the feast** were there out of curiosity (cf. Acts 17:21) or had become proselytes and "accordingly

[215]Macgregor, *op. cit.*, p. 263.
[216]Westcott, *op. cit.*, p. 179.

attended the Jewish festivals."[217] These men had a burning request, one that was perhaps much better than they themselves realized. Their approach to Philip may have been occasioned by the fact that he had a Greek name. In any case, on hearing the request, **Sir, we would** ("wish to," NASB) **see Jesus (21)**, **Philip** told **Andrew (22)** and the two of them told **Jesus** (cf. 1:43-45).

When John wrote that **Jesus answered them (23)**, he left an ambiguity about the antecedent of **them**. There is no indication that it included more than Philip and Andrew, though the possibility of the Greeks having heard is not ruled out. Their question provided the "cue for Jesus' great discourse upon the necessity of his death and the *universal* salvation (32) which resulted from it . . . Though Jesus in the flesh confined himself chiefly to the Jews (Matt. 15:24), yet by the power of his Spirit he will draw also the Gentiles to himself."[218]

Though many times before Jesus had spoken of His hour (2:4; 7:30; 8:20), this is the first time He said, **The hour is come,** and now this expression will persist (12:27; 13:1; 17:1). The purpose of His hour is **that the Son of man should be glorified (23)**. His glorification consists of those events which "we may call the complex of his passion."[219] To some of the Jews at least, the expression **Son of man** "stood for the undefeatable world conqueror sent by God."[220] To those who heard, Jesus' words were most exciting because the people took **glorified** to mean "that the subjected kingdom of the earth would grovel before the conqueror's feet: by *glorified* he meant crucified."[221]

To illustrate exactly what He meant by His glorification, Jesus gave a short parable which would be perfectly obvious to all who heard. **Except a corn** (grain) **of wheat fall into the ground and die, it abideth** (remains) **alone: but if it die, it bringeth forth much fruit (24;** cf. I Cor. 15:36). There could be no clearer allusion to His own death, burial, and resurrection. Likewise He was saying that "the true disciples of the Son of God do not cling to life with passionate affection—this is unproductive

---

[217]Bernard, *op. cit.,* p. 430. "To such proselytes the Court of the Gentiles in the Temple precinct was appropriated" (*ibid.*) (See Chart A.)

[218]Macgregor, *op. cit.,* p. 264.

[219]Lightfoot, *op. cit.,* p. 240.

[220]Barclay, *op. cit.,* p. 142.

[221]*Ibid.*

and permanent death; rather, they hate life in this world, and, by the paradox of the law of God, they preserve it forever."[222] Jesus expanded the obvious meaning of the parable by further paradoxes. Loving one's **life**, the *psyche*,[223] is tantamount to losing it, while **he that hateth**—loves less—**his life in this world shall keep it unto life eternal (25)**.[224] Lightfoot says: "Selfishness is always the death of the true life of man."[225] Likewise when one has to make a choice between Christ and the dearest things of life, the contrast is so great that **he hateth** the latter (cf. Luke 14:26-27). So the believer is a servant, a follower, for whom is reserved the assurance, **Where I am** (*ego eimi*, see comment on 6:20), **there shall also my servant be (26)**. Thus it is that "the Cross is the symbol not only of man's salvation, but also of the Christian way of life."[226]

Barclay provides an interesting outline: (1) Only by death comes life, 24; (2) Only by spending life do we retain life, 25; and (3) Only by service comes greatness, 26.[227]

This discourse about His hour brought Jesus face-to-face with the grim reality of suffering and death.[228] Without any notation of change of time or place by John, Jesus is heard to pray, **Now is my soul troubled; and what shall I say? Father, save me from this hour (27)**.[229] As very man, facing death, this was a wholly natural and necessary prayer. There is no sham here! "The conflict, as in the Temptation, is a real one."[230] Recognition of the purpose of His coming—**for this cause came I unto this hour (27)**—and submission to the will of the Father—**Father, glorify thy name (28)**—brought the heavenly ministration that

[222]Hoskyns, *op. cit.*, p. 424.

[223]The *psyche* here means the physical life of the senses.

[224]The word translated **keep** actually means "watch, guard, defend" (Arndt and Gingrich, *op. cit.*, p. 876).

[225]*Op. cit.*, p. 434.

[226]Howard, IB, VIII, 663.

[227]*Op. cit.*, pp. 143-45.

[228]There is no Gethsemane scene as such in John. However these verses (27-31) carry much the same theme, and some of the details found in the Synoptists' accounts (cf. Matt. 26:39; Mark 14:35-36; Luke 22:42). Why John chose to place these words here is not clear.

[229]Many modern versions take this last clause to be an interrogation. However, both the sentence structure and comparison with the Synoptic accounts seem to indicate that it is a prayer, not a question.

[230]Westcott, *op. cit.*, p. 182.

He had to have in His hour—**Then came there a voice from heaven** (28; cf. Luke 22:43). What Jesus heard was important. The voice said, **I have both glorified it, and will glorify it again** (28). "The Father's 'name', or true character, had already been manifested in Jesus' works, and was soon to be manifested in the Passion and its issue, the triumph of the Resurrection and the victories of the Spirit through the preaching of the Gospel."[231]

Those who **stood by** were aware of something unusual going on, but their reports were quite indefinite. Some said that **it thundered,** while others thought it to be the voice of an angel (29). Things of the Spirit are spiritually perceived. One cannot hear that for which he has made no preparation to understand. "Unhappily the multitude, owing to the half-light in which it lives, cannot discern or appreciate the import of the utterance from heaven."[232] The **voice,** though not understood by the people, **came . . . for** their **sakes** (30; cf. 11:42); that is, in order that they might believe. God has spoken, by both voice and Word, and dull men fail to understand or respond. So **now is the judgment of this world** (31); i.e., "now is the world of men like you being judged."[233] Judgment is a key idea in John. Where there are Word and witness, judgment is inevitable (3:17-19; 5:22-30; 8:15-18, 50; 9:39; 12:47-48; 16:8-11), and in the final issue **the prince of this world** (shall) **be cast out** (31).[234] Hoskyns says: "The concrete obedience of the Son . . . explains the universal significance of the Death of Jesus, and marks the moment of the dethronement of the Devil from his tyranny over men."[235]

This affirmation of the ultimate and final defeat of the prince of this world is balanced with the declaration of the universal drawing power of the Cross. **And I, if I be lifted up from the earth, will draw all men unto me** (32).[236] Westcott commenting on **will draw** (by the Spirit) says: "There is need of this loving

---

[231]Macgregor, *op. cit.,* p. 266.

[232]Lightfoot, *op. cit.,* p. 241.

[233]Bernard, *op. cit.,* p. 441.

[234]Note other references to "the prince of this world": Matt. 4:8-9; Luke 4:6; II Cor. 4:4; Eph. 2:2; 6:12.

[235]*Op. cit.,* p. 425.

[236]The word translated **lifted up** means "to raise high"—as the serpent on the pole (3:44) and Jesus on the Cross (32-33), and also, in a figurative sense, "to exalt" (Acts 5:31). "For John this 'lifting up' is not to be separated from his 'exaltation' into heaven, since the heavenly exaltation presupposes the earthly" (Arndt and Gingrich, *op. cit.,* p. 858).

violence, for men are 'held back by the enemy.' "[237] On the one
hand **lifted up** is an allusion to the lifting up on the Cross, **signifying what death he would die** (33). But there is another meaning implicit in the word **from,** which literally means "out of."
The Cross had an inevitable consequent, the Resurrection!

It was with mixed feelings that the people heard Jesus'
statement about His own death. They could not reconcile Him
as the **Son of man** who **must be lifted up** (i.e., crucified) with
the **Christ** who **abideth for ever** (34; cf. Ezek. 37:25; Ps. 89:4;
110:4; Isa. 9:7). "The Jews did not expect a suffering Messiah."[238] Jesus gave no direct answer to the question, **Who is this
Son of man?** Rather, He spoke to them in figurative terms of the
struggle between **light** and **darkness,**[239] with the imperative to
walk in the light, for **in darkness one knoweth not whither he
goeth** (35). Since **the light** is here for only **a little while** (35),
believe in the light, that ye may be the children of light (36).
Obviously, Jesus is the Light; refusal to believe on Him is the
extinguishing of the light, where darkness and lostness are the
result. Jesus **departed, and** "was hidden" (lit.) **from them.** They
were left in the darkness of their disbelief.

4. *Faith and Unbelief* (12:37-50)

In bold strokes John, using Old Testament scriptures, en-
deavors to show why **they believed not on him . . . though he
had done so many miracles** (signs) **before them** (37). He first
cites Isa. 53:1 verbally from the Septuagint version. **Lord, who
hath believed our report? and to whom hath the arm of the
Lord been revealed?** (38) These are the opening words in the
well-known Suffering Servant prophecy of Isaiah. The **report** was
what the Jews had heard from Jesus, and the **arm of the Lord**
clearly refers to "the mighty actions (Luke 1:51; Acts 13:17) of
Jesus which were the works of His Father (5:19-21) . . . Neither
the truth which Jesus proclaimed nor the miracles which He
wrought moved the Jews to faith."[240]

The second citation is from Isa. 6:9-10. The occasion there
was the vision in the Temple, **when**—the better Greek reading
is "because"—**he** (Isaiah) **saw his glory, and spake of him** (41).

---

[237]*Op. cit.,* p. 183.
[238]Bernard, *op. cit.,* p. 444.
[239]Compare this with the language in 9:4-5; 11:9-10; and 12:46-48.
[240]Hoskyns, *op. cit.,* p. 428.

John prefaced his quotation with **Therefore they could not believe, because that Esaias said** (39). That, with the further citation, **He-hath blinded their eyes, and hardened their heart; that they should not see with their eyes, nor understand with their heart, and be converted, and I should heal them** (40), "reads like the crudest possible statement of a naked doctrine of predestination. And yet it can confidently be stated that this is not the intention of the author."[241] What is really divine foresight reads as though it were divine necessity. But such is not the case. Light rejected becomes darkness. The opportunity to have faith, if ignored, neglected, or refused, becomes callous unbelief. Love spurned turns into the blackness of night and death (13:30). But even though the Jews as a nation rejected Jesus (1:11), and in turn were rejected, there have always been some, the remnant, who have believed. So here, John remarks, **Nevertheless among the chief rulers also many believed on him** (42).

These **chief rulers** who **believed** did not **confess** it, **lest they should be put out of the synagogue** (42). The reason was obvious to John. **They loved the praise of men more than the praise of God** (43). Barclay comments: "Again and again men have failed to support some great cause because it interfered with some lesser interest. When Joan of Arc realised that she stood forsaken and alone, she said: 'Yes: I am alone on earth: I have always been alone. My father told my brothers to drown me if I would not stay to mind his sheep while France was bleeding to death; France might perish if only our lambs were safe.' "[242]

The last seven verses of chapter twelve are a restatement of some of the major themes of the Gospel. John does not say on what occasion, or to whom, Jesus made the statements. But he points up their significance by his introduction: **Jesus cried and said** (44; cf. 7:28, 37), which indicates the importance of the proclamation about to be made. Some of the themes are:

(a) The Son is the Revelation of the Father. To have faith in the Son is to have faith in **him that sent** the Son (44; cf. 3:15-16; 5:36-38, 46; 6:29, 35, 40; 7:38; 8:19, 24, 42, 45-46; 13:20). To have seen the Son is to have seen **him that sent** the Son (45; cf. 1:18; 6:40; 8:19, 42; 10:30, 38; 14:7, 9).

---

[241]*Ibid.*, p. 429. Sometimes in Scripture result is expressed in language we would use to indicate purpose.

[242]Barclay, *op. cit.*, p. 155.

(b) Jesus has "come as light into the world" (46, NASB),[243] and to reject Him is to abide in darkness (cf. 1:4-5; 8:12; 9:5; 12:35-36).

(c) Since Jesus came[244] not to judge the world, but to save the world (47), it is the word which He has spoken that shall judge the one who rejecteth Him and receiveth not His words (48; cf. 3:17-18; 5:24-45; 8:15, 31, 40). Jesus did not come to judge the world in this sense. It is always our Lord's purpose to save men rather than to reject and destroy them. But the very offer of salvation requires decision for or against Him who makes the offer. To reject Christ brings judgment on oneself. Hoskyns comments: "At the last day the criterion of the final judgment is precise; it is the teaching of Jesus, which is the word of God."[245]

(d) The Father who sent the Son also gave Him a commandment, what He should say (49). Jesus' obedient fulfillment of this commandment enabled Him to say, I know that his commandment is life everlasting ("eternal life," Berk., 50; cf. 5:30; 6:38; 7:16-17; 8:28, 38; 10:18; 14:10).[246] God's commandments are expressions of His nature, and none is more essential than the fact that He is holy. One cannot get away from the fact that to aspire to eternal life is to thirst for holiness of heart. One dares not forget the ancient commandment, "Ye shall be holy; for I am holy" (Lev. 11:44), and the warning that without holiness "no man shall see the Lord" (Heb. 12:14).

Thus concludes the section that has been called "The Book of the Signs." Perhaps the reader should recall John's own words about the facts he included: "These signs are written in order that you may have faith that Jesus is the Christ the Son of God, and that having faith you may have life in His name" (20:31, lit. translation).

---

[243]The verb come is in the perfect tense in the Greek and portrays a present state as the result of past action. That is, Jesus *is* "the light of the world."

[244]The verb came is aorist tense in the Greek, and here depicts the Incarnation, once, final, complete.

[245]*Op. cit.*, p. 431.

[246]See section on "Life," in the Introduction.

A. THE SUPPER, 13:1-30

1. *The Theological Setting* (13:1-3)

The setting for the Last Supper is given in theological terminology characteristic of the fourth Gospel. There is a notation
that it took place before **the feast of the passover** (1), but there
is no indication of the physical circumstances, nor is there any
allusion to the instituting of the sacrament of the Lord's Supper
(cf. Matt. 26:17-20; Mark 14:12-16; Luke 22:7-12).[1] Rather,
John's comments are a review of basic theological propositions
in which Jesus is seen to be fully aware of the meaning of all
that has happened in the light of what is about to come to pass.
He **knew that his hour was come** (1; cf. 2:4; 7:30; 8:20; 12:23).
The time for the offering of the sacrifice "once for all" (Heb.
10:10) was not determined by scheming men. No one would take
His life from Him. He would lay it down strictly on His own
initiative (10:18).

There were two things that brought Him to **his hour** and
made it possible. One was that He **loved his own.** Though God's
love for the world has sent the Son (3:16), it is the Son's love
for **his own which were in the world** that made love's sacrifice
an actualization. What kind of love is it that constrained such
action? The KJV translates, **he loved them unto the end.** But
this is quite misleading if we understand that **the end** is simply
the temporal completion of the Incarnation. The words translated
unto the end (*eis telos*) indicate degree, "completely," "fully,"
"absolutely," and here (13:1) combine the meanings "to the
end" and "to the uttermost."[2] Macgregor translates, "to the
utmost limits of love,"[3] and Hoskyns has it, "He loved them com-

---

[1] Bernard makes an attempt to harmonize the Synoptic and Johannine
accounts of the Last Supper (*op. cit.,* pp. 456-58). Also see Ralph Earle,
"The Gospel According to Matthew," *Beacon Bible Commentary;* Kansas
City: Beacon Hill Press, 1964), pp. 233-35.

[2] Arndt and Gingrich, *op. cit.,* p. 228.

[3] *Op. cit.,* p. 274.

pletely and finally, to the uttermost, unto death" (cf. I Thess. 2:16).[4]

Second, Jesus' hour was possible because of His deep awareness of His relationship to the Father. Soon He would **depart out of this world unto the Father** (1). He also knew **that the Father had given all things into his hands, and that he was come from God, and went to God** (3). He was "conscious of his divine mission and his divine destiny."[5]

The theological setting also takes into account the opposition. Heretofore it has been the Jews who have opposed Him and sought to kill Him (7:30, 44; 8:59; 9:22; 10:20, 39; 11:53, 57). But now all that is evil, in the person of **the devil** (2), conspiring with one of Jesus' chosen disciples (6:70), **Judas Iscariot,** constitutes the enemy. The manner in which Jesus met and conquered this opposition provides basic themes for that which is to follow. One is His "amazing act of self-humiliation" (4-5);[6] the other, a display of all-encompassing love which includes one's enemies (13:26, 34).

2. *Jesus' Self-humiliation* (13:4-20)

Because the opening statement of chapter 13 is long and involved, the reader must begin the actual supper scene with the first clause in v. 2, **And supper being ended** (the Gk. says "during supper"), and then continue with the first clause in v. 4, **he riseth from supper.** As He did this, He **laid aside his garments** (4, cf. 10:17; Phil. 2:5-8); that is, the outer robe. Then **he took a towel, and girded himself,** which "marks the action of a slave."[7] Thus prepared, He took **water** and **bason, and began to wash the disciples' feet, and to wipe them with the towel wherewith he was girded** (5). Why one of the disciples did not perform this menial task is not intimated by John, but evidently there had been some "place seeking" among the twelve (Luke 22:24). Further, Jesus was the only One in that room who could carry out even the symbolism of cleansing—for He alone was clean in the theological and moral sense of the word (cf. 17:19; Heb. 13:

---

[4]*Op. cit.,* p. 436.

[5]Macgregor, *op. cit.,* p. 274.

[6]Strachan, *op. cit.,* p. 265.

[7]Hoskyns, *op. cit.,* p. 437. He also quotes a Midrash on Gen. 21:14: "Abraham dismissed her [Hagar] with a bill of divorcement and took a cloth and girded it about her loins, that men might know her to be a slave."

12). He came to make it possible for man to be pure, morally clean, holy.

When Jesus came to wash Peter's feet the disciple said, **Lord, dost thou wash my feet?** (6) Jesus' answer, **Thou knowest not now,** not only affirmed Peter's present ignorance of spiritual things (e.g., the coming of the Spirit), but also promised, **Thou shalt know hereafter** (7).[8] **What I do** would be our Lord's humiliation, symbolized in washing their feet but actually providing all of God's redemptive work for man. Hoskyns comments that Peter's reaction is not a contrast between Peter's pride and Jesus' humility, but rather "between the knowledge of Jesus which is the ground of action, and the ignorance of Peter, who does not as yet perceive that the humiliation of the Messiah is the effective cause of Christian salvation"[9] (cf. 2:22; 7:39; 12:16; 14:25-26; 15:26; 16:13; 20:9). But future understanding was too remote for Peter. He saw only the immediate incongruity of the situation —Jesus washing his feet. Impulsively he declared, "Never at any time will You wash my feet—forever" (lit. translation). Peter had hoped to place a final period to the whole thing. But Jesus knew the way to Peter's heart—the threat of exclusion from the One he loved. **If I wash thee not, thou hast no part with me** (8; cf. Heb. 12:14). "There is no place in the society of Christians for those who have not been purified by Jesus Himself."[10] If fellowship could be gained only by cleansing (cf. I John 1:7), then Peter wanted *all* of that—**feet, hands,** and **head** (9).[11]

Jesus made a general application of the idea about which He and Peter had been conversing. "He who hath bathed does not have need to be washed except for his feet.[12] He is **every whit** (wholly) clean.[13] "You too are clean, but not all of you" (10, lit.

---

[8]The two verbs translated **knowest . . . know** are different words in the Greek. The first is knowledge "absolute and complete" while the second is "the knowledge which is gained by slow experience" (Westcott, *op. cit.,* p. 191).

[9]*Op. cit.,* p. 438.

[10]*Ibid.*

[11]It was Peter who after Pentecost testified that the cleansing had on that occasion reached even to his heart (Acts 15:8-9). So he did know by experience **hereafter** (7).

[12]The phrase "except for his feet" does not appear in some ancient authorities. Some commentators (Macgregor, Westcott) retain the phrase; Hoskyns prefers the shorter reading.

[13]The word translated **clean** is *katharos* (cf. catharsis), and is used of spiritual purity (15:3).

translation). Hoskyns comments that in the act of foot washing Jesus "symbolically declares their complete purification through the humiliation of the death of the Messiah. The faithful Christian is *cleansed by the blood of Jesus*" (I John 1:7; cf. Rom. 6:1-3; I Cor. 10:16).[14] If holiness of heart is at the heart of the *Eucharist* (see comment on 6:53), purity of heart is at the heart of the *Pedilavium* (foot washing). All this was a symbolic foreshadowing of the work of the Spirit which would be made possible with His coming (14:15-17, 25-26; 15:26; 16:7-15).

But what about Judas? Was he clean? Jesus **knew,** and had known (6:70-71), **who should betray him; therefore said he, Ye are not all clean** (11). Bernard says: "As far as bodily cleanliness was concerned, no doubt Judas was on a par with the rest, but not in a spiritual sense."[15]

Having washed the disciples' feet, and having put on His robe, at the table again Jesus asked the disciples, **Know ye what I have done to you?** (12) Macgregor comments: "It is when Jesus 'puts on his robe,' takes up his life again (10:17 ff.) in the power of the Spirit, that he will make all things plain" (7).[16] Without waiting for an answer, Jesus explained that this had been an **example** (15), or model, "as something that does or should spur one on to imitate it."[17] As He, their **Master** (lit., "Teacher") **and Lord,** had done for them, so they ought to do for **one another** (13-14; cf. 34). Hoskyns says: "His action in washing their feet expresses the very essence of Christian authority."[18] There does not seem to be any evidence that Jesus intended the foot washing to be instituted as a sacrament. But it is clear that He was teaching by example the basic and axiomatic though paradoxical principle that the only way to be "the greatest" (Luke 22:24) or to be **happy** (17) is by taking the road of loving service (13:34) and sacrifice (10:15) based on a knowledge of God's will for us. The word for **happy** is *makarioi,* the "blessed" of the Beatitudes (Matt. 5:3-12).

But one of the twelve is excluding himself from the performance of loving service and hence from the blessedness that belongs to such. No doubt thinking of Judas, the Master said,

---

[14]*Op. cit.,* p. 439.

[15]*Op. cit.,* p. 463.

[16]*Op. cit.,* p. 277.

[17]Arndt and Gingrich, *op. cit.,* p. 851.

[18]*Op. cit.,* p. 440.

I speak not of you all (18). Then, as if to emphasize the fact that Judas had himself chosen to play the role of the betrayer as a fulfillment of scripture, He added, **I know whom I have chosen.** Bernard accurately translates this, "I know the *kind of man* whom I chose."[19] The expression **that**[20] **the scripture may be fulfilled** is somewhat misleading. The clear teaching of Scripture is that man's moral choices are left within his own power. Barclay clarifies the issue well when he comments: "All this tragedy which is happening is somehow within the purpose of God . . . It was as Scripture said it would be."[21] The scripture which Jesus quoted is from Ps. 41:9, **He that eateth bread with me hath lifted up his heel against me.** To share bread together was a pledge of friendship. **Lifted up his heel** describes an act of brutal violence, like the sudden kick of a horse. How prophetic! In a few short moments Judas would go, with the taste still in his mouth of the choice morsel shared with him by Jesus. He would then return with a murder-bent mob, thus perpetrating an act of brutal violence never before or since equaled.

Jesus had a special reason for laying out the basic problem before the disciples. This would become to them one more evidence for their understanding of His real nature. He told them before the event so that **when it**—His betrayal by Judas—**is come to pass** they **may believe that I am he** (19). The **I am** (*ego eimi*) is another of Jesus' declarations of His deity (cf. 16:4; 14:29; Ezek. 24:24; Matt. 24:25). Westcott says concerning the **I am:** ". . . that in me is the spring of life and light and strength; that I present to you the invisible majesty of God; that I unite in virtue of my essential Being the seen and the unseen, the finite and the infinite."[22]

Though it is true that the **servant is not greater than his lord** or that the one **sent** is not **greater than he that sent him** (16), Jesus assures His disciples of their relationship to Him and the

[19]*Op. cit.,* p. 467.

[20]The conjunction **that** translates *hina,* which is here used elliptically, and its final meaning (i.e., its indication of purpose) is lost. Arndt and Gingrich (*op. cit.,* p. 378) say: "Very often the final meaning is greatly weakened, or disappears altogether." They also note (p. 379) that sometimes *hina* with the subjunctive is used for an imperative (cf. Phillips, "But let this scripture be fulfilled").

[21]*Op. cit.,* p. 166.

[22]*Op. cit.,* p. 131.

Father. **For he that receiveth whomsoever I send receiveth me; and he that receiveth me receiveth him that sent me** (20).

3. *Jesus' All-encompassing Love* (13:21-30)

Still at the table where He and His disciples were sharing their last meal together, Jesus . . . **was troubled in spirit** (21; cf. 11:33; 12:27; 14:1). As He approached the moment of the separation of Judas, fully aware of His own oneness with God (20), He was nonetheless truly human in His reaction. It might even be said that His hurt was deeper and keener than that of an ordinary man because He knew better than any what separation from God really means.

Jesus prefaced His announcement with **Verily, verily,** thereby calling attention to the gravity of what is to follow. The announcement, **One of you shall betray me** (21), brought into their intimate circle that which heretofore must have appeared only as a distant threat (cf. 11:8; 13:18). It is no wonder that **the disciples looked one on another, doubting** ("at a loss to know," NASB) **of whom he spake** (22).

In order to understand the scene that follows, it is important to picture the "seating" arrangement at the supper table. Actually, the posture of the guests at a feast was that of reclining sideways on divans or couches. Since the table was the same height as the couches, the person placed his left elbow on a cushion on the table, and the right hand was free for taking food. The feet extended away from the table. The table was shaped like a *U* and the couches were around the outside. In the seating arrangement, "the host or principal person was in the centre, and the place of honour was above him, that is, to the left; the next highest place being below him, or to his right. Thus the person on the right of the host would be so placed that his head would be close to the host's breast, and it would be easy therefore to say a word to him confidentially."[23] Thus when we read that **there was leaning on Jesus' bosom one of his disciples** (23), it is easy to understand how this could be.

The one **leaning on Jesus' bosom** is designated as the disciple **whom Jesus loved** (23). This phrase is the writer's indirect method of referring to himself (cf. 19:26; 20:2; 21:7, 20). Traditionally he has been identified as John the son of Zebedee, and the author of the fourth Gospel (see Introduction). This

[23]Bernard, *op. cit.*, p. 471.

would then mean that Jesus was at the center of the table, the place of the host, and John was to His right. The next question concerns the name of the person to Jesus' left, the one in the place of honor. At this point authorities differ. Westcott thinks that it was Peter, on the ground that, being behind Jesus, he could not easily converse with Him, so signaled to John to ask Jesus the name of the betrayer.[24] Barclay, agreeing with Bernard, argues: "Judas was in a position in which Jesus could speak to him privately without the others overhearing it. There is a kind of private conversation here going on between Jesus and Judas . . . He must have been sitting on Jesus' left . . . *The place on the left of the host was the place of highest honour, kept for the most intimate friend.*"[25] If Judas occupied the seat of honor that fateful night, it must have been at Jesus' invitation, for such was the prerogative of the host. To the very last hour Jesus was seeking the lost (Luke 19:10).

When **Peter beckoned** (24, lit., "nodded") to the one **lying on Jesus' breast,** John put the question, **Lord, who is it?** (25) **Jesus answered, He it is, to whom I shall give a sop** ("morsel," NASB), **when I have dipped it** (26). Though this act was to be an answer to John's query, it was so veiled that neither John nor the other disciple caught its full impact. Rather, Jesus' dipping of the morsel and giving it to Judas indicated to them quite the opposite idea. Quimby comments: "In the Orient it was the custom . . . when guests were present, [for] the host, if he wished especially to honor one of them, [to] fold a piece of bread spoon-like, dip it into the dish and, securing some choice morsel, hand it to the guest as a special favor."[26] So this was no move by Jesus to expose Judas; it was an effort to shield him, and He did it well. **No man at the table knew** (28) why Jesus told Judas, who had taken the morsel, **That thou doest, do quickly** (27). John comments that the disciples thought Jesus had given Judas, as the treasurer, some special instructions about purchasing supplies for the Passover **feast** or **that he should give something to the poor** (29).

The shield for Judas' hypocrisy was near perfect. But the exterior was no indication of what was happening to him. For when he took the morsel, professing to accept Jesus' overture of

[24]*Op. cit.,* p. 194.
[25]*Op. cit.,* p. 169.
[26]*Op. cit.,* p. 177.

love, **Satan entered into him** (27). Something terrible happens to the man who spurns the "love to the uttermost" (13:1). So **Judas went immediately out: and it was night** (30; cf. 1:5; 3:19; 9:4; 11:10). When John penned those words he no doubt recalled seeing Judas open the door, walk away from the Light, out into the night. "It is always night when a man goes out from Christ to follow his own purposes."[27]

Here we may clearly see "Love to the Uttermost" outlined: (1) Love that finds a way to serve, 4-9; (2) Love that can know the worst and love the most, 26-29; (3) Love rejected turns to night, 30.

B. THE LAST DISCOURSES, 13:31—16:33

A word needs to be said about the order of the last discourses. Bernard argues that there have been dislocations in the order of the text. His general plan is to place cc. 15 and 16 immediately after 13:31*a*, then 13:31*b*-38, followed by c. 14. This is done to make what seems to him to be a nearer representation of "the intention of the original writer."[28] Macgregor (who follows Moffatt) simply places c. 14 after cc. 15 and 16 on the ground that the allegory of the vine (c. 15) should follow the giving of the new commandment (13:34).[29] There may be reasons to suspect that there have been some dislocations, but most attempts at reordering seem not to help much, mainly because of the highly subjective criteria that provide the basis for the new order. In the final analysis, the best procedure is to follow the textual evidence as found in the objective analysis of textual criticism. There is no textual evidence for the above "reorderings."

1. *The Discourse at the Table* (13:31—14:31)

a. Introduction (13:31-35). Left with the eleven faithful disciples, Judas having **gone out** (31),[30] Jesus told of the "fourfold glory,"[31] or honor. First there is the glory of the Cross, for **now is the Son of man glorified** (31). Second, "in Jesus God

---

[27]Barclay, *op. cit.*, p. 171.

[28]*Op. cit.*, I, xx.

[29]*Op. cit.*, p. 286.

[30]Westcott notes that this indicates Judas left of his own free will (*op. cit.*, p. 196).

[31]Barclay, *op. cit.*, pp. 171-73.

has been glorified"—**God is glorified in him** (31). This is because of Jesus' perfect obedience to the will of the Father and identification with Him even to the extent that Jesus could say, "He that hath seen me hath seen the Father" (14:9). Third, "in Jesus, God glorifies himself." The supreme glory of God is the fact that He came to men as one of them, conquered sin and death on the Cross. Fourth, just as the Incarnation is a glory to God, so it is to Jesus, for **God shall also glorify him in himself, and shall straightway glorify him** (32). It is because of this that "God also hath highly exalted him" (Phil. 2:9). The verb for **glorify** is in both aorist (past) and future tenses in the Greek, and describes "the glorification of the Son of man . . . [as] past, present and future: any logical distinction breaks down, since the significance of the Death and the Coming of the Spirit to the believers, events in time as they are, cannot be limited to this event."[32]

In this aura of glory Jesus called the disciples **little children** (33). "He addresses them tenderly, as the Head of His little family."[33] He then continues with a theme first introduced in 7:33-34, there spoken to the Jews, here to the eleven. The language is almost identical. **Yet a little while I am with you. Ye shall seek me: and as I said to the Jews, Whither I go, ye cannot come; so now I say to you** (33). It is obvious that Jesus is speaking of the proximity of His death and His going to the One who sent Him (7:33).

In 31-32, Alexander Maclaren points out "The Glory of the Cross": (1) The Son of Man glorified in the Cross, 31; (2) God glorified in the Son, 31; (3) The Son of Man glorified in the Father, 32.

In the light of the events that have just transpired Jesus puts into a new wineskin the wine of a new love: **A new commandment I give unto you, That ye love one another; as I have loved you, that ye also love one another** (34). The command of love for one's neighbor was not new (Lev. 19:18; Luke 10:27). But to **love . . . as I have loved you**—that was new! Our Lord's love reached to a Judas (13:5, 26) who would betray Him, and a Peter who would deny Him (13:38; 18:15-18, 27). In fact this kind of love was an event so unique that a new verbal vehicle had to be devised to express it. The *eros* (not in NT) of the

---

[32]Hoskyns, *op. cit.*, p. 450.
[33]Bernard, *op. cit.*, II, 526.

Greeks described only selfish love; and *philia* (in NT only Jas. 4:4) described no more than the friendship love that thinks in terms of getting as well as giving. But the selfless sacrifice of Jesus, His willingness to give all without any guarantee of human response, had to be expressed in a stronger word. So *agape*,[34] a rare word for *love* prior to Paul, came to be used in early Christian literature to describe the kind of love that Jesus demonstrated, and the quality of love that is to characterize the lives of His true disciples.

It is by a love like this, Jesus said, that all men shall **know that ye are my disciples, if ye have love one to another** (35). Macgregor says: "There is to be a new love-circle, the Christian Church, dependent upon a new love-centre, Christ." He then quotes Tertullian as saying: "The heathen are wont to exclaim with wonder, See how these Christians love one another."[35]

b. The Disciples' Questions (13:36—14:14). In this section we find two questions (by Peter and by Thomas) and one request (by Philip).

(1) *Peter's question* (13:36—14:4). It is no wonder that the disciples were filled with questions both about the things that had just happened (e.g., the foot washing and the departure of Judas) and also the fact that Jesus had said He himself was about to go where they could not (33). Peter, true to his impulsive nature, asked, **Lord, whither goest thou?** (36) Jesus' answer, "Where I am going you cannot follow me now; but you shall follow afterward" (36, RSV), carries a dual meaning. The obvious meaning is that Jesus was going to His death and that later Peter would suffer for Jesus' sake and die in defense of His truth (cf. 21:8).[36] The deeper meaning is seen in the use of the word "can." This is a translation of the Greek verb *dynamai*,[37] which means "I can, I am able." The cognate noun is *dynamis* and means "power, might, strength, force."[38]

This verb, with the negative, appears no less than eight times[39] in this general theme context, each time expressing or

[34]The word occurs seven times in this Gospel and eighteen times in I John.

[35]*Op. cit.*, p. 284.

[36]Adam Clarke, *op. cit.*, p. 620.

[37]The English words "dynamite," "dynamic," etc., are derivatives of this word.

[38]Arndt and Gingrich, *op. cit.*, p. 206.

[39]Cf. 7:34; 13:33, 36-37; 14:17; 15:4-5; 16:12.

implying man's utter inability and powerlessness apart from the enabling Spirit of Christ. So the great question is: How could Peter follow Jesus in the full performance of the **new commandment** (34, 36)? This persistent question on the part of the disciples provides much of the setting for Jesus to give the promise of the Spirit, and in the figure of the vine to declare, "Apart from Me you are not able to do one thing" (15:5, lit. translation).

Peter, with strong desire and intent, was willing to try. Thinking only in terms of the impending crisis, he pursued his question. **Lord, why cannot I follow thee now? I will lay down my life for thy sake** (37). Jesus knew His man (cf. 2:25). To intend to do right is important. To want to fulfill the new commandment is essential for spiritual life. But to love to the uttermost (13:1) is not within the ability of human strength. For pre-Pentecost Peter, Jesus had but one prediction. **The cock shall not crow, till thou hast denied me thrice** (38; cf. Matt. 26:31 ff.; Mark 14:27 ff.; Luke 22:31 ff.).

There is a break in the thought between the conclusion of 13:38 and the beginning of c. 14. Jesus has just indicated to Peter his forthcoming denial, and there is no introduction to a new theme. For this reason some commentators have developed various theories of textual dislocations (see comment at beginning of section *B* above).

However, if these opening verses (1-4) had been prefaced by a simple "He said to Peter" or "He said to them," the difficulty would be resolved. It would be easy to find not only a continuity of thought but also a very meaningful purpose in these words as related to what Jesus had just told Peter. Peter's strong affirmation of fidelity had been met by the announcement of his denial. His desire and willingness to follow Jesus even unto death (13:37) seemed to be doomed to failure. So the promise and reassurance of Jesus' words to Peter and the other ten disciples were desperately needed. Jesus, who knew by experience the anguish of a troubled spirit (11:33; 12:27; 13:21), could say with all authority and sympathetic understanding, **Let not your heart be troubled** (14:1). Then, as if to bolster lagging faith in all His hearers, He gave two great imperatives, both in the plural: "Have faith in God, and in Me have faith" (1, lit. translation).[40]

---

[40]The KJV translates the first clause as an indicative **ye believe.** However most commentators agree, on the basis of context, that the imperative is the better translation.

What is it that is prepared for those who have faith? **Many mansions** (rooms) **in my Father's house** (2).[41] Westcott observes that the word **mansions** comes from the Vulgate *mansiones,* "which were resting places, and especially the 'stations' on a great road where travellers found refreshment," suggesting the ideas of both repose and progress.[42] Bernard says that these are "dwelling places," not merely temporary stations on a journey.[43] However, the fact that it is **Father's house** says enough. "The home of God (Matt. 5:34; 6:1), the eternal antitype of the transitory temple in Jerusalem and of the abiding of the Father and the Son in the believer (14:23; 17:21), is capacious and many roomed."[44] On the basis of excellent MS evidence the RSV —along with Strachan, Bauer, Bernard, and Moffatt—translates the remaining part of v. 2 as a question: "if it were not so, would I have told you that I go to prepare a place for you?" The objection to this is that "nowhere in the Gospel has Jesus said that he is 'going to prepare a place.' "[45]

The promise to the disciples was, **I will come again** (3; lit., "I am coming again").[46] The primary reference is to the Second Coming. But it also suggests another thought: "Christ is in fact from the moment of his Resurrection ever coming to the world and to the Church and to men as the Risen Lord."[47]

Peter had asked the question, **Lord, whither goest thou?** (13:36) Jesus' answer had described Peter's weakness (13:36) and his denial (13:38); His answer had also included some great and glorious promises (14:1-3). Now in a concluding statement directed to all the disciples our Lord answered categorically, **And whither I go ye know, and the way ye know** (4).

(2) *Thomas' question* (14:5-7). Jesus' last statement directed to Peter's question only raised another in the mind of Thomas, who has been described as "the type of those who

[41]The Greek word translated **mansions** is *mone,* and means *dwelling (-place), room, abode* (Arndt and Gingrich, *op. cit.,* p. 529).

[42]*Op. cit.,* p. 200.

[43]*Op. cit.,* p. 533.

[44]Hoskyns, *op. cit.,* pp. 452-53.

[45]Macgregor, *op. cit.,* p. 305.

[46]This is a good example of the "prophetic present," which may well be translated as future (cf. RSV, NEB, NASB).

[47]Westcott, *op. cit.,* p. 201.

demand 'tangible proofs and precise definitions.' "[48] He asked,
**Lord, we know not whither thou goest; and how can we know
the way?** (5) This quest for certainty brought from Jesus one
of the most comprehensive and profound statements which He
ever uttered concerning His own nature: **I am the way, the
truth, and the life (6).** The **I am** (*ego eimi*) is here used as
metaphor, at once identifying Jesus with divinity[49] and as the
satisfaction to the basic needs of man. Can lost man find a way?
Christ is the Way, and the only Way, to God (cf. Heb. 10:19-22).
"The road to God is knowledge of the truth, and regeneration,
enlightenment and the possession of Life. Truth and Life are no
ideal abstractions. They are present concretely in the incarnate
Son of God, who is both the Truth and the Life."[50] There is a
kind of glorious exclusiveness about Christ, the Way. **No man
cometh unto the Father, but by me (6).** Its glory is not that any
are excluded. Rather, because of who He is and what He did, the
way is a universal way. "Whosoever will, let him take the water
of life freely" (Rev. 22:17; cf. John 3:16). Thomas à Kempis
wrote in worshipful meditation:

> Without the Way, there is no going; without the Truth, there is
> no knowing; without the Life, there is no living. I am the Way,
> which thou oughtest to follow; the Truth, which thou oughtest to
> believe; the Life, which thou oughtest to hope for. I am the Way
> inviolable, the Truth infallible, the Life unending. I am the Way
> that is straightest, the Truth that is highest, the Life that is true,
> the Life blessed, the Life uncreated. If thou remain in My way,
> thou shalt *know the Truth, and the Truth shall make thee free*,
> and thou shalt lay hold on eternal life.[51]

As much as Thomas and the others loved Jesus, they had not
"really come to know him."[52] With gentle rebuke Jesus said, "If
by acquaintance you had known Me, you would have had a certain and assured knowledge of the Father" (7, lit. translation).
And from henceforth marks "the moment of the Passion. . . . The
Revelation of the Father was not complete until Jesus had re-

[48]Hoskyns, *op. cit.,* p. 454.

[49]See comments on 4:26; 6:20, 35.

[50]*Ibid.,* p. 455.

[51]*The Imitation of Christ,* revised translation (New York: Grosset and
Dunlap, n.d.), p. 253.

[52]Robertson, *op. cit.,* p. 250.

moved His visible presence. Only after that did His disciples begin to understand how much He had revealed of God's nature and purpose."[53]

(3) *Philip's request* (14:8-14). Jesus' assertion that the disciples should have known the Father (7) induced Philip to request some special revelation, perhaps a theophany (cf. Exod. 24:9-11; 33:18). **Lord, shew (show) us the Father, and it sufficeth us** ("we shall be satisfied," RSV, 8). With a hint of pathos and reprimand Jesus said, **Have I been so long time with you, and yet hast thou not known me, Philip?** (9) Bernard observes: "The sheep know their shepherd (10:14), and Philip ought to have 'known' Jesus by this time. But to fail to see God in Jesus was to fail to know Jesus."[54]

There are two reasons why Philip should have known that Father and Son are one (10:30), that Jesus could say, **I am in the Father, and the Father in me** (10). One is the words of Jesus, which are not His own, but are of the Father which sent Him (12:49). The other is the works that Jesus has done. These are wrought by the **Father that dwelleth in me, he doeth the works** (10). Both the word and the works of Jesus are from the Father, and are sufficient reasons for the disciples (note the shift to the plural) to be having faith **that I am in the Father, and the Father in me** (11). If, because of human weakness, a man cannot take Jesus at His word, there is a secondary level of faith—**or else believe me for the very works' sake** (11; cf. 5:36; 10:38). Bernard comments: "The faith which is generated by an appeal like this is not the highest type of faith, but it is not despised by Jesus."[55]

To show that works are secondary and that faith in Him for who He is rather than what He does is primary, Jesus laid it out in plain language. **Verily, verily . . . He that believeth on me** (lit., "he who is putting his faith into Me"), **the works that I do shall he do also** (12). When works are the product of dynamic faith in Him, they are characterized by a certain superiority. The believer is capable of **greater works than these.**

Two questions need to be considered. First, What is the basis for these **greater works?** Three things are evident. There is,

[53]Bernard, *op. cit.*, p. 539.
[54]*Ibid.*, p. 541.
[55]*Ibid.*, p. 542.

first, a rightly placed faith. It is "the one who has faith in Me" who does the works that Jesus does. The second is clearly stated: **because I go unto my Father.** Just as the Father sent the Son, now with His return to the Father He is sending the believers into the world (17:18). They are sent with a commission.[56] In the third place the performance of works is closely related to prayer. With the promise of **greater works** there is also the promise that **whatsoever ye shall ask in my name, that will I do . . . If ye shall ask any thing in my name, I will do it** (13-14); cf. 15:7; 16:23-24).[57] What does it mean to pray in Jesus' name? Though **whatsoever** and **any thing** seem to be all-inclusive, these words are no guarantee that all our prayers will be granted. The great qualifier is **in my name.** This is asking for only that which is within the will of God. Barclay writes: "The prayer which in the end says: Thy will be done, is always answered."[58]

The second question to be answered is, In what sense are these works **greater** than the works done by Jesus? (12) Robertson says: "Greater in quantity."[59] Clarke goes further, and says: "It is certainly the greatest miracle of Divine grace to convert the obstinate, wicked heart of man from sin to holiness. This was done in numberless cases by the disciples."[60] Following in much the same thought, Westcott observes that **greater** means "the wide spiritual effects of their preaching which followed after Pentecost."[61]

"The True Vision of God" may be seen in 8-11. (1) We all need to have God made visible to us, 8; (2) The divine indwelling which makes this sight possible, 9-10; (3) The faith to which Christ invites us, 11 (Alexander Maclaren).

c. *The Promise of the Spirit* (14:15-31). Obedience, love, and faith are the prerequisites for the believer to receive God's greatest gift to man. The one who believes, i.e., has faith, is the one who receives (12; cf. Acts 15:8-9; 26:18). It is to the one who loves that Jesus makes himself real—**He that loveth me . . .**

---

[56]The Greek verb for "send" in 17:18 is *apostello,* and means "to send with a commission."

[57]Some authorities translate v. 14, "If ye shall ask me anything . . . ," on the basis of the Greek pronoun *me* appearing in some MSS.

[58]*Op. cit.,* p. 193.

[59]*Op. cit.,* p. 251.

[60]*Op. cit.,* p. 623.

[61]*Op. cit.,* p. 204.

I will love him, and will manifest myself to him (21). So here,
obedience and love are inseparably bound together. There is no
higher law than the law of love. It does not demand obedience.
Rather, obedience is its inevitable corollary. **If ye love me, keep
my commandments** (15).[62]

In 14:12-18 may be found some "Prerequisites for the Gift of
the Spirit": (1) Faith to receive, 12-14; (2) Enough love to obey,
15; cf. 15:9-10; (3) The reward for obedience, 16-18.

Jesus boldly announced the Gift—the Spirit: **And I will
pray the Father, and he shall give you another Comforter, that
he may abide with you for ever; even the Spirit of truth** (16-17).
Here is the first of several passages in this section describing the
coming of the **Comforter** (cf. 14:26; 15:26; 16:7). The Greek
word translated **Comforter** is *parakletos,* which has been Angli-
cized to "paraclete"—meaning an "advocate," intercessor,"
"pleader"—and personalized as the Holy Spirit. The Greek word
"originally meant in the passive sense 'one who is called to
someone's aid,' " and has the more general meaning *"one who appears in another's behalf, mediator, intercessor, helper."*[63] Various
translations have used different words in an effort to wring from
this Greek word[64] its full and significant meaning—e.g., "Counsel-
or" (RSV), "Helper" (Moffatt, NASB), "Divine Helper" (Phillips), "Advocate" (Weymouth). It is translated "advocate" in
I John 2:1, where it refers to Christ.

The Paraclete is identified as **the Spirit of truth** (17),
"which brings truth and impresses it on the conscience of the
world."[65] But this Gift is not for all men. **The world cannot
receive** Him, for the simple reason that **it seeth him not, neither
knoweth him** (17). "The spiritual can be apprehended not by
worldly men, but only by those whose souls are attuned to the
spiritual realm."[66] But the promise is intimate, personal, and
precious for those who **know him; for he dwelleth with you, and
shall be in you** (17; cf. Acts 2:4; Rom. 8:9; I John 2:27;

---

[62]The literal translation is "you will keep"—simple future indicative—
and is much more in keeping with the sense of the whole passage.

[63]Arndt and Gingrich, *op. cit.,* p. 623.

[64]An excellent and exhaustive discussion of the origin, usages, and
translations of the word may be found in Hoskyns, *op. cit.,* pp. 465-70. Also
see Bernard, *op. cit.,* pp. 496-98.

[65]Bernard, *op. cit.,* p. 499.

[66]Macgregor, *op. cit.,* p. 309.

II John 2). Insofar as the Spirit dwelt in Jesus, He was **with** the disciples. But when Jesus had ascended into heaven and the Spirit had come at Pentecost, He would be **in** them.

Jesus continued His words of encouragement by promising the disciples, **I will not leave you comfortless** ("orphans," NASB):[67] **I will come** (lit., "I am coming") **to you (18)**. The use of the present tense of the verb emphasizes repeated comings of the Lord—in resurrection, Pentecost, judgment, and into the hearts of men who believe on Him—or it may be the futuristic present, "I am coming (soon)." "The life of the Church is the realization of the Pentecostal coming of the Lord, which is to be crowned by His coming to Judgment."[68] With clear reference to His ascension and His eternal presence with men of faith He said, **Yet a little while, and the world seeth me no more; but ye see me (19)**. Such is to be possible because of the power and meaning of the Resurrection—**because I live, ye shall live also (19)**.

In 16-18, Alexander Maclaren speaks of "The Comforter Given." (1) The praying Christ and the giving Father, 16; (2) The abiding Gift, 16-17; (3) The recipient disciples, 17-18.

The phrase **At that day** (20; cf. 16:23, 26) refers "first to the Resurrection,"[69] then to "each victorious crisis of the new apprehension of the Risen Christ."[70] In that day three things will be made clear—**ye shall know (20)**. (1) There will be no doubt about the mutual and reciprocal indwelling of Father, Son, and believer: **I am in my Father, and ye in me, and I in you, 20.** (2) It will be seen that love and obedience are inseparables: **He that hath my commandments, and keepeth them, he it is that loveth me, 21.** (3) The believer who practices loving obedience **shall be loved of my Father, the Son will love him, and will manifest**[71] himself **to him, 21.**

The last statement of Jesus provoked **Judas** (Thaddaeus; see comments on Matt. 10:3 in BBC, VI, 106) to ask, **Lord, how**

---

[67] The Greek word translated **comfortless** is *orphanos*, which means literally, *deprived of one's parents* (Arndt and Gingrich, *op. cit.*, p. 586).

[68] Westcott, *op. cit.*, p. 206.

[69] Hoskyns, *op. cit.*, p. 460.

[70] Westcott, *op. cit.*, p. 207.

[71] The Greek word for **manifest** is *emphanizo*. Literally it means *to reveal*. In a figurative meaning it refers to what transpires within one's soul (Arndt and Gingrich, *op. cit.*, p. 257).

is it that thou wilt manifest thyself unto us, and not unto the
world? (22) In response Jesus reiterated what He had just said.
Love cannot be separated from obedience. If a man love me, he
will keep my words (23). It is in this active relationship that
there is the manifestation of the Son. "The power of receiving
a divine Revelation depends upon active obedience, which rests
upon personal love."[72] Judas had evidently expected that Jesus
would in some way openly manifest himself so that all men
might see Him. But the answer is that "the whole power of the
Godhead is present in the life and witness of the believer"[73]—we
will come unto him, and make our abode with him (23; cf. 17:21).
The Spirit's manifestation is through those who believe in Him,
love and obey Him. The clause we will come, because of the
plural we, "implies necessarily the claim to divinity on the part
of Christ."[74] The we will . . . make our abode with him needs to
be understood in the light of 14:2, for the same Greek word
(*mone*) is used in both verses—there mansions, here abode.
Hoskyns comments: "The sanctuary and home of God, which is
in heaven, and was but incompletely revealed in the temple at
Jerusalem, will descend upon each Christian believer."[75]

Those who make high religious profession and fail to reflect
it consistently in ethical conduct and attitudes need to remember
that "not loving" and "not keeping Jesus' words" are inseparables
(24). "There is no spiritual union with Him which is not also a
moral union."[76]

The second promise of the coming of the Spirit is prefaced
by Jesus' words: These things have I spoken[77] unto you, being
yet present with you (25). In this announcement of the coming
of the Comforter (Paraclete), Jesus identifies Him unequivocally
as the Holy Ghost [Spirit],[78] whom the Father will send in my

[72]Westcott, *op. cit.*, p. 207.
[73]Strachan, *op. cit.*, p. 286.
[74]Westcott, *op. cit.*, p. 208.
[75]*Op. cit.*, p. 460.
[76]*Ibid.*
[77]This expression appears seven times in the Last Discourses (15:11; 16:1, 4, 6, 25, 33).
[78]The Greek word translated Ghost (Spirit) is *pneuma*, whence the English "pneumatic," which means variously *wind, breath, spirit.* The KJV Ghost has present-day connotations that leave something to be desired in a title for the blessed Third Person of the Trinity.

170

name (26). The coming of the Spirit means the realization, on the part of the new Christian community, of the full and true meaning of the life, teaching, death, and exaltation of Jesus. **He shall teach you all things, and bring all things to your remembrance, whatsoever I have said unto you** (26; cf. 16:12-14, 22-23, 25; I Cor. 1:18; 2:13). Though the work of the Spirit is to call to the **remembrance** of the disciples Jesus' teachings, "His work is more than a reminiscence of the *ipsissima verba* [the very words] of the Son of God: it is a living representation of all that He had once spoken to His disciples, a creative exposition of the Gospel."[79] In a very practical vein Barclay says: "The Holy Spirit saves us from arrogance and error of thought."[80]

In 25-27 we see "The Teacher Spirit." (1) The promised Teacher, 25-26; (2) The lesson which this Teacher gives, 26; (3) The pupils of this Teacher, 26-27 (Alexander Maclaren).

To His disciples, and to all who believe in Him, Jesus left a dual bequest. These are much-talked-about aspirations in the present day—peace, **Peace I leave with you;** and freedom from fear, **Let not your heart be troubled, neither let it be afraid** (27). This peace is not mere absence of trouble. It "means everything which makes for our highest good."[81] It is a peace of conquest which is "manifested in unbroken union with the Father, maintained in continuous strife with the world, in persecution, in humiliation, and in death for the glory of God."[82] Could it be that this dynamic peace comes only to those who are possessed by the Holy Spirit? Quimby observes that the coming of the Spirit "is blood transfusion for courageous living. Jesus went away that the Strengthener might come."[83]

Could the disciples have seen ahead, they would have rejoiced that Jesus said, **I go unto the Father: for my Father is greater than I** (28). This clause has caused not a little theological contention. The Arian controversy of the fourth century centered around its interpretation.[84] Bernard argues that the

---

[79]Hoskyns, *op. cit.,* p. 461.

[80]*Op. cit.,* p. 199.

[81]*Ibid.*

[82]Hoskyns, *op. cit.,* p. 461.

[83]*Op. cit.,* p. 185.

[84]See Westcott, *op. cit.,* pp. 213-16, for an excellent review of the views of early representative writers.

greater consists in the fact that "the Father *sent* the Son and *gave* Him all things."[85]

Recognizing that the fulfillment of His hour was at hand, Jesus said, **Hereafter I will not talk much with you** (30). The greater encounter between the cosmic forces of good and evil was at hand: **The prince of this world cometh** (30; cf. Luke 4:13; 22:53). It was "Satan himself . . . whose last assault Jesus now prepared" to meet.[86] But even in anticipation of the final attack, Jesus knew himself to be Victor. The clause **the prince of this world** (Satan) **hath nothing in me** (30) takes on added meaning in the RSV, "He has no power over me." The absolute sinlessness of Jesus is pictured here. There is "no element in Christ's nature which will yield" to Satan.[87] Westcott says: "In others he finds that which is his own, and enforces death as his due; but Christ offered himself voluntarily."[88]

Even in the face of death, loving obedience was the hallmark of Jesus' action. **I love the Father; and as the Father gave me commandment, even so I do** (31). So there is no point in procrastination or delay. There are some problems that time does not solve. **Arise, let us go hence** (31).

2. *The Discourses Along the Way* (15:1—16:33)

a. The Figure of the Vine (15:1-17). There is no indication in John's Gospel of any special place where the discourses of cc. 15 and 16 or the prayer of c. 17 were spoken. After Jesus and the eleven disciples left the room where they had eaten supper, the next notation of place is the brook Cedron, over which Jesus and His disciples passed (18:1; see map 2). There is not even any indication of an event or place that may have prompted the use of the figure of the vine. It has been conjectured that there was a vine growing outside the window of the Upper Room, or that as Jesus and the disciples passed along the road He saw a vineyard, or that they passed the Temple and saw the filigree of golden vines and grapes on the Temple gate. Others take the view that it was the use of the wine in the celebration of the first Eucharist (Matt. 26:26-29; Mark 14:22-25; Luke 22:15-20)

---

[85]*Op. cit.,* p. 555; cf. Mark 13:32; Phil. 2:6; I Cor. 15:27.

[86]Bernard, *op. cit.,* p. 556.

[87]Macgregor, *op. cit.,* p. 313.

[88]*Op. cit.,* p. 210.

that made the figure so appropriate.[89] This does have some
merit, for in the fourth Gospel a feast or sign regularly provides
the basis and/or occasion for a discourse on an important issue
(5:1; 6:4; 7:37; 9:34; and c. 10).[90]

Any of the above situations could have provided the occasion
for this discourse. However, there was no need for such prompt-
ing. The figure of the vine or vineyard appears frequently in the
Old Testament (Isa. 5:1-7; Jer. 2:21; Ezek. 19:10-14; Ps. 80:8-19).
Israel is pictured as a degenerate vine with dried-up fruit, and
a withered vine consumed with fire (Ezek. 19:12), when she
should have been "the choicest vine" bringing "forth grapes"
(Isa. 5:2).

It is against this background that Jesus used the figure, **I am
the true vine** (1). There must be no mistake about it! It is not
Jewish blood but faith in Him that is the way to God's salvation.
If this discourse is best understood in the shadows of the Eucharist and the Cross, then the fruit of the vine, the cup (cf. 6:55-56),
and the blood (19:34) are joined in a figure to portray cleansing
—**Now ye are clean** (3)—bearing **much fruit** (5) and **giving**
loving obedience (9-10).

The purpose of a vineyard is to produce fruit. The responsibility of the **husbandman** (gardener) is to cultivate quality
vines, so they will be productive. To do this two things are necessary: (*a*) **Every branch in me that beareth not fruit he taketh
away** (2; cf. Luke 13:6-9). This may refer specifically to Judas;
certainly, to any apostate. The body of Christ must not be weakened by those who only profess but refuse to bear fruit. (*b*) **Every
branch that beareth fruit, he purgeth** (prunes) **it, that it may
bring forth more fruit** (2).[91] Here it is that the Father's action
"is revealed in the moral purification of the true disciples who
abide in his Son . . . The Father *cleareth away* the unprofitable
branches, and *cleanseth* those that bear fruit."[92]

---

[89]Bernard, *op. cit.*, p. 478.

[90]It should be noted that some take "Arise, let us go hence" (14:31) as
anticipatory. On this view Jesus continued talking, finished His discourse,
and uttered the great high priestly prayer (c. 17) while the group were still
standing in the Upper Room.

[91]There is a play on Greek words in these two clauses of v. 2. The
word for **taketh away** is *airei*, and **purgeth** is *kathairei*. The latter means
literally *make clean*, e.g., of a swept room, or *prune* by removing superfluous
wood (Arndt and Gingrich, *op. cit.*, p. 387).

[92]Hoskyns, *op. cit.*, p. 475.

It is clear that Jesus had the idea of cleansing in mind. He said, **Now** (lit., "already") **ye are clean through the word which I have spoken unto you** (3; cf. 13:10). The question is, "When were the disciples made **clean?**" Westcott says: "The spiritual work represented by this 'cleansing' was potentially completed for the apostles, the representatives of His Church. It remained that it should be realized by them."[93] The record indicates that the cleansing was effected at Pentecost (Acts 15:8-9). Macgregor points out that while "clean" in 13:10 meant "cleansed of sin," here the sense is more of action and "virtually means 'capable of bearing fruits.' "[94] H. Orton Wiley used to say that the cleansing in sanctification involves two things: the initial "making clean," and the continual "keeping clean" (I John 1:7, 9). "It is because of the Word abiding in them (7) that they are kept pure."[95] Hoskyns points out that "there is a double element in the purification of the disciples: the initial purgation occasioned by the Word of Jesus (6:63; cf. Eph. 5:26), and its conservation through the maintaining of a permanent union with Him, which is effected by the abiding of His words in them."[96]

The positive aspect of the continual cleansing is presented in the figure of the attachment of the pruned fruit-bearing branch to the vine. Hence the imperative **Abide in me** with its corollary **and I in you** (4). The command is appropriate, for "in the spiritual sphere this 'abiding' is not maintained without the constant and conscious endeavour of the disciples' own will."[97] At the same time it is because of the empowerment of the **I in you** that the believer is able to abide. **For without**[98] **me ye can do nothing** (5).[99]

If spiritual impotence belongs to those separated from Christ, fruitfulness and productivity characterize those who abide. **He that abideth in me, and I in him, the same bringeth forth much fruit** (5; cf. 8, 16). That the Church should be productive, should bear fruit, is its reason for existence. "The Church without a

[93]*Op. cit.,* p. 217.

[94]*Op. cit.,* p. 287.

[95]Bernard, *op. cit.,* p. 480.

[96]*Op. cit.,* p. 475.

[97]Bernard, *op. cit.,* p. 481.

[98]The Greek word here translated **without** is *choris* and means "apart from" or "separated from."

[99]Cf. 13:33, 36-37; 14:17; 15:4-5; 16:12.

sense of mission is no church."[100] Just as "abiding" is the basis
for fruitfulness, it is also the basis for a successful and satisfying
prayer life. **If ye abide in me, and my words abide in you, ye
shall ask** (ask is an imperative in the Gk.) **what ye will, and it
shall be done unto you** (7; cf. 14:13-14; 15:16; 16:23-24). In
v. 3 the cleansing is **through the word** (*logos*), while here (7) it
is the **words** (*rhemata*) that must **abide**. Westcott comments on
this: "The *words* (*rhemata*), the definite sayings . . . go to make
up 'the word' " (cf. 8:43, 47, 51; 12:47-48; 17:6, 8, 14).[101]

The idea of judgment is also presented in the figure. The
person who does not abide (i.e., the one who by willful attitude
or act severs himself from the true vine) **is cast forth as a branch,
and is withered** (6). Westcott points out of the withering that
"it is not a future consequence, as at the last judgment, but an
inevitable consequence of the separation."[102] However, in the
next clause there is clear reference to final judgment and separation, for the withered branches are gathered, **cast . . . into the fire,
and they are burned** (6). In this universe, which has its moral
as well as its natural law, something terrible happens when a
man separates himself from Christ (cf. 13:30; Matt. 27:5).

There are some significant qualities that characterize the
fruitful vine. It is the pride of the husbandman. **Herein is my
Father glorified, that ye bear much fruit** (8). In the vine is also
the test of discipleship, for in the bearing of **much fruit** you shall
"prove to be My disciples" (8, NASB).[103] In the relationship of
husbandman, vine, and branch, there is suggested the regularly
recurring theme of loving obedience. **As the Father hath loved
me, so have I loved you: continue ye** (abide) **in my love** (9).
The logic of loving obedience is simple: (1) **I have kept my
Father's commandments.** (2) **I . . . abide in his love.** (3) **You
keep my commandments.** (4) **Ye shall abide in my love** (10).
Hoskyns comments: "The fidelity of love is proved and shown
forth in obedience."[104]

[100]Strachan, *op. cit.*, p. 290.

[101]*Op. cit.*, p. 218.

[102]*Ibid.*

[103]Some MSS have the verb *genesthe,* an imperative expressing necessity, which well justifies the above translation. A disciple is a "learner"
and it is hard to conceive of learning without testing or proving. It is reported that Ignatius, when on his way to martyrdom, said, "Now I am
beginning to be a disciple" (Bernard, *op. cit.,* p. 483).

[104]*Op. cit.*, p. 477.

Another theme depicted here is that of joy. It certainly is implied that the fruitful vine is a joy to the husbandman (8). But equally important, it is the vine-branch relationship that guarantees the impartation of joy to the believer. **These things have I spoken unto you, that my joy** (lit., "the joy that is Mine") **might remain** (Gk., "be") **in you, and that your joy might be full** (11; cf. 16:20-24; 17:13).

In 5-8, Alexander Maclaren points out: "The True Branches of the True Vine." (1) Union with our Lord is sure to issue in fruitfulness, 5; (2) Withering and destruction follow separation from Him, 6; (3) Union with Christ is the condition for satisfied desires, 7; (4) Union with Christ brings glory to God and increasing discipleship, 8.

"Abiding in Love" is the theme Alexander Maclaren finds in 9-11. (1) The love in which we are to abide, 9; (2) The obedience by which we are to continue in Christ's love, 10; (3) The joy which follows obedience, 11.

Jesus reiterated what He called the "new commandment" (13:34, see comment), **That ye love one another, as I have loved you** (12). But now, closer to the shadow of the Cross, He introduces another oft-recurring theme: His voluntary death for men (6:51; 10:17-18; 12:24-25), the supreme proof of His love. **Greater love hath no man than this, that a man lay down his life for his friends** (13). What Jesus was about to do for all men (i.e., die on the Cross), He was doing for His friends, the disciples. **Ye are my friends,** He said, **if ye do whatsoever I command you** (14). The word **friend** has special meaning. Abraham "was called the Friend of God" (cf. II Chron. 20:7; Isa. 41:8; Jas. 2:23). Here it emphasizes "the intimacy of the love."[105] This friend relationship is not that of a **servant** (lit., "slave"), for he does not know **what his lord doeth.** But the **friends,** the disciples, know. **For all things that I have heard of my Father I have made known unto you** (15).

The basis of this friend relationship is not of man's merit or working. **Ye have not chosen me, but I have chosen you** (16). This is not to deny man his free moral agency, but it is to affirm that apart from Christ man is impotent (15:1). Hence it is that Christ has **ordained** (appointed) them to **bring forth fruit** that should **remain** ("abide," 16). Westcott observes: "The power of the office of the apostles lay for them in the fact that it was not

---

[105]Macgregor, *op. cit.,* p. 289.

self-chosen."[106] The self-appointed man is doomed to dismal defeat when he tries apart from Christ to produce the fruit that abides.

The major theme reiterated sums up the teaching in the figure of the vine. **These things I command you, that ye love one another** (17), "for as the branches cannot bear fruit apart from the vine, so neither can one branch bear fruit without the assistance of the other."[107]

b. *The Disciples and the Hate of the World* (15:18-27). What is this **world** (18) which hates Jesus and His disciples? The word **world** appears five times in 18-19. One thing is evident right at the outset. It is those who **hate**[108] Jesus. It was not the physical world that rejected Him. It was His own people (see comment on 1:11). Hence the rejection of Jesus was not a mere matter of political expediency or the desire to preserve old and great traditions. It was born of intense hatred against Him because He and His teachings cut right straight across their selfish sinfulness. So it follows that if the world hated Jesus it would hate His followers. There is a vivid contrast between those **not of the world** and **the world** (19). In matters of allegiance there is no middle ground. It is a black-and-white issue. There are no greys. A man is either **of the world** or **not of the world!**

Not only did the Jews hate Jesus. It came to pass, even as Jesus said, that the same hate (of both Jews and pagans) was heaped on those early Christians. Paul was hated by the Jews and he suffered not a little at their hand (II Cor. 11:24). The Jews spread slanderous propaganda among the pagans about the followers of Christ, labeling them as: insurrectionaries, because of their refusal to worship Caesar; cannibals, because of their practice of remembering the Lord's death by eating the broken bread, His body; incendiaries, because of their expectation that "the earth also and the works that are therein shall be burned up" (II Pet. 3:10); immoral, by reporting the love feasts as orgies of sexual indulgence; and as disrupters of the family (in part true) because of the allegiance to Christ of only one member

[106]*Op. cit.*, p. 221.

[107]Hoskyns, *op. cit.*, pp. 478-79.

[108]The Greek word for hate, *miseo*, is a very strong word meaning "detest, abhor, persecute in hatred" (Arndt and Gingrich, *op. cit.*, p. 524).

of the family.[109] It is no wonder that the hate of the Jews inflamed the pagans to persecute the Christians. The very intensity with which the world persecuted the followers of Jesus and the implacable hatred for His friends "is the sign of the verity of that friendship."[110]

There is an interesting corollary to the proposition: **If they have persecuted me, they will also persecute you** (20); namely, **if they have kept my saying, they will keep yours also.** That is, "the disciples could look back and discern what they had to expect: some courageous followers, some faithful hearers . . . [but also some] careless or hostile multitudes."[111]

The argument now shifts. Jesus has been saying that because the world hated Him it would also hate His disciples. Now the same type of argument is applied to the world's hating the **Father also** (23). The reason they will do **these things** for His **name's sake** ("on my account," RSV) is that **they know not him that sent me** (21; cf. 8:55; 14:17; 17:25). Not to know the Son is not to know the Father (14:9). The very fact of the Incarnation, the Word become flesh (1:14), has intensified the guilt and sin of the world. His light only intensified the world's night. The Bible teaches clearly a relationship between our knowledge of God and our responsibility to Him (cf. Luke 12:47-48). So now that He is come **they** (the world) **have no cloke** (excuse) **for their sin** (22; cf. 16:7-9). His life is the perfect exposé of the sin of the world.

It is not only the words of Jesus (22) that condemn the world, but also His works. **If I had not done among them the works which none other man did, they had not had sin** (24). Works, which should have given birth to faith (10:38; 14:11), having been rejected by the world, have gendered hate and sin (24). All the hate and persecutions which the world heaped on Jesus and His followers are seen as the fulfillment of the scripture, **They hated me without a cause** (25; cf. Ps. 35:19; 69:4). Jesus rarely displayed such detachment from the Old Testament as is here suggested by calling the Scripture **their law** (25). The expression probably indicates *their obligation to accept* what is in the Law rather than Jesus' disassociation from it.

[109]Barclay, *op. cit.*, pp. 214-16.

[110]Hoskyns, *op. cit.*, p. 479.

[111]Westcott, *op. cit.*, p. 223.

There will come a time, Jesus said, when there will be ample and true witness to Him. The witnesses are two. The first is the **Comforter,** the Paraclete. **Jesus will send** Him to the disciples **from the Father.** He, the Paraclete, is the **Spirit of truth.** Jesus said, **He shall testify of me** (26). The Paraclete is described as the one who **proceedeth from the Father.** This phrase has been called "the Eternal Procession." It has given rise to "endless disputes between East and West as to the 'Procession' of the Spirit from the Son as well as from the Father."[112] Bernard holds that the clause "does not refer to the mysterious relationships between the Persons of the Holy Trinity, but only that the Spirit . . . has come from God."[113]

It may well be that the Greek word *parakletos* (Paraclete) could be translated "advocate" in this context. For He is introduced as One who **shall testify** in Jesus' behalf. Macgregor says: "The Spirit is the one who will champion the church in her suit against the world and appear as a decisive 'witness' for the defence."[114]

The second witness is to be the disciples themselves. **Ye also shall bear witness** (27). They stand in an exceptionally favorable position to serve as witnesses, for they **have been with** Him **from the beginning.** They also stand to receive special power for this (Acts 1:8) with the coming of the Spirit at Pentecost. As one looks at the whole work and witness of the Spirit, it is seen to be "trebly circumscribed [supported]. His witness is the witness of the Father to the Son through the disciples."[115]

Barclay suggests from this passage (15:26-27) three aspects of the Christian witness. (1) Christian witness comes from long fellowship and intimacy with Christ, 27; (2) It comes from inner conviction, 26; (3) It issues in outward testimony, 27.[116]

c. *Persecutions Promised* (16:1-4a). The oft repeated **These things have I spoken** (1; 14:25; 15:11; 16:4, 6, 25, 33) opens again the theme of coming persecutions. The reason for the advance notice given to the disciples is **that ye should not be offended.**

---

[112]Bernard, *op. cit.,* p. 499.

[113]*Ibid.*

[114]*Op. cit.,* p. 293.

[115]Hoskyns, *op. cit.,* p. 482.

[116]*Op. cit.,* pp. 219-20.

The word translated **offended** is *skandalisthete*, which means "*cause to be caught or to fall*, i.e. *cause to sin*. (The sin may consist in a breach of the moral law, in unbelief, or in the acceptance of false teachings.) The passive can also mean *let oneself be led into sin, fall away*."[117] The NASB translation reads, "that you may be kept from stumbling." Westcott says it is "the image of stumbling over some obstacle in the way."[118] (Cf. 9:22, 34; Matt. 15:12; Mark 4:17; 14:27, 29; Luke 7:23; I John 2:10.) The notice of persecution (cf. Matt. 5:11-12) was also an appropriate and needed warning. Though much is said about the perseverance and heroism of the early Christians, there is evidence that some fell away under the stress of persecution. Pliny, the governor of Bithynia, had been examining people to determine whether or not they were Christians. He wrote to Trajan saying some admitted "that they had been Christians, but they had ceased to be so many years ago, some as much as twenty years ago."[119]

Jesus was specific and prophetic in His statement about what would happen. **They shall put you out of the synagogues: yea (indeed), the time cometh, that whosoever killeth you will think that he doeth God service** (2). **They** no doubt refers to the Jews, and the whole statement alludes "to the murderous hatred of the Jews."[120] Expulsion from the synagogue was feared by every devout Jew (9:22), and those who confessed Christ were **put . . . out** (9:34). There is a Midrash on Num. 25:13 which states, "Every man who pours out the blood of the godless is as one who offers sacrifice."[121] Persecution of the Christians even unto death was thought to be a service, the offering of a sacrifice unto God (cf. Acts 26:9-11). The reason for such rationalized and immoral action on the part of the Jews is, as Jesus said, **they have not known the Father, nor me** (3; 15:21; cf. Luke 19:44). There is hardly an excuse for their not knowing, for the Jews, of all people, "*ought* to have known"[122] (cf. Rom. 9:4-5).

Jesus had a special purpose in telling His disciples about the coming persecution. To be forewarned is to be forearmed. **These**

[117]Arndt and Gingrich, *op. cit.*, p. 760.
[118]*Op. cit.*, p. 225.
[119]Barclay, *op. cit.*, p. 221.
[120]Hoskyns, *op. cit.*, p. 482.
[121]*Ibid.*
[122]Bernard, *op. cit.*, p. 501.

things have I told you, that when the time (lit., "their hour") shall come, ye may remember that I told you of them (4). "The phrase *the hour cometh,* which is used elsewhere of the hour of the crucifixion (12:23; 13:1; 16:32), is here extended to include the hour of the corresponding humiliation of the disciples . . . He foretells their persecution, in order that the memory of His words may provide an additional protection."[123]

d. *The Paraclete Promised* (16:4b-11). The warnings about coming persecutions and the promise of the Holy Spirit were not given to the disciples **at the beginning** for the reason that Jesus was with them (4). **But now** there is sufficient reason. **I go . . . to him that sent me** (5). Jesus' going to the Father is a frequently recurring idea in the last discourses (14:12; 16:10, 17, 28). Earlier the disciples had asked, "Whither goest thou?" (13:36; 14:5), but now, Jesus said, **None of you asketh me, Whither goest thou?** About this lack of spiritual understanding or even wholesome curiosity, Strachan says: "The spiritual world into which Jesus was about to enter was as yet unreal and uncertain to the disciples." Then applying it to the contemporary scene he continues: "Exclusive interest today in the historic Jesus, as distinct from the risen and ascended Lord, still exemplifies this refusal to ask the question He desired His disciples to ask, *Whither goest thou?*"[124]

It was inevitable that, at Jesus' reiteration of His early departure, **sorrow**[125] would fill the hearts of the disciples (6). **Nevertheless,** in spite of the sorrow, **I tell you the truth** (7; cf. Rom. 9:1; I Tim. 2:7). He is the Truth (14:6) and what He speaks is truth (1:17; 8:40, 45-46). The truth is, **It is expedient for you** ("it is to your advantage," Weymouth) **that I go away** (7). Just what are the advantages? There are at least four.

Here we see "The Wonder of the Indwelling Spirit." (1) In the person of Jesus the Spirit has been *with* the disciples. Now the Spirit will be *in* them (14:17), intimate, precious, personal, the very breath of spiritual life. (2) The Incarnation by its very nature was subjected to the limits of space, time, and death (Phil. 2:6-8). But the coming of the Spirit would leap the boundaries of Palestine and the limits of thirty-three and a half years of

---

[123]Hoskyns, *op. cit.,* p. 483.
[124]*Op. cit.,* p. 293.
[125]The word **sorrow** (*lupe*) appears only in this chapter (20-22).

calendar. Through Christ's victory (16:33; I Cor. 15:57) death would have no hold on the universal and eternally present Spirit. Westcott comments: "The withdrawal of His limited bodily Presence necessarily prepared the way for the recognition of a universal Presence."[126] (3) There have been those who have said, "It would have been wonderful to be with Jesus then, i.e., when He was on earth." Bernard says: "There is a better education in discipleship than that which can be supplied by a visible master . . . The braver and more perfect disciple is he who can walk by faith, and not by sight only"[127] (cf. 20:29). (4) Even better acquaintance with and knowledge of Jesus and His words are guaranteed through the coming of the Spirit. The absence of the Son would be filled, but more importantly, His presence would be made complete and meaningful.

The coming of the Paraclete[128] is contingent on Jesus' going away. With this there is the promise, **But if I depart, I will send him unto you** (7). "Jesus will be able to do so, for he himself will now be living in the Spirit in the presence of that Father who is the source of the Spirit's mission" (15:26).[129]

The work of the Holy Spirit, **when he is come** (lit., "that One, having come," 8), is carefully laid out for the disciples to understand. **He will reprove** ("convict," ASV; "bring conviction," Weymouth; "convince," Phillips; "rebuke," Tyndale). In this variety of translations it is evident that the Greek word *elegxei* has two basic meanings: "convince" in the sense of *prove* or *demonstrate,* and "convict" in the sense of *reprove, correct,* or *punish.*[130] "The word is almost exactly equivalent to the English *expose,* which has precisely the same double meaning, *display to the public gaze, expound, explain, unmask, show up, hold up to reprobation.*"[131]

Already seen as the work of the Spirit is His witness to the Son (15:26), His function as Teacher and Reminder of Jesus' words and teachings (14:26), and His constant, abiding inner strength to the believer (14:16-17).[132] But in this role He reaches

---

[126]*Op. cit.,* p. 227.
[127]*Op. cit.,* p. 504.
[128]See comment on 14:16.
[129]Bernard, *op. cit.,* p. 296.
[130]Arndt and Gingrich, *op. cit.,* pp. 248-49.
[131]Hoskyns, *op. cit.,* p. 484.
[132]Cf. Matt. 10:19; Mark 13:11; Luke 12:11-12; 21:15.

outside the circle of believers to **the world** (8). However, note
that He reaches out to the world *only when He has come to believers*. It is by working through believers that the Spirit is convincing and convicting those who do not believe, those who are
in rebellion against God. He convicts them **of sin, and of righteousness, and of judgment.**

He convicts **of sin, because they believe not on** Jesus (9).
In His teachings Jesus had made it clear that to refuse to believe
in Him was tantamount to dying in sins (8:24). Thus the Spirit
shows what sin is in its essence. It is "the selfishness which sets
itself up apart from and so against God. It is not defined by any
limited rule, but expresses a general spirit. To believe in Him, is
to adopt the principle of self-surrender to God. Not to believe
in Him, is to cleave to the legal view of duty and service which
involves a complete misunderstanding of the essence of sin."[133]
Bernard comments: "It is the touchstone of moral character to
discern God in Christ"[134] (cf. 3:18, 36; 20:30-31; Acts 2:36-37;
I John 5:10).

He convinces **of righteousness, because I go to my Father,
and ye see me no more** (10). The Greek word for **righteousness,**
dikaiosune, appears only here in John. It is that quality of moral
character which was perfectly exhibited in every motive and
act of Jesus, which was always in accord with the Father's will.
"Jesus is the *Righteous One* (I John 2:1), no sin can be discovered in Him (8:46; 14:30)."[135] Further, because of Jesus' sinless nature and life among men, it only remains for the Spirit
to demonstrate to men, to convince them, that the righteous life
can be lived in this world. "This revelation once given was finished . . . There was fixed for all time that by which men's estimate of righteousness might be tried."[136]

He convinces **of judgment, because the prince of this world
is judged** (11).[137] These words succinctly describe the cosmic
struggle between good and evil, God and Satan, and at the same

---

[133]Westcott, *op. cit.,* p. 229.

[134]*Op. cit.,* p. 506.

[135]Hoskyns, *op. cit.,* p. 485.

[136]Westcott, *op. cit.,* p. 229.

[137]The verb **is judged** is in the Greek perfect tense, depicting a state
that now exists as a result of past action. Satan is already under the
judgment of God.

time give assurance of the ultimate triumph of God and good. **The prince of this world** is the embodiment of evil (8:44; 13:27; I Cor. 2:8; I John 3:12). His doom is sealed, for judgment has been given (cf. 3:18; 12:31; 16:33; Eph. 2:2-10; I John 2:13-14). "The Devil is fighting a losing battle."[138]

In this section we see "The Gift of the Holy Spirit." (1) He is given especially to Christians who cannot have the physical presence of Jesus, 4; (2) His coming means even more to the Christian than to have known Jesus in the flesh, 5-7; (3) **When he is come** to Christians, God is able to get His work done in the world, 8-11.

e. *"The Spirit of Truth"* (16:12-15). Actually Jesus was nearing the end of His conversations with the disciples. Still He said, **I have yet many things to say unto you** (12), thus indicating the inexhaustible riches of His wisdom and truth for men. At the same time He was laying a foundation for the work of the coming **Spirit of truth** (13). Then too, there was the fact of the inability of the disciples either to comprehend spiritual truth or to "live it out" even if they did understand (13:33, 36-37; 14:17; 15:4-5). But there is One to come who will lead the disciples. **Howbeit**[139] **when he, the Spirit of truth, is come, he will guide you into all truth.** The Greek word for **guide** is *hodegesei* and means literally "to lead or guide along a way or path." So, "Jesus is the Way in which the disciples must be led by the Spirit, and He is also the Truth to which they must be guided"[140] (cf. Num. 24:8; Deut. 1:33; Ps. 25:5, 9; 143:10; Isa. 63:14). The expression **all truth** does not allude to "further new truth, but . . . the whole truth concerning that which was concretely and concisely set forth by the Son of God."[141] It is also quite clear from the context that the phrase **all truth** is not to be construed to mean primarily the discoveries of scientific fact, or even the rapidly expanding knowledge of the works of God in nature, though these should not be excluded. (Consider the testimony of the Negro scientist Dr. George Washington Carver, who simply invited God to go with him to his research laboratory each morning.) The leading of the Spirit is, however, primarily related to the work, teaching, death, and resurrection of Jesus.

---

[138]Strachan, *op. cit.*, p. 298.

[139]This word does not appear in the original.

[140]Hoskyns, *op. cit.*, p. 486.

[141]*Ibid.*, p. 485.

He shall not speak of himself; but whatsoever he shall hear,
that shall he speak . . . He shall glorify me: for he shall receive
of mine, and . . . shew it unto you (13-15). Hoskyns comments:
"The power of the Spirit does not consist in secret and mystical
revelations but in the external preaching of the Gospel, which
makes men revolt from the World and attaches them to the
Church."[142]

In verses 12-15 we see "The Guidance of the Spirit." (1) The
Holy Spirit is given to Christ's followers to be a spiritual Guide,
13; (2) His revelations come as we are ready for them day by
day rather than all at once, 12; (3) There is no realm of truth
closed to the possibility of the Spirit's guidance, 13; (4) His
guidance is always in harmony with the teachings of Jesus, 14-15;
(5) Following the leadership of the Holy Spirit always results in
reflecting honor and glory on our Lord and Saviour, 14.

f. Sorrow Turned to Joy (16:16-24). In repetitive and somewhat veiled language, Jesus spoke to the disciples about His
death and resurrection. A little while, and ye shall not see me:
and again, a little while, and ye shall see me, because I go to
the Father (16). The clause ye shall see me must refer to Jesus'
post-Resurrection appearances to the disciples, but it was probably applicable to Pentecost and the Parousia as well.[143] The
little while no doubt expresses the proximity of the Passion and
the Resurrection (cf. 7:33; 13:33; 14:19). For the first time since
Philip's query in 14:8, there is a question among the disciples
concerning the meaning of Jesus' statement (17). Still not speaking in the open, they said, What is this that he saith, A little
while? we cannot tell what he saith (18). But Jesus knew His
men (2:25) and their desire to ask him (19). For the fourth time
in 16-19 the initial statement of Jesus is given—A little while,
and ye shall not see me: and again, a little while, and ye shall
see me (19). In three of these the verbs see appear twice each.
In each the first see in the Greek is *theoreite* and the second
opsesthe. The first has a wide range of meanings, but is used
primarily in the sense of *observe, perceive, look at* with physical
eyes,[144] while the latter is used by John as "the vision of spiritual
realities."[145] Thus very deftly, by the use of similar yet different

[142]*Ibid.*, p. 486.
[143]Westcott, *op. cit.*, p. 232.
[144]Arndt and Gingrich, *op. cit.*, p. 360.
[145]Bernard, *op. cit.*, p. 513.

words, there is shown the movement of the Lord from incarnation to resurrection and glorification. This provides the basis also for the turning of sorrow into joy.

Knowing fully what would happen in the next few hours, Jesus said to the disciples, **Verily, verily, I say unto you, that ye shall weep and lament, but the world shall rejoice** (20). The enemies of Christ would feel certain that they had won the battle and would engage in their short-lived celebration, while the disciples, certain that all was lost, would engage in the "loud wailings and lamentations customary in the East after a death."[146]

To illustrate the point that there is "beauty for ashes," joy for sorrow for the true disciple, Jesus used the illustration of a woman giving birth to a child. **A woman when she is in travail hath sorrow, because her hour is come: but as soon as she is delivered of the child, she remembereth no more the anguish, for joy that a man** (*anthropos,* "human being") **is born into the world** (21).[147] Just as the woman's **hour is come,** so this is Jesus' hour (12:23; 13:1). The issue of both is new life. His is resurrection life, and it will bring joy to the disciples. **I will see you again, and your heart shall rejoice, and your joy no man taketh from you** (23). "Their joy was stable . . . They would have enemies, but . . . their enemies will not prevail."[148]

In that day when full and abiding joy has come to the disciples, displacing their sorrow, they will be asking Jesus **nothing** ("will ask Me no questions," NASB, 23; cf. vv. 17-19). Their asking will take another form. **Whatsoever ye shall ask the Father in my name, he will give it you.** Many translators and some commentators (Westcott, Macgregor) place the phrase **in my name** at the end of the sentence, where the Greek has it; so "not only is the prayer offered in Christ's name (24; 15:16), but the answer is given in his name."[149]

In a unique way the new economy of prayer which belongs to the Spirit-filled life (23-24; 14:13-14; 15:7) is the basis for a **joy** that is **full** (24). This is prayer that is to be made to the

---

[146]*Ibid.,* p. 514.

[147]Joy in sorrow illustrated by childbirth is an OT figure. See Isa. 26:17-20; 66:7-14; Hos. 13:13-15. "It is O.T. Messianic resurrection imagery" (Hoskyns, *op. cit.,* p. 488).

[148]Westcott, *op. cit.,* p. 233.

[149]*Ibid.,* p. 234.

Father (23) and asked in Jesus' **name** (24; cf. 14:13-14, 26; 15: 16; 16:26).[150]

g. *Victory Assured* (16:25-33). For the sixth time in the Last Discourses the clause **These things have I spoken unto you** (25) is used. Certainly some of Jesus' words have been **in proverbs** (figures)—e.g., the vine (15:1-17) and the sorrow of travail turned to joy (16:16-24).[151] But the time cometh (cf. v. 23, **in that day**) when, in place of **proverbs . . . I shall shew** (tell) **you plainly of the Father** (25). The word **shew** is *apanggelo* in the Greek and "marks the origin rather than the destination of the message."[152] The word **plainly** is *parresia*, which means *"outspokenness, frankness, plainness* of speech, that conceals nothing and passes over nothing."[153]

When the believer prays in Jesus' name, it is not to be with the idea that the Son is the Intercessor who has to plead in behalf of man and to appease the wrath of the Father: **I say not . . . that I will pray the Father for you** (26). The Greek word for **pray** is *erotao;* "it expresses a request made on the basis of fellowship and is used in the Gospel only of the petitions of the Lord."[154] There is a sufficient reason for Jesus' statement: **For the Father himself loveth you** (27). Note the emphatic pronoun **himself.** There is to be no mistake about the Father's love for His children. The reason for the assurance of this love is: **ye have loved me, and have believed that I came out from God.** "To have believed this is to have accepted the central message of the Gospel."[155]

In four compact clauses Jesus gave to the disciples His total "biography." **I came forth from the Father**—His preexistence; **I am come into the world**—His incarnation; **I leave the world** (lit., "I am leaving")—His death; **I go to the Father** (lit., "I am going")—His ascension (28). At this the disciples were persuaded that plain speech had taken the place of **proverb** (29) and affirmed their certainty that Jesus knew **all things** (30; cf. 2:25), even to the extent that "no more questions are needed" (30,

[150]See comment on 14:14.
[151]For comment on the word *proverb* (*paroimia*) see 10:6.
[152]Westcott, *op. cit.,* p. 234.
[153]Arndt and Gingrich, *op. cit.,* p. 635.
[154]Westcott, *op. cit.,* p. 234.
[155]Bernard, *op. cit.,* p. 520.

Phillips).[156] **By this** (cf. I John 2:3, 5; 3:16, 19, 24; 4:9-10, 13, 17; 5:2) **we believe that thou camest forth from God** (30).

The concluding remarks in the discourses are at once an examination of the faith of the disciples and an assuring prediction of certain victory over the forces of evil. Jesus himself answered His question to the disciples, **Do ye now believe?** (31) They had asserted their belief but there were still testing times ahead. At best their faith was unstable. Jesus told them that **the hour** had come (32; cf. 12:23; 13:1) when **ye shall be scattered, every man to his own, and shall leave me alone.** Yet, in spite of their wavering faith and His own sense of being left alone, our Lord assured the disciples of the steadfastness of the **Father—He is with me** (32)—and also promised to give them **peace** (33).[157] To these insecure and unstable disciples there would come a new peace which would be in great contrast to the **tribulation . . . in the world** (33). This peace would come from a clear knowledge of the facts made known to them by Jesus and from a firm faith in their Lord. So He could say to them, just when His public ministry had, "to all seeming, ended in failure,"[158] **I have overcome the world** (33). The Greek verb for **overcome** is *nenikeka*, perfect tense, and indicates a present state which is the result of a past action. Ultimate victory is guaranteed! The pronoun **I** is an emphatic *ego*, and here shows that it is Jesus' own personal victory over the world—unbelief, rebellion, sin, death—that is the basis for the guarantee of ultimate victory. So, **be of good cheer.**

---

[156]Hoskyns cites a reading based on the Sinaitic Syriac—"that thou shouldest ask any man" (*op. cit.*, p. 491).

[157]See comment on 14:27.

[158]Bernard, *op. cit.*, p. 524.

Section V The Lord's Prayer

John 17:1-26

This is the longest of Jesus' recorded prayers, and perhaps it is the most important. Facing **the hour** (1; cf. 12:23; 13:1), it was natural, the habit of His life, to pray as He always had when confronted with a great test or crisis (Mark 1:35; 6:46; Luke 3:21; 5:16; 6:12; 9:18, 28; 11:1; John 11:41; cf. Matt. 11:25-27). The exact place where the prayer was made is not certain, but it was perhaps somewhere between the Upper Room (14:31) and the brook Cedron (18:1; see map 2).

The prayer reflects the victory He has already claimed (16:33), "a victory still to be won on the field of history in the events of chs. 18 to 20, but already achieved in the sphere of the will and spirit."[1] The whole prayer is filled with ideas that have appeared in 13:31—16:33. "Teaching is crowned by prayer."[2]

The different titles given to the prayer are of interest. Most entitle it the High Priestly Prayer. Westcott calls it "The Consecration Prayer."[3]

The prayer has three major themes: (1) Jesus prays for himself, 1-8; (2) Jesus prays for His disciples, 9-19; (3) Jesus prays for the future disciples, 20-26.[4]

A. JESUS PRAYS FOR HIMSELF, 17:1-8

These words (1) would be the words of c. 16. The expression is a brief transition from what immediately precedes. **Jesus lifted up his eyes to heaven, and said, Father.** Here are ease of access, confident approach, and a habit of life (11:41; cf. Mark 6:41; 7:34; Acts 7:55; contrast Luke 18:13). Throughout the prayer the address is repeated (5, 11, 21, 24-25). The additional titles "Holy Father" (11) and "righteous Father" (25) mark "the movement of prayer from the death of Christ to the glorification

---

[1]Lightfoot, op. cit., pp. 295-96.

[2]Westcott, op. cit., p. 237.

[3]Ibid., p. 236.

[4]Though almost all commentators divide the prayer into three parts, Clarke and Westcott, differing from the others at the point of division, conclude part one with v. 5, and begin part two with v. 6.

189

of the Church."⁵ **The hour is** (has) **come** for this work to be
accomplished (cf. 12:23, 27; 13:1; 16:32; Mark 14:41; also cf.
"not yet," 2:4; 7:6, 8, 30; 8:20).

From the point of view of Divinity the whole purpose of **the
hour** is summed up in Jesus' words, **glorify thy Son, that thy Son
also may glorify thee.** Hoskyns comments: "The glorification of
the Son is not to be understood as the reward of virtue. The
glorification of the Son is for the glorification of the Father, and
the glorification of the Father is the salvation of men" (7:39;
8:54; 9:3; 11:4; 12:16, 23, 28; 13:31-32; 14:13; 15:8; 16:14; Phil.
2:11).⁶ Bernard remarks that this prayer, **Glorify thy Son,** is
more than supplication for support or succor in the ordeal of
death. It is more as "a martyr might pray for such signal meas-
ures of grace to be bestowed in the day of trial, that all who
perceive his courage and faith might recognize that he was
honoured of God."⁷

The glorification of Father and Son is possible because the
Father has **given him power** (*exousia*, lit., "authority") **over
all flesh.**⁸ "The *authority* is given in order that Christ may free
men from sin,"⁹ and give them **eternal life.** The clause **to as many
as thou hast given him** is introduced by a neuter pronoun in the
original and is literally "whatsoever thou hast given." "In the
contrast between *all flesh* and *whatsoever thou hast given* is expressed the inevitable tragedy of the mercy of God; it is offered to
all, but received by the few."¹⁰

What is this *eternal life* (2-3) that He gives? It is to **know
thee the only true God,** and **Jesus Christ whom thou hast sent**
(3). The verb **know** (*ginosko*) means to be acquainted with by
experience. It is a present-tense verb and so reflects continued,
growing knowledge. It is knowledge of **the only true God** "in
contrast with the unreal gods of the pagan world."¹¹ The title
Jesus Christ, with both the human and the divine name, appears

⁵Hoskyns, *op. cit.*, p. 495.

⁶*Ibid.*, p. 497.

⁷*Op. cit.*, p. 560.

⁸A Hebrew expression meaning "mankind in its weakness and transi-
toriness, as contrasted with the majesty of God" (Lightfoot, *op. cit.*, p. 300).

⁹Strachan, *op. cit.*, p. 301.

¹⁰Hoskyns, *op. cit.*, p. 498.

¹¹IB, VIII, 744.

in this Gospel only here and in 1:17. That Jesus should thus designate himself in prayer to the Father has seemed awkward to some. However, the expression is appropriate to the One **sent** by **the only true God.**

From Jesus' point of view as He looked back over the years of His earthly sojourn (1:14), there were evident four specific things that He had accomplished which had brought Him to **the hour.** (1) **I have glorified thee on the earth,** 4. He had a **glory** with the Father **before the world was** and He anticipated this to be restored. **Glorify thou me with thine own self** (5; cf. 24). Put in modern speech, He was saying that from every divine perspective the Incarnation was a resounding success. (2) **I have finished the work which thou gavest me to do,** 4. The Greek verb for **finished** is *teleiosas,* meaning *"complete, bring to an end, finish, accomplish . . . bring to its goal or to accomplishment* in the sense of overcoming or supplanting of an imperfect state of things by one that is free from objection."[12] The **work** is man's redemption, and it is **finished** in the most perfect manner (cf. 19:30). Can one help but exclaim, "Hallelujah, 'tis done!" (3) **I have manifested thy name unto the men which** (whom) **thou gavest me out of the world,** 6. The Greek word for **manifested** is *ephanerosa,* which means "to make known by word of mouth . . . though here the teaching is accompanied by a revelation that comes through the deed."[13] In Jewish worship it was forbidden to pronounce the name Yahweh. But now the name **Father** has been made known, and men "no longer need fear to pronounce the sacred name."[14] (4) **I have given unto them the words which thou gavest me,** 8. He, the eternal Living Word, has given to men words which they have **received.** Out of this have come knowledge—they **have known** of Jesus' true nature, **I came out from thee**—and faith—**they have believed** in His mission, **thou didst send me** (8; cf. 18, 21, 23, 25). Strachan comments: "The disciples have been able through listening to the 'words' of Jesus, to keep God's Word (6). 'Keep' means more than obey. It means to guard and to communicate to the world the revelation which God has entrusted to his Church."[15]

[12]Arndt and Gingrich, *op. cit.,* p. 817.

[13]*Ibid.,* p. 860.

[14]Strachan, *op. cit.,* p. 301.

[15]*Ibid.,* p. 302.

B. Jesus Prays for His Disciples, 17:9-19

Though the disciples have been mentioned in the prayer (6-8), only now is the supplication *for them*. **I pray for them** (9). Jesus is himself in the role of Advocate (I John 2:1). Two great forces join on man's behalf, **I**, the Petitioner, and the **Father**, the Petitioned. With that kind of help a disciple need never fall (cf. 10:28; Jude 24).

Who are these disciples in behalf of whom such impassioned intercession is made? They are the eleven (cf. v. 20). They belong to the Father—**they are thine** (9)—and they have been given to the Son, so they belong to both in a mutual ownership: **All mine are thine, and thine are mine** (10). They are **in the world** (11) but **not of the world** (14). It is for these He prays.[16]

What is it that He asks for[17] in their behalf? Three requests are made. (1) Keep them. **Holy Father, keep through thine own name those whom thou hast given me** (11; "keep them in thy name which thou hast given me," RSV). The KJV translation here is based on a poorly attested text, and the RSV is to be preferred. Commenting on the meaning Bernard says: "In Christ God was revealed in His providential love and care, His 'Name,' that is, His essential nature as Father, being exhibited in the Incarnate Son. Thus that 'the Name' of the Father was 'given' to Christ is yet another way of expressing the essential unity of the Father and the Son."[18] The petition is made to our **Holy Father**, and it is through His **name** the disciples are to be kept. Hoskyns says with great clarity: "The holiness of God marks His separation from the unbelief and wickedness of the world, which lies in the power of the Devil (I John 5:19). It is precisely this holiness that marks the true disciples of Jesus, who are in the world but not of it, and which provides the ground of their unity."[19]

There is a moment of tragic reminiscence in the prayer. It is about Judas. All of the disciples have been **kept, and none of them is lost, but the son of perdition** (12). The Greek words for

---

[16]This is not to be interpreted that Jesus never prayed for His enemies but only that on this occasion He prayed especially for His disciples (cf. Luke 13:34; 23:34).

[17]The Greek verb transplated *pray* is *erotao* and means basically to ask for or request.

[18]*Op. cit.*, p. 569.

[19]*Op. cit.*, p. 500.

lost and **perdition** are cognates and refer to "final perishing."
In Mark 14:4 the same noun is used for "waste." "Possibly this
incident was in mind when Judas was called 'the son of loss,'
the man who really wasted what was precious."[20] So it is no
wonder that Jesus prayed, **Keep them from the evil** ("the evil
one," NASB, 15; cf. Matt. 6:13). To be protected from "the evil
one" they are not to be taken **out of the world,** even though **the
world hath hated them** (14). **That the scripture might be fulfilled** probably refers to Ps. 41:9-10.

(2) **That they might have my joy fulfilled in themselves**
(13; cf. 15:11; 16:20-22, 24). Jesus' work in behalf of man is
finished. This is His joy, and now it only remains for that work
to be effected in the disciples—i.e., that they be kept (11, 15),
sanctified (17-18), and united in bonds of love (22, 26).

(3) **Sanctify them through thy truth** (17). The Greek verb
hagiazo, here an aorist imperative, means "consecrate, dedicate,
sanctify, treat as holy, reverence, purify."[21] Its cognate adjective
is *hagios* and means "holy." The plural substantive form *hoi
hagioi* is "the saints." The fact that the verb is an aorist imperative clearly indicates that the sanctification of the disciples was
to be a crisis experience. It "cannot possibly mean an incomplete
process but a definite act of sanctification."[22]

What is the nature of the sanctification for which Jesus
asked the Father for the disciples? (a) It is clear that it could
be wrought only by the power of God. The very fact that the
request was made to the Father and was not a command to the
disciples shows this. Man cannot sanctify himself. He is neither
able nor adequate. (b) It is made effective **through the truth**
(17, 19). Thus one is "truly sanctified."[23] Westcott points out:
"The truth for which they are hated and by which they are
strong (v. 14) is the power by which they are transformed."[24]
Bernard says: "Truth would be the medium of their consecration
as . . . the 'Spirit of Truth' would be the Agent (cf. 16:13)."[25]

---

[20]Bernard, *op. cit.,* p. 571.

[21]Arndt and Gingrich, *op. cit.,* pp. 8-9.

[22]H. Orton Wiley, *The Epistle to the Hebrews* (Kansas City: Beacon
Hill Press, 1959), p. 326.

[23]*Ibid.,* p. 321.

[24]*Op. cit.,* p. 244.

[25]*Op. cit.,* p. 574.

It is also made effective through Jesus' self-consecration. **No one else could have said, For their sakes I sanctify myself (19).** He dedicated, consecrated himself to death, a voluntary Sacrifice (10:18), to make possible the purifying and consecration, the sanctification of believers (cf. Heb. 13:12). Strachan comments: "Jesus is both priest and victim. His is therefore a voluntary sacrifice. In thus 'sanctifying' Himself, Jesus consecrates Himself in death to God."[26] (c) It is preparation for the believers' going out into the world. **As thou hast sent me into the world, even so have I also sent them into the world (18).**

It was Jesus' command that they first tarry (Luke 24:49) and then go and witness (Acts 1:8). It is also a preparation for "living out" the ethical implications of Christian holiness. One must be clean to serve (13:14).[27] "Since Divine consecration must of necessity involve personal moral holiness, He prays that they may not be contaminated by the world, and that they may be preserved from the power of the Evil One."[28] There is sometimes a tendency to put emphasis on the internal experience of sanctification to the neglect or exclusion of its necessary moral implications. To do so is to be false to the teaching of Jesus' words **that they also might be sanctified (19).**[29] According to Bernard the verb "connotes not so much the selection of a man for important work as the equipping and fitting him for its due discharge."[30]

C. Jesus Prays for Future Believers, 17:20-26

When Jesus prayed **not for these alone, but for all them also which shall believe on me through their word,** He showed that "His work is fulfilled in ever-increasing circles of influence."[31] It is *from* the Father and the Son, *through* the Spirit *in* the disciples *into* the world that *His* work must be carried on. In this, there is to be a unity where **they all may be one**—the **Father,** the Son, and **they** (the disciples, 21). The disciples are brought into

---

[26]*Op. cit.,* p. 304.

[27]See comment on 13:4-17.

[28]Hoskyns, *op. cit.,* pp. 501-2.

[29]The Greek *hegiasmenoi* is perfect tense, portraying a present, continued state as the result of previous action (17).

[30]*Op. cit.,* p. 573.

[31]Westcott, *op. cit.,* p. 242.

the unity of the Father and the Son as a result of their sanctification, for which Jesus here prayed. The purpose of this unity is **that the world may believe that thou hast sent me (21).**

What are the characteristics of this unity for which Jesus prayed? (1) It is evident that it is grounded in the ultimate purpose for which Christ was sent into the world, and for which He gave His life—the redemption of man, which is the glorification of the Father and the Son. **And the glory which thou gavest me I have given them; that they may be one, even as we are one (22).**[32] In a very real sense those who are Blood-washed are one, made so by the one perfect Sacrifice (Heb. 10:12-14). (2) It is a unity that issues in perfection or completeness. **I in them, and thou in me, that they may be made perfect in one (23).** The Greek perfect passive participle *teteleiomenoi*, translated **perfect,** is a form of the same word translated "finished" in 4 (see comment, v. 4; cf. Phil. 3:12, 15; I John 2:5; 4:12, 17-18). The perfect participle here portrays a perfection realized in terms of a set goal or purpose. Strachan says that the value of this unity "is in proportion as the presence and influence of the one Spirit takes possession of men's hearts. *I in them and thou in me.* The basis of this unity is religious. Even what is called 'oecumenical' union, the world-wide church remains imperfect without a unity in our doctrine of God and of salvation, and a unity of purpose in our mission. The size and extent of the Church alone will not impress the world. This inward unity expressing itself in a common mission and message will alone impress the world."[33] (3) This unity is to be a demonstration of *agape* love, so **that the world may know that thou hast sent me, and hast loved them, as thou hast loved me (23).** (4) It is a unity pregnant with hope—hope for the future, hope for man, the promise that sometime, someway, somehow **they also, whom thou hast given me, (may) be with me where I am (24;** cf. 7:34; 13:33, 36; 14:3, 5). **Father, this I will,**[34] was Jesus' prayer (cf. Matt. 8:3; 23:37; 26:36-39; I Thess. 4:3). Bernard comments: "At this

---

[32]C. K. Barrett (*The Gospel According to St. John* [New York: Macmillan Co., 1955], p. 428) says: ". . . the glory of Christ is acquired through, and is most completely expressed in the crucifixion. The Church receives glory on precisely the same terms, by unity in faith with the death and resurrection of Jesus, and expresses it in obedience."

[33]*Op. cit.,* p. 304.

[34]Moffatt translates 24: "Father, It is my will that these, thy gift to me, may be beside me where I am."

195

moment of spiritual exaltation, the climax of His consecration of Himself to death, He realizes the perfect coincidence of His will with the Father's, and so can say *thelo* (I will)."[35]

The incomparable love of Jesus for His disciples has been repeatedly declared to them in word and deed. **I have declared unto them thy name** (26); only know it will be from a cross.

[35]*Op. cit.*, p. 579

Section **VI** *Arrest and Trial*

John 18:1—19:16

A. THE ARREST, 18:1-14

1. *In the Garden* (18:1-11)

The hour had come (13:1; 17:1)! The talks with the disciples (13:31—16:33) and the prayer of the Lord for himself, His disciples, and all who would someday believe (c. 17) were finished. **When Jesus had spoken these words, he went forth** (1). Those who reorder the text in cc. 14—16 (e.g., Moffatt, Bernard) say that He went from the Upper Room. However the text as it stands suggests that He had left the Upper Room earlier (14:31). So here He most likely **went forth** from the city of Jerusalem **over the brook Cedron** (Kidron).[1] This notation is peculiar to John. The Kidron gorge (modern name, Wady Sitti Maryam) is between Jerusalem and the Mount of Olives (see map 2).

Across the brook there **was a garden, into the which he entered, and his disciples** (1). The preposition **into** indicates that it was an enclosed area. The mention of the **garden** is important. It was a garden where He was arrested; it was also the place of His resurrection, and "in the place where he was crucified there was a garden" (19:41; cf. 20:15). "The Passion and Resurrection which effected the salvation of the world are contrasted with the Fall in the Garden of Eden."[2] There is no mention of the name Gethsemane in John's account. However, the language of 11, **The cup which my Father hath given me, shall I not drink it?** is similar to the prayer of agony in the garden (Matt. 26:38; Mark 14:36; Luke 22:42). Some have commented that John purposefully omitted the prayer of agony because of his inclusion of the spiritual exaltation in c. 17. Bernard points out: "The moments of greatest spiritual depression and trial often follow close on moods of the highest spiritual exaltation."[3]

An early enemy of the Christian faith, Celsus, said Jesus went to the garden to hide, and "was taken while trying to hide

---

[1]Kidron means literally "winter torrent," pointing out the fact that it is usually dry, carrying water only in the rainy season.

[2]Hoskyns, *op. cit.,* p. 509.

[3]*Op. cit.,* p. 583.

197

himself and to escape in the most disgraceful way."[4] But that is a prejudiced interpretation, for **Judas also, which betrayed him, knew the place** (2). The participle *paradidous,* translated **betrayed,** is in the present tense, indicating action going on. A literal translation would be, "Judas, who is in the act of betraying Him, knew the place." It appears that Jesus deliberately went to a place known to Judas. His giving of himself was altogether voluntary (10:18) and on no account is to be construed as the scheming of man.

The group that came to arrest Jesus was composed of **three** elements: **Judas,** the betrayer, who serves in a very passive role in John (cf. 5; Matt. 26:49; Mark 14:44-45; Luke 22:47-48); **officers from the chief priests and Pharisees** (the two main factions in the Sanhedrin); and **a band of men** (3; the RSV calls them soldiers and suggests that Judas had procured them). The word *speiran,* translated **band of men,** is equivalent to the Latin *cohors* (cf. NASB—"the Roman cohort"). This was comprised of either 600 or 1,000 men. If the latter, there were 240 horses and 760 foot soldiers (cf. Acts 21:31). The whole *speiran* was commanded by a *chiliarchos* **(captain, 12).** It is doubtful that the whole *speiran* came to the garden. In any case it was a detachment of that band. The **officers** were "members of the temple-police, who were under orders of the Sanhedrin."[5] All these came to take Jesus. Hoskyns says: "In the Johannine account the forces of darkness, the Roman and Jewish authorities, and the apostate disciple are arrayed against the Christ from the beginning."[6] In it all they were led by Judas, the embodiment of Satan.[7] Coming to take Him who is the Light of the World (1:9; 9:5), they carried **lanterns and torches** (3). The **torches** were *phanos* made of strips of wood fastened together, and the **lanterns** were *lampas,* ordinary torchlights. They also carried weapons (*hoplon*), which were "swords and staves" (Luke 22:52).

[4]Quoted by Macgregor, *op. cit.,* p. 324.

[5]Westcott, *op. cit.,* p. 252.

[6]*Op. cit.,* p. 509.

[7]A. Plummer (*The Gospel According to St. John* ["Cambridge Greek Testament"; Cambridge: University Press, 1882], p. 308) writes: "There is a suppressed irony in the details of this verse: 'All this force against one; against one who intended no resistance; against one who with one word (v. 6; Matt. xxvi. 53) could have swept them all away.'"

Jesus did not wait to be sought out by the band of men. Because He knew **all things that should come upon him** (cf. 13:1; 17:1), **He went forth** (came forward), **and said unto them, Whom seek ye?** (4) In response to the question they used the name by which He was best known—**Jesus of Nazareth** (7), literally, "Jesus, the Nazarene" (cf. Matt. 26:71; Mark 10:47; 14:67; 16:6; Luke 4:34; 18:37; 24:19; Acts 2:22). Our Lord immediately identified himself as the One they sought. **I am he** (6; cf. 8:24, 28; 13:19).[8] Westcott says that the **I am** (*ego eimi*) only reveals "the person sought, and not his nature."[9] However Macgregor says, "Jesus is pictured as in complete command of the situation, and now the powerlessness of the whole band of his assailants before his divine majesty is still further brought out."[10] This observation carries weight, for John notes that at Jesus' statement **they went backward, and fell to the ground** (6). About this Hoskyns says: "The instruments of evil fall prostrate before their true commander."[11] Westcott modifies his earlier statement somewhat when he explains the falling **to the ground** as "due to the effect which the presence of the Lord, in his serene majesty, had upon those who had come to take him."[12]

The same question as in v. 4 is put by Jesus to the band again in v. 7, and there was the same response. To this Jesus answered, **I have told you that I am he: if therefore ye seek me, let these go their way** (8). It is the hireling that flees when the wolf comes, but "the good shepherd giveth his life for the sheep" (10:12; cf. 15:13). Jesus, soon to be imprisoned and condemned as a common criminal, was directing the affairs that had to do with His own. His providential care for man is made possible through His eternal sacrifice. John saw in Jesus' plea for the safety of the disciples a fulfillment of the saying, **Of them which thou gavest me have I lost none** (9; cf. 6:39; 10:28; 17:12).

In 6-9, Alexander Maclaren speaks of "Christ and His Captors." (1) A remarkable momentary manifestation of our Lord's glory, 6; (2) The voluntariness of our Lord's suffering, 7-8; (3) Christ's self-sacrificing care for us, 8.

---

[8]See comment on 4:26.
[9]*Op. cit.,* p. 253.
[10]*Op. cit.,* p. 375.
[11]*Op. cit.,* p. 509.
[12]*Ibid.*

It must have been at Jesus' bidding that the assailants came to take Him. As the band approached, it was too much for Peter, who had vowed to defend and protect Jesus even at the cost of his own life (13:37). Peter had a sword (Luke 22:38). **He drew it, and smote the high priest's servant, and cut off his right ear** (10).[13] We may be sure that Peter had aimed for more than an ear! **The servant's** ("slave's," NASB) **name was Malchus.** These bits of detail, e.g., **right ear** and **Malchus**—very characteristic of John's account of the Arrest, Trial, Crucifixion, and Burial—add to the evidence that the writer of the fourth Gospel was an eyewitness to these events.[14]

The Master's word to Peter, **Put up thy sword into the sheath** (11), was a clear suggestion as to the nature of the struggle in which Jesus was engaged, and which He himself was to carry through to completion (19:30; cf. Matt. 26:52; Eph. 6:12). Man, it seems, is ever ready to take up some external means of settling deep differences, forgetting that the real struggle is within, and that a satisfactory solution can be found only in the work of the Spirit. Man, like Peter, cries, "Lord, why am I not able to follow Thee?" (13:37, lit. translation.) Jesus told Peter why the sword was not the answer; **The cup which my Father hath given me, shall I not drink it?**[15] Jesus' action was one of "confident acceptance."[16]

2. The High Priests (18:12-14)

When one reads John's account of the Arrest, he is made to feel that on every count Jesus is in full command even though the servants of evil are busily engaged in carrying out their work. So it was that **the band and the captain** (*chiliarchos*) **and the officers of the Jews took Jesus, and bound him** (12). They probably bound[17] His hands behind His back. Now He was at their mercy, or lack of it, but only because He willed it so.

[13]All the Synoptists record the incident (Matt. 26:51; Mark 14:47; Luke 22:50), but only John gives the names of Peter and Malchus. Luke alone mentions the healing of the servant.

[14]See Introduction, "Authorship."

[15]See comment on v. 1 above. Also cf. Matt. 20:22; Mark 14:36; Ps. 75:8; Isa. 51:17, 22; Ezek. 23:31-34.

[16]Strachan, *op. cit.,* p. 307.

[17]The verb is *deo,* meaning "to tie or bind." The noun cognate is *doulos,* meaning "slave," "bond (bound) servant" (cf. Isa. 53:11).

According to a prearranged plan they **led him away to Annas first** (13). John alone mentions the appearance before Annas (cf. Luke 3:2; Acts 4:6). Edersheim says of him: "No figure is better known in contemporary Jewish history than that of Annas; no person deemed more fortunate or successful, but none also more execrated than the late High-Priest."[18] He was fortunate in that, though he himself was high priest only from A.D. 6 to 15, having been deposed by Valerius Gratus, he was succeeded by his five sons, his son-in-law Caiaphas Joseph, and a grandson. Such a family monopoly was not easily sustained. There were bribes, graft, and corruption in the name of religion, and all of it directed toward accumulation of wealth and perpetuation in office. "By the exploitation of the worshippers, by trading on the sacred sacrifices . . . Annas had amassed a fortune."[19] Barclay quotes a passage from the Talmud which reflects the hatred which even the Jews must have had for Annas and his heirs: "Woe to the house of Annas! Woe to their serpent's hiss! They are High Priests; their sons are keepers of the treasury; their sons-in-law are guardians of the Temple; and their servants beat the people with staves."[20]

It is no wonder that Annas was "the real leader in the whole action."[21] His vested interests were seriously threatened by this Man who had driven out from the Temple Annas' merchants and money changers (Matt. 21:12-17; Mark 11:15-19; Luke 19:45-48; John 2:13-17).

Caiaphas Joseph, son-in-law of Annas, was the actual high priest at this time, appointed by the Roman procurator Valerius Gratus. He held office for eighteen years (A.D. 18-36) and was deposed by Vitellius.[22] When it is said that he **was the high priest that same year** (13), it does not refer to his tenure of office but to "that fateful year," the year Christ was crucified. This was evidently prominent in John's thinking as he wrote that **Caiaphas was he, which gave counsel to the Jews, that it was expedient that one man should die for the people** (14; see comment on 11:49-52).

[18]*Op. cit.,* II, 547.
[19]Barclay, *op. cit.,* II, 264-65.
[20]*Ibid.,* p. 265.
[21]Westcott, *op. cit.,* p. 256.
[22]Hoskyns, *op. cit.,* p. 411.

B. THE TRIAL, 18:15—19:16

1. *Peter's First Denial* (18:15-18)

Apparently all the disciples fled (were "scattered," 16:32) at Jesus' arrest except **Simon Peter** and **another disciple (15)** who **followed Jesus.** The unnamed **disciple** is described as being **known unto the high priest.** He was sufficiently well known to be able to go **in with Jesus into the palace of the high priest.** (See map 2.)

Who was this **other disciple?** There have been many conjectures: Nicodemus, Joseph of Arimathaea, or even Judas, on the ground that he had become acquainted there while helping lay the plans for Jesus' arrest. In the case of Judas, it is unimaginable either that Peter would have been conversing with him **(16)** in the light of what had just happened in the garden, or that John would have failed to mention him by name (cf. 6:70-71; 12:4; 14:22). Tradition, well supported, has it that the **other disciple** here was the beloved disciple, John the son of Zebedee.[23]

How did John, a Galilean fisherman, have such close acquaintance with the high priest? Two ideas have been suggested. One is based on a legendary tradition attributed to a statement of "Polycrates, a bishop of Ephesus late in the second century, that 'John who leaned on the Lord's breast was a priest wearing the petalon.' The Greek word *petalon* is used in the Septuagint of Exod. 28:36 for the gold plate fastened in front of the high priest's miter."[24] If the legend were true, it would explain John's easy access. The other idea is that John's father, Zebedee, was a wealthy fisherman with a flourishing business. This involved the merchandising of salt fish, which he sold to the household of the high priest. Barclay tells about an Arab coffeehouse in the back streets of Jerusalem which is purported by certain Franciscans to have been the location of the Jerusalem branch of Zebedee's salt-fish enterprise, "and that is the reason why John had the entry into the High Priest's house."[25]

In any case, John was inside while **Peter stood at the door without (16).** Just as in the early days of discipleship (1:41), John **went out . . . and brought in Peter.** There was a **damsel** (maid) **that kept the door.** Peter had to pass by her. As he did, she said: **Art not thou also one of this man's disciples?**

[23]See Introduction, "Authorship."
[24]Howard, IB, VIII, 440.
[25]*Op. cit.*, II, 268.

(17) These words must have struck an arrow at the heart of Peter. Up to now he had carried out his good and strong intentions (13:37). No other drew a sword, though another disciple had one (Luke 22:38). Others had fled but Peter **followed** (15). Let it be said to Peter's credit that, though he failed, he failed while trying with all his human strength. It is much better to have tried and failed than not to have tried at all.

Peter's answer to the maid, **I am not** (17), seemed to satisfy the maid, but it shook Peter. Uncertain of himself, not sure of his environment, not able to see his Lord, he moved in to lose his identity among the **servants and officers** who in the **cold night warmed themselves. Peter stood with them** (cf. 5), **and warmed himself** (18).

2. *Before Annas* (18:19-23)

These verses appear only in John. The Synoptics make no mention of a hearing before Annas. But it is not difficult to see that **the high priest** (19) Annas,[26] "so long as he lived, presumably held a patriarchal position."[27] It may have been that Caiaphas was present but not in charge. Further, because Jesus had seriously threatened his power, position, and prestige, "Annas wanted to be the first to gloat over the capture, the defeat, the discomfiture of this disturbing Galilaean."[28]

This meeting with Annas was not a formal gathering of the Sanhedrin. No witnesses were called. It appears to have been an attempt to get Jesus to incriminate himself. The questions put to Jesus were **of his disciples, and his doctrine** (19). Jesus' response indicated that His work and teaching had not been secretive or under cover. **I spake openly to the world; I ever taught in the synagogue, and in the temple, whither the Jews always resort; and in secret have I said nothing** (20; cf. 6:59; 7:4, 12, 14, 26; 10:23; 11:54; 12:19). The phrase **in the synagogue** (*en synagoge*) refers to occasions "when people were gathered in solemn assembly."[29] The word **openly** (*parresia*) carries the

---

[26]Some authorities, e.g., Macgregor and Westcott, hold that the high priest mentioned in 19 is Caiaphas. Macgregor transposes 24 to follow 13. However Bernard, following carefully the MS evidence, holds that the scene up to 24 is before Annas.

[27]Hoskyns, *op. cit.*, p. 513.

[28]Barclay, *op. cit.*, II, 265.

[29]Westcott, *op. cit.*, p. 256.

idea of *"frankness, plainness* of speech, that conceals nothing and passes over nothing."[30] Here one is reminded of the words of Socrates: "If any one says that he has ever learnt or heard anything from me in private, which all others could not have heard, know ye that he does not speak the truth."[31]

Since "it was a recognized principle of law that a man's evidence about himself is suspect,"[32] Jesus turned the question to Annas. **Why askest thou me? ask them which heard me, what I have said unto them: behold, they know what I said** (21). It was a fundamental principle in Jewish law that a prisoner should not be asked questions about himself which if answered would incriminate him. Barclay quotes Maimonides, Jewish medieval scholar: "Our true law does not inflict the penalty of death upon a sinner by his own confession."[33] Jesus' attempt to inject a semblance of justice into Annas' illegal procedures was met by immediate rebuff. **One of the officers** of the high priest **struck Jesus with the palm of his hand, saying, Answerest thou the high priest so?** (22) This "use of violence has only shown the officer's weakness."[34] The action of the officer is another indication that this was not a formal meeting of the Sanhedrin. Such action would not have been tolerated there.

The response of Jesus to the blow was a dignified reminder that justice is always in order. **If I have spoken evil, bear witness of the evil: but if well, why smitest thou me?** (23) The word **smitest** (*dero*) literally means "beat." Westcott observes: "The old commentators saw in the calm rebuke a true interpretation of the precept, Matt. v. 39."[35]

3. Jesus Is Sent to Caiaphas (18:24)

The only mention of Caiaphas in connection with the trial of Jesus is that **Annas had sent him bound unto Caiaphas the high priest** (24). The Greek verb for **had sent** is *apesteilen,* an aorist tense, not pluperfect, thus better translated "then sent," as in the RSV. Even if Caiaphas were present during the informal

---

[30]Arndt and Gingrich, *op. cit.,* p. 635.
[31]Plato *Dialogues.* "Apology." 33B.
[32]Bernard, *op. cit.,* p. 601.
[33]*Op. cit.,* p. 265.
[34]Lightfoot, *op. cit.,* p. 307.
[35]*Op. cit.,* p. 257.

proceedings before Annas, there was need for the official action of the Sanhedrin before the case could be submitted to the Roman procurator for final disposition. Caiaphas, being the official high priest, would preside at that hearing (Matt. 26:57; 27:2; Mark 14:53-65; 15:1; Luke 22:54, 63-71). "Nothing is told here of the proceedings . . . which were only formal, as the decision had been already reached at the irregular meeting in the house of Annas."[36] Westcott points out that the meeting was "held to confirm the decision already made, and so to satisfy the form of the law, which however was broken by the infliction and execution of the sentence on the day of trial."[37]

4. *Peter's Second and Third Denials* (18:25-27)

John's account of Peter's denials is interrupted by the record of the episode before Annas. Some have suggested that both Caiaphas and Annas lived in the same court; that is, occupied different apartments surrounding a common court, all of which was the residence of the high priest (see map 2). In any event, the scene of Peter by the fire is continued in 25: **Simon Peter stood and warmed himself.** Even while Peter had hoped to lose his identity by identifying himself with the "servants and officers" (18), **they** (evidently more than one) **said . . . unto him, Art not thou also one of his disciples?** (25) The wording in the original indicates that they expected a negative answer. It was beyond their comprehension that any man would be so foolish as to identify himself with a Man who was already condemned to death. But they had underestimated the drawing power of the love of Christ. It compels men to perform in a manner that is quite incomprehensible to the world. Peter was not in rebellion against his Lord—rather he was incapable (powerless, 13:36) before accusing men. So, **he denied it, and said, I am not** (25).

What had begun as an impersonal and general accusation by the servants and officer ssuddenly became very personal and specific. This time the questioner and accuser was **one of the servants** (lit., "slaves") **of the high priest** and a kinsman ("relative," Weymouth) **of the man whose ear Peter cut off** (26). There was nothing indirect about his question. From the way it is worded in the Greek it is evident that the answer expected was

---

[36]Bernard, *op. cit.,* p. 605.
[37]*Op. cit.,* p. 258.

an affirmative one, **Did not I see thee** (i.e., I, with my own eyes) **in the garden with him?** (26) John, true to fact, but still not elaborating on the weakness of his fellow disciple, wrote simply: **Peter then denied again** (cf. Matt. 26: 74; Mark 15: 71). No sooner had Peter made his third denial than **the cock crew** (27; cf. 13: 38).[38]

5. *Before Pilate* (18: 28—19: 16)

a. The Accusation (18: 28-32). The scene shifts from the formal hearing before Caiaphas and the Sanhedrin to **the hall of judgment** (28). This was the *praitorion,* transliterated as "Praetorium" (NASB). Originally the word designated a general's quarters in camp, later the governor's official residence. The location of the Praetorium in Jerusalem is not certain. Some say that it was the palace built by Herod which was on the hill of Zion in the western part of the city. Others think it to have been the Castle of Antonia, which was located north of the Temple area (see map 2). "The weight of scholarly opinion seems to favor the latter location."[39]

When **they led Jesus** to the Praetorium **it was early.** The word for **early** (*proi*) refers to the fourth watch, 3: 00-6: 00 a.m. Since "a Roman court could be held at any time after sunrise," this move to the governor's quarters must have been as early as possible.[40] But **they** (priests, officers, slaves of the high priest) **themselves went not into the judgment hall, lest they should be defiled; but that they might eat the passover** (28). Since this was Friday, and the Passover began officially at sundown, a Jew, in order to be ceremonially clean, dare not enter a Gentile court or house from which leavened bread had not been removed (Exod. 12: 15). Bernard observes: "These men were about to pollute their souls by unscrupulous testimony which was to bring Jesus to a horrible death, yet were unwilling to incur technical or ceremonial uncleanness while giving that testimony.

---

[38]"An interesting suggestion has been made that this refers to the *gallicinium,* the signal given on the bugle when the change of guard took place in the Roman garrison at the end of the third watch of the night called the 'cock crow,' *alektorophonia*" (Howard, IB, VIII, 766).

[39]George A. Turner and Julius R. Mantey, *The Gospel According to John* ("The Evangelical Commentary"; Grand Rapids: William B. Eerdmans Publishing Co., 1964), p. 360.

[40]Westcott, *op. cit.,* p. 258.

There is no perversion so sinister as that of the human conscience."[41] They were the perfect example of straining out a gnat while gulping down a camel. Hoskyns says of them: "They who pretend to so great devotion are in fact guilty of gross superstition, for the execution of the Messiah becomes the preparation of their solemn festival."[42]

Pilate, to whom Jesus was brought, was well aware of the religious customs and practices of the Jews. He had learned the hard way that failure to recognize and cooperate with these customs brought only trouble—and he did not need any more of that. So he **went out unto them** (29)—he met with them outside of the Praetorium.

Who is this man Pilate and what were his relationships to the Jews? Emperor Tiberius had appointed him Roman procurator in A.D. 26. His province was part of Syria which included Judea, Samaria, and Idumea. His duties were both military and administrative. Although technically under the jurisdiction of the governor of the province of Syria, he had practically absolute jurisdiction in his own province except when a Roman citizen was involved. The policy of Rome was to grant a high degree of self-government to the provinces, and because of the Jews' religious customs and practices this conciliatory policy "was carried to unusual lengths, so that the government of Judaea was exceptionally difficult."[43] Pilate held his position for ten years in spite of periods of severe turbulence. He is depicted as a man who was "obstinate, tactless, and headstrong."[44]

It would appear that Pilate had been apprised of the arrest, probably at the time that the "band" of soldiers was procured. So when they brought Jesus early **he went out**, ready to hear their complaint. He asked, **What accusation** (charge) **bring ye against this man?** (29) In a mood both hostile and insolent they answered, **If he were not a malefactor** (lit., "one who makes a practice of doing evil"), **we would not have delivered him up unto thee** (30). Their reply was designed to indicate to Pilate

[41]*Op. cit.*, p. 606. For a discussion of the problem of harmonizing this with the Synoptic accounts see the comments on Matt. 26:17 (BBC, VI, 233-35).
[42]*Op. cit.*, p. 42.
[43]Lightfoot, *op. cit.*, p. 324.
[44]*Ibid.*

that their judgment had already been passed. All they sought was the necessary ratification for its execution. But Pilate was not easily worked into a corner. Since they had already passed judgment, as their answer implied, the governor challenged them, **Take ye him, and judge him according to your law (31).** If the Jews could have achieved their evil purpose "on their own," they would have done it. No doubt in their clever planning they had given consideration to every possible angle. Their answer reflected their dilemma. **It is not lawful for us to put any man to death (31).**[45]

John, in his characteristic fashion, interprets this as a part of the divine plan previously stated by **Jesus** himself, **signifying what death he should die (32;** cf. 12:32). In considering this, Hoskyns takes the view that, since there must be shedding of blood for the salvation of the world, "the Jews, in insisting upon the crucifixion, are moved by a divine necessity of which they are totally unconscious. The whole narrative leads up to the pregnant conclusion of the trial before Pilate: *then therefore he delivered him unto them—to be crucified* (19:16)."[46]

b. *Where Is Jesus King?* (18:33-38a). Luke records the fact that Jesus had been accused to Pilate of claiming to be a King (Luke 23:2). Though John does not record it, there is evidence that such an accusation had been made. Pilate went **into the judgment hall again, and called Jesus (33).**[47] Immediately he

[45]This verse has been interpreted "to mean that the Jews could not inflict a capital sentence at this particular time (the Passover), or in the particular manner which they desired (crucifixion). But there is nothing in the context to justify such a limitation of the sense . . . The words must be taken as a simple and direct statement that the Jews could not put to death without the governor's authority" (Westcott, *op. cit.,* p. 266). However, Strachan and Hoskyns contend that the extent of the legal competence of the Jews is exceedingly obscure before A.D. 70. Bernard says that crucifixion is "a form of execution never employed by the Jews even when they had the power" (*op. cit.,* p. 334). If the Jews had put Jesus to death, it would have been by stoning (cf. Acts 7:58). But Christ had predicted that He would die by crucifixion (12:32-33), the Roman method. So Jesus had to be turned over to the governor. That is the point of vv. 31-32.

[46]*Op. cit.,* p. 519.

[47]In the context of this Gospel, Jesus' entrance into the pagan court on the eve of the Passover has tremendous significance. The Paschal Lamb was not defiled. There is no boundary of race or time that stops the crimson flow of His blood. He is a universal Sacrifice *once for all.*

asked Him, **Art thou the King of the Jews?** (33)[48] The very fact
that Pilate had raised the question about Jesus' kingship provided
Jesus with the occasion to query Pilate about the nature of his
interest. Had Pilate asked because of his own recognition that
he stood in the presence of sovereignty, or was he asking at the
behest of others? (34) Pilate affirmed in his answer that it
was the suggestion of others. **Am I a Jew? Thine own nation
and the chief priests have delivered thee unto me: what hast thou
done?** (35)

Is Jesus King? He himself gave the affirmative answer. He
has a Kingdom, **my kingdom,** but it is **not of this world** (36). In
it are His **servants,** who because of their nature and purpose (they
are not of this world, 17:16) cannot fight to secure Jesus' deliverance (18:11) from the Jews. Jesus' kingship is not the kind that
can be defended by shield or propagated by sword.[49] Pilate took
this to mean that Jesus did profess to be a King and said, "So
then, You are a King?" (37, lit. translation.) Jesus affirmed
His kingship, **Thou sayest that I am a king** (37), and Pilate
agreed to it. But the question remains: Did Pilate understand
that His kingdom is the Kingdom of truth and that He is Sovereign of truth? **To this end was I born, and for this cause came I
into the world, that I should bear witness unto the truth.**
"The nature of his sovereignty corresponds with the nature of
his mission. He is the King of Truth, and he manifests his royal
power not by force, but by the witness he bears to the Truth"
(3:32; 5:33).[50] As if to put the question pointedly and personally
to Pilate, Jesus said, **Every one that is of the truth heareth my
voice** (37; cf. 10:16, 27).

Here in 37-38 is the age-old conflict between faith and cyni-
cism. Here is a man's opportunity to follow truth and right no
matter what the consequences. And here also is the temptation
to reject truth and honorable action when they are costly. If

[48]The word order in the Greek, *su ei* . . . places the emphasis on the
personal pronoun. Literally it reads, "*Thou* art the King of the Jews?" In
this sense Pilate's remark was much more sarcastic derision than sincere
interrogation. One can almost hear his sneering chuckle.

[49]Bernard takes the view that the **servants** (*huperetai*, 36) were not
the disciples, but the "legions of angels" mentioned in Matt. 26:53.

[50]Hoskyns, *op. cit.,* pp. 520-21.

only men could hear Jesus and believe Him! If only men could join in the faith of Lowell:

> *Truth forever on the scaffold,*
> *Wrong forever on the throne,—*
> *Yet that scaffold sways the future,*
> *And, behind the dim unknown,*
> *Standeth God within the shadow,*
> *Keeping watch above his own.*

("The Present Crisis")

Had Pilate heard Jesus' voice? Evidently not, for his question, **What is truth?** (38), "half sadly, half cynically implies that even in ordinary matters truth is unattainable."[51]

Jesus never gave Pilate a verbal answer to his question. But what our Lord did, for all men to see, was to show the way of truth. Truth is the way to life even when it is the way of the Cross.

c. *The King of the Jews or Barabbas?* (18:38b-40) Pilate was convinced of Jesus' innocence, even if not fully drawn by the Truth. When he went out to the Jews he told them, **I find in him no fault** (*aitia*, "cause for punishment, crime")[52] **at all** (38). Then Pilate tried to slip between the horns of the dilemma on which he found himself. On the one hand, he was persuaded that Jesus was not guilty. On the other, he knew that some favor or clemency would have to be shown the Jews. He reminded them of the custom of releasing a prisoner at the time of the Passover.[53] Should he release unto them **the King of the Jews?** (39) Since Pilate had been so blind to Jesus' true nature and mission, this title may have been only a means of showing his contempt for the Jews.

Pilate's attempt to solve the dilemma by proposing a third solution failed utterly. For they all **cried . . . saying, Not this man, but Barabbas** (40). "There is an impressive pathos in the brief clause"[54] with which John concludes the matter: **Now Barabbas was a robber.**

---

[51]Westcott, *op. cit.*, p. 261.

[52]G. Abbott-Smith, *A Manual Greek Lexicon of the New Testament* (3d ed.; Edinburgh: T. & T. Clark, 1937), p. 14.

[53]Mention of this custom is found only in the Gospels (cf. Matt. 27:15; Mark 15:6; Luke 23:17).

[54]Westcott, *op. cit.*, p. 262.

d. The Scourging and Mockery (19:1-12). Matthew (27:26) and Mark (15:15) indicate that the scourging took place after the Crucifixion had been decreed. John's record places it as a third attempt on the part of Pilate either to shift the responsibility of the decision or to free Jesus (cf. 18:31, 39). When the Jews chose the release of Barabbas, **Pilate therefore took Jesus, and scourged him** (1) "as a punishment likely to satisfy the Jews."[55] The scourging was in itself a bloody and terribly painful ordeal. "The victim was bound in a stooping attitude to a low column and lashed with thongs weighted with lead or bone."[56]

Pilate committed a fatal error in this act, as do all who use expediency alone as the basis for moral judgments. He himself was persuaded that Jesus was completely innocent (18:38), yet by his act he said to the demanding priests and officers that Jesus was worthy of some punishment. The Jews had won their point! The slight compromise with evil is also the beginning of full surrender to its demands.

What happened next was "a soldier's brutal game."[57] **The soldiers platted a crown of thorns** ("twisted some thorns into a crown," Moffatt), **and put it on his head, and they put on him a purple robe** (2), "probably a red military cloak as worn by Roman officers."[58] Having made Jesus as ludicrous and pitiable a sight as their evil imaginations could devise, they filed by with an "Ave" (*chaire*), **Hail, King of the Jews!** Then **they smote him with their hands** (3), exhibiting the callous cruelty so typical of ancient soldiers.

While this mockery was going on, Pilate went out again and announced to the Jews, **Behold, I bring him forth to you, that ye may know that I find no fault in him** (4). At that **Jesus came forth, wearing the crown of thorns, and the purple robe. And Pilate saith unto them, Behold the man!** (*Ecce homo,* 5.) It may have been Pilate's hope that the sight of Jesus in the garb of mockery would show how foolish the charge of sedition really was. By the expression **Behold the man!** (*idou ho anthropos*) he could have meant, "See the poor fellow."[59] Macgregor argues

[55]Westcott, *op. cit.,* p. 267.
[56]Macgregor, *op. cit.,* p. 338. Cf. Isa. 53:5.
[57]Strachan, *op. cit.,* p. 315.
[58]Macgregor, *op. cit.,* p. 339.
[59]Bernard, *op. cit.,* p. 616.

that Pilate intended contempt for Jesus, calling Him "the creature." At the same time he admits that "the definite article (*ho*) lends it dignity and suggests that Pilate's words are an unconscious prophecy of Jesus' uniqueness: 'Here is *the* Man'—the Son of Man, the Man *par excellence* foretold by the prophets."[60] If Macgregor is right, the *Ecce homo* of Pilate is a title of contempt and derision born of a wicked heart and mind totally incapable of recognizing the truth (18:38; cf. 1:29, 36; Isa. 40:9).

But even the sight of the sinless Jesus in mock **robe** and wearing **a crown of thorns** failed to move the **chief priests . . . and officers (6)** to any conciliatory mood. Rather they **cried out** (*ekraugasan*, lit., "screamed excitedly"), **Crucify him, crucify him.** Though the demand that He be crucified had been previously alluded to (18:31), now for the first time it was voiced. These men would not be satisfied with anything short of the life of Jesus and that by crucifixion.

Pilate's response was at once a taunt to the Jews and an affirmation of his belief in Jesus' innocency. **Take ye him, and crucify him.** "In a fit of exasperation [he dares] the Jews to exceed their powers and take the crucifixion into their own hands."[61] "Crucify Him if you dare!" For the third time Pilate declared Jesus to be innocent: **I find no fault in him** (cf. 18:38; 19:4; Luke 23:4, 14, 22). Hoskyns observes: "Both Pilate and the Jews are unconscious witnesses to Christian truth. Pilate proclaims the sinlessness of Jesus, and the Jews declare His death to be the fulfillment of the Law"[62] (cf. 11:50-51).

At that the Jews introduced a new accusation. Since Pilate would not assent to the charge of sedition, a political issue, the matter would have to be pursued on religious grounds. **We have a law, and by our law he ought to die (7).** The law alluded to is: "And he that blasphemeth the name of the Lord, he shall surely be put to death, and all the congregation shall certainly stone him" (Lev. 24:16).[63] The charge, **because he made himself the Son of God** (*huion theou*, 7), was probably intelligible to Pilate, for the expression of divine sonship was "understood in various ways

---

[60]*Op. cit.*, p. 339.

[61]*Ibid.*

[62]*Op. cit.*, p. 523.

[63]The Jews had accused Jesus of blasphemy before (see 10:33, 36).

212

in the Hellenistic world at the time."[64] Westcott observes that
the absence of the article in the Greek "fixes attention upon
the general character of the nature claimed (Son of God) as
distinguished from the special personality."[65]

When Pilate . . . heard that saying, he was the more afraid
(8), or he was "superstitiously afraid."[66] As Macgregor says:
"He is now seized with that superstitious fear which so often
haunts the skeptic."[67] Could it be that he had "ignominiously
scourged one who was in some sense sent by the national divinity?"[68]

Now, driven by fear, not of the Jews, but of an uncertain
Presence, Pilate went again into the judgment hall, and saith
unto Jesus, Whence art thou? (9) His question was not concerned with Jesus' national or geographic origin. He knew that
Jesus was a Jew, and from Galilee (Luke 23:6-7).[69] But Jesus
gave him no answer. Some have said that Jesus was physically unable to answer because of the ordeal of the scourging. But
this position is unlikely in view of the fact that the silence of
Jesus before His accusers was in some instances before the
scourging (cf. Matt. 26:63; 27:14; Mark 14:61; 15:5; Luke 23:9).
Bernard comments: "His refusal to answer questions which were
not asked in sincerity, but out of mere curiosity or with intent
to betray Him into some dangerous admission, is explicable on
moral grounds. Indeed, the dignity of His silence before His
accusers does not need exposition."[70]

Jesus' dignified silence irritated Pilate. Speakest thou not
unto me? He was indignant. The literal word order and translation is, "To me You are not speaking?" thus placing emphasis on
the "to me." Knowest thou not (lit., "You know, don't You")
that I have power to crucify thee, and I have power to release

[64]Lightfoot, *op. cit.*, p. 325.

[65]*Op. cit.*, p. 270. In Greek the use of the article emphasizes individual
identity. The nonuse of the article emphasizes kind or quality—in this case
deity.

[66]Strachan, *op. cit.*, p. 316.

[67]*Op. cit.*, p. 340.

[68]Westcott, *op. cit.*, p. 270.

[69]Pilate had sent Jesus to Herod for examination when he had learned
of Jesus' ministry in Galilee. Only Luke records the hearing before Herod.

[70]*Op. cit.*, p. 619.

thee? (10) There is nothing more brashly presumptive than moral ignorance. This is like the ant saying to the elephant, "Step to one side lest I crush you under my foot."

To set Pilate straight, **Jesus answered, Thou couldest have no power at all against me, except it were given thee from above** (11). The word for **power** is *exousia*, which means *"liberty or power to act; right, authority."*[71] Pilate's "right to exercise authority was derived, not inherent. Human government is only valid as the expression of the divine will."[72] Bernard says: "It is not arbitrary power which can be exercised capriciously without moral blame."[73] Comparing Jesus and Pilate in this respect Strachan says, "Jesus does more than assert His Divine power and origin. He assumes it. In striking contrast, Pilate *asserts* his power."[74]

Jesus here injects a new figure into the picture. **Therefore he that delivered me unto thee hath the greater sin.** Of whom is Jesus speaking? Because of the expression **he that delivered** (*ho paradous*) being frequently applied to Judas (cf. 6:64, 71; 12:4; 13:2, 11, 21; 18:5; 21:20) some have taken this to refer to him. But the fact is that Judas did not deliver Jesus to Pilate. The one who did that was Caiaphas (and those whom he represented). So it is Caiaphas that **hath the greater sin,** and the comparison **greater** is between him and Pilate. Pilate misused a power delegated to him. Caiaphas usurped a judicial power that did not belong to him (cf. 10:1). "The High-Priest was doubly guilty, both in using wrongfully a higher (spiritual) power, and in transgressing his legitimate rules of action."[75] Macgregor has said with point that "the holier the power the more blameworthy the misuse of it."[76]

Thoroughly persuaded of Jesus' innocency (18:38; 19:4, 6), and filled with superstitious fear (8), **from thenceforth Pilate sought** (lit., "was seeking repeatedly") **to release him** (12). The language here suggests that there may have been other unrecorded attempts by Pilate to release Jesus. But all were to no

[71]Abbott-Smith, *op. cit.*, pp. 161-62.
[72]Westcott, *op. cit.*, p. 270.
[73]*Op. cit.*, p. 619.
[74]*Op. cit.*, p. 316.
[75]Westcott, *op. cit.*, pp. 271-72.
[76]*Op. cit.*, p. 341.

avail. **The Jews cried out** ("kept shouting," Weymouth),[77] **saying, If thou let this man go, thou art not Caesar's friend** (lit., "a friend of Caesar"). This may have been a more serious threat to Pilate than appears on the surface. "Friend of the Emperor was an official title, like 'Privy Councillor,' granted to distinguished people."[78] Some, e.g., Strachan,[79] think that Pilate probably held the title. With this personal threat to Pilate involving his political future, the Jews restated their charge of treason and sedition against Jesus. **Whosoever maketh himself a king speaketh against Caesar.**

e. *Pilate Capitulates* (19:13-16). It was evidently **that saying** concerning Pilate's relationship with Caesar which brought the governor to a reluctant decision. The inner encounter with the truth was in conflict with the outside pressures. How a man resolves these encounters reveals his true character. **He brought Jesus forth, and sat down in the judgment seat** (*bema*)[80] **in a place that is called the Pavement, but in the Hebrew, Gabbatha** (13). Moffatt's translation reads, "On hearing this, Pilate brought Jesus out and seated him on the tribunal" (*bemates*). Most authorities agree that the Greek could be accurately translated this way. In defense of this meaning Macgregor says:

> Undoubtedly the meaning is that Pilate set Jesus upon the tribunal, rather than that he took his own seat in order to pronounce final judgment in the presence of the crowd . . . This interpretation makes the scene much more dramatic and alone suits the words "There is your King" . . . Dramatically the Jews are shown rejecting their King. Pilate makes one final attempt to have the case laughed out of court; but John thinks not of the ridicule but of the unconscious prophecy: it is really Jesus who is King and Judge.[81]

Most authorities reject this view. They argue that the verb **sat** (*ekathisen*) is always used intransitively by John, and is so used

---

[77]The Weymouth translation here is based on the imperfect tense form of the verb which appears in some MSS.

[78]Strachan, *op. cit.*, p. 316.

[79]Bernard takes the opposite view on the ground that the title was not known before Vespasian, Roman emperor, A.D. 69-79.

[80]The *bema* was a raised platform, sometimes temporary, sometimes permanent, from which justice was officially administered. This was probably a temporary *bema* hastily erected outside the Praetorium where all the crowd could hear the judgment pronounced.

[81]*Op. cit.*, p. 342.

here. Bernard comments: "It is inconceivable that a Roman
procurator should be so regardless of his dignity, when about to
pronounce sentence of death, as to make a jest of the matter."[82]

John was careful to make note of the time of this part of the
episode, in both its religious and temporal contexts. **It was the
preparation** (*paraskeue*) **of the passover, and about the sixth
hour (14).** Mark (15:25) says that Jesus was crucified at "the
third hour" (9:00 a.m.), using Jewish time. Here John is using
Roman civil time, which began at midnight. Little did the high
priests know that **about the sixth hour** (6:00 a.m.) "the Lamb
slain from the foundation of the world" (Rev. 13:8) was being
prepared as an eternal Sacrifice.

As Jesus stood there on the Pavement or mosaic (*lithostroton*,
lit., "a place spread with stones"), Pilate said **unto the Jews,
Behold your King!** One view about this utterance is that Pilate
unconsciously, yet officially, pronounced the truth about Jesus.
He is King of Kings and Lord of Lords!

Again the Jews **cried out** ("This caused a storm of out-
cries," Weymouth), **Away with him, away with him, crucify
him;** to which Pilate responded, **Shall I crucify your King? (15)**
With great subtilty Pilate had maneuvered the Jews into a position where they would pronounce judgment not only on Jesus
but upon themselves (cf. Matt. 27:25). When **the chief priests**
(Annas and Caiaphas) **answered, We have no king but Caesar
(15),** they "denied the sovereignty of God, and abdicated their
right to be his chosen people."[83] Strachan comments: "Israel
has committed the final apostasy in thus rejecting the ancient
theocratic conception (Ps. 74:12; 84:3; 95:3) that God alone is
King of Israel."[84] The Jews, who have played such a major role
in the fourth Gospel, now disappear from the scene except for
passing reference (19:21, 31; 20:19).

There is no record that Pilate pronounced a formal sentence
of death, but such can be assumed from the setting (the *bema*)
and Pilate's question, **Shall I crucify your King? (15)** Though
16 reads as though it were the Jews who received Jesus from
Pilate, and who **led him away (16),**[85] it was the Roman soldiers

---

[82]*Op. cit.,* p. 622.

[83]Hoskyns, *op. cit.,* p. 525.

[84]*Op. cit.,* p. 317.

[85]Actually the **and led him away** does not appear in the best textual
readings.

who carried out the horrible assignment ordered by the Roman procurator, but instigated by the Jews.

Alexander Maclaren has a narrative exposition of 1-16 under the purely historical title "Jesus Sentenced." (1) Cruelties inflicted in the Praetorium, 1-3; (2) Pilate trying another expedient, 4-8; (3) Again inside the Praetorium, 9-11; (4) **Then delivered he him,** 12-16.

A. THE CRUCIFIXION, 19:17-37

1. *The Crosses* (19:17-22)

The road from the Praetorium to Golgotha is now known as the "Via Dolorosa," the "road of sorrow."[1] Along this road Jesus **went forth . . . bearing his cross** (17). It was the custom that the condemned man, surrounded by a quaternion of Roman soldiers (four), carry his cross to the place of execution. "The fact that Jesus carried his own cross again suggests in symbol the voluntary nature of his sacrifice" (cf. Gen. 22:6).[2] John makes no mention of Jesus' collapse under the weight of the Cross, or of the impressment of Simon, a Cyrenian, to bear the load (Mark 15:21).

At Golgotha they—i.e., the four Roman soldiers—**crucified him** (18). This type of execution was called by Cicero "the most cruel and horrifying death . . . A nefarious action such as that is incapable of description by any word, for there is none fit to describe it."[3] Jesus was executed as a common criminal, and there were two criminals in company **with him, on either side one, and Jesus in the midst.** John gives none of the conversation between Jesus and the robbers (cf. Luke 23:29-43), but the situation of His cross between the other two is noted, thus attesting "His royal dignity."[4]

It was the custom that a **title** (*titlon*), "the technical name for the board bearing the name of the condemned or his crime or both,"[5] should be placed **on the cross.** This Pilate did.[6] He wrote, **JESUS OF NAZARETH THE KING OF THE JEWS** (19). He

---

[1]The exact location of Golgotha is not known, but is generally taken to be a bare hill with skull-like contour, outside but in close proximity to the city (see map 2). "Executions were not allowed within the city walls" (Bernard, *op. cit.*, p. 626). However, the position of the city walls of Jesus' day is not certain (see comments on Matt. 27:33 in BBC, VI, 246-47).

[2]Macgregor, *op. cit.*, p. 344.

[3]Quoted by Barclay, *op. cit.*, p. 291.

[4]Hoskyns, *op. cit.*, p. 528.

[5]Bernard, *op. cit.*, p. 627.

[6]Only John notes that Pilate wrote the title.

was careful to write the title **in Hebrew, and Greek, and Latin, so that all the Jews who passed by could read, for the place where Jesus was crucified was nigh to the city** (20). The fact that the title was written in three languages representing religion, culture, and government was "an unwitting prophecy of Christ's universal kingship."[7] "Thus did Pilate *tell it out among the heathen that the Lord is King*" (Ps. 94:10).[8]

Pilate intended the title to be a thrust and insult to the Jews. As expected, the chief priests of the Jews objected **to Pilate. They said, Write not, The King of the Jews; but that he said, I am King of the Jews** (21). Pilate's response to this request was adamant. **What I have written I have written** (22). The identical verbs *gegrapha* are in the perfect tense and here indicate "a true prophecy."[9] The title, once written and affixed to the Cross, "was the expression of a legal decision."[10]

2. *The Soldiers* (19:23-24)

The persons who actually crucified Jesus were the four Roman **soldiers** (a quaternion). The bounty they received for doing this brutal work was the clothing of the victims. It is not likely that the "take" was much from the two robbers. John, apparently having taken special note as an eyewitness, described in detail how the soldiers divided their spoils. They **took Jesus' garments, and made four parts, to every soldier a part; and also his coat** (tunic, 23). There was something special about His tunic, for it **was without seam, woven from the top throughout** ("in one piece," Weymouth). Seeing that dividing the tunic would destroy its value, the soldiers agreed among themselves, **Let us not rend it, but cast lots for it, whose it shall be** ("to see who gets it," Phillips, 24). The tunic (*chiton*) was the under-robe worn next to the body.

The agreement of the soldiers not to **rend** (*schisomen* is the verb, *schisma* the noun cognate) the tunic seems to have meant something special to John. The same word is used in describing divisions and factions (7:43; 9:16; 10:19; cf. I Cor. 1:10; 11:18; 12:25). Hoskyns suggests: "The indivisible robe, which is closely associated with the body of the Lord, may therefore symbolize

[7]Macgregor, *op. cit.*, p. 345.
[8]Hoskyns, *op. cit.*, p. 528.
[9]*Ibid.*
[10]Bernard, *op. cit.*, pp. 628-29.

the unity of the believers who are joined to the Lord and feed upon His Body, in contrast to the divisions of the Jews, who are torn into factions because of Him."[11]

In all this John saw the fulfillment of Ps. 22:18. In this Hebrew parallelism he found the full explanation for the action of the soldiers. Some of the garments were divided—**they parted my raiment among them;** they gambled for the tunic—**for my vesture they did cast lots** (24). Indicating that he thought the action of the soldiers to be highly significant, and that he had seen it all, he wrote a *finis*—**These things therefore the soldiers did.**

These gamblers at the foot of the Cross highly dramatize the fact that in a sense "Jesus staked everything on His utter fidelity to God; He staked everything on the Cross."[12] Studdert-Kennedy's poem says it well:

> *And, sitting down, they watched Him there,*
> *The soldiers did;*
> *There, while they played with dice,*
> *He made His sacrifice,*
> *And died upon the Cross to rid*
> *God's world of sin.*
> *He was a gambler too, my Christ,*
> *He took His life and threw*
> *It for a world redeemed.*
> *And ere His agony was done,*
> *Before the westering sun went down,*
> *Crowning that day with its crimson crown,*
> *He knew that He had won.*[13]

3. *His Mother* (19:25-27)

The disciples had forsaken their Master (16:32; 18:8) with the exception of Peter and John during the hearing before the high priest (18:15), and John at the Cross (26). But there was a group of loving and faithful women who **stood by the cross of Jesus** (25). There were four of them: **his mother,** Mary; **his mother's sister,** thought to be Salome, wife of Zebedee, hence

---

[11]*Op. cit.,* p. 529.

[12]Barclay, *op. cit.,* p. 295.

[13]Studdert-Kennedy, "The Gambler," *Christ in Poetry;* an anthology, ed. by Thomas Curtis Clark and Hazel Davis Clark (New York: Association Press, © copyright 1952), p. 120.

the mother of James and John;[14] **Mary the wife of Cleophas (better, Clopas); and Mary Magdalene.**

The first words of Jesus from the Cross recorded by John were addressed to His mother. **When Jesus therefore saw his mother, and the disciple standing by, whom he loved, he saith unto his mother, Woman, behold thy son!** (26) Jesus had prayed for forgiveness for those who crucified Him (Luke 23:34). He had given promise and hope to a dying penitent robber (Luke 23:43). But now His gaze is fixed on **his mother.** "It is true to human experience that as death draws nearer, the interest of the dying narrows down to thought regarding those who are nearest and dearest."[15]

The word of address by Jesus to His mother, **Woman,** is neither as cold nor as brusque as the English translation appears (see comment on 2:4). Evidently John was **standing by** Mary, giving her consolation and comfort. The two "beholds"—**Behold thy son!** and **Behold thy mother!** (27)—gave both Mary and John instruction as to their future relationship. John was to care for Jesus' mother. **And from that hour that disciple took her unto his own home.**

4. *"It Is Finished"* (19:28-30)

John provides a profound theological background for Jesus' words, **I thirst** (28). Even in this moment of death Jesus is fully conscious and dedicated to the completion of His mission. **Jesus knowing** (*eidos*, cf. 13:1) **that all things were now accomplished** (*tetelestai*, exactly the same form that is translated, "It is finished," in 30), **that the scripture might be fulfilled** (*hina teleiothe*),[16] **saith, I thirst** (28; cf. Ps. 42:2; 63:1; 69:21). Westcott points out that the verb **fulfilled** "appears to mark not the isolated fulfilling of a particular trait in the scriptural picture, but the perfect completion of the whole prophetic image."[17] "The death of Jesus is the completion of the Scriptures."[18]

---

[14]This would indicate that Jesus and John, the beloved disciple, were cousins (cf. Matt. 27:56; Mark 15:40).

[15]Strachan, *op. cit.*, p. 319.

[16]The usual Greek verb for **fulfilled** is *pleroo*, e.g., 19:24, which means to "make full," "complete." But here the verb *teleioo* has the added idea of "completion in terms of a set goal."

[17]*Op. cit.*, p. 277.

[18]Hoskyns, *op. cit.*, p. 531.

The soldiers must have brought along a **vessel** (jar, bowl) **full of vinegar** (*oxos*, 29). This "*oxos*, or *posea*, was the sour wine which was the usual drink of the legionaries."[19] When Jesus said, **I thirst . . . they filled a spunge with vinegar, and put it upon hyssop, and put it to his mouth.** In view of the fact that **hyssop** is not a plant with a strong enough stem to support a wet sponge, this text has provided some problems. There is an eleventh-century manuscript which has the word *hyssa*, the Greek word for a soldier's javelin, instead of *hyssopo*, **hyssop.** Strachan[20] and Bernard[21] hold that this reading solves the problem. On the other hand, Hoskyns accepts the better authenticated reading, and sees in the use of the **hyssop** (cf. Lev. 14:4, 6; Num. 19:18; Ps. 51:7) a fulfillment of Old Testament symbolism. He says: The hyssop was used for sprinkling blood on "the doors of the Jewish homes during the Passover season in memory of Exod. 12:22. Since Jesus is, in the Fourth Gospel, both the Lamb of God and the Door (10:7), the action of the soldiers is appropriately significant and is of value in reminding the reader that the Jewish Passover is fulfilled in the sacrifice of the true Paschal Lamb."[22]

With marked precision and appropriate dignity, John describes the end. **When Jesus therefore had received the vinegar, he said, It is finished** (*tetelestai*): **and he bowed his head, and gave up the ghost** (*pneuma*, "his spirit," 30). "Every clause in this verse stresses the voluntariness of his sacrifice."[23] The fact that the verb *tetelestai*, meaning "completion in terms of a set goal," is in the perfect tense, gives double emphasis to the idea of perfect completion. The plan of redemption is complete both in the historical sense and in its perfect adequacy to meet every need of sinful man. "*Tetelestai* is not a cry of relief that all is over; it is a shout of victory"[24] (cf. Matt. 27:50; Mark 15:37).

5. *The Open Fountain* (19:31-37)

It was a Roman custom to abandon corpses on the cross, leaving them to the dogs and vultures. But there was a Jewish

[19]Bernard, *op. cit.*, p. 638.
[20]*Op. cit.*, p. 330.
[21]*Op. cit.*, p. 640.
[22]*Op. cit.*, p. 531.
[23]Macgregor, *op. cit.*, p. 349.
[24]Bernard, *op. cit.*, p. 638.

law which "forbade the leaving of a body on the gibbet over-night."[25] For this reason, and because it was the preparation, i.e., the eve of Sabbath,[26] **the Jews ... besought Pilate that the legs of the victims might be broken, and that they might be taken away (31).** This brutal practice, known as the *crurifragi-um,* was used as a means of hastening death. It involved the breaking of the victim's legs with a large mallet. The soldiers did this to first one, then the other of the robbers who were crucified with Jesus (32). **But when they came to Jesus, and saw that he was dead already, they brake not his legs (33).** John notes in this the fulfillment of the scripture, **A bone of him shall not be broken** (36; cf. Exod. 12:46; Num. 9:12). Jesus was the perfect Sacrifice in death as well as in life.

But John saw more than this, for though **they brake not his legs ... one of the soldiers with a spear** (*logche*)[27] **pierced his side, and forthwith came there out blood and water (34).**[28] Hoskyns takes the view that the water and blood are symbolic of the two sacraments, baptism and the Eucharist. He says:

> He [John] perceived that purification (water) and new life (blood) flow from the completed sacrifice of the Lamb of God ... And since, moreover, the benefits of the Sacrifice on Calvary are appropriated by the faithful Christian when he is reborn from above of water and the Spirit (3:3-5), the death of the Christ, and the effusion of the Spirit (v. 30) and of the blood and the water are declared to be the true institution of Christian Baptism and of the Eucharist."[29]

Westcott sees these "as a sign of life in death. It showed both His true humanity and (in some mysterious sense) the permanence of His human life ... As he hung upon the cross He was shown openly to be the source of a double cleansing and vivifying power, which followed from His death and life."[30]

[25]Macgregor, *ibid.*

[26]This was really a "double sabbath," for the next day, beginning at sundown, was the Passover. John describes it as **an high day.**

[27]"The *logche* was a long slender spear, not so heavy as the hyssos" (Bernard, *op. cit.,* p. 645).

[28]This verse, along with I John 5:6-8, has provoked much comment and many theories. For excellent summaries see Westcott, *op. cit.,* pp. 284-86, and Macgregor, *op. cit.,* pp. 644-48.

[29]*Op. cit.,* p. 533.

[30]*Op. cit.,* p. 279.

To this writer it appears that the **blood and water** are a witness to the completed work of the Incarnate One. It has been seen that John has consistently used **water** as a symbol of the best in Judaism which Jesus came to fulfill (see comments on 1:33; 2:6; 3:5; 4:12-14; 5:2; 7:37-39; 9:7). The **blood** is the Incarnation and full redemption which has made life eternal possible for man (6:53-54). Now the work is finished—*tetelestai* (30) and the spear-pierced side bears its witness (cf. I John 5:6-8).

John concludes his remarks about the piercing of our Lord's body by pointing out that it all happened as a part of the fulfilling of the scripture, **They shall look on him whom they pierced** (37; cf. Zech. 12:10).

B. THE BURIAL, 19:38-42

In the hour of Jesus' indescribable humiliation and subjection to death, two of His secret disciples, members of the Jewish aristocracy, came out into the open. How true it is that "Christ on the Cross has a power greater even than Jesus the Rabbi to 'draw men to himself'" (12:32)![31]

First, there was **Joseph of Arimathaea.**[32] Though a member of the Sanhedrin, he had not consented to Jesus' death (Luke 23:50). He asked Pilate **that he might take away the body of Jesus.** With Pilate's permission granted, **he came ... and took the body of Jesus** (38).

Nicodemus is described as the one who came **at the first ... by night** (cf. 3:2) with the implication that there were subsequent visits. He too was a member of the Sanhedrin. Perhaps Nicodemus was a timid man, for it was Joseph who faced Pilate to secure the necessary permission. He must have been wealthy, for **an hundred pound weight**[33] of **myrrh and aloes** would be very costly. What he brought was "the expression of a rich man's homage."[34] The spices were a mixture of the gum of the myrrh tree and powdered aloe wood.

The Jewish mode of burial did not involve embalming of the body, nor cremation, but the wrapping of the bodies "of the

---

[31]Macgregor, *op. cit.,* p. 352.

[32]Arimathaea was located about thirteen miles east-northeast of Lydda, or about sixty miles from Jerusalem.

[33]About seventy pounds on the avoirdupois scale.

[34]Macgregor, *op. cit.,* p. 353.

dead in linen cloths, and to put sweet spices between the folds of the linen. Nicodemus brought enough spices for the burial of a king."[35]

They buried the body of Jesus in **a new sepulchre in a garden . . . in the place where he was crucified** (41). Apparently they did it with some haste because of the swiftly approaching Passover—**the Jews' preparation day** (42). The fact that the **sepulchre was nigh at hand** made it an easier task to perform.

Under the title "Joseph and Nicodemus," Alexander Maclaren discusses 38-42. (1) Secret discipleship and its causes, 38-39; (2) The miseries of secret discipleship—**And after this,** 38; (3) The cure for cowardice—**Then took they the body of Jesus,** 40.

[35]Barclay, *op. cit.,* p. 306.

Section **VIII** *Resurrection and Appearances*

John 20:1—21:25

A. THE RESURRECTION EVIDENCE, 20:1-10

The Christian centuries have rung with the words: **The first day of the week cometh Mary Magdalene early, when it was yet dark, unto the sepulchre, and seeth the stone taken away from the sepulchre** (tomb, 1; cf. Mark 16:1-2). Thus begins John's account of the Resurrection. Whereas his record of "the Passion is the history of the descent of selfishness to apostasy, his history of the Resurrection is the history of the elevation of love into absolute faith."[1] It is highly appropriate that he should begin his account with the experience of Mary Magdalene (Luke 8:2).[2] Much had been forgiven her, and her love for the Lord was great as is evidenced in this story. What Mary saw was of tremendous importance—the first visual evidence of the Resurrection. "The stone had been removed" (Weymouth) from the opening to the tomb.[3]

Without going farther she turned and ran **to Simon Peter, and to the other disciple, whom Jesus loved,** with the disturbing news of what she had seen: **They have taken away the Lord out of the sepulchre, and we[4] know not where they have laid him** (2). Mary, "the great example of bewildered love,"[5] had good evidence but she had come to the wrong conclusion.

When **Peter and that other disciple** (John) **heard this, they ran both together: and the other disciple did outrun Peter, and came first to the sepulchre** (4). There have been many conjectures as to why John won the footrace. The most likely explanation is a matter of agility. John was the younger of the two, and he was only reporting an interesting and eyewitness fact.

[1]Westcott, *op. cit.*, p. 287.

[2]Bernard holds that Mary Magdalene is the Mary of Bethany (*op. cit.*, p. 657). But this is very unlikely.

[3]For a description of an ordinary Palestinian tomb, see comment on 11:38.

[4]The use of the plural **we** reflects that other women had come with her (cf. Matt. 28:1; Mark 16:1; Luke 23:56). Mary speaks for them all.

[5]Barclay, *op. cit.*, p. 309.

An amazing sight struck John. As he stooped (*parakupsas*)[6] to look in, **he saw the linen clothes** (cloths or wrappings) **lying; yet went he not in** (5). The reward for winning the footrace was more than ample, for he had seen the second evidence of the Resurrection, the linen cloths. As soon as Peter arrived, true to his impulsive nature, he went right **into the sepulchre.** Inside, Peter, and John, who followed (8), could see more. Not only did they see **the linen clothes** lie, but also **the napkin, that was about his head, not lying with the linen clothes, but wrapped together** (rolled up) **in a place by itself** (7). Macgregor says that the words **wrapped together** mean properly " 'twirled' turban-like, just as it had been wrapped around the head."[7]

What was the meaning of all these things? There were three evidences of the Resurrection that were cumulatively convincing. First, the stone was removed from the entrance (1). Second, the orderly fashion in which the burial linens were lying. In fact, if Mary's first suspicion had been correct, that someone had **taken away the Lord** (2), there would have been no burial cloths at all, for they would have been taken with the body. Macgregor observes: "The whole language seems to have been carefully chosen to suggest that Jesus' physical body had passed into a spiritual and 'glorified' Risen Body without disturbing the grave-clothes, which had simply settled down on the ledge within the tomb in their original positions."[8] The third evidence, not specifically mentioned but everywhere evident, was the absence of the body of the Lord—the empty tomb.

When John **saw** these things he **believed** (*episteusen*, 8). The verb is in the aorist tense, which indicates a decisive act, not a process. "He had no vision of the Risen Christ, but the sight of the abandoned grave-cloths was sufficient to assure him that Jesus had risen from the dead"[9] (cf. 16:16; Luke 24:12). It is evident from 25, 27, and 29 that "*believed* means belief in the Resurrection of the Lord."[10] In fact, Hoskyns holds that "the pre-eminence of the faith of the Beloved Disciple is the climax of the narrative."[11]

[6]According to Bernard this word in the Septuagint "always means 'to peep' through a door or window" (*op. cit.*, p. 659).
[7]*Op. cit.*, p. 356.
[8]*Ibid.*
[9]Bernard, *op. cit.*, p. 661.
[10]Hoskyns, *op. cit.*, p. 540.
[11]*Ibid.*

At this point John describes the very limited understanding that he and Peter had concerning the Resurrection even when confronted with these apparently unmistakable evidences. He writes: **For as yet they knew not the scripture** (Ps. 16:10), **that he must rise again from the dead** (9). Evidently they "had failed to read the lesson of the Old Testament, even by the help of the Lord's teaching."[12]

B. Personal Appearance to Mary Magdalene, 20:11-18

It would seem that the two disciples left the tomb (10) before Mary was able to get back to the garden after having given them notice about the stone (2). Thus left alone with her sorrow and distress, she **stood without at the sepulchre weeping** ("sobbing," (Moffatt): **and as she wept, she stooped down, and looked into the sepulchre** (11). There is no mention that she saw the linen cloths, or the head napkin "wrapped together in a place by itself" (6-7). Rather, she saw **two angels in white sitting, the one at the head, and the other at the feet, where the body of Jesus had lain** (12). All four Gospels tell of the angelic appearances at the tomb: "the angels" (Matt. 2:5); "a young man" (Mark 16:5); "two men" (Luke 24:4; cf. Rev. 3:4-5; 4:4). These white-robed messengers sat "marking the place where the body had lain, witnesses to the mystery of the Resurrection."[13]

The angels addressed Mary with the question, **Woman, why weepest thou?** (13) She exhibited neither fright nor astonishment at their appearance or address, for only one concern filled her mind—her Lord. She had quite a sufficient reason for her evident sorrow: **Because they have taken away my Lord, and I know not where they have laid him.** She still did not realize the incongruity of her conclusion. The empty grave cloths which had been sufficient evidence to bring John to an active and achieving faith ("he believed"; 8) had not even caught Mary's attention. It is well to remember that God comes to men in various ways according to their different temperaments and unequal abilities to understand and respond. In this sense there is here portrayed a universal gospel. Christ is the risen Lord for all men.

As if to go, Mary **turned herself back, and saw Jesus standing, and knew not that it was Jesus** (14). The question of the

---

[12]Westcott, *op. cit.*, p. 290.
[13]Hoskyns, *op. cit.*, p. 542.

angels to Mary was repeated by Jesus, **Woman, why weepest thou? whom seekest thou?** (15) But she did not recognize Jesus! She thought **him to be the gardener.** Why did she not recognize Him? Barclay suggests two reasons: "The simple and poignant fact is that she could not see Him through her tears . . . She could not take her eyes off the tomb, and she had her back to Jesus. She insisted on facing in the wrong direction."[14]

Gossip gives three reasons why Mary did not recognize Jesus. In outline form they would provide the basis for a sermon based on 20:11-18: (1) Mary was seeking for a dead Christ, 11-13; (2) It was not Mary Magdalene who came on Christ, but Christ who found her, 14-16; (3) Although she was seeking Him with her whole being, Mary did not recognize Christ when she saw Him, 14.[15] He comes in unsuspected ways.

Verse 16 is the record of what has been called "the greatest recognition scene in history."[16] When Jesus said to her, **Mary,** she knew Him at once. "What the word of common interest (*woman*) could not do, the word of individual sympathy does at once."[17] Or as Hoskyns says, "The true, life-giving ruler of the Paradise (Garden) of God has called His own sheep by name, and she knows His voice" (10:3-4).[18] She knew His voice calling her name. She faced Him: **She turned herself, and saith unto him, Rabboni; which is to say, Master** (16). Hoskyns contends, on the authority of Strack-Billerbeck, that **Rabboni** in older Jewish literature is distinct from *Rabbi.* There it is "hardly ever used in reference to men, and never in addressing them. The word is reserved for address to God." Hoskyns then comments: "Mary's use of it here is therefore probably to be understood as a declaration of faith, parallel to that of Thomas (v. 28)."[19]

Though it is not specifically stated by John, it would appear that Mary, in adoration, worship, and deep emotion, had clasped Jesus' feet (cf. Matt. 28:10). At this His word to her was, **Touch me not** ("Cease clinging to me," Moffatt; "Do not hold Me now," Phillips, 17). In the light of 27, when Thomas was invited by the

---

[14]*Op. cit.,* pp. 312-13.

[15]*Op. cit.,* pp. 792-93.

[16]Macgregor, *op. cit.,* p. 358.

[17]Westcott, *op. cit.,* p. 292.

[18]*Op. cit.,* p. 542.

[19]*Ibid.* Macgregor, Westcott, Bernard take the word **Rabboni** to be practically equivalent to *Rabbi* (cf. Mark 10:51).

risen Lord to "thrust" his hand into His pierced side, this verse has perplexed readers and commentators alike. Jesus' word to Mary was, **for I am not yet ascended to my Father** (17; cf. 16:10; also 7:33; 16:5; also 14:12, 28; 16:28). Understandably, Mary wanted never to let Him go again. The word translated **touch** (*haptou*) means "to hold on to an object with the desire to retain possession of it."[20] But this intimate, precious relationship which she and all His followers enjoyed was now to take on a new form and meaning. However, it could **not yet** (cf. 2:4; 7:6, 8, 30, 39; 8:20) be consummated, even as He had said in the promise of the coming of the Paraclete (16:7-8). With keen insight Hoskyns says:

> He now declares to Mary, and through her to the disciples that the time has come for Him to ascend to the Father and therefore for the inauguration of the new order. The command that Mary should cease touching Him refers to the interim period between the Resurrection and the Ascension—and to this period only. So intimate will be the relationship with Jesus that, though Mary must for the time being cease from touching Him, because He must ascend and she must deliver His message, yet, after the Ascension, both she and the disciples will be concretely united with Him in a manner which can actually be described as "touching", and of this the eating of the Lord's Body and the drinking of His Blood (6:51-58) is the most poignant illustration.[21]

Without putting emphasis on the Eucharist as Hoskyns does, Macgregor sees this passage as teaching that "the true proof of the Resurrection and the true possession of the Risen Christ [are] . . . to be realized in the normal spiritual experience of the believer."[22]

Jesus' further word to Mary was, **Go to my brethren, and say unto them, I ascend unto my Father, and your Father; and to my God, and your God** (17). Just as Mary's fellowship with Jesus was henceforth not "to be one dependent on sense-perception,"[23] this was to extend to the disciples—**my brethren** (*adelphous*) with whom He had been united and identified in His incarnation. His perfect humanity is reflected not only in the expression **my brethren** but also **my God**. Strachan comments: "Jesus is now the ladder between heaven and earth (cf. 1:51)

[20]Macgregor, *op. cit.*, p. 359.
[21]*Op. cit.*, pp. 542-43.
[22]*Op. cit.*, p. 359.
[23]Strachan, *op. cit.*, p. 326.

inhabiting both worlds (light and darkness or unbelief), and enabling men to enter the upper world. The Ascension is the final departure of Jesus from the ordinary human life of men to be with the Father. Henceforth He holds communion with His church by means of his *alter ego,* the Spirit."[24]

At Jesus' bidding **Mary Magdalene came** ("Away went Mary of Magdala," Moffatt) **and told the disciples that she had seen the Lord, and that he had spoken these things unto her** (18).

C. PERSONAL APPEARANCE TO THE TEN, 20:19-23

It was early morning (1) when Jesus talked with Mary, "the first day of the week"—Resurrection Day. On **the same day at evening** (19), **the disciples,** ten of them (24), were together in a room, maybe the room of the Last Supper (see map 2). **The doors were shut . . . for fear of the Jews** (19). "The Jewish leaders were doubtless suspicious of any gathering of the disciples of Jesus."[25] Into this setting **came Jesus and stood in the midst** (19). John does not discuss, nor need he, how Jesus came in with the doors all closed. He only notes the fact as he did in the instance of the orderly grave cloths. It might be observed at this point that the stone removed from the entrance to the tomb was for a witnessing evidence to Mary and the disciples, not for an exit for the risen Lord.

Jesus' word, on entering, was, **Peace be unto you,** a normal Hebrew greeting. Yet in this context (21, 26) and in the light of the promise in 14:27, it seems to be a reminder of "His peace as a parting gift to His disciples."[26] It is also a reminder, as Strachan says, that "this *peace* is not at war with all the hard facts of life, but peace won by struggle with and victory over a hostile world."[27]

As witnesses to the intensity of the struggle and the certainty of the victory **he shewed** (showed) **unto them his hands and his side** (20).[28] Having heard Jesus' greeting, and having seen the

[24]*Ibid.,* p. 328.
[25]Bernard, *op. cit.,* p. 672.
[26]Lightfoot, *op. cit.,* p. 335.
[27]*Op. cit.,* p. 329.
[28]It is only in Luke 24:39-40 that the nail-scarred feet are mentioned. The different accounts of the Crucifixion do not give the details of the manner of crucifixion, i.e., whether Jesus was tied by leather thongs or nailed to the Cross, though the wounds indicated here and in Luke clearly imply the nailing.

certain evidences of His resurrection, the **disciples were glad** ("filled with joy," Weymouth), **when they saw the Lord.**

In this appearance to the disciples the Lord came not only to give them assurance of peace (repeated in 21), but also a commission based on the authority of the relationship between Him and the Father. He said, **As my Father hath sent** (*apestalken*) **me, even so send** (*pempo*) **I you** (21). The first clause "is the constant theme of the Johannine Christ when speaking of his authority."[29] In what sense is Jesus here commissioning His disciples? It is instructive to note that the verbs **sent** and **send** are different words and tenses in the Greek. The first, *apestalken*, is perfect, and speaks of the mission of Christ in its enduring aspects. The second, *pempo*, is present, and so emphasizes the continuing activity assigned to the disciples. Westcott comments: "In this charge the Lord presents His own Mission as the one abiding Mission of the Father; this He fulfills through His church. His disciples receive no new commission, but carry out His."[30]

The commission for the disciples to carry on Jesus' work was matched by His assurance of empowerment for the task by the coming of the Spirit. **He breathed** (*enephysesen*) **on them, and saith unto them, Receive ye the Holy Ghost** (*pneuma hagion;* Holy Spirit, 22). The questions immediately arise: What is the relation between this giving of the Spirit and the Pentecostal outpouring? Do they both refer to the same advent of the Spirit? There have been many and various answers to these questions.[31] Hoskyns sees this giving of the Spirit to the disciples in the same light as other Resurrection scenes, i.e., "preparatory for the mission." The Pentecostal outpouring is related to "the mission in public in the power of the Spirit descending from Father and Son in heaven."[32] Westcott calls this (22) the "quickening" Spirit (cf. Gen. 1:7; Ezek. 37:9) and the Pentecostal advent, the "endowing" Spirit.

This bestowal of the Spirit (22) is not the same as that described in Acts 2:4. The first took place while Jesus was with

---

[29]Bernard, *op. cit.*, p. 676.

[30]*Op. cit.*, p. 298. This observation by Westcott is based on an exhaustive study of John's use of the two verbs.

[31]Hoskyns gives a good summary of different views (*op. cit.*, pp. 546-47).

[32]*Ibid.*

His disciples, the latter after His ascension into heaven. The former was a bestowal on disciples who were most certainly God's children (17:9), "an earnest," while the latter was "His manifest coming and permanent abiding in them by His representative, the Paraclete."[33] The former was not the fulfillment of Jesus' promises concerning the coming of the Comforter (7:39; 16:7), but it was a real impartation, an earnest of Pentecost.

The commission to the disciples—**so send I you (21)**—was also accompanied by specific authority concerning the forgiveness or retention of sins. **Whose soever sins ye remit** (forgive), **they are remitted** (forgiven) **unto them; and whose soever sins ye retain** (*kratete*), **they are retained** (23; cf. Matt. 16:19; 18:18). What is the nature of this authority and to whom is it given? There is no indication that it was limited to the ten disciples only. Robertson says: "What he commits to the disciples and to us is the power and privilege of giving assurance of the forgiveness of sins by God by correctly announcing the terms of forgiveness."[34] Strachan says that these words apply to "any disciple of Christ, every member of the Christian community who abides in closest communion with his Lord, who keeps his conscience pure and enlightened by knowledge of other Christian consciences and shares the faith and worship of the community."[35]

Under "The Risen Lord's Charge and Gift," 19-23, we may see (1) The Christian mission, 21; (2) The Christian equipment, 22; (3) The Christian power over sin, 23 (Alexander Maclaren).

D. PERSONAL APPEARANCE TO THE ELEVEN, 20:24-29

Only John records this episode that has to do with the faith—or lack of it—of Thomas. His other name, **Didymus,** means "the twin." John seems to have special interest in his fellow disciple (11:16; 14:5) who is shown to be a man of pessimistic temperament. The events of the last few days seemed to have confirmed Thomas' worst fears. **When Jesus came (19),** for some unknown reason **Thomas . . . was not with** the other disciples (24). He had made a big mistake. "He withdrew from

---

[33]Daniel Steele, *The Gospel of the Comforter* (Boston and Chicago: The Christian Witness Company, 1904), p. 155.

[34]*Op. cit.,* p. 315.

[35]*Op. cit.,* p. 329.

the Christian fellowship. He sought loneliness rather than to-getherness."[36]

When Thomas returned and heard the report of the ten, **We have seen the Lord** (25; cf. 18), his basic attitude toward life shut the door of faith. The fact of Jesus' death was real to him. It was a hard, indisputable fact. Before he could believe the report that Jesus was alive he would have to have evidence that would equal the fact of a cross and a tomb. So he laid down his own criteria for proof: **Except I shall see in his hands the print of the nails, and put my finger into the print of the nails, and thrust my hand into his side, I will not believe** (lit., "never at any time will I believe," 25). Evidently the ten had told of seeing the nail and spear wounds, but Thomas demanded the personal sense experiences of both sight and touch.

The opportunity came **eight days**—meaning "a week"—later. Again (cf. 19) the **disciples were within** ("in the room," NEB), and this time **Thomas** was **with them.** As before, the **doors were shut. Then came Jesus . . . and stood in the midst, and said, Peace be unto you** (26). Immediately Jesus directed His words to Thomas, repeating almost verbatim the demand that Thomas had made before the ten disciples. Then our Lord added the exhortation, **and be not** (*ginou,* lit., "Do not become") **faithless, but believing** (lit., "full of faith," 27). "He knows the very words in which we express our doubts."[37] Thomas must have been shocked to learn that his risen Lord had been present (14:23, 28), though not seen by him or the others at that specific time (cf. 2:25). There is no indication at all that Thomas applied the tests he had demanded. Rather, faith was activated, and Thomas exclaimed, **My Lord and my God** (28). "The keynote with which the Gospel opened (1:1) is struck again at its close: to the Christian believer Christ is none other than *God Himself.*"[38] Westcott says: "The words are beyond question addressed to Christ [and are] a confession as to His Person . . . The words which follow shew that the Lord accepted the declaration of His divinity as the true expression of faith."[39]

The response of Jesus to Thomas indicates that there are levels of faith in the Christian life. Some rely on visible evi-

[36]Barclay, *op. cit.*, p. 321.

[37]Macgregor, *op. cit.*, p. 362.

[38]*Ibid.*, p. 363.

[39]*Op. cit.*, p. 297.

dences, and are not able to realize the blessedness that comes to those who believe in Him for who He is rather than what He does for them. Those who rely on visible evidences alone live their Christian faith in a small world of spiritual values surrounded by the limitations of a temporal order. Those who believe in Christ for who He is have by faith expanded their horizons into a vast world of spiritual values where they enjoy the blessedness that belongs to those **that have not seen, and yet have believed (29).**

E. A DELAYED PREFACE, 20:30-31

Though there is a detailed comment on this passage in the Introduction, Section *D*, it is appropriate to give brief attention to it here. These verses are a declaration of the purpose of the writing of the book. In that sense, they serve the same function as the preface in a modern book.

However, there are some commentators, e.g., Hoskyns, who take the view that the **many other signs** (30) and **these** (31, signs) refer only to the post-Resurrection period. Others, e.g., Westcott, understand the phrases to refer to the whole of the book and then consider 30-31 to be the conclusion of the original writing.

It has also been suggested that 30-31 are misplaced and should appear after 21:23 instead of 24-25. But there is no textual evidence for such a dislocation. Further, words of similar style and location appear in I John 5:13, thus indicating that this style of outline may have been simply the way John thought and expressed himself.

F. PERSONAL APPEARANCE BY THE SEA OF TIBERIAS, 21:1-23

Most authorities hold that the last chapter of John is an appendix or epilogue. Some contend that it was not written by the same man who authored the first twenty chapters. Others see clear evidence, in both language and content, of identical authorship.

Among modern commentators Hoskyns represents a minority who contend that the chapter is an integral part of the Gospel and that it was written by the same author. He comments: "By means of two short scenes its readers are given complete confidence in the catholicity and power of the Church. The capture of 153 fishes, and the patient apostolic care of the sheep and the lambs, form the climax to the gospel, not the faith of Thomas."[40] Westcott, who considers it to be an epilogue but by the same author, says: "The manifestation of the Lord which is given in detail in it is designed to illustrate His action in Society."[41]

1. *The Disciples Go Fishing* (21:1-14)

Prior to His crucifixion Jesus had told His disciples that after He was risen He would go before them into Galilee (Matt. 26:32; Mark 14:28). Synoptic post-Resurrection scenes also refer to meeting the risen Lord there (Matt. 28:7, 10, 16; Mark 16:7). But it is John alone who details the scene at the **sea of Tiberias,**[42] where **Jesus shewed** (*ephanerosen,* lit., "made manifest, revealed") **himself again to the disciples** (1). This language indicates that "he was not visible *continuously* between His Resurrection and final Departure."[43] He revealed himself only as He willed in terms of the needs of His followers (see Chart C).

The scene is introduced by the expression, **and on this wise shewed he himself** (1), which literally translated is, "he revealed himself in this manner." **After these things** would be after the post-Resurrection appearances recorded in c. 20.

Seven of the disciples were together. First named is **Simon Peter** (cf. 1:40-41), indicating his place of leadership among the disciples. Four others are also named: **Thomas, Nathanael,** and **the** two **sons of Zebedee** (James and John) (2).[44] There were **two other of his disciples** but their names are not given.

In spite of the fact that these men had seen and talked with their risen Lord on two different occasions (Thomas only once), they were still as sheep without a shepherd. It was only natural for them to think in terms of their previous occupation. Peter, James, and John had been fishermen by trade. So Peter said, **I go a fishing** (3, lit., "I am going fishing"). He found ready acceptance of his proposal by the other six, who said, "We will go too" (Weymouth). Westcott suggests: "The disciples seemed to have continued their ordinary work, waiting calmly for the sign which should determine their future."[45]

[40]*Op. cit.,* p. 550.
[41]*Op. cit.,* p. 229.
[42]John is the only Gospel writer who uses this name for the Sea of Galilee (cf. 6:1).
[43]Bernard, *op. cit.,* p. 693.
[44]Only here is the name Zebedee mentioned in John.
[45]*Op. cit.,* p. 300.

They . . . entered into a ship[46] **immediately (3).**[47] The best
fishing was during the night hours. But even with the favorable
time **that night they caught nothing** (cf. 9:4; 11:10). If night
and darkness were the occasion of failure, a time when the real
work of life cannot be done, the antidote is to be found in the
coming of the light. It is not merely a matter of style that John
placed the coming of the light—**when the morning was now come**
—in immediate context with the coming of the "true Light" (1:9)
—**Jesus stood on the shore (4).** Jesus was not immediately
recognized. **The disciples knew not that it was Jesus** (cf. 20:14;
Luke 24:16, 31). Some have said that the lack of recognition
by the disciples was due to the distance from shore (about one
hundred yards, 8), the dim light of dawn, or a mist on the lake.
But none of these is needed in view of the fact that Jesus revealed himself only as He willed in keeping with the needs of His
followers. Bernard says: "The risen Lord was not recognizable,
unless He chose 'to manifest Himself.' "[48] Westcott suggests
that they were "preoccupied with their work . . . so that the
vision of the divine was obscured."[49]

Jesus initiated the conversation with a question. A literal
translation would be, "Boys, you have not had any catch, have
you?"[50] **They answered him, No (5).** At that Jesus gave the
unsuspecting disciples specific instructions. **Cast the net on the
right side of the ship** (boat), **and ye shall find (6).** Following
the suggestion (it was really a command) of the unrecognized
Stranger on the shore, **they cast . . . and now they were not able
to draw it for the multitude of fishes.** Some have held that the
great haul of fish was not miraculous. Bernard says: "The Sea of
Galilee still swarms with fish." Further, "This great catch is not
described as a *semeion* (sign, miracle), nor is it suggested that it
was miraculous."[51] However, Trench discusses it under the title
"The Second Miraculous Draught of Fishes"[52] (cf. Luke 5:5-11).

[46]The word here is *ploion*, which is used to describe "large sea-faring
ships," or a "*boat* of the small fishing vessels on Lake Gennesaret" (Arndt
and Gingrich, *op. cit.*, p. 679).

[47]The word **immediately** does not appear in the Greek text.

[48]*Op. cit.*, p. 695.

[49]*Op. cit.*, p. 300.

[50]The way in which the question is worded in the Greek indicates that
Jesus anticipated a negative answer.

[51]*Op. cit.*, p. 697.

[52]*Op. cit.*, pp. 480-504.

In view of the fact that the author of the Gospel, the Beloved Disciple, recalled this as the moment of recognition when he said, **It is the Lord** (7), he must have seen in the catch more than a good haul of fish.

In this episode John and Peter are seen in true character. It was John, keenly perceptive, "a spiritual genius,"[53] (cf. 20:8) who saw Jesus in the miracle. It was Peter, "an eager, impulsive, warm-hearted leader,"[54] who headed for the shore (cf. 18:10; 20:6). "He put on his clothes,[55] for he was stripped for work, and sprang into the sea" (7, RSV).

In a message on 21:1-7, Alexander Maclaren uses as a text and subject John's discovery and exclamation, **It is the Lord** (7): (1) They only see aright who see Christ in everything, 3-4; (2) Only those who love see Christ, 7; (3) They love who know that Christ loves them, 5-6.

Following Peter, **the other disciples came in a little ship** (skiff, dinghy) **dragging the net with fishes** (8). The larger boat (*ploion*) could not come in close to shore because of the shallow water, so the six men took to the skiff, which they used to bring the catch to the shore.

On the shore **they saw a fire of coals there, and fish laid thereon, and bread** (9). Jesus invited them, **Bring of the fish which ye have now caught** (10). Peter took the lead, waded to the skiff, and pulled **the net to land full of great fishes, an hundred and fifty and three** (11). The interpretations of this number (153) have been varied and numerous. Some examples are: three simple elements, 100 + 50 + 3, representing "the full-ness of the Gentiles," "the remnant of Israel," and "the Holy Trinity" respectively (Cyril of Alexandria); *ten* is the Law, *seven* is grace, therefore seventeen is the fullness of the divine revelation, and the numbers 1 through 17 added total 153, which "signifies all those who are included in the saving operation of divine grace (Augustine)."[56] Another interpretation frequently suggested is that the Greeks believed there were 153 kinds of fish.

[53]Bernard, *op. cit.*, p. 698.

[54]*Ibid.*

[55]The verb here is *diezosato*, which "signifies that Peter tucked the garment up into his girdle before he waded ashore in the shallow water" (*ibid.*).

[56]Westcott, *op. cit.*, pp. 306-7. There are several other ingenious but not likely theories described.

Hence, "the disciples make the perfect catch of fish,"[57] thus symbolizing the universality of the gospel. Most modern commentators take it simply as a factual record of the number of fish caught. Hoskyns comments: "There is no symbolical significance in the number itself: it is important as a number, and must have been recognized as such by educated Greeks, and therefore could be used, by transference, to symbolize a perfect and unique catch of fish."[58]

Even with this unusual catch, **yet was not the net broken.** It is quite clear that the whole episode is a portrayal of the Church at work in the gathering of men—men of all "kinds." The unbroken net, an item noted by the ex-fisherman John, says something to this figure. "The Church's resources, with Christ in its midst, are never over-strained."[59]

On the one hand, the scene is quite casual; e.g., in Jesus' question of 5, and here (12) when He said, "Come, eat breakfast" (lit. translation).[60] On the other hand, there was not that ease of communication which had characterized the questions and answers of cc. 13 and 14. **None of the disciples durst** (had the courage to) **ask him, Who art thou? knowing that it was the Lord** (12).

As had been His custom, Jesus presided at the meal. He took **bread,** gave it to **them, and fish likewise** (13). Though some have tried to find in this the Eucharistic meal, there is no good evidence that the author so intended (cf. 6:11). As if to emphasize the purpose of the whole event, John noted that this was **the third time that Jesus shewed** (revealed) **himself to his disciples, after that he was risen from the dead** (14). For a complete listing of our Lord's Resurrection appearances see Chart B.

2. *Jesus and Peter* (21:15-19)

As soon as breakfast was over, Jesus came to the second major concern of the morning. He addressed himself to Peter. **Simon, son of Jonas** (John), **lovest** (*agapas*) **thou me more than these?** Peter responded, **Yea, Lord; thou knowest that I love** (*philo*) **thee** (15). Two questions need to be considered. First, what was the comparison Jesus had in mind when He said **more**

---

[57]Hoskyns, *op. cit.,* p. 554.

[58]*Ibid.,* 556.

[59]Strachan, *op. cit.,* p. 336.

[60]The word *aristao* may mean "to eat breakfast" as well as "to dine."

than these? The language and syntax would admit three possible comparisons. (1) Do you love Me more than you love these disciples? (2) Do you love Me more than you love boats, nets, and catching fish? (3) Do you love Me more than these disciples love Me? (Cf. Mark 14:29; Luke 22:33; John 13:37.) It may well be that what seems to be an ambiguity is really intended to be an implication of full consecration. The Master intended to make clear a general exclusion of everything that would interfere with Peter's love for his Lord. It is abundantly true that the Christian's love for Jesus is to be exclusive, and it is the one response in which there has never been a known excess. In the last analysis, "the questioning has reference to one thing only, and that is Peter's *love* for Jesus . . . If he *loves* that is enough. That is the one essential condition of the apostolic office and ministry."[61] The second question posed here is discussed later (17). It is: What significant difference, if any, is there in the use of different words (*agapao* and *phileo*) for **love?**

It is instructive to note that Peter, even in his first response, was willing to submit his whole intention to the scrutiny of his Lord—**thou knowest.** "With the memory of his failure Peter cannot appeal to his own record, but he can to his Master's understanding."[62] Without any direct indication of either acceptance or rejection of Peter's answer, Jesus said, **Feed** (*boske*) **my lambs** (*arnia*) (15).

A second time Jesus asked the same question, only omitting the comparative **than these,** and using synonyms in the charge, **Feed** (*poimaine,* shepherd) **my sheep** (*probatia*) (16). Jesus put the question **the third time.** Most commentators agree that the three nearly identical questions were asked because Peter had denied in nearly identical fashion three times (18:17, 25-26). The barriers erected by personal denials of the Lord are not hastily broken down. While warming himself at a fire made by the enemies of Jesus, Peter three times denied his Lord. Now, around a fire kindled by his Lord, who loves him, Peter must three times affirm his love.

The third question and response took a slightly different form. **Simon, son of Jonas, lovest** (*phileis*) **thou me?** At this third questioning **Peter was grieved** ("deeply hurt," Phillips), and said, **Lord, thou knowest** (*oidas*) **all things; thou knowest** (*ginoskeis*) **that I love** (*philo*) **thee** (17). It was not only a

[61]Bernard, *op. cit.,* pp. 701-2.
[62]Macgregor, *op. cit.,* p. 373.

matter of divine intuition, absolute knowledge (*oidas*) about Peter; Jesus' knowledge was also based on personal, experiential acquaintance (*ginoskeis*) with him. Again the Lord said, **Feed** (*boske*) **my sheep** (*probatia*).

Most modern commentators hold that the two Greek verbs for "love" (*agapao* and *phileo*) are used synonymously by John, not only here, but also elsewhere in his Gospel.[63] However, Westcott contends that the shift in the use of the words[64] has significance. He comments: "So *Peter was grieved* not only that the question was put again, but that this *third time* the phrase was changed . . . so as to raise a doubt whether he could indeed rightly claim that modified love which he had professed."[65]

In this second part of the episode on the shore of the Sea of Galilee two things stand out clearly. The first is that love, pure love, is the only adequate basis for service—feed my sheep (cf. 13:8-9, 34). The second is that those who are commissioned (20:21) have a God-given command to be pastors of the flock, which is primarily feeding, giving watchful care to the sheep.

Jesus had something more to say to Peter. **When thou wast young, thou girdedst thyself, and walkedst whither thou wouldest: but when thou shalt be old, thou shalt stretch forth thy hands, and another shall gird thee, and carry thee whither thou wouldest not** (18). The end to moral irresponsibility had come for Peter. Hoskyns says: "The boisterous and irresponsible freedom of youth is now at an end. He can no longer act as he had just acted when he girded himself, and left the fish half caught, and swam alone to the shore."[66] The words, **Thou shalt stretch forth thy hands,** were "an unmistakable prediction of martyrdom by the cross."[67] Certainly John understood it to mean this. **This spake Jesus, signifying by what death he should glorify God** (19). According to Westcott "the crucifixion of St. Peter at Rome is attested by Tertullian and later writers. Origen further

---

[63]For an excellent analysis of this see Bernard, *op. cit.*, pp. 702-4.

[64]*Phileo* is taken to mean "the feeling of natural love" and *agapao* is the "loftier word" (*op. cit.*, p. 303). Charles B. Williams points up the essential difference between the two verbs in his translation of v. 16: "Jesus again said to him a second time, 'Simon, son of John, are you really devoted to me?' He said to Him, 'Yes, Lord, you know that I tenderly love you.'" (See also Weymouth.)

[65]*Ibid.*

[66]*Op. cit.*, pp. 556-57.

[67]Bernard, *op. cit.*, p. 709.

stated that he was crucified with his head downwards at his own request."[68] Before Jesus' crucifixion Peter had stoutly maintained his willingness to die for his Lord. But Jesus had declared Peter's inability to follow, and had predicted his denial (13:36-38). Now the test has been one of love—a threefold test (cf. 13:34-35). Apparently, ability to follow Jesus "all the way" is determined not only by one's willingness, but much more by the quality of one's love—perfect love. For now Jesus said to Peter, **Follow me** (19). The fact that this command is in the present tense in the Greek indicates action that is to be continued, habitual, customary. There are to be no more denials.

3. *Jesus and John* (21:20-23)

Commanded and committed to follow Jesus, **Peter, turning about, seeth the disciple whom Jesus loved following** (20). This **following** might be taken in two ways. John was following along with Jesus and Peter on the shore. But this seems unlikely, for there is no indication that they were going anywhere. More plausibly, in view of what has just gone before (18-19) Peter knew John to be one who was spiritually perceptive (cf. 20:8; 21:7), and who in the highest and truest sense was following Jesus.

In view of the fact that following Jesus would mean for Peter death by crucifixion (18), Peter's natural curiosity got the better of him. He asked, **Lord, and what shall this man do?** (21) Jesus answered, "If it is My wish [*thelo*] for him to stay [*menein*] until I come, is that your business, Peter? You must follow Me" (22, Phillips). To come to martyrdom as a follower of Jesus was Peter's destiny. But it is not martyrdom that is a man's glory. It is the doing of God's will—**if I will that he tarry** (23). So it is not a matter of how a follower dies. It is a matter of how he lives, how he fulfills God's will.

G. FINIS, 21:24-25

The conclusion of John's Gospel is an attestation of the authorship—**This is the disciple which testifieth of these things, and wrote these things** (24); it is also a certification of the veracity of the record—**We know that his testimony is true** (24). The first statement, according to conservative scholarship, refers

---

[68]*Op. cit.*, p. 304.

to John. The **we** of the second statement refers to the witness of the Christian community. Quimby says: "But of the truth of his book they were as sure as sunrise . . . Twenty centuries of Christian experience have substantiated this witness. Twenty centuries of Christian life, the *one* place where the truth of the Gospel can be proved, have confirmed it."[69]

The concluding statement is what Hoskyns calls "a most appropriate expression of literary insufficiency."[70] How true it is that the Living Word can never be fully expressed in written words! In this sense **the world itself could not contain the books that should be written (25)**.

[69]*Op. cit.*, p. 203.
[70]*Op. cit.*, p. 561.

Bibliography

I. COMMENTARIES

BARCLAY, WILLIAM. *The Gospel of John,* Vol. II. Second Edition. "The Daily Study Bible." Philadelphia: Westminster Press, 1956.

BARRETT, C. K. *The Gospel According to St. John.* New York: Macmillan Co., 1955.

BERNARD, J. H. *A Critical and Exegetical Commentary on the Gospel According to St. John.* Edited by A. H. McNEILE. Edinburgh: T. & T. Clark, 1928.

CLARKE, ADAM. *The New Testament of Our Lord and Saviour Jesus Christ,* Vol. I. New York: Abingdon Press, n.d.

DODD, C. H. *The Interpretation of the Fourth Gospel.* Cambridge: The University Press, 1954.

GOSSIP, ARTHUR JOHN. "The Gospel According to St. John" (Exposition). *The Interpreter's Bible.* Edited by GEORGE A. BUTTRICK, et al., Vol. VIII. New York: Abingdon-Cokesbury Press, 1952.

HENRY, CARL F. H. "John." *The Biblical Expositor.* Edited by CARL F. H. HENRY, Vol. III. Philadelphia: A. J. Holman Company, 1960.

HOSKYNS, EDWYN CLEMENT. *The Fourth Gospel.* Edited by FRANCIS NOEL DAVEY. London: Faber and Faber, Limited, 1947.

HOWARD, W. F. "The Gospel According to St. John" (Introduction and Exegesis). *The Interpreter's Bible.* Edited by GEORGE A. BUTTRICK, et al., Vol. VIII. New York: Abingdon-Cokesbury Press, 1952.

LIGHTFOOT, R. H. *St. John's Gospel, A Commentary.* Edited by C. F. EVANS. Oxford: At the Clarendon Press, 1957.

MACGREGOR, G. H. C. *The Gospel of John.* "The Moffatt New Testament Commentary." New York: Harper and Brothers Publishers, n.d.

PLUMMER, A. *The Gospel According to St. John.* "Cambridge Greek Testament." Edited by J. J. S. PEROWNE. Cambridge: University Press, 1882.

QUIMBY, CHESTER WARREN. *John, The Universal Gospel.* New York: The Macmillan Company, 1947.

ROBERTSON, A. T. *Word Pictures in the New Testament,* Vol. V. Nashville: Broadman Press, 1930.

STRACHAN, R. H. *The Fourth Gospel.* Third Edition. London: Student Christian Movement Press, 1941.

STRACK, H. L., and BILLERBECK, PAUL. *Kommentar zum N. T. aus Talmud und Midrasch,* Vol. II. Munich: C. H. Beck'sche Verlagsbuchhandlung, 1956.

TURNER, GEORGE A., and MANTEY, JULIUS R. *The Gospel According to John.* "The Evangelical Commentary." Grand Rapids: Wm. B. Eerdmans Publishing Co., 1964.

WESTCOTT, B. F. *The Gospel According to St. John.* London: John Murray, 1908.

II. OTHER BOOKS

ABBOTT-SMITH, G. *A Manual Greek Lexicon of the New Testament.* Third Edition. Edinburgh: T. & T. Clark, 1937.

ARNDT, WILLIAM F., and GINGRICH, F. WILBUR. *A Greek-English Lexicon of the New Testament and Other Early Christian Literature.* Chicago: University of Chicago Press, 1952.

BERDYAEV, NICHOLAS. *Freedom and the Spirit.* New York: Charles Scribner's Sons, 1935.

EARLE, RALPH. "The Gospel According to Matthew." *Beacon Bible Commentary.* Edited by A. F. HARPER, et al. Kansas City: Beacon Hill Press, 1964.

EDERSHEIM, ALFRED. *The Life and Times of Jesus the Messiah,* Vol. II. Grand Rapids: Wm. B. Eerdmans Publishing Company, 1943.

ELIOT, THOMAS STEARNS. *Murder in the Cathedral.* London: Faber and Faber, Ltd., 1935.

HEADLAM, ARTHUR C. *The Life and Teaching of Jesus the Christ.* New York: Oxford University Press, 1923.

HOWARD, W. F. *Christianity According to St. John.* Philadelphia: The Westminster Press, 1946.

JOSEPHUS, FLAVIUS. *Antiquities of the Jews.* Translated by WILLIAM WHISTON. Philadelphia: David McKay, n.d.

KELLY, THOMAS R. *A Testament of Devotion.* New York: Harper and Brothers, 1941.

KEMPIS, THOMAS A. *The Imitation of Christ.* Revised Translation. New York: Grosset and Dunlap, n.d.

LIDDELL AND SCOTT. *Greek-English Lexicon.* Abridged. Twenty-fifth Edition. Chicago: Follett Publishing Company, 1927.

MARSHALL, L. H. *The Challenge of New Testament Ethics.* London: Macmillan and Co., 1950.

PLATO. *The Dialogues of Plato,* Vol. I. Translated by B. JOWETT. New York: Random House, 1937.

STEELE, DANIEL. *The Gospel of the Comforter.* Boston and Chicago: The Christian Witness Company, 1904.

STUDDERT-KENNEDY, G. A. "The Gambler." *Christ in Poetry:* an anthology. Edited by THOMAS CURTIS CLARK and HAZEL DAVIS CLARK. New York: Association Press, 1952.

TRENCH, RICHARD CHENEVIX. *The Miracles of Our Lord.* New York: D. Appleton and Company, 1873.

————. *Synonyms of the New Testament.* New York: Redfield, 1857.

WEYMOUTH, RICHARD FRANCIS. *The New Testament in Modern Speech.* Revised by JAMES ALEXANDER ROBERTSON. Fifth Edition. Boston: The Pilgrim Press, 1943.

WILEY, H. ORTON. *The Epistle to the Hebrews.* Kansas City: Beacon Hill Press, 1959.

WRIGHT, GEORGE ERNEST, and FILSON, FLOYD VIVIAN. *The Westminster Historical Atlas of the Bible.* Philadelphia: The Westminster Press, 1946.

THE ACTS

of the

APOSTLES

Ralph Earle

Introduction

A. Importance

The Book of Acts holds a unique place in the New Testament. It forms a logical link between the Gospels and the Epistles. One would find it much more difficult to read the Epistles of Paul understandably without the background furnished in Acts. Two or three examples from I Thessalonians will illustrate the point. Paul says that he and his companion "were shamefully entreated, as ye know, at Philippi" (I Thess. 2:2). Acts 16:19-24 describes this shameful treatment. Again, Paul writes: "Wherefore when we could no longer forbear, we thought it good to be left at Athens alone; and sent Timotheus . . . to establish you" (I Thess. 3:1-2). Turning to Acts, we learn that Timothy joined the party at Lystra on Paul's second missionary journey (Acts 16:1-3). We also read in the seventeenth chapter how Paul was forced to leave Thessalonica and Berea because of Jewish persecution, and went to Athens. From there he sent Timothy back to Thessalonica. The Book of Acts thus gives us the historical framework for the Pauline Epistles (except the Pastorals). It is the first church history ever written, though covering a period of only about thirty years (A.D. 30-61 or 62).

B. Authorship

The universal voice of the Early Church declares that Acts was written by Luke. This is especially significant because Luke is mentioned only three times in the New Testament. It was common in the second and third centuries to attribute apocryphal Gospels, Acts, and Epistles to the various apostles, but not to obscure men. This alone is a strong argument for the Lukan authorship of Acts.

All three references to Luke are in the Pauline Epistles. In Philem. 24, Paul lists Luke among his "fellowlabourers." In Col. 4:14 he describes him as "Luke, the beloved physician." And in II Tim. 4:11 he writes, "Only Luke is with me." These scriptures show that Luke was a companion of Paul, that he was a physician, and that he alone was with the apostle in the closing years of Paul's life—probably as his attending physician.

The external evidence for Lukan authorship is adequate. Of the testimony of Irenaeus to Acts in the latter part of the second century, Grant writes: "He not only used it but also provided the classical proof that it was written by Luke: the detailed information given in the 'we-passages' (Acts 16:9-18; 20:5—21:18; 27:1—28:16) proves that it was written by a companion of Paul who went with him to Rome; this companion must have been Luke, in prison with Paul at Rome (Colossians 4:14) and later (II Timothy 4:11)."[1] The Muratorian Fragment (ca. A.D. 200) says:

> Moreover, the acts of all the apostles are written in one book. Luke [so] comprised them for the most excellent Theophilus, because the individual events took place in his presence—as he clearly shows [by] omitting the passion of Peter as well as the departure of Paul when the latter went from the city [of Rome] to Spain.[2]

The internal evidence, though not so definite, is strong. Its basic point is the one made by Irenaeus, as noted above. The we-passages prove that the author of Acts was a companion of Paul. There is almost universal agreement among New Testament scholars that these passages show such a unity of style and vocabulary with the rest of Acts as to indicate that the whole book was clearly written by the same individual. Of the companions of Paul mentioned prominently by him in his Epistles, only two are missing in Acts—Titus and Luke. When it comes to a choice between these two we can let the unanimous tradition of the Early Church settle the matter in favor of Luke.

One other piece of internal evidence needs to be mentioned. In 1882, Hobart published a book in which he affirmed that there is enough use of medical language in Luke's Gospel and Acts to prove that the author of these two works was a physician.[3] Harnack, the great German scholar, gave strong support to the thesis. After making a fresh investigation himself of the subject, he wrote: "The evidence is of overwhelming force; so that it seems to me that no doubt can exist *that the third gospel and the Acts of the Apostles were composed by a physician.*"[4] Zahn declared: "W. K. Hobart has proved to the satisfaction of anyone

[1]Robert M. Grant, *A Historical Introduction to the New Testament* (New York: Harper & Row, 1963), pp. 141-42.

[2]"Muratorian Canon," *The New Schaff-Herzog Encyclopedia of Religious Knowledge,* ed. Samuel M. Jackson, VIII (Grand Rapids: Baker Book House, 1950 [reprint]), 56.

[3]W. K. Hobart, *The Medical Language of St. Luke* (Grand Rapids: Baker Book House, 1954 [reprint]).

[4]Adolph Harnack, *Luke the Physician,* trans. J. R. Wilkinson (London: Williams & Norgate, 1907), p. 198.

open to conviction that the author of the Lucan work was familiar with the technical language of Greek medicine, and hence was a *Greek physician.*"⁵ Moffatt felt that Harnack's study "has proved this pretty conclusively."⁶ A. B. Bruce, writing on the Synoptic Gospels in *The Expositor's Greek Testament,* takes Hobart's position in his comments on Luke's Gospel.

In direct opposition to all this, Cadbury asserted that Hobart was wrong, that there is no evidence of a technical medical vocabulary in Luke and Acts. He wrote: "It is doubtful whether his [Luke's] interest in disease and healing exceeds that of his fellow evangelists or other contemporaries who were not doctors, while the words that he shares with the medical writers are found too widely in other kinds of Greek literature for us to suppose that they point to any professional vocabulary."⁷

With all the respect that the present writer has for the scholarship of his former professor at Harvard, he cannot agree with him in this sweeping assertion. Although Hobart went too far in his claims, there is an undeniable residium of evidence that the author of the third Gospel and Acts shows a physician's point of view. The writer would agree with Major when he says: "Nevertheless, there are passages in the Lucan writings, which although they cannot be said to prove, yet do support the hypothesis, that the author was a physician."⁸ In a similar vein, Wikenhauser, after noting that "the linguistic argument by itself" does not prove that "only a physician could have composed the two books," yet goes on to say: "Nevertheless the tradition need not be abandoned, and it may still be sustained, for the author displays familiarity with medical terminology."⁹

C. Place of Writing

There is a tradition that Luke wrote the Book of Acts in Achaia (i.e., Greece).¹⁰ But it seems better to assume that he wrote it in Rome, where he ends the story (Acts 28:16-31).

⁵Theodor Zahn, *Introduction to the New Testament,* trans. John Trout, *et al.* (Grand Rapids: Kregal Publications, 1953 [reprint]), III, 146.

⁶James Moffatt, *An Introduction to the Literature of the New Testament* (3rd ed.; New York: Charles Scribner's Sons, 1918), p. 298.

⁷Henry J. Cadbury, *The Making of Luke-Acts* (New York: Macmillan Co., 1927), p. 358.

⁸H. D. A. Major, T. W. Manson, and C. J. Wright, *The Mission and Message of Jesus* (New York: E. P. Dutton & Co., 1938), p. 253.

⁹Alfred Wikenhauser, *New Testament Introduction,* trans. Joseph Cunningham (New York: Herder & Herder, 1958), p. 209.

¹⁰*Ibid.,* p. 342.

D. DATE

In the nineteenth century many scholars claimed that Acts was written in the middle of the second century. John Knox has propounded that view in recent years.[11] But he has few supporters. Moffatt holds to a date around 100.[12] More popular is the view of Goodspeed[13] and Scott[14] that Acts was written about A.D. 90. Both these men hold to the Lukan authorship. Zahn thought that A.D. 75 was the best date.[15]

On the other hand, Harnack argued strongly for a date before A.D. 70, "perhaps even so early as the beginning of the seventh decade of the first century"[16] (i.e., soon after A.D. 60). Torrey thinks that the third Gospel was written about A.D. 60, and Acts soon after.[17] It seems reasonable to hold that Luke wrote his Gospel during Paul's two years' imprisonment at Caesarea—or at least gathered his materials for it at that time—and that he composed the Book of Acts while Paul was spending two years in prison at Rome. That is the most natural deduction to be drawn from the fact that the story ends at that point. This would place the date of the book at about A.D. 62.

E. PURPOSE

The Tuebingen school of critics in Germany in the latter part of the nineteenth century held that the purpose of Acts was to reconcile the Pauline and Petrine parties in the Church, which were at swords' points with each other. But this "tendential" theory has been largely abandoned in the light of later research. In fact, Henshaw goes so far as to say: "Investigation has now completely refuted the theory."[18]

It is generally held by scholars today that the preface to the

[11]John Knox, *Marcion and the New Testament* (Chicago: University of Chicago Press, 1942), p. 121.

[12]*Op. cit.*, p. 312.

[13]Edgar J. Goodspeed, *An Introduction to the New Testament* (Chicago: University of Chicago Press, 1937), p. 196.

[14]E. F. Scott, *The Literature of the New Testament* (New York: Columbia University Press, 1936), p. 94.

[15]*Op. cit.*, III, 159.

[16]Adolph Harnack, *The Acts of the Apostles*, trans. J. R. Wilkinson (New York: G. P. Putnam's Sons, 1909), p. 297. Cf. also Harnack's *The Date of the Synoptic Gospels*, trans. J. R. Wilkinson (New York: G. P. Putnam's Sons, 1911), p. 99.

[17]C. C. Torrey, *The Composition and Date of Acts* (Cambridge: Harvard University Press, 1916), p. 68.

[18]T. Henshaw, *New Testament Literature* (London: George Allen and Unwin, 1952), p. 185.

Gospel of Luke (1:1-4) applies also to Acts. If so the primary purpose, as stated there, was that Theophilus might "know the certainty of those things, wherein thou hast been instructed." A reading of the book itself seems clearly to support Clogg's assertion that Luke's aim was to show: " (1) the power possessed by the Apostles through the Holy Spirit . . . (2) the gradual expansion of the Church partly in numbers, through this power of the Apostles, partly in geographical extent."[19]

Kirsopp and Silva Lake suggest a threefold purpose, which perhaps forms a more adequate statement of the case. They state that among the motives for writing the book were:

> a. A desire to prove the supernatural inspiration and guidance given to the Church on the day of Pentecost . . . b. A desire to show that the best Roman magistrates never decided against the Christians . . . c. A more purely historical desire to show how the Church ceased to be Jewish and became Greek, because the Jews rejected and the Greeks accepted the message of salvation.[20]

F. Text

A word needs to be said about the text of Acts. It has peculiar features not found in any other book of the New Testament.

Four types of text of the New Testament are generally distinguished by scholars. The first is the Byzantine Text found in the bulk of the late manuscripts. This was the basis of the so-called *Textus Receptus* (Received Text) which the King James translators used. There is almost universal agreement that this is the poorest Greek text.

The best text is what Westcott and Hort called the Neutral (unedited) Text. This question-begging name has been largely abandoned now in favor of the more accurate designation, Alexandrian Text. In general, this is what is found in the two great fourth-century manuscripts, Vaticanus and Sinaiticus. Only papyrus manuscripts of parts of the New Testament are older than these two. Modern translators use this text based on the oldest manuscripts.

The third text is known as the Western Text. It is found in Codex Bezae (designated as *D*), from the fifty century, and also in the Old Latin version of North Africa.

[19]F. B. Clogg, *An Introduction to the New Testament* (New York: Charles Scribner's Sons, 1937), p. 247.

[20]Kirsopp Lake and Silva Lake, *An Introduction to the New Testament* (New York: Harper & Brothers, 1937), p. 66.

The fourth family, more recently isolated by scholars, is called the Caesarean Text. But that is not particularly significant for the study of Acts.

In Acts the Western Text is characterized by longer readings not found in the Alexandrian Text. The great problem facing textual scholars is the question as to which, if any, of these Western readings may be genuine. Some of them probably represent authentic traditions. But it seems doubtful if any actually belong to the original text. A full comparison of the texts of Acts in Vaticanus and Bezae, with copious notes, will be found in Vol. III of *Beginnings of Christianity*.

Philip preached. This is *kerysso*, "herald" or "proclaim," not *euangelizo* (cf. 4). To the Samaritans he "was proclaiming" (imperfect of continuous action) **Christ**—literally, the Christ; that is, "the Messiah." The Samaritans, along with the Jews, were looking for the Messiah to come (John 4:25).

Philip's hearers **gave heed** (6) to his preaching. They were hearing the words he said and **seeing the miracles** (lit., "signs") which he performed. The working of miracles played an important role in the ministry of Jesus and in the early evangelization of Jews and Samaritans. Paul declared: "For the Jews require a sign, and the Greeks seek after wisdom" (I Cor. 1:22). As the preaching of the gospel reached out into the Gentile world, the working of miracles assumed less importance.

These "signs" consisted mainly of casting out **unclean spirits** (demons) and healing the afflicted (7). **Many taken with palsies, and that were lame** is in the Greek simply "many paralyzed and lame ones" (cf. Phillips).

The result of this manifestation of divine power was **great joy in that city** (8). When God comes in blessing, rejoicing always follows.

3. *Philip and Simon* (8:9-13)

But (9) there was a sad contrast to this almost universal joy. **A certain man, called Simon, had bewitched the people with his sorcery** (magic). He claimed to be **some great one.** The inhabitants of the city, **from the least to the greatest** (10), were taken in by this charlatan, so that they were saying: **This man is the great power of God.** The Greek says: "This one is the power of God which is called Great" (cf. ASV). The rabbis sometimes referred to God as "the Power." There has been much discussion as to whether all this reflects a pagan point of view or a Hebrew background. Since the Samaritans were a mixed race, it may well be that they had mixed theological concepts and that the answer to the debate is "both."

To this false magician the people **had regard** (11). The Greek says "gave heed"—exactly the same form as in 6 and 10. For a long time Simon had **bewitched them with sorceries**—literally, "amazed them with his magical arts."

But now **they believed Philip** (12). He was **preaching** (*evangelizing*) **concerning the kingdom of God**—as John the Baptist and Jesus had done. Philip was now also preaching in

351

the name of Jesus Christ. Salvation was only through the name of **Jesus,** the "Saviour" (cf. 4:12).

Those who believed **were baptized.** This showed that they no longer depended on faithful adherence to the Law as the means of salvation, but that they put their trust in Christ alone. The believers consisted of **both men and women.**

Amazingly, even **Simon himself believed** (13). Inevitably the question arises as to whether this was genuine faith in Jesus Christ or merely mental assent to the truths of Christianity. In favor of genuine faith is the fact that the same word is used as in 12. Certainly Simon gave all the outward appearance of being a true believer, for he was baptized. Evidently Philip accepted his conversion as sincere. Furthermore, **he continued with Philip.** The verb is a strong one, meaning "to attend constantly, continue stedfastly."[10] **Beholding the miracles and signs**—literally, "signs and powers"—which were being done, he **wondered,** or "was amazed."

On the nature of Simon's conversion Meyer has this to say: "He was, by the preaching and miracles of Philip, actually moved to faith in Jesus as the Messiah. Yet this faith of his was only historical and intellectual, without having as its result a change of the inner life."[11]

4. *Samaritan Pentecost* (8:14-17)

When the apostles . . . at Jerusalem (14) heard about what had taken place in **Samaria,** they dispatched **Peter and John** to look into the situation. These two men had been closely associated in some of the earlier activities described in Acts (cc. 3—4). But John is not mentioned again in the book.

When the two apostles arrived, they **prayed** for the Samaritans **that they might receive the Holy Ghost** (15). It is clear that these new converts, though definitely saved through believing in Jesus Christ and already baptized (12), had not been filled with the Holy Spirit. There must come to them the same experience which had come to the 120 in the Upper Room on the Day of Pentecost.

This fact that, though converted and baptized with water, the Samaritans had not yet been baptized with the Holy Spirit

[10]Abbott-Smith, *op. cit.*, p. 385.
[11]*Op. cit.*, p. 169.

(cf. Matt. 3:11) is further underscored in parentheses. Luke explains why the apostles prayed thus: **For as yet he was fallen upon none of them: only they were baptized in the name of the Lord Jesus (16).** The Greek suggests that they were continuing (imperfect tense) in a state of having been baptized with water (perfect participle). They had not yet experienced their personal Pentecost. Here is certainly reflected clearly Luke's understanding that the gift of the Holy Spirit is an experience subsequent to conversion.

Peter and John laid . . . their hands on them, and they received the Holy Ghost (17). Many scholars have maintained that the reference is not to the reception of the Holy Spirit himself, but rather to the bestowal of miraculous gifts of the Spirit. But this is not what the narrative says. It declares clearly: **they received the Holy Ghost.** That there were some outward manifestations connected with this seems implied by the statement in the following verse that Simon was aware of what had taken place. There is no mention in the narrative, however, of speaking in tongues.

Knowling objects to the interpretation of **Holy Ghost** here as meaning special gifts of the Spirit. He says: "In a book so marked by the working of the Holy Spirit . . . it is difficult to believe that St. Luke can mean to limit the expression *lambanein* [receive] here . . . to anything less than a bestowal of that divine indwelling of the Spirit which makes the Christian the temple of God."[12]

This passage in Acts is very significant. The Samaritans were converted to Christ through the preaching of Philip and at a later time filled with the Holy Spirit under the ministry of Peter and John. For them, unquestionably, the receiving of the Spirit was subsequent to conversion.

It might be asked why Philip, who was himself filled with the Spirit (cf. 6:3, 5), could not consummate this work without the coming of Peter and John. The answer to this is probably that it was necessary to establish the unity of the Church of Jesus Christ at the beginning by this act of apostolic authority. There were not to be separate movements springing up here and there, but one united Church founded by the men whom Jesus commissioned for this task.

[12]EGT, II, 216.

5. *Simon and Simony* (8:18-24)

Simony—a word derived from this incident—means the buying or selling of ecclesiastical office or authority. **When Simon saw** that the Holy Spirit was given **through the laying on of the apostles' hands,** he **offered them money** (18) if they would share with him this power to bestow the Spirit (19). This was better magic than anything he possessed! He wanted to retain his hold on the people.

In reply Peter said to Simon: **Thy money perish with thee** (20). This could be interpreted as a prayer that his money, which was threatening to bring him to destruction, might perish. Knowling says: "The words are no curse or imprecation, as is evident from verse 22, but rather a vehement expression of horror on the part of St. Peter, an expression which would warn Simon that he was on the way to destruction."[13] After noting other interpretations, Alexander concludes: "The true solution seems to be, that Peter spoke by direct divine authority, and also that the wish is to be qualified by the exhortation in v. 22."[14] He adds: "The sin and folly of the sorcerer's offer lay not merely in the thought of bribing God, but in that of purchasing what, from its very nature, could be only a free gift."[15]

Peter went on to assert: **Thou hast neither part nor lot in this matter** (21). **Part** indicates a share or portion. **Lot** means what is obtained by casting lots; that is, an assigned part. The Greek word for **matter** is *logos*, which literally means "word." Hackett prefers that translation here and explains it as meaning: "doctrine or gospel, which we preach."[16] This is the sense conveyed in the Peshitta Syriac version (5th cent.), which has "in this faith." But *logos* can mean "that which is spoken of," and so "matter, affair, thing."[17]

Peter also declared: **Thy heart is not right**—literally, "straight," and so in a moral sense "straightforward"[18]—**in the sight of God.** This shows that if Simon had experienced a true conversion, which seems to be implied in 13, his love of money

---

[13]*Ibid.,* p. 218.
[14]*Op. cit.,* p. 334.
[15]*Ibid.*
[16]*Op. cit.,* p. 111.
[17]Abbott-Smith, *op. cit.,* p. 271.
[18]*Ibid.,* p. 186.

had by now caused him to backslide. He was no longer sincere, and no man can be saved without being sincere.

But it was not too late for Simon to be forgiven. Peter admonished him to **repent** of his **wickedness, and pray**—"beg, request, beseech"[19]—**God**,[20] **if perhaps the thought of thine heart may be forgiven thee** (22). **If perhaps** might seem to suggest an uncertainty as to whether Simon could be forgiven. But the Greek says literally "if therefore"; that is, as a result of your repenting. The only uncertainty—and it was a very real one— was whether Simon would repent. Apparently he did not. Gloag puts it well: "Peter here . . . expresses no doubts of God's forgiveness, no limitation of His mercy; but the doubt refers to Simon's repentance."[21]

The Greek for **thought** (only here in NT) comes from the verb meaning "to continue." So it means a conscious "plan" or "project,"[22] a "plot."[23]

Peter went on to describe Simon as being **in**—literally, "into" (*eis*)—**the gall of bitterness, and . . . the bond of iniquity** (23). Bruce writes: "In the papyri *eis* used thus after *einai* expresses destination."[24] It suggests that Simon had fallen into this state. Meyer paraphrases the passage thus: "I recognize thee as a man who has fallen into bitter enmity against the gospel as into gall, and into iniquity as into binding fetters."[25] Gloag says: "Gall here signifies 'poison,' as, according to the opinion of the ancients, the poison of serpents resided in their gall."[26]

Simon's reaction to Peter's warning gives no evidence of true repentance. He was not concerned with his sin, but only with its consequences. Peter had bade him pray the Lord to forgive him (22). Now Simon asks the apostles to **pray** (same word as in 22) that none of the things mentioned by Peter **come upon** him (24). There was no godly sorrow for sin, but only a fear for his own safety.

[19]*Ibid.*, p. 101.
[20]The best Greek text has "the Lord."
[21]*Op. cit.*, p. 292.
[22]Meyer, *op. cit.*, p. 172.
[23]*Beginnings*, IV, 94.
[24]*Acts*, p. 188.
[25]*Op. cit.*, p. 172.
[26]*Op. cit.*, p. 293.

In Simon we see (8:8-13, 18-24) "An Unacceptable Candidate for the Baptism with the Holy Ghost." (1) Simon was rejected because he had a wrong conception of the price to be paid, 18, 20; (2) He had a wrong motive in seeking for the Holy Ghost, 19; (3) His heart was not right in the sight of God, 21-23. (G. B. Williamson).

6. *Samaria Evangelized* (8:25)

This verse seems to constitute a transitional paragraph between what precedes and what follows. **They**—probably just Peter and John—**when they had testified** (thoroughly witnessed) **and preached** (the Gk. says simply "spoken") **the word of the Lord, returned to Jerusalem.** The last part of this verse has two imperfects, so that literally it reads: "they were returning to Jerusalem and were evangelizing many villages of the Samaritans." This suggests a continuous campaign of evangelism during a protracted return journey.

Peter's fellow evangelist was the same John who had once desired to call down fire from heaven to destroy a Samaritan village (Luke 9:52-56). Jesus had rebuked him for having the wrong spirit. But now, after Pentecost, he had the Spirit of Christ. Gloag wisely observes: "It was a different kind of fire which he now prayed might descend from heaven upon the Samaritans—the fire of the Holy Ghost."[27]

B. Witnessing to the Ethiopian Eunuch, 8:26-40

Philip was a Spirit-filled, Spirit-led, versatile evangelist. He could preach to the great crowds in "a city-wide revival." But he could also do personal work with a single individual out on a desert road. Eternity may reveal that the second of these activities was just as fruitful in its ultimate consequences as the first. The essential lesson to be learned is that when the Holy Spirit prompts us to some ministry to others He empowers us to carry out the commission. Where God guides, God provides. Another lesson is that in the eyes of the Lord no Spirit-directed task is small. Only divine omniscience can foresee the results of a few moments of witnessing to one whose heart the Holy Spirit has prepared to receive that witness.

[27]*Op. cit.,* p. 297.

1. A Seeking Pilgrim (8:26-31)

In the midst of Philip's activities in the Samaritan city, with many converts to care for, **the angel**—literally, "an angel"—**of the Lord** called him to a new task. The context suggests that this is another way of saying that the Spirit led him (cf. 29, 39). The command was: **Arise**—aorist tense of immediate action—**and go**—imperfect tense of continuous action, "be going"—**toward the south** (26). In the only other place in the New Testament where the Greek word for **south** occurs it is translated "noon" (22:6). Some scholars favor that rendering here. But "southward" seems to be the correct meaning of the phrase.

Philip was to go **unto the way that goeth down from Jerusalem unto Gaza, which is desert. Gaza** was about sixty miles southwest of Jerusalem. It was the southernmost city of Palestine, almost on the border of Egypt (see map 1). In Old Testament times it was one of the five cities of the Philistines. **Which is desert** may refer to **way**; that is, "Take the desert road," rather than another route. This is the opinion of Schuerer[28] and Gloag.[29] But Lake and Cadbury would apply the phrase to the city. The old Gaza, which was situated about two and a half miles from the Mediterranean, had been destroyed by Alexander the Great (332 B.C.) and was still deserted. It might well be called Desert Gaza. The new Hellenistic Gaza was on the coast.[30] Bruce accepts this interpretation.[31] In either case, the assignment involved several days' journey. It was perhaps thirty-five miles from Samaria to Jerusalem and sixty miles farther to Gaza.

Philip **arose and went** (27). Both verbs are in the aorist tense and suggest prompt obedience. Because he went at once, he met his man. Had he delayed for any reason, he would have missed his divinely made appointment with the eunuch.

Following divine directions, Philip saw **a man of Ethiopia,** who **had come for to worship,** or "on a pilgrimage," and was now returning home. **Ethiopia** was the name of a kingdom on the Nile, between modern Aswan and Khartoum. Most recent scholars feel that the reference here is not to Abyssinia, commonly known today as Ethiopia. However, the *Westminster Dictionary*

[28]*Op. cit.*, II, i, 71.
[29]*Op. cit.*, pp. 300-302.
[30]*Beginnings*, IV, 95.
[31]*Acts*, p. 190.

of the Bible asserts that the prophecy of Ps. 68:31—"Ethiopia shall soon stretch out her hands unto God"—"was fulfilled in the conversion of the Ethiopian eunuch (Acts 8:26-40) and the introduction of the gospel into Abyssinia."[32]

The traveler whom Philip met was **an eunuch**[33] **of great authority under Candace queen of the Ethiopians.** The Mosaic law barred a eunuch from being a member of the congregation of the Lord (Deut. 23:1). But the prohibition seems to have been lifted at a later time (Isa. 56:3-5). **Of great authority** is *dynastes*, meaning "prince." **Candace** was a title, like Pharaoh. Lake and Cadbury note: "The title was given to the queen mother, who was the real head of the government.[34] The eunuch had **charge of all her treasure.** He was thus a man of high office and great responsibility.

As befitted a man of his position, the eunuch was provided with the best means of transportation in that day. He was **sitting in his chariot,** and was reading the prophet Isaiah (28). Handwritten scrolls were rare and expensive, but he was a wealthy man and so could possess one. According to the custom of the times, he was reading aloud, for Philip **heard him** reading (30). The rabbis held that the Law should be read aloud by one who was traveling.[35]

In obedience to the inner voice of the Spirit (29), Philip **ran** (30) to catch up with the chariot. Hearing the eunuch reading from the scroll of Isaiah, he asked the question: **Understandest thou what thou readest?**—a very pertinent question at any time. **Understandest** is literally, "Do you know?" **Thou readest** is literally, "You know again." There is a play on words in the Greek which cannot be brought over into English. The same two verbs occur together in II Cor. 3:2—"known and read of all men."

The reply of the Ethiopian eunuch was almost pathetic: **How can I, except some man should guide me? (31) Guide** is the same verb used by Jesus in John 16:13—"Howbeit when he, the Spirit of truth, is come, he will guide you into all truth." Philip, Spirit-filled, was able to give guidance in the Scriptures.

---

[32]WDB, p. 173.
[33]For the meaning of **eunuch,** see comments on Matt. 19:12.
[34]*Beginnings,* IV, 96.
[35]*Ibid.*

Eager to learn the true meaning of the prophetic passage, the eunuch **desired** Philip to join him in the chariot. The verb **desired** (*parakaleo*) is a strong one, meaning "call for" or "entreat."[36]

2. *A Strange Prophecy* (8:32-33)

The place of the scripture (32) is better translated "the passage of Scripture." **Place** (*perioche,* only here in NT) is the word used by the Church Fathers for a Scripture lesson to be read in public. It literally means "a portion circumscribed, a section."[37]

The quotation in 32-33 is taken almost verbatim from the Septuagint of Isa. 53:7-8. It is a part of one of the "Servant Songs" of Isaiah, found in an outstanding Messianic chapter of the Old Testament. **So opened he not his mouth** was fulfilled when Jesus "answered nothing" as He was falsely accused before Pilate (Matt. 27:12). The difficult clause **his judgment was taken away** probably means "justice was denied him" (RSV). Gloag thus interprets it: "His judgment—the judgment due to Him—His rights of justice—were withheld by His enemies."[38]

The next clause, **who shall declare his generation?** has caused even more difficulty. Gloag thinks it means: Who shall "set forth the wickedness of His contemporaries?"[39] But Meyer says that, while he formerly held that view,[40] he finally chose this interpretation: "How indescribably great is the multitude of those belonging to Him."[41] The final clause, **for his life is taken from the earth,** admittedly seems to fit better with the first of these explanations than the second.

3. *A Spirit-filled Preacher* (8:34-40)

The question that concerned the Ethiopian eunuch was: **Of whom speaketh the prophet this? of himself, or of some other man?** (34) Lumby writes: "Some of the Jews interpreted this passage of a suffering prophet, but most generally it was applied

[36]Abbott-Smith, *op. cit.,* p. 340.
[37]*Ibid.,* p. 356.
[38]*Op. cit.,* p. 306.
[39]*Ibid.* So Lumby, *op. cit.,* p. 186.
[40]*Op. cit.,* p. 177.
[41]*Ibid.,* p. 176.

to the suffering nation."[42] The eunuch seemed to sense that the application should be made to an individual. But to whom?

Philip was equal to the demands of the situation. He **opened his mouth, and began at the same scripture, and preached unto him Jesus** (35). This was the answer. The Suffering Servant of the Lord, of whom Isaiah spoke, was none other than Jesus, God's chosen Messiah.

Doubtless the chariot covered considerable ground while Philip was expounding the passage in Isaiah and exposing Jesus in it. Finally **they came unto a certain water** (36), and the eunuch requested baptism. Perhaps Philip had echoed Peter's words on the Day of Pentecost: "Repent, and be baptized . . . in the name of Jesus Christ for the remission of sins" (2:38).

Verse 37 is sound New Testament theology, but it is omitted from the revised versions because it is not in the oldest and best Greek manuscripts. It may represent an authentic tradition, but it gives every appearance of being a marginal gloss, added by some scribe to furnish an answer to the question of 36 and finally finding its way into the text.

The eunuch ordered his charioteer to stop (38), while he and Philip **went down** into the pool or brook. Running water was considered preferable for Christian baptism in the Early Church (*Didache* 7:1).

When the two men came up out of the water, **the Spirit of the Lord caught away Philip** (39). He disappeared from sight. **The eunuch . . . went on his way rejoicing,** as do all who find Christ as Saviour. This is in striking contrast to the rich young ruler, who "went away sorrowful" (Matt. 19:22).

Philip was found—that is, appeared—**at Azotus** (40). This is the Old Testament Ashdod, one of the five cities of the Philistines. It was situated about twenty miles north of Gaza, about halfway between that city and Joppa (see map 1). On his way northward up the coast, Philip **preached in all the cities** —literally, "was evangelizing all the cities." These would include Lydda and Joppa, where believers are mentioned soon after this (9:32-42). Philip evangelized the coastal cities as far north as **Caesarea,** where we find him the next time he appears in Acts (21:8). This city was built by Herod the Great and named Caesarea Sebaste, after the Emperor Augustus of Rome. Com-

---

[42]*Op. cit.,* p. 187.

pleted about 13 B.C., it was the seat of Roman government in Judea in the days of Jesus.

This chapter might be used to emphasize the importance of "Two Kinds of Evangelism": (1) Mass evangelism, 4-25; (2) Personal evangelism, 26-40. Under the first could be pointed out: (*a*) The *method* is preaching, 5: (*b*) The *message* is Christ, 5: (*c*) The *motive* is to get people both saved and sanctified, 12-17. Under personal evangelism attention could be called to: (*a*) The importance of prompt obedience, 27 (see comments); (*b*) The opportunity provided, 27-29; (*c*) The place of prophetic scripture, 30-32; (*d*) The interpretation of the passage, 34-35; (*e*) The application to personal need, 36-39.

C. WITNESS CONVERTED, 9:1-31

Without question the most important event in the Book of Acts was the coming of the Holy Spirit on the Day of Pentecost. If this had not happened, the book would never have been written. Some have maintained that it was the Resurrection which transformed cowardly disciples into courageous witnesses. But there is not any evidence for this in the New Testament. What the sacred account does clearly show is that it was Pentecost which made the difference.

In some ways it would seem that the second most important event in the Book of Acts was the conversion of Paul. More than half the book (cc. 13—28) deals mainly with his activities. He wrote thirteen of the twenty-seven books of the New Testament. One can hardly imagine what first-century Christianity would have been like had Saul not been converted. He became the most effective witness of the Early Church.

1. *Saul Saved* (9:1-9)

Up to this point Saul has been mentioned only briefly. He was present at the stoning of Stephen (7:58) and gave his approval to that awful act (8:1), then spearheaded the persecution of the Church at Jerusalem (8:3).

Now comes the story of Saul's conversion, which takes up most of chapter 9. The importance of this event is evidenced by the fact that it is related at some length again in chapters 22 and 26. It is the only event which is thus described three times in Acts.

Saul was still **breathing out threatenings and slaughter against the disciples of the Lord** (1). The Greek says "breathing in." The phrase is probably best translated as simply "breathing." The very breath of Saul's life was hot with anger against the believers.

Intent on pursuing the fugitives from the Jerusalem persecution, Saul went to **the high priest**—Caiaphas, who held that office A.D. 18-36—and asked for **letters** (*epistolas*) to the **synagogues** of **Damascus** (2). If he found there **any of this way**—literally, "the Way," one of the earnest names for Christianity —he wanted to **bring them bound unto Jerusalem**. The Roman government had given the high priest authority to require the return of Jews who had broken the Law, so that they could be tried by the Sanhedrin (I Maccabees 15:15-17).

Damascus is one of the most ancient cities in the world still standing today. Situated about seventy miles from the Mediterranean, over the Lebanon and Anti-Lebanon Mountains, it is an oasis on the edge of the desert. The main caravan route from Egypt to Mesopotamia passed through it, so that it was always a busy trading center. Many thousands of Jews lived there at this period. A strict Jewish sect, called the "Covenanters of Damascus," is described in the Zadokite Fragment. Many scholars today connect this group with the Qumran Community made famous by the Dead Sea Scrolls.

It was a long way from Jerusalem to Damascus, some two hundred miles northward by way of the Sea of Galilee or eastward via Philadelphia (modern Amman, see map 1). Walking this distance would take at least a full six days between Sabbaths. Saul had plenty of time to think. He may well have remembered the stoning of Stephen, whose face shone like that of an angel (6:15). Could it possibly be that Stephen was right? No; away with the thought! On to Damascus! This new heresy that was threatening the true religion must be rooted out before it spread any further. Those **of this way** (lit., "of the Way") must be imprisoned.

But God had other plans for Saul. As he neared Damascus, something happened: **suddenly there shined round about him a light from heaven** (3). This symbolized the spiritual revelation which was to break in upon the soul of the proud young Pharisee. As if struck by lightning, he **fell to the earth** (4). Probably he had been walking, not riding a horse. The strict Jews were averse to riding horseback, a mode of travel which was popular with the Romans.

Smitten to the ground, Saul heard his name called: **Saul,**

Saul, why persecutest thou me? Astonished at the accusation,
he demanded: Who art thou, Lord? (5) Bruce says of Lord:
" 'Sir', 'my lord'; a title of respect, as Saul did not yet know who
was speaking to him."[43] The voice answered: I am Jesus whom
thou persecutest.[44] When Paul punished the Church, he was
persecuting the Head of the Church, Jesus Christ himself. This
is a solemn warning not only to outsiders who might attack the
church, but also to church members if they deliberately hurt a
fellow church member. In doing so, they are hurting Christ.

Saul was instructed: Arise, and go into the city, and it shall
be told thee what thou must do (6). New light would come as
he obeyed the divine command.

His companions stood speechless (7). This does not conflict with Paul's statement in 26:14 that they "all" fell "to the
earth." It would not take long for the other men to get to their
feet again. Or stood may primarily mean "stopped." Gloag
thinks the best solution is that stood speechless "does not refer
to posture at all, but merely intimates that they remained fixed,
were panic-struck, were overpowered by what they heard and
saw."[45] In any case, the leader of the party was smitten with
blindness and continued to lie prostrate on the ground.

The thing his companions could not understand was that
they were hearing a voice, but seeing no man. There is a significant difference in the form of the Greek between hearing a
voice (7) and the statement above that Saul "heard a voice" (4).
In 4 the word "voice" (*phone*) is in the accusative case, seeming
to indicate an intelligible voice and emphasizing the hearing of
the content. But here voice is in the genitive case. It seems clear
that the genitive indicates the hearing of a sound, without any
understanding of what was spoken.

This takes care of the apparent contradiction between this
verse and Paul's assertion in 22:9 that his companions "saw

---

[43]*Acts*, p. 198.

[44]The last clause of 5—it is hard for thee to kick against the pricks—
and the first half of 6—and he trembling and astonished said, Lord, what
wilt thou have me to do? And the Lord said unto him—are not in the
Greek text at this place. The words were apparently translated by Erasmus
from the Latin Vulgate (EGT, II, 232). "It is hard for thee to kick against
the goad" is genuine in 26:14, but not here. "What shall I do, Lord?" is
found in the Greek text of 22:10, but it does not belong here. These facts
are thus true to the account of Saul's conversion but they derive their
authenticity from the other records of this epochal event.

[45]*Op. cit.*, p. 323.

indeed the light . . . but they heard not the voice [accusative case] of him that spake to me." They heard a sound, but only Saul caught the words uttered by the voice.

A somewhat similar situation seems to be described in John 12:28-29. When a voice came from heaven the unbelieving multitude "said that it thundered." Some, with more spiritual discernment, thought an angel had spoken. But apparently only Jesus and His disciples understood the words uttered.

When Saul finally staggered to his feet, he discovered that he was blind. Though his eyes were open, **he saw no man (8).** Paul himself says, "I could not see for the glory of that light" (22:11). His companions **led him by the hand, and brought him into Damascus.** Gloag appropriately observes: "Thus Paul entered Damascus in a very different manner from that which he had planned: instead of haling men and women, and committing them to prison, he himself is led, humbled, afflicted, and blind, the prisoner of Jesus Christ."[46]

2. *Saul Filled with the Spirit* (9:10-19a)

Ananias (10) means "The Lord is gracious"—a fitting name for this Jewish **disciple** (Christian) at Damascus, who ministered graciously to the convicted Saul. **The Lord**—Jesus (cf. 17)— spoke to him **in a vision,** a frequent means of communication of the divine will in both the Old and New Testaments.

When **Ananias** heard his name called, he answered: **Behold, I am here, Lord** (lit., "Behold, I, Lord"). Thus he expressed his consecration. He was ready for orders to be given.

But the command that came was a startling one. He was to **go into the street which is called Straight, and enquire in the house of Judas for one called Saul, of Tarsus (11).** There is still a Straight Street in Damascus, running from east to west through the main bazaar of that busy city. The house of Judas is pointed out today near the west end.

The voice added: **Behold, he prayeth.** This suggests, what we would already assume, that Saul spent those three sightless days in prayer, seeking to bring his heart and mind into conformity with his soul-shaking experience on the road.

The Lord went on to tell Ananias that He had already prepared the way for his visit by giving Saul a vision. A certain Ananias would come to him, lay his hand upon him, and cause

[46]*Ibid.,* p. 325.

him to **receive his sight** (12)—literally, "see again." This aspect of divine guidance—preparing the heart of both messenger and recipient—should be a constant encouragement to prompt obedience.

Understandably, Ananias protested. He had **heard** from many people a report of Saul's persecution of the **saints at Jerusalem** (13). This implies that Ananias had not himself fled from Jerusalem, but that he was a longtime resident of Damascus.

The term **saints** occurs here for the first time in Acts as a name for Christians. It is found again in 32, 41, and 26:10. Paul uses it forty times as a designation for those who belong to the Church of Jesus Christ. The Greek word is the plural of *hagios* (holy), and so literally means "holy ones." It emphasizes the fact that all Christians are set apart to Christ and are to be cleansed from acquired depravity. The word is translated "holy" about 165 times and "saints" 61 times in KJV.

Ananias went on to remind the Lord that, even here in Damascus, Saul had **authority from the chief priests to bind all that call on thy name** (14). Prayer to Jesus was considered a serious offense by the Jews because it seemed to them to deny their belief in monotheism.

In reply to Ananias' objections, the Lord still said, **Go** (15). Things had changed for Saul. Now **he is a chosen vessel unto me.** Since Christ had chosen him, Ananias was not to reject him. Saul was to bear the name of Christ **before the Gentiles, and kings, and the children of Israel.** The order here may seem strange. But Paul's preaching mission was primarily to the Gentiles, rather than to the Jews. Kings before whom Paul witnessed were Herod Agrippa II (c. 26) and probably Nero (cf. 27:24). It is also indicated that Paul's ministry was to be a suffering ministry (16).

Obediently **Ananias went his way** (17). Coming into the house where Paul was praying, he laid **his hands on him**—either for receiving his sight or receiving the Holy Spirit. Bruce wisely suggests both.[47]

Ananias greeted the humbled Pharisee as **Brother Saul.** These words, coming from the lips of one whom Saul had planned to persecute, must have brought immense comfort to his soul. He was already being loved by those whom he had hated.

---

[47]*Acts,* p. 202.

The older Christian informed his new brother in Christ that he had been sent by the same One who appeared to Saul on the road. In view of the fact that *kyrios* (Lord) is the regular translation of *Jehovah* (or Yahweh) in the Septuagint, the phrase **the Lord, even Jesus** furnishes a strong affirmation of the deity of Jesus.

Saul had both a physical need and a deeper spiritual one. Both would be met. Ananias had come **that thou mightest receive thy sight, and be filled with the Holy Ghost.**

Immediately—Saul was now ready—something like scales **fell from his eyes** (18). With this **he received sight**—the same word used when Jesus healed the blind—**and was baptized.** He was now officially a member of the new community of Christians. For the first time in three days he **received meat** (took food), **and was strengthened** (19).

There are remarkable parallels between the visions of Ananias and Saul in this chapter and those of Peter and Cornelius in the next. Howson describes it thus: "The simultaneous preparation of the hearts of Ananias and Saul, and the simultaneous preparation of those of Peter and Cornelius—the questioning and hesitation of Peter, and the questioning and hesitation of Ananias—the one doubting whether he might make friendship with the Gentiles, the other doubting whether he might approach the enemy of the Church—the unhesitating obedience of each, when the divine will was made clearly known—the state of mind in which both the Pharisee and the Centurion were found—each waiting to see what the Lord would say unto them—this close analogy will not be forgotten by those who reverently read the two consecutive chapters."[48]

The story of Saul's conversion (1-19) shows that "Divine Power Needs Human Cooperation." Under (1) Divine power we note: (*a*) The light, 3; (*b*) The voice, 4-7; (*c*) The blindness, 8-9. Under (2) Human cooperation we see concerning Ananias: (*a*) His orders, 10-12; (*b*) His objections, 13-16; (*c*) His obedience, 17; (*d*) His objectives realized, 18.

3. *Saul Preaching Christ* (9:19b-22)

After his conversion Saul spent **certain days with the disciples which were at Damascus** (19). Evidently Ananias "went

---

[48]W. J. Conybeare and J. S. Howson, *The Life and Epistles of St. Paul* (New York: Charles Scribner's Sons, 1894), I, 93.

bond" for him and so he was fully accepted in the Christian community.

Straightway (20)—same word as "immediately" (18)—Saul began preaching at Damascus. How are we to harmonize this with his own statement that after his conversion he went into Arabia (Gal. 1:15-17)? The simplest solution is to assume that he began at once to preach his newfound faith. When he discovered that he needed to think through some of the theological implications of his message, he retired into Arabia for a period of meditation and prayer. This Arabian sojourn would seem to fall somewhere after v. 21 and before 26.

Saul **preached** . . . **in the synagogues.** As a rabbi trained in Jerusalem at the feet of Gamaliel, he would be more than welcome in any Jewish synagogue and invited to speak. But now it was not just giving a rabbinical interpretation of the Law: **he preached Christ . . . that he is the Son of God.** How startled his hearers must have been! It was well known that Saul had persecuted the Christians in Jerusalem and had come to Damascus with the express purpose of rooting out this new heresy. He had come to arrest those of "the Way" and take them in chains to Jerusalem for trial before the Sanhedrin (21). Now he himself was preaching this "heresy"! One can hardly imagine the astonishment and consternation that would come over his Jewish audiences when they discovered what this disciple of Gamaliel was preaching to them. No wonder it says: **all that heard him were amazed (21)!**

Doubtless there were many arguments with the scribes in the synagogues (cf. 6:9). **But Saul increased the more in strength, and confounded the Jews which dwelt at Damas-cus. Proving** is literally "joining together," and so means here deducing or demonstrating. That is, he put Old Testament prophecies alongside their fulfillment in Jesus' ministry and thus demonstrated **that this is very Christ** (22). Paul's main message, like Peter's (2:36; 3:13-21), was that Jesus was the Messiah. The Jews could not refute Paul's Spirit-empowered preaching.

4. Saul Escaping the Jews (9:23-25)

It was inevitable that Paul's life should soon be in danger. He could not hope to escape being threatened with the same fate as that of his Lord and of the martyr Stephen. So it is not surprising to read that after **many days were fulfilled**—including maybe several months spent in Arabia (Gal. 1:18)—**the Jews took** counsel—same verb as in Matt. 26:4—to kill him (23). Fortunately their laying await (plot, the same word as in the Septuagint of Esther 2:22, in connection with the plot to assassinate the king) became known of Saul. Meanwhile the Jews watched the gates day and night to kill him (24).

But Saul made his escape. This difficult feat was achieved only because the disciples took him by night, and let him down by the wall in a basket (25). By the wall is literally "through the wall." Paul himself tells us: "But I was let down in a basket through a window in the wall, and escaped his hands" (II Cor. 11:33, RSV). Hackett reports that just to the left of the East Gate of Damascus he saw two or three windows in the wall, which opened into houses inside the city.[49] Josephus uses the phrase "through the wall" to describe the escape of the spies from Jericho.[50] The natural way to lower a man would be in a basket fastened to a rope. That method is still used in Bible lands today.

While Acts seems to say that the Jews "were watching" (imperfect tense) the gates day and night to kill Saul, he himself writes: "In Damascus the governor under Aretas the king kept the city of Damascenes with a garrison, desirous to apprehend me" (II Cor. 11:32). Until recently scholars held that Damascus was under Roman rule at this time. It could not be understood how an ethnarch (Gk. for "governor") of Aretas IV, who was king of the Nabatean Arabs from 9 B.C. to A.D. 40, could have maintained a garrison in that city. But there have not been found in Damascus any Roman coins for the period A.D. 34-62. The government of Damascus may have been turned over to the Nabateans for this time.[51] Or perhaps the ethnarch was "an Arab sheik or chieftain who headed the Arabian community in that mixed city."[52] Probably the Jews and Nabateans worked together in the attempt to prevent Saul's escape.

5. Saul Preaching in Jerusalem (9:26-31)

When the fugitive left Damascus he returned to Jerusalem (26). On his arrival there he assayed (attempted) to join . . . the disciples. It would seem that his reason for going back to Jerusalem was that he wanted to atone for his previous persecu-

---

[49]*Op. cit.*, p. 123, n. 2.
[50]*Ant.* V. 1. 2.
[51]Cadbury, *The Book of Acts in History*, p. 20.
[52]*Ibid.*

tion of the church there by bearing witness for Christ in that hotbed of opposition. But the Christians were afraid of him, not believing that he was a true disciple.

Bighearted **Barnabas**, "son of consolation" (4:36), **took** Saul, **and brought him to the apostles** (27). He told them of Saul's conversion and his preaching the gospel in Damascus. The result of Barnabas' sponsorship was that the new convert **was with them coming in and going out at Jerusalem** (28). He was able to move freely in Christian circles there.

Some have sought to find a contradiction between these two verses and Paul's own statement: "Then after three years I went up to Jerusalem to see Peter, and abode with him fifteen days. But other of the apostles saw I none, save James the Lord's brother" (Gal. 1:18-19). But there is nothing in the Acts account which conflicts with the statement in Galatians that Saul saw only two of the apostles. The others may have been away from Jerusalem at this time.

The former foe of Christ's followers now **spake boldly in the name of the Lord Jesus, and disputed against the Grecians** (29) —"Hellenists" or Greek-speaking Jews. These were the same ones who had disputed with Stephen and finally brought about his death. Now they were seeking to kill Saul.

When the believers in Jerusalem learned of this, **they brought him down to Caesarea**—the main seaport of Palestine at this time—**and sent him forth to Tarsus** (30), his hometown, 300 miles north of Caesarea. The only thing we know about Saul's activities during the next half-dozen years or more is his own statement: "Afterwards I came into the regions of Syria and Cilicia" (Gal. 1:21, see map 3). It appears from this that he spent these years evangelizing his native province of Syro-Cilicia. Ramsay speaks of them as "ten years of quiet work within range of the synagogue and its influence."[53]

Tarsus was the capital of Cilicia. In Paul's day it was the third greatest university center, after Athens and Alexandria.

The result of Paul's leaving Jerusalem was twofold. In the first place, his own life was spared, and that was a great boon to his own century and to all generations to come. In the second place, the Christian movement in Palestine was relieved for the time from further persecution. The account declares: **Then had the churches**—"church" (sing. in the oldest MSS)—**rest**

---

[53]*Op. cit.*, p. 47.

throughout all Judaea and Galilee and Samaria (31)—the three
main divisions of Palestine in that day (see map 1), given in the
order of their Jewish importance. This is the only mention of the
Christian church in Galilee until the time of Eusebius (4th cent.),
a strange phenomenon in view of the fact that Jesus devoted the
major part of His public ministry to that area.

The record goes on to say that the church in Palestine was
being **edified**—literally, "built up"—and **multiplied.** With Saul
gone, the contention with the Hellenistic Jews ceased and the
Church enjoyed a period of peace and prosperity.

D. WITNESSING IN JUDEA, 9: 32-43

So far the entire ninth chapter has been taken up with
Saul's conversion and subsequent career for perhaps a dozen
years. Now the narrative returns to Peter, who is the leading
figure in Acts 1—12. The rest of this chapter describes two
incidents in his ministry, both of them in Judea.

1. *Peter at Lydda* (9: 32-35)

As Peter passed throughout all quarters, i.e., "in the course
of travelling about among them all" (Phillips)—probably super-
vising the evangelization of the Jews in Judea—**he came down
also to the saints which dwelt at Lydda** (32). This city, mentioned only here (32, 35, 38) in the New Testament, was situated near the seacoast, a short distance inland from Joppa. It
was about thirty miles from Jerusalem (see map 1).

There Peter **found a certain man named Aeneas** (33), who
had been a helpless paralytic for eight years. His case was thus
considered hopeless.

But no case is hopeless with God. Peter said to the man:
Jesus Christ maketh thee whole: arise, and make thy bed (34).
He obeyed immediately and was healed. All the people in **Lydda**
and nearby **Saron**—the Plain of Sharon, stretching from Lydda
northward to Mount Carmel—saw the former bedridden paralytic
walking about. The result was that many **turned to the Lord**
(35). The Church was continuing to grow.

2. *Peter at Joppa* (9: 36-43)

Joppa was the ancient seaport for Jerusalem, though it has
no natural harbor. Its modern name is Jaffa, now united with
Tel Aviv—a new, all-Jewish city built just north of it.

At Joppa there was **a certain disciple** (feminine form only here in NT) called **Tabitha** (Aramaic) or **Dorcas** (Gk.). Both words mean "gazelle"—a beautiful, fleet-footed animal. Dorcas **was full of good works and almsdeeds**—"abounding with deeds of kindness and charity" (NASB).

But one day **she . . . died** (37). In keeping with the customs of the time, they **washed** her body and **laid her in an upper chamber.** Outside Jerusalem it was permitted to hold a body three days for burial.[54]

Since Joppa was less than ten miles from Lydda, two men were sent to ask Peter to come without delay (38). It would seem probably that the believers at Joppa had heard about the healing of Aeneas at Lydda.

Promptly **Peter arose and went with them** (39). He found in the upper room many **widows** who had gathered to mourn the death of Dorcas. They showed Peter **the coats and garments** (Gk., under and outer clothes, or tunics and robes) which Dorcas "was making" while alive. It is not clear whether these **widows** were the recipients of these clothes or whether they were workers in the church who helped to distribute the clothing which Dorcas made.

Peter put the mourners out of the room, as his Master had done at the house of Jairus (Mark 5:40). Kneeling down, he **prayed** (40). Then he said very simply, but in full faith: **Tabitha, arise.** The woman who had been dead **opened her eyes** and **sat up.** Calling **the saints and widows**—the widows were almost certainly Christians—he **presented her alive** (41). News of this spread **throughout all Joppa** (42), with the result that **many believed in the Lord.** These two miracles of Peter at Lydda and Joppa greatly increased the accessions to the Church.

Peter stayed on in Joppa **many days,** living in the house of **Simon a tanner** (43). Tanning was considered by the Jews to be an unclean occupation, because it involved handling dead bodies. Apparently Peter was becoming a bit more flexible in his thinking or he would not have stayed in such a place.

E. Witnessing to Gentiles, 10:1—11:30

Samaria, as already noted (on 8:5), was a sort of halfway house between Jews and Gentiles. The carrying out of Christ's commission involved the evangelization of the Jews in Jerusalem

---

[54]EGT, II, 247.

first, then the Samaritans, and finally the Gentiles. But all the events recorded in this chapter took place in Judea. So we are still in the fulfillment of the second part of Acts 1:8 (see comments on that verse).

1. *Visions* (10:1-16)

Two visions are recorded in this section: that of Cornelius in Caesarea and that of Peter in Joppa. In each case the recipient of the vision was prepared for contact with the other man. God was working at both ends of the line.

a. Cornelius in Caesarea (10:1-8). **Caesarea** (1) was the main seaport of Palestine and the capital of the Roman government there. Herod the Great had built on the site of Strato's Tower a magnificent city and splendid harbor, protected by a long breakwater. In spite of its prominence, the city is mentioned in the New Testament only in the Book of Acts (fifteen times).

Cornelius was a very common name in the Roman Empire. This was due in part to the fact that, in 82 B.C., Cornelius Sulla had freed 10,000 slaves and called them after his own name.[55] This **Cornelius** was a **centurion**—literally, "chief of a hundred"; that is, an officer over a hundred soldiers. He was a centurion in **the Italian band,** or "cohort." A cohort normally consisted of 600 men—a tenth part of a legion.

Four things are said of Cornelius. First, he was **devout** (2). The adjective, meaning "pious" or "godly," is found (in NT) only here, 7, and II Pet. 2:9. In the second place, he was **one that feared God with all his house.** Bruce says that these two expressions, "though not strictly technical terms . . . are generally used in Acts to denote those Gentiles who, though not full proselytes . . . attached themselves to the Jewish religion, practising its monotheistic and imageless worship, attending the synagogue, observing the Sabbath and food-laws, etc."[56] Such people are sometimes referred to as "proselytes of the gate." But in an article on "proselytes and God-Fearers," Kirsopp Lake insists that the expression "proselyte of the gate" must be abandoned as having no historical validity. People were either proselytes or not proselytes.[57] Gloag agrees with this when he writes: "The

[55]Lumby, *op. cit.,* p. 208.
[56]*Acts,* p. 215.
[57]*Beginnings,* V, 74-96.

only proselytism which the Jews seem to have recognized was when the Gentiles adopted the whole law. . . . We judge, then, that there was, at least in apostolic times, no such class as 'proselytes of the gate.' "[58] Cornelius was not a proselyte, as Peter's words in 28 show. A proselyte was considered inside the Jewish fold; Cornelius was not.

The third thing that is said about this man is that he **gave much alms to the people;** that is, to the Jews. The fourth thing is that he **prayed to God always.** He was a devout worshiper of the true God. But he was not a member of either the Jewish community or the Christian Church.

One day Cornelius was praying (cf. 30) in his house **about the ninth hour** (3:00 p.m.)—the time for the offering of the evening sacrifice in the Temple, when devout Jews and God-fearers would be engaged in prayer (cf. 3:1). He **saw in a vision . . . an angel of God coming in to him** and calling his name, **Cornelius** (3). **Evidently** means "clearly" (NEB). **When he looked on him**—better, "fastening his eyes upon him" (ASV)— **he was afraid** (4). This is normally the reaction of those confronted by angels, as noted in Scripture. But the heavenly messenger spoke with words that were both complimentary and comforting: **Thy prayers and thine alms are come up for a memorial before God.** The name **memorial** was given to "the portion of the meal-offering which the priest was commanded to burn upon the altar to be an offering of a sweet savour unto the Lord (Lev. ii.2)."[59] The **prayers** and **alms** of Cornelius had been like this offering, pleasing to God.

The angel instructed Cornelius to **send men to Joppa, and call for**—literally, "send for," or "summon"—**Simon, whose surname is Peter** (5). **Simon** is said to have been the most common name among the Jews of that time. So this Simon had to be identified by his surname, **Peter.** Actually he was lodging with **Simon a tanner** (6), which made the identification all the more necessary. The house of the tanner was **by the sea side.**[60] There were probably two reasons for this. One was that his occupation, involving the handling of dead bodies, rendered him unclean; so

---

[58] *Op. cit.,* p. 363.

[59] Lumby, *op. cit.,* pp. 209-10.

[60] The rest of the verse—**he shall tell thee what thou oughtest to do**— is not in the early Greek MSS, and so is not included in recent translations.

he was required to live outside the town. The other was that his business probably involved the use of seawater.

When the angel had left, Cornelius **called two of his household servants** (7)—the single Greek word signifies those dwelling in the house—**and a devout soldier of them that waited on him continually.** His own godly life had influenced even his servants and soldiers. He told these three trusted men about his vision and then **sent them to Joppa** (8). They were to find Simon Peter and bring him back.

b. Peter in Joppa (10:9-16). **On the morrow**—the day after these messengers left Caesarea—**they . . . drew nigh unto the city** (9); that is, Joppa. It was the **sixth hour** (noon) and **Peter went up upon the house top to pray.** This was not one of the regularly appointed hours of prayer. But devout souls may well have engaged in private prayer at this time (cf. Ps. 55:17). Such prayer is always appropriate.

It was thirty miles from Caesarea to Joppa. There has been considerable difference of opinion as to when the servants left Caesarea—whether the day of the vision or the next morning. Also there have been discussions as to how they traveled—whether by foot or on horseback—and how long it took them to make the journey. The facts stated in the narrative are that they arrived in Joppa about noon **on the morrow** (9), stayed overnight with Peter there, and left "on the morrow" (23), and then "the morrow after" (24) arrived back in Caesarea—probably after midafternoon. Since a day's travel on foot was normally about twenty miles, the best reconstruction seems to be this: The servants of Cornelius left Caesarea the morning after his vision, traveled twenty miles, and stopped for the night. The next day they covered the remaining ten miles, arriving in Joppa about noon. After staying overnight there, they started the return trip the next morning (the third day after the vision). Stopping for the night again, they would travel the last ten miles or so on the fourth day. This accords perfectly with the statement of Cornelius to Peter: "Four days ago . . . a man stood before me in bright clothing" (30).

As Peter was praying on the housetop in Joppa, **he became very hungry** (10) and wanted to eat. While waiting for the noon meal to be prepared, **he fell into a trance.** The Greek word, which has been taken over into English as "ecstasy," literally means "a standing outside oneself."

In this trance Peter **saw heaven opened** (11) and the appearance of **a great sheet knit** (tied) **at the four corners,** being lowered to the earth. In it **were all manner of fourfooted beasts of the earth**[61] **... and creeping things, and fowls of the air** (12) —"whatever walks or crawls or flies" (NEB). Lumby observes: "The significance of the outstretched sheet, as a figure of the wide world, and the four corners as the directions into which the Gospel was now to be borne forth into all the world has often been dwelt upon."[62]

A voice commanded him: **Rise, Peter; kill, and eat** (13). But Peter protested strongly: **Not so, Lord; for I have never eaten any thing that is common or unclean** (14). The use of **common** (*koinos*) in the sense of **unclean** is thus explained by Lumby: "All persons who were not Jews were viewed as the 'common' rabble, shut out from God's covenant ... then whatever practices of these outcasts differed from those of the chosen people were called 'common' things, and as these 'common' things were those forbidden by the Law, all such prohibited things or actions became known as 'common.' "[63] The laws concerning clean and unclean foods are found in the eleventh chapter of Leviticus.

Again the voice spoke. This time it said: **What God hath cleansed, that call not thou common** (15). The significance of these words is thus explained by Gloag: "The Jews looked upon unclean animals as an image of the Gentiles, whom they called dogs. But now Peter was taught that all men were on the same footing in the sight of God."[64] There was also another implication: "The distinction between clean and unclean meats which formed so considerable a part of the Mosaic law was abolished; and thus one of the great barriers of separation between Jews and Gentiles was removed."[65] This was necessary for the evangelization of the world, as well as for the unity of the Church.

This was done thrice (16), apparently the whole performance being repeated. Alexander comments: "This repetition of the revelation, no doubt in precisely the same form, may have

[61]**And wild beasts** is not in the best Greek text.
[62]*Op. cit.,* p. 211.
[63]*Ibid.,* p. 212.
[64]*Op. cit.,* p. 369.
[65]*Ibid.*

been intended partly to impress it on the memory, but chiefly to preclude the suspicion of its being a mere dream of fancy."[66]

This section (1-16) illustrates the need of "Preparation for Revelation." If we would hear from heaven we must meet the conditions fulfilled by both Cornelius and Peter: (1) They were godly men, 1-4, 9; (2) They had laid everything else aside to pray, 9, 30; (3) They waited on God until they heard from Him, 3-6, 13-15, 19-20.

2. Visits (10:17-29)

a. Servants in Joppa (10:17-23a). **While Peter doubted in himself** (17), i.e., was "much perplexed" (ASV), as to **what this vision** might **mean,** the servants sent by Cornelius reached the outside door of the house where he was staying. Since they were "unclean" Gentiles they did not presume to enter the house, but **called** to ask whether Simon Peter lodged there (18). If the door was locked, any visitor would have to call from the outside. Actually it is the common custom today in Eastern lands to call out rather than to knock.

While Peter thought—strong compound (only here in NT) meaning "pondered"—about **the vision, the Spirit** informed him that **three men**[67] were seeking him (19). He was commanded to **go with them, doubting nothing** (20). **Doubting** is a compound verb meaning "be divided in one's mind or hesitate." So here **doubting nothing** means "without hesitation" (RSV). God had sent these messengers, and Peter was to go with them.

Obediently Peter went down and talked with the men (21). They told him of Cornelius' vision. The latter had been **warned** (22)—or "instructed"—to send for Peter. The apostle took them in and **lodged them** (23), in spite of the fact that they were Gentiles. Already Peter's vision was producing results.

b. Peter in Caesarea (10:23b-29). **On the morrow** the apostle started out with the messengers from Cornelius. Fortunately for Peter, **certain brethren from Joppa accompanied him.** When challenged soon by some in the Jerusalem church, he would need the witness of these men to testify exactly what happened in the house of Cornelius. So their presence was providential.

On the **morrow after** (24)—the fourth day since Cornelius

---

[66]*Op. cit.,* p. 396.

[67]The oldest Greek MS of NT, Vaticanus (4th cent.), has "two." If this reading (adopted by Nestle) is correct, it refers to the two servants, with the soldier acting as guard.

received his vision (see comment on 9)—the small party reached Caesarea. Besides the soldier and two servants from Cornelius, there were Peter and "six brethren" (cf. 11:12) who accompanied him. It is very unlikely that a group of ten men would have gone on horseback. Evidently they walked, as was the custom of that day. Thus the journey of thirty miles would take them at least a day and a half.

When they reached their destination, they found that **Cornelius waited for them.** The Greek suggests that he "was continuing to wait expectantly for them." He doubtless had assumed that his servants would stay overnight in Joppa and so would be reaching Caesarea soon after noon of the fourth day.

Furthermore, he had **called together his kinsmen and near friends.** The fact that Cornelius had **kinsmen** in Caesarea implies that he had been stationed there a long time, as does also the statement that he was "well spoken of by the whole Jewish nation" (22, RSV). The adjective **near** means literally "necessary." Here alone (in NT) it signifies "intimate, familiar." The idea seems to be that friends who are so near and dear to one are felt to be necessary. Cornelius was obviously a man with a large heart.

When Peter came in, **Cornelius met him, and fell down at his feet, and worshipped him** (25). Lumby comments: "This act of obeisance in the Roman officer marks most strongly his sense that Peter was God's messenger. Such acts were not usual among Roman soldiers."[68] While it was common in the East for men to fall down at the feet of their superiors, "the idea of prostration was alien to the western mind, and the custom was not introduced into the imperial court till the reign of Diocletian."[69] Alexander says: "Having been directed by an Angel to send for the Apostle, with a promise of divine communications from him, it is not surprising that Cornelius should have supposed him to be more than a mere man."[70]

But Peter took him up, saying, Stand up; I myself also am a man (26). This implies that Cornelius was trying to pay him religious worship, against which Peter protested. Similarly an angel refused worship from John (Rev. 19:10).

While conversing the two men entered the house. Peter

---

[68]*Op. cit.,* p. 215.
[69]Rackham, *op. cit.,* p. 154.
[70]*Op. cit.,* pp. 401-2.

must have been surprised to see the **many** who had gathered to hear him (27). He reminded them of the fact that it was **unlawful** for a Jew to associate with people of **another nation** (28). With a fine touch of courtesy Peter used a rare word which literally means "another tribe" (only here in NT). He graciously avoided the offensive term *ethnoi,* which commonly connoted "heathen."

Peter had been compelled to set aside this Jewish prohibition, because **God hath shewed me that I should not call any man common or unclean** (cf. 15). It is impossible for us to realize the terrific change that this involved in the thinking of a devout Jew of that day. His whole religious training had taught him that the Israelites were God's chosen people and that the rest of mankind was unclean and outside the divine covenant.

Because of the vision on the housetop at Joppa, Peter had come to these Gentiles **without gainsaying** (29). This is one word in the Greek (only here in NT). It means literally "not spoken against," and so "without even raising any objection" (NASB). Peter then asked **for what intent**—literally, "for what reason"—they had sent for him.

3. Verification (10:30-48)

The last part of this chapter tells the story of the verification of the visions seen by Peter at Joppa and by Cornelius at Caesarea. By pouring out His Spirit in the house of Cornelius, God proved to everyone concerned that the Gentiles as well as the Jews were to be the recipients of His favor.

a. Presentation by Cornelius (10:30-33). Peter was presented to the audience by Cornelius, who recounted the story of his vision as an explanation for the gathering. Said he: **Four days ago I was fasting until this hour; and at the ninth hour I prayed in my house, and, behold, a man stood before me in bright clothing** (30). The word **fasting** is not in the best Greek text. Probably the best rendering of the first part of this is: "Four days ago, until this hour, I was keeping the ninth hour of prayer in my house" (ASV). This would seem to indicate that Peter and his companions reached the home of Cornelius about three o'clock on the fourth day after the vision.[71]

The report of Cornelius that **a man** appeared to him does not

---

[71]The so-called Western text has "three days ago" (cf. Phillips). But this seems to be based on a misapprehension of the time involved in the journeys to and from Joppa (see comment on 9).

conflict with the other statement that it was "an angel of God" (3). It was an angel in the form of a man, as was true at the empty tomb (Matt. 28:5; Mark 16:5).

Verses 31-32 are an echo of 4-6. Cornelius went on to express his gratitude for Peter's coming and to assure him that they were **all ready to hear** (implies "obey") **all things that are commanded thee of God** (33). Peter had a receptive audience, ready and willing to walk in the light. That is the secret of the results that took place in this historic meeting at Cornelius' house.

b. *Preaching of Peter* (10:34-43). In view of his own vision, as well as of that given to Cornelius, Peter was forced to conclude: **Of a truth I perceive that God is no respecter of persons: but in every nation he that feareth him, and worketh righteousness, is accepted with him** (34-35). Cornelius was just as much accepted before God as any physical descendant of Abraham.

After this introduction Peter gave a brief summary of Jesus' ministry (36-41). It is almost an epitome of Mark's Gospel, which the Early Church held to contain the preaching of Peter.[72]

The apostle began by referring to the **word** (*logos*) which came to the nation of Israel through the preaching of Jesus (36). It was a message of **peace,** but it was rejected. Peter takes time to emphasize the deity of Jesus: **he is Lord of all.**

He says that his hearers know **that word** (*rhema*), **which was published** (37). Since *rhema* is sometimes translated "thing" (5:32; Luke 2:15), the phrase here may be rendered, "the event which happened."[73] Cornelius and his friends, in common with most of the people of that country, knew about the ministry of Jesus.

That ministry covered **all Judaea**—all Palestine. This takes **Judaea** in the wider sense as the country of the Jews. **And began from Galilee**—literally, "having begun from Galilee," which is thus included in **Judaea. The baptism which John preached** would be the baptism of repentance. It is with the ministry of John the Baptist that Mark's Gospel begins.

It was at the baptism of Jesus by John (cf. Luke 4:1, 14) that **God anointed Jesus of Nazareth with the Holy Ghost and with power** (38). **Who went about doing good, and healing all that were oppressed of the devil** summarizes a large part of the Gospel of Mark.

[72]See Introduction to "Mark," BBC, VI, 264-66.
[73]*Beginnings*, IV, 120.

Peter affirms that **we**—he and his six companions from Joppa—**are witnesses of all things which he did both in the land of the Jews** (same as "Judaea" in v. 37) **and in Jerusalem (39)**, in the closing part of His ministry. It was there that He was **hanged on a tree** (crucified). On **the third day** God **raised** Him, and **shewed him openly (40)**—literally, "gave him to be made manifest" (ASV). Yet this was **not to all the people, but unto witnesses chosen before of God . . . who did eat and drink with him after he rose from the dead (41)**. This statement agrees perfectly with what is found in the Gospels.

The risen Christ **commanded** His disciples to **preach unto the people** (Matt. 28:19), **and to testify** that Jesus Christ was divinely **ordained . . . to be the Judge of quick** (living) **and dead (42)**.

The closing note of Peter's message was pointedly evangelistic: **To him give all the prophets witness, that through his name whosoever believeth in him shall receive remission of sins (43)**. In the Greek, **whosoever believeth in him** is placed last, for emphasis. This gospel of forgiveness of sins through faith in Jesus Christ is for all who will believe, both Jews and Gentiles.

c. Pouring Out of the Spirit (10:44-48). While Peter was still preaching, the Holy Spirit fell on those who were hearing the Word (44). **Spake these words** is probably to be rendered: "was speaking these things" (*rhemata*).

At the Jerusalem Council, Peter compared this "Gentile Pentecost" with the original Pentecost of Acts 2. He said: "And God, which knoweth the hearts, bare them witness, giving them the Holy Ghost, even as he did unto us; and put no difference between us and them, purifying their hearts by faith" (15:8-9). Just as God had cleansed the hearts of the 120 in the Upper Room when they were filled with the Spirit (2:4), so He had cleansed the hearts of Cornelius and his associates when the Holy Spirit fell on them. This is the experience commonly known as entire sanctification.

The Christian Jews who had accompanied Peter to Caesarea **were astonished**—"stood out of themselves with amazement"— when they saw that **the gift of the Holy Ghost**—genitive of apposition, the Gift which was the Holy Spirit himself—**was poured out** on these **Gentiles (45)**. They heard these people **speak with tongues (46)**, as had the 120 on the Day of Pentecost.[74]

---

[74]For the historical and theological implications of this see comments on 19:6.

In spite of his Jewish prejudices, Peter sensed that God had fully accepted these Gentiles into the Kingdom. So he proposed that Christian baptism should be administered to them (47). Cornelius and his friends were **baptized in the name of the Lord** (48); that is, in the name of Jesus. This formula was apparently used in the Early Church as well as the Trinitarian form (Matt. 28:19). The main emphasis here is on the fact that it was Christian baptism.

4. Vindication (11:1-18)

Chapter 10 has the story of Peter's visit to the house of Cornelius and the outpouring of God's Spirit on the group assembled there. Chapter 11 gives Peter's vindication of his entering a Gentile home and associating with "heathen."

a. Peter Criticized (11:1-3). Word of what had happened at Caesarea filtered out to **the apostles and brethren that were in Judaea** (1). They heard the startling news that **the Gentiles had also received the word of God.**

When Peter returned to Jerusalem, **they that were of the circumcision** (2)—the Christian Jews who emphasized the continued keeping of the Law—**contended with him.** Their complaint was: **Thou wentest in to men uncircumcised, and didst eat with them** (3). To the strict Jew the **uncircumcised** man was unclean, and contact with him would defile a person. But the most serious thing that Peter did was to **eat with them.** This was something no rigid son of Abraham would do.

b. Peter Cleared (11:4-18). If a man knows that he is right, his best defense is a straightforward explanation of what he did, and why. This was the method that Peter followed. **He rehearsed the matter from the beginning, and expounded it by order unto them** (4). He gave his critics the whole story. The fact that the story of what happened is repeated here shows the great importance attached to this significant event. A new epoch had dawned —that of the evangelization of the Gentiles.

The narrative of 5-10 is almost exactly the same as 10:9b-16, except that Peter's account here, told in the first person, is rather more vivid. For instance, he says that the vessel let down from heaven **came even to me** (5). This is the sort of added touch that one might expect him to give.

Peter recounted the fact that there were **three men** (11) from Caesarea who came to the house where he was (cf. 10:7,

17). He told how **the Spirit bade me go with them, nothing doubting** (12). It was the Holy Spirit who told him to go with these men to Cornelius' house, so that he had no choice in the matter. If people wanted to criticize him for going, they would have to quarrel with the Spirit about it.

Nothing doubting is the same as "doubting nothing" (10: 20). But the Greek has the active form of the verb here; it is the middle-passive form in 10:20. The difference has been well expressed by adopting "without hesitation" in 10:20 and "making no distinction" here (RSV). As a reason for the change, Lumby suggests: "The vision had given no hint of a journey to be taken; now [10:20] Peter is informed of it, and so too when the end of the journey is reached the 'nothing wavering' is shewn to mean 'putting no distinction between Jews and other men,' and thus the vision was made intelligible little by little and the perplexity removed."[75]

Not only did the Spirit direct him to go, but **these six brethren accompanied me** (12). In 10:23 we were not told how many, but only that "certain brethren" accompanied Peter. Did Peter have some premonition that the strict Christian Jews at Jerusalem might criticize him? If so, he had ample witnesses to corroborate the story he told. Perhaps the six men added their enthusiastic testimony concerning the wonderful outpouring of the Spirit in the house of Cornelius.

Peter made a significant addition to Cornelius' report of his vision (cf. 10:32). He quoted the centurion as saying that the angel told him to send for Peter, **who shall tell thee words, whereby thou and all thy house shall be saved** (14). Adam Clarke interprets this as meaning: "He shall announce to you all the doctrine of salvation."[76] That Peter understood his mission to be that of telling Cornelius how to be saved is clearly evident from his discourse in the centurion's home (10:34-43). He laid the elementary foundations of Christian experience by preaching the Crucifixion, the Resurrection, and the Judgment. His final words were: "To him give all the prophets witness, that through his name whosoever believeth in him shall receive remission of sins" (10:43). What Peter was preaching was forgiveness through faith in Jesus. Obviously it was his understanding that this was what Cornelius and his companions needed.

[75]*Op. cit.,* p. 214.
[76]*Op. cit.,* p. 769.

How are we to explain, then, the statement: **As I began to speak, the Holy Ghost fell on them, as on us at the beginning (15)**? That is, the people in Cornelius' house received the same experience as had the 120 disciples on the Day of Pentecost. This may have been the first salvation sermon that opened hearts for the gift of the Holy Spirit, but it was certainly not the last. Perhaps the explanation which best accords with Scripture is that while Peter was only getting well started with his sermon **(as I began to speak)** his hearers in their hearts believed on Jesus Christ and experienced evangelical conversion—as did John Wesley while sitting in a society meeting on Aldersgate Street on the evening of May 24, 1738. Then, because their hearts were fully open for all of God's will, these listeners who had walked devoutly in the light of Judaism (10:2), and had now accepted Christ, were suddenly filled with the Holy Spirit. This reconstruction of what took place does not ignore or suppress any statements in the biblical account.

Peter went on to tell his critics in Jerusalem: **Then remembered I the word of the Lord, how that he said, John indeed baptized with water; but ye shall be baptized with the Holy Ghost (16)**. This is quoted from 1:5. In the Gospels it is John the Baptist who is reported as saying these words. But Acts indicates that Jesus repeated them.

Peter completed his defense by posing a question that effectively silenced his critics. Said he: **Forasmuch then as God gave them the like gift as he did unto us, who believed on the Lord Jesus Christ, what was I, that I could withstand God? (17)** To this there was no possible answer. When Christian Jews heard Peter's recital, **they held their peace, and glorified God, saying, Then hath God also to the Gentiles granted repentance unto life (18)**. This was to them an astounding fact, but they were compelled to accept it. Some of the implications of Gentile salvation would be discussed later at the Jerusalem Council (c. 15). But an important victory was won at this point.

5. *Voyages in Evangelism* (11:19-30)

This section tells of two movements of the Early Church along the Mediterranean Sea. The first was northward from Jerusalem to Antioch in Syria. The gospel was preached freely in that far-off city. The other was southward from Antioch to Jerusalem (see map 3). The first carried the spiritual blessings of salvation to those in the north. The second bore material blessings from the new converts there to the needy brethren in Jerusalem. Since mention is made of **Cyprus** (an island), it may well be that they travelled by boat.

a. Northward (11:19-26). The opening words of this paragraph—**Now they which were scattered abroad** (19)—are exactly the same in the Greek as the beginning clause of 8:4. Another strand of the Christian diaspora is here picked up and recounted. This dispersion started with **the persecution that arose about Stephen** (cf. 8:1).

The dispersed Christians traveled north to **Phenice**—Phoenicia (the cities of Tyre and Sidon), modern Lebanon, on the coast north of Palestine (see map 3)—**and Cyprus**—the largest island at the eastern end of the Mediterranean Sea—**and Antioch.** This city, founded in 300 B.C., had become the third greatest city in the Roman Empire, surpassed only by Rome and Alexandria.[77] Its walls are said to have enclosed a larger area than did those of Rome. Five miles out of the city was the grove of Daphne, a leading center for the worship of Apollo and Artemis. Partly as a result, Antioch was notorious for its immorality. Yet many Jews and proselytes lived there.[78] These were evangelized first. For it is stated that the early missionaries were **preaching the word to none but unto the Jews only.** This was probably before Peter's experience at Caesarea.

Fortunately there were some men from **Cyprus and Cyrene** (North Africa) who were a bit more open-minded. When they reached Antioch, they preached the Lord Jesus to the Grecians (20). While the early Greek MSS differ between *Hellenas* ("Greeks," ASV) and *Hellenistas* (**Grecians**), the context makes it clear that this new preaching was to the Gentiles. The evangelists—**preaching** is *euangelizomenoi*—were announcing the Good News about **the Lord Jesus,** or proclaiming that Jesus is Lord.

Because they were carrying out Christ's command (Matt. 28:19), they saw the fulfilling of His promise (1:8)—**the hand of the Lord was with them** (21). That is, His power was manifested in their ministry. The result was that a **great number believed, and turned unto the Lord.** Antioch soon became the leading center of Christianity.

[77]Josephus, *War* III. 2. 4.
[78]*Ibid.* VII. 3. 3.

Tidings of what was going on in Antioch reached **the cars of the church which was in Jerusalem** (22). Concerned as to whether this evangelization of the Gentiles was in divine order, the leaders sent out **Barnabas to go as far as Antioch.** This may imply that he was to check up on the work in **Phenice** (19, Phoenicia) on his way north.

The Jerusalem church could not have made a wiser choice for this special mission than Barnabas. He was a true "son of consolation" (4:36) wherever he went. A narrow-minded, legalistic Jewish Christian would almost certainly have hindered the wonderful moving of the Spirit of God at Antioch. But Barnabas encouraged it: **Who, when he came, and had seen the grace of God, was glad, and exhorted them all, that with purpose of heart they would cleave unto the Lord** (23). Bighearted Barnabas was so fully consecrated to his Lord that he rejoiced to see anyone—even a Gentile—accepting Christ. Instead of criticizing the new movement, he gave it his approval and blessing. He rejoiced to see the grace of God at work in this very needy city. Barnabas was himself a Cyprian Jew (4:36), and he fitted in perfectly with the evangelists from Cyprus and Cyrene. He **exhorted** the new converts, thus fulfilling the meaning of his name as "son of exhortation" (see comments on 4:36).

The description of Barnabas is about as noble a one as could be made of any man: **For he was a good man, and full of the Holy Ghost and of faith** (24). The three things here stated of Barnabas have formed the main points of many a funeral sermon. The consecrated pastor is always happy when he can say these things about a deceased member of his church. The result of the character and ministry of this good, Spirit-filled, faith-inspired man of God was that **much people was added unto the Lord.**

But Barnabas needed help. The task in Antioch was too great for him. This cosmopolitan, Greek-speaking metropolis demanded the services of an intellectual giant as well as a Spirit-filled exhorter. So Barnabas went to **Tarsus,** about one hundred twenty-five miles northwest of Antioch, to **seek Saul** (25). Happy is the man who realizes his limitations and is willing to bring in an associate who is equal to the situation. Unselfish Barnabas desired only what was best for the Kingdom. So he sought out Saul, the brilliant, highly trained young Jewish rabbi who had been converted some years before. Saul had made a good start in his ministry, and then had been shipped home by the church at Jerusalem (9:30) when his life became endangered.

When he had found him, he brought him unto Antioch (26).
The words **seek** and **found** suggest that Barnabas had to search
for some time before he found Saul. Probably the latter was
busy evangelizing his province of Syria and Cilicia, as he himself
intimates (Gal. 1:21). **For a whole year** Barnabas and Saul **assembled themselves with the church, and taught much people.**
It must have been a year of fruitful ministry for them both—
bighearted Barnabas exhorting and encouraging the people, keen-
minded Saul expounding the Scriptures and exalting Christ. They
made a wonderful team.

A very interesting statement occurs at the end of this verse:
And the disciples were called Christians first in Antioch. Hitherto they had been designated as "believers," "brethren," "saints,"
"of the Way," and, as here, "disciples." But since the Jews commonly used "brethren" and "disciples," it was necessary to assign
a more distinctive name that would unquestionably indicate the
disciples of Christ.

The term **Christian** occurs only twice again in the New
Testament. Agrippa said to Paul: "Almost thou persuadest me
to be a Christian" (26:28). And Peter wrote: "If any man suffer
as a Christian [being persecuted by the world for carrying that
name], let him not be ashamed" (I Pet. 4:16). In both of these
other places the indication is that the name was used by outsiders.
The history of name-fixing, taken together with this fact, suggests that **Christians** was not a self-chosen designation, but one
assigned by those outside the church. Furthermore, it is very
unlikely that the Jews called the believers by this name. Gloag
observes: "It is not to be imagined that they would give the
sacred name *Christos* to those whom they regarded as heretics
and apostates."[79] The Jews called them "Nazarenes" (24:5), a
term of contempt.

It seems clear that the designation **Christians** was given to
the disciples by the Gentiles at Antioch, as Meyer affirms.[80] It
has often been assumed that this term was used in derision. But
Meyer insists: "There is nothing to support the view that the
name was at first a *title of ridicule*."[81] Rather, as the Greeks and
Romans commonly designated political parties by the names of

[79]*Op. cit.*, I, 403.
[80]*Op. cit.*, p. 223.
[81]*Ibid.*

the founders, so they would refer to this group as **Christians.**
Lake and Cadbury rightly observe that the term "implies that
Christos was already taken by the Gentile population as a proper
name—a custom to which Christians surprisingly soon submitted
as is shown by Paul's use of the word."[82] Originally "Christ"—
literally, "the Christ"—meant "the Messiah." It was a title added
to the name Jesus, "Jesus the Christ," when preaching to the
Jews. But the Gentiles would naturally take it as a proper name.

The fact that the people of Antioch found it necessary to
assign a name to the new movement in their city shows how
large it had become. It had to be recognized and designated.
Gloag writes: "So long as Christianity was confined to the Jews
and Jewish proselytes, the Christians would not be distinguished
from them, and would be regarded by the Gentiles as a Jewish
sect; but now the fact that numerous Gentiles were received
without circumcision into the church was a proof that Christianity was different from Judaism; and thus the disciples could
no longer be regarded in the same point of view as the Sadducees, Pharisees, Essenes, and other Jewish sects."[83]

The story of the evangelization of Antioch illustrates "When
the Gospel Succeeds": (1) When it is preached to new people,
19; (2) When it is preached to all classes and races, 20-21;
(3) When it is preached by Spirit-filled men, 22-26.

b. *Southward* (11:27-30). Doubtless the report of what was
going on at Antioch continued to spread (cf. 22). As a result
there came **prophets from Jerusalem unto Antioch** (27). Among
them was **Agabus** (28), who is mentioned again in 21:10. In the
New Testament **prophets** seems to mean primarily "preachers."
But occasionally one would make a prediction. So Agabus **signified by the Spirit that there should be great dearth throughout
all the world: which came to pass in the days of Claudius Caesar,**
who reigned A.D. 41-54. Lake and Cadbury note: "The evidence
of Suetonius (*Claudius* xix.) and Tacitus (*Ann.* xii. 43) shows
that widespread famine was a feature of the reign of Claudius."[84]
Josephus tells of a famine in Palestine in A.D. 44-48,[85] which is
probably the same one mentioned here.

[82]*Beginnings,* IV, 130.
[83]*Op. cit.,* I, 404.
[84]*Beginnings,* IV, 131.
[85]*Ant.* III. 15. 3; XXII. 2. 5.

The disciples (29) at Antioch, **every man according to his ability**—literally, "even as he had plenty"—**determined to send relief**—literally, "arranged to send for a ministry" (*diakonia*)— **unto the brethren which dwelt in Judaea.** Thus they repaid with much-needed material goods their Jewish brethren who had sent them the spiritual blessings of the gospel.

The relief was sent **by the hands of Barnabas and Saul** (30). This was a wise move, cementing more closely the Gentile church at Antioch to the Jewish church at Jerusalem.

F. WITNESSES PERSECUTED, 12:1-25

1. *Peter Imprisoned* (12:1-5)

Without question Peter is the leading character of the first twelve chapters of Acts, as Paul is of chapters 13—28. It was Peter who held the election of the twelfth apostle to take the place of Judas Iscariot (c. 1); preached on the Day of Pentecost, with 3,000 converted (c. 2); healed the lame man and preached another sermon (c. 3); addressed the Sanhedrin (c. 4); exposed Ananias and Sapphira, and acted again as defense attorney before the Sanhedrin (c. 5). Then Stephen becomes the central figure (cc. 6—7), followed by Philip (c. 8). After Saul's conversion Peter again comes to the front, this time at Lydda and Joppa (c. 9). Next comes the story of Peter's preaching to Gentiles in the house of Cornelius (c. 10), and his defense of that action (c. 11). Finally there is given the account of Peter's imprisonment and deliverance (c. 12). For the first fifteen years of its history (A.D. 30-45), Peter was the dominant figure in the Church. For the next twenty years (A.D. 45-65), Paul was the great leader in the evangelization of the Roman Empire.

The persecution of the Church started almost immediately after Pentecost. Peter had healed a lame man at the Beautiful Gate of the Temple, and vast crowds had witnessed the results. When the miracle-worker took advantage of the gathered multitudes to preach about Jesus, the priests of the Temple moved in on the situation and arrested him (c. 4). Freed from that imprisonment, he was soon locked up again, with other apostles (c. 5). Stephen was the next victim; only this time it was death (c. 7). This martyrdom triggered a veritable barrage of violent persecution of the believers in Jerusalem (c. 8). Saul attempted to carry this general scourging of the Church to foreign parts, but was himself arrested by the Lord on the road to Damascus. Now Herod begins the bloody work of liquidating the leaders of the Church (c. 12).

He is called **Herod the King** (1). This was Herod Agrippa I, who is mentioned (in NT) only in this chapter. He was a grandson of Herod the Great and nephew of Herod Antipas, the one who killed John the Baptist.

At the death of Herod the Great in 4 B.C. his son Antipas became tetrarch of Galilee and Perea, ruling until A.D. 39. Another son, Archelaus, became ethnarch of Judea (including Samaria and Idumea), but was recalled to Rome in A.D. 6 and deposed. For a period of thirty-five years Judea was ruled by seven different procurators (Roman governors), of whom the best known was Pontius Pilate (A.D. 26-36).

Finally, for a brief three years (A.D. 41-44) the whole of Palestine was ruled by Herod Agrippa I; the country was thus united for the first time since the death of Herod the Great in 4 B.C. Agrippa was determined to keep in the good graces of his Jewish subjects—a fact which led to the persecution of the Christians. Josephus says of him: "He loved to live continually at Jerusalem, and was exactly careful in the observance of the laws of his country. He therefore kept himself pure, nor did any day pass over his head without its appointed sacrifice."[86]

About that time (1) refers to the last events described in chapter 11. Herod Agrippa exerted himself **to vex**—literally, "to ill-treat, afflict, distress"[87]—some of the members **of the church.** The first thing he did was to execute **James the brother of John** (2). These two sons of Zebedee had requested the highest places of honor on either side of Jesus. The Master's reply was: "Ye know not what ye ask. Are you able to drink of the cup that I shall drink of, and to be baptized with the baptism that I am baptized with? . . . Ye shall drink indeed of my cup, and be baptized with the baptism that I am baptized with" (Matt. 20: 22-23). Now this prophecy, as it related to James, was fulfilled. John's sufferings were evidently not so sharp, but probably stretched over a period of years. There is no solid historical support for the late tradition that John was martyred at the same time as James. Alexander comments: "It is remarkable that, so

[86]*Ant.* XIX. 7. 3.
[87]Abbott-Smith, *op. cit.,* p. 227.

far as we know, one of these inseparable brothers was the first, and one the last, that died of the Apostles."[88]

Though nothing has been said in the Book of Acts about any activity of James, the fact that he was singled out as the first of the twelve apostles to be martyred would suggest that he was recognized as an outstanding leader in the Church. Neutral, passive men are not persecuted. Doubtless his selection by Jesus as a member of the inner circle of three disciples—with their Master at the raising of Jairus' daughter, on the mount of Transfiguration, and in the Garden of Gethsemane—would cause him to be highly honored by the early believers in Jerusalem.

When Herod Agrippa saw that his execution of James **pleased the Jews, he proceeded further to take Peter also** (3). He may well have known of this apostle's dominant place in the earliest years of the new movement. To execute him would be to strike a massive blow against the Church of Jesus Christ.

So he **apprehended him** and **put him in prison** in the care of **four quaternions of soldiers** (4)—sixteen men. The Romans divided the night into four watches of three hours each. For each of these watches one squad of four men would have charge of the prisoner. The same would be true in the daytime. The frequent change of watch was intended to help make sure that no one went to sleep on duty.

The king planned to bring Peter out of prison for public execution **after Easter.** This translation is an odd anachronism. The Greek is *to pascha.* Alexander remarks: "There is no imaginable reason why it should not be translated here, as in every other place where it occurs, by the exact equivalent, *the Passover.*"[89]

Since in the strictest sense the seven days of the Feast of Unleavened Bread followed the one day of the Passover (Exod. 12:3-19), some have criticized the account for saying, **Then were the days of unleavened bread (3)** and later stating that Herod planned to bring Peter out to the people for public execution "after the Passover" (4). The simple solution of the problem is the fact that both terms—"unleavened bread" and "passover"— were loosely applied to the whole period of eight days. That the two terms were used interchangeably at this time is fully attested

[88]*Op. cit.,* p. 443.
[89]*Op. cit.,* p. 445.

by Josephus.[90] Luke identifies the two in his Gospel (Luke 22:1), and it is altogether reasonable to assume that he does so here. Thus the passage would mean that in the general period of **unleavened bread** Herod arrested and imprisoned Peter, intending to bring him out right at the close of the feast, when the great Passover crowd would acclaim Herod for his zeal for the Law in executing a leading "heretic."

So **Peter . . . was kept in prison** (5). But **the church** was making prayer to God for him **without ceasing**—one word, meaning "earnestly" (ASV).

2. *Peter Delivered* (12:6-11)

Finally the time came when the next day Herod **was going to bring him forth** (6)—literally, "lead before." But **the same night**—just in the "nick of time"—God intervened in answer to prayer.

Peter was sleeping between two soldiers, bound with two chains: and the keepers before the door kept the prison. This indicates how the four soldiers of each "quaternion" (4) were stationed. Two of them were chained to the prisoner, one on either side. The other two stood duty as sentries. Lake and Cadbury note: "The custom of fastening a prisoner to a soldier is mentioned by Seneca."[91] Peter had escaped once from prison, when the chief priests locked him up (5:19), and Herod Agrippa was taking no chance this time.

Suddenly something changed the situation. **And, behold, the angel**—rather, "an angel"—**of the Lord came upon him, and a light shined in the prison** (7). The angel tapped Peter on the side and told him to get up quickly. As he obeyed, the **chains fell off from his hands.**

Since the Greek word *angelos* means "messenger," some have contended that it was a human messenger who released Peter. But the whole tenor of the narrative is against this interpretation. The expression **angel of the Lord** is exactly the same as in Luke 2:9, where clearly a heavenly visitor is intended (cf. 5:19; 8:26). Also the statement that **a light shined in the prison** is paralleled in Luke 2:9—"An angel of the Lord stood by them, and the glory of the Lord shone round about them" (ASV). In the third

---

[90]See comments on Matt. 26:17 (BBC, VI, 233)

[91]*Beginnings*, IV, 135.

place, a human messenger could not have freed him from the chains that held him bound to a guard on each side.

Peter was immediately commanded to dress and to slip on his **sandals** (8). God does not do for us what we can do for ourselves. Then the angel told the freed prisoner to put on his **garment** (outer cloak) and follow him. Peter obeyed, still dumbfounded. He thought he was seeing **a vision** (9). It did not seem possible that it could actually be true.

They went **past the first and the second ward** (10)—probably the two sentries who stood guard. These would be in addition to the two soldiers to whom Peter was chained. Finally **they came unto the iron gate that leadeth unto the city;** that is, the outside gate of the prison compound. This **opened to them of his own accord**—one word in Greek, *automate;* that is, automatically. The term occurs elsewhere (in NT) only in Mark 4:28.

Passed on through one street suggests that the prison was located inside the city. Passing **through one street** may suggest that they went down a street past an intersection. This would be far enough to be a safe distance from the prison. Perhaps Peter had been held in the Tower of Antonia, just north of the Temple area (see map 2). When they were away from the prison, **the angel departed from him.** His miraculous intervention was no longer needed. Peter could now make his own way. To expect God to do for us what we can do for ourselves is fanaticism.

When Peter was come to himself (11) is literally "Peter having become in himself." He had in a sense been out of himself, in a sort of trance. Now he became fully conscious of his surroundings. He recognized that it was the Lord who, through His angel, had delivered him **out of the hand of Herod, and from all the expectation of the people of the Jews.** The Jewish leaders had doubtless assumed that his death was certain.

3. *Peter Reporting* (12:12-17)

When he had considered the thing (12) is all one word in the Greek, *synidon* (found only here and in 14:6). It means "to see in one view . . . to comprehend, understand."[92] Here it suggests: when he "had taken in all the circumstances and decided what was best to be done."[93] His decision made, he went to the

[92]Abbott-Smith, *op. cit.,* p. 427.
[93]Lumby, *op. cit.,* p. 232.

home of **Mary the mother of John, whose surname was Mark.**
John was a common Jewish name; **Mark** (Marcus), a Roman
name (cf. Marcus Aurelius). This is the first of four times that
Mark is mentioned by name in Acts; he was probably the young
man who fled from the Garden of Gethsemane (Mark 14:51-52).

In the home of John Mark's mother **many were gathered together praying.** The implication is that Mark's father was dead
but that his mother owned a house sufficiently large to serve as
one meeting place for a Christian congregation in Jerusalem. It
is altogether possible that it was in the large upper guest room
of this home that the Last Supper was held and that Pentecost
occurred.

When **Peter knocked at the door of the gate** (13)—the outside door fronting on the street—a girl **named Rhoda**—Greek for
"Rose"—**came to hearken.** That is, she would ask who it was
and make sure that it was a friend before she opened the door at
this hour of the night. Doubtless the Christians in Jerusalem
had become wary during the time that young Saul was "entering
into every house" to arrest and imprison the followers of Jesus
(8:3). Now that Herod Agrippa had launched another period of
persecution, they would be on their guard again.

When Peter answered, Rhoda recognized his **voice** (14). So
excited was she that **she opened not the gate for gladness, but
ran** back into the house to report that Peter himself was standing
at the door. The reaction of the praying disciples was, **Thou art
mad** (15)—out of your mind. When she insisted that Peter was
really there, they said: **It is his angel.** Lumby notes: "The Jewish belief was that each man had a guardian angel assigned to
him."[94] Jesus himself seemed to reflect that view (Matt. 18:10).
Gloag also states: "This notion, that each individual has his
guardian angel, was strongly maintained by the early Fathers."[95]
He goes on to say, however: "The word of our Saviour may be
interpreted as asserting the guardianship of angels in general, and
not that a particular angel is attached to each individual."[96]

Meanwhile, **Peter continued knocking** (16). When the people inside finally opened the door and saw that it was really he,
they were astonished. Where was their faith? It certainly seems
that they did not expect the Lord to answer their prayers. But

[94] *Op. cit.,* p. 233.
[95] *Op. cit.,* I, 420.
[96] *Ibid.*

twentieth-century Christians sometimes are just as surprised when their petitions are actually granted.

Peter beckoned to the excited—and perhaps dangerously noisy—people **to hold their peace (17)**. This is one word in the Greek, *sigan,* meaning "to be silent." Time was precious. Peter **declared**—literally, "led the way through" the matter—how the Lord had delivered him from prison. He finished with this injunction: **Go shew**—one word, "report"—**these things unto James, and to the brethren**. This **James** was not the son of Zebedee, who had just been killed (2). He evidently was the one whom Paul identifies as "James the Lord's brother" (Gal. 1:19). This is the James who acted as moderator of the Council of Jerusalem (15:13-21) and was evidently considered to be the head pastor of the church in Jerusalem (cf. 21:18). The passage here seems to imply that position. It is not clear whether **brethren** refers to the leaders of the church or simply to other members of the church not present at Mary's home. It seems obvious that "pastor and people" were to be notified of Peter's release.

Then Peter **departed, and went into another place**. Where he went is not told. Any suggestions would be sheer guesswork. But it was altogether necessary that the escaped prisoner go into hiding. All we know is that he apparently left the city.

4. *Prison Guards Executed* (12:18-19)

"When it became day" (lit. rendering), **there was no small stir**—"trouble" or "disturbance"—**among the soldiers, what was become of Peter (18)**. There was reason for these guards to be disturbed, as the next verse shows.

Herod searched for Peter, but could not find him (19). Thereupon **he examined**—the verb indicates judicial investigation (cf. 4:9)—**the keepers**—literally, "the guards"—and ordered that they should be **put to death**. This is all one word in Greek, literally meaning "to be led away"; that is, to execution. Lake and Cadbury write: "According to the Code of Justinian, which doubtless represents Roman custom, a guard who allowed a prisoner to escape was liable to the penalty which the prisoner would have paid."[97]

Thereupon Herod—perhaps disgusted and upset—**went down from Judaea to Caesarea, and there abode**. This city was the headquarters of the Roman government of Palestine.

---

[97]*Beginnings,* IV, 139.

5. *Persecutor Punished* (12:20-23)

Herod was highly displeased (20)—a strong, rare word meaning "have a hot quarrel"[98]—with the people of **Tyre and Sidon,** the two main cities of ancient Phoenicia (modern Lebanon, see map 1). Josephus tells how Herod Agrippa built beautiful buildings in Berytus,[99] or Beirut (now capital of Lebanon). This city is only a few miles north of Tyre and Sidon. It may be that the commercial supremacy of the two older cities was being endangered by the favor which Herod was showing to the newer city.

Tyre and Sidon joined in coming **with one accord**—in a common embassy. Having secured the friendly help of **Blastus the king's chamberlain**—the one in charge of his bedroom, and so very close to Herod—they **desired peace;** that is, a cessation of the quarrel. The reason for their concern was that **their country was nourished by the king's country.** This may have two meanings. First, Phoenicia—a narrow, mountainous country—was literally fed by grain and fruits from Galilee. In the second place, Tyre and Sidon depended on commerce from Herod's territory to help keep their foreign trade and shipping at a high level. If Beirut became prosperous, they would suffer because of it.

The **set day** (21) is identified by Josephus as one appointed for holding a festival in which vows would be made for the safety of the Roman emperor, and in which Herod Agrippa "exhibited shows in honour of Caesar."[100] He was **arrayed in royal apparel.** Josephus is more explicit. He says: "He put on a garment made wholly of silver, and of a contexture truly wonderful, and came into the theatre early in the morning; at which time the silver of his garment being illuminated by the fresh reflection of the sun's rays upon it, shone out after a surprising manner, and was so resplendent as to spread a horror over those that looked intently upon him."[101]

Arrayed thus, Herod Agrippa **sat upon his throne, and made an oration unto them.** Overcome with his appearance and words, and eager to get into his good graces, the people shouted: **It is the voice of a god, and not of a man** (22). Josephus confirms this

---

[98]Abbott-Smith, *op. cit.,* p. 210.
[99]*Ant.* XIX. 7. 5.
[100]*Ant.* XIX. 8. 2.
[101]*Ibid.*

fully when he writes: "And presently his flatterers cried out . . . that he was a god; and they added, 'Be thou merciful to us; for although we have hitherto reverenced thee only as a man, yet we shall henceforth own thee as superior to mortal nature."[102] This contemporary Jewish historian adds that the king "did neither rebuke them, nor reject this impious flattery."[103]

Herod had killed James and intended to kill Peter. Divine retribution for this and the acceptance of blasphemous worship decreed his death. **And immediately the angel of the Lord smote him, because he gave not God the glory: and he was eaten of worms, and gave up the ghost (23)**—literally, "expired." Again Josephus furnishes general agreement. He says: "A severe pain also arose in his belly, and began in a most violent manner."[104] He further records that Herod continued in pain for five days before he finally died.[105]

6. Preaching Progress (12:24-25)

In spite of all the efforts of Satan to hinder the work of the Church, **the word of God grew and multiplied (24).** This is the third such progress report in the Book of Acts (cf. 6:7; 9:31). Regardless of opposition, the work prospered.

When they had fulfilled their ministry, **Barnabas and Saul returned from Jerusalem (25).** The two oldest Greek MSS, Vaticanus and Sinaiticus, have "to Jerusalem." But this does not seem to make sense. These two men had gone up to Jerusalem with the famine relief (11:29-30). It would be expected that now they would be returning to Antioch. Furthermore, the home of **John . . . Mark** was in Jerusalem. It would seem natural for him to be accompanying the older men to Antioch. At the beginning of the next chapter we find these three men in Antioch. So in spite of the textual difficulties it seems best to accept **from Jerusalem** as the correct reading.[106] "To Jerusalem" may be an early scribal error.[107]

---

[102]*Ibid.*

[103]*Ibid.*

[104]*Ibid.*

[105]*Ibid.*

[106]It is found in the Nestle text and in the new British and Foreign Bible Society edition (1958).

[107]Bruce, *Acts,* p. 252.

Section IV *Witnessing in the Gentile World*

Acts 13:1—28:31

Jesus had announced that the disciples would receive the power of the Holy Spirit and be His witnesses (*a*) in Jerusalem, (*b*) in all Judea and Samaria, and (*c*) unto the uttermost part of the earth (1:8). We have followed the course of this outreach from Jerusalem (cc. 2—7) to all Judea and Samaria (cc. 8—12). The rest of the Book of Acts (cc. 13—28) describes the carrying of the gospel around the eastern end of the Mediterranean world and westward to Rome, the capital of the empire. Peter had been the main figure in the first twelve chapters of the book, but Paul holds the central place for the rest of the story of what Harnack called "the mission and expansion of Christianity."

A. CYPRUS, 13:1-12

1. *The Commission* (13:1-3)

Literally v. 1 says: "Now there were at Antioch, in the church that was there" (ASV; cf. NEB). In the Book of Acts the word **church** is used almost exclusively for the local congregation, whereas in the Epistles—particularly Ephesians—it often refers to the entire Church of Jesus Christ. So far in Acts it has had reference to the believers at Jerusalem (5:11; 8:1, 3; 11:22), except for two instances (7:38; 9:31).

Antioch in Syria was the third largest city in the Roman Empire (after Rome and Alexandria). It was the place where the followers of Christ had first been called Christians, thus differentiating them from the Jewish worshipers in the synagogue. Hence this was the logical location from which to launch the great Gentile mission. The narrow-minded, strongly Jewish attitude of many of the disciples at Jerusalem (cf. 15:1; 21:17-25) would have proved a great hindrance to any worldwide movement with Jerusalem as its headquarters. So Antioch became the main base for the evangelization of the Gentile world. Its situation (see map 3) at the northern extremity of Syria, facing Asia Minor and Europe, was also fortunate. Psychologically and geographically Antioch was providentially fitted to be the launching pad for the attack on the pagan world beyond Judaism. Christianity was no longer a sect of Judaism but a world-conquering religion.

397

Mention is made of **certain prophets and teachers** in the church at Antioch. In the New Testament the term **prophets** seems to be used mainly for "preachers." The Greek word *prophetes* (from *prophemi*, "speak forth") means "one who acts as an interpreter or forth-teller of the Divine will."[1] So far in Acts it has been used for the Old Testament prophets (e.g., 3:22-23; 7:37; 8:28). But now, as in Paul's Epistles, the term is applied to those who preached the gospel. **Prophets** were considered as second only to apostles, with **teachers** listed in third place (I Cor. 12:28). After the office of apostle had ceased, the prophets and teachers comprised the two main groups of workers in the Church worthy of receiving support, as the second-century *Didache* (c. 13) clearly shows.

In the Greek the particle *te* is placed before **Barnabas** and with **Manaen.** This fact led Ramsay to suggest that the list of five names should be divided into two parts, with the first three designated as **prophets** and the last two as **teachers.**[2] Lake and Cadbury doubt the validity of this distinction.[3] Alexander thinks it probable that "the two words are generic and specific terms, applied to the same persons, one denoting their divine authority, the other the precise way in which it was exercised."[4] But since prophets and teachers are treated as distinct classes in both the New Testament and the *Didache* (see above), Ramsay's interpretation deserves some consideration.[5]

Barnabas has already played a minor but significant role in Acts. He is first cited for his generous gift to the Church (4:36-37). It was he who became the sponsor of Saul before the suspicious congregation at Jerusalem (9:27). When confronted with the tremendous challenge at Antioch in the beginnings of the work there, Barnabas hunted up the intellectual giant and fervent convert, Saul, and brought him to Antioch as the main teacher in the church (11:22-26). He had been sent, with Saul, to Jerusalem with a relief offering for the famine-stricken Chris-

---

[1]Abbott-Smith, *op. cit.,* p. 390.

[2]*Op. cit.,* p. 65.

[3]*Beginnings,* IV, 141.

[4]*Op. cit.,* p. 464.

[5]See Charles W. Carter and Ralph Earle, *The Acts of the Apostles* ("Evangelical Commentary on the Bible"; Grand Rapids: Zondervan Publishing House, 1959), pp. 173-74.

tians (11:30). He is named first here as doubtless the main leader in the church at Antioch.

Simeon (or Symeon) was a very common Hebrew name. He was called **Niger,** which is Latin for "black." This man is sometimes identified with Simon of Cyrene (Mark 15:21), though the identity cannot be proved. **Lucius of Cyrene** (North Africa) may be the same one who is mentioned in Rom. 16:21. He is probably not Luke, the author of Luke and Acts. It will be remembered that it was men from Cyprus and Cyrene who preached freely to the Gentiles at Antioch (11:20).

Manaen is connected with **Herod the tetrarch**—Herod Antipas, who ruled Galilee and Perea (4 B.C.—A.D. 39). The entire phrase **which had been brought up with** is all one word in the Greek, *syntrophos.* This comes from *syn,* "with," and *trepho,* "bring up." Abbott-Smith defines it thus: "1. properly, *one nourished* or *brought up with, a foster-brother:* Ac 13:1 EV. 2. In Hellenistic usage, as a court term, *an intimate friend* of a king."[6] Bruce writes: "The title *syntrophos* was given to boys of the same age as princes, who were brought up with them at court."[7] Similarly Bicknell says: "Manaen was the foster-brother, or more accurately playmate, of Herod Antipas."[8] But after noting that the literal meaning, "foster-brother," is found in a second-century papyrus, Moulton and Milligan say: "From its widespread use as a court title, it is better understood as 'courtier' or 'intimate friend.' "[9] So rather than "foster brother" (ASV, Phillips) probably the word should be translated "a member of the court of" (RSV), or "a companion-of-honour to" (C. K. Williams).

On the combination of men named here Lumby makes this interesting comment: "One a Cypriote, another a Cyrenian, another a Jew, but from his double name accustomed to mix among non-Jews, one a connection of the Idumean house of Herod, and Saul, the heaven-appointed Apostle of the Gentiles—the list may

---

[6]*Op. cit.,* p. 434.

[7]*Acts,* p. 253.

[8]E. J. Bicknell, "The Acts of the Apostles," *A New Commentary on Holy Scripture,* ed. Charles Gore, H. L. Goudge, and Alfred Guillaume (New York: Macmillan Co., 1928), p. 353.

[9]VGT, p. 615.

be deemed in some sort typical of 'all the world,' into which the Gospel was now to go forth"[10]

These leaders were evidently having a special season of waiting on the Lord. **Ministered** (2) is the verb *leitourgeo*, from which comes "liturgy." Abbott-Smith points out the original meaning of the word, as follows: "1. in classics, at Athens, *to supply public offices at one's own cost, render public service to the State*, hence, generally, 2. *to serve the State, do a service, serve.*"[11] In the first century B.C., Diodorus (I. 21) used the term to describe service to the gods. In the Septuagint it is employed for the service of the priests and Levites in the Tabernacle and the Temple (cf. Heb. 10:11). Only here and in Rom. 15:27 is it used in connection with Christian service. Probably a majority of commentators hold that the reference here is to "ministry in organized worship."[12] However, there is no indication in the text that such was the case. It may very well be that this was a "staff" prayer meeting of the leaders of the local congregation. The Church later used the term mainly with reference to the sacrament of the Lord's Supper. But it has a more general sense here. It may be translated "worshiping" (Phillips; cf. NEB).

In connection with this ministering they **fasted**. This exercise is spiritually of value only in relation to prayer. When engaged in for the purpose of giving oneself to uninterrupted, intensive praying it can be invaluable. The custom of waiting on the Lord in prayer and fasting at times of important decisions has been practiced by the saints of all ages.

So here, as the five faithful leaders **ministered to the Lord, and fasted, the Holy Ghost said** . . . How, we are not told. But presumably it was by making an impression distinctly on their minds, as He does today.

The command of the Spirit inaugurated a new era in the expansion of Christianity. He said: **Separate me**—better, "Set apart for me"—**Barnabas and Saul for the work whereunto I have called them.** God asked for the two best men in the congregation for the task of "foreign missions." Too often the church has selfishly kept her most gifted men at home. But the divine call is for the best equipped and most talented Christians to carry on the greatest enterprise in the world—missionary evan-

[10]*Op. cit.,* p. 239.
[11]*Op. cit.,* p. 266.
[12]Bicknell, *op. cit.,* p. 353. Cf. also Alexander, *op. cit.,* p. 466.

gelism. Once more the Spirit needs to speak, and again His voice needs to be heard and heeded. In these days of international ferment the work of world missions demands the best the Church can give.

When God's will had been indicated, again **they . . . fasted and prayed** (3). Who is meant by **they**? Normally the antecedent would be the five men mentioned above, as it apparently is the antecedent for **they** in v. 2. But here the probability is that there is an awkward change in subject—a feature found in both the Old Testament and the New Testament—and that the reference is to the whole congregation. As a simple matter of fact, the five men could not have **laid their hands** on two of themselves. It seems unlikely that the remaining three would lay hands on their two colleagues who had been called, without involving the whole church. It may well be assumed, though not stated, that the congregation was called together for a special service of fasting and prayer. This was an epochal moment in the history of the Church—the launching of the great world missionary program—and it was necessary to seek earnestly God's guidance and power. Also the two called ones must be ordained to this special mission.

In this story of the inauguration of foreign missions one cannot fail to see a parallel with the famous "haystack prayer meeting" in Williamstown, Massachusetts. Several students at Williams College were caught in a sudden rainstorm and sought shelter under a typical New England haystack. Instead of wasting their time, or doing worse, they engaged in a serious discussion of the need of the heathen that had never heard the gospel. This led to prayer for these needy, unevangelized millions. Later, some of these praying college students were to offer themselves to go as the first foreign missionaries to leave the shores of America. Out of this concern came the first foreign missionary society in the United States. The missionary enterprise was born in a prayer meeting at Antioch and it is in many prayer meetings since then that it has received a fresh start.

At the conclusion of the special season of prayer and fasting, **they sent them away.** Everywhere else that this verb occurs in the New Testament it is rendered (KJV) as "let go." The church released these men from home duties for foreign service.

The teaching of verses 1-3 may be summed up under the topic "Secrets of Successful Service": (1) Waiting on God, 2; (2) Listening to His voice, 2; (3) Obeying His call, 3; (4) Enlisting the cooperation of the church, 3.

2. *The conquest* (13:4-12)

The two missionaries were not only "set . . . free for this work" (Phillips) by the church, but they were also **sent forth by the Holy Ghost (4)**. This is the combination that counts. To be called by God and sent forth by His Spirit, while at the same time being ordained by the church and sent with its blessing—this is the norm for Christian service.

The missionaries **departed**—literally, "went down"—**unto Seleucia**. This was the seaport of Antioch, sixteen miles west of the city and five miles north of the mouth of the Orontes River, on which Antioch was situated. Bruce comments: "Luke is usually careful to note the ports of departure and arrival"[13] (cf. 14: 25-26; 16:11; 18:18). This is one of the many evidences in this book that he had traveled widely.

From Seleucia they **sailed** —literally, "sailed away." The verb is found only in Acts (here; 14:26; 20:15; 27:1). It is one of the many nautical terms used by Luke, a seasoned voyager on the Mediterranean.

They sailed in a southwesterly direction **to Cyprus**, a large island about one hundred fifty miles long and forty miles wide. It was situated some sixty miles off the coast of Syria, but about one hundred miles from Antioch (see map 3). In earlier times it was noted for its rich deposits of copper, which formed one of its main exports. This was the origin of its name; in the Greek *kypros* means "copper." Barnabas was from Cyprus (4:36), and it was natural that he should want to go there.

The missionaries landed **at Salamis (5)**, "the chief town of Cyprus,"[14] and the main seaport at the east end of the island. There **they preached the word of God in the synagogues of the Jews**. The mention of **synagogues** (plural) shows that there was a sizable colony of Jews there. Already many of them had heard the gospel (11:19). But the work of evangelism had only been started. Now it must be pushed farther. So the missionaries **preached**—"were declaring" (*katengellon*)—**the word of God** (cf. 11:19—"preaching the word").

It is a striking phenomenon that at the very beginning of their missionary enterprise these preachers found waiting for them an open door in the form of Jewish synagogues. Since Barnabas and Saul were both good Jews, they could attend the

---

[13]*Op. cit.*, p. 254.
[14]*Beginnings*, IV, 143.

Sabbath services and preach the gospel to those who worshiped there.

The two missionaries had **John to their minister**—better, "John as their attendant" (ASV). In religious circles today **minister** usually means pastor or preacher. Here the word is *hyperetes;* literally, "under rower." The term indicates a servant who is subordinate to authority. John Mark (cf. 12:12, 25) was not the preacher of the party but the one who waited on the two older men.

After Barnabas and Saul had declared the Word of God in Salamis, they made a missionary tour of the island. **When they had gone through** (6) is one word in the Greek, *dielthontes.* Ramsay says that this verb is "the technical term for making a missionary progress through a district"[15] (cf. 15:41). Instead of **the isle** the best Greek text has "the whole island." Ramsay thinks the statement here indicates that they visited all the Jewish communities on the island, preaching in the synagogues.

The missionaries evangelized their way across the island from east to west, finally arriving at **Paphos,** the seat of the Roman government in Cyprus. Here they found a **sorcerer.** The word is *magos,* which occurs in v. 8, and elsewhere in the New Testament only in Matt. 2:1, 7, 16. There it is translated "wise men" and probably indicates astrologers from Media or Persia. Here it has a different connotation. Bruce writes: "As this man was a Jew, *magos* is not used here in its original or technical sense (see on viii. 9), but in the sense of 'magician.' "[16] That is the correct translation in this passage.

This magician is also labeled as **a false prophet;** that is, one who was "falsely claiming inspiration."[17] Jesus had warned that false prophets would appear (Mark 13:22).

In the third place this man is identified as **a Jew.** It seems surprising that the Jews would indulge in magic, in view of the Old Testament denunciations of this practice. But there is ample evidence that they did. Josephus mentions a Jewish sorcerer from Cyprus.[18] He also says that some Roman officials were fascinated with another Jewish magician.[19] It was one of the signs of the

15*Op. cit.,* p. 384.
16*Acts,* p. 256.
17Alexander, *op. cit.,* pp. 469-70.
18*Ant.* XX. 7. 2.
19*Ant.* VIII. 2. 5.

decadence of Judaism that magic was making inroads among the Jews.

The magician at Paphos was named **Bar-jesus. Bar** is the Aramaic word for "son." So this man was called "son of Jesus" (Heb., Joshua).

Bar-Jesus was with the **deputy** (7)—"proconsul," Roman governor—**of the country** of Cyprus. Nineteenth-century critics asserted that Luke had made a mistake here. They maintained that Cyprus was an imperial province, governed by a propraetor, and not a senatorial province, governed by a proconsul. So Luke was wrong. But subsequent discoveries have completely vindicated his accuracy. Cyprus was made an imperial province in 27 B.C. But five years later the emperor gave it to the senate, and it remained a senatorial province. As at many other places in Acts, archaeology has confirmed Luke's accuracy.[20]

The proconsul sent for Barnabas and Saul, and **desired to hear the word of God.** He was **a prudent**—"intelligent" or "understanding"—**man,** and he wanted to know the nature of this teaching that was being propagated in his province.

Bar-Jesus, the magician, was also called **Elymas** (8). With regard to the statement, **for so is his name by interpretation,** Bruce says: "The meaning cannot be that Elymas is the translation of Bar-Jesus, for the two names have quite different meanings."[21] The Greek says: "Elymas the magician (for that is the meaning of the name)."

The magician **withstood**—"resisted" or "opposed"—the missionaries, **seeking to turn away** the proconsul **from the faith.** Bruce comments: "Elymas seems to have been one of the pet magicians whom great men sometimes kept in their entourage . . . and he had a shrewd suspicion that if the proconsul paid heed to Barnabas and Saul, his own services were likely to be dispensed with."[22]

Saul (a common Hebrew name) was also called **Paul** (9)— a Latin word (cf. Sergius Paulus).[23] Because Paul was born a Roman citizen (22:27-28), but of Jewish parents (22:3), he was given both Hebrew and Roman names. Since he was proud

---

[20]See A. T. Robertson, *Luke the Historian in the Light of Research* (New York: Charles Scribner's Sons, 1920), pp. 179-82.

[21]*Acts,* p. 257.

[22]*Ibid.*

[23]*Paul* and *Paulus* are the same in the Greek.

of the fact that he was "of the tribe of Benjamin" (Phil. 3:5), it is probable that he was named after Israel's first king, Saul, who was also of that tribe. He would naturally be known by that name in Jewish circles. But now that he is going to work mainly in the Gentile world he calls himself Paul. The fact that he was with Sergius Paulus may also have influenced him. Paul could say to the Roman governor: "My name is also Paul."

Filled with the Holy Ghost—literally, "having been filled with the Holy Spirit" (exactly the same expression as in 4:8)— is the keynote of the Book of Acts. The indwelling Spirit gave Paul special inspiration and power for this occasion.

Set his eyes is a strong verb in the Greek. With the exception of II Cor. 3:7, 13 it is used only by Luke in the New Testament (ten times in Acts). Coming from an adjective meaning "strained, intent," it means "to look fixedly."[24].

Paul looked intently at the magician and charged him with being **full of all subtilty** (10). This is best translated "deceit." "The Greek word primarily means a bait for fish; then any deception; then a desire or disposition to deceive."[25] Paul also said that Elymas was full of **all mischief**—"unscrupulousness, recklessness, facility in doing evil, which is the original and etymological import of the word."[26] The **all** before both nouns emphasizes the depth and breadth of the magician's evil character.

Paul also called Elymas **child**—rather, "son"—**of the devil** (slanderer, false accuser). The magician was known as Bar-Jesus ("son of Jesus"), but he was really a "son of the devil." He was also an **enemy of all righteousness.** When would he **cease to pervert**—same word translated "turn away" in 8—**the right ways of the Lord**—the way of salvation?

Because of his opposition to the true light the magician would be **blind, not seeing the sun for a season** (11). This suggests that his blindness would be only temporary. He was not punished as severely as Ananias and Sapphira, because they sinned against greater light and also their action threatened to influence the whole Church adversely by setting an example of deceitfulness. **There fell on him a mist**—the beginning of dimness of sight (Gk. word only here in NT)—**and a darkness**—the climax of total blindness. **He went about seeking some to lead him by the hand**

---

[24] Abbott-Smith, *op. cit.,* p. 67.
[25] Alexander, *op. cit.,* p. 474.
[26] *Ibid.*

(three words in Gk.) is literally "going about [present participle of continued action] he was seeking [imperfect indicative of continuous action] hand-leaders." The picture is that of a helpless blind man groping around, begging people to take his hand and guide him home. Probably most of the onlookers were afraid to help him.

The effect on the proconsul is not surprising. He **believed, being astonished at the doctrine** (Gk., "teaching") **of the Lord (12)**. **Being astonished** is a strong verb meaning "to strike with panic or shock, to amaze, astonish."[27] The governor was overwhelmed by what had happened. It was the combination of Paul's teaching and God's judgment which "struck" the proconsul so forcibly. Lumby comments: "He was convinced by the miracle and by the words with which it was accompanied that the Apostles were teachers of that way of the Lord after which he had been seeking in vain from Elymas."[28] **Believed** in the context of Acts means accepted Christ as his Saviour and thus became a Christian.

B. Asia Minor, 13:13—14:28

1. *Pisidian Antioch* (13:13-52)

a. *The Synagogue* (13:13-15). The expression **Paul and his company (13)**—literally, "those around Paul"—is exceedingly significant. It suggests a new leadership for this missionary party. Hitherto it had been "Barnabas and Saul." But hereafter it will be "Paul and Barnabas." The only two exceptions are in connection with the Jerusalem Council (15:12, 25), where the Jewish leaders would naturally name Barnabas first, and at Lystra (14:14), where Barnabas was taken as the chief god, Jupiter.

Paul's party **loosed from Paphos.** The verb literally means "put out to sea." Luke alone uses this verb in a nautical sense (thirteen times in Acts and once in Luke 8:22). It is one of the many indications of his familiarity with the sea. The Jews were notoriously poor sailors. But Luke, who was probably the only non-Jewish writer of the New Testament, apparently loved to travel the high seas.

The missionaries **came to Perga in Pamphylia** (see map 3). This was a voyage of about one hundred seventy miles to the

---

[27]Abbott-Smith, *op. cit.,* p. 141.
[28]*Op. cit.,* p. 243.

mainland of Asia Minor. **Perga** was about eight miles up the Cestrus and perhaps five miles back from the river. The probability is that they landed at the main harbor of Attalia (cf. 14: 25) and then walked inland to Perga. **Pamphylia** was a territory between the Taurus Mountains and the Mediterranean Sea in what is now Turkey. In A.D. 43 it had been united with Lycia (in the west) to form an imperial province.

Once again (cf. 5) John Mark is mentioned. The sad note is here appended: **and John departing from them returned to Jerusalem** (13). We are not told why he did so. It may well be that a combination of factors influenced him. There may have been a lurking homesickness that drove him back to his mother's home in Jerusalem. It is altogether possible, even probable, that he resented Paul's taking over the leadership of the party, as reflected in the phrase, **Paul and his company.** Had not the Holy Spirit designated "Barnabas and Saul" as the missionaries (2)? What right did Paul have to usurp first place? The fact that John Mark was a cousin of Barnabas (Col. 4:10, NEB) would tend to make him solicitous for his relative. Perhaps the young attendant had assumed that the missionary tour would include only Cyprus, the home territory of Barnabas, and he was not happy about the move to the mainland.

Another possibility is suggested in the next verse. Paul and Barnabas left the swampy lowlands and went up into the mountainous region of Galatia. Why? In his Epistle to the Galatians, Paul suggests an answer. He says: "You know it was because of a bodily illness that I preached the gospel to you the first time" (Gal. 4:13, NASB). Sir William Ramsay thinks that in Pamphylia the apostle had a recurrence of chronic malaria.[29] Lake and Cadbury comment: "The generally malarious nature of the coast and the far more healthy climate of Antioch (3600 feet above the sea) render very probable Ramsay's guess that Paul had fever in Perga."[30] One can imagine that Paul told Barnabas of the necessity for his moving to a higher altitude. Bighearted, unselfish Barnabas agreed to go. But his young cousin refused. If Paul was calling the signals, he was going home. Besides it was too dangerous to go up into hills infested with robbers and laced with treacherous mountain torrents. He was not going to risk *his* life. And so home he went.

[29]*Op. cit.*, pp. 91–97.
[30]*Beginnings*, IV, 148.

With their attendant gone, Paul and Barnabas **departed from Perga** (14)—literally, "having gone through [see comment on 6] from Perga"—**they came to Antioch in Pisidia.** The best Greek text reads: "Pisidian Antioch." Actually, "Antioch was not in but near to Pisidia."[31] It is called Pisidian Antioch to differentiate it from Syrian Antioch, from which the missionary party had come. Ramsay says that "Pisidian Antioch" denotes "a Phrygian city towards Pisidia."[32] Bruce writes: "Pisidian Antioch was actually in the region probably called Phrygia Galatica, and was the civil and military centre of that part of the province."[33] Later on, in A.D. 295, Antioch became a part of Pisidia. Earlier, Augustus had made it a Roman colony.[34] From the very beginning of his missionary career Paul followed the policy of evangelizing the great metropolitian centers.

At Pisidian Antioch the two missionaries **went into the synagogue on the sabbath day, and sat down.** In so doing they were following the example set by their Master (Luke 4:16). With regard to the form of worship, Bruce says: "The synagogue service in the first century consisted of (1) the Shema ('Hear, O Israel: the Lord our God the Lord is one'), (2) prayer by the leader, (3) reading of the Law (and, on Sabbath and feast days, of the Prophets), (4) a sermon by any suitable member of the congregation."[35]

The law (15) consists of the Pentateuch, the first five books of Scripture. In the Hebrew canon **the prophets** include the so-called "former prophets"—Joshua, Judges, I & II Samuel, I & II Kings—and the "latter prophets"—Isaiah, Jeremiah, Ezekiel, and the Book of the Twelve (Minor Prophets). The rest of the Hebrew canon was grouped in the third division, called the Hagiographa ("Holy Writings").

After the reading of the stated lessons from the Law and the Prophets, word was sent to the visitors by the **rulers of the synagogue**—the plural suggests that more than one man officiated. Adam Clarke describes **Men . . . brethren** as "a Hebraism

---

[31]*Ibid.*

[32]*Op. cit.*, p. 174.

[33]*Acts*, p. 260.

[34]Lystra, Philippi, and Corinth were also Roman colonies.

[35]*Acts*, p. 260.

for, 'Ye men who are our brethren,' i.e. *Jews,* as we ourselves are."[36]

The message to the missionaries was: **If ye have any word of exhortation for the people, say on.** Exhortation may just as accurately be translated "encouragement" (Phillips) or "comfort." In view of the fact that the Jews called their coming Messiah "the Consolation of Israel" (cf. Luke 2:25), Clarke says: "*Paraklesis* is to be understood here as meaning *consolation,* and this in reference to the Messiah . . . Paul shows the care and protection of God towards his people Israel, and the abundant provision he had made for their salvation by Jesus Christ."[37]

b. The Sermon (13:16-41). This first recorded sermon by the Apostle Paul is strikingly similar to that of Stephen (7:2-53) in that both give a historical resumé of God's dealings with His people. Yet Paul's discourse is not at all a repetition of the other. Whereas Stephen begins with Abraham and the patriarchs, Paul starts with the Exodus.

Alexander summarizes the content of the sermon thus: "Beginning with a brief sketch of the early history of Israel, as the ancient church or chosen people, from their first vocation to the reign of David (17-22), the Apostle suddenly exhibits Jesus, as the heir of that king and the promised Saviour (23), citing John the Baptist as his witness and forerunner (24-25); then makes the offer of salvation through Christ to both classes of his hearers (26), describing his rejection by the Jews at Jerusalem (27), his death, burial, and resurrection (28-31); all of which he represents as the fulfilment of God's promise to the fathers (32), and of specific prophecies, three of which he quotes, interprets, and applies to Christ (33-37); winding up with another earnest offer of salvation (38-39), and a solemn warning against unbelief (40-41)."[38]

(1) *Moses to John* (13:16-25). Jesus followed the custom of the Jewish rabbis in being seated while teaching the people (cf. Matt. 5:1; Luke 4:20). But here at Pisidian Antioch **Paul stood up** (16), after the manner of the Greek and Roman orators. **Beckoning with his hand** to gain the attention of his audience (cf. 21:40), he addressed his hearers as **men of Israel**—literally,

---

[36]*Op. cit.,* p. 783.
[37]*Ibid.,* p. 784.
[38]*Op. cit.,* p. 481.

"men, Israelites"; that is, "fellow Israelites"—**and ye that fear God.** The God-fearers were those who worshiped in the Jewish synagogue and observed the Sabbath. The term could perhaps include Gentile proselytes (see comments on 10:2).

One of the main emphases of the Old Testament is the fact that God **chose** (17) Abraham and his descendants to be His covenant people (cf. Exod. 6:1, 4, 6; 13:14, 16). The same Greek verb for **chose** is used repeatedly in the Septuagint to express this idea (e.g., Deut. 7:7; 14:2; Ps. 33:12; 77:70). He **exalted the people** by making them numerous and strong. **With an high arm**—Hebrew expression for great power—God brought them out of Egypt.

For about **forty years suffered he their manners in the wilderness** (18)—or, "as a nursing-father bare he them in the wilderness" (ASV). The difference between these two renderings is a matter of only one letter in the Greek. The KJV translates *etropophoresen,* the ASV *etrophophoresen* ("nourish, bear like a nurse"). The evidence of the MSS is so nearly balanced that it is almost impossible to be certain as to which is correct. The KJV rendering is followed essentially by the RSV and NEB. The confusion in the text goes back to the Septuagint of Deut. 1:31, which Paul is evidently quoting. Both readings are found in different MSS of the Septuagint. Bruce writes: "The Heb. word is *nasa,* which may mean 'to carry' or 'to endure', and could be represented by either of the Gk. words."[39] Adam Clarke gives what is probably the best conclusion when he writes: "Both, when rightly understood, speak nearly the same sense; but the latter [ASV] is the most expressive, and agrees best with Paul's discourse, and the history to which he alludes."[40]

Rapidly Paul surveys the subsequent history of Israel to the time of David. God **destroyed seven nations** (19)—Hittites, Girgashites, Amorites, Canaanites, Perizzites, Hivites, and Jebusites (Deut. 7:1)—**in the land of Chanaan** (Canaan), and **divided** their territories to the tribes of Israel **by lot**—or "as an inheritance."

And after that he gave unto them judges about the space of four hundred and fifty years, until Samuel the prophet (20). This presents a chronological problem, which is reflected in the variant readings in the MSS. The best Greek text places the

[39]*Acts,* p. 263.
[40]*Op. cit.,* p. 784.

phrase, **about the space of four hundred and fifty years,** with 19 rather than 20. Bruce says of this reading: "It is best explained as covering the 400 years' sojourning . . . the 40 years in the wilderness, and the time that elapsed between the entry into Canaan and the distribution of the land in Josh. xiv."[41] The problem with KJV rendering is that it cannot be harmonized with the statement in I Kings 6:1 that the fourth year of Solomon was 480 years after the Exodus. This could not be true if the period of the judges was 450 years. Rackham holds that the period of 450 years began with the promise to Abraham that his seed should inherit the land.[42]

The period of the **judges** ended with **Samuel the prophet,** who was considered by the Jews to be the first prophet since Moses. But after Samuel there continued to be prophets in Israel throughout the rest of the Old Testament age. Lake and Cadbury note: "As in the early chapters of I Samuel he is the connecting link between Judges and Prophets and can be reckoned with either."[43]

Before Samuel died the Israelites **desired a king** (21). So God gave them **Saul the son of Cis** (Kish). He was **of the tribe of Benjamin,** as was the speaker himself (see comments on 9). The length of Saul's reign is given here as **forty years.** This is not indicated definitely in the Old Testament. But it is confirmed by Josephus, who writes: "Now Saul, when he had reigned eighteen years while Samuel was alive, and after his death two and twenty, ended his life in this manner."[44] In another place, however, he says that Saul ruled for twenty years.[45] But may this not be a round figure for the length of his reign after the death of Samuel, who might still be thought of as judge?

Because Saul disobeyed, God **removed him** (22) from being king (by his untimely death) and put **David** in his place. Divine election is subject to human obedience. God chose Saul but rejected him when he disobeyed. In the same way the nation of Israel would be **removed** for its disobedience and the Church of Jesus Christ would take Israel's place as God's people.

[41]*Acts,* p. 264.
[42]*Op. cit.,* p. 211.
[43]*Beginnings,* IV, 151.
[44]*Ant.* VI. 14. 9.
[45]*Ant.* X. 8. 4.

The divine **testimony** to David consists of three Old Testament quotations, combined into one—a feature which is common in the New Testament. **I have found David** is from Ps. 89:20, **a man after mine own heart** from I Sam. 13:14, and **which shall fulfil all my will** from Isa. 44:28.

Of this man's seed (descendants, cf. Rom. 1:3) God had **raised unto Israel a Saviour, Jesus** (23). This was the heart of Paul's message, for which the historical introduction only paved the way.

John the Baptist had "proclaimed before the face of His entrance a baptism of repentance" (lit., 24). **Coming** probably refers to Jesus' entrance upon His public ministry. John had declared: **I am not he** (25)—i.e., the Messiah. Rather, **there cometh one after me, whose shoes of his feet I am not worthy to loose** (cf. Luke 3:16).

(2) *Messiah crucified and resurrected* (13:26-41). Again (cf. 16) Paul addresses both the Jews—**children of the stock of Abraham** (26)—and the Gentile God-fearers. To them **is the word of this salvation sent.** But the Jerusalemites **and their rulers** (27), because they were ignorant of both Jesus and **the voices of the prophets which are read every sabbath day** in the synagogue services, had **fulfilled** those very prophecies in **condemning** Christ. **Though they found no cause of death in him** (28), yet they prevailed on Pilate to put Jesus to death. When they had **fulfilled** the Old Testament prophecies concerning Him (29), they removed His body from the Cross and placed it in a sepulcher. Specifically it was Joseph of Arimathaea who buried Him (Matt. 27:57-60).

Then comes one of the central emphases of apostolic preaching: **But God raised him from the dead** (30). It was necessary that the early Christians should present the Resurrection to prove that Jesus was the Messiah and Saviour. But since Christ's resurrection is the guarantee of our victory in Him, it may well be that the Resurrection should bulk larger in gospel preaching today.

The risen Christ **was seen many days**—actually forty (cf. 1:3)—by His disciples who came with Him **from Galilee to Jerusalem** (31). This agrees with the accounts in the Gospels and in Acts 1. Those who saw Him **are his witnesses unto the people.**

Paul went on to **declare . . . glad tidings** (32; *evangelizometha*), that the divine promise to **the fathers** God had **fulfilled**

(33) **unto us their children**[46] in raising up Jesus. The promise which Paul quotes is: **Thou art my Son, this day have I begotten thee** (Ps. 2:7). It would seem most natural to take **raised up** as referring to Jesus' resurrection "from the dead" (NEB). But many good scholars think that the reference is to the Incarnation. Bruce insists that it is the Incarnation which is meant here, whereas the Resurrection comes in 34.[47]

I will give you the sure mercies of David (34) represents the Hebrew text of Isa. 55:3. But the Greek text here is a quotation of the Septuagint of that passage: "to you . . . the holy things of David, the sure things." Lake and Cadbury comment: "It is important to notice that the whole argument is based on the LXX, and disappears if the speech be not in Greek."[48] The quotation in 35 is from Ps. 16:10. In 36, Paul argues that, since David has died, these passages must apply to the Messiah. He only is the One who **saw no corruption** (37).

The conclusion of all this is that **through this man is preached unto you the forgiveness of sins: and by him all that believe are justified from all things, from which ye could not be justified by the law of Moses** (38-39). This is the point that Paul labors at great length in Galatians and Romans. It is the heart of his message to the Jews.

The sermon closes with a warning to his hearers lest by their rejection of the gospel they should bring upon themselves the prophetic prediction of Hab. 1:5.

c. *Hungry Hearts* (13:42-43). **The Jews** left **the synagogue** (42), but **the Gentiles** tarried to beg the missionaries to preach more of this truth to them **the next sabbath.** Their hearts were hungry to hear more about Jesus as Saviour. **Many of the Jews and religious** (devout) **proselytes followed Paul and Barnabas** (43). The apostles urged them **to continue in the grace of God** already at work in their hearts.

d. *Jealous Jews* (13:44-47). Such interest was stirred up by the visit of the two missionaries that **the next sabbath day came almost the whole city together to hear the word of God** (44). **But when the Jews saw** the great crowd which had gathered to

---

[46]There is a very complicated textual problem here (see Carter and Earle, *op. cit.*, p. 188). But the KJV rendering seems to give the right meaning (cf. RSV).

[47]*Acts*, p. 269 (see further Carter and Earle, *op. cit.*, p. 188).

[48]*Beginnings*, IV, 156.

hear Paul and Barnabas, **they were filled with envy** (45). It was the same jealousy that had caused Jesus' death. Refusing to accept the Word of God, these religious leaders opposed the apostles' preaching, **contradicting** (speaking against) **and blaspheming.** They doubtless blasphemed the name of Jesus as an impostor.

Paul and Barnabas informed the Jews that **it was necessary** (46) that the gospel should have first been preached to them (cf. Rom. 1:16). But since they had rejected it and thereby judged themselves **unworthy of everlasting life, lo, we turn to the Gentiles.** This was the thing that would now take place in city after city—Jews rejecting the gospel, Gentiles accepting it. It was all a fulfillment of the prophecy (47) in Isa. 49:6—words originally addressed to Israel but in Luke 2:32 applied to Christ. Here Paul claims them for himself as God's appointed **light of the Gentiles,** to carry the gospel to **the ends of the earth**—i.e., the boundaries of the Roman Empire (in Paul's case).

e. Revival and Riot (13:48-52). The Gentiles rejoiced at this good news, **and glorified the word of the Lord** (48), which was now to be preached to them. The note is added: **as many as were ordained to eternal life believed.** Adam Clarke emphasizes the fact that the simple verb translated **ordained** "includes no idea of *pre*-ordination or *pre*-destination of any kind."[49] He goes on to say that *tasso* "signifies to *place, set, order, appoint, dispose;* hence it has been considered here as implying the *disposition* or *readiness of mind* of several persons in the congregation, such as the *religious proselytes* mentioned in ver. 43, who possessed the reverse of the *disposition* of those Jews who *spake against those things, contradicting and blaspheming,* ver. 45."[50] In other words, the proselytes, "in this good *state* and *order* of mind, believed."[51] Lumby calls attention to the military use of *tasso* for arranging troops in order, and says: "Thus the Gentiles were ordering themselves, and were ordered unto eternal life. The text says no word to warrant us in thinking that none could henceforth change sides."[52] The Jews and Gentiles had ordered themselves on opposite sides over the issue of the apostolic preaching, but this did not unalterably settle their destiny.

---

[49]*Op. cit.,* I, 790.
[50]*Ibid.*
[51]*Ibid.*
[52]*Op. cit.,* p. 251.

Not only did many Gentiles accept Christ, but **the word of the Lord was published**—literally, "carried about" or "spread abroad"—**throughout all the region** (49). Paul's policy was to concentrate on the large cities and let the work of evangelism spread out from these centers.

Not content with opposing the apostles' preaching in the synagogue, **the Jews stirred up the devout and honourable women** (50). **Honourable** may mean "wealthy." These were devout; i.e., worshipers in the synagogue. They were incited, along with **the chief men of the city,** to persecute Paul and Barnabas. They finally **expelled** the missionaries—literally, "drove them out"—from their **coasts** (district).

The apostles **shook off the dust of their feet against them** (51). This was in obedience to Christ's command (cf. Matt. 10:14; Mark 6:11; Luke 9:5; 10:11). The Jews often did this when returning from Gentile territory. So here it may have signified that Paul and Barnabas considered these Christ-rejecting Jews to be "heathen."

Driven out of Pisidian Antioch, the two missionaries came to **Iconium.** Today the place is called Konia. Because it is situated at the junction of several roads it has always been an important city. In New Testament times it was in the Phrygian region of the Roman province of Galatia.

In spite of all that had happened, **the disciples were filled with joy, and with the Holy Ghost** (52). This statement is often, if not usually, applied to Paul and Barnabas. But Alexander suggests: *"The disciples* who were thus affected were no doubt the converted Jews and Gentiles, whom the missionaries left behind at Antioch . . . and against whom the persecution was perhaps continued for a time."[53] The disciples **were filled with joy** precisely because they were filled **with the Holy Ghost.**

Alexander Maclaren uses this text (52) as the basis for a sermon, "Full of the Holy Ghost." (1) May be the experience of every Christian; (2) The result of that universal, abundant life; (3) The way by which we may be thus filled.

2. Iconium (14:1-7)

At Iconium (see map 3) the two missionaries followed the same policy as at Pisidian Antioch: they entered the synagogue.

[53]*Op. cit.,* p. 507.

Together (1) means "after the same manner" or "in the same way" (cf. Phillips—"Much the same thing happened at Iconium"). The expression **the synagogue of the Jews** shows that Luke is writing for Gentiles. Here Paul and Barnabas **so spake, that a great multitude both of the Jews and also of the Greeks believed.** Apparently more Jews were saved in Iconium than in Pisidian Antioch.

Again here opposition came from the **unbelieving Jews** (2). This word could very properly be translated "disobedient" (ASV). Lumby says: "The word is stronger than 'unbelieving', it expresses unbelief breaking forth into rebellion, and so exactly describes the character of these Jews who were persecuting Paul and Barnabas."[54] He adds: "It is noteworthy throughout the Acts that persecution seems nearly in every case to have originated with the Jews."[55] The Jewish opponents **stirred up the Gentiles** and "poisoned their minds" (NEB) **against the brethren.**

In order to combat this Jewish opposition (or in spite of it) the missionaries "spent"[56] a **long time** in Iconium, **speaking boldly in the Lord** (3). **In** is literally "upon" (*epi*). A good translation is, "in reliance on the Lord" (NEB). Alexander comments: "*In the Lord*, or rather *on him*, i.e. in reliance on him, and by his authority, both of which ideas are suggested by the next clause."[57]

The Lord **gave testimony unto the word of his grace.** Probably this means that the Holy Spirit witnessed to the hearts of the hearers that what the missionaries were preaching was true. He also **granted signs and wonders to be done by their hands.** The miracles were to convince those who "require a sign" (I Cor. 1:22).

The result of the preaching was that **the multitude of the city was divided** (4). This is the inevitable result of proclaiming the gospel. The presenting of Christ provokes a crisis; men either accept Him or reject Him. This is the explanation of Jesus' strange words: "Suppose ye that I am come to give peace on earth? I tell you, Nay; but rather division" (Luke 12:51).

So in Iconium **part held with the Jews,** rejecting the gospel, **and part with the apostles.** Both Paul and Barnabas are here

---

[54]*Op. cit.,* p. 257.

[55]*Ibid.*

[56]**Abode** literally means "rub away" or "consume."

[57]*Op. cit.,* pp. 509-10.

referred to as **apostles.** At first the term was applied only to the Twelve. But Paul calls himself an apostle at the beginning of nine of his thirteen Epistles. Only here is Barnabas designated as such. Alexander suggests: "Paul and Barnabas are both here called Apostles, not in the technical distinctive sense, but in the primary and wider one of *missionaries,* ministers sent forth upon a special service."[58]

Finally the conflict came to a climax. **An assault (5)** was made by both **Gentiles** and **Jews.** Probably this is too strong a translation for the noun, which means "a violent impulse" or "hostile movement." Lumby comments: "It rather refers to the excitement, urging, and instigation which the Jews were applying to their heathen companions, and which was likely to end in violence."[59] The implication of the next verse is that the apostles sensed this growing opposition and left town before an actual assault was made on them.

The intention of the **Gentiles . . . Jews,** and **their rulers** was **to use them despitefully**—"to outrage, insult, treat insolently"[60] —**and to stone them.** This shows that the opposition was instigated by the Jews, for this was the Jewish form of punishment. Probably the Jews held these missionaries to be guilty of blasphemy in their preaching of Jesus.

When the apostles became aware of what was being planned, they **fled**[61] **unto Lystra and Derbe** (see map 3), **cities of Lycaonia (6)**—a region of the province of Galatia. This implies that Iconium was at this time not Lycaonian but Phrygian. Ramsay points out the fact that this was true only between A.D. 37 and 72,[62] when Paul and Barnabas were there. Once again Luke has been proved to be historically accurate.

From Iconium to Lystra was a distance of about twenty miles, or about one day's journey on foot. The site of **Lystra** was identified in 1885 by an inscription which states that Augustus had made it a colony of Rome. There **they preached the gospel (7)**—literally, "were evangelizing."

[58]*Ibid.,* p. 510.

[59]*Op. cit.,* p. 257.

[60]Abbott-Smith, *op. cit.,* p. 453.

[61]The compound verb means "flee for refuge."

[62]*Op. cit.,* pp. 110-11.

3. *Lystra* (14: 8-19)

In this city the missionaries found a man who had been a **cripple** from birth (8), never having walked. He was **impotent in his feet**. The adjective is generally translated "impossible" in the New Testament. Here alone it has the connotation "power-less" physically, a sense found frequently in medical writers.[63] From a human point of view the man's case was hopeless.

The cripple **heard Paul speak** (9)—literally, "was hearing Paul as he was speaking." Evidently the man was listening care-fully. The preacher, **stedfastly beholding him**—*atenisas*, same form used of Peter looking at the cripple in 3:4—and seeing that he "was having" (lit.) **faith to be healed, commanded with a loud voice, Stand upright**—*orthos*, "straight"—**on thy feet** (10). This was asking the impossible. But when the man *willed* to obey, God furnished the power. The helpless cripple suddenly **leaped** to his feet (aorist tense) and "kept on walking" (imperfect tense). As in many other cases in the Gospels and Acts, faith was demonstrated in obedience and rewarded with divine power.

The usual public reaction followed. Paul had been speaking in Greek, which was commonly used throughout the Roman Empire. But when the people of Lystra became excited, they cried out **in the speech of Lycaonia** (11), their mother tongue. Apparently this point is mentioned to explain why the apostles did not realize at once what these people were saying and doing.

The conclusion the populace drew from the miracle was: "The gods, having become like men, descended to us" (lit. trans-lation). Alexander writes: "This language agrees perfectly, not only with the general belief in such epiphanies or theophanies, divine appearances in human form, as found in Homer and the later classics, but also with the local superstitions and traditions of the very country where the words were spoken, *Lycaonia,* so called from *Lycaon,* whose fatal entertainment of Jupiter is one of Ovid's fables in the first book of his Metamorphoses, while in the eighth he tells the fabulous but interesting story of the visit paid to Philemon and Baucis, in the adjacent province of Phrygia, by Jupiter and Mercury, the very gods mentioned in the next verse."[64]

[63]Hobart, *op. cit.,* p. 46.
[64]*Op. cit.,* p. 516.

By these superstitious Lycaonians, **Barnabas (12)** was called **Jupiter,** and **Paul** was identified with **Mercurius** (Mercury). These were the Roman names for the Greek gods Zeus and Hermes. Paul was called **Mercurius, because he was the chief speaker**—literally, "was the one leading the word" (or discourse). The belief of that day was that Hermes was the spokesman for Zeus. In typical Oriental fashion it was held that a chief god would communicate only through a subordinate. The distinction pointed out here does not necessarily indicate any difference in appearance. It simply means that Paul **was the chief speaker.**

The priest of Jupiter (Zeus), **which was before their city (13)**—apparently this means, "whose temple was before the city" (ASV; cf. RSV, Phillips, NEB)—**brought oxen and garlands.** The **garlands** were "sometimes put on the heads of the victims, and sometimes used by the worshippers for their own decorations at religious rites."[65] They brought these **unto the gates** (a public place), **and would have done sacrifice with the people.** Concerning the worship of Zeus and Hermes, Bruce writes: "Of two inscriptions of Sedasa, near Lystra, dating from c. A.D. 250, discovered by Prof. W. M. Calder, one records the dedication to Zeus of a statue of Hermes along with a sundial, by men with Lycaonian names, the other mentions 'priests of Zeus.' "[66]

When Paul and Barnabas heard about what was happening, **they rent their clothes (14)**—with horror at the blasphemy of this attempted worship of them as gods—**and ran in**—the best Greek text says "sprang forth"—**among the people.** Lumby thinks that "sprang forth" makes it impossible to take "gates" (13) as meaning the gates of the city, but rather that the reference is to "the entrance of the house where the Apostles lodged."[67] But probably the idea is that they rushed out through the city gates into the space between the gates and the temple of Zeus.

The apostles' speech to the Lycaonians (15-17) bears striking resemblance to Paul's discourse before the Areopagus at Athens (17:22-31). In neither case was reference made to the divine revelation in the Scriptures, with which the heathen audience would have been unfamiliar, but the appeal was to God's

[65]Lumby, *op. cit.,* p. 261.
[66]*Acts,* p. 281.
[67]*Op. cit.,* p. 261.

revelation in nature. This is the first occurrence in Acts of preaching the gospel to a purely pagan audience.

Courteously the missionaries cried: **Sirs** (Gk., "men") , "why are you doing this?" (15) **We also are men of like passions with you;** or, "We are only human beings with feelings just like yours" (Phillips). The main emphasis to this heathen audience was that they should **turn from these vanities** (idols, lit., "useless things") **unto the living God.** This is the One who **made heaven, and earth, and the sea, and all things that are therein**—a quotation from Exod. 20:11 (exactly the same in 4:24).

In His great mercy and forbearance God did not destroy the heathen in their false worship, but **in times past**—literally, "in generations gone by" (ASV)—**suffered all nations to walk in their own ways (16).** This is closely parallel to Paul's statement in 17:30—"And the times of this ignorance God winked at" (i.e., "overlooked").

But God did not leave himself **without witness (17).** His providential goodness to all men—**rain . . . and fruitful seasons**— is a constant reminder of His love and power. The heathen gods were powerless to give rain—"Are there any among the vanities of the Gentiles [cf. **vanities, 15**] that can cause rain?" (Jer. 14: 22)

Even with these arguments **scarce**—"with difficulty, hardly" —**restrained**—"caused to cease"—**they the people, that they had not done sacrifice unto them** (18). When religious fervor is roused, it is difficult to control. Too often people do not appreciate being enlightened when the truth presented conflicts with their purposes and desires.

While the people of Lystra were perhaps smarting under their disappointment that Barnabas and Paul were not really Zeus and Hermes, **there came thither certain Jews from Antioch (19)**—over 100 miles away—**and Iconium.** These jealous Jews (cf. 13:45, 50; 14:2) showed their extreme hatred of the apostles by following them all this distance on foot. **They persuaded the people** of Lystra—perhaps attributing the healing miracle to demonic power (cf. Matt. 12:24)—and succeeded in getting Paul **stoned** (cf. II Cor. 11:25). Then they **drew**—better, "dragged"— **him out of the city, supposing he had been dead.** The fanatical opponents of Christianity seemed to have accomplished their purpose. The main resentment was evidently aimed at Paul because he was the chief speaker.

4. *Derbe and Return* (14:20-28)

a. Organizing Churches (14:20-23). In the divine plan Paul's life work was not yet complete. A group of **disciples stood round about him** (20)—"encircled" (*cyclosanton*). In the short time that he had been in Lystra he had won some converts, among whom was doubtless young Timothy (cf. 16:1; I Tim. 1:2). These risked their lives to stand guard around Paul's body. Suddenly, to their joy and astonishment, **he rose up.** On the significance of this verb Lumby writes: "The word *anastas* conveys the impression that this was a resurrection from the dead, and that the restoration of the Apostle, and his immediate exhibition of vigour, and boldness to enter again into the city, was the effect of a miracle."[68] He adds: "That one stoned and left for dead by a savage mob should revive and go about as if nothing had befallen him must have been a still more striking evidence of the mighty power of God present with these teachers than what the people had seen before in the restoration of the cripple."[69]

The next day—after perhaps spending the night in the home of Timothy, where he observed the deep piety of the young man's mother and grandmother (II Tim. 1:5)—Paul **departed with Barnabas to Derbe.** The fact that he was able to walk this distance of about sixty miles shows that he had recovered fully from the effects of the stoning. Years later, just before his death, Paul reminded Timothy of the "persecutions, [and] afflictions, which came unto me at Antioch, at Iconium, at Lystra; what persecutions I endured: but out of them all the Lord delivered me" (II Tim. 3:11).

Only a few years ago (1933) Lake and Cadbury could say that the site of **Derbe** is "not yet completely identified."[70] But recent discoveries have fixed the location with greater certainty at about sixty miles southeast of **Lystra.**[71]

The evangelization of Derbe **is** described in only two clauses: **And when they had preached the gospel to that city, and had taught many** (21)—better, "made many disciples" (ASV). The verb *matheteuo* comes from *mathetes,* "disciple"; its proper meaning is "make a disciple." The correct translation (cf. NEB—

---

[68]*Op. cit.,* p. 264.
[69]*Ibid.*
[70]*Beginnings,* IV, 163.
[71]IDB, III, 195; I, 826.

"gained many converts") emphasizes the success of the apostolic mission in Derbe.

Having finished their task in Derbe, the missionaries **returned again to Lystra, and to Iconium, and Antioch.** A casual reading may fail to note the tremendous implications of this statement. Adam Clarke well remarks: "Behold the *courage* of these Christian men! They counted not their lives dear to them, and returned to do their Master's work in the *very places* in which they had been so grievously persecuted, and where one of them had been apparently stoned to death!"[72]

Tarsus, Paul's hometown, was only 160 miles away, and right on the return route to Antioch in Syria, from which they had been sent. It would have been much safer and simpler to go east to Tarsus, enjoy a brief rest there, and then continue on to Syrian Antioch to report. They had won many converts to Christ, and certainly would have been justified in returning home. But instead Paul and Barnabas headed back north and west right into the jaws of hate and death. Why? The following two verses give the answer: they must take care of the converts they had won.

Two main ministries are here described. The first (22) was that of comfort and encouragement. The second (23) was that of organization. Both were necessary.

They began by **confirming**—"strengthening, establishing" **the souls of the disciples (22).** These new converts must become "fixed and settled"—the root meaning of the word—in the Lord. This purpose was achieved by **exhorting them to continue** (on) **in the faith,** which "seems clearly here to mean "Christianity.' "[73] **And that** is better translated "and, saying," the *hoti* being equivalent to quotation marks introducing a direct quotation. Paul's own life was a perpetual example of the fact that **we must through much tribulation**—"literally, *many tribulations,* which expresses not mere quantity or number but variety"[74]—**enter into the kingdom of God.** Bruce comments: "The kingdom of God is to be understood here in the sense of a consummation yet future (cf. II Tim. iv. 18; II Peter i. 11), not as something already realized."[75]

[72]*Op. cit.,* p. 796.
[73]*Beginnings,* IV, 167.
[74]Alexander, *op. cit.,* p. 526.
[75]*Acts,* p. 286.

Tribulation literally means "pressure." The plural here suggests the pressures which all Christians must endure.

Verse 22 deals with "How to Conserve Converts": (1) Strengthening the soul; (2) Exhorting to steadfastness; (3) Warning of tribulation.

A certain amount of organization is necessary to preserve the continuity of any movement. These early missionaries adopted the simple framework familiar to them in Jewish circles of appointing a group of **elders** (23) in each congregation.

The word **ordained** has caused endless discussion. It is better translated "appointed" (ASV, NEB, etc.). The Greek verb is *cheirotoneo.* It comes from *cheir,* "hand," and *teino,* "stretch"; i.e., "stretch out the hand." Its original meaning was "to vote by stretching out the hand,"[76] as was done in the Athenian *ecclesia,* or free assembly of voting citizens. That is apparently the connotation of the word in the only other place where it occurs in the New Testament (II Cor. 8:19). The term was also used in the more general sense of "appoint."[77] Ramsay thinks that the congregations in these Galatian cities had a voice in the selection of elders.[78] The First Epistle of Clement—written about A.D. 95— says that the apostles appointed the elders. After discussing the matter at some length, Alexander expresses his preference for what he calls "the true meaning between the opposite extremes."[79] He writes: "This middle ground is, that the verb itself, expressing as it clearly does the act of Paul and Barnabas, can only mean that they appointed or ordained these elders, without determining the mode of election or the form of ordination; but that the use of this particular expression, which originally signified the vote of an assembly, does suffice to justify us in supposing that the method of selection was the same as that recorded . . . in 6,5.6, where it is explicitly recorded that the people chose the seven and the twelve ordained them."[80] Perhaps that is the best conclusion we can reach.

In connection with the appointment of elders, they **prayed with fasting**—literally, "with fastings," probably meaning a time

[76]Abbott-Smith, *op. cit.,* p. 481.
[77]*Ibid.*
[78]*Op. cit.,* p. 122.
[79]*Op. cit.,* p. 527.
[80]*Ibid.*

of fasting in each church. This was a feature of the setting apart of Paul and Barnabas for their missionary work (13:3). In later times also the appointment of elders was always accompanied by fasting. Such times of waiting upon the Lord are certainly appropriate in connection with important decisions in the church.

As a final act, the apostles **commended**—the verb means "deposit" or "place in charge of"—**them to the Lord** (cf. 20:32), **on whom they** had **believed** (pluperfect), when the missionaries first preached there.

b. *Reporting to Home Base* (14:24-28). Having **passed throughout**—*dielthontes*, "preached their way through" (cf. 13:6) —**Pisidia, they came to Pamphylia** (24), on the coast of the Mediterranean. Bruce writes: "Pisidia was the southernmost 'region' of the province of Galatia; it lay across the northern boundary of Pamphylia"[81] (see map 3).

They **preached the word in Perga** (25). They had visited this city earlier (cf. 13:13-14), but Paul's illness may have prevented their preaching there. After evangelizing Perga, **they went down into Attalia**—"the chief port of Pamphylia, now called Adalia, at the mouth of the Catarractes."[82] From here they **sailed**—literally, "sailed away"—**to Antioch** (26). This was Syrian Antioch, **from whence they had been recommended** (better, "committed") **to the grace** (care) **of God for the work which they fulfilled.** They could honestly say, "Mission accomplished."

They evidently called for a special meeting of **the church** (27). To the congregation **they rehearsed**—the verb appropriately means "to bring back word, report"[83]—**all that God had done with them, and how he had opened the door of faith unto the Gentiles.** That is, God had provided that the Gentiles also could be saved through simple faith in Jesus Christ.

There (28)—at Syrian Antioch—**they abode long time**— literally, "spent time" (see comment on 3)—**with the disciples.** No indication is given as to the length of time. But the language implies a matter of months, perhaps a year or so.

C. JERUSALEM COUCIL, 15:1-35

The first general Church council, held in Jerusalem probably in A.D. 48, is one of the most important events recorded in Acts.

---

[81]*Acts,* p. 286.
[82]*Beginnings,* IV, 168.
[83]Abbott-Smith, *op. cit.,* p. 28.

The question was: Are the Gentile Christians to be required to keep the Jewish law? On the answer to this question hung, to a great extent, the fate of the Church. If the answer was, "Yes," Christianity would be simply another sect of Judaism; if the answer was, "No," it would be free to fulfill its divinely ordained mission of being a world religion.

1. *Pharisaic Christianity* (15:1-5)

Certain men (1) who **came down from Judaea**—one always came "down" from Jerusalem—**taught the brethren**—literally, "were teaching" (RSV) the Gentile Christians at Antioch—**Except ye be circumcised after the manner** (custom) **of Moses, ye cannot be saved.** But there were many Gentiles in Antioch who had been enjoying salvation for years, and yet had never been circumcised. Naturally, this new teaching was disturbing.

Paul and Barnabas (2) recognized the real issue at stake and the seriousness of it. If this teaching prevailed, their work among the Gentiles, which God had blessed so abundantly, could well be ruined. Many Christian converts would renounce their faith rather than subject themselves to this offensive rite. On the other hand, those who did submit to circumcision would thereby renounce Christ. That was the position that Paul took with the Galatian converts in his letter to them (Gal. 5:2).

So these two missionaries to the Gentiles **had no small dissension and disputation**—"questioning" or "debate"—with these false Judaistic teachers. Finally the church at Antioch **determined**—"appointed"—**Paul and Barnabas, and certain other of them**—probably including some who agreed with the Judaizers, so that both sides would be represented—to **go up to Jerusalem unto the apostles and elders about this question.** Lumby notes: "Peter, John and James we find were now at Jerusalem, and they seem, from other notices in the N.T. (Gal. i. 18, 19, and ii. 9), to have been the Apostles who continued to live in the holy city. These with the elders appear now as the governing body of the infant church."[84] However, the statement that in the early persecution at Jerusalem the apostles remained in the city (8:1) may suggest that all of the twelve who were yet alive, including Matthias, were still there.

These emissaries were **brought on their way by the church** (3). It was a courteous custom in those days for members of a

[84]*Op. cit.*, p. 270.

church to "escort"[85] their respected teachers on the beginning of their journeys (cf. 20:38; 21:16). The delegates **passed through**—literally, "were passing through" on a missionary tour (same verb as in 13:6; 14:24)—**Phenice** (Phoenicia) **and Samaria, declaring the conversion of the Gentiles** (see map 1). Paul was not one to be deterred from continuing to preach salvation through faith in Jesus Christ, apart from the Law, even though there may have been some Judaizers in the party. **Declaring** literally means "telling in detail." Lumby observes: "The verb *ekdiegeisthai* implies that he gave his story with all details, and we may be sure that he dwelt on the way in which the Spirit of God had set a seal upon the work, though the converts of whom he spake were all uncircumcised."[86]

This report **caused great joy unto all the brethren.** Doubtless many of the Christians in Phoenicia and Samaria were Gentiles, and they rejoiced at this good news.

When the emissaries reached **Jerusalem** (4), after a journey of nearly three hundred miles, **they were received of the church**—better, "welcomed by the church." They were welcomed, in particular, by **the apostles and elders, and they declared**—"reported"—**all things that God had done with them** (same phrase as in 14:27; see comments there).

When Paul and Barnabas finished giving the report of their missionary work—telling how a great number of Gentiles had been saved through simple faith in Jesus Christ, without being circumcised—**there rose up certain of the sect of the Pharisees which believed** (5). Saul himself had been a zealous Pharisee, so he could understand how they felt. But his loyalty to Jesus Christ was so complete that he had been able to divorce himself from the Law, as evidently these Judaistic Christians had not.

The Pharisaic Christians asserted publicly that it was necessary **to circumcise them**—the Gentiles converts—**and to command them to keep the law of Moses.** Bruce says: "For those to whom the Church was but another party within the Jewish fold, the answer was simple enough: Gentiles should be admitted into the Church in the usual manner in which proselytes were adopted into the Jewish commonwealth, by circumcision and obedience to the whole Mosaic law."[87] These Pharisees were steeped in the Penta-

---

[85]One meaning given by Abbott-Smith (p. 382) for the verb here.
[86]*Op. cit.,* p. 271.
[87]*Acts,* p. 287.

teuch, but they had not read the Prophets with sufficient understanding. Had they done so they would have recognized that the teaching of Paul was a logical deduction from the teaching of the Prophets. Hosea (6:6), Amos (5:21-24), and Micah (6:6-8) had clearly declared that God desired righteousness rather than ritual. Ezekiel (36:25-27) and Jeremiah (31:31-34) had shown the spiritual nature of true religion, that it is a matter of the heart rather than legal observances. But there was a dearth of prophets in Israel in Jesus' day, and legalism reigned supreme.

2. *Peter's Speech* (15:6-11)

It would appear that Paul and Barnabas reported to a general gathering of the Church at Jerusalem (4), but that when the Judaizers raised their objection (5), **the apostles and elders came together for to consider**—literally, "to see about"—**this matter** (6). This was the group to which the Antioch church had asked that the question be carried (2). The large crowd of church members would have neither the time nor the ability to weigh the question adequately and arrive at a wise decision.

When there had been much disputing (7)—"after a long debate" (NEB)—**Peter rose up.**[88] In view of the chief place that he had held in the very earliest days of the Church (Acts 1—5), it may be presumed that he still commanded a large measure of deferential respect. So his speech would be heard with eagerness.

Fortunately, because of his housetop vision at Joppa (10:9-16), Peter was prepared to take the right side of the issue. He reminded his hearers how **a good while ago**—literally, "from beginning days," and so "in the early days" (NEB)—God had chosen him to introduce the gospel to the Gentiles. This he had done in the house of Cornelius (10:34-48).

Verses 8 and 9 are among the most important in the Book of Acts. It is often asserted that, while Acts has much to say about being filled with the Holy Spirit, it has no teaching on sanctification—although the word "sanctified" occurs in 20:32 and 26:18. The answer to that objection is to be found in this passage. Peter declared that "God, the heart-knower" (cf. 1:24), **bare them witness** (8)—i.e., the people gathered in Cornelius' house—**giving them the Holy Ghost, even as he did unto us**—at Pentecost (c. 2);

[88]This is the only place in Acts in which Peter is mentioned after the first twelve chapters, where his name occurs fifty-seven times.

**and put no difference between us and them, purifying their
hearts by faith (9).** Peter affirmed that two things happened
both to the Jews at Pentecost and to the Gentiles at Caesarea:
they were filled with the Holy Spirit, and their hearts were
cleansed. Thus we affirm, with Peter, that when a person is filled
with the Holy Spirit he not only receives power (1:8), but he
also is cleansed from sin (15:8-9). These two verses comprise a
key passage for the preaching and teaching of entire sanctification.
When the Spirit fills one's heart, He necessarily cleanses it; for
He is the *Holy* Spirit, the sanctifying Spirit.

Knowling makes a pertinent observation about **purifying—**
"cleansing," *katharisas*—**their hearts.** He says: "Here it stands
in contrast to the outward purification of circumcision upon which
the Judaizers insisted."[89]

The modern counterpart is found in those who put much
emphasis on water baptism but completely ignore the baptism
with the Holy Spirit. Water baptism is an outer act, but Spirit
baptism is an inner action—a cleansing of the heart from sin by
the inward purging of the sanctifying Spirit. **Giving** and **purifying** are here both aorist participles, suggesting a crisis rather than
a process.

The essential truths of "Entire Sanctification" may be seen
in this passage. (1) God knows the human heart and is concerned that its deepest needs be satisfied, 8; (2) He has made
the Holy Spirit available to all believing Christians—Jew and
Gentile alike—to satisfy the heart's need, 8-9; (3) The gift of the
Holy Spirit is a heart-cleansing experience, 9; (4) God's gift and
the experience of cleansing may be had in a moment of time—it
is the result of faith, and is described by the aorist (**giving** and
purifying), suggesting a crisis rather than a process, 8-9 (A. F.
Harper).

At the close of his speech Peter made his plea. Why tempt
God by putting **a yoke upon the neck of the disciples (10)**? "The
yoke of the Law" (Torah) was a familiar rabbinical expression.[90]
Lake and Cadbury say that **yoke** "was commonly used by Jewish
writers in the sense of 'obligation.'"[91]

Peter declared, in contrast to Jesus' "easy" yoke (Matt. 11:
29-30), that the yoke of the Law was one **which neither our fa-**

---

[89]EGT, II, 319.
[90]*Ibid.,* p. 320.
[91]*Beginnings,* IV, 173-74.

thers nor we were able to bear. Schuerer documents this statement when he writes: "Life was a continual torment to the earnest man, who felt at every moment that he was in danger of transgressing the law; and where so much depended on the external form, he was often left in uncertainty whether he had really fulfilled its requirements."[92]

Peter ended his speech with a declaration that there is only one way of salvation for both Jews and Gentiles (cf. 4:12). He said: **But**—in contrast to the unbearable yoke of the Law—**we believe that through the grace of the Lord Jesus Christ we shall be saved, even as they (11).** That is, Jews cannot be saved by obedience to the law of Moses, but only through the grace of Christ. In this Peter was in perfect agreement with Paul.

3. *Joint Session* (15:12)

Peter's speech, especially his conclusion, apparently stunned the group into silence. We read: **Then all the multitude kept silence** (became silent). The mention of the **multitude** poses something of a problem. Paul and Barnabas apparently reported on their missionary activities to the whole church (4). Then there was held a special meeting of the apostles and elders to discuss the question that had risen (6). How does the **multitude** come into the picture again?

It is not impossible to apply this term to a meeting of the apostles and elders,[93] as the same word is used for the Sanhedrin (23:7). But "the whole church" is mentioned in 22. So it may be best to assume that the apostles and elders had summoned the congregation together for a final decision. Rackham suggests: "Though the initiative rested with the apostles, the consent of the whole church was required."[94]

The assembled group now **gave audience to**—"were hearing" —**Barnabas and Saul.** Once more (cf. 14:14) Barnabas is named first (also in 25). This is perhaps because he was held in higher esteem than Paul by the Jerusalem church, and Luke was influenced by this fact in his description of the events.

Paul and Barnabas were **declaring** ("unfolding") **what miracles and wonders God had wrought among the Gentiles by them.**

---

[92]*Op. cit.,* II, ii, 124.
[93]*Beginnings,* IV, 172.
[94]*Op. cit.,* p. 249.

This was the thing for which the Early Church had prayed (4:30), and now God had answered in abundant measure.

4. James's Conclusion (15:13-21)

When Barnabas and Paul **had held their peace** (13)—same verb as "became silent" (12)—**James**, the brother of Jesus, who was evidently bishop (head pastor) of the Jerusalem church and now acting as moderator of the Jerusalem Council, summed up the matter and stated the conclusion. He called Peter by his Hebrew name **Simeon** (cf. II Pet. 1:1), by which he would be known among the Jews. James noted Peter's reference to the fact that under his ministry **God at the first did visit the Gentiles, to take out of them a people for his name** (14). No longer was Israel alone the people of God. The believing Gentiles were also His people. This was a bitter pill for the proud Jew to swallow, but it was so.

James then declared that **the prophets** supported this truth (15). In proof he cited (16-18) the words of Amos 9:11-12. The quotation is from the Septuagint, which differs considerably from the Massoretic (Hebrew) text. **After this** (16) is, in the Book of Amos, "in that day" (both Heb. and Gk.). The reference is evidently to the day of the Messiah.

The quotation in 17 is the most problematical. The Old Testament Massoretic text reads: "That they may possess the remnant of Edom and all the nations which are called by my name"—a prophecy of the restoration of the Davidic kingdom to its ancient strength. Apparently the Septuagint translators adopted *yidreshu* (will seek) in place of *yireshu* (will possess), and *adam* (man) in place of *Edom*. The Hebrew also makes **residue** (remnant) the object, not the subject.

Lumby offers this solution of the problem:

> The original paints the restored tabernacle, and of course the people of David restored along with it, as possessors of the remnant of Edom and all the heathen. The nations shall be joined unto the Lord's people. The LXX, as an exposition, speaks of "the residue of men seeking unto the restored tabernacle." St. James makes both clear by shewing that "to seek after the Lord" is to be the true up-building both of the house of David and of all mankind besides.[95]

[95]*Op. cit.*, p. 277.

There is considerable confusion in the text of 18. The oldest MSS have simply: "Known from eternity" (or "from creation"). Perhaps the best we can do is to combine the last part of 17 with the short text of 18 and translate it: "Saith the Lord, who maketh these things known from of old" (ASV). The suggestion has been made that 16 was fulfilled by the presence of Jews in the Church, and 17 by the presence of Gentiles.

Wherefore my sentence is (19)—literally, "Wherefore, I for my part judge"—shows that James spoke with authority as moderator of the council. The *ego* is expressed for emphasis (*ego krino*). The decision which James handed down was **that we trouble not them, which from among the Gentiles are turned to God.** The Gentiles were to be free from keeping the Jewish law. **Trouble not,** a rare verb, is a double compound which means, literally, "stop annoying."

Erdman suggests that the decision of James includes three points: (1) Liberty, 19; (2) Purity, 20; (3) Charity between both Jews and Gentiles, 21.[96]

Only four restrictions were placed on the Gentile Christians (20). They were to **abstain from pollutions of idols**—i.e., things offered to idols (cf. 29; 21:25)—**and from fornication, and from things strangled, and from blood.**

The first of these restrictions concerned a real problem in the Early Church, which Paul dealt with at length (I Cor. 8:1-10; 10:19). Animals were sacrificed to heathen gods, and then their meat was sold in the markets. In the council decision the Gentile converts were forbidden to eat this meat knowingly. Paul took the same stand.

Fornication was an exceedingly common sin among the heathen, and was often practiced as a part of their worship. The Jews prided themselves on their high moral standards. The Church was of course justified in making this demand of Gentile members.

The eating of what was **strangled** was evidently forbidden primarily because the blood was not drained out of the meat. So this is closely connected with the fourth prohibition, against eating **blood.** This command goes back to Noah's time, when men were first allowed to eat animals (Gen. 9:4). It was repeated in the Mosaic law (Lev. 3:17; 7:26; 17:10, 14; 19:26).

[96]Charles R. Erdman, *The Acts* (Philadelphia: Westminster Press, 1919), p. 113.

The very close connection of these last two prohibitions may explain why **things strangled** is omitted from the Western Text. With this left out, however, **blood** is often interpreted as meaning murder. In that case all the prohibitions would be moral, none of them ceremonial. Bruce writes: "Idolatry, fornication, and murder were the three cardinal sins in Jewish eyes."[97]

For the Jewish Christians who still wanted to worship in the synagogue, **Moses** was proclaimed **in every city . . . being read in the synagogues every sabbath day** (21). Those who wished could attend. The Law would not suffer. Adam Clarke suggests the sense of this verse as being that the converted Jews could attend the synagogue and hear the Law read. So it would not be necessary to write them. But the Gentile converts needed these basic instructions.[98] The Gentile Christians, however, should be free from the Mosaic law. The decree of the Council of Jerusalem was a veritable Emancipation Proclamation for the Gentile members of the Church.

5. *Joint Decision* (15:22-29)

The decision of James was endorsed and published by **the apostles and elders, with the whole church** (22). Thus the decrees went out with the full authority of the mother church at Jerusalem. For a discussion of **apostles and elders** see comment on 23.

Then pleased it is better translated, "Then it seemed good" (ASV). Lumby writes: "The expression is one often used in the official announcements of public resolutions, or decrees made by authority. (Cf. Herod I.3; Thuc. IV. 118.)"[99] Lake and Cadbury say: "*Edoxe* is the technical term in Greek of all periods for 'voting' or 'passing' a measure in the assembly."[100] They translate it here, "It was voted."[101]

The Church decided **to send chosen men of their own company to Antioch with Paul and Barnabas.** This was a wise move. It would tend to cement together the Jewish church at Jerusalem and the Gentile church at Antioch. Also these Jerusalem Christians who returned with Paul and Barnabas would

[97]*Acts,* p. 299.
[98]*Op. cit.,* p. 803.
[99]*Op. cit.,* p. 280.
[100]*Beginnings,* IV, 178.
[101]*Ibid.*

offset the bad impression made by the Judaizers who had previously gone to Antioch from Judea. Then to have two Jerusalem men together with two Antioch men would present a united front for the Jewish-Gentile Christian Church—something that was very much needed, as Paul's Epistles show.

So they chose **Judas surnamed Barsabas, and Silas, chief men among the brethren,** i.e., "leading men among the brethren" (the Jerusalem Christians). Because **Judas** was an exceedingly common name in those days, he is identified as "the one called Barsabas." In 1:23 we read of a "Joseph called Barsabas." So it has been conjectured that these two men may have been brothers (*bar* is Aramaic for "son"), belonging to a prominent family in the Jerusalem church. Nothing further is known about this Judas.

The case of **Silas** is different. He was Paul's main companion on the second missionary journey, so that his name occurs frequently in the next three chapters. Also he is doubtless the Silvanus mentioned in several of Paul's Epistles (II Cor. 1:19; I Thess. 1:1; II Thess. 1:1) and in I Pet. 5:12.

They wrote letters by them after this manner (23) is in the Greek simply: "Having written through their hand." Every English version paraphrases this in some way, such as "and gave them this letter to deliver" (NEB). The four men evidently acted as letter carriers rather than stenographers. The letter was probably composed by James, at the request of the Church.[102]

The writers of the letter are identified as: **The apostles and elders and brethren.** But the oldest Greek MSS have: "The apostles and the elders, brethren." Lumby would translate this: "the Apostles and elder brethren." He comments: "Hitherto, though the whole church came together only two sets of persons have been spoken of as to be consulted or as having authority. These are *hoi apostoloi kai hoi presbyteroi* (verses 2, 6 and 22)."[103] So the decree was written "in the names of these two bodies."[104] This does not rule out the idea that the whole church may have voted its agreement with the decision (see above comment on 22).

The letter was addressed to the **brethren which are of the Gentiles in Antioch and Syria and Cilicia** (see map 3). It was sent only to the Gentile Christians, for it was evidently assumed

[102]Bengel, *op. cit.*
[103]*Op. cit.*, p. 281.
[104]*Ibid.*

433

that the Jewish Christians would continue to observe the Law. The decree was a special concession to the Gentile converts. **Antioch** was the chief city of the double Roman province of *Syria et Cilicia*. But it is here named specifically because the church at Antioch had requested guidance from the apostles and elders at Jerusalem.

Greeting[105] is found in the Greek at the end of the verse, after the designation of the addressers and addressees. This is always the order in the thousands of Greek papyrus letters from this period which have been dug up from the dry sands of Egypt. Furthermore, all of them have exactly the same word as here, *chairein*. That the Epistle of James was written by the same James as the one who composed this letter from the Jerusalem Council is given significant support by the fact that it is the only New Testament Epistle which has this common Greek form, *chairein*. Elsewhere in the New Testament it is found only in the letter of Claudius Lysias to Felix (23:26). Paul, Peter, and John (II John) have all replaced this with *charis*, "grace." This comes from the same root as *chairein* but carries a richer spiritual and theological connotation. The literal meaning of *chairein* is "to rejoice, be glad."[106]

The letter proper begins with 24: **Forasmuch as we have heard, that certain**[107] . . . **from us have troubled you with words, subverting your souls**—or "unsettling your minds" (RSV)[108]— **to whom we gave no such commandment.** The word **such** is in italics, indicating that it is not in the original. It distorts the meaning. It is not that the Jerusalem church had given these unaccredited Judaizers **no such commandment,** but that they had given them no commandment at all—literally, "where we did not command." The supposed emissaries from Jerusalem were completely unauthorized.

Subverting (*anaskenazo,* only here in NT and not at all in the LXX) is a strong term. It was used in classical Greek for "an entire removal of goods."[109] The application here is obvious:

---

[105]**Send** is in italics, which means that it is not in the original. It should be omitted.

[106]Abbott-Smith, *op. cit.,* p. 477.

[107]**Which went out** (*exelthontes*) is not in the earliest Greek MSS.

[108]The added words, **saying, Ye must be circumcised, and keep the law,** are not in the oldest MSS.

[109]Lumby, *op. cit.,* p. 282.

"The devastation wrought in the minds of the Gentile converts through the new teaching is compared to an utter overthrow."[110] The danger was that mental confusion might be followed by spiritual death.

In view of the wrong influence that had gone out unofficially from the Jerusalem church, the leaders of that congregation felt it their duty to rectify the situation. **It seemed good (25)**—*edoxe*, same word translated "pleased it" in 22—**unto us, being assembled with one accord,** i.e., being unanimous—**to send chosen men unto you**—literally, "having chosen men, to send to you"—**with our beloved Barnabas and Paul.** The Jerusalem leaders showed a Christian spirit in referring to these two missionaries to the Gentiles as **our beloved** representatives. This showed the true spirit of *homothymadon,* **of one accord.**

Beloved, only here in Acts, occurs frequently in the Epistles of Paul, Peter, James, and John. It may have been at this very time that Peter, James, and John gave to Paul and Barnabas "the right hands of fellowship" (Gal. 2:9).[111]

Barnabas and Saul are further described as **men that have hazarded their lives for the name of our Lord Jesus Christ (26).** This had been brought home forcibly to the Jerusalem believers as the two missionaries had recounted their experiences in Cyprus and Asia Minor. **Have hazarded** is literally "have given over" or "have given up." The primary meaning is that they had devoted their lives to Christ, and in so doing they had risked their lives on behalf of His name.

The two men chosen to accompany Barnabas and Saul, as representatives of the Jerusalem church, were **Judas and Silas (27). We have sent therefore** is the epistolary perfect, stating the case from the standpoint of those who will be reading the letter. It means, "We are therefore sending" (NEB), along with this letter. The two emissaries would verbally confirm and explain what was in the epistle.

Then comes the heart of the message. **It seemed good**—*edoxe*, cf. 22, 25—**to the Holy Ghost, and to us (28).** Thus the apostles and elders express their conviction of divine authority for the

[110]*Ibid.*

[111]The much-debated question as to whether Gal. 2:1-10 refers to the Jerusalem Council (Acts 15) or to the so-called Famine Visit (Acts 11:27-30) belongs properly to the commentary on Galatians and so will not be discussed here. The present writer prefers the identification with Acts 15 (contra Bruce, *Acts,* p. 38).

decision they had reached. Peter and John may have recalled Jesus' promise to the disciples: "Howbeit when he, the Spirit of truth, is come, he will guide you into all truth" (John 16:13). They had been filled with the Spirit at Pentecost and now they could claim divine guidance.

The decision was **to lay upon you no greater burden than these necessary things**—the things necessary to avoid giving offense to their Jewish brethren in Christ. Lumby puts it this way: "And as they [in Jerusalem] at the suggestion of the Spirit were laying aside their long-standing prejudices against intercourse with Gentiles, they claim that the Gentiles in their turn should deal tenderly with the scruples of Jews."[112]

The four prohibitions decided upon (cf. 20) are now stated (29), but in a different order and with "pollutions of idols" changed to **meats offered to idols**. Possibly someone had suggested that this point needed to be made more specific. If the readers observed these few simple restrictions, they would **do well**. The letter ends with **Fare ye well**; literally, "Be strong, or in good health."[113]

This incident shows the Church "Averting a Crisis." The three stages were: (1) Dissension, 1-5; (2) Debate, 6-12; (3) Decision, 13-29.

6. *Joy over the Outcome* (15:30-35)

When the four men **were dismissed** (30)—"released, let go" —**they came**—literally, "came down" (from Jerusalem)—**to Antioch: and when they had gathered the multitude together**— (*synagogontes*) meaning here "the congregation"—**they delivered the epistle**. Bruce says that the verb was "technical in later Greek for sending in a report or handing over a letter."[114]

When the Christians at Antioch had heard the letter read, **they rejoiced for the consolation** (31). They were much relieved to learn that they, as Gentiles, would not be required to keep the Jewish law.

Judas and Silas (32) were also **prophets**; i.e., preachers. So they **exhorted**—or "encouraged" (NASB)—**the brethren . . . and confirmed them**—literally, "made them stronger" (cf. 14:22).

---

[112]*Op. cit.*, pp. 282-83.
[113]Only here in the best text of the New Testament.
[114]*Acts*, p. 304.

They helped to make the Church "firm and compact after its recent shaking and division."[115]

After Judas and Silas **had tarried there a space** (33)—literally, "had done time"—**they were let go**—same word as "dismissed" in 30—**in peace**—"i.e., with the words 'Go in peace' . . . or 'Peace to you.' "[116] **Unto the apostles** may be read, "to those who had sent them" (*aposteilantos autous* in the oldest MSS instead of *apostolous*).

Verse 34 is omitted in recent versions because it is not found in the majority of the best Greek MSS. Bruce explains the matter well when he writes: "The insertion, which contradicts *ver.* 33, was no doubt intended to explain why Silas appears again at Antioch in *ver.* 40; as, however, the plain sense of *ver.* 33 is that both Judas and he returned to Jerusalem, we must infer that Silas later came back from Jerusalem to Antioch."[117]

But **Paul . . . and Barnabas** (best Gk. text, 35)—usual order resumed, now that they are away from Jerusalem (cf. 12, 25)—**continued in Antioch, teaching and preaching the word of the Lord.** The church at Antioch was fortunate indeed to enjoy the rich ministry of the Apostle Paul.

D. Asia Minor Again, 15:36—16:10

1. *Separation of Paul and Barnabas* (15:36-41)

Some days after (36)—lit., "after some days," probably implying a short period of time[118]—**Paul** suggested to **Barnabas** that they revisit the churches they had founded on their first missionary journey. The apostle was becoming concerned for the welfare of their converts; it was time to check up on them. The verb **visit** means first of all "to inspect, examine," and then, "to visit."[119] Here it may carry something of its original thoughts of a visit for inspection. Paul wanted to look in on his converts and **see how they do.**

Barnabas evidently gave his hearty approval to the idea, but he **determined to take with them John . . . Mark** (37). Rather than **determined,** the best Greek favors "desired" or "wished" (cf. "wanted," Phillips).

---

[115]Rackham, *op. cit.*, p. 257.
[116]Bruce, *Acts*, p. 305.
[117]*Ibid.*
[118]Hackett, *op. cit.*, p. 179.
[119]Abbott-Smith, *op. cit.*, p. 173.

Paul, however, **thought not good to take him with them** (38) —literally, "thought it fit not to take this one along with them." He felt that John Mark was not worthy to go on this missionary tour after he had **departed from them from Pamphylia, and went not with them to the work.** This implies that Paul felt Mark was either lazy or cowardly, or both. The work was too great to have it hindered by the presence of anyone who was not fully consecrated to the task.

Barnabas evidently insisted that John Mark, his cousin (Col. 4:10, NASB), should go. He felt that the younger man should be given another chance. Paul, with his extreme zeal and dedication, could not understand or sympathize with a "quitter."

These were men with strong wills, as all great leaders are. Apparently neither would give in, because each was fully convinced that he was right.

Finally things came to a climax (39). **The contention was so sharp between them** is only two words in the Greek, *egeneto paroxysmos*—literally, "there arose a 'paroxysm.'" But what does this noun mean? It occurs elsewhere in the New Testament only in Heb. 10:24, where it means "provocation"—"Let us consider each other for a provocation of love" (lit. translation). For this particular passage Abbott-Smith suggests "irritation."[120] Lake and Cadbury translate it "quarrel."[121] The word is used twice in the Septuagint (Deut. 29:28; Jer. 32:37) of God's righteous anger against His disobedient children.

Perhaps the best treatment of this problematical passage is that found in Alexander. He writes: "It is not to be magnified, however, into anything beyond a sudden and a temporary irritation (*sharpening*, as the Greek words primarily signify), sufficient to account for the effect here mentioned, and, we may add, to carry out the divine purpose of multiplying labourers and even missions by a painful but momentary alienation between Paul and Barnabas."[122]

That the alienation was not permanent is shown by Paul's later references to Barnabas in his Epistles (I Cor. 9:6; Col. 4:10). Also John Mark was restored to Paul's confidence. He recommended him to the Colossian church (Col. 4:10) and mentioned him as one of "my fellowlabourers" (Philem. 24). Finally, he

[120]*Ibid.*, p. 347.
[121]*Beginnings*, IV, 183.
[122]*Op. cit.*, p. 560.

wrote to Timothy in his last Epistle: "Take Mark, and bring him with thee: for he is profitable to me for the ministry" (II Tim. 4:11). John Mark was at last completely exonerated.

The result of the dispute between Paul and his colleague of several years was that **they departed asunder one from the other.** This separation of old friends must have left many a pang. **Barnabas took Mark,** his cousin, **and sailed**—literally, "sailed out"—**unto Cyprus.** This was his old home territory. Barnabas is never mentioned again in the Book of Acts. Tradition has it that he stayed on Cyprus until his death. It may be that he was already getting along in years and that this was his last trip. There is a possibility that he might not have been equal to the rigors of Paul's extended journeys into Europe. At any rate, Barnabas deserves the highest commendation for his generous Christian spirit and for the tremendous contribution he made to the life of the Early Church. Except for his magnanimous spirit, Paul might never have been accepted by the Jerusalem church. Also, it was Barnabas who rescued Paul from oblivion by bringing him to Antioch, from which he set out on his missionary journeys. More than to any other human being, Paul owed the greatness of his career to Barnabas. Paul's life and labors are the finest memorial that this great soul could have had. His epitaph reads: "He was a good man, and full of the Holy Ghost and of faith" (11:24). Every generation of the Church needs more men like Barnabas.

After Barnabas left, **Paul chose Silas** (40). This was a wise choice. Silas was probably a younger man than Barnabas. He was mentioned by name in the letter Paul was taking from the Jerusalem Council. The fact that he was a member of the Jerusalem church would make him more acceptable to some Jews in the cities where Paul was going. The fact, too, that Silas was, like Paul, a Roman citizen (cf. 16:37) would be a tremendous asset as they moved into Macedonia and Greece.

Paul departed, **being recommended**—literally, "having been committed" (cf. 14:26)—**by the brethren unto the grace of God.** The absence of this note in connection with Barnabas' departure does not necessarily mean that he left without the church's blessing. And yet one cannot rule out this possibility. He may have left rather suddenly, whereas Paul took time to choose Silas and have a farewell service—perhaps partly for the sake of his new missionary companion.

In 37-40 we find "A Good Man's Faults." (1) The imperfect goodness of men; (2) The possible evil lurking in our best qualities; (3) The grave issues of small faults (Alexander Maclaren).

Paul, accompanied by Silas, **went through Syria and Cilicia** (see map 3), **confirming the churches** (41). This was Paul's home territory, around Tarsus. It was also the area where the Judaizers had probably been hard at work. The first need was to make sure that the Gentile converts in this Roman province (*Syria et Cilicia*) were confirmed (strengthened) in the faith and established in Christ. Paul had evangelized this area soon after his conversion (Gal. 1:21). Now it was time to confirm the work. Doubtless Paul and Silas read the letter from the Jerusalem Council to the Gentile Christians and encouraged them to enjoy their freedom in Christ.

2. *Selection of Timothy* (16:1-5)

Leaving his hometown of Tarsus and going up over the Taurus Mountains through the famous Cilician Gates (a pass eighty miles long), Paul finally **came . . . to**—"arrived at"—**Derbe and Lystra** (1). Having gone overland this time, he was approaching the cities of southern Galatia in the opposite direction from his first journey (see map 3).

At Lystra[123] he found a **disciple** named **Timotheus,** or Timothy, who had been saved under his ministry (I Tim. 1:2). He was the son of a **Jewess** who **believed**—i.e., had been converted to Christianity, probably on Paul's first visit to this city (14:8-20)—**but his father was a Greek,** and apparently unconverted.

Timothy was **well reported of**—"well spoken of"—**by the brethren that were at Lystra and Iconium** (2). Since Iconium was twenty miles from Lystra, this indicates that the young man had made an outstanding impression as an exemplary Christian. His reputation had traveled beyond the bounds of his own city.

Paul admired Timothy so much that he desired to have him go with him (3). Because all the Jews of that area knew that Timothy's father was a Greek, Paul had him **circumcised.** This act does not conflict with Paul's attitude toward circumcision as reflected in Gal. 2:3 and 5:3, nor with the decree of the

---

[123]The best Greek MSS have "to Derbe and to Lystra," implying that there means Lystra. This is further supported by the mention of Lystra again in the next verse.

Council of Jerusalem. Both of those dealt with the case of Gentile converts. But Timothy had been brought up in the Jewish religion by a pious mother and grandmother (II Tim. 1:5; 3:14-15). Evidently his father had refused to let the boy be circumcised. Apparently the father was now dead—the tense of the verb in **was a Greek** implies this.[124] If Timothy was going to be received by the Jews in the synagogues where Paul went, he would have to be circumcised, "For by the Rabbinical code the child of a Jewish mother was reckoned as a Jew."[125] Thus in order to be considered a good Jew he had to be circumcised. "It could be no offence to the Gentiles, and would render the labours of Timothy more acceptable to the Jews."[126] On another occasion Paul evidently refused to have his associate, Titus, circumcised (Gal. 2:3), even under heavy pressure from the Jews. But that was because Titus was a Gentile, and Paul was standing by his principle of Gentile freedom from the Jewish law. The apostle's action here was an extension of his own policy: "And unto the Jews I became as a Jew, that I might gain them that are under the law" (I Cor. 9:20). The one question that mattered with Paul was: What is best for the kingdom of God?

As they were going through (imperfect tense) **the cities** (Lystra, Iconium, Pisidian Antioch), the missionaries **delivered them** (4)—the Gentile Christians—**the decrees**—literally, "dogmas," used for imperial decrees (17:7; Luke 2:1)[127]—**that were ordained of the apostles and elders which were at Jerusalem. That were ordained** is literally, "which had been judged." This is the only place in the New Testament where this common verb *krino* is translated **ordained.** In the light of the context (c. 15) probably the best translation for the whole phrase is: "the decisions which had been reached" (Phillips), or "the decrees which had been decided on."[128]

Apparently the promulgation of the decrees of the Jerusalem Council helped rather than hindered the work, for we read: **And so were the churches established in the faith, and increased in**

[124]Bruce, *Acts,* p. 308.

[125]Lumby, *op. cit.,* p. 287.

[126]*Ibid.*

[127]The Greek word *dogma* is derived from the verb *dokeo,* used in 15:28 ("it seemed good"). First meaning "opinion" (from *dokeo,* "I think"), it came to be used for public decrees and ordinances.

[128]*Beginnings,* IV, 185 (cf. NASB).

number daily (5)—literally, "were being strengthened" and "were increasing" (imperfect tenses). This is the fourth brief progress report of the missionary work (cf. 6:7; 9:31; 12:24).

3. *The Spirit's Restraint* (16:6-10)

Now when they had gone throughout (6) is better rendered, "They made their way through" (Phillips) [129]—i.e., made a missionary tour (cf. 8:4; 13:6). These preachers of the gospel worked their way through **Phrygia and the region of Galatia**—rather, "the Phrygian and Galatic country" (Gk.). Probably Ramsay is right when he renders this: "the Phrygian region of *the province* Galatia."[130] Bruce translates the phrase, "the Phrygian and Galatian region," but interprets it as meaning "the border district between ethnic Phrygia and Galatia."[131]

At this point they **were forbidden of the Holy Ghost to preach**—literally, "to speak"—**the word in Asia**—the Roman province of Asia, at the west end of Asia Minor. The literal Greek, "having been forbidden," suggests that they received this command while they were still at work in the cities of southern Galatia. Probably Paul had planned to head next for the great metropolis Ephesus, the leading city of Asia, for it was his policy to evangelize the large cities first. But Ephesus must wait for a later time. On his third missionary journey, he preached there for about three years (c. 19).

After they were come to Mysia (7)—better, "when they came opposite Mysia,"[132] the northwest part of the province of Asia (see map 3)—**they assayed**—"were trying"—**to go into Bithynia**—a senatorial province in northwest Asia Minor—**but the Spirit suffered them not.** The best Greek text has, "and the Spirit of Jesus[133] did not allow them."

Since they were forbidden by the Spirit—presumably by a strong inward impression—to preach the gospel either westward in Asia or northward in Bithynia, the missionaries did the only thing which was left to them. **Passing by Mysia (8)**—rather than

---

[129] The best Greek text has the indicative rather than the participle "having gone through."

[130] *Op. cit.,* p. 194.

[131] *Acts,* p. 309.

[132] *Beginnings,* IV, 186 (cf. RSV).

[133] Only here in NT.

preaching through it (contra 8:4; 13:6), because it was a part of the province of Asia—they **came down to Troas.** That is, they took a middle course westward to this Roman colony on the seacoast. The city was at "land's end," facing across the water toward Macedonia in Europe.

This incident furnishes a valuable lesson in divine guidance. Paul was somewhat in the position of a man walking down a corridor. He wants to enter doors on the right or left, but finds them all marked, "Do not enter." So he keeps on down the corridor, feeling tempted to frustration as he approaches what seems to be a blank wall. But as he comes to the end, suddenly double doors open and he finds himself entering a large auditorium filled with many people.

Paul must have wondered why he was forbidden by the Spirit to go to the left (Asia) or to the right (Bithynia). But when he kept on straight ahead to land's end, suddenly a great door swung open and he found himself facing a vast harvest field in Europe. God had closed smaller doors because he had a bigger work for His apostle to do. So it is sometimes in our lives.

Nothing is said about Paul and his party preaching in Troas. It would appear that at this time the apostle was moving ahead with sealed orders, not knowing his destination. But soon the seal would be broken as his next destination was revealed.

In a vision at **night** Paul saw a Macedonian man beseeching him: **Come over into Macedonia, and help us** (9). Macedonia was at this time a Roman province. In spite of its dominance over Greece under Philip, and its conquests of Egypt and Syria under the brilliant leadership of Alexander the Great, it was finally conquered by the Romans in 168 B.C. and made into a Roman province in 146 B.C.

After the vision, **immediately we endeavoured**—"sought," suggesting the seeking of means of transportation (cf. NEB—"we at once set about getting a passage"). **Assuredly gathering**—better, "concluding" (ASV)—**that the Lord had called us . . . to preach the gospel unto them** (10)—"to evangelize [*euangelisasthai*] them."

This is the beginning of the first of the so-called "we-sections" in Acts, where the first person plural is substituted for the third person. This we-section extends through v. 17. If one marks in his Bible all the occurrences of "we" and "us" in vv. 10-17 he will find them numerous.

After v. 17 the "we" ceases until Paul returned to Philippi on his third journey (20:5). It seems a justifiable assumption to hold that Luke, the author of Acts, joined the Pauline party at Troas, sailed across with the missionaries to Europe, and remained at Philippi as the first pastor of that church for some half a dozen years until Paul's return. Then he rejoined the party and stayed with Paul for most of the time until the great apostle's death (cf. II Tim. 4:11—"Only Luke is with me").

The question as to how these two men met is an intriguing one. Did Paul take sick—with chronic malaria on the coastlands again (see comments on 13:13)—and have to seek medical care? Did he thus find "Luke, the beloved physician" (Col. 4:14)? The foremost medical school of that day was at Tarsus, Paul's hometown, and Paul may very well have attended the university there—third greatest, after Athens and Alexandria. Therefore one is tempted to speculate that Paul and Luke may have known each other there and have recognized each other in Troas. Luke then decided to cast in his lot with Paul's evangelistic team.

Ramsay, indeed, goes a step further. He thinks that Luke was the "man of Macedonia,"[134] although he suggests that they "met accidentally as strangers,"[135] perhaps when Paul sought the services of a physician.[136] It is not impossible that Luke may have been acquainted with Philippi and may have urged Paul to go there. This may have been the background, but it must not be taken as a substitute for the clear statement (9) that the call to Macedonia came to Paul at night in the form of a vision.

In 16:6-10, under the subject, "Divine Direction," one might note: (1) God guides by checks as well as promptings, 6-7; (2) When we obey the checks, the proper opening will come in due time, 8-9; (3) Though we may be tested, God will always make His will clear to those who obey, 10.

E. MACEDONIA, 16:11—17:15

1. *Philippi* (16:11-40)

This city was captured by Philip of Macedon, who fortified it as a frontier stronghold, developed its gold mines, and named

---

[134]*Op. cit.*, p. 203.
[135]*Ibid.*
[136]*Ibid.*, p. 205.

it after himself. It was made a Roman colony, which means that its citizens had the same rights and privileges as if their land were a part of Italy. In Paul's day it was a prosperous city, but today is only a cemetery. "The decay of Philippi, now entirely deserted, is probably due largely to malaria."[137]

a. *Conversion of Lydia* (16:11-15). The voyage from **Troas** to **Neapolis** (see map 3) is described in one short sentence, but with graphic touches. **Loosing,** in the middle voice, is a nautical term used only by Luke (Luke 8:22, and thirteen times in Acts). **Came with a straight course** (11)—literally, "ran a straight course"—is another nautical term, found only here and in 21:1. Conybeare and Howson suggest the translation, "sailed before the wind."[138] The fact that they made this run (about one hundred forty miles) from **Troas** to **Neapolis** in two days is evidence that they had favorable winds. Coming in the opposite direction against contrary winds took them five days (20:6).

The one night on their way they stopped at **Samothracia** (or Samothrace), a mountainous island with an elevation of 5,000 feet, "the great landmark in this corner of the Levant."[139] Since the Aegean Sea is filled with rocks jutting above the water—or, worse still, near the surface—it was not safe to sail at night in those days of neither compass nor charts.

At the end of the second day they came to **Neapolis** (Gk. for "New City"), called Cavalla today. Lake and Cadbury say: "Cavalla is the only real port on the south coast of Macedonia except Salonica, and for sailing boats it is far safer than Salonica."[140] For this reason it was the eastern terminus of a much-traveled road, the Egnatian Way, in Europe.

From the seaport Neapolis the missionaries walked ten miles up over the hills and down onto the plain to **Philippi** (12). It is described as being **the chief city of that part of Macedonia, and a colony** (Gk., *kolonia*). Macedonia was divided into four administrative districts. But the capital of this eastern region was Amphipolis, not Philippi. **Chief** is *prote* (lit., "first"). Lake and Cadbury say: "*Prote* . . . was an honorary title given to or claimed by many of the more important cities in the eastern

---

[137]*Beginnings,* IV, 187.
[138]*Op. cit.,* p. 246.
[139]*Beginnings,* IV, 186.
[140]*Ibid.,* p. 187.

provinces."[141] But they conclude: "It is more probable . . . that the meaning of *prote* in this passage is simply 'a leading city.' "[142]

The Greek word *kolonia* is a transliteration of the Latin *colonia*, which has been taken over into English as **colony.** Lake and Cadbury present rather fully the significance of this term. They write: "The Roman colonies were originally settlements of Roman citizens in captured territory as garrisons . . . later . . . used to provide for the needs of veteran soldiers."[143] Roman colonists had three main rights: (*a*) autonomous government; (*b*) immunity from taxation; (*c*) the same legal privileges as those living in Italy.

The question has sometimes been raised as to why Philippi alone is described in Acts as a **colony** when Pisidian Antioch, Lystra, Troas, Ptolemais, Corinth, Syracuse, and Puteoli all had this honor. Ramsay thought the reason for this was that Luke was showing pride in his native city, Philippi.[144] But in the fourteenth edition (1920) of his famous work, *St. Paul the Traveler and the Roman Citizen,* Ramsay finally accepted the strong tradition of the Early Church that Luke was a native of Antioch in Syria. He then explained Luke's attitude here in these terms: "His love for Philippi was due to the long and successful evangelization which he carried out there."[145] This seems a reasonable explanation. **Abiding certain days** would be "some days."

On the sabbath (13)—Jewish Sabbath, Saturday—the missionaries **went out of the city**—the best Greek text has "gate" —**by a river side**—the Gangites or Angites, a tributary of the Strymon. Here they found a place **where prayer was wont to be made**—better, "where we were supposing that there would be a place of prayer" (NASB). Apparently a place beside a river or on the seashore was preferred because of the Jewish ceremonial washings. Finding some women who had gathered there, Paul and his companions sat down and talked with them. The mention of **women** implies that there was no synagogue at Philippi. The traditional rule was that there must be at least ten Jewish men in a community before a synagogue could be formed.[146] Because

[141]*Beginnings,* IV, 188.
[142]*Ibid.*
[143]*Ibid.,* p. 190.
[144]*Op. cit.,* p. 206.
[145]*Ibid.* (14th ed.), p. xxxviii.
[146]Bruce, *Acts,* p. 314.

male Gentiles were required to submit to circumcision before entering Judaism, it was easier for women to become proselytes. Often women are more religious than men, and more conscientious about attending worship. The fact that no men are mentioned here suggests that most of these women may have been proselytes.

In the group was a **woman named Lydia** (14). She was a **seller of purple**—"a seller of purple fabrics"[147] (one word, only here in NT)—**of the city of Thyatira,** in the province of Asia. This city was famous for its purple dye, procured from a shellfish. Cloth tinted with this dye was valued very highly in the ancient world. Since Thyatira had a Jewish colony, Lydia may well have become a proselyte there. It is stated here that she **worshipped God.** **The Lord opened** her heart, so that she gave careful attention to the things being spoken by Paul.

After she had been **baptized** (15) as a Christian, she begged the missionaries to stay at her house while in Philippi. It is obvious she was a successful businesswoman with a large home where the party of four men could be entertained. **Her household,** baptized with her, would probably be her retinue of servants. Nothing is said about husband or children.

Constrained is a strong word. In classical Greek it meant "to compel by force."[148] Lumby comments: "The force used was that of a prayer which would accept no 'Nay.' "[149] Meyer makes the helpful suggestion that here it describes "the vehement urgency of the feeling of gratitude."[150]

Under the narrative title "Paul at Philippi," Alexander Maclaren points out from v. 13: (1) The apparent insignificance and real greatness of Christian work; (2) The law of growth in Christ's kingdom; (3) The simplicity of the forces to which God entrusts the growth of His kingdom.

b. *Casting Out a Demon* (16:16-18). **As we went to prayer** (16) is more accurately rendered, "as we were going to the place of prayer" (ASV). This was probably another trip to the riverside meeting place. **Damsel** should be "slave girl." Moulton and Milligan say that the Greek word "from meaning originally

---

[147]Abbott-Smith, *op. cit.,* p. 374.

[148]*Ibid.,* p. 337.

[149]*Op. cit.,* p. 291.

[150]*Op. cit.,* p. 312.

'a young woman' came in later Greek to denote 'a female slave.' "[151]

This slave girl who met the missionaries on their way to prayer was **possessed with a spirit of divination**—literally, "a spirit, a Python." Bruce writes: *"Pythones were inspired by Apollo, the Pythian god, who was regarded as embodied in a snake (the Python) at Delphi (also called Pytho)."*[152] The girl **brought her masters much gain**—"work" or "business"—**by soothsaying** (used only here in NT)—better, "fortune-telling" (NASB).

The demon-passessed girl **followed Paul and us** (17). This marks the end of the first "we-section" (10-17). **Followed** is a strong compound (only here and in Luke 23:55), meaning "followed after." She "kept crying out" (imperfect tense): **These men are the servants of the most high God, which shew**—"proclaim"—**unto us**[153] **the way of salvation.** One is reminded of the demon-possessed men shouting that Jesus was the Messiah and Son of God (Mark 1:24; Luke 4:41).

Paul was no more eager to have testimony coming from this quarter than was Jesus. So he did the same thing that Christ did: cast out the demon. As the slave girl kept up her unwelcome nuisance **many days** (18), **Paul, being grieved**—"worn out"—commanded the spirit **in the name of Jesus Christ to come out of her.** The cure was immediate and complete: **he came out the same hour.** The first difficulty in Philippi had been met and vanquished.

c. *Cast into Prison* (16:19-24). In almost all the cases of persecution described in Acts, the opposition came from the Jews and was related to religion. There were two exceptions, here and in Ephesus (19:23-41). In both of these instances the opposition was stirred up by Gentiles for financial reasons.

When the slave owners **saw that the hope of their gains was gone** (19)—since the girl could no longer tell fortunes—**they caught**—"laid hold on"—**Paul and Silas, and drew**—better, "dragged"—**them into the marketplace**—the Agora—**unto the rulers. Was gone** is literally "had gone out." It is exactly the same form as "came out" in the previous verse. Bruce comments:

---

[151]VGT, p. 474.

[152]*Acts,* p. 315.

[153]The best Greek text has "you."

"Luke's sense of humour appears in his choice of *exelthen* here after its use in *ver.* 18; their 'hope and profit' was in fact the expelled spirit itself."[154] Because the demon had "gone out," their hope of gain had "gone out."

Rulers (19) is a general term (*archontes*). **Magistrates** (20) is a more specific one (*strategoi*), referring to the Roman praetors. Lake and Cadbury say: "Probably . . . *archontes* is merely a general term defined more closely by the following *strategoi*."[155] There were two praetors in each colony, ruling jointly.

The charges which the offended slave owners brought against Paul and Silas were serious. First of all, they appealed to racial prejudice: **these men, being Jews.** Then they leveled two charges at them. The first was: **do exceedingly trouble our city.** The compound verb, **do exceedingly trouble,** is a strong one. Meyer translates it, "bring into utter disorder."[156] One thing that the Roman government would not tolerate was any disturbance of the public peace. *Pax Romana* was the watchword of the empire.

The second charge was: **teach customs, which are not lawful for us to receive, neither to observe, being Romans** (21)—in contrast to "being Jews" (20). Judaism had been acknowledged by the Roman government as a legal religion. Not so Christianity. The new movement could be sure of legal protection only so long as it was considered a sect of the Jews. Rome was unfriendly to the rise of new religions.

Capitalizing on this fact and on ever-present racial prejudice, the plaintiffs scored immediate success. **The multitude** (22) of onlookers **rose up together against them**—in a spontaneous outburst of anti-Semitism. **The magistrates rent off their clothes.** Ramsay thinks that the praetors tore their own clothes "in loyal horror."[157] But Alexander is probably correct when he says: "Not their own, as some would imagine, which would be wholly out of character in Romans, but those of Paul and Silas."[158] The magistrates then **commanded to beat them**—literally, "to beat them with rods."

After **they had laid many stripes** (23) upon them, they cast **them into prison, charging the jailor to keep them safely** (23),

[154]*Acts*, p. 316.
[155]*Beginnings*, IV, 195.
[156]*Op. cit.*, p. 314.
[157]*Op. cit.*, p. 219.
[158]*Op. cit.*, p. 581.

since they might be dangerous political prisoners. With such strict orders, the jailer **thrust them into the inner prison** (24)—or "the inmost prison"—**and made their feet fast in the stocks**—literally, "the wood." Lake and Cadbury write: "It was apparently made like the traditional village stocks, but had more than two holes for the legs so that they could be forced widely apart into a position which soon became intolerably painful."[159]

d. Conversion of the Jailer (16:25-34). The incident that follows is one of the glorious memorials to the triumph of Christianity in the human spirit. Instead of grumbling and complaining because they could not sleep for pain, **at midnight Paul and Silas prayed, and sang praises unto God** (25)—literally, "praying, they were hymning God" (*hymnoun*, "singing the praises of"). When they prayed, they felt a joy rising within their hearts. This caused them to break forth into singing. Sincere prayer always leads ultimately to praise. And praise dispels the gloom. In this dark dungeon a light shone in the hearts of the two missionaries. They prayed and sang aloud, for **the prisoners heard them**—literally, "were listening to them."

Suddenly there was a great earthquake (26). God could not leave His servants suffering there while they were singing His praises. So He shook open the prison doors and shook off the shackles from the prisoners' hands and feet. The **keeper of the prison** (27)—one word in Greek, translated "jailor" in 23—wakened by the earthquake, was horrified to see the prison doors open. Presuming that the prisoners had fled, **he drew out his sword** to commit suicide—"either as a point of military honour or perhaps to avoid the punishment due to a jailer who let prisoners escape."[160] (Cf. 12:19; 27:42.)

Acting quickly, Paul **averted** the suicide by loudly crying out: **Do thyself no harm: for we are all here** (28). The one really in command of the situation was God's man, Paul, not the jailer. The latter **called for a light** (29)—Greek, "lights"—**and sprang in**—"rushed in"—**and came trembling**—badly shaken by the whole affair—**and fell down before Paul and Silas**, recognizing that the earthquake was connected with them.

Then he **brought them out** (30)—one Greek MS (D) adds "having fastened up the others"—and asked, **Sirs, what must I**

[159]*Beginnings,* IV, 196.
[160]*Ibid.,* p. 198.

do to be saved? He may have heard the words of the demon-possessed slave girl (cf. 17), and the earthquake made him believe they were true.

The answer of the missionaries was: **Believe on the Lord Jesus Christ,**[161] **and thou shalt be saved, and thy house** (31). Nothing is said about repenting, as in 2:38 in answer to the question, "What shall we do?" The reason probably is that Paul sensed a true repentance already in the jailer's attitude. He was ready to believe. **House** here means "household," which may have included the man's servants as well as his immediate family.

What the jailer and his household needed was instruction in **the word of the Lord** (32), and this the missionaries proceeded to give. Perhaps Paul spoke to the men, and Silas to the women and children.

The same hour of the night (33), the jailer **washed their stripes.** Then he **was baptized, he and all his, straightway.** Bruce says: "The washing and the baptism took place after he brought them out of the prison (*ver.* 30) and before he took them into his house (*ver.* 34), probably at a well in the courtyard."[162]

When the jailer had brought the two prisoners into his house, **he set meat before them** (34)—literally "set a table"—**and rejoiced, believing in God with all his house.** Instead of the threatened funeral there was a time of feasting and rejoicing.

From vv. 30-31, Alexander Maclaren lifts up "The Great Question." (1) The question that we should all ask, **What must I do to be saved?** 30; (2) The clear answer, **Believe on the Lord Jesus Christ,** 31; (3) The blessing we may all receive, **Thou shalt be saved,** 31.

e. Complete Vindication (16:35-40). **When it was day** (35), **the magistrates**—praetors—**sent the serjeants**—lictors, literally, "rod-bearers." Lumby comments: "These were the lictors, that attended on the praetors . . . probably the same persons who on the previous day had scourged Paul and Silas, and were now sent to see that they were got rid of."[163] It is altogether likely that the magistrates had been so frightened by the earthquake

---

[161]**Christ** is omitted in the very oldest MSS.
[162]*Acts,* p. 321.
[163]*Op. cit.,* p. 297.

that they had decided they had better not detain the missionaries further.

The message the "policemen" (NASB) brought was, **Let those men go.** The jailer reported this to Paul and bade the former prisoners depart **in peace** (36).

But Paul had something else in mind. He replied: **They have beaten us openly uncondemned, being Romans, and have cast us into prison; and now do they thrust us out privily** (secretly)? **nay verily; but let them come themselves and fetch us out** (37). On the surface this seems like personal retaliation. What must be realized is that Paul made a strategic move at this point. The founders of the new Christian church in Philippi had been publicly accused as criminals. Without any semblance of a trial or legal condemnation, they had been cast into prison as dangerous characters. For the sake of the church and *its* reputation, not his, Paul demanded that the magistrates give them a complete vindication, which would tell the whole town that the founders of the church were not criminals or troublemakers. If he had been seeking revenge, he would have sued the slave owners who had slandered him and Silas. This he did not do.

When the magistrates heard that Paul and Silas were Roman citizens **they feared** (38), as well they might. As Roman citizens, the two missionaries could have appealed to the emperor, and the magistrates would have been severely punished. "Citizens were protected against flogging,"[164] and in any case could not be bound until after they had been officially condemned in court.

The question as to why Paul and Silas did not claim their citizenship and thus escape the beating—as Paul did later in Jerusalem (22:24-29)—cannot be answered with certainty. The most likely explanation is that there was such confusion in the Agora that they could not make themselves heard. The whole matter seems to have been a rushed affair.

At any rate, the magistrates came and humbly **besought** the missionaries **to depart out of the city** (39). They wanted no more riots, for their careers were already endangered by what had happened.

Paul and Silas left the prison, went to **the house of Lydia** to see **the brethren** (40), that is, the new converts, **comforted them**—or "exhorted them"—**and departed.** They evidently felt that it was best for the new church that they should leave town.

---

[164]*Beginnings,* IV, 200.

2. *Thessalonica* (17:1-9)

Paul and his party "took the road"—the famous Egnatian Way that linked Rome with the East—**through Amphipolis and Apollonia** on their way to **Thessalonica** (1, see map 3). This was a distance of about one hundred miles and so would take the best part of a week between Sabbaths to walk it. From Philippi it was thirty-three miles to Amphipolis, thirty more to Apollonia, and another thirty-seven to Thessalonica—rather too far apart for one day's walk, so they may have ridden. Because Luke was not along we do not have any particulars of the trip.

It was Paul's policy to follow the main roads. Bruce has aptly observed: "The highways of Empire became for Paul the highways of the Kingdom of Heaven."[165]

Amphipolis—"on-both-sides city"—was so called because it was almost surrounded by the Strymon River, about three miles from the sea. It was the capital of the first district of Macedonia, which included Philippi. We are not told why Paul did not stop to preach here or at Apollonia.

Thessalonica was an important seaport on the Aegean and is still a thriving commercial center. It was the capital of Macedonia and its largest city. Unlike Philippi, it had **a synagogue of the Jews.** This gave the missionaries a strategic place to begin evangelization of this community.

a. Progress (17:1-4). **Paul, as his manner**—"custom"—**was** (2), attended the synagogue services, and for **three sabbath days reasoned**—"discussed" or "argued" (NEB)—**with them out of the scriptures.** Since the Jews were keen on the study of the Scriptures and loved to argue, Paul had a golden opportunity.

Two verbs are used to describe the apostles' arguments from the Scripture. The first is **opening** (3); literally, "opening thoroughly." The basic task of a preacher is to open the Bible to the understanding of people. The second verb is **alleging.** This verb literally means "place beside." So Paul was placing specific scriptures by the side of his arguments to support them. For this passage Abbott-Smith suggests the meaning "to bring forward, quote as evidence."[166] Paul was bringing forward passages from the Jewish Scriptures to prove his points.

The main point that he had to present and prove was that

---

[165]*Acts,* p. 324.
[166]*Op. cit.,* p. 343.

Christ must needs have suffered, and risen again from the dead.
Until the Jews could see that their Scriptures taught a suffering,
resurrected Messiah they could not be expected to accept Jesus
as their Messiah. Having established the fact that the Old Testament Scriptures teach that the Messiah would suffer (Psalms 22;
Isaiah 53) and die, but rise again (Ps. 16:10), Paul could make
his final point: **this Jesus, whom I preach unto you, is Christ**
(the Messiah).

A typical result followed Paul's preaching: **some of them
believed** (4), or "were persuaded" (ASV). These **consorted
with Paul and Silas.** The verb literally means "to allot to, assign
to by lot"[167] (cf. Phillips—"threw in their lot"). Alexander explains it thus: *"Consorted with* (or more exactly, *were allotted
to) Paul and Silas,* by divine grace, as their portion, or the fruit
of their ministry."[168] Besides these Jews who were persuaded
and "joined" (NEB) Paul and Silas, there were **of the devout
Greeks**—worshipers in the Jewish synagogue—**a great multitude,
and of the chief women**—or possibly, "wives of the leading men"
—not a few. Since the Jews required circumcision of proselytes
and the Christians made no such demand of their converts, the
Gentile worshipers in the synagogue would be attracted to the
new religion. Christianity offered everything which drew these
Gentiles to Judaism—belief in one God, high moral standards,
etc.—without the offensive legal requirements. This is not to
deny that Christianity makes higher demands in terms of real
consecration and sacrifice; but these are primarily in the spiritual
realm.

b. Persecution (17:5-9). It was inevitable that the popularity
of the new preachers should provoke opposition. The situation
was the same as it had been several times before: "the Jews were
jealous."[169] So they **took unto them certain lewd**—"wicked" or
"worthless"—**fellows of the baser sort**—literally, loungers in
the Agora (marketplace). Lake and Cadbury think that this etymological meaning may not have held at this time. They translate
baser sort as "lower class."[170] However, it is probably best to
let the original meaning carry through (cf. Phillips—"unprinci-

---

[167]Abbott-Smith, *op. cit.,* p. 385.

[168]*Op. cit.,* p. 598.

[169]The clause **which believed not** is omitted in the best MSS, though the
truth of the phrase is obvious.

[170]*Beginnings,* IV, 204.

pled loungers of the market place"; NEB—"low fellows from the dregs of the populace"). Bruce goes so far as to suggest "gangsters."[171]

Picking such people, the Jewish opponents having **gathered a company**—literally, "having made a crowd" or "formed a mob" (NASB)—**set all the city on an uproar** (cf. same word in 20:10). Having **assaulted**—"mobbed" (NEB)—**the house of Jason**— where apparently the missionaries had been staying—they **sought** —"were seeking" (imperfect tense)—**to bring them out to the people.** The term used here is not the usual word for "people" (*laos*), but *demos*. It has the special meaning of "the people assembled" (cf. 12:22; 19:30, 33). Bruce says: "As Thessalonica was a free city, its citizen-body (*demos*) discharged legislative and juridical functions."[172] The Jews intended to bring the missionaries before the town assembly.

For some unknown reason Paul and his party were not at Jason's house at the time. So the mob **drew** (6)—lit., "were violently dragging"—**Jason and certain brethren unto the rulers of the city.** The term *politarches* (lit., "city-ruler," only here and in v. 8) had not until recently been found anywhere in Greek literature. So earlier critics accused Luke of having invented this word. But once more Luke has been completely exonerated by archaeology as being an accurate historian. No less than nineteen inscriptions have been discovered, ranging from the second century B.C. to the third century A.D., which contain this word. Fourteen of these inscriptions belong to Macedonia, and five of them refer to Thessalonica itself. In the time of Augustus, Thessalonica had five politarchs; later it had six. Lake and Cadbury write: "*Politarches* is mainly if not exclusively a Macedonian title for the non-Roman magistrates of a city."[173] Luke was a widely traveled man and a careful investigator. He walks through the complex history of the first century with a sure step.

The measure of the impact that Paul and his associates were making is shown by the accusation brought against them: **These that have turned the world upside down are come hither also.** The term **world** (*oikoumene*) means the civilized world. **Turned . . . upside down** is a strong verb (in NT only here, in 21:38, and in Gal. 5:12). Here it may mean "stir up sedition." This

---

[171]*Acts*, p. 326.
[172]*Ibid.*
[173]*Beginnings*, IV, 205.

was a most serious offense in the eyes of the Roman government. The accusation may have been intended to carry political overtones that would alarm the rulers and incite them to take drastic action. This is made more specific by the further charge: **and these all do contrary to the decrees of Caesar, saying that there is another king**—"emperor"—[174] . . . **Jesus** (7). This was nothing less than treason. Jason's offense was that he had **received** ("harboured") [175] these political agitators in his home.

Naturally this accusation **troubled the people** (8)—*ochlon,* "crowd"—**and the rulers of the city** (*politarches*). So the **rulers took security** (9) from Jason and the others, and released them. Ramsay suggests that this may have been a guarantee that Paul would leave town and not return, and that this was the hindrance the apostle refers to in I Thess. 2:18.[176]

3. *Beroea* (17:10-15)

Either because of some such pledge, or the danger of further rioting, **the brethren immediately sent away Paul and Silas by night unto Berea** (10). This necessity to escape detection shows how serious the situation was. Did young Timothy quietly stay for a short time? That is possible. But if so he soon joined the other two at Beroea (cf. 14).

Berea—the correct spelling is Beroea (cf. RSV, NEB)—is the modern Verria, about fifty or sixty miles west of Thessalonica and south of the Egnatian Way (so that it was spoken of at that time as "off the road"). Arriving there, the missionaries **went into the synagogue of the Jews**. Once more Paul found a "pulpit" awaiting him.

The Jews at Beroea are described as being **more noble**—or "generous-minded" (Phillips)—**than** those in Thessalonica (11). This was evidenced by the fact that they **received the word**—the preaching of Paul—**with all readiness of mind**—*prothymia,* "eagerness, willingness, readiness."[177] They **searched the scriptures**—our Old Testament—**daily, whether these things were so. Searched** is literally "examining" or "investigating" (present participle of continuous action).

---

[174]*Ibid.,* p. 206.
[175]*Ibid.,* p. 205.
[176]*Op. cit.,* pp. 230-31.
[177]Abbott-Smith, *op. cit.,* p. 381.

The result of this eager, honest examination of the Scriptures day by day was that they found the things spoken by the missionaries **were so.** Obedient to the truth, **many of them**— i.e., Jews—**believed** (12). Also there was a considerable number of Gentile men and women who accepted Christ. The word for **honourable** in late Greek meant "wealthy, influential."[178] **Not a few** is masculine, and so may refer primarily to the men. But it is more likely that it and **Greeks** (feminine) refer to both men and women.

These two verses (11-12) indicate "The Price of Learning": (1) Eagerness to know, 11; (2) Earnestness in study, 11; (3) Acceptance of truth, 12.

At Beroea the same thing happened that had taken place in the province of Galatia. Just as the Jews of Pisidian Antioch and Iconium followed Paul to Lystra and made trouble for him there (14:19), so now **the Jews of Thessalonica** (13), when they heard **that the word of God was preached** by Paul at Beroea, **came thither also, and stirred up the people.** The best Greek text has, "stirring up and inciting the crowds."

The result was that Paul had to leave town. **Immediately (14),** to protect his life, **the brethren sent away Paul to go as it were to**—the better Greek text has "as far as"—**the sea.** In this case Silas and Timothy stayed behind to establish the new converts.

Some of the Christians from Beroea **conducted Paul** to **Athens** (15, see map 3). This was a courteous, thoughtful act, especially as his life was in danger. Whether they went by land or by sea is not stated. The fact that his escorts conducted Paul all the way to Athens favors the idea that they went by land. Presumably they would have returned from the seaport had they put him on a ship. As it was, they made the long journey over 200 miles southward. Then, having received orders for Silas and Timothy to come to Athens **with all speed** (as quickly as possible), they returned to Beroea.

It appears that Silas and Timothy joined Paul at Athens, and that he sent Timothy back to Thessalonica (I Thess. 3:1-3) and Silas to either Philippi or Beroea (18:5). By the time they again joined Paul he had gone on to Corinth (18:5). It was then that Paul wrote the two Epistles to the Thessalonians.

[178]*Ibid.*, p. 190.

F. GREECE, 17:16—18:17

1. *Athens* (17:16-34)

¶This was the greatest center of culture and education in the ancient world. Bruce says: "The sculpture, literature and oratory of Athens in the fifth and fourth centuries B.C. have never been surpassed; in philosophy, too, she took the leading place, being the native city of Socrates and Plato, and the adopted home of Aristotle, Epicurus and Zeno."[179] Athens is still, as is Rome, one of the great capitals of the world.

a. *Arraigned Before the Areopagus* (17:16-21). While Paul was waiting at Athens for Silas and Timothy to rejoin him, **his spirit was stirred in him** (16)—"provoked, roused to anger"— **when he saw the city wholly given to idolatry**—better, "full of idols" (ASV). Lake and Cadbury write: "The abundance of statues in Athens, and in general the evidences of the Athenian religiosity, were remarked by other visitors."[180] All this shows how little impression had been made on the populace by even their best philosophers, such as Socrates.

Paul had a twofold ministry in Athens: the first with the Jews, primarily in the synagogue, and the second with the Gentiles in the marketplace. He **disputed** (17)—"argued," same word as in 2 (see comments there)—**in the synagogue with the Jews, and with the devout persons**—Gentile worshipers of the true God—**and in the market**—the Agora—**daily with them that met him**—literally, "those who happened to be present." He thus adapted himself to the conditions of each city where he ministered. Since the favorite method of teaching in Athens was the "free for all" discussion in the Agora, Paul adopted that technique here. He would become "all things to all men" (I Cor. 9:22) to win them to Christ. Few other men of his day could have carried on the twofold ministry which he had at Athens. For the first (to the Jews) he had been trained at the feet of Gamaliel in Jerusalem. For the second (to the philosophically minded Athenians) he had probably been educated at the great university of Tarsus, which was surpassed only by Athens and Alexandria. God had prepared His man for this broad ministry in a most amazing way. Filled with the Holy Spirit, Paul was able to take the re-

---

[179]*Acts*, p. 331.
[180]*Beginnings*, IV, 209.

vealed Word of God and the wisdom of the Greek philosophers and thus establish a rapport with both Jews and Gentiles.

In his daily discussions in the Agora, Paul chanced to meet some **philosophers** (the word is found only here in the NT)— **Epicureans** and **Stoicks** (18). Of the former Bruce says: "The Epicureans took their name from Epicurus (341-270 B.C.), whose ethical system, founded on the atomic theory of Democritus, presented pleasure (*hedone*) as the chief end of life, the pleasure most worth having being a life of tranquillity (*ataraxia*), free from pain, disturbing passions, and superstitious fears."[181]

Of the **Stoicks** he writes: "The Stoics regarded Zeno (340-265 B.C.) as their founder, and took their name from the *Stoa Poikile* in Athens, where he taught."[182] The Stoics' belief was pantheistic, rationalistic, and fatalistic. In practice they laid emphasis "on the supremacy of the rational over the emotional faculty in man, and on individual self-sufficiency."[183] They thus denied the heart of true religion, which is dependence on God. Prominent Stoics in Roman times were Seneca, Epictetus, and Marcus Aurelius.

These Epicureans and Stoics **encountered** Paul—"i.e. met him in disputation, argued with him."[184] Someone asked: **What will this babbler say?** The expression **what will** is more accurately rendered "what would" (ASV); that is, "What might he be wishing to say?" **Babbler** is literally "seed-picker." Of this term Lake and Cadbury write: "It would seem that the word was used first of birds that pick up grain, then of men who picked up odds and ends in the market; it was then transferred to men who were zealous seekers of the second-rate at second hand, and finally to generally worthless fellows."[185] Phillips gives a good translation of the question—"What is this cock sparrow trying to say?"

This was the question of some. But **other some** (18; others) observed: **He seemeth to be a setter forth of strange gods,** or "foreign deities." The word for **gods** is *daimonia*, which is used in the Gospels fifty-two times for demons, as also elsewhere in the New Testament. In the Septuagint it is used for heathen deities.

[181] *Acts*, p. 332.
[182] *Ibid*.
[183] *Ibid*.
[184] Lumby, *op. cit.*, p. 307.
[185] *Beginnings*, IV, 211.

It is essentially an adjective meaning "divine." In classical Greek it meant "the Divine power." That is what it signifies here.

The reason for this talk about foreign deities was that Paul **preached unto them Jesus, and the resurrection.** Some commentators have held that the Athenians took *Jesus* and *Anastasis* **(resurrection)** as meaning a god and goddess. But Lake and Cadbury think this "improbable."[186]

Those who had been disputing with Paul in the Agora brought him to the **Areopagus (19).** This is two words in Greek, *Areios pagos,* which means "Hill of Ares," or Mars. Since the ancient court of Athens met on Mars' Hill, the court itself came to be called after the name of the hill, *Areopagus.* As the government of Athens became more democratic, this aristocratic court lost some of its prerogatives, but still kept the right to try murder cases and other serious moral crimes. Bruce says: "It had supreme authority in religious matters and seems to have had the power at this time to appoint public lectures and exercise some control over them in the interest of public order."[187] Probably Paul was brought "before the Court of Areopagus" (NEB).

Lake and Cadbury make a pertinent observation at this point. They write: "According to Acts, therefore, just as Paul is brought before the *strategoi* at Philippi, the *politarchai* at Thessalonica, the *anthupatos* at Corinth, so at Athens he faces the Areopagus."[188] They add: "The local name for the supreme authority is in each case different and accurate."[189] Luke writes carefully and correctly, as a reliable historian.

The request presented to Paul was: **May we know what this new doctrine** ("teaching"), **whereof thou speakest, is?** The NASB reads: "May we know what this new teaching is which you are proclaiming?" Paul was bringing **strange things (20)** to their ears, and they wanted an explanation of what he was talking about.

The parenthetical statement of 21 was very true to life in the Athens of Paul's day. It is abundantly corroborated by contemporary writers.

b. Arguing Before the Areopagus (17:22-31). Then **Paul stood in the midst of Mars' Hill (22).** But **Mars' Hill** is the same

---

[186]*Ibid.,* p. 212.
[187]*Acts,* p. 333.
[188]*Beginnings,* IV, 213.
[189]*Ibid.*

expression which is translated "Areopagus" in 19 (see comments there). Practically all scholars are agreed that "Areopagus" is the correct translation in both places. Lake and Cadbury note that **in the midst** "is obviously more appropriate to the council than to the hill."[190] Cadbury, in his later work, *The Book of Acts in History,* says that in the first century the Court of the Areopagus met in a portico northwest of the Agora, which was "called alternately the Stoa Basileios and the Stoa of Zeus Eleutherios."[191] But he goes on to say: "The possibilities must be left open that the council sometimes met on the hill Areopagus and not in the Agora even in later times, or that Paul spoke on the hill but not to an official group."[192]

Courteously Paul addressed his audience as **men of Athens.** But his opening statement as it appears in KJV seems less than tactful: **I perceive that in all things ye are too superstitious.** Probably it would be better to translate the last expression "very religious" (ASV) or "extremely religious" (Phillips, following Deissmann). The Greek word used here basically means "fearers of the gods." Lake and Cadbury translate it "very superstitious," but leave the matter somewhat open.[193] Bruce favors "very religious."[194] Knowling seems justified when he writes: "It is incredible that St. Paul should have commenced his remarks with a phrase calculated to offend his hearers."[195] The apostle certainly did not have high respect for either Felix or Agrippa, yet he began his speeches before both these men with utmost courtesy (24:10; 26:2-3). Paul was not the kind of man to show disrespect for such an audience as he faced at Athens. Ned Stonehouse finishes his discussion of the question by saying: "It does appear definitely more satisfactory in the present connection to conclude that Paul is underscoring their religiosity rather than their superstition."[196]

Paul goes on to explain why he said this: **as I passed by** (23) —literally, "while I was going through" (the streets)—**and beheld your devotions**—rather, "objects of worship"—**I found an altar**

[190]*Ibid.,* p. 214.
[191]*Op. cit.,* p. 57, n. 43.
[192]*Ibid.*
[193]*Beginnings,* IV, 214.
[194]*Acts,* p. 335.
[195]EGT, II, 370.
[196]*Paul Before the Areopagus* (Grand Rapids: Wm. B. Eerdmans Publishing Co., 1957), p. 17.

with this inscription, TO THE UNKNOWN GOD. Knowling well expresses the significance of this when he says: "In such an inscription Paul wisely recognized that there was in the heart of Athens a witness to the deep unsatisfied yearning of humanity for a clearer and closer knowledge of the unseen power which men worshipped dimly and imperfectly."[197]

Paul continued: **Whom therefore ye ignorantly worship**— better, "worship as unknown" (RSV), connecting this with **unknown** in the inscription, as the Greek does—**him declare I unto you.** The apostle was glad to identify for these people the unknown God they unknowingly worshiped. This was a tactful approach and definitely favors the translation "religious" rather than "superstitious" in Paul's opening remark.

The apostle goes on to describe this "unknown god." He is the **God that made the world**—*cosmos,* "orderly universe"—**and all things therein** (24). He is also **Lord of heaven and earth.** Consequently He cannot dwell in handmade temples. Neither can He be **worshipped**—Greek, "served"—**with men's hands,** for He is the One who **giveth to all life, and breath, and all things** (25). God has **made of one**[198]—literally, "out of one"; i.e., Adam—**all nations** (26). Thus Paul asserted the unity of the human race and suggests God's displeasure with all racial prejudice, whether it be that of the Greeks and Jews of the first century or the white and colored peoples of the twentieth century.

The purpose of all this was **that they should seek the Lord.**[199] **Haply** (27) means "perhaps." Paul goes on to assert that God is **not far from every one of us.**

In him we live, and move, and have our being (28) is treated as a quotation in the RSV. Kirsopp Lake thinks it is quoted from Epimenides.[200] The last clause of the verse, **For we are also his offspring,** comes from the poet Aratus. **His** refers to Zeus.

Since we are the **offspring of God** (29)—by creation—it is foolish to think that the **Godhead**—"the divine," or "deity"— is like the images of gold or silver made by men.

The former **times of this ignorance God winked at**—better, "overlooked" (ASV)—**but now commandeth all men every**

---

[197]EGT, II, 372.

[198]**Blood** is not in the oldest MSS.

[199]The earliest MSS have "God" instead of **Lord.**

[200]*Beginnings,* V, 250.

where to repent (30). Paul is now coming to his evangelistic conclusion.

Why do men need to repent? **Because he hath appointed a day, in the which he will judge the world in righteousness by that man whom he hath ordained** (31); that is, Jesus Christ. Of this, God **hath given assurance**—better, "has provided proof"— **unto all men, in that he hath raised him from the dead.** This is a part of the Easter message that is seldom proclaimed. The Resurrection is the proof to men, God's guarantee, that there will be a judgment day, when all mankind will be judged. It is a sobering thought.

c. *Acceptance by an Areopagite* (17:32-34). The mention of the **resurrection** produced an immediate reaction: **some mocked** (32). Others said they would hear more some other time. The Greeks had a belief in immortality, but denied any bodily resurrection. The Jews were stronger on the resurrection than on immortality. It is the glory of Christianity that it emphasizes both truths. Feeling he could accomplish nothing more with these skeptical Greeks, **Paul departed from among them** (33).

However, there were a few who **believed** (34). Among them was **Dionysius the Areopagite.** It was a great victory to win one convert out of this very select group of about thirty persons. "There may even be a note of triumph in the epithet 'Areopagite' written after one of the convert's names."[201] About **Damaris** we know nothing further, but she was probably well known as a member of the church in Athens.

2. *Corinth* (18:1-17)

Athens was a center of culture, but Corinth was a center of commerce. Its situation made this inevitable. It was located on a narrow isthmus connecting the mainland section of Greece with the Peloponnesus to the south (see map 3). It was dangerous to go around the southern tip of Greece because of the multitude of small, rocky islands jutting out of the sea and also because the prevailing winds were from the north and tended to drive ships toward the coasts of Africa. Corinth had an eastern harbor, Cenchreae, and a western harbor, Lechaeum. Sailors and travelers from all over the Mediterranean were to be found on the streets of Corinth. That is probably one reason why Paul spent

[201]*Beginnings*, IV, 219.

a year and a half in this great metropolis. The gospel would spread out from this center over the then known world.

But Corinth was also infamous for its low morals. To Corinthianize meant to corrupt morally. The temple of Aphrodite at Corinth was said to have had a thousand sacred prostitutes. With immorality as a part of religious worship, it is no wonder that the morals of Corinth were deplored far and wide.

Politically, Corinth was the capital of the Roman province of Achaia (Greece). It was Paul's regular policy to establish a strong church in each provincial capital, so that the evangelization of the province would take place from its main center.

a. Ministry in the Synagogue (18:1-4). As at Athens, Paul had a twofold ministry in Corinth—to the Jews and to the Gentiles. But whereas they were simultaneous in Athens—teaching in the synagogue on the Sabbath days, and talking with people in the marketplace during the week—in Corinth one followed the other. Paul taught in the synagogue until he was ousted from there. Then he ministered particularly to Gentiles in the house of a Gentile who had been worshiping in the synagogue.

Paul **departed from Athens, and came to Corinth** (1)—a distance of about sixty miles. Again we are not told whether he went by land or sea. There he found a Jew named **Aquila, born in Pontus**—northeastern part of Asia Minor (see map 3)—**lately come from Italy, with his wife Priscilla** (2). She is usually called Prisca in the Epistles (Rom. 16:3; I Cor. 16:19; II Tim. 4:19). It appears that she was the stronger character of the two, for her name usually precedes her husband's.

Luke gives an explanation as to why Aquila and Priscilla had left the capital city. It was because **Claudius had commanded all Jews to depart from Rome.** This is probably the decree mentioned by Suetonius in his *Life of Claudius* (25.4)—"He [Claudius] expelled the Jews from Rome, because they were in a state of continual tumult at the instigation of one Chrestus" (probably misspelling of "Christus," Christ). This was A.D. 49, the year before Paul came to Corinth. Since the conversion of Aquila and Priscilla is not mentioned here, it seems likely that they were Christians before they left Rome.

Because Paul **was of the same craft** (3)—*homotechnon*, "of the same trade"—**he abode with them, and wrought: for by their occupation**—*techne*, "trade"—**they were tentmakers.** Some recent scholars have preferred the translation "leather-workers."

Lake and Cadbury write of "felted cloth made of goat hair . . . which was so specially a product of Cilicia that it was called *Cilicium* in Latin, *kilikion* in Greek."[202] They continue: "It is of course tempting to connect Paul of Tarsus in Cilicia with the special product of his own province. Possibly this is what he really worked at."[203] Yet they go on to say: "But it is impossible to resist the weight of ancient testimony that to the Greeks it meant a 'leather-worker.' "[204] The present writer would prefer to follow the leading English versions (KJV, ERV, ASV, RSV, NEB) in designating Paul's trade as tentmaking.

In addition to working at his trade during the week, Paul **reasoned**—"was discoursing"—**in the synagogue every sabbath, and persuaded**—"was persuading," a gradual process—**the Jews and the Greeks** (4). It appears that in most, if not all, the synagogues of the Dispersion there were Gentiles worshiping with the Jews.

b. Ministry Opposed by the Jews (18:5-6). When Silas (last mention of him in Acts) and Timothy arrived from Macedonia (see comments on 17:15), **Paul was pressed in the spirit** (5). The best Greek text reads "was held together [or 'constrained'] by the word." The meaning of this is probably expressed correctly by Phillips: "was completely absorbed in preaching the message." Bruce gives an excellent explanation and interpretation: " 'proceeded to devote himself entirely to the preaching'; perhaps supplies brought by Timothy and Silas from Thessalonica and Philippi (cf. II Cor. xi. 8; Phil. iv. 15) released him from the necessity of manual labour."[205] Under this constraint, he **testified** —"solemnly protested"—**to the Jews that Jesus was Christ**—"the Messiah was Jesus."

When the Jews **opposed themselves** (6)—rather, "set themselves against" or "resisted"—**and blasphemed**—probably better, "reviled him" (RSV), although it may be that they cried out, "Anathema Jesus"[206]—**he shook his raiment,** probably as a sign that God had rejected them. "The act is figurative of entire renunciation."[207]

[202]*Beginnings,* IV, 223.
[203]*Ibid.*
[204]*Ibid.*
[205]*Acts,* p. 344.
[206]Rackham, *op. cit.,* p. 325.
[207]Lumby, *op. cit.,* p. 319.

Then Paul announced: **Your blood be upon your own heads; I am clean: from henceforth I will go unto the Gentiles.** The first statement here is a very solemn one (cf. Ezek. 33:4). These Jews must bear their guilt. Paul had done his duty and was **clean** (i.e., free from blame). The last statement of this verse had been made by Paul and Barnabas in virtually the same form at Pisidian Antioch (13:46). The **henceforth** here perhaps suggests a more settled policy. Yet Paul continued to minister first in the synagogues (cf. 19:8). But as he was "squeezed out" of the synagogues, he devoted more and more time to the Gentiles. At Ephesus he taught in the synagogue for three months, but two years in a Greek hall (19:8, 10). Always the Jews were given the first opportunity (cf. Rom. 1:16—"to the Jew first, and also to the Greek").

c. *Ministry in the House of Justus* (18:7-11). Because of the severe opposition of the leaders in the synagogue, Paul **departed** —literally, "changed his place"[208]—and went into the house of a man **named Justus** (7). Of the two oldest Greek MSS, Sinaiticus has "Titus Justus" (ASV); and Vaticanus has "Titius Justus." Most translators today adopt the latter (e.g., NASB, NEB, Phillips). Bruce writes: "The name Titius Justus suggests that he was a Roman citizen."[209] This would give Paul and the new Christian congregation a good status in the city, which was important.

Justus was **one that worshipped God;** i.e., a devout Gentile worshiping in the Jewish synagogue. His **house joined hard to the synagogue.** It may seem a bit odd that Paul should hold services right next door to the synagogue from which he had been practically ousted. But two reasons may have led him to do it. The first was that he wanted to be conveniently situated where the Gentile worshipers could easily find him. The second was that the advantage of staying in the home of a Roman citizen was one that could not be passed up.

The success of the move is shown in part by the fact that **Crispus . . . believed on the Lord with all his house** (8). The expression **the chief ruler of the synagogue** "does not mean that he was the head of the synagogue, but that he was one of the prominent men who had the title of archisynagogue."[210] His action

---

[208]Ramsay, *op. cit.*, p. 255.

[209]*Acts*, p. 345.

[210]*Beginnings*, IV, 225.

probably caused a considerable sensation in the city, **and many of the Corinthians hearing believed, and were baptized.** Because of the later party divisions in Corinth, following human leaders, Paul thanked God that he baptized none in that city except Crispus, this outstanding convert, and Gaius (I Cor. 1:14). Gaius is probably to be identified with Justus, Paul's host (Rom. 16:23). (Every Roman citizen had three names, a nomen, praenomen, and cognomen. His full Latin name would be Gaius Titius Justus.) As an afterthought Paul says that he also baptized the household of Stephanas, but he cannot recall any others (I Cor. 1:16). Evidently his assistants, Silas and Timothy, took care of baptizing the many who were being converted.

It may well be imagined that the leaders of the synagogue were becoming furious about what was happening next door. Apparently Paul also was becoming fearful about the growing opposition, which may well have threatened his life. Perhaps he had decided that it was about time for him to move on. The apostle had a naturally restless spirit, and he had not stayed long in any place so far.

That some such situation existed is shown by the fact that the Lord spoke to His apostle in a night vision with this message: **Be not afraid, but speak, and hold not thy peace** (9)—literally, "Stop being afraid, but go on speaking, and do not become silent." The Lord continued: **For I am with thee, and no man shall set on thee to hurt thee: for I have much people in this city** (10). There were many yet to be converted. Bruce notes: "The word regularly used of the Jewish people [*laos*] as distinct from the Gentiles is here used of the new 'chosen people.' "[211]

The vision had the desired effect. Paul **continued there a year and six months, teaching the word of God among them** (11). **Continued** is literally "sat"; i.e., for teaching. Knowling aptly observes: "The word may be purposely used here instead of the ordinary *menein* [remain] to indicate the quiet and settled work to which the Apostle was directed by the vision which had calmed his troubled spirit."[212] (Cf. "settled down," Phillips.)

Our spirits may be strengthened by "The Word of the Lord" in 9-10. (1) The divine consolation, **Be not afraid . . . no man shall set on thee to hurt thee,** 9-10; (2) The divine commission,

[211]*Acts*, p. 346.
[212]EGT, II, 389.

467

speak, and hold not thy peace, 9; (3) The divine concern, **I have
much people in this city,** 10 (A. F. Harper).

d. Ministry Protected by Gallio (18:12-17). When **Gallio
was the deputy**—"proconsul"—**of Achaia, the Jews made insurrection with one accord against Paul, and brought him to the
judgment seat** (12). The Greek word *bema*, judgment seat,
can be seen today inscribed on the wall at this spot in the ruins
of ancient Corinth. This is the regular word for the official tribunal of a Roman ruler.

An inscription found at Delphi and dated probably A.D. 52
refers to "Gallio . . . proconsul of Achaia."[213] Kirsopp Lake
thinks this evidence shows that Gallio became proconsul in the
summer of A.D. 51 or 52.[214] Since Paul was probably arraigned
before Gallio soon after he came as proconsul—the Jews would
naturally take advantage of a new man who did not know anything about the missionaries—it seems best to date Paul's year
and a half in Corinth from the spring of 50 to the fall of 51. Bruce
concludes: "Probably from the late summer of 50 to the early
spring of 52."[215]

In the past some critics have claimed that in the first century
Achaia was an imperial province, governed by a propraetor. And
so it was from A.D. 16 to 43. But from A.D. 44 it was a senatorial
province, governed by a proconsul.[216] Once more Luke has been
proved to be a reliable historian.

The charge brought against Paul before Gallio was: **This fellow persuadeth**—in the papyri this verb carries the sense of evil
persuasion,[217] and in Herodotus it means "seduce, mislead"[218]—
men to worship God contrary to the law (13). What they meant
was "contrary to the Mosaic law." But they hoped that Gallio
would take it as meaning "contrary to Roman law."

Gallio saw through their duplicity. As Paul was about to
make his defense (14), the proconsul said to the Jews: **If it were**

[213]*Beginnings,* V, 461.

[214]*Ibid.,* p. 464. G. B. Caird ("Chronology of the NT," IDB, I, 604) says
that "the obvious interpretation of the Delphi inscription is that Gallio's
term of office in Achaia extended from July, 51, to June, 52."

[215]*Acts,* p. 346.

[216]Ramsay, *op. cit.,* p. 258.

[217]Moulton and Milligan, VGT, p. 37.

[218]Liddell and Scott, *op. cit.,* I, 115.

a matter of wrong—a *civil* case, "injury done to others"[219]—**or wicked lewdness**—a *criminal* case, "crime, villainy"—**O ye Jews** —expresses exasperation—**reason would that I should bear with you**—"I might reasonably be expected to put up with you" (Phillips).

The proconsul went on: **But if it be a question (15)**—plural, "questions," in the oldest MSS—**of words and names, and of your law**—literally, "the law according to you folk"—**look ye to it**—the Greek is emphatic: "you *yourselves* see to it"—**for I will be no judge of such matters.** Ramsay gives an excellent paraphrase of the first part of this verse: "If they are questions of word, not deed, and of names, not things, and of your law, not Roman law."[220]

Because the charge which the Jews made had nothing to do with Roman law, Gallio threw the case out of court. When the Jews probably tried to continue pressing the matter, **he drave them**—literally, "drove them away"—**from the judgment seat (16)**—"he had them ejected from the court" (NEB).

The mention of **Sosthenes** as **the chief ruler of the synagogue (17)** has led some to suppose that he had been elected to take the place of Crispus, who had been converted to Christianity. But they may both have had this honorable title simultaneously (see comments on 8). It is entirely likely that this is the same Sosthenes who is mentioned in I Cor. 1:1 as an associate of Paul. Perhaps his beating at this time influenced him toward Christ. This possibility is involved in the question as to who it was that beat Sosthenes. Instead of **all the Greeks,** the oldest MSS have "they all." Since the last "them" (16) referred to the Jews, it has been suggested that it was the Jews, not the Greeks, who beat Sosthenes—in anger because he had lost the case or because he may have shown some sympathy for Paul. John Wesley translates it: "Then they all took Sosthenes . . . and beat him," and adds: "It seems because he had occasioned them so much trouble to no purpose."[221] Many scholars reject this idea as being too farfetched. But Lake and Cadbury write: "Possibly Sosthenes was beaten by both parties—by the Jews for mismanaging the case,

---

[219]Rackham, *op. cit.,* p. 331.

[220]*Op. cit.,* p. 257.

[221]John Wesley, *Explanatory Notes upon the New Testament* (London: Epworth Press, 1954 [reprint]), p. 469.

and by the Greeks on general principles."[222]   (Cf. NEB—"Then there was a general attack on Sosthenes.")

The last statement, **Gallio cared for none of those things,** has led some to speak of "the careless Gallio." But the governor was only performing his duty in refusing to have anything to do with a case which did not belong in a Roman court. Gallio was the brother of Seneca, who praises him highly for his noble character.

G. Asia, 18:18—20:38

1. *Ephesus* (18:18—19:41)

This was "the greatest commercial city of Asia Minor" and "the capital of the province of Asia."[223] Paul had probably wanted to preach here early on this second journey (see comments on 16:6-8). Even now he could make only a brief visit. Not until his third journey was he able to evangelize the city (c. 19), but he then spent three years doing it.

a. Paul's Brief Visit (18:18-21). The apostle remained in Corinth **yet a good while** (18)—literally, "sufficient days." There is no indication as to how long this was. Then, having taken his leave of the Christians—**the brethren**—he **sailed thence into Syria** —a general name for Syria and Palestine. With him were **Priscilla and Aquila** (note her name first). It is not clear whether **having shorn his head in Cenchrea**—eastern harbor for Corinth— **for he had a vow** refers to Paul or to Aquila. Meyer thinks it was Aquila's vow.[224] But most commentators hold that Paul is meant. Lumby writes: "For some reason, either during sickness or in the midst of his conflict at Corinth, he had taken a vow upon himself of the nature of the Nazirite vows (Numb. vi. 1-21)."[225] Since the same Greek words are used here as in 21:23, Bruce thinks it was "a temporary Nazirite vow. The minimum duration of such a vow was 30 days."[226] The cutting of the hair marked the end of the vow. Since these vows were ordinarily terminated in Jerusalem, this may have been the reason for Paul's trip back there at this time—to offer his hair in the Temple, as Lumby suggests.

[222]*Beginnings,* IV, 228.
[223]Bruce, *Acts,* p. 349.
[224]*Op. cit.,* pp. 352-53.
[225]*Op. cit.,* p. 324.
[226]*Acts,* p. 349.

Stopping off at Ephesus (see map 3) after a two or three days' voyage,[227] Paul left Priscilla and Aquila there (19). **He himself entered into the synagogue, and reasoned with the Jews.** The use of **himself** seems to imply that Priscilla and Aquila did not go to the synagogue at this time, which seems odd. Alexander treats this as a sort of parenthesis: "As if he had said, Aquila and Priscilla went no further, leaving Paul to complete his voyage alone, but not until he had gone into the synagogue and there addressed the Jews, showing how far he was from having abandoned the desire and hope of their salvation."[228]

Paul was asked to stay longer, but declined (20). It has been suggested that his vow, evidenced by his hair cut short, may have favorably impressed the Jews at Ephesus so that they begged him to remain.

Verse 21 reads literally: "But having taken his leave [same verb as in 18] and saying, 'I will return again to you, God willing,' he put to sea [cf. 13:13; 16:11] from Ephesus." **I must by all means keep this feast that cometh in Jerusalem** is not in the oldest MSS. **If God will** is, in the Latin, *Deo volente* (God willing), often abbreviated today into D.V.

b. Paul's Return to Syria (18:22-23). When Paul **had landed at Caesarea, and gone up, and saluted the church, he went down to Antioch** (22, see map 3). The big question is: What church is meant? Lake and Cadbury favor Caesarea: Paul "went up" from the port to the city.[229] But most commentators prefer Jerusalem. The expression **went down to Antioch** favors this interpretation and suggests a trip from Jerusalem to Antioch. Jews always went "up" to Jerusalem and "down" from it (cf. 8:5; 15:2).

After Paul **had spent some time**—how long we do not know —at Antioch, **he departed, and went over all the country of Galatia and Phrygia in order, strengthening all the disciples** (23). This is generally taken as marking the beginning of Paul's third missionary journey. He took the same route as that with which he had begun his second journey, doubtless traveling through his hometown, Tarsus, and going over the mountains through the Cilician Gates. He visited the churches which he had

[227]Knowling, *op., cit.,* p. 393.
[228]*Op. cit.,* p. 640.
[229]*Beginnings,* IV, 230.

founded on his first journey and revisited on his second journey. These were in the southern part of the province of Galatia (see map 3).

Bruce says of this paragraph: "In these two verses and xix. 1 is compressed a journey of 1500 miles. Note how quickly Luke can cover the ground when describing a journey on which he did not accompany Paul."[230]

c. *Apollos' Eloquent Ministry* (18:24-28). Before beginning the account of Paul's long ministry at Ephesus (c. 19), the author briefs his readers on recent happenings at that city. Particularly he tells about the ministry of Apollos there.

Four things are stated about **Apollos** (24). First, he was a **Jew.** Second, he was **born at Alexandria** (see map 3), an Egyptian city which was founded by Alexander the Great in 332 B.C. and named after him. For a long time there had been a large settlement of Jews there, filling two out of its five wards. Alexandria was second only to Athens as a great center of culture and learning. Here the Septuagint had been translated, and here Philo (a Jew) was famous in the first century as an intellectual genius who combined Greek philosophy with the Hebrew Scriptures, interpreting the Scriptures allegorically.

In the third place, Apollos was **an eloquent man.** The exact meaning of *logios* is disputed. In classical Greek, and again in modern Greek, it meant "learned." But in koine Greek it meant "eloquent." Abbott-Smith prefers the latter for this passage,[231] as do the standard English versions.

In the fourth place, Apollos was **mighty in the scriptures.** In the Greek this phrase is placed at the end, after **came to Ephesus.** This may emphasize the fact that this cultured, well-trained man came to Ephesus and there he especially demonstrated his unusual power of expounding the Scriptures.

This man was instructed—*katechemenos*, "catechized," used of oral instruction—**in the way of the Lord** (25). On this expression Alexander writes: "*The way of the Lord* is a phrase used elsewhere only in relation to the ministry of John the Baptist, as our Lord's forerunner (see Matt. 3,3. Mark 1,3. Luke 3,4. John 1,23), and as John's baptism is expressly mentioned in the last

[230]*Acts*, p. 350.
[231]*Op. cit.*, p. 270.

clause, it has been suggested, and it is not impossible, that it here means the religion taught by John, i.e. the doctrine of a Messiah come or coming, and of his kingdom as at hand (see Matt. 3,1.2. 11.12)."[232] He notes, however, that the phrase is commonly taken as meaning the gospel. It is impossible to be sure which is meant here.

Apollos **taught diligently**—Greek, "accurately"—**the things of the Lord.** Instead of **Lord,** the best Greek text has "Jesus" (cf. ASV). This might give the impression that he knew about salvation through Jesus. But immediately a significant modification is added: **knowing only the baptism of John.** This sounds as though he knew and taught the facts of Jesus' life and ministry. Did he know about the Crucifixion and Resurrection? We are not told. Rather clearly he knew nothing of Pentecost.

When **Aquila and Priscilla (26)**—the best Greek text reverses this order (cf. ASV)—heard Apollos speaking boldly in the synagogue, **they took him unto them**—probably into their home— **and expounded unto him the way of God more perfectly**—Greek, "more accurately." Because we do not know precisely what previous knowledge Apollos had, we cannot tell exactly what is implied in this statement. But it is rather certain that the main thing this eloquent preacher needed to be told about was the Holy Spirit. This was probably his greatest lack.[233]

When Apollos wished to cross (the Aegean) to **Achaia** (meaning Corinth), **the brethren wrote, exhorting (27)**—rather, "encouraged him and wrote to the disciples to welcome him" (NASB). The Christians at Ephesus commended Apollos to the Christians at Corinth.

When Apollos arrived at Corinth he **helped them much which had believed through grace.** He immediately took Paul's place as a Christian leader, at least in a measure, at Corinth.

Apollos, with his unusual knowledge of the Scriptures, **mightily convinced (28)**—better, "powerfully confuted" (ASV) —**the Jews . . . publickly, shewing**—"proving"—**by the scriptures that Jesus was Christ** (the Messiah).

d. *Paul's Ministry of the Spirit* (19:1-7). After Apollos had left Ephesus, Paul came there, **having passed through**—having made a missionary tour through (cf. 13:6)—**the upper coasts.** The Greek word for **upper** has not been found anywhere except

---

[232]*Op. cit.,* p. 644.
[233]Rackham, *op. cit.,* p. 343.

in medical books (where it is used for the upper part of the body), as Lake and Cadbury admit.[234] **Upper coasts** means "hinterland" from the standpoint of Ephesus.[235] Paul simply came overland, and, arriving at Ephesus, found **certain disciples** (1).

The identity of these disciples is one of the most vexing questions in the study of Acts. The older prevailing view, beginning with Chrysostom (4th cent.), was that they were disciples of John the Baptist. This idea is expressed by Adam Clarke in these terms: "It is likely that these were Asiatic Jews, who, having been at Jerusalem about twenty-six years before this, had heard the preaching of John, and received his baptism, believing in the *coming* Christ, whom John had proclaimed; but it appears that till this time they had got no farther instruction in the Christian religion."[236] He also says: "Those who have not received these blessings from the Holy Spirit, whatever their profession may be, know nothing better than John's baptism: good, excellent in its kind, but ineffectual to the salvation of those who live under the meridian of Christianity."[237]

Over against this may be placed the interpretation of Alexander: "*Certain* (i.e. some, a few) *disciples,* not of Apollos, or of John the Baptist, but of Christ, as the word always means when absolutely used . . . and as appears from the way in which Paul treated them."[238] Similarly Lake and Cadbury say of **disciples:** "This must mean Christians, both from the use of *mathetas* in Acts and from the context."[239] Bruce echoes this and adds a point, when he comments: "Presumably disciples of Christ, in accordance with the meaning elsewhere of *mathetes* thus used absolutely; had they been disciples of John, we should have expected this to be explicitly stated."[240]

To these disciples Paul posed the question: **Have ye received the Holy Ghost since ye believed** (2; or "were converted")?[241] The Revised rendering is: "Did ye receive the Holy

---

[234]*Beginnings,* IV, 237.

[235]*Ibid.,* p. 236.

[236]*Op. cit.,* p. 841.

[237]*Ibid.*

[238]*Op. cit.,* p. 648.

[239]*Beginnings,* IV, 237.

[240]*Acts,* p. 353.

[241]Alexander, *op. cit.,* p. 648.

Spirit when ye believed?" (ASV) Which is correct? The Greek literally reads: "Did you receive [the] Holy Spirit having believed?" The question is: Does the aorist participle, "having believed," indicate action antecedent to, or simultaneous with, that of the main verb? The best grammarians of the Greek are agreed that the aorist participle usually indicates antecedent action. But in a few places in the New Testament the aorist participle unquestionably expresses simultaneous action. Most scholars maintain this to be the case here. Actually the matter is decided, not on the basis of scientific grammar, but of theological presupposition. Obviously Paul's question in itself cannot be used as a proof text either for or against the doctrine of the infilling of the Spirit as a second work of grace, subsequent to conversion. The whole passage (1-7), however, seems clearly parallel to the experience of the disciples on the Day of Pentecost.

The answer of these "disciples" was: **We have not so much as heard whether there be any Holy Ghost.** This is a correct translation of the Greek. But in John 7:39 the same construction in the Greek is translated, "The Holy Ghost was not yet given." Perhaps that is the best translation here (cf. ASV—"Nay, we did not so much as hear whether the Holy Spirit was *given*"). As has often been pointed out, John the Baptist talked about the Holy Spirit (Matt. 3:11 and parallels). But what these men clearly did not know was that the Spirit had been poured out at Pentecost. It seems that these "disciples" had not been in contact with the Christian Church. Perhaps they had left Palestine before Pentecost and had been isolated from the followers of Jesus ever since.

There is still something to be said for the literal translation here (KJV, RSV, NEB, Phillips). Page insists that "the only possible rendering of the Greek" is: "We did not even hear of the existence of a Holy Spirit."[242] Bruce suggests a solution which is true to the Greek and yet makes place for the above interpretation, when he writes: "Possibly *pneuma hagion* is to be understood here in a special sense, of the Holy Spirit as sent at Pentecost with outward manifestation."[243]

Paul expressed his surprise at their answer by asking a second question: **Unto what then were ye baptized?** (3) They

---

[242]T. E. Page, *Acts of the Apostles* (London: Macmillan and Co., 1886), p. 203.

[243]*Acts*, p. 354.

replied: **Unto John's baptism.** Paul pointed out that John's baptism was a **baptism of repentance (4),** but that the Baptist himself had told the people **they should believe on him which should come after him, that is, on . . . Jesus** (the oldest MSS omit **Christ** here).

When they heard this, they were baptized in the name of the Lord Jesus (5). It is clear that these "disciples" had not before received Christian baptism.

And when Paul had laid his hands upon them, the Holy Ghost came on them; and they spake—literally, "were speaking" —**with tongues, and prophesied**—"were prophesying." As at Samaria (8:17) the Holy Spirit was bestowed by the laying on of apostolic hands. Regarding the speaking in tongues here, Adam Clarke writes: "They received the miraculous gift of different languages; and in those languages they *taught* to the people the great doctrines of the Christian religion; for this appears to be the meaning of the word *epropheteuon, prophesied,* as it is used above."[244]

The question of speaking in tongues has been an issue in the Christian Church in modern times. It is mentioned only three times in Acts: in connection with the original Pentecost (2:4), the Gentile Pentecost (10:46), and the Ephesian Pentecost (19:6). In each of these instances it is connected with the receiving of the Holy Spirit. On the other hand, nothing is said about speaking in tongues when the Samaritan converts received the Spirit (8:17).

The thing that should be stressed is that the account of the original Pentecost seems clearly to indicate that the disciples spoke in some fifteen different languages on the Day of Pentecost (2:5-11). Since Peter established a very close connection between what happened at Pentecost and what happened in Cornelius' house (15:8-9), it would seem justifiable to assume that the Spirit-filled believers at Caesarea also spoke intelligible languages. As Adam Clarke points out (in the above quotation), it appears that this is what happened also here at Ephesus.

These "disciples" at Ephesus furnish a good example of "Walking in the Light": (1) They repented under the preaching of John the Baptist, 3-4; (2) They were baptized as Christians under the ministry of Paul, 5; (3) They were filled with the Holy Spirit, 6.

[244]*Op. cit.,* p. 842.

It is in verses 5 and 6 rather than in the question of v. 2 that one may find the most substantial evidence for two works of grace. Here the picture is clear and incontrovertible, as it is in c. 8. These **disciples (2)** were **baptized in the name of the Lord Jesus (5)**. After that, Paul **laid his hands upon them,** and the Holy Ghost came on them **(6)**. Here are two distinct experiences, clearly portrayed. Here is evidence that those who have believed and entered the Christian faith still need to be filled with the Holy Spirit as a subsequent experience.

Luke says that **all the men,** who thus received the Spirit, **were about twelve (7)**. It seems strange that **about** should be used with such a small figure. Alexander suggests a good explanation: "It may have been intended to preclude the false impression, that all the brethren in Ephesus . . . were in this infantile state of ignorance and backwardness. *All* may then be understood to mean *all told,* or at the most."[245]

This section (1-7) may be presented under the title of Paul's question, "Have Ye Received the Holy Ghost?" (1) A searching question for all disciples, 1-2; (2) The proper preparation, 2-5; (3) A second blessing for believers, 5-6 (A. F. Harper).

e. Paul's Ministry in the Synagogue (19:8-10). After his encounter with this small handful of disciples, Paul **went into the synagogue, and spake boldly for the space of three months (8)**. This was an unusually long time for him to continue teaching in the synagogue without being ousted. It would appear that for some unknown reason the Jews at Ephesus were more receptive to Paul's ministry than were the Jews elsewhere. Even in his first, brief visit with them, they had "desired him to tarry longer time with them" (18:20). He seems to have made a favorable impression on them, which in this case lasted for a number of weeks.

Paul's synagogue teaching is described as **disputing and persuading the things concerning the kingdom of God.** Of these two verbs Alexander writes: *"Disputing* (or *discoursing*) *and persuading* may describe his teaching as both doctrinal and practical, didactic and hortatory; or the first term may describe his preaching, and the second its effect."[246] Cf. NEB—"using argument and persuasion.")

Paul was nothing if not aggressive. It was inevitable that his

[245]*Op. cit.,* p. 653.
[246]*Op. cit.,* pp. 53-54.

bold, forceful preaching should provoke a crisis. Finally, **divers** **(9)**—literally, "certain ones"—**were hardened**—"became obstinate," or stubborn—**and believed not.** The verb is "in Greek a single word which may be rendered *disbelieved,* denoting not a mere negation, but a positive refusal. The Greek verb also suggests the idea of disobedience or resistance to authority."[247] When Paul's opponents **spake evil of that way**—Greek, "the Way" (cf. 9:2)—**before the multitude**—probably the congregation in the synagogue—**he departed from them.** Once again the Jews had rejected their Messiah and Saviour. Almost invariably a majority of them did so. Perhaps the only exception was at Beroea (17:11-12).

But there were many who had believed during this period of three months. So Paul **separated the disciples.** That is, when he left the synagogue he took with him the new converts. Instead of disputing in the synagogue (cf. 8), he was now **disputing daily** **in the school of one Tyrannus.** This **school** (Gk., *schole*) was "a hall used for lectures or other meetings."[248] After **Tyrannus** one important Greek MS (D) adds: "from the fifth to the tenth hour"—i.e., from 11:00 a.m. to 4:00 p.m., the time devoted to the midday meal and the afternoon siesta. Lake and Cadbury say: "It may be suggested that Tyrannus himself used the hall for teaching from early morning (Martial ix. 68, xii. 57, Juvenal vii. 222 ff.) until the fifth hour, and that during the same time Paul was engaged in his own labour (xx. 34)."[249] They add: "Martial iv. 8 indicates that the fifth hour was the usual time for stopping work . . . Then Paul could secure the use of the building for his mission."[250]

This preaching in the hall of Tyrannus **continued by the space** **of two years (10).** As at Corinth, Paul's ministry was divided into two parts. There the apostle "reasoned in the synagogue every sabbath" (18:4) for an unstated length of time, and then taught the Word of God in the house of Justus for a year and a half (18:7-11). Here he carried on a ministry in the synagogue for about three months and then preached in the hall of Tyrannus for two years. It is characteristic of Paul that he should rise

---

[247]*Ibid.,* p. 654.
[248]*Beginnings,* IV, 239.
[249]*Ibid.*
[250]*Ibid.*

early and do a day's work with his hands—presumably working with Aquila at his trade of tentmaking to support himself and his colleagues (20:34)—and then preach and teach for five hours while he could have the use of a building. He evidently spent his evenings still ministering to the converts, for he reminded the Ephesian elders: "by the space of three years I ceased not to warn every one night and day with tears" (20:31). Paul was one of the most consecrated, hardworking preachers of all time. He once said: "I have worked harder than any of them" (II Cor. 11:23, Phillips). His life and work are a challenge to every God-called minister today.

As a result of his prolonged ministry in Ephesus, **all they which dwelt in Asia**—the province—**heard the word of the Lord,**[251] **both Jews and Greeks.** One reason why this sweeping generalization could be made was that people from all over the province came to the famous Temple of Diana at Ephesus (27). Those who were converted while visiting Ephesus would carry the gospel back to their home communities. It is also probable that Paul's associates, Silas and Timothy, may have done some evangelizing of the surrounding cities. The statement here, more than any other in the Book of Acts, explains the reason for Paul's policy of concentrating on the provincial capitals and largest cities, making them centers of evangelism for the whole regions. It also demonstrates the success of this procedure.

f. Paul's Ministry to the Sick (19:11-20). In addition to his preaching, the apostle had a healing ministry: **God wrought special**—literally, "not ordinary"—**miracles by the hands of Paul** (11). It is evident from the life of Christ and the description here that God is interested in both the bodies and the souls of men. For this was a divinely ordained ministry, not just something that Paul was attempting.

Some of the methods used may seem a bit surprising to us. From Paul's **body** (12)—not *soma,* but *chrotos,* meaning "the surface of the body, skin" (one of Luke's medical terms)[252]— there were carried to the sick **handkerchiefs**—kerchiefs worn on the head—**or aprons** (lit., "workmen's aprons"). These pieces of cloth, which Paul wore at his work, did not cause any healing. But God accommodated himself to the human demand for something tangible, even as Jesus used clay and spittle (John 9:6).

---

[251] Jesus is not in the oldest Greek MSS.
[252] Hobart, *op. cit.,* p. 242.

These were material props to limited faith (cf. 5:15; Luke 8:44).
God can work with or without material intermediaries. In this
case, not only were people healed of diseases, but demons were
cast out.

Some **vagabond**—literally, "itinerant" (Phillips)—**Jews, exorcists** (13), decided to capitalize on the situation to gain some
publicity and perhaps financial reward. So they **took upon them
to call over them which had evil spirits the name of the Lord
Jesus, saying, We adjure you by Jesus whom Paul preacheth.**
Orkizo, **adjure,** is from the same root as *exorkiston,* **exorcists**
(only here in NT), which literally means "one who administers
an oath." Josephus tells of a Jewish exorcist who cast out demons
by pronouncing the name of Solomon.[253] A very striking parallel
to the present passage is found in a magical papyrus scroll from
this period (now in Paris) which contains the words: "I adjure
you by the God of the Hebrews, Jesus."[254]

Lake and Cadbury say about the exorcism and magic described here: " (i.) Such practices were especially associated with
Ephesus . . . (ii.) In the magic of the ancient world the Jews
played a prominent part."[255] When men forsake true religion,
they gravitate toward senseless superstition.

One group of exorcists was composed of the sons of **Sceva,
a Jew,** and **chief of the priests** (14)—one word, meaning "high
priest." Since only the high priest had a right to go into the
holy of holies, on the Day of Atonement, and utter the sacred
name, Yahweh, Sceva claimed special knowledge of the magical
name. Thus he hoped to gain unusual prestige. His sons adjured
a demon to come out of some person. The **evil spirit** (15) replied
(using the man's vocal cords), **Jesus I know, and Paul I know;
but who are ye?** Two different Greek words are used for **know.**
Alexander suggests this paraphrase: "I know who Jesus is, and
as for Paul, I am well acquainted with him."[256] The question is
literally: "But you, who are you?"

The demon-possessed man **leaped on them, and overcame
them.**[257] Evidently he tore off their clothes, for **they fled out of**

[253]Ant. VII. 2. 5.

[254]Deissmann, LAE, p. 252.

[255]*Beginnings,* IV, 240.

[256]*Op. cit.,* p. 659.

[257]The ASV, following the best Greek text, has "both of them." But
the Greek word for "both" sometimes means "all."

that house naked and wounded (16). When **the Jews and Greeks** living in Ephesus learned of this, **fear fell on them all, and the name of the Lord Jesus was magnified (17)**.

Fear often produces conviction, and creates honesty. Many of the new converts **came, and confessed (18)**—literally, "were coming, confessing, and declaring their deeds." Lake and Cadbury state that the Greek word for **deeds** "has the technical meaning of 'magic spell,' so that the probable meaning here is that the former exorcists now disclosed the secret formulae they had used."[258]

The converts who had practiced **curious arts (19)**—"a technical term for magic"[259]—having brought together their **books**, burned them publicly. Concerning **books** Lake and Cadbury say: "The *bibloi* of the magicians were doubtless parchments or papyri of relatively small size with magical charms written on them."[260] The value of these magical papyri which were burned was "counted up" as being **fifty thousand pieces of silver**—about $10,000. People in those days paid a high price to be fooled by magic.

So mightily grew the word of God and prevailed (20) is the fifth of six brief progress reports in Acts (cf. 6:7; 9:31; 12:24; 16:5; 28:31).

g. Paul's Purpose in the Spirit (19:21-22). Verse 21 is a summary of the rest of the Book of Acts. Paul's plan was to revisit Macedonia and Achaia (cf. 20:1-3), then go to Jerusalem (c. 21), and finally to Rome (c. 28).

There is some question whether **in the spirit (21)** means Paul's human spirit (KJV, ASV; cf. NEB, "made up his mind") or the Holy Spirit (RSV, "in the Spirit"). As is frequently the case, the best answer is, "Both." Alexander expresses the combination thus: *"In the spirit,* i.e. under the divine direction, or in his own mind as determined by the Holy Ghost."[261]

Much as he wanted to take this trip, Paul felt that he should stay in **Asia** (i.e., Ephesus) **for a season (22)**. It is altogether possible that right at this time he was much concerned about developments in the church at Corinth, including the attitude of some members toward himself. Fearful that his own presence at this stage might cause an undesirable crisis, he dispatched Timo-

---

[258]*Beginnings,* IV, 242.

[259]Adolph Deissmann, *Bible Studies,* trans. A. Grieve (Edinburgh: T. & T. Clark, 1901), p. 223, n. 5.

[260]*Beginnings,* IV, 243.

[261]*Op. cit.,* p. 663.

thy and Erastus to Macedonia. It is altogether possible that
Timothy went on to Greece and that this is the visit he made to
Corinth on behalf of Paul (cf. I Cor. 4:17; 16:10).[262] Whether or
not **Erastus** is the same one who is mentioned in Rom. 16:23 is
not certain.

h. Paul's Opposition (19:23-41). Usually two things happened when Paul spent much time in a city: first a revival, and
then a riot—and then he left town! That was the Pauline pattern
in Pisidian Antioch (13:50), Iconium (14:5-6), Lystra (14:19-
20), Philippi (16:14-23), Thessalonica (17:4-10), Beroea (17:
11-14), and Corinth (18:1-18). About the only city where Paul
preached and did not suffer persecution was Athens, and there he
was, in effect, laughed out of town (17:32). Probably the cruel
Athenian mockery hurt Paul more than the violent mobs elsewhere.

(1) *Demetrius the silversmith* (19:23-27). The inevitable
finally happened: **there arose no small stir about that way** (23)
—"the Way." The opposition was headed by Demetrius. In most
places it was the Jews who opposed Paul for supposedly religious
reasons. But here at Ephesus, as in Philippi (16:19-24), the opposition came from Gentiles and for economic reasons.

Demetrius (24) was **a silversmith** who made **silver shrines
for Diana** (Gk., Artemis). **Shrines** is literally "sanctuaries."
Terra-cotta images of temples have been discovered by archae-
ologists, but none made of silver. This has led Lake and Cadbury
to suggest that what is really meant here is silver statuettes of
Artemis, such as have been found.[263] But Knowling makes the
sensible suggestion that because of their size and value the silver
shrines were probably melted down later for use as silver.[264]
Bruce says that they "naturally were not allowed to survive."[265]
Gain is the same word which is translated "craft" in 25. Probably
the best translation in both places is the more usual one, "business." **Craftsmen** is *technitais* (cf. technicians).

Having gathered together these craftsmen with "workers in
allied trades" (25, NEB), Demetrius reminded them that their
living depended on making these sacred objects. But now Paul

[262]Rackham, *op. cit.*, p. 362.
[263]*Beginnings*, IV, 245-46.
[264]EGT, II, 411.
[265]*Acts*, p. 363.

was threatening their business by attacking idol worship (26). Not only so, but there was also the danger that the Temple of Diana would no longer be revered, **and her magnificence should be destroyed** (27)—better, "should even be dethroned from her magnificence" (NASB). **Whom all Asia and the world worshippeth** sounds like an exaggeration. But Lily Ross Taylor writes: "Not only was the cult the most important of the province of Asia: it had a fame throughout the Greek and Roman world that probably no divinity except Apollo of Delphi could surpass."[266] Archaeology has discovered "over thirty places where the reverence for Ephesian Artemis is attested."[267] The Temple of Diana at Ephesus was so large and magnificent that it was considered one of the seven wonders of the ancient world.

(2) *Diana of the Ephesians* (19:28-41). It was a clever speech that Demetrius made to these craftsmen. He first touched their pocketbooks and roused them to anger over the financial peril. Then he added the religious appeal. The result was that his hearers **were full of wrath** (28). With typical mob hysteria they began to shout, **Great is Diana of the Ephesians.** Soon **the whole city was filled with confusion** (29). With mob-like spirit, the crowd seized **Gaius and Aristarchus,** Paul's companions from **Macedonia,** and rushed into the **theatre** (Gk. *theatron*). The theater, recently excavated, is said to have held 25,000 people.

Paul wanted to go in to the **people** (30). The Greek word *demos* (cf. 12:22; 17:5) had special reference to "the people assembled"[268] (cf. NASB, "Paul wanted to go in to the assembly"). Moulton and Milligan think that in the New Testament "it suggests merely a rabble."[269] It is true that when the town clerk had quieted the crowd he reminded them that such things should be handled in a **lawful assembly** (39). Nevertheless it is also stated that **he dismissed the assembly** (41). It appears that this was in a sense an **assembly**—the Greek word is used for an assembly of the voting citizens—but that it was not a "regular assembly" (39, RSV). At any rate, the crowd was so inflamed that **the disciples** (30) would not allow Paul to enter the place.

Also he was warned by **certain of the chief of Asia** (31),

[266]*Beginnings*, V, 251.
[267]*Ibid.*, IV, 247.
[268]Abbot-Smith, *op. cit.*, p. 104.
[269]VGT, p. 144.

some prominent friends, not to **adventure himself**—better, "venture" (NASB)—**into the theatre.**

The crowd was so disorganized that **some ... cried one thing, and some another: for the assembly was confused (32).** The word for **assembly** is *ekklesia.* This chapter (vv. 32, 39, 41) is the only place in the New Testament where the term is used in its original sense of *"an assembly* of citizens regularly convened"— and here that meaning attaches clearly only to v. 39. The etymological sense of the word is "called out." The voting citizens were called out from the mass of the whole population to govern a Greek city-state. The word is also used in the Septuagint for the "congregation" of Israel. Both of these uses combined to form the background of the New Testament ecclesia, which sometimes means the local Christian congregation, sometimes the Church of Jesus Christ in its entirety.

On the use of *ekklesia* in this verse Bruce makes this interesting observation: "Luke is perhaps being ironical; the town-clerk at any rate did not regard this as a regular meeting of the 'assembly'—the Demos gathered in its legislative capacity."[270] There is clear evidence, however, that the ecclesia at Ephesus did meet in the theater.[271]

The Jews tried to put **Alexander** forward (33). Who he was or why they did it, we do not know. The most plausible guess is that he was trying to make a **defence** for the Jews by declaring that they had no connection with Paul. The Jews were as much opposed to idolatry as were the Christians, and so would come under the ire and fire of Demetrius and his associates. The only difference was that Paul was far more aggressive in his preaching and far more successful in winning converts than were the Jews.

When **Alexander beckoned** for silence and tried to speak, the people, learning that he was a Jew, shouted him down. In fact for two hours they insanely yelled: **Great is Diana of the Ephesians (34).** Apparently the crowd was as anti-Semitic as it was anti-Christian. This accords well with the statement in 32 that the greater part of people **knew not wherefore they were come together.** It was a typical mob, in which reason had been tossed to the winds.

Finally the yelling crowd was brought under control by the **townclerk (35).** The Greek word is *grammateus,* which elsewhere

[270]*Acts,* p. 366.
[271]Deissmann, LAE, pp. 121-22.

in the New Testament (mostly in the Gospels) is translated "scribe." In the papyri it means a military officer. Here it means "secretary." **Appeased** is better rendered "quieted" (ASV). It is obvious that this secretary carried much authority. Bruce writes: "The 'town-clerk' or executive officer who published the decrees of the Demos was an Ephesian, not a Roman official, but as the most important native official of the provincial capital, he was in close touch with the Roman authorities, who would hold him responsible for the riotous assembly."[272]

When order was restored so that he could be heard, the **townclerk** spoke with some sternness to the crowd. Who was there that did not know that **the city of the Ephesians is a worshipper of the great goddess Diana, and of the image which fell down from Jupiter?** The Greek word for **worshipper** is *neokoros*. It means "temple keeper," an honorary title for a city. Ephesus is mentioned on an inscription as the "Temple keeper of Artemis."[273]

Image which fell down from Jupiter is all one word in Greek, *diopetes* (only here in NT). It is an adjective meaning "fallen from heaven." There is no reference in the Greek to either **image** or **Jupiter.** The object which fell from the sky was probably a meteorite, which the people proceeded to worship as a sacred stone (cf. RSV).

The town clerk went on to reprove the people for doing something **rashly** (36)—or "recklessly." **Cannot be spoken against,** i.e., they were "undeniable facts" (Phillips). The mob leaders had brought in men who were neither **robbers of churches** (37)—literally, "temple robbers" (cf NASB), but probably here meaning "sacrilegious"—nor **blasphemers of your goddess.** (The best Gk. text reads "our goddess.") If **Demetrius, and** his fellow **craftsmen . . . have a matter against any man, the law is open** (38)—"court-days are kept"[274]—**and there are deputies**—"proconsuls"—**let them implead one another**—better, "let them bring charges against one another" (NASB). If there are any **other matters** (39), they will be taken care of **in a lawful assembly.** That was what this meeting was not. It had not been regularly called, but rather precipitated by spontaneous mob action.

The town clerk warned the crowd of the seriousness of its actions: **For we are in danger to be called in question for this**

---

[272]*Acts*, p. 367.
[273]*Beginnings*, IV, 250.
[274]Abbott-Smith, *op. cit.*, p. 7.

day's uproar (40)—literally, "accused of riot concerning this day." One of the things which the Roman government demanded most strongly of its rulers was that they must maintain peace and order. Rioting was a cardinal sin in the eyes of Rome. This the town clerk realized full well, and he was much concerned. **Concourse** is better rendered "commotion," or "riotous gathering."[275]

Having reproved the people, the town clerk **dismissed the assembly** (41)—the *ekklesia*. Knowling suggests that he may have wanted to regularize this meeting, to avoid trouble with the proconsul for allowing an irregular gathering.[276]

2. *Trip to Macedonia and Greece* (20:1-6)

After the riotous meeting in the theater at Ephesus, Paul left town. In the best Greek text the first verse reads: "After the uproar had ceased, Paul, having sent for the disciples and exhorted them,[277] having farewelled, went out to go to Macedonia."

And when he had gone over (2)—"gone through," evangelizing (cf. 13:6)—**those parts**—Macedonia—**and had given them much exhortation**—literally, "had exhorted them much by speech"—**he came into Greece.** This is the only place in the New Testament where *Hellas,* **Greece,** occurs. It was the popular name for Achaia (see map 3).

Without doubt it was Corinth where Paul spent **three months** (3)—probably in the winter, when there was no sailing on the Mediterranean. In the spring he was ready to **sail** ("put to sea") for **Syria** (Palestine) when he discovered a plot against his life. The Jews planned to get rid of him on board ship, either by assassinating him when he could not escape or by secretly shoving him overboard. But when Paul learned of this, he decided to take the land route back through Macedonia. That was safer.

Several men **accompanied** Paul (4). These men were evidently chosen representatives of the various churches to carry the contributions of those churches to Jerusalem (cf I Cor. 16:3). **Sopater,** perhaps the Sosipater of Rom. 16:21, was from **Berea.** There were two men from Thessalonica: **Aristarchus** (cf. 19:29)

---

[275]*Ibid.,* p. 435.

[276]EGT, II, 419.

[277]This item is missing in the late MSS and so in KJV, which is based on them.

and **Secundus** (not mentioned elsewhere). Then there was **Gaius of Derbe,** who would probably be well acquainted with Timothy, who lived in nearby Lystra. From **Asia,** to represent Ephesus, were **Tychicus** and **Trophimus.** These men had crossed over into Asia and were waiting for Paul at Troas (see map 3; cf. 16:8-11).

Verse 6 begins the second "we-section." Paul had left Luke at Philippi soon after founding the church there, and presumably Luke had acted as its pastor in the intervening years. **We sailed away from Philippi** (6)—i.e., from Neapolis, ten miles away (cf. 16:11-12). They sailed **after the days of unleavened bread—** i.e., the Passover, in March or April (like our Easter). They came **to Troas in five days.** This shows that they had faced contrary winds. Going in the other direction they had once made the distance in two days (16:11). At Troas, Paul and his party stayed for a week.

3. *Troas* (20:7-12)

This incident at Troas is especially significant as the first clear indication of Christians worshiping on Sunday. **Upon the first day of the week** (7) is literally "in the one of the Sabbaths" (essentially the same expression as in Luke 24:1 and John 20:1). In the New Testament, "sabbaths" is commonly used for the interval between two Sabbath days, and so means "week." Scholars are agreed that the expression above means "on the first day of the week." Alexander cites this as "a striking illustration of the fact, that literal translation is not always the most faithful."[278]

Since the Jewish Sabbath began at sunset, some commentators have interpreted the phrase here as meaning "on the Saturday night" (NEB).[279] But Lake and Cadbury note that the expression **the morrow** refers to time after the late night meeting. So they conclude: "The context seems to show that Luke did not follow the Jewish rule at this point . . . for Luke the day began at dawn, or at least not at sunset."[280] Bruce agrees with this, suggesting that Luke was using "the Roman reckoning from midnight to midnight."[281] Alexander thinks that "the observance of the first day of the week, as that of our Lord's resurrection, had already become customary, so that the assembling of the

[278]*Op. cit.,* p. 689.
[279]So Rackham, *op. cit.,* p. 377.
[280]*Beginnings,* IV, 255.
[281]NIC, p. 408, n. 25.

church at that time for the purposes here mentioned, was a matter of course."[282]

When the disciples—the earliest MSS have "we" instead of **the disciples**—**came together to break bread**—probably the celebration of the Lord's Supper, or at least the agape (love feast). It is not fully known whether the love feast and the Lord's Supper were held together or separately. Since on the night before His crucifixion it appears that Jesus instituted the Lord's Supper at the conclusion of the Last Supper, some have thought that the early Christians may have celebrated the Eucharist at the close of the agape.

In connection with this service **Paul preached unto them, ready to depart on the morrow.** The word **preached** is *dialegomai* (cf. "dialogue"), which means "to converse with, discourse, discuss, argue."[283] It has already occurred in 17:2, 17; 18:4, 19; 19:8-9 and is found in 20:9; 24:12, 25. Perhaps the best meaning here is the first, "conversed with." Lumby says: "The meeting was one where reasoning and conversation were used to solve doubts and clear away difficulties which might be in the minds of the Christians at Troas."[284] **Ready to depart** is literally "being about to depart." **Speech** (*logos*) is sometimes used for "discourse."

There were many lights—*lampades,* "lamps"—**in the upper chamber, where they**—"we" in best Greek text—**were gathered together** (8). Probably the lamps in the upper room helped to make it hot and stuffy. Also the place was apparently crowded, for **Eutychus** (9) was sitting in a window—a mere latticed opening. All this resulted in the young man being **fallen into a deep sleep, and sunk down with sleep.** Both these expressions have the same verb, but in different tenses. The first (present) suggests a gradual process, the second (aorist) a final climax. Rackham expresses it well: "The tenses in the Greek exactly paint the continuous struggle and the moment of defeat."[285] Eutychus **fell down from the third loft**—"third story"—**and was taken up dead** (cf. RSV). The Greek does not say "as dead" (Phillips) or "for dead" (NEB).

Nothing daunted, Paul **went down, and fell on him, and embracing him said, Trouble not yourselves; for his life is in him**

---

[282]*Op. cit.,* p. 689.

[283]Abbott-Smith, *op. cit.,* p. 108.

[284]*Op. cit.,* p. 354.

[285]*Op. cit.,* p. 380, n. 5.

(10). This description has led some to say that the young man just "had the breath knocked out of him," and that by using the present method of mouth-to-mouth resuscitation Paul revived him. But Luke, the physician, was present and he pronounced him dead.

After taking this brief interruption "in stride," Paul went back up to the third-floor hall.

Everyone was "immensely comforted" when they **brought the young man alive** (12), which implies that he had been dead. Whether he was brought back into the service in the upper room,[286] or recovered consciousness only shortly before Paul left town,[287] is not stated.

When he returned to the room, Paul broke bread and ate (11). In 7 it was stated that the congregation had gathered "to break bread." It would appear that only now did they actually get around to eating the Lord's Supper. Even after that, Paul **talked . . . till break of day.** He evidently felt that this would be his last opportunity to minister to the Christians at Troas. When daybreak came, **he departed,** "went out."

4. *Down the Coast* (20:13-16)

Luke, who was a good sailor, accompanied by all the members of the party (cf. 4) except Paul, **went before to ship** (13)— i.e., on board the ship (Gk.). Evidently the rest of the party left town before the apostle did. They **sailed**—"put to sea" (cf. 13:13; 16:11; 18:21)—**unto Assos,** intending to pick up Paul at that point. He had made this arrangement, preferring to walk the twenty miles or so to Assos (see map 3). The voyage by ship was at least twice as long, around jutting Cape Lectum. The reason for Paul's decision may be explained by supposing that "he was a bad sailor, and to such the open water from Troas to Assos in the stormy north-east wind, prevalent about five days out of seven, can be most unpleasant in a small boat."[288] Perhaps Paul also wanted time for quiet meditation while he walked alone.

Paul and the voyagers met **at Assos,** where **we took him in** (14). Though it is not so stated, it is very likely that they anchored at Assos for the night.[289] Because of the many rocks jutting out of the water it was not safe to sail after dark. The next day,

[286]Lumby, *op. cit.,* p. 355.
[287]Bruce, *Acts,* p. 374.
[288]*Beginnings,* IV, 257-58.
[289]Contra, Lumby, *op. cit.,* p. 356.

sailing southward, they **came to Mitylene,** about thirty miles away. This city was "the capital of Lesbos, on the east side of the island, famous as the birthplace of Sappho and Alcaeus, described by Cicero as noble, by Horace as beautiful, by Vitruvius as magnificent."[290]

The next day, having **sailed**—"sailed away"—the ship came **over against Chios** (15)—apparently meaning a point on the mainland opposite the island of Chios, which is five miles offshore. For some reason they chose to anchor this night close to the mainland.

The next day they **arrived at**—"crossed over to"—**Samos.** This island, southwest of Ephesus, was famous as the birthplace of Pythagoras. The clause **and tarried at Trogyllium** is found in only one Greek uncial MS (D, 5th or 6th cent.) and Papyrus 41 (8th or 9th cent.). Though it is rejected by a majority of scholars, Bruce comments: "an addition probable in itself, and not likely to have been interpolated."[291] Ramsay defends its genuineness and explains its implication thus: "When the wind fell, they had not got beyond the promontory Trogyllia at the entrance to the gulf, and there, as the Bezan text mentions, they spent the evening."[292] Lake and Cadbury conclude: "There is no obvious reason for inserting this statement, unless it be that the run from Samos to Miletus seemed too long. Possibly it is the true text."[293]

The next day they **came to Miletus.** This place, famous as the birthplace of Thales, had once been the leading commercial city of Asia Minor, but it was now eclipsed by Ephesus, about thirty miles away.

Alexander has called attention to "a curious circumstance, that *the next day,* thrice repeated in this verse, answers to three different Greek phrases, meaning *the coming,* or *ensuing* (day); *the other* (day); and *the adjoining* or *adjacent* (day)."[294] This is a typical example of the variety of Greek expressions used to convey the same idea.

Paul had determined (16)—"decided" (NASB)—**to sail by Ephesus,** even though, as Alexander comments, "it really lay in his way."[295] But Lake and Cadbury have pointed out the fact that

---

[290]Alexander, *op. cit.,* p. 698.
[291]*Acts,* p. 375.
[292]*Op. cit.,* p. 294.
[293]*Beginnings,* IV, 258.
[294]*Op. cit.,* p. 699.
[295]*Ibid.*

this is not quite correct. To have gone to Ephesus the ship would have had to turn eastward, against the prevailing northeast winds, and then return westward to get around the promontory Trogyllium. They affirm: "The natural course was the one taken, which keeps close to the north of Samos and so comes in to the coast at Miletus."[296]

There appear to have been two reasons why Paul bypassed Ephesus. The first was that it would have been somewhat out of his way. The second was that he feared if he went to Ephesus it would be hard to leave town soon, because of his three-year "pastorate" there. Luke gives as the reason; **because he would not spend the time in Asia** (the province of Asia, and particularly Ephesus).

His haste was due to the fact that he wanted, if possible, **to be at Jerusalem the day of Pentecost.** This came in late May or early **June.**

There is one characteristic of this paragraph (13-16) which should not go unnoticed. Nowhere else do we have the day-by-day log of a voyage given in such detail. We are told where the ship stopped each night to anchor. This is in sharp contrast to some parts of Acts, where long land trips or sea voyages are summarized in a few words. But Luke was a seasoned traveler who kept a careful log. The "we-sections" are the passages that give the movements of Paul's party in great detail. Even apart from the "we," one could tell when Luke is along. The same phenomenon is found in the final voyage to Rome (cc. 27—28).

Another factor perhaps enters in. Most of the places mentioned by Luke in the week's voyage down the coast were connected with Greek literature, some as the homes of great poets or philosophers. The details of this section reflect the fact that Luke was widely read as well as widely traveled.

5. *Miletus* (20:17-38)

Much as Paul would naturally have liked to visit Ephesus again, he chose the safer course of stopping at Miletus. He may purposely at Troas have chosen a ship which would stop at Miletus, and not at Ephesus; that is, a faster ship which would get him to Palestine more quickly.

a. Solemn Warning (20:17-35). **From Miletus,** Paul, having sent to Ephesus, a distance of some thirty miles, **called (17)**—a

---

[296]*Beginnings,* IV, 259.

compound verb meaning "to call from one place to another"[297]— **the elders**—*presbyterous*—**of the church.** He had an important, parting message for them. But he did not feel he could take time to visit the whole church. Since a day's walk was normally twenty miles, it would presumably have taken three days to send a messenger and bring the Ephesian elders to Miletus.

When they arrived, Paul poured out his heart to them in the only recorded message of his to church leaders, although there are many parallels in the Epistles he wrote to the churches he had founded. It appears that Ephesus may have become the foremost church center in the last third of the first century, superseding Jerusalem and Antioch. Paul, quick to recognize the strategic importance of this leading city of Asia Minor, would be concerned to see that the elders of the church there were warned to preserve a high purity of doctrine and conduct. That this policy paid off is evidenced by the position which Ephesus held in the days that followed. Dr. Cell, of Boston University School of Theology, used to say that in the second century whatever Rome and churches of Asia Minor agreed upon was considered of highest authority for the general Church. This parting message of the apostle, plus the ministry of Timothy (I Tim. 1:3) and that of the Apostle John after A.D. 70, all helped to make Ephesus a bulwark of the faith (cf. Rev. 2:2).

Paul reminded the Ephesian presbyters that from the day he first **came (18)**—"set foot" (ASV)—**into Asia** (Ephesus) he had been with them **at all seasons.** The apostle was not a "fair weather" Christian nor a hireling preacher. He had **been with** his people whenever they needed his pastoral ministrations. That is the test of a good pastor.

In all of this he was constantly (present tense) **serving the Lord (19).** He who serves the real needs of people best serves his Lord (cf. Matt. 25:34-40). The verb *douleuo* literally means "to be a slave, be subject to, serve."[298] Paul was the *doulos*, "slave," of Jesus Christ, as he calls himself at the beginning of Romans (1:1). He was **serving the Lord with all humility of mind**— literally, "lowly-mindedness," a favorite word in Paul's Epistles, though the Romans held this attitude in contempt.

He also served **with many tears**—he was tenderhearted (cf. I Thess. 2:7-8). There were **temptations**—better, "trials" (NASB)

---

[297]Abbott-Smith, *op. cit.*, p. 287.

[298]*Ibid.*, p. 122.

—**which befell** him **by the lying in wait**—"plots"—**of the Jews.**
They were still hounding his trail, as they had done in Galatia
on his first journey and at Thessalonica and Beroea on his second.

Paul then went on to describe his ministry at Ephesus (20-
21). He had **kept back nothing that was profitable** (20). Lumby
says of the verb here: "*Hypostello* is applied to the wrapping up
of anything to keep it out of sight or to stow it away . . . Hence
it has the metaphorical sense of 'cloaking' what ought to be spoken out."[299] Paul did not temper his preaching to suit the tastes
of the people, but gave them what they needed. That is the test
of a good preacher.

Paul had carried on at Ephesus both **publickly, and from
house to house.** He did not consider that he had discharged his
responsibilities when he preached in the pulpit. This needed to
be supplemented by teaching in the homes.

He was busy **testifying** (21)—intensive compound, meaning
"solemnly protesting"[300]—**both to the Jews, and also to the Greeks**
—he did not neglect either group—**repentance toward God, and
faith toward our Lord Jesus Christ.** This is the evangelical combination. We have sinned against God, so our attitude toward
Him must be one of repentance. But we can be saved only as
repentance is mixed with **faith toward our Lord Jesus Christ**—
acceptance of His atoning death on our behalf.

Paul next told the conditions under which he was making this
trip (22-24). He was going to Jerusalem **bound in the spirit** (22).
Does this mean his human spirit (KJV) or the Holy Spirit
(RSV)? Since the modern device of capital letters to indicate
Deity was not used in the Greek, the matter is open and must be
decided in harmony with the context. Equally good scholars
argue for both sides. **In the spirit** may with equal accuracy be
translated "by the Spirit." Probably the only satisfactory solution is to accept both ideas. Paul felt bound in his spirit by the
constraint of the Holy Spirit.

He was concerned as to what would happen to him in Jerusalem, because the Holy Spirit **witnesseth** (23)—"solemnly pro-
tests" (c. 21)—**in every city**—probably Corinth, Philippi, and
Troas—**saying that bonds**—i.e., imprisonment—**and afflictions**—a
more general term, usually rendered "tribulations"—**abide me**—
better, "await me."

[299]*Op. cit.,* p. 359.
[300]Abbott-Smith, *op. cit.,* p. 109.

The Greek text of 24 varies considerably in the different MSS. Perhaps the best rendering is that found in NASB: "But I do not consider my life of any account as dear to myself, in order that I may finish my course, and the ministry which I received from the Lord Jesus, to testify solemnly of the gospel of the grace of God." Bruce makes this apt observation: "It is evident from a comparison of this verse with the next that the preaching of this Gospel is identical with the proclamation of the Kingdom."[301]

The apostle had a strong feeling that these people would never see his face again (25). This creates somewhat of a problem. "The Pastoral epistles imply, though they do not explicitly assert, a later visit to Ephesus (cf. I Tim. i.3; II Tim. i.15 ff.)."[302] Also, toward the end of his first imprisonment at Rome, Paul intimated that he had hopes of being released and of revisiting the province of Asia. The Greek of the present passage could be taken to mean that not **all** of his hearers would see him again. But the natural way to translate it would be as we have it in the standard English versions. Lumby wisely says: "It seems better to take the words as the conviction of the Apostle's mind at the moment. He was impressed with the belief that he would never come back."[303] The fact that the Holy Spirit had warned him that imprisonment awaited him at Jerusalem (cf. 23) would give him sufficient reason for thinking this.

In the light of his conviction that this was the last time he would ever speak to the Ephesian elders Paul said: **I take you to record** (26)—literally, "I testify to you"—**this day, that I am pure from the blood of all men.** Why? **For I have not shunned**—*hypesteilamen,* which is rendered "I kept back" in 20—**to declare unto you all the counsel of God** (27). This means "the whole plan of salvation, what God offers and what he asks from men."[304] It includes not only the doctrines of "repentance toward God, and faith toward our Lord Jesus Christ" (21), but also regeneration and entire sanctification (cf. I Thess. 5:23). One must not only have his sins forgiven but also have his heart cleansed from all sin (cf. I John 1:7) and filled with the Holy Spirit. To neglect to preach all of this is to fail to declare all the counsel of God.

[301]*Acts,* p. 379.
[302]*Ibid.,* p. 380.
[303]*Op. cit.,* p. 361.
[304]*Ibid.*

As a faithful "general superintendent" of the Gentile church, Paul exhorted the Ephesian elders: **Take heed therefore unto yourselves, and to all the flock, over which the Holy Ghost hath made you overseers** (28). The order here is important. One cannot minister properly to others unless his own soul is blessed with God's presence. A man's first responsibility is to take care of his own spiritual condition. If he fails in this, and thus loses his soul, it will have done him no good to try to watch over those whom God has entrusted to his care.

Overseers is the noun *episkopos* (from which comes "episcopal"). Elsewhere in the New Testament (Phil. 1:1; I Tim. 3:2; Titus 1:7; I Pet. 2:25) it is translated "bishop." It literally means "one who watches over," and so a "superintendent" or "guardian." The fact that these men are called "elders" (*presbyteroi*) in 17 implies that presbyters and bishops were one and the same in the Apostolic Church.

The responsibility of these leaders was to **feed**—literally, "shepherd"—**the church of God.** Some Greek MSS have "the church of the Lord" (cf. ASV). Those who feel that "church of God" is genuine (cf. Westcott and Hort, Nestle) think that the change to the other was made because of the implication that it was the blood of God which purchased the Church. Admittedly this is the impression one gets from reading the KJV—**the church of God, which he hath purchased with his own blood.** Bruce, taking the cue from Lake and Cadbury, would translate the last phrase, "by means of the blood of His own One."[305] The Greek word for **purchased** means essentially "acquired for himself."

Then Paul sounded a sad note. He knew that after his departure **grievous wolves** (29)—"fierce wolves," in contrast to the true shepherds of the flock—would enter in, **not sparing the flock.** He seems to refer to false teachers coming in (cf. Rev. 2:6). **Departing** (*aphixis*, used only here in NT) in classical Greek meant "arrival," but in the papyri sometimes meant "departure."

Worse still, **of your own selves** (30)—meaning "from within the church," but perhaps also implying "out of the very group before me"—**shall men arise, speaking perverse things, to draw away disciples,** i.e., the disciples of Christ. Phillips emphasizes the phrase **after them,** by translating, "trying to draw away the disciples and make them followers of themselves." Apparently the apostle is referring to the Judaizers who were already work-

[305]*Acts,* p. 381.

ing in this general area, as we know from the Epistle to the Galatians (cf. I Tim. 4:1-6; II Tim. 3:1-13). In the province of Asia the churches were also threatened with Gnostic influences, as is evidenced in Colossians and I John. That the Ephesian elders profited from the warning given here is implied by Rev. 2:2.

Paul urged these leaders of the church to **watch** (31)—"be awake," or "be on the alert"—remembering that for **three years** —the approximate length of his time at Ephesus (cf. 19:8, 10, 22) —he had not ceased **to warn**—literally, "putting in mind," and so "admonishing, exhorting"—**every one night and day with tears** (cf. 19). Paul had one passion: to serve Christ by serving others.

The apostle commended these presbyters **to God,**[306] **and to the word of his grace** (32). "It is as if he said: "I am to leave you, but I leave you to the care of One who will help you as He has helped me, and who will not leave you."[307] Alexander says: *"The word of his grace* may mean either the doctrine of salvation . . . or his gracious word of promise."[308] **Which**—or "who"—**is able to build you up** perhaps modifies "God," rather than "the word." God is able **to give you an inheritance among all them which are sanctified.** There is a sense in which all Christians are sanctified; that is, "set apart to God" (cf. I Cor. 1:2; 3:1-3). In a higher sense, those are sanctified who have consecrated themselves completely to Christ, have surrendered their wills unreservedly to the will of God, and have had their hearts cleansed from all sin and filled with the Holy Spirit. It is the privilege of every Christian to have **an inheritance** among the sanctified. The Greek word for **inheritance** literally means "a possession obtained by lot." The biblical background is that of the Israelites obtaining by lot their inheritance in the land of Canaan, which is a type of the sanctified life.

Paul reminds these men: **I have coveted no man's silver, or gold, or apparel** (33). Greed for money has ruined the spirituality of many men. But the apostle had gone further than merely avoiding covetousness: **these hands have ministered unto my necessities, and to them that were with me** (34). As at Thessalonica (II Thess. 3:7-12) and Corinth (I Cor. 9:11-15; II Cor. 11:7-12; 12:13-16), so at Ephesus, Paul had earned his own living by the labor of his hands. He did this so as not to give occasion

---

[306]Nestle has "the Lord" (Vaticanus, 4th cent.; cf. Phillips).

[307]Lumby, *op. cit.,* p. 364.

[308]*Op. cit.,* p. 715.

for any criticism by his Judaistic opponents that he was preaching for personal gain.

In all of this unselfish service the apostle had given these church leaders an example, **how that so labouring ye ought to support the weak** (35). On the word **support** Alexander writes: " 'To support,' a most expressive Greek verb which, according to its etymology, originally signifies to lay hold of anyone (or something) opposite, as if to hold it up."[309] Some have interpreted **weak** as meaning legalists with an overscrupulous conscience (cf. Rom. 4:19; 14:1-2, 21; I Cor. 8:9-12). But the context here suggests a more general sense.

The saying here attributed to the Lord Jesus, **It is more blessed to give than to receive,** is not found in the Gospels. However it agrees perfectly with the spirit and tone of Christ's teaching (cf. Luke 6:38). Lake and Cadbury write: "The sentiment suits the character of Jesus in the Gospels, and accords with Luke's interest in giving."[310]

Paul's discourse to the Ephesian elders might be labeled "A Pastor's Parting Words to His Congregation." Four main notes are sounded: (1) Reminder of (a) His earnest care, 19, 31; (b) His faithful preaching, 20-21, 26-27. (2) Warning of (a) Persecution, 29; (b) Apostasy, 30. (3) Exhortation to (a) **Take heed,** 28; (b) Be alert, 31. (4) Commendation to (a) God; (b) **The word of his grace,** 32.

b. Sad Farewell (20:36-38). Having finished his farewell speech, **Paul kneeled down, and prayed with them all** (36)—a fitting example for any time of parting. **They all wept sore, and fell on Paul's neck, and kissed him** (37). The verb **kissed** is a compound, literally meaning "to kiss fervently, kiss affectionately." It is also in the imperfect: "kept on kissing fervently." It was hard to let him go.

The Ephesian elders were **sorrowing most of all** (38) over Paul's announcement that they would not see him again. With courteous kindness, **they accompanied him unto the ship.** The verb means literally "sent him forward," and so "escorted."

H. TRIP TO JERUSALEM, 21:1-16

Chapter 20 related the journey of Paul from Ephesus through Macedonia to Greece, then back through Macedonia to Philippi (see map 3). Here he picked up Luke, whom he had left there on

---

[309]*Op. cit.,* p. 717.
[310]*Beginnings,* IV, 264.

the second missionary journey. "We" sailed to Troas, where the party spent a week. From there "we" sailed down the coast to Miletus, with each night's anchorage noted (13-16). The chapter ends with a description of Paul's farewell to the Ephesian elders. This is one of Paul's few recorded speeches which Luke himself heard.

Chapter 21 describes the remaining portion of the trip to Jerusalem and tells what happened when Paul arrived for his last recorded visit there. Luke is with the party, as indicated by the use of "we" through this section. His presence is also reflected in the continuance of the detailed, almost daily, record of each move that was made. It is obvious that Luke kept a day-by-day log of his voyages, and he here shares the gist of his travel diary with his readers.

1. *Tyre* (21:1-6).

Regarding the clause **after we were gotten from them** (1), Bruce writes: "One is disposed to continue the atmosphere of clinging affection in the previous verses by giving this word its literal force, 'tore ourselves away.' "[311] It must always be remembered that the Greek MSS had no chapter divisions, such as break up the text today. The careful student of the Bible should ignore the chapter separations when they do not coincide with the author's units of thought. The system of paragraphing in the revised versions will help one to do this.

After the touching farewell, Paul's party **launched**—"set sail" (cf. 13:13; 16:11; 18:21; 20:3, 13)—**and came with a straight course**—literally, "having run a straight course, we came." The participial phrase (all one word in Gk.) is found only here and in 16:11. Lake and Cadbury say: "This implies that the wind, as usual in this district in the summer, was north-east, and this again explains why it was much easier for Paul to send for the Ephesian elders than to go to them."[312] They also remark: "It is not too much to guess that Paul reached Miletus from Troas on one 'wind,' spent the intervening calm with the Ephesians, and then went on with the next wind."[313] These winds usually blow for four or five days, followed by two or three days of calm.[314]

---

[311]*Acts*, p. 384.
[312]*Beginnings*, IV, 264.
[313]*Ibid.*
[314]*Ibid.*

The first day the party reached **Coos** (or **Cos**), which was "about forty nautical miles from Miletus."[315] This is the name of both the island and its capital city. The same is true of **Rhodes** (see map 3), where they anchored the next night. In both cases the name probably refers here to the city itself. On the island of Cos there was a temple of Aesculapius, the god of healing, and a medical school attached. It was also supposed to be the home of Hippocrates, the father of medical science. The Hippocratic Oath, still required of all physicians and surgeons, can be seen today hanging in doctors' offices.

Rhodes, some eighty miles from Cos, was famous for the Colossus of Rhodes, a gigantic bronze statue, 150 feet high, of the sun-god Apollo. The legs of the statue once spanned the entrance to the harbor. One of the seven wonders of the ancient world, it was already in ruins when Paul visited the place, having been destroyed by an earthquake in 224 B.C. But the city was still a great commercial port and a free city under the Roman Empire.

The third day out of Miletus the boat reached **Patara,** about seventy miles from Rhodes. This was a seaport on the south coast of Lycia, at the southwestern extremity of Asia Minor. Here we are told that **finding a ship sailing over** (2)—literally, "crossing over"—**unto Phenicia, we went aboard.** Alexander remarks: "The minuteness and exactness of this narrative evince that it proceeds from an eye-witness, while the nauticale phraseology shows him to have been familiar with the sea."[316]

One Greek MS (D) complicates the matter by adding "and Myra" after **Patara** (1). This would make the change from a coastwise vessel to the other ship bound for Phoenicia take place at Myra rather than **Patara.** In favor of this reading is the fact that "Myra seems to have been the great port for the direct cross-sea traffic to the coasts of Syria and Egypt."[317] In spite of this, Ramsay prefers the more common text as we have it.[318] Apparently Lake and Cadbury also do.[319] Bruce is noncommittal.[320] There does not seem to be sufficient justification for adding "and

[315]Knowling, EGT, II, 441.
[316]*Op. cit.,* p. 720.
[317]Ramsay, *op. cit.,* p. 298.
[318]*Ibid.,* p. 299.
[319]*Beginnings,* IV, 264-65.
[320]*Acts,* p. 384.

Myra," especially since that would require a voyage of some fifty miles east against the prevailing northeast winds.

The next lap of the journey was about four hundred miles across the sea to Tyre. As a good log-keeper, Luke notes: **Now when we had discovered** (3)—"come in sight of" (ASV)—**Cyprus, we left it on the left hand**—i.e., passed to the southwest of it—**and sailed into Syria**—a general name for all the area along the Mediterranean coast between Asia Minor and Egypt. They **landed at Tyre**—main seaport of Phoenicia—**for there the ship was to unlade her burden**—"unload its cargo" (NASB). Typical of Luke, this verse has four nautical terms—**discovered, sailed, landed, unlade.**

Finding (4)—literally, "having found," implying a search—**disciples, we tarried there seven days.** It would appear that no one in Paul's party was acquainted with Tyre. They probably knew that there were Christians in the city (cf. 11:19; 15:3) but did not know where to find them. It must be remembered that there were as yet no church buildings; the Christians met in private homes. The reason the party stayed **seven days** was probably that it took that time to unload the ship.

During the week that Paul spent in Tyre the believers **said to Paul through the Spirit, that he should not go up to Jerusalem.** And yet he went! Did he disobey the Spirit in doing so? Alexander gives a good answer to the question when he writes: "This was not a divine command to Paul, but an inference of the disciples from the fact, which was revealed to them, that Paul would there be in great danger."[321] Bruce agrees with this interpretation, and concludes: "We must not infer that his continuing the journey was contrary to God's will; it was 'under the constraint of the Spirit' (xx. 22) that he was going to Jerusalem."[322] Of one thing we are certain: Paul felt that it was God's will that he should go on, regardless of danger.

At Tyre today there is a beautiful, smooth beach several miles in length, on which one can see camel caravans traveling. Here the farewell took place. Portions of verses 5 and 6 literally read: "And having knelt on the beach, having prayed, we took leave of one another, and embarked in the boat, and those returned home." "The boat" identifies it as the same one on which they had arrived.

---

[321]*Op. cit.,* p. 722.
[322]*Acts,* p. 385.

2. *Caesarea* (21: 7-14)

And when we had finished (7)—perhaps, "continued"[323]—
our course—"voyage"—**from Tyre, we came to Ptolemais**, a distance of about twenty-five miles, a short half day's sail southward. **Ptolemais** was the ancient Accho (Judg. 1:31), now called
Acre. Today it lies across the Bay of Acre from Haifa, which is
now the greatest port on the coast of Palestine. At Ptolemais
Paul's party **saluted the brethren, and abode with them one day.**

Luke continues the narrative: **And the next day we**[324]
. . . departed, and came unto Caesarea (8)—a distance of about
thirty-five miles. We are not told whether they travelled by
land or sea. Caesarea had succeeded Ptolemais as the leading
seacoast city of Palestine, because Herod the Great had built a
great harbor there and erected magnificent buildings. It was the
seat of Roman government in Judea at this time.

In Caesarea, Paul and his party stayed at the home of **Philip
the evangelist** (*euangelistes,* only here, in Eph. 4:11, and II Tim.
4:5). He was **one of the seven** (cf. 6:5). He had acted as evangelist to the Ethiopian eunuch and to the people of Samaria (c. 8).
Evidently he had so distinguished himself in this field that he
has the honor of being the only man in the New Testament to
carry that title.

Philip had **four daughters, virgins, which did prophesy.** This
probably means simply that they preached. Lumby comments:

> The English word "prophesy" has come to have, since about the
> beginning of the seventeenth century, only the one sense of "to
> predict what is yet to come." In the time of Queen Elizabeth
> "prophesyings" meant "preachings," and Jeremy Taylor's famous
> work on the "Liberty of Prophesying" was written to uphold the
> freedom of preaching.[325]

The party stayed at Caesarea **many days** (10). Paul had
been hastening to get to Jerusalem in time for the Day of Pentecost (20:16). In those times of uncertain sailing schedules, the
ships being entirely dependent on the variable winds, one would
have to allow a wide margin of time in figuring any arrival date.
It would seem that Paul had made better progress to this point
than he had anticipated, and now he had several days to spare

---

[323]Bruce, *Acts,* p. 386.
[324]**That were of Paul's company** is not in the oldest MSS.
[325]*Op. cit.,* p. 370.

before Pentecost. Also he apparently preferred to spend them at Caesarea, where he could evangelize the Gentiles, rather than at Jerusalem, where many of the Jews were unfriendly to him.

While Paul was at Caesarea, the Gentile capital of Judea, **there came down from Judaea (10)**—i.e., Jerusalem, the Jewish Judea—**a certain prophet, named Agabus.** Since this name is not a common one, it is altogether likely that this is the same Agabus who had earlier predicted the famine under Claudius Caesar (11:28). He was a foreteller as well as a forthteller.

Agabus **took Paul's girdle**—a sash-like belt—**and bound his own** (Paul's) **hands and feet (11).** Then he uttered the divinely inspired prediction that Paul would thus be bound by the Jews at Jerusalem, and handed over to the Gentiles (i.e., the Roman rulers). It is to be noted that Agabus did not tell Paul not to go up to Jerusalem. He simply warned him of what would happen to him if he did.

When this prediction had been heard, **both we, and they of that place, besought him not to go up to Jerusalem (12).** It is evident that Luke, together with the others from Greece, Macedonia, Asia, and Galatia (cf. 20:4), urged Paul not to go on to Jerusalem. In this plea they were joined by the Christians of Caesarea. There is no doubt about the love which these Gentile believers had for the great apostle.

However, Paul was not to be deterred. He replied: **What mean ye to weep (13)**—this shows the earnestness of their plea—**and to break mine heart?**—or weaken my purpose. Alexander comments: *"To break* (literally, *crushing,* shivering) *my heart,* i.e., weakening, as far as in you lies, my courage, and endeavouring to shake my resolution, by working on my own fears and my sympathy with your distress."[326] The apostle declared his readiness not only to be bound, but also to die at Jerusalem **for the name of the Lord Jesus.** That was the name that he once had cursed at Jerusalem. Now he was ready to make amends by dying for it.

When Paul's friends saw that he would not be persuaded to change his course, they **ceased** pleading with him, only saying: **The will of the Lord be done (14).** This must always be the conclusion to which consecrated Christians come. After all the discussion is ended, this is the final word.

---

[326]*Op. cit.,* p. 729.

This passage suggests: (1) Christian concern for others, 12; (2) Christian courage in oneself, 13; (3) Christian consecration to God, 14.

3. *Journey to Jerusalem* (21:15-16)

Having spent some time at Caesarea, **we took up our carriages** (15). It is obvious that **carriages** meant something different to the KJV translators from what it does to us today. Then it meant something carried; now it means something that carries. The expression is all one word in Greek, an aorist participle which literally means "having made our preparations." Probably "packed our baggage" (NEB) is the thought. This done, they **went up to Jerusalem,** a rugged trip of over 60 miles, (see map 1) including the climb to an elevation of 2,500 feet. It would take three days to walk this. If they hired horses, as suggested by Ramsay[327] and Rackham,[328] and endorsed by Bruce ("a very reasonable supposition"),[329] the trip would probably be made in two days.

The latter view finds some support in the so-called Western text (see Introduction) of 16, which reads: "And these brought us to those with whom we should lodge, and we reached a village, and were with Mnason, a Cypriote, an early disciple." The general thought of this is suggested by the RSV rendering: "And some of the disciples from Caesarea went with us, bringing us to the house of Mnason of Cyprus, an early disciple, with whom we should lodge." If it is objected that this lodging must have been in Jerusalem, since the statement has already been made, **We ... went up to Jerusalem** (15), it should be noted that **went up** is in the imperfect tense and so should be translated "were going up." This fits in perfectly with the idea of stopping halfway there to stay overnight with Mnason, who had a home in a village on the road to Jerusalem. This also accords with the opening clause of **17, when we were come to Jerusalem** (aorist participle indicating final arrival).

Paul would have had numerous friends in Jerusalem with whom he could have stayed. Also he would not have needed disciples from Caesarea to guide him around the very familiar city

[327]*Op. cit.,* p. 302.
[328]*Op. cit.,* p. 413.
[329]*Acts,* p. 389.

of Jerusalem. "The accompanying, on the other hand, was quite natural, if Mnason lived in a village known to these disciples, but not known to Paul."[330]

It will be noted that **old disciple** is correctly rendered "early disciple" in recent versions. The Greek adjective is *archaios,* from which comes "archaic." It means "original, ancient." Rackham thinks this implies that Mnason was probably one of the 120 at Pentecost[331] (cf. Phillips—"one of the earliest disciples").

I. JERUSALEM, 21:17—23:35

1. *Paul in Trouble* (21:17-40)

The apostle had been warned on the way up to Jerusalem that imprisonment and tribulations awaited him there (cf. 20: 22-24; 21:4, 11-12). So it is not surprising to learn that trouble overtook him soon after his arrival.

a. Paul Makes a Vow (21:17-26). Paul and his party were given a warm welcome by **the brethren** (17) at Jerusalem. **Received us gladly** is doubly emphatic in the Greek. The verb itself is a compound, meaning "to accept gladly, welcome, receive."[332] To this is added the adverb **gladly.**

The following day **Paul went in with us unto James** (18). This was James the brother of Jesus, who was apparently the bishop or main pastor of the Jerusalem church (12:17) and moderator of the Jerusalem Council (15:13-20). **Went in** is a rare verb in the New Testament. Rackham notes: "The uncommon form of this verb in the Greek marks the solemnity of the occasion."[333] The same form is found in 26.

Luke adds: **and all the elders were present.** They were probably on hand to receive the offering which Paul and his companions had brought to the poor saints at Jerusalem from the Gentile churches of Achaia, Macedonia, Asia, and Galatia (20:4; I Cor. 16:1-4; II Cor. 8:1-22; 9:1-5).

The apostle had brought with him representatives of the churches which had given these offerings (cf. I Cor. 16:3). There were two reasons for this. The first was that Paul wanted to

---

[330]Frederick Blass, *Philosophy of the Gospels* (London: Macmillan Co., 1898), p. 130.

[331]*Op. cit.,* p. 413.

[332]Abbott-Smith, *op. cit.,* p. 49.

[333]*Op. cit.,* p. 414

protect himself against any charges of misappropriation of funds. His attitude is reflected in what he wrote to the Corinthian church: "Avoiding this, that no man should blame us in this abundance which is administered by us: providing for honest things, not only in the sight of the Lord, but also in the sight of men" (II Cor. 8:20-21). The representatives of all the churches could report back home that the offerings given by their churches were actually delivered to the Jerusalem church. One cannot be too careful about the handling of church funds. There must be no opportunity for criticism or suspicion.

The second reason was that Paul wanted the elders at Jerusalem to see and meet these representatives of his missionary churches. The apostle had a twofold object in raising the generous offering for the Jerusalem saints. It was not only the altruistic motive of meeting the economic needs of the poverty-stricken Christians in the mother church. Uppermost in Paul's mind was the desire to bind together the Jewish and Gentile churches in a closer unity and fellowship. He hoped that the love offering from the Gentiles would help the Jewish Christians to feel more kindly toward them. Also he wanted the leaders at Jerusalem to feel the spirit of his converts in the provinces. A personal contact was essential for bringing this about.

Luke was evidently one of these representatives. It is at least possible, if not probable, that he is the one to whom Paul refers as "that brother whose services to the gospel are universally praised in the churches" (II Cor. 8:18, RSV). Doubtless Luke's own church at Philippi had been among the most generous in giving to this need (cf. Phil. 4:14-16). A sense of modesty may have led Luke to omit any reference here to the presentation of the offering.[334]

Having **saluted** the elders (19), Paul **declared particularly** —"gave them a detailed account" (Phillips)—of the **things God had wrought among the Gentiles by his ministry.** When they heard the report, the elders **glorified the Lord** (20)—the best Greek text has "glorified God." Lake and Cadbury comment: "The implication is that they were not merely thankful, but relieved. The facts were not what had been reported."[335]

Then the elders made a proposition to Paul. One cannot escape the feeling that these legalistic Jewish Christians at

[334]*Ibid.*
[335]*Beginnings,* IV, 270.

Jerusalem were pathetically narrow-minded in their attitude. They wanted Paul, the apostle to the Gentiles, to prove that he was still a good Jew! He had been rejoicing for years in the glorious freedom of salvation through faith in Jesus Christ, and preaching this to the Gentiles. Now they wanted him to conform to an item in the law of Moses in order to placate the Judaizers in the Church. We can admire their motive of wanting to avoid any danger of rupture between the Jewish and Gentile Christians, without endorsing the method they used.

The elders began by calling attention to **how many thousands**—Greek *myriades,* "myriads" (lit., "tens of thousands")—**of Jews there are which believe; and they are all zealous of the law.** The last clause posed the problem. Most of the Jewish converts to Christianity still observed the law of Moses. In their minds this did not conflict with faith in Christ for salvation. In this view the Law was not a means of salvation, but a divinely ordained way of life for God's people.

These Jewish converts had been **informed** (21). The Greek verb is *katecheo,* from which comes the English "catechize," and signifies oral instruction. Alexander claims that the word "is here descriptive, not of mere report or rumour, but of careful inculcation on the part of Paul's opponents. The Christian zealots of Jerusalem . . . had been not simply *told* but *taught* by his calumniators what here follows."[336] Lumby agrees with this interpretation, and adds: "We can hence understand the great hostility which the Apostle experienced, and his strong language about these Judaizers. They must have had their partisans at work in preparation for his visit, and have poisoned men's minds against him."[337]

The accusation brought against Paul was false. The Judaizers claimed that he was teaching **all the Jews which are among the Gentiles to forsake Moses**—literally, teaching them "an apostasy from Moses." The Greek word *apostasia* is used in I Maccabees 2:15 concerning those who were being compelled to forsake the Law and sacrifice to idols. This forms a striking parallel to its use in this passage.

They also said he was teaching the Jews **that they ought not to circumcise their children**—literally, "to stop circumcising their children"—**neither to walk after the customs.** There is no

[336]*Op. cit.,* p. 736.
[337]*Op. cit.,* p. 375.

evidence in Acts or the Pauline Epistles that the apostle taught any of these specific things to the Jews. It is clear that he did tell the Gentile Christians that they were free from the Law. And he did write to his "brethren": "Ye also are become dead to the law by the body of Christ; that ye should be married to another, even to him who is raised from the dead" (Rom. 7:4). But nowhere is it indicated that he told the Jews to stop observing the regulations of the Law.

What is it therefore? (22) This literal translation means, "How stands the matter?" or, "What then is to be done?" (NASB) The clause **the multitude must needs come together** is perhaps not a part of the original text (cf. ASV). In any case, the Jewish Christians would hear that Paul had arrived.

So the elders outlined a plan. They had four men under **a vow** (23). This is the same word (*euche*) as in 18:18, though it is translated "prayer" in Jas. 5:15 (the only other place in the NT where it occurs). Temporary Nazirite vows usually lasted thirty days. It was suggested that Paul should **purify** himself—literally, "be purified"—with these four men, **and be at charges with them** (24)—"literally, *spend (money) on them,* i.e. pay the expenses of their offerings and other ceremonial forms attending the conclusion of their vow"[338]—**that they may shave their heads.** Lumby comments: "The shaving of the head took place at the conclusion of the vow, and when the victims were offered, the hair was burnt in the fire which was under the sacrifice of the peace-offering."[339]

The result would be that all would know the falsity of the things they had been taught concerning Paul, and that **thou thyself also walkest orderly**—a military term, meaning "walk in line" or "keep in step"—**and keepest the law.** The question has sometimes been raised as to whether Paul could honestly subscribe to this idea that he observed the Mosaic law. Of one thing we are certain: that the apostle acted conscientiously, in accordance with what he felt to be best for the cause of Christ. Once more he followed his policy of being all things to all men (see comments on 18:18).

The elders agreed (25) that the matter of Gentile Christian practice had already been settled at the Council of Jerusalem (c. 15). Only four restrictions had been placed on the Gentile

---

[338]Alexander, *op. cit.,* p. 739.
[339]*Op. cit.,* p. 376.

converts, the same as those specified in 15:29 in the letter which they had **written**—literally, "sent."

So Paul took the four men who were under a vow, and having been purified with them he **entered** (26)—see comment on "went in" (18)—**into the temple, to signify the accomplishment** —literally, "announcing the completion"—**of the days of purification, until that an offering should be offered for every one of them.** Hackett thinks that Paul stayed in the Temple until each one's offering was presented.[340] Rackham suggests that he went into the Temple on four different days, one for each of them.[341] The offering for the end of the Nazirite vow was one male lamb, one ewe lamb, and one ram, with the appropriate meal and drink offerings (Num. 6:13-15). The total cost of these for four men would run into considerable money.

b. Paul Mobbed and Arrested (21:27-36). **When the seven days** (27)—of purification (cf. 26)—**were almost ended, the Jews which were of Asia**—i.e., from around Ephesus, and so most apt to recognize "Trophimus an Ephesian" (29)—**when they saw him in the temple, stirred up**—"threw into confusion" (cf. 19:32)— **all the people, and laid hands on him.** This was violent mob action.

The attackers cried out: **Men of Israel, help** (28). They were posing as defenders of the sacredness of the Temple. Loudly they yelled that Paul was the one who was teaching **all men every where against the people** (the Jewish people), **and the law, and this place: and further brought Greeks also into the temple, and hath polluted this holy place.**

This, of course, was untrue. The basis of their accusation was a typical piece of illogical reasoning. They saw Paul in the Temple. They had previously seen him in a city street in the company of **Trophimus an Ephesian** (29). They put these two premises together and drew the fallacious deduction that he must have had this Gentile with him in the Temple. This is a good example of how some false rumors get their start.

All the city was moved (30)—"excited, stirred up"—**and the people ran together**—Arndt and Gingrich say that the Greek suggests the forming of a mob.[342] **They took Paul, and drew**— literally, "were dragging" (imperfect tense)—**him out of the**

[340]*Op. cit.,* p. 251.
[341]*Op. cit.,* p. 415.
[342]*Op. cit.,* p. 793.

temple, beating him as they dragged him (cf. 32). **Forthwith the doors were shut.** Presumably this was done by the priests and Levites to prevent the desecration of the sacred enclosure by mob action.

As they went about (31)—literally, "while they were seeking"—**to kill him, tidings**—the word means *"information,* especially against fraud or other crime"[343]—**came** (lit., "went up") to the military barracks overlooking the Temple. Word came to **the chief captain**—*chiliarchos, "the commander of a thousand,* especially a Roman *military tribune,"*[344]—**of the band**—"cohort" —**that all Jerusalem was in an uproar.** Lake and Cadbury write: "The garrison of Jerusalem consisted of one cohort of auxiliaries, made up—at least on paper—of 760 infantry with a detachment of 240 cavalry."[345] They add: "It was stationed in the Antonia, connected by two flights of steps with the temple, which it overlooked from watchtowers."[346] (See map 2.)

The tribune **immediately took soldiers and centurions, and ran down unto them** (32). Since a **centurion,** as the name signifies, was an officer in charge of a hundred men, the implication is that at least two hundred soldiers rushed down to suppress the mob. The Feast of Pentecost, which Paul had hurried to Jerusalem to attend (20:16), was the time of the year when there were the most Jews in Jerusalem from outside Palestine. This was because the other main feast, the Passover, came too early for comfortable sailing on the Mediterranean. So Pentecost was the favorite feast with the non-Palestinian Jews. There would be a large contingent from the province of Asia, and they spearheaded the attack on Paul. But when they saw the tribune and his soldiers, they stopped beating the apostle.

Since Paul was clearly the center of the uproar, the tribune arrested him and order him **bound with two chains** (33). The tribune evidently thought Paul to be a dangerous criminal.

When the tribune inquired who Paul might be and what he had done, the people yelled in such confusion that he had to order the prisoner taken **into the castle** (34)—rather, "the barracks" (NASB). When they reached the stairs leading up to the barracks, the soldiers had to carry Paul because of **the violence** of

[343]Abbott-Smith, *op. cit.,* p. 467.
[344]*Ibid.*
[345]*Beginnings,* IV, 275.
[346]*Ibid.*

the mob (35). The people followed hard after him, yelling, **Away with him** (36). They were determined to have him killed.

c. *Paul Makes a Plea* (21:37-40). As Paul was about to be led into the barracks, he sai‍d to the tribune: **May I speak unto thee?** (37) Obviously he addressed him in correct Greek, for the tribune answered in surprise: **Canst thou speak Greek?**—literally, "Do you know Greek?" The tribune thought he was **that Egyptian** (38) who had raised an **uproar** (insurrection) and **led out into the wilderness four thousand men that were murderers.** Josephus tells of this same insurrection, but says that there were 30,000.[347] Knowling suggests that there may have been 4,000 armed men, but 30,000 followers altogether.[348] **Murderers** here is assassins (*sicarii*). They carried small, hidden daggers and killed people even in broad daylight.

Paul assured the tribune that he was no such person. Without hesitation he proclaimed his origin: **I am a man . . . a Jew of Tarsus . . . in Cilicia, a citizen of no mean city** (39). He was justly proud of his native city, one of the three leading intellectual centers of that day (after Athens and Alexandria). Pressing the point home, Paul asked permission to address the crowd. When the tribune had given him permission—**suffer** (39) and **given . . . licence** (40) are the same verb in Greek—**Paul stood on the stairs, and beckoned with the hand unto the people.** Surprisingly, the howling mob fell silent. Then he addressed the crowd **in the Hebrew tongue** (*dialektos*, "dialect"). **Hebrew** probably means Aramaic, the language commonly spoken in Palestine in the time of Christ.

2. *Paul's Speech to the Jews* (22:1-29)

Saul's conversion is recorded in 9:1-18. Here Paul recounts the story (cf. c. 26). There are some slight differences of wording.

a. *His Birth and Early Life* (22:1-5). **Men, brethren, and fathers** means simply, "Brothers and fathers" (Moffatt). This is exactly the way Stephen began his defense (7:2). **Fathers** (cf. 3) would refer to Jewish elders and teachers. Paul pleaded for a hearing: **Hear ye my defence which I make now unto you.** The word **defence** is *apologia*. The English word "apology" originally meant defense, and this sense still appears in the theological term "apologetics." But already in Shakespeare (contemporary

[347]*War* II. 13. 5; *Ant.* XX. 8. 6.
[348]EGT, II, 454.

with KJV) "apology" had taken on its modern sense of "an explanation offered to a person affected by one's action that no offence was intended, coupled with the expression of regret for any that may have been given."[349]

When the Jews heard Paul addressing them in their own **Hebrew (2)**—probably Aramaic—**tongue** ("language, dialect"), they listened quietly. The clear implication is that they had expected him to speak in Greek. Probably most of the mob did not know his identity (cf. 19:32). On the apostle's general approach here Blaiklock makes this fitting remark: "Nothing more clearly indicates Paul's fine education and superb powers of mind than his ability to make immediate and effective contact with any audience, and to present his message, without loss of content, in the terms of their thought and experience."[350]

Paul began his defense by identifying himself as a **Jew (3)**. Then he gave the place of his birth—**Tarsus, a city in Cilicia**— of which he was justly proud (cf. 21:39). In the third place he was **brought up**—"educated"—**in this city** (Jerusalem) **at the feet of Gamaliel.** Schuerer notes: "The pupils sat on the ground during the instruction of the teacher, who was on an elevated place."[351]

Gamaliel is named elsewhere in the New Testament only in 5:34, where he appears as a mild, fair-minded person. Bruce comments: "His tolerant attitude there contrasts with the persecuting zeal of his pupil; it is by no means unusual for the pupil to be more extreme than his master."[352]

Under Gamaliel young Saul was **taught**—literally, "trained" —**according to the perfect manner**—literally, "exactness" or "strictness"—**of the law of the fathers.** The Pharisees were noted for being extremely strict in their interpretation and application of the Law, while the Sadducees were considered lax.

This verse emphasizes Paul's two significant backgrounds. In his hometown of Tarsus he was exposed to Greek culture, language, and learning. In Jerusalem he received a thorough training in the Old Testament Scriptures, particularly the Torah (Pentateuch). This combination fitted him preeminently to invade such Greek cities as Athens and Corinth with a twofold

---

[349]*Oxford English Dictionary* (Oxford: Clarendon Press, 1933), I, 389.

[350]*Op. cit.,* p. 173.

[351]*Op. cit.,* II, i, 326.

[352]*Acts,* p. 400.

ministry: first to the Jews in the synagogue, and then to the Gentiles in the marketplace (Athens), a home (Corinth), or a hall (Ephesus). Everywhere he went the apostle was well prepared to move into any situation with the gospel of Jesus Christ.

Tactfully Paul told his audience that he had been **zealous toward God**—literally, "a zealot of God"—**as ye all are this day.** So fanatical had been his zeal that he had **persecuted this way unto the death, binding**—"putting in chains"—**and delivering into prisons both men and women** (4). The speaker could understand and appreciate the attitude of his audience, for he had once been in the same position.

Saul's persecution of the Christians could be corroborated by **the high priest** (5)—Ananias (cf. 23:2), who was doubtless a member of the Sanhedrin at that earlier time—as well as by **all the estate of the elders**—literally, the *presbyterion,* meaning the Sanhedrin (cf. Luke 22:66). From this body Saul had **received letters unto the brethren** (the Jews) and had gone **to Damascus, to bring** the Christians **bound unto Jerusalem, for to be punished.**

b. *His Birth from Above* (22:6-11). **About noon** Saul had been nearing Damascus, when **suddenly there shone from heaven a great light round about me** (6). This significant introduction to his conversion is related in all three accounts (cf. 9:3; 26:13). Paul told Agrippa that this light was brighter than the midday sun (26:13). The shock of the blinding light knocked Saul to the ground. As he lay there, stunned into quietness, he heard a voice asking: **Saul, Saul, why persecutest thou me?** (7) It has been suggested that Paul's doctrine of the Church as the body of Christ (Eph. 1:23) may have originated in this experience. In persecuting the body, Saul was hurting the Head—**I am Jesus of Nazareth, whom thou persecutest** (8).

As proof that the vision was not a personal hallucination Paul declared: **They that were with me saw indeed the light** (9). This is not mentioned specifically in the other accounts. For a solution to the apparent contradiction between the latter half of this verse and 9:7 see the comments on 9:7-8 and 26:14.

Saul's first question was: **Who art thou?** (8) His second was: **What shall I do?** (10) The first answer was, **I am Jesus;** the second, **Arise, and go.** The first emphasizes acceptance of Christ; the second, consecration to His service. Taken together, these make an excellent sermon outline: (1) We must know who Jesus is: Son of God and Saviour; (2) We must also obey Him as Lord and Master.

Still blind because of **the glory of that light** (the dazzling brilliance from above), Saul was **led by the hand . . . into Damascus (11)**. He had planned to come as conqueror of the Christians. Instead he arrived as the captive of Christ.

c. His Baptism by Ananias (22:12-16). This person is described as **a devout man according to the law, having a good report of all the Jews which dwelt there (12)**. It is the consensus of commentators that this Ananias was a Jew. That he kept the Law carefully is indicated by his high reputation among the Jews of Damascus. It seems clear that Jewish converts to Christianity still worshiped in the synagogue and observed the requirements of the Mosaic law. The point that Paul was making with his Jewish audience, as he spoke from the stairs of Antonia, was that a good, law-abiding Jew had endorsed his conversion to Christ.

Ananias came to the blind, praying man (cf. 9:11) and greeted him as **Brother Saul (13)**. These words must have brought immense comfort to the heart of one who was caught in the transition from Judaism to Christianity. Here was a man whom he had come to persecute calling him **Brother**.

Receive . . . sight and **looked up** are both the same verb, *anablepo*. *Blepo* means "see" and *ana* has the dual meaning of "again" and "up." The attempt of RSV and NEB to translate the verb the same way in both places required the addition of "and saw," and is probably less satisfactory than the KJV use of two different expressions.

Ananias informed Saul that God had chosen the former persecutor to **know his will, and see that Just One, and . . . hear the voice of his mouth (14)**—three aorist infinitives in the Greek, referring to what had taken place on the road to Damascus. The purpose of this was that the converted Pharisee should be God's **witness unto all men of what thou hast seen and heard (15)**. Saul was admonished to rise and **be baptized, and wash away thy sins (16)**. Both of these verbs are in the aorist middle. This particular usage is explained by Blass-Debrunner as "the middle in the sense 'to let oneself be . . .' "[353] The sense is correctly indicated in the familiar translation of the KJV.

[353]*Op. cit.*, p. 166.

The Jews required all Gentile proselytes to Judaism to be baptized, because they were considered unclean. It was a very humbling experience for Saul, who had been a strict observer of the Law, to acknowledge his uncleanness in God's sight by submitting to Christian baptism.

This verse does not teach baptismal regeneration, as some have claimed. Alexander comments: "As his body was to be baptized by man, so his sins were to be washed away by God."[354] He continues: "The identity, or even the inseparable union, of the two effects, is so far from being here affirmed, that they are rather held apart, as things connected by the natural relation of type and antitype, yet perfectly distinguishable in themselves and easily separable in experience."[355]

Calling on the name of the Lord is in the best Greek text "calling on his name." This probably means the name of Jesus.

d. His Mission to the Gentiles (22:17-21). The purpose of this entire speech was "to prove that the course of Paul had been divinely ordered and thus to imply that those who oppose Paul are, in reality, placing themselves in opposition to God."[356] Erdman finds three steps in this argument: "(1) By birth, education, and earlier experience Paul has been in perfect agreement with his hearers . . . (2) The divine power which suddenly transformed Paul from a persecutor to an apostle had been manifested by a vision of Jesus . . . and further by a miracle wrought upon him by a devout Jew named Ananias . . . (3) Paul states that his relation to the Gentiles, his work among them, and his message to them, are wholly due to a divine purpose."[357]

In line with this he called attention to the fact that **when he** returned to **Jerusalem, and while** he was praying **in the temple** —this happened in the Holy Land, in the Holy City, and in the Holy Temple, where he was piously worshiping God—he fell into **a trance** (17). The Greek word is *ekstasis,* from which comes "ecstasy." Only in Acts does it have this meaning (cf. 10:10; 11:5, both in connection with Peter's vision on the house-top in Joppa). Arndt and Gingrich say it means: *"trance, ecstasy,*

---

[354]*Op. cit.,* p. 764.
[355]*Ibid.*
[356]Erdman, *op. cit.,* p. 148.
[357]*Ibid.*

a state of being brought about by God, in which consciousness is wholly or partially suspended."[358]

In this trance Paul **saw him** (18)—rather obviously Christ. Why is it not so stated? Alexander makes this suggestion: "His name may be suppressed because Paul was unwilling to offend his hearers by an unnecessary repetition or obtrusion of what he believed but they did not, and because he was still more unwilling to expose that name to their irreverence and even blasphemy, if they should be so offended."[359]

The Master bade His servant: **Make haste, and get thee quickly out of Jerusalem.** Paul remonstrated. He reminded the Lord that he had **imprisoned and beat in every synagogue them that believed on thee** (19). This shows the extent of his ravaging of the church at Jerusalem in those early days (cf. 8:3). He had also consented to the death of Stephen (20), and **kept the raiment of them that slew him** (cf. 7:58). **Martyr** is literally "witness."

But the Lord answered His servant: **Depart: for I will send thee far hence unto the Gentiles** (21)—literally, "Be going because I myself will send you on a mission far away to Gentiles." Lenski comments: *"Ego* is emphatic with authority: *I* am doing this, no matter what thou thinkest."[360] It was not the divine will that Paul should be slain by angry Jews before he got started on his Gentile mission.

Since this vision of Saul in the Temple (17-21) is not recorded elsewhere, there has been some disagreement as to when it occurred. But it seems most natural to assume that it took place on Saul's first visit to Jerusalem after his conversion (9:26; Gal. 1:18). This is the view of Lenski[361] and of numerous others, including Lake and Cadbury.

Paul's speech to the Jews (3-21) suggests the topic "Before and After." *Before* his conversion Paul was: (1) A zealous Jew, 3; (2) A cruel persecutor, 4-5; (3) A convicted sinner, 6-11. *After* his conversion he was: (1) A commissioned witness, 14-15; (2) A fearless preacher, 17-20; (3) An appointed missionary, 21.

e. *His Plea of Citizenship* (22:22-29). "The suggestion of the preaching to the Gentiles was the last straw to the mob."[362]

[358]*Op. cit.,* p. 244.
[359]*Op. cit.,* p. 766.
[360]*Op. cit.,* p. 913.
[361]*Ibid.,* p. 910.
[362]*Beginnings,* IV, 281.

The account says: **And they gave him audience**—literally, "were hearing him"—**unto this word** (22). Then they began shouting: **Away with such a fellow from the earth: for it is not fit that he should live. It is** . . . **fit** is in the imperfect tense. Robertson writes: "Verbs of propriety, possibility, obligation or necessity are also used in the imperfect when the obligation, etc., is not lived up to, has not been met."[363] Lenski paraphrases the passage thus: "He should not have been permitted to live this long, should have been removed from the earth long ago."[364]

The mob was now almost in a frenzy. The people **cast off their clothes**—perhaps waving them above their heads—**and threw dust into the air** (23). So the **chief captain** (*chiliarch*) ordered Paul to be brought up into the barracks and **examined**[365] **by scourging** (24). C. S. C. Williams comments: "It was customary for Romans to use the barbarous scourge on slaves and aliens to beat the truth out of them."[366]

As they bound him with thongs (25) is thus interpreted by Thayer: "when they had stretched him out for the thongs, i.e., to receive the blows of the thongs, (by tying him up to a beam or a pillar; for it appears from vs. 29 that Paul had already been bound)."[367] The victim's body was stretched tightly over a low pillar, with his hands and feet fastened to rings in the floor, while his back was stripped bare for the lash. The literal meaning of the verb **bound** is "stretch out," which suggests that this is what is meant here. Many prisoners died as a result of Roman scourging.

While this was going on, Paul said to the centurion in charge: **Is it lawful for you to scourge a man that is a Roman**—i.e., a Roman citizen—**and uncondemned?** For this immunity privilege of Roman citizenship see the comments on 16:38.

As soon as he heard the question, the centurion hurried off to the tribune to inform him that Paul was a Roman citizen (26).

[363]A. T. Robertson, *A Grammar of the Greek New Testament in the Light of Historical Research* (5th ed., New York: Harper & Brothers, n.d.), p. 886.

[364]*Op. cit.,* p. 915.

[365]Arndt and Gingrich (p. 64) say that the rare verb is a technical judicial term and that with the modifying phrase here it means: *"give a hearing, and use torture* (in the form of a lashing) *in connection with it."*

[366]*Op. cit.,* pp. 245-46.

[367]*Op. cit.,* p. 552.

The tribune came in and asked the prisoner for "a solemn affidavit"[368] that he actually was a Roman citizen. When Paul affirmed that he was, the tribune apparently became friendly,[369] and remarked: **With a great sum obtained I this freedom** (28). Paul answered: **But I was . . . born** (a citizen). Lenski notes: "Under the emperors the Roman citizenship was sold in order to fill their exchequer; Dio Cassius (LX,17) reports that the wife of Claudius thus accumulated money."[370] It is likely that the tribune's name was Lysias and that he adopted the additional name Claudius (cf. 23:26) when he purchased his citizenship (perhaps from the wife of the Emperor Claudius). The fact that Paul was born a Roman citizen means that his father or grandfather had purchased it, or else that one of them had been granted citizenship because of some special service to the state.[371] Ramsay writes: "It is clear from the preceding account that Pompey, Julius Caesar, Antony, and Augustus are likely to have given the Roman citizenship to a certain number of important Tarsians."[372] This suggests the possibility that Paul's father or grandfather may have been a leading citizen of Tarsus.

The question may be raised as to how Paul could have proved that he was a Roman citizen. Apparently there is no evidence that citizens carried special papers to this effect. But Paul had relatives in Jerusalem (cf. 23:16) who could have substantiated his claim. Since a false claim of Roman citizenship was punishable by death,[373] an impostor would be slow to say that he was a citizen.

Immediately the soldiers who were about to examine Paul by torture **departed from him** (29). Also the tribune was fearful for his political future, **because he had bound him.**

---

[368]Blaiklock, *op. cit.*, p. 174.

[369]C. S. C. Williams (p. 246) calls attention to the fact that the Western text "suggests a cynical remark by the chief chaptain, 'I know at what a sum I obtained this citizenship,' meaning, 'Even a disreputable-looking person like you can obtain it nowadays', but Paul's reply suggests that the Alexandrian text is correct."

[370]*Op. cit.*, p. 919.

[371]*Ibid.*, p. 688 (on 16:37).

[372]W. M. Ramsay, *The Cities of St. Paul* (New York: A. C. Armstrong, 1908), p. 198.

[373]*Ibid.*

3. Paul Before the Sanhedrin (22:30—23:10)

In his earlier days Paul had brought many a Christian before the Sanhedrin to be tried for his belief in Christ. Now it was his turn to endure this experience.

a. The Sanhedrin Summoned (22:30). The next day after Paul's arrest—and after a safe night in the Roman barracks— the tribune **commanded the chief priests and all their council** (the Sanhedrin) to convene. He then brought Paul down before the group. His purpose was to ascertain the prisoner's crime.

b. Paul Versus the High Priest (23:1-5). As a prisoner of the Roman government, **Paul, earnestly beholding**—the verb (cf. 3:4, 12; 6:15; 10:4; 13:9; 14:9) means "looking intently at"— **the council** (1), i.e., the Sanhedrin, addressed its members as **brethren**—fellow Jews though not fellow Christians. Then he made the somewhat startling assertion: **I have lived in all good conscience before God until this day.**

The verb **lived** is *politeuomai*, which literally means "to be a citizen, live as a citizen."[374] Finally it came to have the more general sense of "live, conduct oneself, lead one's life."[375]

Paul's declaration appears to mean that he had always been sincere and conscientious, even in his violent persecution of the Christians. We have the apostle's own statement that he did this "ignorantly in unbelief" (I Tim. 1:13). It is difficult for us to realize how strongly the young Pharisee felt that it was God's will for him to root out this dangerous heresy.

It should be noted, however, that Lenski objects to this interpretation. He holds that Paul's assertion related only to the charges brought against him (cf. 21:28). "By appealing to his conscience regarding these charges and naming God as its arbiter Paul does what Luther did at Worms."[376]

Alexander feels that the emphasis of the verb is on *theocratic citizenship* and that **before God** should be translated "to God"— "I have lived as a citizen to God." He goes on to say: "Thus understood, the clause before us is not a vague profession to have acted conscientiously, either before or after his conversion, but a definite and bold claim to have acted theocratically, i.e., as a faithful member of the Jewish church, from which they repre-

---

[374]Abbott-Smith, *op. cit.*, p. 371.
[375]Arndt and Gingrich, *op. cit.*, p. 693.
[376]*Op. cit.*, p. 928.

sented him as an apostate."[377] In a similar vein, Hervey says
that the Greek phrase means "to live in obedience to God," and
continues: "St. Paul boldly asserts his undeviating compliance
with the Law of God, as a good and consistent Jew (Phil. iii.6)."[378]

The reaction to Paul's statement before the Sanhedrin was
sudden and strong. **The high priest Ananias commanded them
that stood by him to smite him on the mouth** (2). Secular
records show that this Ananias was cruel and rapacious, utterly
unworthy of his office. Lenski thinks that the high priest resented Paul's calm and confident attitude before the Sanhedrin.
"This fellow Paul should have cringed and quavered: instead
he presumed to speak of his good conscience and blameless conduct even in the very presence of his majesty, the high priest."[379]

Paul's reaction was forceful: **God shall smite thee, thou
whited**—"whitewashed"—**wall** (3). The apostle has often been
criticized for having "lost his temper." But Lake and Cadbury
comment: "This form of 'predictive curse' was held by the
Rabbis to be correct on the basis of Deut. xxviii. 20 ff."[380] It is a
striking fact that Ananias was assassinated ten years later, in
September of A.D. 66.

The bystanders were horrified. They cried: **Revilest thou
God's high priest?** (4) The fact that the high priest was considered to be God's special representative (cf. Deut. 17: 8-13) was
precisely what made the act of Ananias so diabolical, calling
forth the prediction of divine judgment. The attitude of the
Jewish people toward the office of the high priest is well expressed by Josephus when he writes: "He that does not submit
to him shall be subject to the same punishment as if he had been
guilty of impiety towards God himself."[381]

In a more conciliatory tone Paul replied: **I wist not, brethren,
that he was the high priest** (5). Lumby sums up very well
the various views that have been expressed to account for this
surprising assertion of the apostle. He says: "Some think that
it may have been true that St. Paul from defect of sight, with

[377]*Op. cit.*, p. 781.

[378]A. C. Hervey, "The Acts of the Apostles" (Exposition), *The Pulpit
Commentary*, ed. H. D. M. Spence and Joseph S. Exell (Grand Rapids:
Wm. B. Eerdmans Publishing Co., 1950 [reprint]), II, 211.

[379]*Op. cit.*, p. 929.

[380]*Beginnings*, IV, 287.

[381]*Against Apion*, II. 24.

which he is supposed to have been afflicted, could not distinguish that the speaker was the high priest; others that the high priest was not in his official position as president of the court; or that owing to the troublous times, and St. Paul's recent arrival in Jerusalem, he was not aware who was high priest; or that he was speaking in irony, and meant to imply that the action of the judge was of such a character that none would have supposed him to be high priest; or that he meat by *ouk eidein* that for the moment he was not thinking of what he was saying."[382] Lumby adds: "It is most consonant with St. Paul's character to believe that either his own physical deficiency, or some lack of the usual formalities or insignia, made him unable to distinguish that he who had given the order was really the high priest."[383] With this conclusion we would heartily agree. It might not be out of order to call attention at this point to Lenski's strong contention that this was not a regular meeting of the Sanhedrin in its usual place of assembly, but that the tribune had summoned the members of the Sanhedrin to come to the Antonia barracks.[384] If this was actually the case, it is understandable how the apostle would fail to know who the high priest was.

But when Paul realized that he had spoken thus to the high priest, he in effect apologized for his action; that is, he acknowledged that he had inadvertently done wrong. He quoted Exod. 22:28—**Thou shalt not speak evil of the ruler of thy people.** Paul had not intentionally broken this commandment, and he was sorry for having unintentionally done so.

    c. Pharisees vs. Sadducees (23:6-10). **When Paul perceived (6)**—literally, "when Paul came to know"—**that the one part were Sadducees, and the other Pharisees, he cried out in the council**—*synedrion,* Sanhedrin. **Men and brethren** simply means "brethren." **I**—literally, "I myself"—**am a Pharisee, the son of a Pharisee**—the best Greek text has "of Pharisees." Paul went on to say: **of the hope and resurrection of the dead I am called in question.**

    Some have questioned Paul's ethics in making this the real issue at stake. But Knowling puts the matter in proper perspective. He writes: "It is possible that the Pharisees might have

[382]*Op. cit.,* p. 395.
[383]*Ibid.,* pp. 395-96.
[384]*Op. cit.,* pp. 924-29.

attracted the attention of the Apostle by their protest against the behaviour of Ananias and their acceptance of the words of apology . . . but it is equally probable that in St. Luke's apparently condensed account the appeal to the Pharisees was not made on a sudden impulse . . . but was based upon some manifestation of sympathy with his utterance."[385] He also suggests: "May we not even say that to the Pharisees he became as a Pharisee in order to save some, to lead them to see the crown and fulfilment of the hope in which he and they were at one, in the Person of Jesus, the Resurrection and the Life?"[386] Barnes pictures the apostle as addressing himself particularly to the Pharisees at this point: "Brethren, the doctrine which has distinguished you from the Sadducees is at stake . . . Of that doctrine I have been the advocate . . . for my zeal in urging the argument in defence of it . . . —the resurrection of the Messiah—I have been arraigned, and now cast myself on your protection."[387]

The desired effect resulted. The Pharisees immediately championed Paul's case against the Sadducees. **There arose a dissension—dispute—between the Pharisees and the Sadducees (7)**.

The main difference in belief between these two groups is stated clearly in 8: **For the Sadducees say that there is no resurrection, neither angel, nor spirit: but the Pharisees confess both.** The use of **both** for three items here may be explained in either of two ways. **Angel** and **spirit** may be thought of as referring to the same thing. Or the Greek word for **both** may be used for more than two (cf. 19:16). Arndt and Gingrich note that the term *amphoteroi* sometimes means "all, even when more than two are involved," and translate the phrase here: "believe in them all."[388] Moulton and Milligan furnish support from the papyri for this usage.

The distinction stated here between the beliefs of the Pharisees and Sadducees is abundantly confirmed by Josephus, the Jewish historian of the first century. With regard to the Pharisees he writes: "They also believe that souls have an immortal

---

[385]EGT, II, 466-67.

[386]*Ibid.*, p. 467.

[387]Albert Barnes, *Notes on the New Testament: Acts of the Apostles* (Grand Rapids: Baker Book House, 1949 [reprint]), p. 323.

[388]*Op. cit.*, p. 47.

vigour in them, and that under the earth there will be rewards or punishments, according as they have lived virtuously or viciously in this life; and the latter are detained in an everlasting prison, but the former shall have power to revive and live again."[389] Schuerer says of Josephus' statement: "What is here represented in a philosophizing style as the doctrine of the Pharisees, is merely the Jewish doctrine of retribution and resurrection, already testified by the Book of Daniel (Dan. xii.2), by all subsequent Jewish literature, and also by the New Testament, as the common possession of genuine Judaism."[390] In making his appeal Paul was thus placing himself in the mainstream of Jewish orthodoxy, as the Pharisees well knew.

Of the Sadducees, Josephus says: "They also take away the belief of the immortal duration of the soul, and the punishments and rewards in Hades."[391] And again: "The doctrine of the Sadducees is this: That souls die with the bodies."[392]

On the matter of **angel** and **spirit,** Josephus is not specific. But Schuerer properly observes: "This statement of the Acts, though not confirmed by other testimony, is nevertheless thoroughly trustworthy, as in entire accordance with the picture which we elsewhere obtain of the two parties."[393] He adds: "That in this respect also the Pharisees represented the general standpoint of later Judaism needs no proof."[394]

Rapidly the confusion increased. The account says: **There arose a great cry** (9)—"a loud outcry." **The scribes** belonging to the Pharisaic party, as apparently most of them did, **arose, and strove,** or "contended sharply." Their contention was: **We find no evil in this man.** The clause **let us not fight against God** is not found in the earliest MSS, and so should be omitted. One modern translation has it, "Perhaps an angel or spirit has spoken to him" (NEB).

Finally the **dissension** ("dispute," cf. 7), became so violent that the **chief captain** (10), or "commander" (NASB), fearful

[389]*Ant.* XVIII. 1. 3.
[390]*Op. cit.,* II, ii, 13.
[391]*War* II. 8. 14.
[392]*Ant.* XVIII. 1. 4.
[393]*Op. cit.,* II, ii. 14.
[394]*Ibid.*

for Paul's life, ordered **the soldiers**—literally, "army," meaning "a detachment of soldiers on duty"[395]—**to go down** and bring him back into the barracks. This would seem to suggest that the meeting of the Sanhedrin was taking place outside this building.

4. Paul's Life in Danger (23:11-35)

The tribune had feared that his prisoner might be torn in pieces by the two quarreling factions in the Sanhedrin. But now there arose a far more serious threat to the apostle's life.

a. Comfort (23:11). Paul was undoubtedly deeply disturbed by the uproar in the Sanhedrin and greatly concerned for his personal safety. But before the worst news reached him (cf. 16) the Lord prepared him for the shock by ministering to him with comfort and assurance. The very night after the unpleasant experience before the council, **the Lord stood by him.** While the primary sense probably is that Jesus "appeared to him" (NEB), one cannot forego mentioning the common force of the expression "stood by him." In this hour of severe strain and trial the Lord stood by His servant and strengthened him.

To the distraught apostle Jesus said: **Be of good cheer**[396]— "Have courage! don't be afraid!"[397] Then the promise was given: **as thou hast testified of me in Jerusalem, so must thou bear witness also at Rome.** This was doubly consoling. In the first place, Paul had the divine assurance that he would not die at Jerusalem. That must have been a great comfort, especially in view of the information he was soon to receive about the plot against his life. In the second place, he knew now that his desire to visit Rome (cf. 19:21) would be fulfilled.

This verse records how Jesus gave to Paul: (1) Consolation —**Be of good cheer;** (2) Commendation—**as thou hast testified of me in Jerusalem;** (3) Confirmation—**so must thou bear witness also at Rome.**

Doubtless the apostle was tempted to feel that he had failed in his witness in Jerusalem, even after doing his best to cooperate with the Jewish Christian leaders there. In fact, it was while fulfilling their request that he was mobbed and almost killed.

---

[395]*Beginnings*, IV, 290.

[396]**Paul** is omitted in the earliest MSS, but this sense of a very personal ministry of the Holy Spirit is a well-attested fact of Christian experience.

[397]Arndt and Gingrich, *op. cit.*, p. 352.

But the Lord intimated that his witness had not been in vain. Then, too, Paul probably felt that his purpose to witness in Rome was doomed to failure. Now he was given the assurance that it would be carried out. The Lord knew that His servant greatly needed a boost to his morale, and lovingly He gave it to him.

b. *Conspiracy* (23:12-15). While the Lord was working for Paul, Satan was working against him. But God is never late. He got to the man in prison even before the plot against his life was made. The next morning, however, over forty Jews having **banded together** (12)—literally, "having made a conspiracy"— **bound themselves under a curse**—literally, "anathematized themselves." They solemnly bound themselves to this oath: "May God curse us if we **eat** or **drink** before we have killed Paul." This was desperate religious fanaticism, and Paul's life was now in serious danger.

The conspirators **came to the chief priests and elders** (14). It is noticeable that the scribes (the Pharisees), who with the chief priests and elders made up the Sanhedrin (cf. Matt. 16:21), are not mentioned. In the meeting of the council the day before they had taken Paul's side. So it would not be safe to let them know about this plot. Lenski doubtless portrays the correct picture when he writes: "We conclude that at first a few of the leaders were approached by the conspirators who then confided in those whom they could trust to keep secret their scheme."[398] Significantly he adds: "This [their scheme] is stated outright just as though these murderous fellows knew what kind of men their great religious leaders were."[399]

To these godless leaders the men said: **We have bound ourselves under a great curse**—literally, "with an anathema we anathematized ourselves"; that is, "we have most solemnly sworn." Did these men then starve themselves to death? Edersheim shows how easily the priests sometimes absolved a man from such a rash vow, assuring him that no punishment would follow his failure to carry it out.[400]

The plotters asked the chief priests to have **the council**

---

[398]*Op. cit.,* p. 943.

[399]*Ibid.*

[400]Alfred Edersheim, *Sketches of Jewish Social Life in the Days of Christ* (London: Religious Tract Society, 1876), p. 229.

signify—"inform, give a report"[401]—**to the chief captain (15)**, asking him to bring Paul down again the next day before the Sanhedrin, **as though ye would inquire something more perfectly concerning him.** The Greek word for **inquire,** *diaginoskein,* occurs (in NT) only here and in 24:22. There it clearly has the technical judicial sense, "determine." But does it have that meaning here? Arndt and Gingrich think so. They translate the phrase in this passage: "determine his case by thorough investigation."[402] Lenski prefers the meanings, "decide for the benefit of the chiliarch more accurately these matters regarding Paul."[403] It will be remembered that the tribune had previously brought his prisoner before the Sanhedrin in order to determine the exact nature of the crime alleged against him by the Jews (22:30). So Lenski is probably correct when he says: "The idea was to let the chiliarch know that the Sanhedrin was now in a better position than it had been on the day before to procure the desired information for him."[404]

The forty-odd conspirators planned to assassinate Paul on his way across the Temple area to the meeting place of the Sanhedrin. With sharp daggers hidden under their cloaks, that number of fanatically desperate men could have accomplished their purpose successfully in spite of a considerable detachment of soldiers. That the chief priests would endorse such a plot, which might even have endangered the life of the tribune himself, shows how determined they were to do away with Paul.

c. Chiliarch Informed (23:16-22). A nephew of the apostle **heard of their lying in wait (16)**—literally, "ambush." It is generally assumed that he was living with his parents in Jerusalem. But it is possible that he was a theological student there, as his uncle had been at an earlier date, and that his home was in Tarsus. Also it has often been said that probably Paul's wealthy parents disowned him when he became a Christian. That is altogether possible. But in this case the nephew was concerned for his uncle's safety.

How he obtained his information we do not know. Edersheim suggests that the young man was a member of a Pharisaic

---

[401]Arndt and Gingrich, *op. cit.,* p. 257.

[402]*Ibid.,* p. 181.

[403]*Op. cit.,* pp. 943-44.

[404]*Ibid.,* p. 944.

guild ("Chabura"), and thus learned of the plot.[405] The nephew **entered into the castle**—the barracks—**and told Paul.** Knowling comments: "Evidently Paul's friends were allowed access to him, and amongst them we may well suppose that St. Luke himself would have been included."[406] Hackett makes the further observation: "Lysias may have been the more indulgent, because he would atone for his fault in having bound a Roman citizen."[407]

Paul requested one of the centurions on duty to take his nephew to the commandant (17). The latter took the young man aside and inquired what he had to tell him (19). When he heard the report of the oath-bound conspiracy (20-21), the chiliarch let his informant leave with the injunction not to tell anyone (22). **Tell** is a compound in Greek meaning "to speak out, divulge." **Shewed** is the same verb which is rendered "signify" in 15 (see comments there); in 24:1; 25:2, 15 it is translated "informed."

d. *Centurions Summoned* (23:23-25). The tribune realized that the situation was indeed serious. So he summoned 2 centurions and ordered them to make ready 200 infantry, 70 cavalry, and 200 spearmen and have them prepared to leave at nine o'clock that evening for Caesarea. In those more primitive times, without street lights, it would be safe to start out at that hour, for all would be dark and quiet.

The word translated **spearmen** has not been found elsewhere in Greek literature until the sixth century. Arndt and Gingrich, in the latest authoritative lexicon, say: "A word of uncertain meaning, military technical term according to Joannes Lydus . . . a light-armed soldier, perhaps *bowman* or *slinger*."[408] Knowling thinks that this term, *dexiolabous*, is "probably from *dexios* and *lambano*, grasping their weapons by the right hand, so here of those who carried their light weapon, a lance, in their right hand."[409] Schuerer concluded: "This much only is certain, that it designated a special class of light-armed soldiers (javelin-throwers or slingers)."[410] Anyone wishing a full discussion of the

---

[405]*Op. cit.,* p. 227.
[406]EGT, II, 471.
[407]*Op. cit.,* p. 266.
[408]*Op. cit.,* p. 173.
[409]EGT, II, 472.
[410]*Op. cit.,* I, ii, 56.

question will find it in Meyer.[411] Bruce gives what is probably the best summary of the matter: "The escort was composed of heavy infantry, cavalry, and light-armed troops . . . the three constituents of the Roman army."[412]

The centurions were also to provide **beasts (24)**—better, "animals"; i.e., horses or mules—for **Paul,** and probably the soldiers immediately responsible for him, to **bring him safe unto Felix the governor.** Having given these orders, the tribune composed **a letter** to h.'s superior **(25). After this manner** is literally "having this form" (*typon*), which means "this wording"—"not merely this approximate form or content."[413]

e. *Communication to the Governor* (23:26-30). The letter began with the name of the sender, as was the custom in those days. **Claudius Lysias (26)** probably adopted the first of these two names when he became a Roman citizen (see comment on 22:28). After giving his own name, with no titles, Lysias courteously addressed his letter to **the most excellent governor Felix,** or "His Excellency the Governor Felix" (NEB). **Governor** is *hegemon,* which literally means "leader." In the New Testament it is used mostly for the Roman procurators of Judea.

Felix had apparently become the governor of Judea in A.D. 52. He was a cruel, wicked ruler. The Roman historian Tacitus, playing on the fact that Felix had once been a slave, wrote of him: "Antonius Felix, indulging in every kind of barbarity and lust, exercised the power of a king in the spirit of a slave."[414]

Greeting is *chairein* (see comment on 15:23). This was the regular word in the secular papyrus letters of that day.

As might be expected, Lysias places himself in the best possible light in this letter to the governor. It is true that he rescued Paul from the mob that was about to lynch him **(27).** But he stretched the truth when he added: **having understood that he was a Roman.** The account (21:31-40; 22:24-29) clearly

---

[411]H. A. W. Meyer, *Critical and Exegetical Handbook to the Acts of the Apostles,* trans. Paton Gloag (New York: Funk & Wagnalls, 1883), pp. 433-34.

[412]*Acts,* p. 416.

[413]Lenski, *op. cit.,* p. 950.

[414]*Histories* V, 9, in P. Cornelius Tacitus, *The Annals and the Histories* (Chicago: Encyclopaedia Brittanica, Inc., 1952), p. 297. Tacitus also says that, because Felix had a brother who was a favorite of the emperor, he "thought that he could do any evil act with impunity, backed up as he was by such power" (*Annals* XII. 54; *op. cit.,* p. 122).

indicates that he did not know of Paul's citizenship until some time after he had arrested him. But the story sounded better this way.

Lysias went on to tell how he brought his prisoner before the Sanhedrin in an effort to ascertain his crime (28). But he soon discovered that it was a matter of Jewish religion, not Roman law (29). When he learned of the plot against Paul's life, immediately he sent the prisoner to the governor, telling his accusers to make any further complaints directly to the procurator. Thus Lysias had rid himself of a most unpleasant problem and protected himself from the possibility of getting into trouble over Paul's case.

f. Convoy to Caesarea (23:31-35). In obedience to the tribune's command, the soldiers took Paul, and **brought him by night to Antipatris** (31, see map 1). Lake and Cadbury find a difficulty here. After noting that a day's march for a Roman legion was "traditionally fixed at twenty-four miles," they go on to say: "Auxiliaries, being less heavily armed, would go somewhat faster, but forty miles, the distance of Antipatris from Jerusalem, is an impossible night-march for infantry, and quite a severe task for cavalry."[415] They do admit, however, that "the exact location of Antipatris is uncertain."[416]

There are two possible solutions. It is stated that the infantry **on the morrow** (32) let the cavalry convoy the prisoner the rest of the way to Caesarea. They **returned to the castle**; i.e., to their barracks at Jerusalem. But it does not say what time the next day. It could have been noon or afternoon. Some scholars stress **by night** as meaning that the convoy traveled only at night and may have taken two nights on the way.[417] Hackett himself would allow taking the phrase **by night** "as applying only to the greater part of the journey," and adds: "It would be correct to speak of the journey, in general terms, as a journey by night, although it occupied two or three hours of the following day."[418] Hervey thinks they could make it during the one night since they would reach Gophna (three hours' march from Jerusalem) at midnight, and would be walking downhill the

[415]*Beginnings*, IV, 293.
[416]*Ibid.*, p. 295.
[417]Hackett, *op. cit.*, p. 269.
[418]*Ibid.*

rest of the way to the Plain of Sharon, on which Antipatris was situated.[419]

When the convoy of cavalry reached **Caesarea** (sixty miles from Jerusalem), the letter and prisoner were both presented **to the governor** (33). Having read the letter, Felix inquired from what province Paul had come. When he learned that it was **Cilicia** (34), he declared: **I will hear thee . . . when thine accusers are also come** (35). Lake and Cadbury say of the compound verb rendered **I will hear:** "It was apparently a legal term for 'hold a hearing,' being so used in Hellenistic historians, inscriptions, and papyri, and is appropriately employed here."[420]

The governor then ordered that Paul should be **kept**—"guarded"—**in Herod's judgment hall**—Herod's "praetorium." This was the palace built at Caesarea by Herod the Great. When the Herods were succeeded in Judea by Roman procurators, the palace became the governor's residence and the seat of Roman government. Paul was probably kept in some kind of guardroom in the *praitorion,* but not this time in a dungeon.

J. CAESAREA, 24:1—26:32

After a hectic week in Jerusalem, pressured by the Christians and persecuted by the Jews, Paul spent two quiet years in prison at Caesarea, followed by two years in prison at Rome. One is tempted to wonder if the great apostle made a mistake when he refused to be stopped by the warnings of prophets (20:22-24; 21:4, 10-11) and the pleadings of friends (20:12-14). If he had not gone on to Jerusalem he would have missed the persecution and imprisonment that overtook him there. He presumably would have been able to spend the next four years in preaching rather than in prison.

But perhaps the Lord knew that His zealous apostle was "going too hard" and needed a rest. Did Paul's remark to the high priest (23:3) reveal a man whose nerves were a bit frayed by the too heavy schedule of preaching, traveling, and the constant care of the many churches he had founded (cf. II Cor. 11:28)? It is only fair to ask the question. For Paul was perfectly human, as well as Spirit-filled.

The decision as to whether or not the apostle did the right thing in going up to Jerusalem hinges somewhat on whether we

[419]*Op. cit.,* II, 215-16.
[420]*Beginnings,* IV, 296.

translate the clause in 20:22 as "bound in the spirit" (KJV, ASV) or "bound in the Spirit" (RSV)—cf. "under the binding force of the Spirit" (Moffatt); "the Spirit compels me to go there" (Goodspeed); "compelled by the Spirit" (Phillips); "bound by the Spirit" (Berk.); "under the constraint of the Spirit" (NEB). It is obvious that the bulk of modern translators[421] take this passage as Paul's testimony that the Holy Spirit was leading him to go on to Jerusalem, regardless of the predicted consequences. And there we probably do well to let the matter rest.

One thing should always be kept in mind: Out of those four years of enforced physical inactivity and so opportunity for quiet meditation there came the richest of Paul's writings. Had he not been arrested—by the Spirit as well as by the Roman government—we would not today have his Prison Epistles with their profound depths of spiritual truth. It was because of these experiences that Paul could write that he was "the prisoner of Christ Jesus" (Eph. 3:1, NEB), not just the prisoner of Rome. As Christ's prisoner he was held in the grip of the Spirit in a closer fellowship with his Lord than ever before. Thus he was able to perform his highest service.

1. Paul Before Felix (24:1-27)

At Caesarea, Paul made three main appearances: before Felix (c. 24), before Festus (c. 25), and before Agrippa (c. 26). This man who had the reputation of turning the world upside down (cf. 17:6) could not be ignored. He was now being brought before "governors and kings" (Matt. 10:18) for the sake of Christ.

Foakes-Jackson makes the general observation concerning this incident: "The account of the trial before Felix is a model report. Condensed as the speeches for the prosecution and defence are, they give all the necessary points, and leave nothing to be desired."[422]

a. *Presentation of the Charge* (24:1-9). As a historian, Luke was fond of chronology. So here he begins the account by saying, **after five days** (1). But there is a difference of opinion as to how this is to be counted. Knowling says: "Most probably to be reckoned from the arrival of St. Paul at Caesarea, not from his apprehension in Jerusalem, or from his start from Jerusalem on

---

[421]NASB, "bound in spirit," is an exception.
[422]*Op. cit.*, p. 213.

the way to Caesarea."[423] Lake and Cadbury agree with this,[424] as do many others. Hackett thinks it means on the fifth day after Paul left Jerusalem. He writes: "The escape from the Jewish conspiracy is nearest to the mind here after what has been related; and further, according to Roman usage, a case referred like this should be tried on the third day, or as soon after as might be possible."[425]

The high priest, Ananias, came down from Jerusalem, accompanied by some **elders** and **a certain orator named Tertullus.** The Greek word for **orator** originally meant a public speaker (the Gk. suggests "rhetorician"). But it came to be used for a "lawyer" (Phillips) or "attorney" (NASB). Whether **Tertullus** was a Jew,[426] a Roman, or a Greek is uncertain. "In vss. 3, 4, 6 he speaks of himself and his clients as 'we,' but in vs. 2 he speaks of 'this nation,' and in vs. 5 of 'the Jews.' "[427] The reference to "our law" (6) and the language of 7 would certainly imply that Tertullus was a Jew. But the last clause of 6, all of 7, and the first clause of 8 are omitted in the earliest and best MSS. So this section cannot be used as evidence. The customs of the time would support the idea that the lawyer was a Gentile. Knowling says: "Tertullus was apparently one of the class of hired pleaders, often employed in the provinces by those who were themselves ignorant of Roman law."[428] The trial was probably conducted in Greek.

Informed occurs again in 25:2, 15. Knowling says: "The verb appears to be used in these passages as a kind of technical term to indicate laying formal information before a judge."[429] It is used that way by the contemporary Josephus.[430]

Tertullus began his speech with eloquent flattery (2-3), which is all the more offensive because so utterly untrue. Felix was hated, not appreciated, by the Jews. His life history is anything but praiseworthy. Born as slaves, he and his mother were apparently freed by Antonia, the mother of Emperor Claudius.

[423]*EGT,* II, 476.
[424]*Beginnings,* IV, 296.
[425]*Op. cit.,* p. 270.
[426]So Bruce, *Acts,* p. 321.
[427]*Beginnings,* IV, 297.
[428]*EGT,* II, 476.
[429]*Ibid.,* pp. 476-77.
[430]*Ant.* XIV. 10. 8.

His brother became a great favorite with Claudius and as a result Felix was made procurator of Judea. He ruled with a heavy hand. Lumby writes: "The character of Felix, as gathered both from Roman and Jewish historians, is that of a mean, profligate and cruel ruler, and even the troublous times in which he lived are not sufficient to excuse the severity of his conduct."[431] The only grain of truth in what Tertullus said was the reference to **great quietness**. Felix did suppress bands of robbers in Judea. But even in this he went to excess. Knowling comments: "His severity and cruelty was so great that he only added fuel to the flame of outrage and sedition, Jos., *Ant.*, xx., 8, 6 *B.J.*, ii., 13, 6, whilst he did not hesitate to employ the Sicarii to get rid of Jonathan the high priest who urged him to be more worthy of his office."[432] Schuerer goes so far as to say: "This man's term of office constitutes probably the turning-point in the drama which had opened with A.D. 44 and reached its close in the bloody conflicts of A.D. 70."[433] During the administrations of other procurators there had been sporadic uprisings against Rome. But "under Felix rebellion became permanent."[434]

Very worthy deeds (2) is one word in Greek. It literally means "reforms." The phrase is properly rendered "reforms are being carried out" (NASB).

The language here is in keeping with the customs of that day. **That I be not further tedious unto thee** (4) is better rendered "not to take up too much of your time" (NEB). Of **clemency**—"gentleness, graciousness"[435]—Lake and Cadbury say: "The word *epieikeia* is very frequent in the papyri in just such complimentary expressions in the appeals to officials."[436] **A few words** is an adverb meaning "briefly."

Then came the first accusation: **We have found this man a pestilent fellow** (5). The last expression is one word in Greek; literally, "pestilence." When used of a person it means "a pest."[437]

The second accusation was that Paul was **a mover of sedition** —"one who is stirring up insurrection"—**among all the Jews**

[431]*Op. cit.*, p. 402.
[432]EGT, II, 477.
[433]*Op. cit.*, I, ii, 174.
[434]*Ibid.*, p. 175.
[435]Arndt and Gingrich, *op. cit.*, p. 292.
[436]*Beginnings*, IV, 298.
[437]Abbott-Smith, *op. cit.*, p. 272.

throughout the world (*oikoumene,* the inhabited earth). That is exactly what the apostle was not doing. Instead of agitating people to revolt against the Roman government—which is the implication of this false charge—he was teaching that Christians should be in subjection to governmental authority (cf. Rom. 13:1-7).

The third accusation was that Paul was **a ringleader of the sect of the Nazarenes.** The word for **ringleader,** *protostates* (only here in NT) is used "properly, of soldiers, *one who stands first, one in the front rank* (Thucydides, Xenophon); hence, metaphorically, a leader."[438] **Sect** is *hairesis,* from which comes "heresy." But in the New Testament, as in Josephus, it means a sect or party. It is used of the Pharisees (15:5) and the Sadducees (5:17). The Jews considered Christianity to be just another sect within Judaism, but a dangerous one.

This is the only place in the New Testament where **the Nazarenes** is used as a designation for Christians. Elsewhere it occurs in the singular, mostly in the phrase "Jesus of Nazareth" (lit., "Jesus the Nazarene"). Probably **Nazarenes** here means simply "followers of the Nazarene." In a special note on "Names for Christians and Christianity in Acts," Cadbury writes: "The context of Acts allows us to suppose that it was a term of reproach."[439] In agreement with this Knowling says: " 'The disciple is not above his Master,' and the term is applied as a term of contempt to the followers of Jesus, as it had been to Jesus Himself."[440] Other names used for Christians in Acts are disciples, brothers, saints, believers, Christians, the church, the fellowship (*koinonia*), and those of "the Way."

The fourth accusation was that Paul **had gone about**—literally, "tried" or "attempted"—**to profane the temple** (6). It is interesting to note that the Jews did not charge him with actually having done it, but with attempting it. Previously the Jews from the province of Asia had accused the apostle of having brought into the Temple a Gentile from Ephesus named Trophimus (21:28-29). But this false charge was based on the ridiculous reasoning that, since they had seen Trophimus with Paul on one of the city streets and since they now saw Paul in the Temple, therefore he must have brought this Gentile into the

[438]*Ibid.,* p. 392.
[439]*Beginnings,* V, 386.
[440]EGT, II, 478.

sacred enclosure—a good example of drawing a wrong conclusion from two right premises. But apparently the Jewish leaders recognized that there was no sound evidence to support such a charge, and so they modified it before the court.

It must be realized that the matter of a Gentile going beyond the so-called Court of the Gentiles (see Chart *A*) was an extremely serious one. Ordinarily the Jews were not allowed by the Romans to put any man to death. "But the Jewish law, that no Gentile should be allowed to enter the inner court of the temple, was recognized by the Roman authorities, and anyone who transgressed it was punished with death, even if he were a Roman citizen."[441] So Paul was not exempt. But if the accusation of 21:28 were true, which it was not, it would be Trophimus, not Paul, who should be put to death.

As already noted (see comments on 1), the last clause of 6, all of 7, and the first clause of 8 are omitted in most of the best Greek MSS. Macgregor writes: "It must, however, be admitted that the longer Western reading improves the sense, and it is defended by many scholars as genuine."[442] No competent scholar would assert dogmatically either that this passage does or that it does not belong in the New Testament. But the preponderance of evidence is against it.

Tertullus was confident that when Felix examined Paul— **whom** (8) is singular in the Greek—he would find the accusations lodged against him to be true. **The Jews also assented** (9) —literally, "joined in the attack"—**saying**—literally, "affirming" —**that these things were so.** It looked as though a strong case had been made against Paul.

b. Presentation of the Defense (24:10-21). The prosecuting attorney having presented his case, opportunity was now given for the defense to answer. Paul had no lawyer, so he pleaded his own case.

In contrast to the fulsome flattery of Tertullus, Paul made a courteous but restrained introduction. He was sincerely thankful that he was being tried before an official who had **been of many years a judge unto this nation** (10), and so would be familiar with Jewish customs. Josephus indicates that Felix succeeded Cumanus as governor in A.D. 52.[443] But Tacitus says that "Galilee

---

[441]Schuerer, *op. cit.*, I, ii, 74. See also Josephus, *War* VI. 2. 4.
[442]IB, IX, 309.
[443]*War* II. 12. 8; *Ant.* XX. 7. 1.

was governed by Cumanus, Samaria by Felix."[444] Bruce comments: "We may infer, by comparing the two accounts, that Cumanus was procurator of Judaea from 48 to 52, while Felix occupied a subordinate post in Samaria, and that when Cumanus was disgraced in 52, Felix was promoted to procuratorship of the whole province, an unprecedented honour for a freedman."[445] Since Paul's trial took place in 56 (or possibly 57), Felix had been living in Palestine for eight or nine years. The apostle later (c. 25) found himself at a disadvantage before Festus, who had just come fresh from Rome and was unacquainted with Jewish ways.

Answer for myself (*apologeomai*) is literally "make my defense." It is a technical judicial term.

Because that thou mayest understand (11) means, "As you may ascertain" (RSV). Felix could "easily verify the fact" (Phillips) that only twelve days had passed since Paul went up to Jerusalem to worship. That would mean that he had spent only about a week in Jerusalem (see comments on 1). The significance of this chronological reference is thus explained by Knowling: "The shortness of the time would enable Felix to gain accurate knowledge of the events which had transpired, and the Apostle may also imply that the time was too short for exciting a multitude to sedition."[446] Lumby reckons the **twelve days** as follows: "the day of St. Paul's arrival, the interview with James on the second day, five days may be given to the separate life in the Temple during the vow, then the hearing before the council, next day the conspiracy, the tenth day St. Paul reached Caesarea, and on the thirteenth day (which leaves five days, xxiv. 1, as Jews would reckon from the conspiracy to the hearing in Caesarea) St. Paul is before Felix."[447]

Paul followed this with a flat denial of the charge that he was "a mover of sedition" (cf. 5). Verse 12 is worded awkwardly. Much more clear and correct is the reading in RSV—"and they did not find me disputing with any one or stirring up a crowd, either in the temple or in the synagogues, or in the city." It was the antagonistic Jews who had stirred up a crowd (cf. 21:27).

[444]*Annals,* XII, 54 (*op. cit.,* p. 122).
[445]*Acts,* p. 416.
[446]EGT, II, 481.
[447]*Op. cit.,* p. 410.

The prisoner challenged his accusers to **prove** their charges against him (13).

One thing Paul would confess: **After the way which they call heresy (14)**—"a sect" (ASV); see the same word in 5—**so worship I the God of my fathers, believing all things which are written in the law and in the prophets**—literally, "all the things which are according to the law and which have been written in the prophets." The point Paul is making is that it is he, not his Jewish accusers, who has stayed true to the Hebrew Scriptures. As Maclaren says, "He hints that they did not believe in either law or prophets, else they would have been Nazarenes too."[448] Furthermore he held to the hope of the **resurrection of the dead, both of the just and unjust (15)**. This was a belief which he shared with the Pharisees, though they were clearer and stronger on the resurrection of the righteous than on the resurrection of the unrighteous.

Then Paul made a mighty affirmation: **Herein do I exercise myself, to have always a conscience void of offence toward God, and toward men (16)**. Alexander writes: "*I exercise (myself)*, a verb originally denoting any kind of hard work; then specially applied to athletic strife or training; and then to moral discipline, especially that of the severest kind."[449] He adds: "It here denotes, not only constant or habitual practice, but methodical and systematic effort."[450]

The Greeks were perhaps the first to develop a concept of **conscience.** The English word comes from the Latin *con* (*cum*), meaning "with," and *scio*, "know." Hence it means "knowing with"—"properly 'co-knowledge,' a second reflective consciousness which a man has alongside his original consciousness of an act."[451] The Greek word *syneidesis* has exactly the same meaning as the Latin *conscientia*—"co-knowledge." It first meant "consciousness." Thornton-Duesbery maintains that the modern idea of a moral conscience is not found in classical Greek philosophy

[448] Alexander Maclaren, *Expositions of Holy Scripture: The Acts* (Grand Rapids: Wm. B. Eerdmans Publishing Co., 1944 [reprint]), II, 283.

[449] *Op. cit.*, p. 827.

[450] *Ibid.*

[451] J. P. Thornton-Duesbery, "Conscience," *A Theological Word Book of the Bible*, ed. Alan Richardson (London: SCM Press, 1950), p. 52.

but appeared "where Jew and Greek met and exchanged ideas in the last three centuries B.C."[452]

On **void of offence** Alexander makes this helpful comment: "In Greek a single word, suggestive of two ideas, *unoffended* and *unoffending,* i.e. a conscience neither wounded by transgression nor allowing me to be the means of tempting others."[453] Paul sought to avoid either taking or giving offense. It is of interest to note that, besides its use here in Paul's speech before Felix, this adjective is found elsewhere in the New Testament only in Paul's Epistles (I Cor. 10:32; Phil. 1:10).

In the Greek text **always** comes at the very close. Knowling says that it is "emphatic here at the end of the sentence, implying that the Apostle's whole aim in life should free him from the suspicion of such charges as had been brought against him."[454] Furthermore, in the Greek **always** is a phrase, "through all." It means not only "at all times"—the modern sense—but "in all ways"; literally, "through everything." Paul is again insisting (cf. 23:1) that he was and always had been a conscientious and consistent Jew.

The next point in the apostle's defense was: **Now after many years I came to bring alms to my nation, and offerings** (17). He had not been in Jerusalem for four or five years—assuming that "the church" (18:22) means the church in Jerusalem, as 18:21 definitely implies. And when he did finally return, it was not for selfish reasons or with malicious motives. He had come **to bring alms to my nation**—the Christian Jews at Jerusalem. This is the only place in Acts where specific reference is made to this offering which Paul had gathered from the Gentile churches of Achaia, Macedonia, Asia, and Galatia (Rom. 15:25-26; I Cor. 16:1-4; II Cor. 8:1-4). Bruce expresses clearly the apostle's reason for doing this. He writes: "Paul took it very seriously; not only was it in his eyes a requital in some measure of the spiritual debt owed by the Gentile churches to those from whom the Gospel first proceeded, but a means of conciliating the Judaistic extremists in the Jerusalem church, and of thus welding Jews and Gentiles in the Church into one body, by making each section feel dependent on, and grateful to, the other."[455]

[452]*Ibid.*
[453]*Op. cit.,* p. 827.
[454]EGT, II, 484.
[455]*Acts,* p. 425.

Of **offerings** Lumby says: "These were the sacrifices connected with the vow which he had undertaken. They must be offered in the Temple."[456]

The fact that in the Greek **alms** comes early in the verse, while **offerings** comes at the end, supports this interpretation that the two do not refer to the same thing. This is brought out well in the literal translations in KJV and ASV, but glossed over too smoothly in RSV. The correct thought is given in NEB, "After an absence of several years I came to bring charitable gifts to my nation and to offer sacrifices."

Paul continued: **Whereupon** (18)—the Greek suggests that it was while he was offering his sacrifices (cf. Phillips, "It was in the middle of these duties")—**certain Jews from Asia found me purified**—perfect participle of *hagnizo*, "ceremonially purified"—**in the temple, neither with multitude, nor with tumult**—"not polluting it by my own presence, and neither gathering a crowd nor raising a stir."[457] Maclaren says: "They called him a 'Nazarene'; he was in the Temple as a 'Nazarite.' Was it likely that, being there on such an errand, he should have profaned it?"[458]

In the Greek text the phrase **certain Jews from Asia** occurs at the beginning of 19, not 18 (cf. Phillips, "There was no mob and there was no disturbance until these Jews from Asia came"). It was the Jews who excited a tumult, not Paul. A dash (—) following **Asia** (ASV and RSV) represents the force of the Greek. Lumby finds the implication of this to be: "Of these Asiatic Jews St. Paul was now about to speak, but he checks himself and does not say any word against them, only that they ought to have been here to explain the offence for which he had been assailed."[459] **Who ought to have been here before thee, and object, if they had ought against me** (19). This was one of the strongest legal points that Paul made in his trial before Felix. Why had not the prosecution produced its star witnesses to prove its case? Was this not a tacit confession that the accusations were unfounded?

---

[456]*Op. cit.*, p. 142.

[457]David Brown, "Acts-Romans," *A Commentary Critical, Experimental and Practical on the Old and New Testaments,* by Robert Jamieson, A. R. Fausset, and David Brown (Grand Rapids: Wm. B. Eerdmans Publishing Co., 1948 [reprint]), VI, 167.

[458]*Op. cit.*, p. 284.

[459]*Op. cit.*, p. 412.

Then the apostle challenged the Jews who were there to mention one single crime of which they had found him guilty when he **stood before the council** (20), **except it be for this one voice, that I cried standing among them, Touching the resurrection of the dead I am called in question by you this day** (21). If he were really guilty, why had not the Sanhedrin condemned him? Why had Tertullus and the Sadducean accusers not told Felix what actually happened in that meeting of the Sanhedrin? As Maclaren notes, "The Pharisees in the Council had acquitted him when they heard his profession of faith in a resurrection. That was his real crime, not treason against Rome or profanation of the Temple."[460]

It has sometimes been held that in this verse Paul confessed that he made a mistake in saying what he did to the Sanhedrin. For instance, Farrar writes: "In the remark of St. Paul before the tribunal of Felix I seem to see—though none have noticed it —a certain sense of compunction for the method in which he had extricated himself from a pressing danger."[461] Numbers of writers have followed Farrar's suggestion. But Lake and Cadbury declare: "The meaning is that if the Jews speak the truth they must admit that they had no case against him except theological difference, which in the eyes of Felix would be none at all."[462] Bruce agrees with this when he writes: "He does not blame himself . . . he simply insists that the only valid charge that can be brought against him is a theological one."[463] This was what Lysias had said in his letter (23:29).

Pauls' defense before Felix is a model for Christians to follow today when falsely accused or otherwise persecuted by the world. He was (1) Fair, 10; (2) Factual, 11; (3) Firm, 12; (4) Forceful, 13; (5) Affirmative, 14-15.

c. *Procrastinating Judge* (24:22-27). Felix,[464] "having a rather accurate knowledge of the Way" (RSV), **deferred them** (22). Arndt and Gingrich note that this verb is a technical legal term, meaning to "adjourn" a trial.[465] Felix stated that when Lysias

---

[460]*Op. cit.*, II, 285.

[461]F. W. Farrar, *The Life and Work of St. Paul* (New York: E. P. Dutton Co., 1896), p. 543.

[462]*Beginnings*, IV, 304.

[463]*Acts*, p. 426.

[464]The oldest MSS omit **heard these things.**

[465]*Op. cit.*, p. 50.

came down from Jerusalem the case would be resumed. But Maclaren calls attention to the fact that Lysias had said nothing about coming down, and comments about the governor's procrastination: "Prompt carrying out of all plain duty is the only safety. The indulgence given to Paul, in his light confinement, only showed how clearly Felix knew himself to be doing wrong, but small alleviations do not patch up a great injustice."[466]

The procurator turned his prisoner over to the care of a centurion, with orders that he should **let him have liberty (23) —** *anesin,* "some freedom"[467]—**and that he should forbid none of his acquaintance to minister or come unto him.** Among those who would minister to Paul's needs, making him as comfortable as possible, would be Philip the evangelist and his four prophesying daughters (21:8). It also may be taken as certain that Luke frequently visited his cherished friend, and doubtless acted as his personal physician.

After some days **Felix came with his wife Drusilla . . . a Jewess (24).** There is a story behind this simple reference. Felix married three times, into three royal families. Drusilla was the daughter of Herod Agrippa I (12:1) and the sister of Herod Agrippa II (25:13). When she was sixteen years of age—some say fourteen—she was married to the king of Emesa. Schuerer thus describes what happened then: "Soon after her marriage Felix saw the beautiful queen, became inflamed with passion, and determined to possess her. By the help of a magician of Cyprus called Simon, he prevailed on her to marry him."[468]

Probably to satisfy the curiosity of his Jewish wife, Felix with Drusilla **sent for Paul, and heard him concerning the faith in Christ.** The oldest Greek MSS add "Jesus" after **Christ.** Lumby points out the significance of this: "What St. Paul would urge was not only a belief in the Christ, for whose coming all Jews were looking, but a belief that Jesus of Nazareth was the Messiah whom they had so long expected."[469]

[466]*Op. cit.,* II, 285.

[467]Arndt and Gingrich, *op. cit.,* p. 64. In the article on this word in the *Theological Dictionary of the New Testament,* edited by G. Kittel and translated by G. W. Bromiley (Grand Rapids: Wm. B. Eerdmans Publishing Co., 1964), Bultmann writes: "*Anesis* in the strict sense occurs in Ac. 24:23 as 'mitigation,' i.e., of imprisonment . . . Elsewhere it is found only in the metaphorical sense of 'refreshment' or 'rest'" (I, 367).

[468]*Op. cit.,* I, ii, 176-77.

[469]*Op. cit.,* p. 414.

Paul **reasoned of righteousness** (25)—righteous principles and practices in daily living—**temperance**—"self-control," especially continence from sensual pleasures—**and judgment**—literally, "the judgment"—**to come.** As the apostle talked, Felix "became alarmed" (Phillips) and said to Paul: **Go thy way for this time; when I have a convenient season, I will call for thee.**

It has often been said that this **convenient season**—one word in Greek; literally, "time" or "season"—never came. But this is contradicted by the statement that **he sent for him the oftener, and communed with him** (26). Paul had many other opportunities to speak to Felix about moral and spiritual matters. But it is doubtless true that Felix failed to repent of his wickedness.

The description of Felix in v. 25 underscores the thought of "Procrastination, the Thief of Souls": (1) He was faithfully warned; (2) He trembled with conviction; (3) He put off his salvation.

The main reason Felix kept Paul in prison was that **he hoped also that money should have been given him of Paul.** So the apostle was unjustly retained in custody for **two years** (27), until **Porcius Festus came into Felix' room,** i.e., "Felix was succeeded by Porcius Festus" (NASB). Even then, **Felix, willing to shew the Jews a pleasure**—literally to lay down or deposit a favour with the Jews as a deposit for which a due return might be expected"[470]—**left Paul bound.** That Roman governors sometimes took bribes for the release of prisoners is evidenced by Josephus. He tells how Albinus, the successor of Festus, "permitted the relations of such as were in prison for robbery . . . to redeem them for money; and nobody remained in the prisons as a malefactor but he who gave him nothing."[471]

Felix was evidently motivated by two desires: to secure a bribe from Paul, and to gain favor with the Jews. But he failed in both purposes. A delegation of Jews filed accusations against Felix before the emperor at Rome. So he gained nothing by his shocking miscarriage of justice in handling Paul's case.

Porcius Festus was evidently a better character than his predecessor, although not much is known about him. In fact, Knowling affirms: "We know nothing of him except from the N.T. and Josephus."[472] Schuerer describes him as "a man who,

[470]Knowling, EGT, II, 490.
[471]*War* II. 14. 1.
[472]EGT, II, 489.

though disposed to act righteously, found himself utterly unable to undo the mischief wrought by the misdeeds of his predecessor."[473]

2. *Paul Before Festus* (25:1-22)

Paul was rightfully the responsibility of Felix. But that governor had failed to discharge his obligation, and so Festus was left with a prisoner whose fate he must decide.

a. Accusation Against Paul (25:1-5). **When Festus was come into the province** could be taken as meaning either "when Festus had entered upon his office as governor" (cf. NEB) or "when Festus had entered his province" which he was to govern. "But the point is of only linguistic importance, as in this case there is no real difference between the office of Festus and the district in which he held office. When he entered on one he also entered the other."[474]

The question as to exactly when Festus became procurator of Judea is still being debated. Older writers commonly placed it at A.D. 60. Kirsopp Lake[475] went to the other extreme, as did also Harnack,[476] in placing the beginning of Festus' administration in A.D. 56 (Lake would even allow 55). A date midway between these opposing views is probably best. In his famous article on "Chronology of the NT" in Hastings' *Dictionary of the Bible,* C. H. Turner holds to a date of A.D. 58, making Paul arrive in Rome in the spring of A.D. 59.[477] Bruce suggests "58 or 59" as the time when Festus became procurator.[478] G. B. Caird, in his article on "Chronology of the NT" in *The Interpreter's Dictionary of the Bible,* prefers A.D. 59.[479] But A.D. 58 seems to us most reasonable.

According to the Jewish way of reckoning, **after three days he ascended from Caesarea to Jerusalem** could mean that he arrived in Caesarea one day, spent the next day there, and then went up the hills to Jerusalem on the third day (see map 1). The point is that he lost no time in paying a visit to the Jewish capital after he arrived at the Roman headquarters in Caesarea.

[473]*Op. cit.,* I, ii, 184.
[474]*Beginnings,* IV, 306.
[475]*Ibid.,* V, 471.
[476]*Acts of the Apostles,* p. 7, n. 1.
[477]HDB, I, 425.
[478]*Acts,* pp. 428-29.
[479]IDB, I, 605.

The high priest and the chief of the Jews informed—for the meaning of this verb see the notes on 24:1—**him against Paul** (2). This was the main thing they had on their minds. They **besought him, and desired favour against him, that he would send for him to Jerusalem** (2-3)—literally, "they were beseeching him, asking [as] a favor against him that he would summon him to Jerusalem." The use of the imperfect, "were beseeching," suggests that they were urgent and persistent. The NASB reads: "They were urging him, requesting a concession against Paul."

But they were **laying wait in the way to kill him;** literally, "making an ambush to kill him on the way." It is probable that the forty original conspirators, having been previously robbed of their prey, were determined to get him this time.

Fortunately for Paul, Festus refused the request. He stated categorically that the prisoner "was being kept" (lit.) in Caesarea, to which he planned soon to return (4). He added: **Let them therefore . . . which among you are able, go down with me** (5). This gives the impression that the elders of the Jews who were able to make the trip should go with him. But this is not what the Greek means. It is rather "those empowered among you,"[480] or "the influential men" (NASB). Josephus uses the term to designate "the principal men" of the Jews.[481] These could accuse Paul, if there was **any wickedness**—literally, something "out of place" or "improper"—**in him.**

b. Arraignment of Paul (25:6-12). Festus stayed in Jerusalem **more than ten days** (6). But the best Greek text says: "not more than eight or ten days," which makes much better sense. The day after he arrived in Caesarea he sat down **on the judgment seat**—"took his seat" translates the aorist here more accurately than **sitting**—and ordered **Paul to be brought** before him.

Concerning the significance of **the judgment seat,** Schuerer writes: "The judge's sitting upon the *sella* was a necessary formality, without which the decision would have no legal effect."[482]

---

[480]Lenski, *op. cit.,* p. 990: "the duly empowered representatives of the Sanhedrin."

[481]*War* I. 12. 5.

[482]*Op. cit.,* I, ii, 15, n. 8.

When the prisoner was brought in, the Jews from Jerusalem **stood round about** (7)—the best Greek text adds "him," making the scene more vivid—**and laid many and grievous**—literally, "weighty"—**complaints**—"charges"—**against Paul, which they could not prove.** Meanwhile Paul **answered for himself** (8)— literally, "was defending himself"—with the straightforward assertion: **Neither against the law of the Jews, neither against the temple, nor yet against Caesar, have I offended any thing at all** —literally, "did I commit any sin." He had not been guilty of breaking the laws of either the Jews or the Romans. Therefore there was no true charge against him. The case should have been dismissed.

But **Festus** was **willing to do the Jews a pleasure** (9). This expression is almost exactly the same in the Greek as that used of Felix, "willing to shew the Jews a pleasure" (24:27). These Roman governors were primarily politicians concerned with their own interests. So Festus asked the prisoner if he would be willing to go up to Jerusalem for a trial there.

Paul had had enough of Jewish prevarication and Roman procrastination. He had one way of escape left open to him, and he took it. He did not intend to let Festus throw him to the wolves who were waiting to devour him. So he stood firmly on his rights as a Roman citizen. It would be interesting to know how the governor, acting as judge, felt when his prisoner firmly, and perhaps sternly, declared: **I stand at Caesar's judgment seat**— literally, "I am standing [emphatic in the Gk.] before the judgment seat of Caesar." "Paul means to say that he is a Roman citizen before a Roman tribunal."[483] This is **where I ought to be judged,** not at Jerusalem. **To the Jews have I done no wrong, as thou very well knowest** (10). Lenski writes: "Festus has mistaken his man. Here is a man who looks him squarely in the eye and is not afraid of his unjust judge."[484] Did the governor wince? If not, he should have. He knew that Caesarea was the proper place to try Paul's case. And he also knew fully (*epiginosko*) that his prisoner was innocent. The apostle reminded him bluntly of these things. Again Lenski comments: "Festus had to take these rebukes in open court. One wonders how the Jews eyed

[483]Robertson, *Word Pictures*, III, 430.

[484]*Op. cit.*, p. 966.

him and took his measure when he heard these plain facts spoken by Paul."[485]

The apostle was not afraid of death. If guilty of any capital crime, **I refuse not to die** (11). But if all the accusations are false, **no man may deliver me unto them.** How those words must have stung Festus! In them Paul revealed that he knew what the governor's purpose was. Festus was fast becoming ready to give in to the Jews' demand. For Paul that meant almost certain death. But **no man,** not even the Roman procurator, could deliver this Roman citizen over to the Jewish mob. Paul stood his ground, without mincing words.

He closed his challenge with the declaration: **I appeal unto Caesar.** Schuerer says: "In the earlier days of the empire, it would seem that a Roman citizen accused of an offence constituting a capital charge had the important privilege of appealing to the emperor . . . at the beginning of the proceedings [or at] any subsequent state of the trial, claiming that the investigation be carried on at Rome and the judgment pronounced by the emperor himself."[486]

Festus conferred with the council (12)—not *synedrion*, Sanhedrin, but *symboulion*. Its first meaning is "counsel" and then "council." Bruce writes: "These were the governor's assessors, of whose advice he might avail himself, though the decision lay in his hands alone."[487] After talking with them, Festus turned back to Paul and said: **Hast thou appealed unto Caesar? unto Caesar shalt thou go.** Bruce comments: "If we understand Paul's appeal in the usual way, as an appeal to the Emperor in person, we may conclude that it was made not so much for the sake of his personal safety, as from a desire to win recognition for the churches in the Empire as practising a *religio licita* distinct from Judaism."[488]

c. *Appeal to Agrippa* (25:13-22). "After some days had passed" (lit. Gk.), **king Agrippa and Bernice came unto Caesarea to salute Festus** (13); i.e., "pay their regards" to him. This **Agrippa** was Herod Agrippa II, son of Herod Agrippa I (12:1),

[485]*Ibid.,* p. 997.
[486]*Op. cit.,* II, ii. 59.
[487]*Acts,* p. 432.
[488]*Ibid.,* p. 433.

545

who was grandson of Herod the Great (Matt. 2:1). He was the brother of **Bernice,** and also of Drusilla (24:24).

Herod Agrippa II was only seventeen years old when his father died in A.D. 44. Because of this he was not given his father's kingdom, but stayed on in Rome as a favorite with the emperor Claudius. He finally (A.D. 50) received the small kingdom of Chalcis, which he later exchanged for a larger territory.

His sister **Bernice** had been married to her uncle, the king of Chalcis. When he died in A.D. 48 she went to live with her brother, Agrippa. Schuerer says that she "soon had the weak man completely caught in the meshes of her net, so that regarding her, the mother of two children, the vilest stories became current. When the scandal became public, Bernice, in order to cut away occasion for all evil reports, resolved to marry Polemon of Cilicia."[489] This marriage did not last long, and she was soon back at her brother's house, where she "seems to have resumed her old relations with him. At least this somewhat later came to be the common talk of Rome."[490]

The emperor Claudius had given to Herod Agrippa II the right to appoint the Jewish high priests and to supervise the Temple. So Festus was particularly happy to see him at this time. The first trial in his new domain had ended in an embarrassing way for the governor, with the prisoner appealing from him to Caesar. As Rackham says, "The arrival of Agrippa was a godsend for Festus."[491] On the one hand Agrippa was "fully conversant with Jewish customs and theology" and on the other he was "thoroughly Roman in tastes and sympathies."[492]

So after **many days** (14) of feasting, Festus mentioned Paul's case to the king. The Jews had wanted the governor at once to give a **judgment**—strong word meaning "condemnation" (only here in the NT)—**against him** (15).

Verse 16 expresses well the high principles of Roman justice, which have made it the main foundation of modern jurisprudence. But unfortunately the best of systems break down because of the frailty of the human factor. The New Testament gives eloquent testimony to the fact that Roman justice often failed and became a farce. "Pilate 'made a present of' Jesus to the Jews:

[489]*Op. cit.,* II, ii, 195.
[490]*Ibid.,* pp. 195-96.
[491]*Op. cit.,* p. 456.
[492]*Ibid.*

Felix expected a bribe from St. Paul and left him in prison in order to curry favour with the Jews: Festus himself, though convinced of the apostle's innocence, kept him in prison, also to please the Jews—a motive which he naturally suppresses in the account he gives Agrippa."[493]

Deliver (16) is literally "bestow freely," or "make a present" (see paragraph above). **To die** is not in the oldest MSS. **Licence,** literally "place," is better translated "opportunity" (ASV). **Crime laid against him** is one word in Greek, meaning "accusation" or "charge." The entire last clause literally reads "receive a place of defense (*apologia*) concerning the accusation."

The optative mood is rare in the New Testament and completely missing in modern Greek, though fairly common in the classics. But it occurs twice in 16 and once in 20. This would be in keeping with the culture and education of the governor.

Festus related to Agrippa how he had promptly—**without any delay on the morrow** (cf. 6)—conducted Paul's trial (17). But instead of the accusations which Festus had expected to hear in a Roman court (18), the accusers brought up **certain questions against him of their own superstition** (19)—*deisidaimonias*. This noun is related to the adjective translated "too superstitious" in 17:22 (see comments there). Originally it meant "fear of the gods." Liddell and Scott give this meaning first, and then "superstition."[494] The best New Testament Greek lexicons (Thayer, Abbott-Smith, Arndt and Gingrich) give three senses: (*a*) a good sense, "fear of the gods," or "piety"; (*b*) a bad sense, "superstition"; and (*c*) an objective sense, "religion"—with literary examples of all these usages. Cremer gives only this definition: "*dread of the gods,* usually in a condemnatory or contemptuous sense=*superstition.*"[495] But Moulton and Milligan write: "It is in this general sense of 'religion,' without any pronouncement as to whether it was right or wrong, that the word is to be understood."[496] In line with this, but somewhat more specific, is Thayer's conclusion: "Festus in the presence of Agrippa the Jewish king employs the word ambiguously and cautiously, in Acts xxv. 19, of the Jewish religion, viz. so as to

[493]*Ibid.,* p. 460.
[494]*Op. cit.,* I, 375.
[495]*Op. cit.,* p. 172.
[496]VGT, p. 139.

leave his own judgment concerning its truth in suspense."[497] That seems to be a sensible explanation of the matter.

Festus said that there were questions also about **one Jesus, which was dead, whom Paul affirmed to be alive.** Rackham observes that these words "exactly represent the idea which a Roman would have about the Lord."[498] The Greeks (and Romans) scoffed at the thought of a resurrection (cf. 17:32). If Christ had died, only a fool would say that He was alive.

"Being at a loss how to investigate these questions" (20, RSV), Festus had asked Paul if he was willing to go up to Jerusalem and be tried there. But the prisoner **appealed to be reserved** (21)—"kept in custody"—**unto the hearing**—Greek *diagnosis*, "decision," a law term—**of Augustus** ("most reverend," a title adopted by Octavius Caesar and copied by his successors). The governor had then commanded him to be kept in custody until he could "send him up" (so best Gk. text) **to Caesar**—another title for the emperor (cf. Czar, Kaiser).

In response to this recital of Festus, Agrippa said, **I would also hear the man myself** (22). The expression **I would** is not an adequate translation. Burton writes: "In Acts 25:22 the use of the Imperfect *eboulomen* rather than a Present softens the request for politeness' sake, and may well be rendered *I should like*."[499] Festus answered that a hearing would be held the next day.

3. Paul Before Agrippa (25:23—26:32)

Many commentators call attention to the dramatic picture drawn here by the author. For instance, Winn writes: "This is the last major speech in Acts, and Luke intends it to be the climax. He carefully paints the scene."[500] Rackham observes: "It is one of the most finished passages in the Acts, adorned with rare words [thirteen found only here in NT] and with an elaboration of style, not to say grandiloquence."[501]

a. Festus' Introduction (25:23-27). **Agrippa** and **Bernice** came **with great pomp** (23). The Greek word is *phantasia*,

[497]*Op. cit.*, p. 127.

[498]*Op. cit.*, p. 460.

[499]Ernest D. Burton, *Syntax of the Moods and Tenses in New Testament Greek* (2nd ed.; Chicago: University Press of Chicago, 1893), p. 16.

[500]*Op. cit.*, p. 125.

[501]*Op. cit.*, p. 462.

which means "show, showy appearance, display, pomp."[502] Bruce comments: *"Fantasia* is still used in Palestinian Arabic for a procession."[503]

The royal couple entered the **place of hearing**—one word in Greek, equivalent to the Latin *auditorium*—**with the chief captains**—there were five of these *chiliarchs* or tribunes (cf. 21:31) stationed at Caesarea, each in charge of a cohort—**and principal men of the city,** most, if not all, of whom would be Gentiles.[504]

The contrast between Agrippa and Paul is vividly pointed up in v. 23. One might speak of "Potentate and Prisoner": (1) Agrippa came, Paul was brought; (2) Agrippa entered with great pomp, Paul entered in chains; (3) Agrippa was accompanied by Bernice, while Paul stood alone. Yet there was another side: (1) Agrippa was a slave to sin, whereas Paul was a free man in Christ; (2) Agrippa was accompanied by a wicked woman, whereas Paul was escorted by his unseen Lord; (3) The contrast will be most acute at the final judgment.

When Paul had been brought in, Festus introduced him to the crowd. Concerning this prisoner **all the multitude of the Jews** (24)—to be taken in an official, political sense as meaning "people"[505]—had **dealt with**—"made petition to"—the governor, **both at Jerusalem** and at Caesarea, **crying that** Paul **ought not to live any longer.** They were desperate for his death.

But when Festus had examined the prisoner, he had found **nothing worthy of death** (25). Paul had appealed to Augustus, and Festus had **determined**—"decided"—to send him to Rome. Alexander comments: "It was because Festus, though convinced of his innocence, instead of giving judgment in his favour, weakly and unreasonably asked him to submit to a new trial, at another and most prejudiced tribunal . . . that Paul found himself compelled to gain deliverance from both by an assertion of his civil rights."[506]

The dilemma in which Festus found himself was that he had **no certain thing to write unto my lord** (26). The title **my lord** was a bold one for the governor to apply to Nero (A.D. 54-68). It

---

[502]Thayer, *op. cit.,* p. 649.
[503]*Acts,* p. 437.
[504]*Ibid.*
[505]Deissmann, *Bible Studies,* p. 232.
[506]*Op. cit.,* p. 865.

had been refused by Augustus and Tiberius, but was accepted by Caligula (37-41).[507] Deissman notes, concerning the use of **lord** (*kyrios*) in the Greek papyri and inscriptions, that in the time of Nero "the number of examples suddenly rushes up tremendously."[508] This is indirect evidence for Luke's accuracy here.

Because Festus was at a total loss as to what to write the emperor, he had brought Paul in for an **examination.** The Greek word is *anakrisis*. Thayer defines it thus: *"an examination;* as a law-term among the Greeks, the preliminary investigation held for the purpose of gathering evidence for the information of the judges . . . this seems to be the sense of the word in Acts xxv.26."[509] Lumby says: "So Festus uses the technical term in its proper sense."[510] On the other hand, Rackham writes: "This preliminary examination was not a legal, but an informal, hearing."[511] That seems to be a correct statement of the case. Apparently Paul could now be tried only before Caesar.

Festus felt the irony of his situation. It was obviously **unreasonable to send a prisoner** (27) without indicating any charges against him. The governor hoped that Agrippa would be able to clarify the issues for him.

b. Paul's Apologia (26:1-23). When Agrippa gave the prisoner permission **to speak for thyself**—literally, "on behalf of"— Paul **stretched forth the hand** in salutation to the king and **answered for himself,** or "made his defense." This is the verb *apologeomai,* related to the noun *apologia.*

(1) *Introduction* (26:2-3). The apostle began, as always, with a courteous introduction. To the king he said: **I think myself happy** (2). The adjective is *makarios,* "blessed" (Matt. 5:3-12). The verb is *hegeomai,* which in classical Greek meant "consider, regard."[512] Moulton says that this usage here "is one of the literary touches characteristic of the speech before Agrippa."[513] It seems clear that Paul had a strong educational

[507]Knowling, EGT, II, 499.

[508]LAE, p. 353.

[509]*Op. cit.,* p. 39.

[510]*Op. cit.,* p. 423.

[511]*Op. cit.,* p. 462.

[512]Blass and Debrunner, *op. cit.,* p. 176 (#341).

[513]James Hope Moulton, *A Grammar of New Testament Greek,* I (3rd ed.; Edinburgh: T. & T. Clark, 1908), 148.

background. The prisoner considered himself fortunate to be able to **answer for myself** (*apologeisthai*, same verb as in previous verse).

Paul was happy especially because Agrippa was **expert in all customs and questions**—"disputes" or "controversies"—**which are among the Jews** (3). This characterization of Agrippa finds documentary support in a statement by Schuerer: "The rabbinical tradition tells of questions pertaining to the law which were put by Agrippa's minister or by the king himself to the famous scribe Rabbi Elieser."[514] Yet Schuerer adds: "Judaism was indeed as little a matter of heart conviction with Agrippa as it had been with his father."[515]

(2) *The issue stated* (26:4-8). The first point which Paul made was that all the Jews knew about his early life **at Jerusalem** (4). They knew, though they were unwilling to acknowledge it, that he had lived as **a Pharisee** according to the **straitest** (strictest) **sect,** or party (see comments on 5:17), in Judaism (5).

Then Paul stated the issue clearly. It was not Temple desecration or insurrection against Rome of which he was guilty. Rather he was being **judged for the hope of the promise made of God unto our fathers** (6). **Instantly serving God** (7) is literally "worshipping with zeal or earnestness." In a general sense the reference here is to the Messianic hope, as indicated by v. 7. But v. 8 suggests that it includes the resurrection. Knowling puts it this way: "A hope not merely of the resurrection of the dead, but of the Messiah's kingdom with which the resurrection was connected, as the context points to the national hope of Israel."[516] Alexander insists on a narrower interpretation. He writes: "The hope described in this verse cannot be that of a general resurrection, which is only partially revealed in the Old Testament, and was not held by all the Jews at this time."[517] He continues: "The only hope answering to the description, as an ancient, national, and still intense one, is the hope of the Messiah, as promised to the Patriarchs, prefigured in the Law, predicted in the Prophets, and still ardently expected by the People."[518] But

---

[514]*Op. cit.*, II, ii, 197.
[515]*Ibid.*
[516]EGT, II, 502.
[517]*Op. cit.*, p. 874.
[518]*Ibid.*

it would seem that v. 8 requires us to include the resurrection of Jesus as proof that He really was the Messiah, not an impostor.

Twelve tribes (7) is one word in the Greek. Knowling comments: "The expression was full of hope, and pointed to a national reunion under the Messiah."[519] Bruce aptly observes: "Paul knows nothing of the fiction of the ten 'lost' tribes."[520] The prisoner expresses his surprise that for the sake of this hope,[521] held by the community of Israel, he should be **accused of the Jews**—literally, "by Jews," of all people!

Verse 8 reads literally: "Why is it judged unbelievable with you if God raises dead people?" In the Greek "if" means "if, as He does." Knowling says that this question should be considered "in connection with the great truth to which the whole speech was meant to lead up, ver. 23, *viz.*, that Jesus, although crucified, had risen again, that He was at this moment a living Person, and by His resurrection had been proved to be the Messiah, the fulfiller of the hope of Israel."[522]

(3) *The zealous Pharisee* (26:9-11). **I** (9) is emphatic in the Greek—literally, "I indeed then." Bruce helpfully brings out the force of this: "Pharisee though I was, and thus in theory a believer in the resurrection of the dead, I yet judged it incredible in this particular case, and thought it my duty to oppose such a heresy."[523]

Paul here describes in more detail than anywhere else his campaign of persecution against the Christians. On the authority of the high priests he imprisoned **many of the saints** (10). **When they were put to death,** as in the case of Stephen, **I gave my voice against them,** or, better, "cast my vote against."[524] The Greek noun literally means "a small, smooth stone" or "pebble," sometimes used as an amulet (see Rev. 2:17). But it was also "used in voting, in juries and elsewhere, a black one for conviction, a white one for acquittal."[525]

The last clause of v. 10 is often taken as indicating that Paul was a member of the Sanhedrin, and so a married man. But Hack-

---

[519]EGT, II, 502.

[520]*Acts*, p. 442.

[521]**Agrippa** is not in the oldest MSS.

[522]EGT, II, 503.

[523]*Acts*, p. 442.

[524]Arndt and Gingrich, *op. cit.*, p. 901.

[525]*Ibid.*

ett notes that the Greek word "signified also opinion, assent, and accompanied various verbs, as *to place* and *to cast down,* as meaning to think, judge, sanction, with a figurative allusion to the act of voting."[526] Bruce writes: "The phrase may be used officially or unofficially . . . and cannot be said to *prove* that Paul was a member of the Sanhedrin."[527] Lenski goes a step further and says: "The record shows so many contacts of Paul with the Sanhedrin that, if he had been one of the members, that fact would undoubtedly have been stated."[528] The moderate statement of Bruce is probably the best that can be made.

Paul went on to say that he had **punished** the Christians **oft in every synagogue, and compelled them to blaspheme** (11). But the imperfect tense here means: "I tried to compel them." Bruce rightly declares: "He does not say that he succeeded in making them blaspheme, as AV implies."[529]

Being exceedingly mad against the followers of Jesus, Saul had **persecuted**—the Greek word also means "pursued" (cf. Phillips, "hounded")—**them even unto strange** (lit., "outside") **cities.** The correct meaning is "foreign cities."

(4) *The converted Christian* (26:12-18). This is the third time that the conversion of Saul has been described (cf. 9:1-9; 22:6-16). That fact alone should prove its importance in the Book of Acts. **Chief priests** (12) means ex-priests and sons of the high priest.

Verse 13 is closely parallel to 22:6, but a bit more vivid. Only here (14) is it stated that Paul's companions, as well as he himself, fell to the ground. There he heard a voice addressing him **in the Hebrew tongue,** which means the Aramaic dialect.

It is hard for thee to kick against the pricks—rather, "the goads"—was a common proverb in classical Greek, but has not been found in Aramaic. The picture is that of a stubborn ox kicking back against the goad and so only hurting itself. The ox goad was a sharp stick, or a pole with a sharp metal end, with which a man would prod his oxen to move forward.

In his valuable book, *The Origin of Paul's Religion,* Machen takes the position that there was no psychological preparation for the dramatic moment of Saul's conversion. Specifically he main-

[526]*Op. cit.,* p. 284.
[527]*Acts,* p. 443.
[528]*Op. cit.,* p. 1033.
[529]*Acts,* p. 443.

tains that the reference here to kicking against the goads does not mean that the young Pharisee was at all aware of his fighting against God or that he entertained any doubts as to the rightness of his actions in persecuting the Christians.[530]

The true picture seems to this writer to have been somewhat different. Saul was kicking against the goads of: (1) a decent human conscience, that must at all times have told him that his cruel treatment of Christians was wrong; (2) the godly lives of the Christians, that could not fail to impress him; (3) the face of Stephen (6:15) and his prayer for the forgiveness of his persecutors (7:54-60). It is reasonable to believe that the haunting memory of this scene hounded him all the way to Damascus.

For further discussion of Saul's conversion see the comments on 9:1-9 and 22:6-16. It is significant that Paul always looked back to this as the great turning point of his life and the source of his authority to speak as one who had been captured by Christ. It was also the source of his unshakable conviction that **Jesus** (15) was really the Messiah, the Son of God.

So set was young Saul in his persuasion that Jesus of Nazareth was an impostor and His followers dangerous heretics that he had pursued relentlessly his persecution of the Christians. He had stifled all questions of conscience and memories of Stephen as being delusions of the devil, who was trying to turn him aside from his God-appointed task of preserving the faith of Judaism, the true religion. It finally took the climactic crisis of a light from heaven and the audible voice of Jesus to show him that he was mistaken. When he was really convinced by the Damascus road experience that Jesus was the Christ, he accepted Him as Saviour and Lord and never wavered from this. He drove on just as vigorously and wholeheartedly in his propagation of Christianity as he formerly had in his persecution of it.

In 13-19 we see clearly indicated some basic experiences of "Christian Conversion." (1) Christ takes the initiative in sending convicting power, 13; (2) There is a consciousness of personal encounter with God, 14; (3) Sincere desire to know God's will brings inner assurance of God's salvation purpose for one's life, 15-18; (4) Obedience to God's known will brings the life of blessing, 19 (A. F. Harper).

[530]J. Gresham Machen, *The Origin of Paul's Religion* (New York: Macmillan Co., 1921), pp. 60-62.

Then came Paul's commission from Christ. He was told, **Rise, and stand upon thy feet** (16). The bright light from heaven had knocked him, blinded, to the ground. But now that he had been humbled and was willing to listen to the voice of the despised Nazarene, he was told to stand up. There is a time to fall on our faces before Christ and receive our commission from Him. Then it is our duty to stand on our feet and carry out the commission. God wants humble, submissive servants who will at the same time be bold and courageous to fulfill His will.

Christ told Paul that he had **appeared** to him for one **purpose**: to make him a **minister**—better, "servant"; literally, "under rower"—**and a witness** (*martyra*). **Delivering** (17) is perhaps best rendered "rescuing." Lake and Cadbury say: "*Exairoumenos* has this meaning everywhere else in Luke's work and usually in the LXX and similar Greek."[531] God promised to rescue His servant **from the people, and from the Gentiles.** How applicable these words were to Paul just now! Again Lake and Cadbury comment: "*Laos* [people] is as idiomatic in the sense of 'the Jews' as *ta ethne* [literally, 'the nations'] is for the Gentiles."[532]

The last clause of 17—**unto whom now I send thee**—may indicate that Paul's mission was particularly to the Gentiles,[533] though Bengel thinks (on the basis of v. 20) that **whom** refers to both Jews and Gentiles.[534] Other commentators agree with him.[535] Lechler even goes so far as to say: "The mission of Paul refers, primarily, to Israel (*ho laos*, ver. 17); the Gentiles are mentioned only in the second place: it is precisely in this manner that Paul likewise expresses himself in his Epistles."[536] This view is supported by such passages as Rom. 1:16, as well as by the apostle's regular practice of preaching first to the Jews in the synagogues wherever he went.

Send is the verb *apostello,* a cognate of the noun *apostolos.* Paul was Christ's apostle to both Jews and Gentiles. His minis-

---

[531]*Beginnings,* IV, 319.

[532]*Ibid.*

[533]Lumby, *op. cit.,* p. 429.

[534]John Albert Bengel, *Gnomon of the New Testament,* trans. Andrew R. Fausset (4th ed.; Edinburgh: T. & T. Clark, 1860), II, 717.

[535]E.g., Lenski (p. 1040), Alexander (p. 880), Knowling (p. 507), Alford (II, 280).

[536]*Op. cit.,* p. 443.

try was: **To open their eyes, and to turn them from darkness to light, and from the power of Satan unto God, that they may receive forgiveness of sins, and inheritance among them which are sanctified by faith that is in me** (18). Bengel observes: "There is in this passage a noble description of the whole process of conversion."[537] But it also includes sanctification.

Verse 18 provides excellent material for a textual sermon: (1) Salvation opens the spiritual eyes of those who have been blinded by sin; (2) Conversion is turning from the darkness of sin to the light of God's presence; (3) Salvation brings one out from under the power (Gk., "authority") of Satan into the freedom which God gives; (4) Forgiveness of sins comes to those who turn from Satan to God; (5) Those who are forgiven may receive an inheritance among the sanctified.

It should be emphasized that sanctification comes by faith in Christ, not by our own works. One does not become sanctified by striving and struggling, but by surrendering to Christ. Therefore it is an instantaneous experience. When one surrenders fully, he is sanctified wholly. John Wesley wrote: "I believe this perfection is always wrought in the soul by a simple act of faith; consequently in an instant"; and added, "But I believe [in] a gradual work, both preceding and following that instant."[538]

Inheritance among them which are sanctified is the same, in English, as in 20:32. But in the Greek a different word is used for **inheritance.** In 20:32 it is *kleronomia,* which properly means an inheritance obtained by lot (i.e., by someone casting lots). But here it is simply *kleros.* This word first meant the "lot" that was cast, and then that which was obtained by casting lots. The distinction between these two Greek words is thus pointed out by Lenski: "An inheritance awaits its possessor, a lot is at once his."[539] Entire sanctification can be the present possession of those who will accept it by faith.

Since the verb *hagiazo* occurs in Acts only here and in 20:32[540]—and the Greek nouns for "holiness" or "sanctification" (*hagiasmos, hagiotes, hagiosyne*) not at all—this would be a good place to discuss the meaning of the verb. It comes from the

[537]*Op. cit.,* p. 717.

[538]John Wesley, *Works* (Grand Rapids: Zondervan Publishing House, n.d.), XI, 446.

[539]*Op. cit.,* p. 1041.

[540]Out of a total of twenty-nine times in the New Testament.

adjective *hagios,* "holy," and so properly means *"to make holy, consecrate, sanctify . . .* 1. *to dedicate, separate, set apart for God . . .* 2. *to purify,* make conformable in character to such dedication."[541]

In his article on *hagiazo* in the monumental *Theological Dictionary of the New Testament,* Procksch says: "The verb *hagiazo* belongs almost exclusively to biblical Greek or Greek influenced by the Bible."[542] He also declares: "Sanctification is not a moral action on the part of man, but a divinely effected state."[543]

Cremer says that *hagiazo* signifies "to place in a relation with God answering to his holiness."[544] He also states: "To sanctify means, to make anything a participator, according to its measure, in God's holiness, in God's purity as revealed in His electing love."[545]

The exact form of **sanctified** in the two passages in Acts is *hegiasmenois* (dative plural of the perfect passive participle). Thayer writes: "In general Christians are called *hegiasmenoi,* as those who, freed from the impurity of wickedness, have been brought near to God by their faith and sanctity, Acts xx. 32; xxvi. 18."[546]

In its broadest sense the term **sanctified** includes all Christians as being set apart to God. But it is also true that the term has a narrower, more specific use as applied to those who have made a full surrender of their wills to God's will, have been crucified with Christ (cf. Rom. 6:6; Gal. 2:20), and have been filled with the Holy Spirit (cf. 15:8-9).

Verse 18 is one of the most significant passages in this part of Acts. Ladd writes: "This verse, which is the summary of Paul's message, is very similar to Col. 1:12-14."[547]

In 26:13-18 we see "God's Purpose for Paul." (1) It was

---

[541] Abbott-Smith, *op. cit.,* pp. 4-5.

[542] *Theological Dictionary of the New Testament,* ed. Gerhard Kittel, trans. and ed. G. W. Bromiley, I (Grand Rapids: Wm. B. Eerdmans Publishing Co., 1964), III.

[543] *Ibid.,* p. 112.

[544] *Op. cit.,* p. 53.

[545] *Ibid.,* p. 54.

[546] *Op. cit.,* p. 6.

[547] George E. Ladd, "The Acts of the Apostles," *Wycliffe Bible Commentary,* ed. Charles F. Pfeiffer and Everett F. Harrison (Chicago: Moody Press, 1962), p. 1173.

active, 16*a*; (2) It was progressive, 16*b*; (3) It was effective, 17-18 (G. B. Williamson).

(5) *The consecrated Christian* (26:19-23). Verse 19 is one of the great declarations of obedient consecration: **I was not** (lit., "I did not become") **disobedient unto the heavenly vision.** In spite of the obvious dangers and hardships that confronted him in carrying out such a commission, Paul never wavered in his faithful obedience to the vision and call that Christ gave him.

The young Saul began his ministry right in the city where (or near which) he received his conversion and call. He preached in **Damascus** (20), mainly to Jews (9:19-22), and then **at Jerusalem,** where he ran into conflict with the Hellenists (9:26-29).

In his speech before Agrippa, Paul says that he also preached **throughout all the coasts**—Greek, "country"—**of Judaea.** There is no specific mention of this in Acts 9, though the statement "then had the churches rest throughout all Judaea . . ." (9:31) might seem to imply it. But the real problem is Gal. 1:22. There he says that when he left Jerusalem for Syria and Cilicia he was "unknown by face unto the churches of Judaea which were in Christ."

How is this seeming contradiction to be resolved? Alexander says of 26:20: "If this is related to the beginning of his ministry, it would be inconsistent with his statement in Gal. 1,22; but he here puts together his whole ministry among the Jews, before proceeding to the other and chief part of his commission, to the nations, i.e. other nations, Gentiles."[548] Hervey points out the fact that Paul would have had opportunity to preach widely in Judea on the so-called "famine visit" (11:27-30) and on his way to the Council of Jerusalem (15:1-3). He adds: "So there is no contradiction whatever between the statement in this verse and that in Gal. i.22."[549]

First to the Jews, and then to the Gentiles, Paul **shewed**— literally, "was announcing" or "declaring"—**that they should repent and turn to God, and do works meet for repentance.** Charles Kingsley Williams translates it this way: "I carried my message, that they should repent and turn to God and live in a manner to match such repentance." These three emphases in

[548]*Op. cit.,* pp. 882-83.
[549]*Op. cit.,* II, 267.

Paul's message could well be used as the three main points of a sermon. For the meaning of **repent** see the comments on Matt. 3:2 (BBC, VI, 42-43). In the Greek **repentance** has the definite article. It means "that repentance," or "such repentance" (Williams). **Meet for** means "befitting" or "worthy of."

It was **for these causes** (21)—telling both Jews and Gentiles that they needed to repent—that the Jews had mobbed Paul in the Temple and tried to kill him. But he had **obtained help of God** (22). The Greek word for **help** suggests the "aid" or "assistance" given by an ally.[550] **God** was Paul's Ally in his campaigns of preaching the gospel. With God on his side, he had been able to **continue**—Greek, "stand"—**unto this day, witnessing both to small and great**—like King Agrippa. He had been **saying none other things than those which the prophets and Moses did say should come.** Paul always insisted that nothing which he said was contrary to what the Jewish Scriptures (our OT) taught, and so the Jews should accept it. His gospel was simply the fulfillment of Old Testament prophecy. **The prophets and Moses**—or, more usually, "Moses and the prophets" (cf. Luke 24:27; John 1:45)—was an expression used by the Jews to signify the entire Old Testament.

An interesting modern parallel to Paul's position here is the case of John Wesley. When accused of preaching some strange, new doctrine, he maintained emphatically that he taught nothing contrary to the Thirty-nine Articles of the Church of England.[551] Upon being challenged by Bishop Gibson of London as to what he meant by perfection, Wesley told him exactly what he preached. The bishop's response was: "Mr. Wesley, if this be all you mean, publish it to all the world."[552]

What did Moses and the prophets say should come? Paul's answer gives the heart of his gospel message: **That Christ should suffer, and that he should be the first that should rise from the dead, and should shew light unto the people**—the Jews (cf. 17)—**and to the Gentiles** (23). Particularly in preaching to the Jews, Paul's main emphasis was that the Old Testament teaches a suffering and resurrected Messiah (cf. 17:3).

c. *Reaction and Response* (26:24-29). To Festus, a Roman, all this talk about the sufferings and resurrection of the Messiah

---

[550]Abbott-Smith, *op. cit.*, p. 171.
[551]Cf. Wesley, *Works*, VIII, 55-56.
[552]*Ibid.*, XI, 374.

seemed to be silly nonsense (cf. 17:32). He suddenly interrupted the speaker. **With a loud voice** he shouted: **Paul, thou
art beside thyself**—"you are raving" (Goodspeed)—**much learning doth make thee mad** (24)—literally, "is turning [you] to
madness." This noun is from the verb translated **thou art beside
thyself.** The meaning is perhaps brought out best in the translation by Charles B. Williams: "You are going crazy, Paul! That
great learning of yours is driving you crazy."

The relation between the two meanings for "mad" in English
shows up in the Greek verb here. *Mainomai* first meant "to rage,
be furious" and then "to rave, be mad."[553] The line between
"raging" and "raving" is sometimes hard to draw.

On this verse Lake and Cadbury comment: "Paul has been
talking to Agrippa as one Jew to another, and naturally the
Roman Festus thought that anyone who had eschatological ex-
pectations must be mad. . . . Many educated persons hold the
same view about eschatology today, but history is against them
and Festus. . . . Moreover it [the eschatological hope] was as
central in the Christianity of Paul as it had been in that of
Jesus."[554]

Courteously but firmly Paul responded: **I am not mad, most
noble Festus; but speak forth the words of truth and soberness**
(25). Then, in a transition from the rude, ignorant Festus to the
well-informed Agrippa, Paul continued: **For the king knoweth
of these things, before whom also I speak freely** (26)—or, "boldly."[555] In other words, "He will listen to me, even if you will
not; he knows what I am talking about"—**for this thing was not
done in a corner,** but out in the open.

Then Paul turned squarely to the one before whom he had
been asked to defend himself. Addressing him simply, but directly, he asked: **King Agrippa, believest thou the prophets?**
(27) When the king hesitated to reply, the prisoner answered for
him: **I know that thou believest.** Probably this means that
Agrippa gave mental assent to the truth of the Holy Scriptures,
since he had some Jewish blood in his veins.

The king's only response was: **Almost thou persuadest me
to be a Christian** (28). This has been the text for hundreds of
sermons, as well as the basis of the well-known invitation hymn

[553]Abbott-Smith, *op. cit.*, p. 275.
[554]*Beginnings,* IV, 321.
[555]Abbott-Smith, *op. cit.*, p. 347.

"Almost Persuaded." But the exact meaning of the words has been the subject of endless discussion. Was Agrippa serious or sarcastic? If we could have heard his tone of voice and seen the look on his face, we probably would have the answer. Failing this, we can only look carefully at the text in the light of its context.

One problem is that the Greek seems a bit ambiguous. Literally it reads: "In a little you are persuading me to make [or, 'to do'] a Christian." After considerable discussion, Alexander concludes: "The idea then is, 'thou persuadest me a little (or in some degree) to become a Christian,' i.e., I begin to feel the force of your persuasive arguments, and if I hear you longer, do not know what the effect may be."[556] Brown gives a similar interpretation.[557]

But this is not the view of the majority of commentators today. Alford states the case correctly when he says: "Most of the ancient commentators . . . take the words as implying some effect on Agrippa's mind, and as spoken in earnest: but this I think is hardly possible, philologically or exegetically."[558] Hackett writes: "Agrippa appears to have been moved by the apostle's earnest manner, but attempts to conceal his emotion under a jest."[559] Lechler says: "It is indeed possible that for a moment a serious impression was made on the king; still, he immediately replies in derisive terms . . ."[560] Lumby comments: " 'With little labour' or 'in a little time' implies that the king despised the attempt which had been made to convince him, and mocked at the language of St. Paul in so readily taking for granted that he was in accord with him."[561] It may well be that Agrippa was embarrassed in the presence of the Gentile notables by Paul's Jewish appeal to him. Maclaren writes: "His ironical words are no confession of being 'almost persuaded,' but a taunt."[562]

Many more similar opinions could be quoted, but these will suffice. Lenski presents somewhat of a mediating position, which may have value. He rejects the translation "almost" as

[556] *Op. cit.*, p. 891.
[557] *Op. cit.*, pp. 175-76.
[558] *Op. cit.*, II, 283.
[559] *Op. cit.*, p. 289.
[560] *Op. cit.*, p. 444.
[561] *Op. cit.*, p. 433.
[562] *Op. cit.*, p. 326.

impossible. Yet he does not think that Agrippa spoke ironically or contemptuously. His conclusion is this: "Agrippa imagines that he sees through Paul's scheme and with an air of lofty superiority that is intended to impress the company lets Paul know that he sees through his plan of operation."[563] In other words, the king was not speaking sarcastically, but he was firmly rejecting the apostle's evangelistic approach.

There is no doubt, of course, about the serious earnestness of Paul's reply (29). **I would to God,** or "I could pray," is "the classical use of the optative with *an* to express a softened assertion, the 'potential' optative."[564] Bruce adds: "The whole sentence is very elegantly expressed."[565] Paul possessed the education and culture for using the best Greek, and would certainly employ it before this type of audience.

Both almost, and altogether may mean " 'with few words or with many,' 'with ease or with difficulty.' "[566] In the Greek text this double phrase is placed before **not only thou, but also all that hear me this day,** and that should be the order in an English version. The correct translation is: "I would to God, that whether in a short or long time [margin, 'with a little or with much'], not only you, but also all who hear me this day, might become such as I am, except for these chains" (NASB, cf. ASV). In connection with this last clause Maclaren asks the pertinent question: "Did Festus wince a little at the mention of these, which ought not to have been on his wrists?"[567]

d. *Paul's Vindication* (26:30-32). Agrippa had no desire to prolong the situation that was becoming too unpleasant for him. So he **rose up** (30). Lenski writes: "Agrippa had felt Paul's touch upon his heart, and from this strange and unexpected power he withdrew. It was his hour of grace, and when he withdrew he left salvation behind him."[568]

The group rose and left in order of rank. First it was **the king,** then **the governor,** then **Bernice,** then the rest. It was a state occasion, and protocol was observed.

---

[563]*Op. cit.,* p. 1057.
[564]Bruce, *Acts,* p. 449.
[565]*Ibid.*
[566]*Ibid.*
[567]*Op. cit.,* II, 327.
[568]*Op. cit.,* p. 1059.

In the consultation that followed, everyone agreed that Paul was innocent of any crime (31). Finally Agrippa gave the verdict of acquittal: **This man might have been set at liberty, if he had not appealed unto Caesar** (32). Paul was fully vindicated. Actually it was Festus who was found guilty, because he had refused to release a prisoner whom he knew to be innocent. Before the bar of his own conscience, as well as before the audience that day, he stood condemned for his crime.

K. Voyage to Rome, 27:1—28:16

The last two chapters of Acts are filled with nautical terms, many of which are not found elsewhere. In his book *Luke the Historian in the Light of Research*,[569] A. T. Robertson devotes a whole chapter to "Nautical Terms in Acts 27." James Smith, a noted Scottish yachtsman and authority on ancient ships, became interested in the subject. He checked carefully Luke's narrative against his own thorough knowledge of the Mediterranean—he spent the winter of 1844-45 on Malta—and wrote a book on Paul's journey. In this he says: "St. Luke, by his accurate use of nautical terms, gives great precision to his language, and expresses by a single word what would otherwise require several."[570]

Foakes-Jackson characterizes this account of Paul's voyage as "among the finest pieces of descriptive writing in the New Testament."[571] Macgregor calls it "much the most dramatic piece of writing in the whole book."[572]

1. Caesarea to Malta (27:1-44)

The party set out from Caesarea with the intention of going directly to Rome. But a severe storm prevented their doing so, and they spent the winter on the island of Malta.

a. Caesarea to Crete (27:1-8). **When it was determined—** better, "decided"—**that we should sail into Italy** brings Luke back into the picture. The last mention of "we" or "us" is in 21:18, when Paul and his companions arrived at Jerusalem. What

---

[569]New York: Charles Scribner's Sons, 1920.

[570]James Smith, *The Voyage and Shipwreck of St. Paul* (4th ed.; London: Longmans, Green, and Co., 1880), p. 61, n. 1.

[571]*Op. cit.*, p. 227.

[572]IB, IX, 331.

had Luke been doing in the intervening two years, while Paul
was a prisoner at Caesarea? The answer is that he was probably
collecting the materials for his Gospel. It may well be that at this
time he had an interview with the aged mother of Jesus, the
only human being who could furnish him with some of the
information found in the first two chapters of Luke's Gospel.

It has often been noted that the narrative of Acts is most
vivid and detailed when Luke is along. That is certainly true
of this chapter, which could have been written only by an eyewitness.

Sail—literally, "sail away"—is the first nautical term in this
account of the voyage. The Greek word occurs only in Acts
(cf. 13:4; 14:26; 20:15).

They—indefinite reference to Festus and his soldiers—**delivered Paul and certain other prisoners unto one named Julius.**
As a Roman citizen who had appealed to Caesar, Paul had special status. "The others had been in all probability already condemned to death, and were going to supply the perpetual demand
which Rome made on the provinces for human victims to amuse
the populace by their death in the arena."[573]

Julius was **a centurion of Augustus' band.** This expression
has created considerable discussion. In an article on "The Roman
Army," T. R. S. Broughton identifies it as "a Syrian auxiliary
Cohors Augusta,"[574] which was stationed in Palestine in the
first century. Several commentators have suggested that the
reference is to a special courier service (*frumentarii*), responsible directly to the emperor. Concerning the problem Blaiklock
writes: "The *frumentarii*, or special military agents of the Emperor, sent abroad on duties of inspection, seem to have been a
later invention; but information is far from complete, and those
who regard the otherwise unidentified *Augustus' band* (1) as a
corps of picked troops detached from the regular formations for
special services, may indeed be correct."[575] That is the best
conclusion to which one can come. As Broughton says, "The
question must be left open."[576]

Entering (2)—literally, "having embarked"—in **a ship of
Adramyttium**—a harbor on the west coast of Asia Minor, south

[573]Ramsay, SPT, p. 314.
[574]*Beginnings*, V. 443-44.
[575]*Op. cit.*, p. 189.
[576]*Beginnings*, V, 444.

of Troas (see map 3)—**we launched,** or "set sail." This is another nautical term, found six times in the narrative of this voyage to Rome (27:2, 4, 12, 21; 28:10-11). It means "put to sea" (cf. 13:13).

Aristarchus, a Macedonian of Thessalonica, being with us. How can it be explained that he and Luke were allowed to accompany an imperial prisoner? Moe suggests: "The governor must have given Luke and Aristarchus special permission to join in the voyage, and this probably on the ground that they should function as the apostle's servants."[577] The expression **with us,** however, seems to suggest a different status for Luke. May he not have attended Paul as his personal physician, as he seems later to have done in the apostle's final imprisonment (II Tim. 4:11—"only Luke is with me")? **Aristarchus** seems to have been one of Paul's especially faithful friends (cf. 20:4) and was with the apostle during his first imprisonment at Rome (Col. 4:10; Philem. 24).

The day after they left Caesarea they **touched at Sidon** (3). This verb (*katago*) literally means "bring down." Luke alone uses it as a nautical term in the sense of "bring to land" (cf. 28:12; Luke 5:11). So a good translation here would be "put in" (most recent versions) or "landed" (Berk.). Sidon was nearly seventy miles north of Caesarea. The prevailing west winds of that season of the year had pushed them along in good time.

Julius courteously entreated—rather, "treated"—**Paul.** Nowhere else in the New Testament does the Greek verb have this sense, but the meaning is found clearly in the papyri of that period.[578] **Courteously** is an adverb, *philanthropos,* meaning "humanely, kindly." It is a striking fact that every Roman centurion mentioned in the New Testament is presented in a favorable light (cf. Matt. 8:5-13; 27:54; Acts 10:1-4). So here Julius treated Paul kindly and **gave him liberty**—"permitted him"—to visit **his friends** in the city and **to refresh himself**—literally, "to obtain care." Apparently the ship stayed in the harbor for a day or two while loading or unloading.

Having **launched** (4)—"put to sea"—from Sidon, the ship **sailed under**—"under the lee of"—**Cyprus;** that is, to the east and

---

[577]Olaf Moe, *The Apostle Paul,* trans. L. A. Vigness (Minneapolis: Augsburg Publishing House, 1950), p. 441.

[578]VGT, p. 690.

north of that island, between it and the mainland. The shortest route would have been to the west of it, across the open sea (see map 3). Barclay comments: "The prevailing wind at that time of the year was the west wind and they could only make Myra by slipping under Cyprus and then following a zigzag course up the coast."[579] This is what is called "tacking" against the wind. They adopted this procedure **because the winds were contrary.**

They **sailed over** (5)—literally, "sailed through" and so, "sailed across"—**the sea**—literally, "the deep"—**of Cilicia and Pamphylia.** Thus they were going westward, against the wind. The Western text (see Introduction) says that they sailed "for fifteen days," which may well have been true.[580] Finally they **came to Myra,** in **Lycia** (see map 3).

There the centurion found a ship of Alexandria sailing into Italy (6). A glance at the map will show that for a ship to go from Alexandria (Egypt) to Italy by way of Myra was to travel two sides of a triangle (sailing north and then west). The direct route would be to follow the hypotenuse almost straight northwest to Italy. In his excellent article on "Roads and Travel [in NT]," Sir William Ramsay describes the situation thus:

> The voyage from Alexandria to Rome was a much more difficult and tedious matter than the voyage from Rome to Alexandria, owing to the prevalence during summer of westerly winds in the Mediterranean. The ships had to help themselves by the uncertain and fitful breezes on the coasts. Now it was unsafe to keep too southerly a course owing to the great quicksands, Syrtes, on the African coasts: even if the winds permitted, ships could not venture from Alexandria on a course which would keep them near the Cyrenaic shore lest the wind might shift around towards the north and drive them too far south (Ac 27:17). They were compelled to take a northerly course, keeping as much to the west of north as the wind would allow. Thus they might fetch the Lycian coast . . . but it may be regarded as absolutely certain that they could never attempt a course across sea from the Egyptian coast direct to Italy or Sicily.[581]

Now the picture becomes clear. Since the prevailing winds were from the west, it was impossible to sail directly to Italy. Ships would go straight north, trying to keep as far west as

[579]William Barclay, *The Acts of the Apostles* ("The Daily Study Bible"; Philadelphia: Westminster Press, 1953), p. 199.

[580]*Beginnings,* III, 241.

[581]HDB, V, 379-80.

possible. Sometimes they cleared the west end of Cyprus. But strong west winds made it necessary for Paul's ship to sail under the lee of Cyprus and tack along the shore of Asia Minor to Myra. Then the ship would head west for Crete, making use of such offshore north winds as might be blowing.

The **ship of Alexandria** would be loaded with wheat. Winn notes: "Egyptian grain was the staple diet of Rome, and its uninterrupted transportation was so important to the life of the city that the government itself owned and operated a fleet of grain ships."[582]

The centurion put his prisoners on board the Alexandrian ship. The reason for changing vessels was that the first would soon be turning north toward its home port of Adramyttium while the centurion and his prisoners had to continue on to the west. But the contrary winds still impeded their progress—**when we had sailed slowly** (7). This is all one word in the Greek, found only here in the New Testament. James Smith lists seven compounds of *pleo* which are used only by Luke in a nautical sense.[583] After sailing slowly for **many days**, tacking against a west wind, they **scarce were come over against Cnidus**—rather, "with difficulty had arrived off Cnidus" (NASB). They had come a distance of about one hundred thirty miles from Myra. **Cnidus** (see map 3) was at the southwest corner of Asia Minor, forming the dividing line between the western and southern coasts.

Up to this point the ship would be protected to a great extent from the northwest winds. But when it passed Cnidus and headed out into the open sea it would catch their full strength. This is suggested by the expression, **the wind not suffering us;** literally, "the wind not permitting us further." This clause belongs with what follows, not with what precedes. The correct meaning of the verse is: "And when we had sailed slowly for a good many days, and with difficulty had arrived off Cnidus, since the wind did not permit us to go farther, we sailed under the shelter of Crete off Salmone" (NASB). The shortest route to Italy lay north of Crete (see map 3). But apparently a northwest wind forced this ship to sail east and south of Crete. Smith gives adequate documentation for his assertion that "this is precisely

[582]*Op. cit.,* p. 128.
[583]*Op. cit.,* p. 28.

the wind which might have been expected in those seas towards the end of summer."[584] With a northwest wind blowing strongly, the ship's "only course was to run under the lee of Crete, in the direction of Salmone . . . which is the eastern extremity of that island."[585]

The narrative continues: **And, hardly**—"with difficulty"—**passing it, came unto a place which is called The fair havens (8).** Arndt and Gingrich say the Greek word for **passing** is a technical nautical term meaning "sail past, coast along."[586] "Sailing past" is the translation in NASB. Since the idea of "coasting along" (RSV, Phillips) is that of keeping close to the coast for safety, NEB has "hugging the coast."

Of the harbor mentioned here, Smith writes: "Now Fair Havens is the last harbour before arriving at Cape Matala, the farthest point to which an ancient ship could have attained with north-westerly winds."[587] So they were almost forced to put in there. While **fair havens** "is not mentioned in any ancient writer,"[588] yet there is a bay on the south shore of Crete which still carries a name almost exactly like the Greek expression used here. The ruins of **Lasea,** some four miles east of Fair Havens, were identified with some certainty in 1856.

b. *Dangerous Decision* (27:9-12). The ship stayed at Fair Havens for **much time (9).** Hackett takes the expression "By now much time had been lost" (NEB) as including "since the embarkation at Caesarea."[589] He writes: "On leaving Palestine they expected to reach Italy before the arrival of the stormy season, and would have accomplished their object had it not been for unforeseen delays."[590] Knowling, however, says: "not since the commencement of the voyage . . . but since they lay weatherbound."[591] This is the view of Ramsay.[592] In agreement with James Smith he holds that a ship could not proceed safely past

[584]*Ibid.,* p. 76.
[585]*Ibid.,* p. 77.
[586]*Op. cit.,* p. 625.
[587]*Op. cit.,* p. 77.
[588]*Beginnings,* IV, 328.
[589]*Op. cit.,* p. 295.
[590]*Ibid.*
[591]EGT, II, 520.
[592]SPT, p. 321.

Cape Matala, six miles west of Fair Havens, as long as the northwest wind blew.

Due to the delay, **sailing was now dangerous, because the fast was now already past.** The reference is to the great annual Day of Atonement, the only fast prescribed in the Mosaic law (Lev. 16:29-31). Since the Jews used a lunar, rather than solar, calendar the date of this annual fast day falls in September or October. In A.D. 59, the date held by Ramsay for this voyage, the fast came about the fifth of October. In A.D. 58, the Day of Atonement fell on about the fifteenth of September.[593] Concerning conditions at this time of the year, Ramsay writes: "The dangerous season for navigation lasted from Sept. 14 to Nov. 11, when all navigation on the open sea was discontinued."[594] He continues: "The ship reached Fair Havens in the latter part of September, and was detained there by a continuance of unfavourable winds until after Oct. 5."[595] He thinks the original voyage began at Caesarea about August 17.[596] This agrees well with Hackett's observation that in his day (about 1850) the active shipping season at Alexandria began about the first of August. He writes: "The rise of the Nile is then so far advanced that the produce of the interior can be brought to that city, where it is shipped at once and sent to different parts of Europe."[597]

As to the date of Paul's journey to Rome, the present writer has always preferred the conclusion of C. H. Turner in his monumental article on "Chronology of the New Testament" in Hastings' *Dictionary of the Bible*—that Paul arrived at Rome in the spring of A.D. 59, and so left Caesarea in 58.[598] This is the view of Moe in his helpful work on the life of Paul.[599]

G. Ogg, in his article on "Chronology of the New Testament" in *The New Bible Dictionary*, places Paul's departure from Caesarea at A.D. 61 and his first Roman imprisonment at 62-64.[600] But this is altogether too late. Most American New Testament schol-

---

[593]EGT, II, 520.
[594]SPT, p. 322.
[595]*Ibid.*
[596]*Ibid.*, p. 321.
[597]*Op. cit.*, p. 294.
[598]HDB, I, 424.
[599]*Op. cit.*, p. 18.
[600]Wm. B. Eerdmans Publishing Co., 1962, p. 227.

ars today would date Paul's two years in prison at Rome A.D. 59-61 or 60-62.

In favor of A.D. 60-62 is G. B. Caird in his article "Chronology of the NT" in *The Interpreter's Dictionary of the Bible*.[601] He places Paul's trial before Festus in A.D. 59 and his arrival at Rome in 60. F. F. Bruce makes out a rather strong case for A.D. 59 as the time for the voyage from Caesarea to Malta (with Paul reaching Rome in 60). He says that it was only about fifty or sixty miles to the island of Cauda (16), and fourteen more days took them to Malta (27), where they spent three months. He concludes: "The seas were closed until the beginning of February at the earliest. . . . The three months spent in Malta must therefore have been (roughly) November, December and January; they must have left Fair Havens not much earlier than the middle of October, and this reckoning accords with the date of the Fast in A.D. 59 (Oct. 5), but not in any of the neighboring years from 57 to 62, when it fell earlier."[602]

Bruce may be right. Cadbury has added one supporting item for this date in his recent work, *The Book of Acts in History*. After noting that "a new Judean coinage begins in the fifth year of Nero, that is before October A.D. 59," he asks: "Is it not probable that it is due to the arrival of a new procurator?"[603] If so, A.D. 59 is the accession year of Festus and the time when Paul left for Rome. The best we can do is to settle for either 58 or 59 as the date for Acts 25—27, and 59-61 or 60-62 for the two years' imprisonment at Rome (28:30).

Paul **admonished them** (9). But whom? Alexander comments: "*Paul admonished* (or *exhorted*), a Greek verb used only in this chapter [see below, on v. 22], but originally meaning to commend, and then to recommend, advise, especially in public, as a speaker in the Greek assemblies."[604] He adds: "It is probable, therefore, that this exhortation was addressed to the whole company, not merely to the chiefs and officers."[605]

Paul warned that **this voyage will be with hurt and much damage, not only of the lading** (cargo) **and ship, but also of our lives** (10). Later on, the apostle received a divine revelation that

[601]Ed. G. A. Buttrick (New York: Abingdon Press, 1962), I, 607.
[602]*Acts*, pp. 455-56.
[603]*Op. cit.*, p. 10.
[604]*Op. cit.*, p. 906.
[605]*Ibid.*

no lives would be lost (24), and so it happened. This suggests that **I perceive** in this verse refers to human intuition or observations, not to divine inspiration.

Unfortunately, rather than taking Paul's advice, **the centurion believed the master and the owner of the ship (11).** The Greek word for **master** means "steersman, pilot," as attested by writers all the way from Homer and the Septuagint to contemporary inscriptions and papyri, together with Philo and Josephus.[606] The translation **owner of the ship** (only here in NT) is attested by Arndt and Gingrich. However they add: "But it can also mean *captain,* since the sailing-master of a ship engaged in state service was called a *naukleros.*"[607] Ramsay feels strongly that "captain" rather than "owner" is the correct translation here, since "the ship belonged to the Alexandrian fleet in the Imperial service."[608] He also says: "The centurion . . . is represented as the commanding officer, which implies that the ship was a Government ship, and the centurion ranked as the highest officer on board."[609]

The harbor at Fair Havens **was not commodious (12)**—literally, "not well placed" or "not suitable" (NASB)—**to winter in.** Bruce comments: "It is protected by small islands, but was not a very good winter harbour, as it stands open to nearly half the compass."[610]

So **the more part**—"the majority"—**advised** leaving this inadequate harbor and trying to make **Phenice** (Phoenix), forty miles to the west. Lake and Cadbury note: "Unlike other place names in this section, Phoenix is mentioned by ancient geographers and without much variation of spelling."[611]

The harbor at Phoenix **lieth toward the south west and north west.** Perhaps no other expression in Acts is so uncertain as to its exact meaning. The Greek literally means "looking down the southwest wind and down the northwest wind." A glance at the versions will underscore the confusion in which translators find themselves. Contrary to the KJV, the ASV, RSV, and NASB all have "looking (facing) northeast and southeast."

[606]Arndt and Gingrich, *op. cit.,* p. 457.
[607]*Ibid.,* p. 536.
[608]SPT, p. 324.
[609]*Ibid.,* p. 323.
[610]*Acts,* p. 454.
[611]*Beginnings,* V, 329.

But the last two have in the margin "or *southwest and north-west*," which is the accepted reading in Phillips and the NEB. Obviously both cannot be correct. What is right?

The two nouns in the Greek are *lips* and *choros*. In an article on "The Winds," Lake and Cadbury write: "In the LXX *lips* generally means south, but in the papyri—far more important for our purpose—it invariably means west."[612] Of *choros* they say: "This word appears not to be found elsewhere in Greek."[613] It is a Latinism. After citing a passage in Pliny (in Latin), they conclude: "Thus in Acts xxvii. 12 *kata liba* either means west or west with a tendency to south, and *kata choron* ought to mean west with a tendency to north."[614] So they would agree with the KJV and NEB in favoring a harbor which faced west. They also make an interesting observation about the language used here: "The combination of Greek and Latin words in Luke's description of the storm and of the harbour of Phoenix suggests the possibility that he was influenced by the mixed speech of sailors, partly Alexandrian and partly Italian."[615] The former spoke Greek, the latter Latin. This may account for the odd double expression (one Gk., one Lat.) used here to describe the harbor of Phoenix.

In the face of all this evidence it may well be asked how the ASV, RSV, and NASB came to adopt a translation which has the harbor facing east. The answer lies in James Smith's interpretation of the passage. He takes the preposition *kata* as meaning "in the same direction as," and continues: "If I am right, *bleponta kata liba* does not mean, as is generally supposed, that it is open to the point *from* which that wind (*Libs*) blows, but to the point towards which it blows—that is, it is not open to the south-west but to the north-east."[616]

At the agreed general location of Phoenix there is a promontory which juts a considerable distance out from the coast. On the east side is the harbor of Lutro, which Smith identifies with Phoenix. On the west side is Phineka. The similarity of this modern name to Phoenix, as well as the more natural meaning

[612]*Ibid.,* V, 342–43.
[613]*Ibid.,* p. 343.
[614]*Ibid.*
[615]*Ibid.*
[616]*Op. cit.,* p. 88.

of the Greek words, seems to favor the identification with Phineka, with its harbor facing west.[617]

c. *The Storm* (27:13-20). **When the south wind blew softly** (13)—the Greek verb literally means "to blow underneath," and so "to blow gently."[618] **Loosing** is literally "having lifted up" or "having taken up." Arndt and Gingrich say that in this passage the verb may have the nautical sense of "weigh anchor"[619] (cf. ASV, NASB).

Having weighed anchor, **they sailed close by Crete. Sailed** is the same verb as in 8. **Close** is literally "closer." The clause is best translated, "began sailing along Crete, close inshore" (NASB). Thus they felt safe.

But when they had gone about three or four miles westward, they passed Cape Matala and found themselves unprotected on the north. Suddenly they were struck by a **tempestuous**—Greek, typhonic—**wind, called Euroclydon** (14)—better, "Euraquilo" (ASV). This is another combination of Greek and Latin: *euros,* Greek for east wind, and *aquilo,* Latin for north wind. So it means "a Northeaster" (Goodspeed).

The clause **when the south wind blew softly** has significant homiletical application. When young people are lured out of the safe harbor of home, the church, and the standards of the New Testament by the softly blowing south winds of seductive worldly pleasure, they are apt to be caught by howling hurricanes and find their frail barks driven furiously across life's sea to be wrecked somewhere on the shores of time. On the basis of this passage one could well say: "Watch out for those south winds that blow softly."

The ship was caught (15)—a strong compound meaning "seized violently," or "seized and carried away"—**and could not bear up into the wind.** The verb literally means "to look in the face." Here it is used as a nautical term, with the sense "to beat up against the wind."[620] So **we let her drive**—literally, "having given way, we were being carried." That is, they were helpless before the wind. Smith summarizes these two verses thus: "The ship was 'caught' (*synarpasthentos*) in a typhoon (*anemos ty-*

[617]So Bruce, *Acts,* p. 457.
[618]Abbott-Smith, *op. cit.,* p. 42.
[619]*Op. cit.,* p. 23.
[620]Abbott-Smith, *op. cit.,* p. 42.

phonikos), which blew with such violence that they could not face it, but were forced . . . to scud before it, for such is the evident meaning of the expression—*epidontes epherometha*—'yielding to it we were borne along by it.' "[621]

And running under (16)—i.e., "under the lee of"—**a certain island**—literally, "small island"—**which is called Clauda**—or Cauda, today called Gaudo in Greek and Gozzo in Italian, about twenty-five miles southwest of Fair Havens—**we had much work to come by the boat;** i.e., "we were scarcely able to get the boat under control."[622] This was the small dinghy that was towed behind the ship. By now this was doubtless waterlogged and perhaps banging dangerously against the stern. The **we** may suggest that Luke helped to haul it in.

When they finally succeeded in hoisting the skiff on deck, **they used helps (17).** This is "probably a nautical technical term . . . *they used supports* (perhaps cables)."[623] In a strikingly parallel passage, Aristotle (fourth century B.C.) uses the word in connection with a storm at sea. He says: "Thus when in danger at sea people may feel confident about what will happen . . . because their experience gives them the means of dealing with it"[624]—literally, "having the helps."

The exact meaning of **undergirding the ship** is uncertain. Some have maintained that ropes were stretched from stem to stern. But it seems much more likely that ropes (or cables) were dropped over the bow, looped under the hull, and secured crosswise across the deck. James Smith gives the following quotation from *Falconer's Marine Dictionary:* "To frap a ship . . . is to pass four or five turns of a large cable-like rope around the hull or frame of a ship, to support her in a great storm . . . when it is apprehended that she is not strong enough to resist the violent efforts of the sea; this expedient, however, is rarely put in practice."[625] Smith also quotes from Sir George Back's description of frapping his ship in this way when it was leaking badly on his return from an arctic voyage in 1837.[626]

---

[621]*Op. cit.,* pp. 98–99.

[622]Arndt and Gingrich, *op. cit.,* p. 654.

[623]*Ibid.,* p. 144.

[624]Aristotle *Rhetoric* II. 5 (*The Works of Aristotle* [Chicago: Encyclopaedia Britannica, 1952], II, 629).

[625]*Op. cit.,* p. 108.

[626]*Ibid.,* p. 109.

Cadbury accepts this view as the most likely one. He says: "The planks ran lengthwise of the ship's hull, and a rope passed under the keel and fastened either at the gunwale on opposite sides, or joined on deck and pulled tight by twisting, or by a windlass, would hold the planks as the hoops hold the staves of a barrel."[627]

Ramsay has pointed out the special danger which confronted this ship. He writes: "An ancient ship with one huge sail was exposed to extreme danger from such a blast; the straining of the great sail on the single mast was more than the hull could bear; and the ship was exposed to a risk which modern vessels do not fear, foundering in the open sea."[628] Later ships had three masts, to distribute the strain.

Luke continues: **and, fearing lest they should fall into the quicksands, strake sail, and so were driven.** The Greek for **quicksands** is *Syrtis*. This refers to shoals off the coast of Africa west of Cyrene (see map 3). They were called Syrtis Major to differentiate them from Syrtis Minor, farther east. Lake and Cadbury note: "It was about three times as far as they had already come [i.e., from Cnidus], and dead to leeward with the wind from the northeast, so that the danger was a serious one."[629]

Fall literally means "fall out from." Here (as in 26, 29) it is a "nautical technical term," meaning "drift off course, run aground."[630]

Strake sail is more accurately rendered "lowered the gear" (RSV). The verb is the same as that used in 30 for lowering the skiff. Concerning the noun Smith writes: "*Skeuos*, which I have translated 'gear,' when applied to a ship, means appurtenances of every kind, such as spars, sails, rigging, anchors and cables, etc."[631] This noun *skeuos* is translated "vessel" nineteen of the twenty-three times it occurs in the New Testament (including 9:15; 10:11, 16; 11:5). Only here is it rendered "sail." The clause may mean "lowered the mainsail" (NEB). Smith thinks that the "gear" was "not the mast, but the yard with the sail attached to it."[632] In order to use the rudder effectively in heading

---

[627]*Beginnings*, V, 348.
[628]SPT, p. 328.
[629]*Beginnings*, IV, 333.
[630]Arndt and Gingrich, *op. cit.*, p. 243.
[631]*Op. cit.*, p. 111.
[632]*Ibid.*, p. 112.

westward, to keep from being blown southwestward on the African sandbanks, they would need to have a small storm sail unfurled. Ramsay describes the situation thus: ". . . leaving up just enough sail to keep the ship's head to the wind, and bringing down everything else that could be got down."[633]

They were now at the mercy of the sea, **driven** (lit., "carried") by the storm. Smith made a very careful computation of the distance between Cauda and Malta (about 475 miles) and the time lapse (13½ days, cf. 27) and came up with the conclusion that they drifted at the rate of about 1½ miles per hour. Two captains in the Royal Navy, both stationed in the Mediterranean, independently agreed that this would be the average rate of a ship's drift in a severe storm. Thus Luke's accuracy in this narrative has been strikingly confirmed.[634]

The best translation of 18 is: "The next day as we were being violently storm-tossed, they began to jettison the cargo" (NASB). But they left some wheat in the bottom of the hold for ballast (cf. 38). **On the third day we cast out with our own hands the tackling of the ship** (19). The best Greek text reads "they" rather than **we**. As to the meaning of **tackling**, Smith says: "I suppose the main-yard is meant; an immense spar, probably as long as the ship, which would require the united efforts of passengers and crew to launch overboard."[635]

Verse 20 describes the situation when morale on board ship reached an all-time "low." **Neither sun nor stars in many days appeared.** It must be recalled that in those days there was no compass, and mariners were entirely dependent on celestial navigation. With no sun by day or stars at night, they were lost. It is probable, too, that the ship was leaking. As **no small tempest lay on** them, it is not to be wondered at that **all hope that we should be saved was then taken away**—literally, "was being taken away entirely."

d. *The Assurance* (27:21-26). During the grueling days of the storm there was a **long abstinence** (21). The Greek word is *asitia,* which is made from *a* (negative) and *sitos,* "wheat" (as in 38). So it literally means "wheatlessness." The term seems ironical in the light of the fact that this was a ship carrying wheat.

[633]SPT, p. 329.
[634]Smith, *op. cit.,* pp. 124-28.
[635]*Ibid.,* p. 116.

Smith cites several descriptions of a ship in a storm to buttress his conclusion that either the food was spoiled or the cooking facilities out of order, because of water leaking in.[636] A more likely explanation is that of Arndt and Gingrich: *"Almost nobody wanted to eat* because of anxiety or seasickness."[637] Both the noun *asitia* and the adjective *asitos* ("fasting") in 33 occur only here. They are "much employed in medical language . . . the noun often meaning 'want of appetite.' "[638]

It should be noted that practically all commentators and recent translators take the going without food as applying to the whole group. This was not a religious fasting by Paul alone, as might be inferred from the KJV.

Paul now reminds his co-sufferers that they should have listened to him when he warned against leaving Fair Havens. The Greek word for **hearkened** literally means "obey." Arndt and Gingrich translate the clause here: "You ought to have followed my advice and not to have sailed"[639] (cf. NASB). If they had stayed at Fair Havens, as he had advised (cf. 9-10, RSV, NASB), they would have saved themselves **this harm**—"damage" or "injury"—**and loss.**

Paul continued: **And now I exhort**—"advise" or "urge"[640]—**you to be of good cheer** (22)—"to cheer up" or "keep up your courage." While the ship was doomed, there would be no loss of life—"not a single one of you will be lost."[641]

What was the basis of Paul's confident assurance? **This night** (23)—i.e., "last night"—there had stood by him **the angel of God**—rather, "an angel of the God to whom I belong and whom I serve" (NASB). This angel bade him: "Stop being afraid, Paul!" He **must be brought before Caesar** (24)—God had ordained it—and so he would not fail to reach Rome alive.

As a special favor, **God hath given thee**—the verb means "has graciously given," or "has given as a present"[642]—**all them that sail with thee.** It seems evident that Paul had prayed not

[636]*Ibid.,* pp. 117-19.
[637]*Op. cit.,* p. 115.
[638]EGT, II, 527.
[639]*Op. cit.,* p. 644.
[640]*Ibid.,* p. 621.
[641]*Ibid.,* p. 88.
[642]Bruce, *Acts,* p. 462.

only for himself but for all on board. Lumby says: "In the midst of such peril, though no mention is made of the fact, we cannot doubt that the Apostle cried unto the Lord in his distress, and the gracious answer was vouchsafed that all should be preserved."[643]

On the basis of this divine revelation Paul exhorted his hearers to be of good courage, **for I believe God** (25). Faith asserts itself most significantly in the face of the worst circumstances. Apparently the angel had further informed him that they **must be cast upon a certain island** (26).

In this passage there are some worthwhile observations which may be gathered around the title "Hearing from God in the Storm." (1) God may be found by those who serve Him, 21-23; (2) Hearing brings personal assurance and strength, 24; (3) Hearing from God brings reflected reassurance and courage to those around us, 22, 25 (A. F. Harper).

e. Nearing Land (27:27-32). On the **fourteenth night** (27) since leaving Fair Havens, they were being **driven up and down in Adria**—better, "drifting across the sea of Adria" (RSV), for they were evidently being blown in the same direction all the time. Of **Adria,** Knowling writes: "not in the narrower sense of the Adriatic, the Gulf of Venice, or as we now speak of 'the Adriatic,' but as including the whole sea which lay between Malta, Italy, Greece and Crete; St. Luke probably used the term as it was colloquially used by the sailors in this wider sense."[644]

About midnight the shipmen deemed—better, "began to surmise" (NASB)—**that they drew near to some country**—literally, "that some land was approaching." Smith observes: "St. Luke here uses the graphic language of seamen, to whom the ship is the principal object, whilst the land rises and sinks, nears and recedes."[645] Ramsay follows Smith in thinking that they heard the breakers, as they passed the low, rocky point of Koura on their way into St. Paul's Bay, the traditional site of the shipwreck.[646]

When the sailors **sounded** (28)—literally, "having heaved the lead"—they **found it twenty fathoms.** A fathom is 6 feet; so

[643]*Op. cit.,* p. 441.
[644]EGT, II, 529.
[645]*Op. cit.,* p. 120, n. 1.
[646]SPT, pp. 334-35.

the water was 120 feet deep at this point. Taking another sounding, they found it only **fifteen fathoms** (90 feet). Smith has carefully checked the probable course of Paul's ill-fated ship, and found that the lapse of time between the two sounds would be about half an hour.[647]

Realizing that they were fast nearing the rocky shore, **they cast four anchors out of the stern** (29). Ordinarily a ship riding at anchor prefers to be anchored at the bow. But this was a peculiar situation. The ship was being driven before the wind. A bow anchorage would have let her swing around, so that she could not be maneuvered properly (cf. 39). When everything possible had been done for the safety of the ship, those on board **wished**—literally, "prayed"—for day to come.

But the crew members decided to abandon ship (30). They lowered the skiff into the sea, **under colour**—under "pretence" or "pretext"—that they were about to lay out anchors from the bow.

The most important man on board was Paul. He sensed the deceptive plans of the sailors and told the centurion and soldiers that they would all be lost unless the crew stayed with the ship (31). By now the centurion, and probably also the soldiers, realized that Paul was the man to listen to. So the soldiers cut the ropes that held the skiff, and the small boat drifted away (32). From here on, the crew and passengers were involved together in whatever happened.

f. Courageous Example (27:33-38). By now it was getting near daybreak. Probably no one was sleeping; all were on deck. Paul knew that everyone would need strength for the arduous hours just ahead. So he **besought them all to take meat** (food, 33). He reminded them that they had eaten nothing for fourteen days.

He continued: **Wherefore I pray** (34)—the verb means "beseech," "exhort," or "encourage" (same word as "besought" in 33)—**you to take some meat: for this is for**[648] **your health**—literally, "salvation," and so "safety" or "preservation." He reminded them: **there shall not an hair fall from the head of any of you.** This was a common ancient proverbial expression to describe

---

[647]*Op. cit.*, p. 131.

[648]Bruce (*Acts*, p. 465) comments: "This use of *pros* with the genitive is literary, and is the one NT occurrence." Blass and Debrunner (*op. cit.*, p. 125) say it means "on the side of," and so "in the interest of, to the advantage of."

complete deliverance (cf. I Sam. 14:45; II Sam. 14:11; I Kings 1:52; Matt. 10:30; Luke 21:18).

Then Paul set the example. **He took bread, and gave thanks to God in the presence of them all: and when he had broken it, he began to eat (35)**. It does not seem necessary to treat this as a sacramental meal. **Bread** is literally "loaf," the size of a small biscuit.

With Paul's encouragement and example, all were **of good cheer, and they also took some meat (36)**. This was to prove important for the unexpected ordeal of swimming ashore.

In this whole time of severe testing the apostle had shown himself "An Example for All Christians" in three ways: (1) Courage in danger, 21-22; (2) Confidence in God, 23-25; (3) Command in crisis, 31-36.

The ship is stated to have had 276 persons on board (37). Lumby writes: "The occasion for the numbering was probably the near expectation of coming ashore, and so it was needful to have all told, for the captain, in respect of the crew, and for the centurion, that of his prisoners and soldiers none might be allowed to escape or be missing."[649] He adds: "The mention of the number at this point of the history is one of the many very natural features of the narrative."[650]

Instead of 276, the oldest Greek uncial MS (Vaticanus) and the Sahidic version have "about seventy-six." Westcott and Hort, who gave highest authority to Vaticanus, adopted the latter reading. Lake and Cadbury also chose it for their translation. Yet they admit: "But there is nothing impossible in the larger number."[651] Bruce says that the reading of Vaticanus is "probably to be rejected" in favor of the other, which is "much better attested."[652] It is true that Luke is fond of using "about" (*hos*) before round numbers. But "about seventy-six" does not seem sensible.

As justification for the reasonableness of the larger number here, many commentators call attention to Josephus' account of his voyage to Rome on a ship with about six hundred on board. The passage also gives a bit of parallel to Paul's shipwreck. It reads: "Accordingly I came to Rome, though it were through a

[649]*Op. cit.*, p. 444.
[650]*Ibid.*
[651]*Beginnings*, IV, 336.
[652]*Acts*, p. 466.

great number of hazards by sea; for as our ship was drowned in the Adriatic Sea, we that were in it, being about six hundred in number, swam for our lives all the night; when, upon the first appearance of the day, and upon our sight of a ship of Cyrene, I and some others, eighty in all, by God's providence, prevented [preceded] the rest, and were taken up into the other ship."[653]

When the people on Paul's ship **had eaten enough** (38)— literally, "were filled" or "satisfied"—**they lightened the ship** by throwing its cargo of **wheat into the sea.** The reason for this is obvious. They wished the ship to ride high in the water that it might go as far up on the beach as possible, so that they might be within easy swimming distance of shore.

g. *Shipwreck and Escape* (27:39-44). When daybreak came, all eyes eagerly scanned the shore. But no one **knew** (39)— "recognized"—**the land.** However, **they discovered**—literally, "noticed" or "observed"—**a certain creek with a shore**—better, "certain bay with a beach" (NASB). Lumby comments: *"Aigialos* is used to signify such a sandy beach as might allow a ship to be run aground upon it without the danger of her immediately coming to pieces."[654] On this beach **they were minded**—literally, "were resolving" or "deciding"—**if it were possible, to thrust in the ship**—"run the ship ashore."

When they had taken up the anchors (40) should probably be "cast off . . . the anchors."[655] **They committed themselves unto the sea** should be united with the previous clause. The two together will then read correctly: "And casting off the anchors, they left them in the sea" (NASB). At the same time they **loosed the rudder bands**—or "loosened the lashings of the steer-ing-paddles" (NEB). Lake and Cadbury comment: "Ancient ships had a rudder, or rather a steering oar, on each side."[656] Then they **hoised up** (hoisted) **the mainsail to the wind.** All recent versions have "foresail." Lake and Cadbury write: "The word is not known elsewhere in Greek, except in lexicographers probably dependent on this passage."[657] But Smith seems to have demonstrated satisfactorily that the *artemon* was the "fore-

[653]Josephus *Life* 3.
[654]*Op. cit.*, p. 445.
[655]Arndt and Gingrich, *op. cit.*, p. 651.
[656]*Beginnings*, IV, 338.
[657]*Ibid.*

sail" on the ship.[658] Having made all these preparations, they
made toward shore.

And falling into a place where two seas met—where the sea
waves met the current between the beach and a tiny island close
to shore—**they ran the ship aground** (41). Smith describes
vividly the probable identification of this place, calling attention
to the accuracy of Luke's account.[659] He notes: "The rocks of
Malta disintegrate into extremely minute particles of sand and
clay, which, when acted upon by the currents or by surface agi-
tation, form a deposit of tenacious clay."[660] He says that a large
ship would draw about three fathoms (eighteen feet) of water,
which is just about the depth at which mud is found, unruffled by
the surface currents. He concludes: "A ship, therefore, impelled
by the force of a gale into a creek with a bottom such as that laid
down in the chart, would strike a bottom of mud graduating into
tenacious clay, into which the fore part would fix itself and be
held fast, whilst the stern was exposed to the force of the
waves."[661]

This is exactly what is described in Luke's account. Ramsay
remarks: "One of the completest services that has ever been
rendered to New Testament scholarship is James Smith's proof
that all these circumstances are united in St. Paul's Bay."[662]

Of the waves (41) is not found in most of the earliest MSS.
Ramsay well observes: "In v. 41 'the violence' is the expression
used by a person standing on the shore and watching the waves
smash up the ship: he does not need to specify the kind of violence."[663] He adds: "The humblest scribe can supply *kymaton*
['of the waves'] here, and most of them have done so"[664] (cf.
italics in ASV, NASB).

The soldiers wanted to **kill the prisoners,** for whom they
were responsible, **lest any . . . should swim** to shore **and escape**
(42). **But the centurion,** wishing to **save Paul, kept**—"prevented"—**them from their purpose** (43). Instead he commanded
that those who could swim should jump into the water and head
for shore. The rest were to make it in on planks or on **pieces of**

---

[658]*Op. cit.*, pp. 136-41.
[659]*Ibid.*, pp. 142-43.
[660]*Ibid.*, p. 144.
[661]*Ibid.*
[662]SPT, p. 341.
[663]*Ibid.*
[664]*Ibid.*

the ship (44). The swimmers would be on the shore to help these stragglers reach land safely. The result was that **they escaped all safe to land**—better, "all came safely to land" (NEB). It was only because of Paul's bold leadership, under God, that this agonizing voyage came to such a satisfactory end. The centurion had the good sense and fairness to save the life of his prisoner who was instrumental in saving the whole number on board.

An outline that suggests itself for this chapter might be titled "Warning to the Careless": (1) The false seduction, 13; (2) The furious storm, 14-38; (3) The fateful shipwreck, 39-44.

2. *Winter on Malta* (28:1-10)

After the horrors of two weeks on the stormy sea, solid land must have felt very comforting to the escapees from the ship. There would be no more sailing for several months, because the season was closed for the winter.

a. Miracle of Preservation (28:1-6). **When they were escaped** (1)—literally, "having come safely through"—**they**—the best Greek text has "we"—**knew that the island was called Melita.** This is to be identified with Malta (see map 3), which belonged at that time to the province of Sicily.

Barbarous people (2) is literally "barbarians" (exactly the same expression as that translated "the barbarians" in 4). Since these were civilized people, perhaps "the natives" (Phillips) would be a fairer rendering. Luke, being a Greek, reflects the Greek point of view. Just as the Jews called all foreigners "Gentiles," so the Greek applied the epithet "barbarians" to all who did not speak Greek. Alford says that it is "a term implying very much what our word *natives* does, when speaking of any little-known or new place."[665] The Maltese spoke a Phoenician dialect.

The natives treated the shipwrecked people with **no little kindness**; literally, "with no common humanity" (*philanthropia*, only here and Titus 3:4). **They kindled a fire** and welcomed the escapees to it, because of the prevailing **rain** and **the cold.** This implies that the northeaster was still blowing.

Paul joined in gathering firewood. When he laid a bundle of sticks on the fire, suddenly a roused **viper . . . fastened** itself **on his hand** (3). The objection has been raised that there are now

---

[665]*Op. cit.*, II, 301.

no vipers on Malta. Smith rightly comments: "Upon this point I would merely observe that no person who has studied the changes which the operations of man have produced on the fauna of any country, will be surprised that a particular species of reptiles should have disappeared from that of Malta."[666]

Based on information from the great Professor Agassiz of Cambridge, Hackett says that vipers become torpid in chilly weather, and this one was evidently roused by **the heat** (Gk., *therme*), when thrown with the wood on the bonfire. Vipers lurk in rocky areas, such as mark this region. Hackett continues: "They are accustomed, also, to dart at their enemies, sometimes several feet at a bound; and hence the one mentioned here could have reached the hand of Paul as he stood in the vicinity of the fire."[667] Lake and Cadbury say that **fastened on his hand** means that the snake bit him.[668] The verb **fastened** "was employed by all the medical writers."[669]

The natives observed the **beast** (*therion*)—literally, "wild beast"—hanging on Paul's hand (4). Hobart writes: "St. Luke uses this word here exactly in the same way as the medical writers, who employed it to denote venomous serpents, and of these they applied it in particular to the viper (*echidna*)."[670]

The inhabitants of the island decided that Paul must be **a murderer.** Though he had **escaped the sea**, yet he was finally caught by **vengeance**—literally, "the justice." Probably this was thought of as a goddess, "Justice" (NASB).

Naturally the onlookers expected to see Paul drop **dead** (6). But when considerable time passed and he was obviously unharmed, **they changed their minds, and said that he was a god.** Lake and Cadbury call attention to the significant variation back and forth between the aorist and imperfect tenses in this verse and translate it: "But they waited, expecting that he was going to swell up or fall down suddenly; but when they waited a long time and saw that nothing amiss was happening to him, they changed their minds and began to say that he was a god."[671] One

---

[666]*Op. cit.*, p. 151.
[667]*Op. cit.*, p. 314.
[668]*Beginnings*, IV, 341.
[669]Hobart, *op. cit.*, p. 288.
[670]*Ibid.*, p. 51.
[671]*Beginnings*, IV, 342.

is reminded of the same reaction on the part of the people of Lystra (14:11).

A striking feature of this paragraph is the copious use of medical terms, as the scene was viewed through the eyes of Luke, the physician. Harnack says: "The whole section, xxviii. 3-6, is tinged with medical colouring."[672]

b. Miracles of Healing (28:7-10). In the same quarters (7) —better, "in the neighborhood of that place"—were possessions —"lands" or "estates"—of the chief man of the island. The Greek word for chief is *protos,* "first." Lake and Cadbury write: "The discovery of two inscriptions using it to denote an official of the Maltese gives colour to the suggestion that it is the name of the chief representative of the Roman government on the island (which belonged to the province of Sicily) or some native officer."[673] They add: "If so, the word in Acts is another instance of correct local nomenclature comparable to the politarchs in Thessalonica."[674]

The official's name was Publius. He received—"welcomed" —us, and lodged—"entertained"—us three days courteously— Greek, *philophronos,* meaning "kindly, with friendliness." "Perhaps the suggestion is that after these three days they moved into the town in the interior of the island."[675]

The father of Publius was bedridden with a fever (8)— plural in the Greek, perhaps suggesting "intermittent attacks of fever"[676]—and a bloody flux (Gk., *dysenterion,* "dysentery"). Paul prayed, and laid his hands on him, and healed him.

The result was that others also . . . in the island (9)—literally, "the rest of the people on the island"—which had diseases —literally, "weaknesses" or "frailties," and so "sicknesses"—came —"were coming" (imperfect tense)—and were healed—"getting cured" (NASB). This is a different word for healed than in 8. Here it is *therapeuo,* basis of many medical and psychological terms in English.

Barclay makes a typically appropriate observation at this point. He notes that, while Paul had the gift of healing, he him-

[672]*Luke the Physician,* p. 179.
[673]*Beginnings,* IV, 342.
[674]*Ibid.*
[675]*Ibid.*
[676]EGT, II, 541.

self had to put up with his "thorn in the flesh." Barclay says: "He healed others while he could not heal himself. Like his Master in another sense, he saved others when he could not save himself."[677] He also gives an interesting illustration: "Beethoven, for instance, gave to the world immortal music, which he himself, being stone-deaf, never heard."[678] That is unselfish creativity.

In appreciation for Paul's healing ministry the people of Malta **honoured us with many honours** (10). Lumby comments: "No doubt these included gifts of money and such things as would be needed by travellers who had lost everything in the shipwreck."[679] When the party left, **they laded us with such things as were necessary.** That is, they supplied the people with ample provisions for the remaining voyage to Italy. The nearly three hundred people in the group were now more deeply than ever indebted to Paul, who, under God, had made all this possible—their very survival, and now the supply of their needs.

3. Malta to Rome (28:11-16)

The time spent on the island of Malta was **three months** (11). This was probably November, December, and January. During this time there was no sailing on the Mediterranean. Pliny, in his *Natural History* (ii. 47), says that navigation began on February 7, with the advent of spring.[680] Another Roman writer, Vegetius, declares that the seas were closed from November 11 to March 5, and were dangerous as early as September 14.[681] It is obvious that there was some difference of opinion as to the exact length of the sailing season. But all are agreed that during November, December, and January it was unsafe to venture out on the Mediterranean. Josephus speaks of messengers sent from Rome to Palestine, who "were tossed by a storm, and were detained on the sea for three months."[682]

At the end of the three months on Malta, Luke says, **we departed**—"set sail" (NASB)—**in a ship of Alexandria**—another ship carrying wheat from Egypt to Italy, like the one on which they had suffered shipwreck (cf. 27:6)—**which had wintered in**

[677]*Op. cit.,* p. 208.
[678]*Ibid.*
[679]*Op. cit.,* p. 450.
[680]*Beginnings,* IV, 343.
[681]*Ibid.*
[682]*War* II. 10. 5.

the isle—probably in the main harbor of Valetta. **Whose sign was Castor and Pollux** is only two words in Greek. The first is an adjective meaning "marked with a sign," here used as a substantive, "figurehead."[683] The second is *Dioskouroi,* meaning "The Twin Brothers." So the correct translation is: "which had the Twin Brothers for its figurehead" (NASB). The reference is to the two sons of Zeus, Castor and Pollux. These twin gods "were favourite objects of worship by sailors. They were called on for aid or vowed to in time of storm."[684] Their images were apparently carved on either side of the bow of the ship, **Castor** on one side and **Pollux** on the other.

Apparently the ship set sail from Malta in February. Ramsay suggests: "As the autumn was unusually tempestuous, it is probable that fine weather began early."[685] Evidently a steady south wind began to blow, for they sailed almost straight north to Syracuse (see map 3)—"not more than a day's sail from Melita"[686] (about eighty miles). **Syracuse** (12), on the east coast of Sicily, was the chief port and main city of that island. There they stayed **three days,** presumably because the favorable wind ceased.

From Syracuse they **fetched a compass** (13)[687]—"made a circuit" (RSV) or "tacked round" (Phillips)—**and came to Rhegium.** This was a city on the extreme southern toe of Italy about seven miles across the strait from Messina in Sicily. It would seem that, after vainly waiting for three days at Syracuse for the south wind to blow again, they finally started out and tacked against a northwest wind, making a circuitous run to Rhegium.

But here fortune favored them. **After one day**—of added delay at Rhegium—**the south wind blew, and we came the next day to Puteoli,** "having accomplished a distance of about 180 miles in less than two days."[688] Sailing before the wind, they had made excellent time. Smith writes: "Puteoli was then, as it is

[683]Abbott-Smith, *op. cit.,* p. 343.

[684]*Beginnings,* IV, 343.

[685]SPT, p. 345.

[686]Smith, *op. cit.,* p. 156.

[687]The bulk of the MSS have *perielthontes,* which literally means "having gone around." Vaticanus and Sinaiticus (fourth-century MSS) have *perielontes.* Of the latter Bruce writes: "This seems to be a technical nautical term whose meaning we cannot determine" (*Acts,* p. 474). But the general meaning of the statement seems to be well represented in recent translations.

[688]Smith, *op. cit.,* pp. 156-57. A nautical mile is about 6,080 feet.

now, the most sheltered part of the Bay of Naples. It was. the principal port of southern Italy, and . . . the great emporium for the Alexandrian wheat-ships."[689]

At Puteoli **we found brethren** (14). This must have been a great comfort to Paul, Luke, and Aristarchus, who had probably not seen any other Christians for about six months. The centurion graciously allowed Paul to spend a week with these believers. Instead of **were desired**—literally, "besought" (the word can also mean "comforted")—some MSS read: "were comforted, because we remained."

And so we went toward Rome is literally, "and thus we came to Rome" (NASB). This seems strange when compared with "we came to Rome" (16). Ramsay thinks that **Rome** means the whole district in 14 but the city itself in 16.[690] But Lake and Cadbury reject this theory because of the **thence** (from Rome) in 15. They suggest a simpler and more satisfactory interpretation: "Therefore the probable meaning is merely 'and from Puteoli we went straight to Rome.' "[691] They add: "After this general statement, in which *houtos* [so] emphasizes the fulfilment of prophecy, the writer goes on to give the details of this last stage of the journey."[692]

On the clause, "and so we came to Rome," Knowling makes this pertinent observation: "There is a kind of triumph in the words: like an emperor who has fought a naval battle and overcome, Paul entered into that most imperial city; he was nearer now to his crown; Rome received him bound, and saw him crowned and proclaimed conqueror."[693]

The words **and so we went toward Rome** could well be the basis of a sermon on "The Cost of Obedience." One could note: (1) The prospect, 19-21 (cf. Rom. 1:15); (2) The promise, 23:11; (3) The price (at Jerusalem, Caesarea, and on the sea). But finally **we came to Rome** (16). Ultimately, regardless of the trials on the way, every obedient soul reaches God's appointed destination. This applies both to goals in this life and to our eternal home.

[689]*Ibid.,* p. 157.
[690]SPT, p. 347.
[691]*Beginnings,* IV, 345.
[692]*Ibid.*
[693]EGT, II, 544.

It was about one hundred forty miles from Puteoli to Rome, a rather long journey for those days. But some of **the brethren (15)** at Rome, having learned of Paul's arrival in Italy, **came to meet us as far as Appii forum**, forty-three miles from Rome on the old Appian Way. Other Christians met the party at **The three taverns**, thirty-three miles from Rome.

Concerning **meet**—literally, "for a meeting"—Bruce writes: "*Apantesis* appears to have been a sort of technical term for the official welcome of a newly arrived dignitary by a deputation which went out from the city to greet him and to escort him there; there is thus deep significance in the use of this word to describe the welcome received by Paul from the Roman church."[694]

When Paul saw these Christians who had come to meet him, **he thanked God, and took courage.** He may well have wondered what kind of reception he would have from the Roman church. If he had entertained any doubts or fears, they were quickly dispelled in the warm welcome given him. The presence of these friendly believers must have brought great comfort to the apostle.

When we came to Rome (16)—more accurately, "when we entered Rome" (NASB)—**the centurion delivered the prisoners to the captain of the guard.** This was probably the commander of the Praetorian Guard. As a special favor to this extraordinary prisoner, he was allowed **to dwell by himself with a soldier that kept him.** We may be sure that the centurion put in a good word for him. Also the letter which Festus sent would indicate that Paul was no dangerous criminal.

The last **we** of the book occurs here. Lake and Cadbury note: "Verse 16 ends the 'we-sections,' and the writer adds a concluding paragraph, summarizing the next two years, which Paul spent in Rome."[695]

L. ROME, 28:17-31

1. *Conference with Jewish Leaders* (28:17-22)

After three days (17)—probably spent in visiting with Christians who came to see him—**Paul called the chief of the Jews together.** Claudius had decreed the banishment of all Jews

[694]*Acts*, p. 475.
[695]*Beginnings*, IV, 345.

from Rome (18:2) but clearly many had returned. The apostle was following, even in Rome, his policy of ministering first to the Jew.

To these local Jewish leaders he said that though he had done **nothing against the people, or customs of the fathers,** yet he had been **delivered . . . into the hands of the Romans.** When **examined** by them, he would have been released (18), but when the Jews seemed determined to have him killed, he had appealed to Caesar (19). Then he added: **not that I had ought to accuse my nation of.** What he evidently means is that he was entirely on the defensive in his trials before Felix and Festus; he brought no counter suit against those who had mobbed him. The Jews were still his own people.

Paul then announced the reason for his wishing to speak to them: **because that for the hope of Israel I am bound with this chain** (20). This was the Messianic hope and the belief in the Resurrection (cf. 23:6; 26:6-8).

In response the Jewish leaders at Rome said that they had not received any letters from Jerusalem concerning him, nor had any Jews from Judea reported anything against him (21). This may seem a bit surprising, in view of Paul's two years in prison at Caesarea. Bruce makes a helpful suggestion: "Roman law was severe on unsuccessful prosecutors; it is likely, therefore, that they allowed the case to go by default."[696]

The Jews wanted to hear Paul speak for himself (22). All they knew was that **this sect** (*hairesis;* cf. 5:17; 15:5; 24:5, 14) was **every where . . . spoken against.**

2. Rejection of Jesus (28:23-29)

A day was set when Paul could explain his religious position (23). On the appointed day **many** came **into his lodging;** or "as his guests" (NEB). To them **he expounded**—"explained" or "set forth"—**and testified**—literally, "confirmed by testimony"[697]—**the kingdom of God.** He had firsthand knowledge of the Kingdom in his own heart.

From morning until evening Paul discoursed, **persuading them concerning Jesus, both out of the law of Moses, and out of the prophets.** This must have been a magnificent exposition,

---

[696]*Acts,* p. 477.
[697]Thayer, *op. cit.,* p. 140.

second only to that of Jesus himself to the disciples on the way to Emmaus (Luke 24:27).

As always, the response was mixed: **some believed**—literally, "were persuaded of"—**the things which were spoken, and some believed not** (24). Even today the preacher of the gospel experiences the same double reaction of his audiences. Maclaren reminds us that "to one or other of these two classes we each belong."[698] He continues: "The same fire melts wax and hardens clay; the same light is joy to sound eyes and agony to diseased ones; the same word is a savour of life unto life and a savour of death unto death; the same Christ is set for the fall and for the rising of men, and is to some the sure foundation on which they build secure, and to some the stone on which, stumbling they are broken, and which, falling on them, grinds them to powder."[699]

When the Jews began to argue among themselves, Paul gave them **one word** before they left. **Well spake the Holy Ghost by Esaias**—Isaiah—**the prophet** (25) is one of the many New Testament testimonies to the divine inspiration and authority of the Old Testament.

The quotation in 26 and 27 is from Isa. 6:9-10. Paul had already used this in Rom. 11:8. In a similar way Jesus applied it to the Jews who rejected Him (Matt. 13:13-15; see BBC, VI, 132-33).

Then Paul repeated a declaration he had made, in substance, twice before (cf. 13:46; 18:6). He said: **Be it known therefore unto you, that the salvation of God is sent unto the Gentiles, and that they will hear it** (28). Bruce comments: "Thus, while Acts records the expansion of the Gospel among the Gentiles, it also records progressively its rejection by the greater part of the Jewish nation."[700]

Verse 29 is missing in the oldest Greek MSS. So it is omitted by most versions today (ERV, ASV, RSV, NEB, NASB).

3. *Two Years at Rome* (28:30-31)

Why does the Book of Acts close with the mention of Paul's spending two years in prison at Rome? The most natural inference is that he was released at the end of the **two whole years** (30). Some think he may have been acquitted. For instance,

[698]*Op. cit.*, II, 380-81.
[699]*Ibid.*, p. 381.
[700]*Acts*, p. 479.

Ramsay writes: "That he was acquitted is demanded both by the plan evident in *Acts* . . . and by other reasons well stated by others."[701] However, in a later article Ramsay adopted the view of Lake,[702] given below. Lake suggests that the Jewish prosecutors failed to appear, and so Paul was released. He speculates —there is not certain knowledge at this point—that two years may have been the statutory limit for holding a prisoner awaiting trial.[703] Bruce concludes: "After two years the case probably went by default."[704] In a similar vein Winn says: "It is not unlikely that the case lapsed for want of accusation."[705]

During these two years **Paul dwelt . . . in his own hired house.** Lake and Cadbury prefer "at his own expense" (cf. RSV, NEB). They say: "There is no evidence that *misthoma* ever meant 'a hired house' (A.V.)."[706]

Paul **received all that came** to **him, preaching (30-31)**— "proclaiming"—**the kingdom of God, and teaching those things which concern the Lord Jesus Christ.** Thus his ministry was a combination of preaching and teaching. He did this **with all confidence.** The Greek noun *parresia* is an interesting word (cf. 4:13, 29, 31). It means: "1. *outspokenness, frankness, plainness* of speech, that conceals nothing and passes over nothing . . . 2. 'Openness' sometimes develops into *openness to the public,* before whom speaking and actions take place . . . 3. *courage, confidence, boldness, fearlessness,* especially in the presence of persons of higher rank."[707]

No man forbidding him is one word in Greek, an adverb meaning "without let or hindrance."[708] Arndt and Gingrich would translate the last two phrases together as "quite openly and unhindered."[709] This was the final triumph of Paul in the Book of Acts. He had stood boldly before Felix and Festus and Agrippa, fearlessly witnessing for his Lord. Now as a Roman

[701]SPT, p. 360.
[702]*Beginnings*, V, 326.
[703]*Ibid.*, p. 330.
[704]*Acts*, p. 480.
[705]*Op. cit.*, p. 194.
[706]*Beginnings*, IV, 348.
[707]Arndt and Gingrich, *op. cit.*, pp. 635-36.
[708]*Ibid.*, p. 33.
[709]*Ibid.*, p. 636.

prisoner he still preached the everlasting gospel. He was not free to go out, but he ministered to all who came to him.

From this closing scene of Acts two significant points are suggested by Alexander Maclaren: (1) God's unexpected and unwelcome ways of fulfilling our desires, and His purposes. Paul had for a long time wanted to preach at Rome (Rom. 15:23). But he would not have chosen this way of going there—a prisoner in chains. "Jewish fury, Roman state-craft and law-abidingness, two years of a prison, a stormy voyage, a shipwreck, led him to his long-wished-for goal." (2) The world's mistaken estimate of greatness. Maclaren writes: "Who was the greatest man in Rome at that hour? Not the Caesar but the poor Jewish prisoner."[710]

Since it was Luke's purpose to describe the spread of the gospel from Jerusalem to Rome, he stopped with a brief summary of Paul's ministry in the imperial city. Why the book ends here we do not know. Any answer would be only speculation.

Some think that Luke intended to write a third volume. But this is doubtful. Others think that Paul was executed. But it is difficult to harmonize this with Luke's silence about it. The most natural conclusion is that Paul was released and Luke simply ended the story.

[710]Maclaren, *op. cit.*, p. 384.

Bibliography

I. COMMENTARIES

ALEXANDER, JOSEPH A. *Commentary on the Acts of the Apostles.* Grand Rapids: Zondervan Publishing House, 1956 (reprint).

ALFORD, HENRY. *The Greek Testament.* Revised by EVERETT F. HARRISON. Chicago: Moody Press, 1958.

BARNES, ALBERT. *Notes on the New Testament.* Grand Rapids: Baker Book House, 1949 (reprint).

BENGEL, JOHN ALBERT. *Gnomon of the New Testament.* Translated by ANDREW R. FAUSSET. Fourth Edition. Edinburgh: T. & T. Clark, 1860.

BICKNELL, E. J. "The Acts of the Apostles." *A New Commentary on Holy Scripture.* Edited by CHARLES GORE, H. L. GOUDGE, and ALFRED GUILLAUME. New York: Macmillan Co., 1928.

BLAIKLOCK, E. M. *The Acts of the Apostles.* "The Tyndale New Testament Commentaries." Wm. B. Eerdmans Publishing Co., 1959.

BLUNT, A. W. F. *The Acts of Apostles.* "The Clarendon Bible." Oxford: Clarendon Press, 1923.

BROWN, DAVID. "Acts-Romans." *A Commentary Critical, Experimental and Practical on the Old and New Testaments.* By ROBERT JAMIESON, A. R. FAUSSET, and DAVID BROWN. Grand Rapids: Wm. B. Eerdmans Publishing Co., 1948 (reprint).

BRUCE, F. F. *The Acts of the Apostles:* The Greek Text with Introduction and Commentary. Chicago: Inter-Varsity Christian Fellowship, 1952 (1st Am. ed.). Cited as *Acts.*

————. "The Acts of the Apostles." *The New Bible Commentary.* Edited by F. DAVIDSON. Grand Rapids: Wm. B. Eerdmans Publishing Co., 1953. Cited as NBC.

————. *Commentary on the Book of Acts.* "The New International Commentary on the New Testament." Grand Rapids: Wm. B. Eerdmans Publishing Co., 1954. Cited as NIC.

CALVIN, JOHN. *Commentary upon the Acts of the Apostles.* Edited by HENRY BEVERIDGE. 2 vols. Grand Rapids: Wm. B. Eerdmans Publishing Co., 1949 (reprint).

CARTER, CHARLES W., and EARLE, RALPH. *The Acts of the Apostles.* "Evangelical Commentary on the Bible." Grand Rapids: Zondervan Publishing House, 1959.

ERDMAN, CHARLES R. *The Acts.* Philadelphia: Westminster Press, 1919.

FOAKES-JACKSON, F. J. *The Acts of the Apostles.* "The Moffatt New Testament Commentary." New York: Harper & Brothers, n.d.

GLOAG, PATON J. *A Critical and Exegetical Commentary on the Acts of the Apostles.* 2 vols. Edinburgh: T. & T. Clark, 1870.

HACKETT, H. B. *A Commentary on the Acts of the Apostles.* Revised Edition. Philadelphia: American Baptist Publication Society, 1882.

HERVEY, A. C. "The Acts of the Apostles" (Exposition). *The Pulpit Commentary*. Edited by H. D. M. SPENCE and JOSEPH S. EXELL. Grand Rapids: Wm. B. Eerdmans Publishing Co., 1950 (reprint).

JACKSON, F. J. FOAKES, and LAKE, KIRSOPP. *The Beginnings of Christianity*. Part I: *The Acts of the Apostles*, Vol. IV. London: Macmillan & Co., 1933.

KNOWLING, R. J. "The Acts of the Apostles." *The Expositor's Greek Testament*. Edited by W. R. NICOLL. Grand Rapids: Wm. B. Eerdmans Publishing Co., n.d.

LADD, GEORGE E. "The Acts of the Apostles." *Wycliffe Bible Commentary*. Edited by CHARLES F. PFEIFFER and EVERETT F. HARRISON. Chicago: Moody Press, 1962.

LECKLER, G. V. "Acts" (Exegesis). *Commentary on the Holy Scriptures*. Edited by J. P. LANGE. Grand Rapids: Zondervan Publishing House, n.d.

LENSKI, R. C. H. *The Interpretation of the Acts of the Apostles*. Columbus, Ohio: Wartburg Press, 1944.

LUMBY, J. RAWSON. *The Acts of the Apostles*. "Cambridge Greek Testament." Cambridge: University Press, 1885.

MACGREGOR, G. H. C. "The Acts of the Apostles" (Exegesis). *The Interpreier's Bible*. Edited by G. A. BUTTRICK, Vol. IX. New York: Abingdon-Cokesbury Press, 1954.

MACLAREN, ALEXANDER. *Expositions of Holy Scripture: The Acts*. Grand Rapids: Wm. B. Eerdmans Publishing Co., 1944 (reprint).

MEYER, H. A. W. *Critical and Exegetical Handbook to the Acts of the Apostles*. Translated from the fourth German edition by PATON GLOAG. Revised and edited by W. P. DICKSON. American edition by WILLIAM ORMISTON. New York: Funk & Wagnalls, 1883.

PAGE, T. E. *Acts of the Apostles*. London: Macmillan and Co., 1886.

PLUMPTRE, E. H. "The Acts of the Apostles." *Commentary on the Whole Bible*. Edited by CHARLES JOHN ELLICOTT. Grand Rapids: Zondervan Publishing House, n.d.

RACKHAM, R. B. *The Acts of the Apostles*. Eighth Edition. "Westminster Commentaries." London: Methuen & Co., 1919.

ROBERTSON, A. T. *Word Pictures in the New Testament*, Vol. III. New York: Richard R. Smith, 1930.

WESLEY, JOHN. *Explanatory Notes upon the New Testament*. London: Epworth Press, 1954 (reprint).

WILLIAMS, C. S. C. *A Commentary on the Acts of the Apostles*. "Harper's New Testament Commentaries." New York: Harper & Brothers, 1957.

WINN, ALBERT C. "The Acts of the Apostles." *The Layman's Bible Commentary*. Edited by BALMER H. KELLY, Vol. XX. Richmond, Va.: John Knox Press, 1960.

II. OTHER BOOKS

ABBOTT-SMITH, G. *A Manual Greek Lexicon of the New Testament*. Second Edition. Edinburgh: T. & T. Clark, 1923.

ANDREWS, SAMUEL. *The Life of Our Lord upon the Earth*. Grand Rapids: Zondervan Publishing House, 1954 (reprint).

ARNDT, W. F., and GINGRICH, F. W. *A Greek-English Lexicon of the New Testament and Other Early Christian Literature.* Chicago: University of Chicago Press, 1957.

BLASS, FREDERICK. *Philology of the Gospels.* London: Macmillan Co., 1898.

BLASS, F., and DEBRUNNER. *A Greek Grammar of the New Testament and Other Early Christian Literature.* Translated and revised by ROBERT W. FUNK. Chicago: University of Chicago Press, 1961.

BOWEN, C. R. *Studies in the New Testament.* Edited by R. J. HUTCHESON. Chicago: University of Chicago Press, 1936.

BURTON, ERNEST D. *Syntax of the Moods and Tenses in New Testament Greek.* Second Edition. Chicago: University Press of Chicago, 1893.

CADBURY, HENRY, JR. *The Book of Acts in History.* New York: Harper & Brothers, 1955.

———. *The Making of Luke-Acts.* New York: Macmillan Co., 1927.

CLOGG, F. B. *An Introduction to the New Testament.* New York: Charles Scribner's Sons, 1937.

CONYBEARE, W. J., and HOWSON, J. S. *The Life and Epistles of St. Paul.* New York: Charles Scribner's Sons, 1894.

CREMER, HERMANN. *Biblico-Theological Lexicon of New Testament Greek.* Translated by WILLIAM URWICK. Edinburgh: T. & T. Clark, 1878.

DEISSMANN, ADOLPH. *Bible Studies.* Translated by ALEXANDER GRIEVE. Edinburgh: T. &. T. Clark, 1901.

———. *Light from the Ancient East.* Translated by L. R. M. STRACHAN. New York: George H. Doran Co., 1927.

FARMER, W. R. *Maccabees, Zealots, and Josephus.* New York: Columbia University Press, 1956.

FARRAR, F. W. *The Life and Work of St. Paul.* New York: E. P. Dutton Co., 1896.

GOODSPEED, EDGAR J. *An Introduction to the New Testament.* Chicago: University of Chicago Press, 1937.

GRANT, ROBERT M. *A Historical Introduction to the New Testament.* New York: Harper & Row, 1963.

HARNACK, ADOLPH. *The Acts of the Apostles.* Translated by J. R. WILKINSON. New York: G. P. Putnam's Sons, 1909.

———. *The Date of the Acts and of the Synoptic Gospels.* Translated by J. R. WILKINSON. New York: G. P. Putnam's Sons, 1911.

———. *Luke the Physician.* Translated by J. R. WILKINSON. London: Williams & Norgate, 1907.

HENSHAW, T. *New Testament Literature.* London: George Allen & Unwin, 1952.

HOBART, W. K. *The Medical Language of St. Luke.* Grand Rapids: Baker Book House, 1954 (reprint).

KITTEL, GERHARD (ed.). *Theological Dictionary of the New Testament.* Translated and edited by GEOFFREY W. BROMILEY, Vol. I. Grand Rapids: Wm. B. Eerdmans Publishing Co., 1964.

KNOX, JOHN. *Marcion and the New Testament.* Chicago: University of Chicago Press, 1942.

596

LAKE, KIRSOPP, and LAKE, SILVA. *An Introduction to the New Testament.* New York: Harper & Brothers, 1937.

LIDDELL, HENRY G., and SCOTT, ROBERT. *A Greek-English Lexicon.* Revised by HENRY S. JONES. Oxford: Clarendon Press, 1940.

LIGHTFOOT, J. B. *St. Paul's Epistle to the Galatians.* Grand Rapids: Zondervan Publishing House, n.d.

MAJOR, H. D. A., MANSON, T. W., and WRIGHT, C. J. *The Mission and Message of Jesus.* New York: E. P. Dutton & Co., 1938.

MAYOR, JOSEPH B. *The Epistle of St. James.* Grand Rapids: Zondervan Publishing House, 1954 (reprint).

MOE, OLAF. *The Apostle Paul.* Translated by L. A. VIGNESS. Minneapolis: Augsburg Publishing House, 1950.

MOFFATT, JAMES. *An Introduction to the Literature of the New Testament.* Third Edition. New York: Charles Scribner's Sons, 1918.

MOULTON, JAMES HOPE. *A Grammar of New Testament Greek,* Vol. I, "Prologomena." Third Edition. Edinburgh: T. & T. Clark, 1908.

MOULTON, JAMES HOPE, and MILLIGAN, GEORGE. *The Vocabulary of the Greek Testament Illustrated from the Papyri and Other Non-literary Sources.* Grand Rapids: Wm. B. Eerdmans Publishing Co., 1949.

RAMSAY, W. M. *The Cities of St. Paul.* New York: A. C. Armstrong & Son, 1908.

------. *St. Paul the Traveller and the Roman Citizen.* Grand Rapids: Baker Book House, 1949 (reprint).

ROBERTSON, A. T. *A Grammar of the Greek New Testament in the Light of Historical Research.* Fifth Edition. New York: Harper & Brothers, n.d.

------. *Luke the Historian in the Light of Research.* New York: Charles Scribner's Sons, 1920.

SCHUERER, EMIL. *A History of the Jewish People in the Time of Jesus Christ.* Edinburgh: T. & T. Clark, 1885.

SCOTT, E. F. *The Literature of the New Testament.* New York: Columbia University Press, 1936.

SELWYN, E. G. *The First Epistle of Peter.* Second Edition. London: Macmillan & Co., 1947.

SMITH, JAMES. *The Voyage and Shipwreck of St. Paul.* Fourth Edition. London: Longmans, Green, and Co., 1880.

STONEHOUSE, NED. *Paul Before the Areopagus.* Grand Rapids: Wm. B. Eerdmans Publishing Co., 1957.

THAYER, JOSEPH H. *A Greek-English Lexicon of the New Testament.* Corrected Edition. New York: American Book Co., 1889.

TORREY, C. C. *The Composition and Date of Acts.* Cambridge: Harvard University Press, 1916.

WESLEY, JOHN. *Works.* 14 vols. Grand Rapids: Zondervan Publishing House, n.d.

WIKENHAUSER, ALFRED. *New Testament Introduction.* Translated by JOSEPH CUNNINGHAM. New York: Herder & Herder, 1958.

ZAHN, THEODOR. *Introduction to the New Testament.* Translated by JOHN TROUT, et al. 3 vols. Grand Rapids: Kregel Publications, 1953 (reprint).

III. ARTICLES

BLUNT, A. W. F. "Pentecost, Feast of." Revised by D. R. JONES. *Dictionary of the Bible*. Edited by JAMES HASTINGS. Revised Edition by F. C. GRANT and H. H. ROWLEY. New York: Charles Scribner's Sons, 1963.

DOSKER, HENRY E. "Pentecost." *The International Standard Bible Encyclopedia*. Edited by JAMES ORR. Revised Edition. Chicago: Howard-Severance Co., 1929.

PURVES, G. T. "Pentecost." *A Dictionary of the Bible*. Edited by JAMES HASTINGS, Vol. III. New York: Charles Scribner's Sons, 1900.

RAMSAY, W. M. "Roads and Travel (in NT)." *A Dictionary of the Bible*. Edited by JAMES HASTINGS. New York: Charles Scribner's Sons, 1904.

TAYLOR, F. J. "Passion." *A Theological Word Book of the Bible*. Edited by ALAN RICHARDSON. London: SCM Press, 1950.

WHEATON, DAVID H. "Passion." *Baker's Dictionary of Theology*. Edited by EVERETT F. HARRISON. Grand Rapids: Baker Book House, 1960.

Map 1

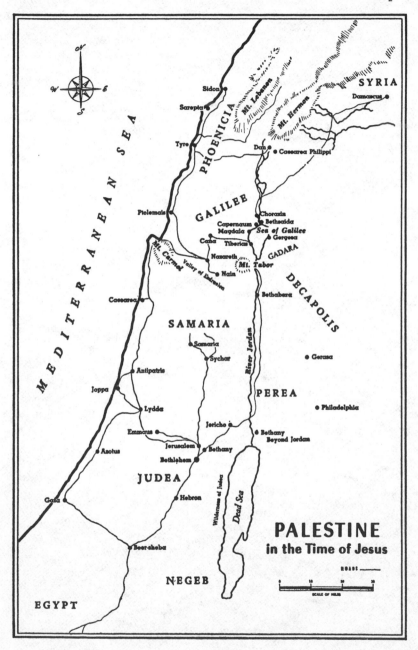

PALESTINE
in the Time of Jesus

Map 2

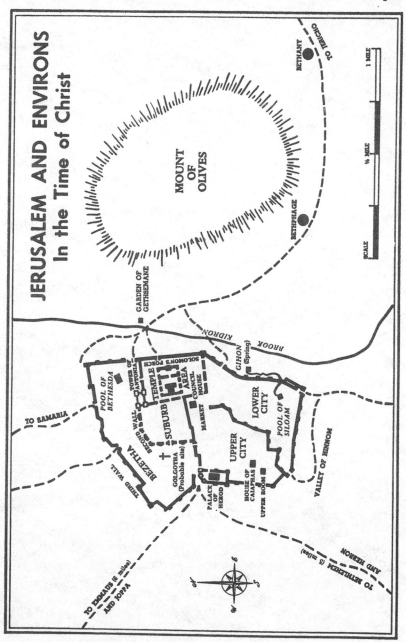

JERUSALEM AND ENVIRONS
In the Time of Christ

Map 3

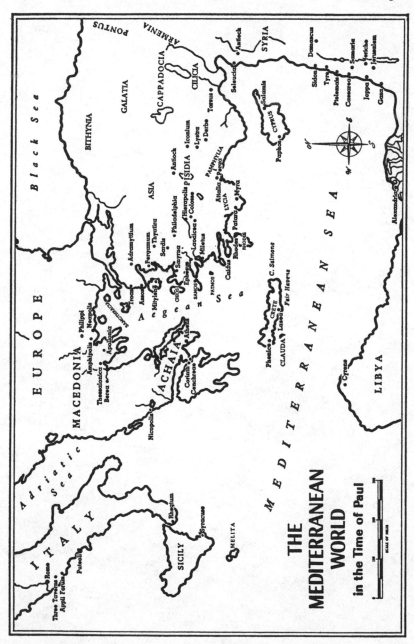

THE
MEDITERRANEAN
WORLD
in the Time of Paul

HEROD'S TEMPLE

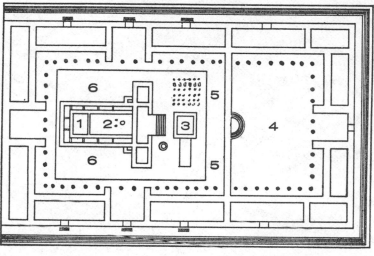

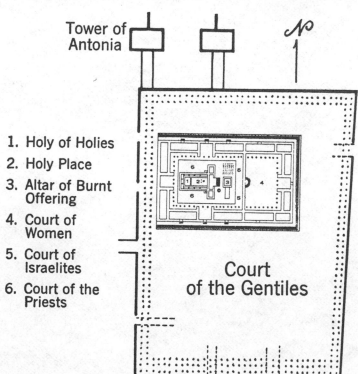

Tower of Antonia

1. Holy of Holies
2. Holy Place
3. Altar of Burnt Offering
4. Court of Women
5. Court of Israelites
6. Court of the Priests

Court
of the Gentiles

RESURRECTION APPEARANCES

(1) To MARY MAGDALENE
(Mark 16:9-11; John 20:11-18)

(2) To the OTHER WOMEN
(Matthew 28:9-10; Luke 24:9-11)

(3) To the TWO DISCIPLES on the WAY to EMMAUS
(Mark 16:12-13; Luke 24:13-35)

(4) To SIMON PETER
(Luke 24:33-35; I Corinthians 15:5)

(5) To the DISCIPLES (Thomas Absent)
(Mark 16:14; Luke 24:36-48; John 20:19-25)

(6) To THOMAS and the OTHER DISCIPLES
(John 20:26-31; I Corinthians 15:5)

(7) To the SEVEN DISCIPLES by the SEA of GALILEE
(John 21:1-23)

(8) To MORE THAN FIVE HUNDRED
(I Corinthians 15:6)

(9) To JAMES
(I Corinthians 15:7)

(10) To the ELEVEN (Great Commission)
(Matthew 28:16-20; Mark 16:15-18)

(11) To the DISCIPLES on OLIVET (The Ascension)
(Mark 16:19-20; Luke 24:50-53; Acts 1:9-12)

(12) To the APOSTLE PAUL
(I Corinthians 15:8)